On Jaspers vs. RB on myth: pp 451-53 and

Rudolf Bultmann

A Biography

Rudolf Bultmann

A Biography

Konrad Hammann

Translated by Philip E. Devenish

POLEBRIDGE PRESS
Salem, Oregon

Design and production by Robaire Ream

Printed in the United States of America

10 9 8 7 6 5 4 3 2 1

First English Edition

Library of Congress Cataloging-in-Publication Data
Hammann, Konrad.
[Rudolf Bultmann. English]
Rudolf Bultmann : a biography / Konrad Hammann ; translated by Philip E. Devenish. -- First English edition.
pages cm
Includes bibliographical references and index.
ISBN 978-1-59815-118-3 (alk. paper)
1. Bultmann, Rudolf, 1884-1976. 2. New Testament scholars--Germany--Biography. 3. Theologians--Germany--Biography. I. Devenish, Philip E., translator. II. Title.
BX4827.B78H26613 2013
230.092--dc23
[B]

2012034525

"Rudolf Bultmann's special field of competence as a theologian was the New Testament, and it is entirely possible that he is the preeminent scholar in this field in our time. But it is not only or even primarily as a New Testament scholar that Bultmann is significant for theology and religious studies. In his own mind, certainly, he was, first and last, a Christian theologian, who did all of his work, including his historical work, in service of the church and its witness. And as the years have passed, it is in this capacity that he is also widely regarded as one of the three or four Protestant theologians of the twentieth century whose impact on Christian witness and theology promises to be lasting. The value of Konrad Hammann's fine biography is the extent to which it illumines the life and work of this extraordinary human being."

—**Schubert M. Ogden**, University Distinguished Professor of Theology Emeritus at Southern Methodist University

Table of Contents

Acknowledgments

I wish to pay hearty thanks to the friendly people who have rendered outstanding services to the making of this book. Mrs. Anna-Elisabeth Bruckhaus of Tübingen gave me considerable help by sharing her extensive knowledge of Bultmann's unpublished works. She generously placed at my disposal all the materials from the Estate that I requested and was also successful in obtaining the plates. Mrs. Kirsten Fromm of Münster drew up the typesetting copy in her usual accurate fashion and coordinated enquiries for and securing of literature, for which the student assistants of the Institute for Protestant Theology and Teaching in Münster assumed responsibility. My wife helped me by continuously listening to and commenting on the individual chapters of the book in their various stages of formation.

For sharing valuable communications I thank Mrs. Gesine Diesselhorst of Göttingen and my colleagues Helmut Koester of Harvard, Heinrich Leipold of Niederweimar bei Marburg, Otto Merk of Erlangen, Jürgen Schlienbecker, Esq. (of Marburg), and the now deceased Bishop Christian Zippert (of Michelbach bei Marburg). My colleagues Andreas Frossmann of Hamburg and Christof Landmesser of Tübingen afforded me advance access to their edition of Bultmann's correspondence with Martin Heidegger. My colleague Martin Vialon of Istanbul made it possible to consult his study of Erich Auerbach and Rudolf Bultmann prior to its publication. The publishing house of Mohr Siebeck, which has always fostered the work of Rudolf Bultmann and with which Bultmann was closely affiliated, and especially the Managing Director of the press, Dr. Henning Ziebritzki, have shown a lively and helpful interest in this book. Mrs. Jana Trispel and her co-workers saw to the printing of this biography with the accustomed quality of the house of Mohr Siebeck. I heartily thank all of these for their support.

Münster, November 2008
Konrad Hammann

Preface to the Second Edition

For this second edition, some printing errors and oversights have been corrected. Now and then I added to the text or clarified language. The pagination remains substantially unchanged. For the professional support of this new edition, I would like to thank Mrs. Anna K. Krueger of Mohr Siebeck.

Münster, August 2009
Konrad Hammann

Abbreviations

Dates are listed in the European format: Date. Month. Year (August 20, 1884 = 20. 8. 1884).

German Abbreviations follow S. M. Schwertner, *Internationales Abkürzungsverzeichnis für Theologie und Grenzgebiete*, 1992 (2d ed.), as well as *Redaktion der RGG* (2d ed.), *Abkürzungen Theologie und Religionswissenschaft nach RGG*, 2007 (4th ed).

In addition, the following abbreviations have been employed in the text and notes:

1,2 Cor	1,2 Letter to the Corinthians
1 Sam	Book of 1 Samuel
1 Thess	Letter to the Thessalonians
AEKR Boppard	Archiv der Ev. Kirche im Rheinland, Archivstelle Boppard [Archive of the Protestant Church in the Rhineland, Boppard Branch]
AHRp	Arbeiten zur Historischen Religionspädagogik [journal]
Bl.	Blatt, Blätter [sheet (of paper)]
BVB	Beiträge zum Verstehen der Bibel
Cant	Canticles (Song of Solomon)
Cnfd.	Confidential; not meant to be shared publicly
DLA Marbach	Deutsches Literaturarchiv Marbach a.N. [Archive of German Literature in Marbach]
Est.	Estate
FAZ	Frankfurter Allgemeine Zeitung [periodical]
FS	Festschrift [collection of commemorative essays]
FZ	Frankfurter Zeitung [periodical]
Gal	Letter to the Galatians
Gen	Book of Genesis
GStA PK Berlin	Geheimes Staatsarchiv Preussischer Kulturbesitz Berlin [Secret State Archives, Prussian Cultural Heritage Foundation]
GuV	R. Bultmann, *Glauben und Verstehen*, 4 vols, 1933–1975.
HAZ Oldenburg	Hannah-Arendt-Zentrum der Universität Oldenburg [Hannah Arendt Centre at the University of Oldenburg]
Isa	Book of Isaiah
Jb.	Jahrbuch [yearbook]

JEA Wuppertal	Julius-Ebbinghaus-Archiv der Bergischen Universität Wuppertal [Julius Ebbinghaus Archive at the University of Wuppertal in Bergisches Land]
Jer	Book of Jeremiah
Matt	Book of Matthew
MP	R. Bultmann, *Marburger Predigten*, 1968 (2d ed)
PhAU Konstanz	Philosophisches Archiv der Universität Konstanz [Philosophical Archive at the University of Constance]
Phil	Letter to the Philippians
Ps(s)	Book of Psalm(s)
RB	Rudolf Bultmann
Rev.	Review
RGG	Die Religion in Geschichte und Gegenwart
Rom	Book of Romans
SS	Summer semester
StA Oldenburg	Niedersächsisches Staatsarchiv Oldenburg [State Archives of Lower Saxony in Oldenburg]
UA	Universitätsarchiv [University Archive]
UB	Universitätsbibliothek [University Library]
UCLA Library	University of California Los Angeles Library
ULB	Universitäts- und Landesbibliothek [University and State Library]
VW	R. Bultmann, *Das verkündigte Wort*, 1984.
WS	Winter semester

I. Formative Years (1884–1907)

1. Family

My father, who was born in Freetown, Sierra Leone (West Africa), was a descendant of farming folk from the district of Bremen; his father was a missionary. My grandfather on my mother's side was a pastor in Baden.[1]

On August 20, 1884, Helene Bultmann, née Stern, the thirty-year-old wife of a Lutheran pastor of the same age, Arthur Kennedy Bultmann, brought her first child, a son, into the world in Wiefelstede, in the Grand Duchy of Oldenburg. The boy's father had just become pastor in Wiefelstede in May of 1884, formerly having been pastor in Neuenburg for just five years, since 1879. So it was that one of his first official pastoral actions in his new domain was to baptize his son with the name of Rudolf Karl on September 23, 1884. The parents had chosen these names in honor of the child's godfathers, Rudolf Stern and Karl Eggerking, whom Elise Stern joined as godmother.[2] In Wiefelstede the Bultmann couple had two additional children, Helene (b. 1885) and Peter (b. 1888). The sibling group became complete when Arthur, a latecomer, was born in Oldenburg in 1897.

The Bultmann family, which traced its roots to the rural countryside, had already produced several teachers and pastors in the nineteenth century. At the turn of the twentieth century, other Oldenburg Bultmanns besides Arthur Kennedy were active in religious callings. Arthur Kennedy Bultmann's father had dedicated himself early on to the mission of the revival movement, and Fritz Bultmann served as a missionary in Kent, Sierra Leone (West Africa). After his second wife died in childbirth, he proposed marriage to Elise Ramsauer in 1846, his deceased wife's best friend. Elise agreed and journeyed to West Africa, without ever having seen her husband-to-be beforehand,[3] though to be sure, this was in accord with the customs typical of revivalist missionary circles. Fritz and Elise Bultmann returned to Oldenburg in 1860 with a total of ten children, among them the above-mentioned Arthur Kennedy, who had been born in Freetown in 1854.

1. "Autobiographische Bemerkungen Rudolf Bultmanns," 28. 1. 1956, in B. Jaspert, *Barth-Bultmann Briefwechsel* (2d ed.), 303.

2. Data from the baptismal registry of 1884, in the Archive of the Evangelical-Lutheran Church Parish Wiefelstede.

3. Cf. H. Ramsauer, "Johannes Ramsauer und Pestalozzi," 81; P. Ramsauer, *Zieh,* 270f.

And while Fritz Bultmann's missionary work in Africa had enriched the spiritual and cultural name of his otherwise rather settled family, his marital connection with Elise Ramsauer meant an additional gain for the family reputation, for she was a daughter of a student and close confidant of Johann Heinrich Pestalozzi, one Johannes Ramsauer. Beginning in Stuttgart in 1817, this Swiss teacher from the canton of Appenzell had tutored the Princes Alexander and Peter, sons of Queen Katharina of Württemberg's first marriage to Prince Georg of Oldenburg. In 1820, when the princes moved to Oldenburg after Katharina's death, Ramsauer followed them in order to continue their education and, after 1826, that of the children of the Grand Duke Peter Friedrich Ludwig, as well as to establish several elementary schools for girls. Through his widespread educational activity in Oldenburg, Johannes Ramsauer sought to carry out the pedagogical ideas and principles of Pestalozzi, and indeed to develop them further, especially in the area of preschool education. In matters of religion, he was increasingly influenced by the revival movement, but since this played little if any role in the church life of Oldenburg, Ramsauer and his wife cultivated close contacts with the revival circles around Gottfried Menken and Friedrich Ludwig Mallet in Bremen.[4] This integration into the revivalist network no doubt helps explain the marriage of the missionary Fritz Bultmann to Ramsauer's daughter Elise.

A peculiar combination of pietistic-revivalist religiosity and education in the spirit of Pestalozzi thus shaped the familial environment in which Arthur Kennedy Bultmann spent his childhood and youth. After attending the academy in Oldenburg, he finished his theological studies in Erlangen, Tübingen, and Göttingen. In Erlangen, he became versed in the experiential theology of the Erlangen School; in Tübingen, Johann Tobias Beck's speculative-biblical kingdom-of-God theology had a strong influence on him. Ordained at the age of twenty-four after passing his exams brilliantly in 1878, Arthur Kennedy Bultmann naturally supposed that his immediate pastoral duties would proceed along the lines laid out for him by his parents and his theological teachers. At first, therefore, he remained "more on positive, biblical ground."[5] This is illustrated by a sermon he preached at a harvest thanksgiving festival in Wiefelstede in 1888, a homily that exhibits a clearly biblicist style.[6]

Like his father's family, the maternal line into which Rudolf Bultmann was born also drew its spiritual profile from the revival movement of the

4. Cf. H. Ramsauer, "Johannes Ramsauer," 33–45; P. Ramsauer, *Zieh*, esp. 216f.

5. Obituary: "Kirchenrat Bultmann," 51.

6. Cf. sermon preached at Wiefelstede at the harvest thanksgiving celebration on 19 October 1888, by the pastor of the congregation at that time, A. Bultmann, in W. Zager, *Liberale Exegese*, 149–55.

nineteenth century. Helene Bultmann was a daughter of the pastor Ludwig Rudolf Stern, who, after studies in theology in Erlangen, Tübingen, and Heidelberg, filled various pastoral posts in the province of Baden near Leiselheim am Kaiserstuhl from 1860 until 1882, and from then until his death in 1899 in Denzlingen, near Freiburg. Rudolf Bultmann's maternal grandfather was a son of Wilhelm Stern, a central figure in the revival movement in Baden. He was born in 1792, the son of a baker from Mosbach, and in 1814 took up a position in Pestalozzi's school in Yverdon after theological study in Heidelberg and Tübingen—a striking parallel to the history of Bultmann's paternal line. Beginning in 1817 Stern served in various educational capacities in Karlsruhe and Gernsbach until 1823, when Johann Peter Hebel called him to the newly established teacher's college in Karlsruhe. Thereafter Stern strove for more than forty years to enhance both the theoretical and practical aspects of teacher training, and after 1837 served as Director of the college. His pedagogical views especially reflected the philanthropic ideals of the Enlightenment. Following inner religious struggles and influenced by an encounter with Aloys Henhöfer, he aligned himself with the Baden revival movement; and from that time forward pietistic-revivalist religiosity became an integral component, indeed the guiding impulse, of his pedagogical endeavors.[7] Therein we find further parallel to the path that Johannes Ramsauer was pursuing in Oldenburg at about the same time.

Helene Stern, the mother of Rudolf Bultmann, brought into her marriage with Arthur Kennedy Bultmann the spiritual inheritance her grandfather had bequeathed to her family, and she stood firm in this her whole life. But it was a different matter with her husband, for, in the years after 1900, Arthur Kennedy Bultmann underwent a change of direction in his theological views.[8] As early as the sermon that had failed to secure for him the pastorate of Oldenburg II, he had developed a concept of the kingdom of God that closely resembled a kind of liberal eschatology. To be sure, the kingdom of God is finally realizable only in the eternal future of the day of Christ, but the Christian is called to play a part in the ongoing building of the historical kingdom of God through his religio-ethical activity.[9] What motives led Arthur Kennedy Bultmann to join ranks with free Protestantism, we do not know. He evidently expected liberal theology to provide more help in overcoming the contemporary problems afflicting the church than biblical positivism was able to provide. During the course of a round of pastoral

7. Cf. G. Silberer, "Wilhelm Stern," 139–53.

8. Cf. in this regard M. Evang, *Frühzeit,* 107f; W. Zager, *Liberale Exegese*, 140–42.

9. Cf. A. Bultmann, "Zeichen," 12–20. Although A. Bultmann had been elected by a majority of the people, another applicant received the pastorate at Oldenburg II at the intervention of the Grand Duke.

Plate 1: Rudolf Bultmann's Parents, Arthur Kennedy Bultmann and Helene Bultmann, née Stern, ca. 1900

inspections carried out in Oldenburg in 1905, he responded to a question about the theological studies he had pursued in his final years by stating that he had devoted himself to the writings of such liberal theologians as Wilhelm Bousset, Otto Baumgarten, and Paul Drews on matters of biblical and practical theology.[10]

In 1904 Arthur Kennedy Bultmann attested his theological course-correction by joining the Oldenburg Evangelical Association of Preachers, the alliance of liberal theologians in the Grand Duchy. And in these later years he left the pietistic Bremen North German Missionary Society and joined the yet more liberally oriented General Evangelical-Protestant Missionary Association. Arthur Kennedy Bultmann also served as a journalist to further the aims of this missionary association: the spread of "Christian religion and culture among non-Christian peoples . . . in connection with the elements of truth already present therein." A contemporary mission, as he explained citing Ernst Troeltsch, must take into account the findings of critical theological scholarship and place the message of Jesus rather than the doctrines of the church at the center of its activities.[11] And from the time of its official

10. Cf. W. Zager, *Liberale Exegese,* 140n7.
11. Cf. A. Bultmann, "Mission," 53f (quotation 53); cf. E. Troeltsch, "Mission."

founding in 1903, Arthur Kennedy Bultmann also belonged to the Alliance of the Friends of *Die Christliche Welt* [*The Christian World*], an organization of the laity, clergy, and theologians of free, modern Protestantism.

Arthur Kennedy Bultmann's theological adoption of liberal positions led to a mutually painful alienation from his former friends and even caused tensions within his own household, for Helene Bultmann was not ready to follow her husband and give up her pietistic religiousness. As a result, as he became elderly and his health declined, he withdrew into himself, and the couple's religious differences remained until his death on April 28, 1919. Although the pastor at St. Lambert in Oldenburg, Bultmann refused to allow a funeral sermon so as to guarantee that "he would not be gossiped about at his coffin,"[12] and in place of a sermon at his burial, the pastor read a prayer that the deceased had offered daily during the last years of his life—a paraphrase of the Lord's Prayer that breathed the spirit of liberal theology.[13] The headstone that marks the graves of Bultmann and his wife in the New Cemetery in Oldenburg still indicates what separated them religiously. Under the name of Arthur Kennedy Bultmann stands the credo of the liberal theology that Adolf Harnack had succinctly enunciated in his *Wesen des Christentums* [*What Is Christianity?*]: "I believe in God my father." Under the name of Helene Bultmann, who died in 1935, stands the personal confession of her pietistic faith, Job 19:25: "I know that my redeemer lives."

12. Obituary: "Kirchenrat Bultmann," 51.
13. Cf. Obituary: "Kirchenrat Bultmann," 99.

Plate 2: The Bultmann Siblings: Rudolf, Peter, Arthur and Helene, ca. 1901

Rudolf Bultmann was to outlive his younger sisters. His brother Peter led a turbulent life. For a time he was editor of the communist newspaper *Spartakus* but later converted to Roman Catholicism. A teacher in Oldenburg and a librarian in Leipzig, he emigrated during the Third Reich for political reasons. With his wife Frieda and their children he went first to Vienna, then, as a result of the Nazi occupation of Austria, to Prague. During this period Rudolf Bultmann and his wife, as well as the Catholic Church, supported him and his family. But in the end Peter Bultmann could not escape Nazi pursuit, and in 1942 he died under unknown circumstances in a concentration camp in the French Pyrenees. His sister Helene married the Oldenburg pastor August Pleus in 1906 and for many years was the pastor's wife and mother of three children in Dedesdorf on the Lower Weser River. Rudolf Bultmann was godfather to her daughter Elisabeth, born in 1908, who later became a deaconess or parish nurse. On his fiftieth birthday, August 20, 1934, he officiated at the marriage in Dedesdorf of Marianne Pleus, his sister's second daughter, and his student, Kendrick Grobel, a New Testament scholar who taught from 1934 on in the United States, ending his career at Vanderbilt University.[14] Helene Pleus died in 1974, two years before her oldest brother. The youngest of the Bultmanns, Arthur, was allotted only a brief life. An Army volunteer, Arthur Bultmann fell in France at age twenty in February of 1917, a sacrifice of the First World War.

2. Childhood and Youth

> *As a child I was a very spirited boy, endowed with a rich imagination, so that even now I can envy myself in this. I experienced everything very intensely, and, for that reason I have very vivid memories back into my earliest childhood, of which I could tell much.*[15]

Rudolf Bultmann spent the first five years of his life in Wiefelstede, a small farming village in Oldenburg's Ammerland, some "sixteen kilometers north of Oldenburg, situated on the Geest, amidst fields and woodlands." The village idyll in which he grew up, the house in which he was born, the large garden of the parsonage with trees, under which he, along with other children, performed "The City-Musicians of Bremen," remained vivid memories in his later life. Of course, by the time he recorded these childhood memo-

14. Cf. RB, *VW*, 74–78.

15. UB Tübingen, RB est., RB to H. Feldmann, 19. 9. 1915, Mn 2-2739; quotations in the passage that follows also come from this letter.

ries in 1915, much had changed in Wiefelstede. The old parsonage where he was born had given way the year before to a new building, and some trees—among them the "big walnut tree behind the house" and "the pink hawthorn that glowed behind the kitchen"—had been felled in the meantime. And yet, when he visited the house of his birth in September of 1915, Bultmann still saw "not the new, but the old . . . , as it had been"; and as he looked back on untroubled childhood days, what came to mind was "how beautiful" the churchyard was "among the old thatched houses and the luxuriant cottage gardens!" In the later images of his adulthood, something still shines through, and so it appears that the young Rudolf must have experienced during his first years such a delightful home life that "allen in die Kindheit scheint und worin noch niemand war" ["all my childhood shines like a never-never land"].[16] His earliest memories also included the following episode. Rudolf often stayed in the old Brügges farmhouse across from the church and the parsonage. The family had a daughter "whose name was Liese and whose hair was completely ash-blond. My mother still tells how once I was at home and sitting at the window looking out. Outside in front of the house Liese was standing in the wind, and I cried, 'Look, Mother! The Brügges' Liese has sauerkraut on her head!'"[17]

In 1890, the Bultmanns moved from Wiefelstede to the vicinity of Rastede, where Arthur Kennedy Bultmann assumed his third pastorate. Rastede, as Rudolf Bultmann reported in 1915, "has a somewhat more urban appearance, but is beautifully situated and has magnificent woods. . . . Here I spent my real youth (up to my thirteenth year), stole apples and broke windows, commanded the village youth on Indian raids, helped the farmers with the potato harvest, received my first thrashing in elementary school, fell in love for the first time."[18] The change of location caused the young Bultmann to broaden his perspective on the world around him, for in 1895 Rastede, a town of about five thousand predominantly Lutheran inhabitants, was the summer residence of the Grand Duke of Oldenburg. One day the eight-year-old reported proudly to his mother, who was staying in Denzlingen with her parents, "Today, as I was coming out of church, the Grand Duke walked by me, and I touched my hat. In reply he said, 'Good day, my boy!'"[19] To be sure, the uplifting encounter did not prevent the lad with a special attraction to the Grand Duke from stealing apples and plums in his lordship's

16. E. Bloch, *Prinzip*, 1628.
17. UB Tübingen, RB est., RB to H. Feldmann, 19. 9. 1915, Mn 2-2739.
18. UB Tübingen, RB est., RB to H. Feldmann, 19. 9. 1915, Mn 2-2739.
19. UB Tübingen, RB est., RB to H. Bultmann, n.d. (1892), Mn 2-2740.

extensive park or from occasionally getting chased by the garden's watchmen.[20] But despite a hip problem that had troubled him from birth, he was evidently nimble enough to escape the watchman's clutches; nor did any physical impairment prevent him from taking part in the adventures typical of youngsters of his age.

A letter from the time in Rastede has been preserved in which the eleven year-old depicts in detail the festivities that took place here as everywhere in the Kaiser's Germany on Sedan Day, commemorating the Prussian victory over Napoleon III in 1870. In his report, the patriotic views that would have been affirmed in the official address given on this occasion play no role. Instead, he enumerates the dramatic events of the day: the twenty-five cannon rounds that were fired early in the morning, the children's entertainment, the gymnastic competitions in the marketplace, the evening torchlight procession, and the concluding fireworks. But most important to him was the delightful prospect that "Fried Heinen means to give me a torch."[21]

Even in old age he fondly recalled the camaraderie with his fellow-students in the elementary school in Rastede, which he attended until 1895. "I see it," he notes in looking back on those years, "as a great gain for my life and in particular for my scholarly work as well, that I was allowed to spend my early youth in the rural landscape of my home, that I was familiar with the rural lifestyle, that I spoke Low German with my schoolmates, took part in their games, and was thoroughly involved in their interests. From this has grown not only a strong feeling for home, but also . . . a sense for popular and rural ways of thinking and speaking, and an impulse to base the investigation of the history of spirit on language."[22] He was able to quench his thirst for knowledge not only at school but also at the home of a noble lady, and this became a special point of attraction for the boy. Miss von Wicht, a "very distinguished lady," owned many pictures and books and often read aloud to Rudolf. "There I was introduced for the first time to the German sagas and became enthused with Siegfried and Beowulf. . . . In our garden, which was nearly as large as a park, and which for that reason was largely given over to us to do as we liked, I immediately converted everything that had been heard and read into reality. There I defeated dragons and knights." As they benefitted from the powerful influence of nature on walks they took

20. Cf. UB Tübingen, RB est., RB to H. Feldmann, 19. 9. 1915, Mn 2-2739.

21. UB Tübingen, RB est., RB to H. Bultmann, 23. 8. 1895 (in prospect of letter dated 2. 9. 1895), Mn 2-2740.

22. RB, resume (fragment), Mn 2-3437; cf. H. Fischer-Barnicol, "Freiheit zur Zukunft," Mn 2-323.

together, Miss von Wicht also impressed upon him "this lesson: Whenever one sees something beautiful, one must also show it to other people. So, this I also decided to do and am thankful to the elderly lady for this and for much besides."[23] Bultmann was to observe this counsel his whole life, as one sees not least in the thousands of letters by which he communicated with his friends and conversation partners, and in which he shared with them what he was doing and how he was getting on.

As concerns his correspondence, the already mentioned letter to his mother, written three days after his eleventh birthday, offers a presentiment that its author was to become decidedly an *homme de lettres.* In it, Bultmann not only reports the details of Sedan Day and his own birthday, not only mentions the presents, but also illustrates the letter with a sketch of his sailboat so as to give his mother an impression of its condition—with an eye to negotiating a necessary improvement in the mast. Other than that he asks his mother to assure Peter, who had also gone along, that his little garden was being tended. For his own part, he reports that things are going well in school and that "I have not been homesick for you in quite some while." Asides such as these are precious: "I don't at all miss being bathed by Grosselehne" and, as a postscript, "Might Grosselehne, to whom I also send many greetings, wash my school socks?" The writing is stylistically flawless: "And now I will close my wonderful letter, containing not a single dictated word. Greetings to all, and especially Peter, and you most of all, and kisses from Your Rudolf."[24]

According to the preserved sources, Bultmann shared an affectionate relationship with his sisters. Around 1902 he corresponded with his sister Helene, who lived for a time in a boarding school for girls, on how the play *Über die Kraft* [*On Strength*], by the Norwegian playwright Bjørnsterne Bjørnson, was to be interpreted.[25] And in hardly a single one of the letters that he later sent to his parents from university did he neglect to make inquiries about his sisters and to show an interest in what was happening to them. And was Peter actually to be confirmed at Easter? Was Arthur still reading Grimms' tales? He would like to write to him again sometime. Writing from Tübingen in January, 1904, he wishes Lene "a good recovery from her toothaches."[26] Arthur in particular waited longingly for his eldest brother's

23. UB Tübingen, RB est., RB to H. Feldmann, 19. 9. 1915, Mn 2-2739.

24. UB Tübingen, RB est., RB to H. Bultmann, 23. 8. 1895, Mn 2-2740.

25. Cf. UB Tübingen, RB est., RB to H. Bultmann (later Pleus), 8. 12. 1901, Mn 2-2747; cf. A. Bultmann Lemke, "Unveröffentliche Nachlass," 13f.

26. UB Tübingen, RB est., RB to H. Bultmann, 20. 1. 1904, Mn 2-2740

semester vacation so that Rudolf could help him overcome his deficiencies in Latin and Greek and earn an ever-endangered promotion.[27]

Bultmann had attended the Grand Ducal Academy in Oldenburg since 1895. In 1897, he moved to Oldenburg with his family, since his father had been named incumbent of the pastorate at Oldenburg V (and, in 1901, that of Oldenburg III). Two years later, on March 26, 1899, Rudolf was confirmed there in St. Lambert's Church.[28] How he experienced the instruction prior to confirmation—did it come from his father?—we do not know. In a later missive he refers to his father's well-informed view that the instruction of confirmands was "very worthwhile," though the rite of confirmation itself was to be regarded as "foolish and shameful," for the misunderstanding too readily arose "that one was presenting to the confirmands a decisive step, as if they had to make a vow, as if they were in a certain sense 'finished.'" All the more necessary, then, to ensure a "better form of instruction" offered by better-educated pastors.[29]

During his time at school in the Oldenburg Academy, a new world opened to Rudolf: the cultural world of the humanities. Stimulated by his teachers, he developed a pronounced interest in art and literature. Besides instruction in religion, he absorbed Greek, Latin, and the history of German literature. For his birthdays and for Christmas he increasingly treasured the German classics and Shakespeare. "Homer and the Greek classics I read in school. That was just the world in which I lived."[30] As part of the middle-class cultural atmosphere of his home, it was understood that Rudolf should learn to play a musical instrument, the piano. His passion for the performing arts, however, did not meet with undivided agreement, since his mother wished to keep him and his sisters from visiting the opera and the theatre. But she was unable to enforce her will; indeed, despite her pietistic rigor she was remembered by her children and grandson as an affectionate and warmhearted woman. All in all, Bultmann preserved a lifelong gratitude to his parents for "the awakening of imagination, the joy of nature and of the beautiful, and the urge to read and to question, out of which over the course of time grew the passion for critical questioning and research."[31]

27. Cf. H. Ramsauer, "Rudolf Bultmann als Mensch und Lehrer," 12.

28. Cf. Archive of the Evangelical-Lutheran Oberkirchenrat Oldenburg, confirmation register, confirmed 1899.

29. UB Tübingen, RB est., RB to W. Fischer, 23. 4. 1908, Mn 2-2198.

30. Statement of Bultmann's in interview with H. Fischer-Barnicol, "Freiheit zur Zukunft"; cf. also Bultmann's autobiographical remarks of 1956 in B. Jaspert, *Barth-Bultmann Briefwechsel*, (2d ed.), 303.

31. RB, resume (fragment), Mn 2-3437.

As he looked back on his religious training, Bultmann said he "had been brought up as a child in very 'orthodox' fashion"; nevertheless, in "the final years in the academy" he also developed an inner urge to test ideas, during the course of which "the old conceptions gradually" fell away, "unconsciously at first, as I was defending them against others, and then consciously." About the time that his father gradually opened himself to a more liberal Protestantism—in the course of which he presumably discussed with his son the new religious orientation that faced them—Bultmann likewise freed himself from a number of old notions. Among these, surely, was the orthodox concept of faith mediated by his religious education, which held that any religion must necessarily contain objective content. This process of change was not an easy one. It would be "difficult, after all, to forget the old," confesses Bultmann to a friend at the end of 1904, alluding to Phil 3:13, and adds by way of explanation, "by the gleam of the Christmas candles, the voices of childhood come back to life, and one sees oneself again as a small child sitting on a stool at his mother's feet and hears her tell of the Savior." Bultmann appraised his own emancipation from the received interpretation of religion in a letter cited as a case in point of a general process of transformation taking place in history as a whole.[32] In a later autobiographical reflection, he said it came to him "as a deliverance" to have separated himself "without compromise . . . from false approaches, from deceitful conceptions of the beyond," and from the "magic of that old ecclesiasticism."[33]

Sometime after his seventh year of secondary school, Bultmann developed a close friendship with Leonhard Frank, one of his schoolmates. During the time of his spiritual and religious self-discovery, "the years when criticism of what has been handed down awakens, and the interest in philosophical questions becomes vivid," Frank was his most important conversation partner. The friends shared a variety of interests, read "a great deal together," discussed "free will or the immortality of the soul," and reconnoitered the surroundings of Oldenburg in their wanderings. It was specifically during these wanderings that Bultmann discovered "for the first time the beauty of the landscape of [his] native land," and he retained a deep love of his north German homeland all his life. The friendship with Leonhard Frank was supported by a trust that grew from "an insistence on the true and the good": and that included the readiness to resolve differing opinions. When Bultmann read aloud something of one of his poems, Frank was "in his

32. UB Tübingen, RB est., RB to E. Teufel, 31. 12. 1904, Mn 2-2393.
33. RB, *VW*, 106f.

sensible way . . . always an incorruptible judge and also able to be ironic in all friendship and goodness."[34]

On school vacations and later during semester vacations, Bultmann regularly visited his friend's home. Leonhard Frank was a Jew, the son of a cattle-dealer from Westerstede. Being few in number, the Jews of Westerstede did not have their own synagogue, and except for the high holy days they gathered for worship in a room in the Franks' home.[35] It is likely but not certain that the young Bultmann occasionally attended Jewish worship there while visiting his friend.[36] In any case, religious themes played a considerable role in the relations between the two friends. While students in Berlin in 1904–05, they read the Old Testament together and presented each other with Adolf Harnack's *What Is Christianity?*[37]

Through his relationship with Leonhard Frank, Bultmann was confronted early on with the questions regarding an independent status and future for Judaism in imperial Germany. After admission to legal studies in Leipzig, his friend joined a Jewish fraternity, thinking that this would best enable him to confront the widespread anti-Semitism in student circles. Bultmann was hesitant about this step because he thought that for Jewish students to organize themselves into a fraternity would be ineffective in overcoming the anti-Semitism that was rooted "deeply in the German people." But his friend countered that because of its nationalistic sentiment and a decision to distance itself from Zionism, his fraternity would avoid the risk of severing relations with other fraternities.[38] In December, 1905, Frank admitted to his friend that because of the recent persecutions of Jews in White Russia he had toyed with the idea "of converting to Christianity." Since clearly there was no prospect that the centuries-long hatred of Jews would soften in the future, Jews had only one way out of this miserable situation, and that was to be completely absorbed into the nations that had taken them in. In any case, they could hardly become an independent people, "since they no longer had a common language, culture, and ethnicity." In the course of their assimilation, Frank proposed, Jews would "in matters of morality and religion" enrich the nations that accepted them through the prominence of their spiritual accomplishments and their splendid sense of family, and

34. UB Tübingen, RB est., RB to H. Feldmann, 12. 7. 1917, Mn 2-3447.

35. Cf. W. Vahlenkamp, *Geschichte*, 34–38.

36. On what follows, cf. K. Hammann, "Rudolf Bultmanns Begegnung mit dem Judentum," 40–42.

37. UB Tübingen, RB est., RB to W. Fischer, 8. 12. 1904, Mn 2-2198; RB to H. Feldmann, 12. 7. 1917, Mn 2-3447.

38. Cf. UB Tübingen, RB est., L. Frank to RB, 25. 5. 1903 and 5. 8. 1903, Mn 2-765.

would thus make an important contribution to what was lacking in national unity.[39]

Even if Frank did not undertake the conversion to Christianity he had considered under duress, his considerations illustrate the severity of the pressure to acculturate that affected those Jews who, as part of academic culture, were especially exposed to the anti-Semitism of the empire of Kaiser Wilhelm. Like German Jewry as a whole, Frank struggled for the social recognition and equal rights of Jews by emphasizing his unequivocal national loyalty. And while on the basis of experience with Frank the young Bultmann recommended the acculturation of the Jews, he characteristically repudiated the condition that Jews give up their religious identity through baptism but rather declared himself in favor of their ethnic and social acculturation.[40] For him, Frank represented with "his strong sense of family," with his high view of vocation "that he regarded as service for the general public," and "in his pronounced sense of justice . . . a typical Jew in the best sense."[41]

Another student who likewise completed his studies in the upper classes of the Oldenburg Academy at the turn of the century was Karl Jaspers. He certainly saw the year-and-a-half-younger Bultmann on the school grounds—or so he recalled fifty years later through the roseate prism of a past during which both had become famous—but did not venture to admit having had closer contact with him. Jaspers found it sufficient to recall noticing the "shining eyes" of Bultmann and being glad of the presence of his fellow student.[42] In his senior year, Jaspers strenuously inveighed against the spirit of the school, which he perceived as an amalgam of humble submissiveness to secular authority and philological sophistry with a coat of scholarly paint. For this criticism he came into sharp conflict with the school administration.[43] Although such a rebellion against the academy's authorities was not in Bultmann's nature, he did criticize faulty pedagogical methods, the spiritless drumming-in of subject matter, and the teachers' lack of personal attention to their students.[44] But, all in all, he found school a happy experience. On February 23, 1903, the examination board of the Grand Ducal Academy awarded him his diploma, noting good or very good performance

39. UB Tübingen, RB est., L. Frank to RB, 3. 12. 1905, Mn 2-765.

40. Cf. UB Tübingen, RB est., RB to W. Fischer, 8. 10. 1905, Mn 2-2198.

41. UB Tübingen, RB est., RB to H. Feldmann, 12. 7. 1917, Mn 2-3447.

42. K. Jaspers, "Erwiderung auf Rudolf Bultmanns Antwort," in K. Jaspers and RB, *Die Frage der Entmythologisierung*, 138.

43. Cf. H. Saner, *Karl Jaspers*, 15f.

44. Cf. UB Tübingen, RB est., RB to W. Fischer, 22. 12. 1906, Mn 2-2198.

Plate 3: Rudolf Bultmann as a Graduate

in all subjects, and he maintained his amicable relations with several teachers long after he had left Oldenburg.[45]

During his time at school, Bultmann often vacationed with his family in the Black Forest, where he and his father enjoyed hiking. This helpful arrangement allowed them to visit the maternal grandparents, who lived in Denzlingen near Freiburg. He recorded his impressions in several drawings of the ruins at Zähringen and such motifs from Freiburg as the Swabian gate, both of which bespeak his artistic gift. On Christmas in 1906 he composed a poem there for his brother Peter, entitling it "New Year's Eve on Kandel [the highest hill in the Black Forest]: A Black Forest Poem."[46] In July, 1901, the sixteen-year-old first went alone to the health resort on the island of Wangeroog that had belonged to the Grand Duchy of Oldenburg since 1818. The isle and the sea made such an overwhelming impression on him that in the years to follow he traveled often to his island in the sea. When in 1908 he again followed this yearning, he depicted to a student friend the deep feelings that the North Sea kindled in him: "How everything works in harmony—the sea, shore, and dunes, and the sky with its sublime

45. Cf. UB Tübingen, RB est., correspondence of H. Böhnke (Mn 2-490) and H. Gerken with RB (Mn 2-824).

46. Cf. RB, poems, undated, Mn 2-247; Mn 2-3057.

Plate 4: A Drawing of Bultmann's from 1901

clouds! And from the wide, sweeping line of the horizon the scene obtains its incomparable calm and majesty. And the sound of the roar of the waves is constant, as beautiful as the loftiest fugue of Bach, with a thousand voices in ever-new gradations and combinations repeating the same mighty theme! And then—is it really so, or does it just seem to me that here the scenery, and above all that of the coast, is so much richer in color than that of the mountains? . . . [It] is a wondrous harmony of delicate, pure colors of the finest gradations."[47]

In 1901, during his first stay at Wangeroog, Bultmann artistically rendered the quintessential charm arising from the beauty of the island world in such picturesque motifs as a fishing boat on the shore, the old church tower, the dunes, the lighthouse of Wangeroog.[48] Two years later he entered a competition sponsored by the Oldenburg *Nachrichten für Stadt und Land* [*News of City and Country*], and received a first prize for his poem "Island Churchyard," with the epigraph "Wangeroog," and even though the newspaper divided the award between him and a fellow contestant, his poem appeared in the *News of City and Country* for July 11, 1903,[49] and he received twenty-five Reichsmarks.

47. UB Tübingen, RB est., RB to W. Fischer, 31. 8. 1908, Mn 2-2198.

48. Cf. Mn 2-3057. Bultmann's drawing, "The Old Church Tower on Wangeroog," is reproduced here and in R. Rittner, *Rudolf Bultmann und Oldenburg*, 8.

49. RB, "Inselkirchhof," in *Nachrichten*; cf. K. Müller, *Rudolf Bultmanns Erste Veröffentlichung*, 235f.

Island Churchyard

Grave and still the broad expanse,
Still in moonlit gleam
Peace above it hovers,
Like a blessed dream.

On the little hillocks,
Sway the grass and reed,
While black crosses tower,
Still and grave their deed.

White dunes in their silence,
Circling round, the sea
In the distance, calmly
Sounds eternally.

Happy, he to whom these
Peace and quiet bring;
Happy he to whom the sea
Its funeral song does sing.

Plate 5: Eduard Thurmann, Anna Bultmann (later Thurmann), Maria Bultmann (later Cold) and Rudolf Bultmann on Wangeroog in 1911

Bultmann composed the poem, his first publication, during his first semester of study in Tübingen. Soon after his arrival there he visited the Wurmlinger chapel nearby.[50] It may be that this visit and Ludwig Uhland's well-known popular poem, "Die Kapelle" ["The Chapel"], inspired him to make his own poetic effort. To be sure, both poems treat the theme of the transience of human life, though in quite different ways. Uhland contrasts the idyllic life of the shepherd boy in the valley with the sad tones of bells and the awful funeral dirge from the chapel on the mountain above in order to announce the inexorable *Memento mori*. Bultmann, in contrast, sees finite human life surrounded by the everlastingness of eternity, as it becomes visible and audible in the sight and sound of the waves. This poem certainly expresses the author's melancholy mood in crossing the threshold into adulthood. At the same time, one can perhaps read between the lines both the homesickness that Bultmann overcame during the first semester in Tübingen and his longing for the scenes of his early life in the Oldenburg Ammerland, in the Wesermarsch, and on Wangeroog. But "Island Churchyard," with its pantheistic echoes, was not to remain Bultmann's last word on a future hope that transcends death.

3. Theological Studies in Tübingen, Berlin, and Marburg

In 1903, I passed the academy's graduation examination and began to study theology at the University of Tübingen. After two semesters, I went to Berlin for two semesters and finally for two more to Marburg, attending lectures in philosophy and the history of philosophy, as well as in theology. During the time in Berlin, I also enjoyed visits to the theatre, concerts, and museums. The theological teachers to whom I am especially grateful were these: in Tübingen, the church historian Karl Müller; in Berlin, the Old Testament scholar Hermann Gunkel and the historian of doctrine Adolf Harnack; and in Marburg, the New Testament scholars Adolf Jülicher and Johannes Weiss and the systematic theologian Wilhelm Herrmann.[51]

On May 7, 1903, Bultmann matriculated at the University of Tübingen. He moved into his student quarters at 8 Neckarhalde, below the castle. He

50. Cf. UB Tübingen, RB est., RB to A. Bultmann, 24. 4. 1903, Mn 2-2735.

51. "Autobiographische Bemerkungen," B. Jaspert, *Barth-Bultmann Briefwechsel* (2d ed.), 303.

did not like the new surroundings at all, at least not during the first weeks. The city in itself was "extremely ugly."[52] He was always glad when he "met a North German, for it [seems to me] that anyone who would move to Tübingen without having to should have his head examined. In contrast, Oldenburg is so beautiful!" Only because of his professors could he imagine staying longer than one semester.[53] To be sure, the Tübingen summer brought a definite revision of his first impressions. At the end of October, 1903, Bultmann sent his sister Helene a detailed description of how he had furnished his room. The interior was done to remind him of home: on the walls were scenes of Oldenburg and Wangeroog framing twin portraits of his parents; on the chest of drawers he placed pictures of his youngest brother Arthur, Goethe, and Schiller; and in front of these his smoking paraphernalia. Finally, the view overlooking the huge seminary buildings, the Neckar, the Platanenallee, and the Swabian mountains gradually reconciled him to the less favorable local conditions.[54]

Bultmann quickly found a placed in Tübingen student life. He sang in the university choir, took part in the performances of the academic musical society, and his cousin Peter Ramsauer from Oldenburg, who was studying jurisprudence in Tübingen, introduced him to the liberal student fraternity *Igel* [*Hedgehog*] in the summer semester of 1903. Even if at first Bultmann was only a guest,[55] he nevertheless still belonged to a group of students who took a lively part in the activities of the fraternity. He was enthusiastic about the communal life and the pub-going in *Igel*. This non-dueling fraternity, which had been founded in 1871, had in the summer of 1902 just moved into a new house on the castle mount, "the most beautiful building in Tübingen."[56] Here Bultmann found a group of friends with whom he would remain connected his whole life: the theologians Wilhelm Gottschick, Hermann Lahusen, Hermann Noltenius and Eberhard Teufel, as well as the physician Walther Fischer. During the semester they walked in and all around the university city, the valley of the Neckar, and the Swabian mountains. In the spring of 1904, Bultmann traveled with these companions to Florence, where he surveyed Renaissance art in the many churches, the Uffizi Gallery, and the Palazzo Pitti. He developed a particularly strong relationship with Walther Fischer, and during their time together as stu-

52. UB Tübingen, RB est., RB to H. Bultmann, 25. 4. 1903, Mn 2-2740.
53. UB Tübingen, RB est., RB to H. Bultmann, 10. 5. 1903, Mn 2-2740.
54. UB Tübingen, RB est., RB to (his sister) H. Bultmann, 28. 10. 1903, Mn 2-2747.
55. Cf. M. Evang, *Frühzeit*, 12f.
56. UB Tübingen, RB est., RB to H. Bultmann, 10. 5. 1903, Mn 2-2740.

dents they carried on many long and deep discussions of art, literature, and music.[57]

Bultmann's keen desire for cultivated conversation was met by the Tübingen theological professors' habit of taking a personal interest in their students, whom they regularly invited to their homes in the evening.[58] But that was not all, for even early on Bultmann did not limit himself to taking courses in the department of theology.[59] He listened to Karl Voretzsch on the folkloric study of folksongs and folktales, and Hermann von Fischer, his friend's father, introduced him to the history of German literature, as well as to the life and work of Lessing. The philosopher Christoph von Sigwart, whose course on metaphysics Bultmann attended in the summer semester of 1903, influenced the young student the most: "To be sure, he is very old, but his lecturing is wonderful. The language is rich, flowing, perfect, and everything is full of spirit and ideas. I have to pay extraordinarily close attention in order always to be able to follow him. Sigwart is, as everyone knows, the most important professor of this place and the pride of the University of Tübingen."[60]

On the Protestant theological faculty at the beginning of the twentieth century, representatives of the school of Albrecht Ritschl—people like Johannes Gottschick, Theodor Haering, and Karl Müller—set the tone. To be sure, pietist circles within the Württemburg State Church had in 1897 made arrangements for an additional theological professor, who was to provide a counterweight to the dominant historical orientation of the faculty. Adolf Schlatter, who had filled this professorship since 1898, had a hard job in Tübingen at first. This Swiss New Testament scholar, who was in various respects an outsider to academic theology, was seen by many students as a biblically pious but not really critical theologian. Bultmann, too, found Schlatter unappealing: "After what I heard from Schlatter, I was *very* disappointed. He *bores* me to an extraordinary degree. He does speak freely and spiritedly, but he is pedantic and the thoughts are poor."[61] Bultmann simply

57. Cf. A. Bultmann Lemke, "Unveröffentliche Nachlass,“ 16–18. W. Fischer, son of the Tübingen historian of literature Hermann von Fischer, was evidently Bultmann's "big brother," who familiarized his "little brother" with fraternity life. Cf. also V. Hoffmann, *Leben*.

58. Cf. UB Tübingen, RB est., RB to H. Bultmann, 20. 1. and 28. 2. 1904, Mn 2-2740.

59. Cf. the lists of the courses Bultmann attended in Tübingen, Berlin, and Marburg in M. Evang, *Frühzeit*, 8f, 13f, 20f.

60. UB Tübingen, RB est., RB to H. Bultmann, 25. 4. 1903, Mn 2-2740; this passage is also in A. Bultmann Lemke, "Unveröffentliche Nachlass," 15.

61. UB Tübingen, RB est., RB to H. Bultmann, 25. 4. 1903, Mn 2-2740.

could not warm up to Schlatter's lectures,[62] and so he temporized by sending his pietist mother two of Schlatter's printed sermons.[63] Later, all of this criticism notwithstanding, he came to understand more fully and to respect Schlatter's contribution to New Testament exegesis.[64]

Bultmann attended two sets of lectures by the Ritschlian Johannes Gottschick, "Theological Encyclopedia" and "Luther's Theology." Bultmann's correspondence gives no information regarding his impression of Gottshick, even though this man was the father of his student friend Wilhelm Gottschick, and was the first publisher of *Zeitschrift fur Theologie und Kirche* [*Journal for Theology and Church*], the Ritschlian school's academic journal that he headed until 1906. Looking back on his student days at Tübingen, Bultmann recorded with restraint, "What I got from Gottschick is only now gradually becoming clear to me."[65] A more lasting influence on the young theological student was that of Theodor Haering, who sought in his thinking to add a personal, mostly pietistic surface to the structure of Christian faith and ethics he had taken over from Albrecht Ritschl. Bultmann attended three systematic and two exegetical courses of lectures by Haering, whom he found to be, "a thoroughly hearty, simple person. His delivery is attractive, deeply inward, and often full of humor besides."[66] Clearly, Bultmann was deeply affected by Haering's sermons,[67] for he later prepared for the first-level exams in systematic theology with the dogmatics and ethics of Haering at hand.[68]

And Haering's dogmatics led Bultmann to corroborate the judgment of Wilhelm Herrmann that this exposition best fulfills "the requirements of a doctrine of faith—a *Glaubenslehre*."[69] Haering explained "with marvelous clarity what faith is about; what personal faith means, how it is grounded in the revelation of the personal God, who is love and holiness." For Bultmann, the conceptual transparency of Haering's dogmatics ultimately reflected the "personality that stands behind the book and that one ever hears speaking to oneself."[70] It was also the systematician Haering who, with his lectures on Romans in the winter semester of 1903/04, gave Bultmann his introduction

62. UB Tübingen, RB est., RB to H. Bultmann, 10. 5. 1903, Mn 2-2740.

63. Cf. UB Tübingen, RB est., RB to H. Bultmann, 20. 1. 1904, Mn 2-2740.

64. Cf. RB, "Vier neue Darstellungen," in RB, *Theologie als Kritik*, 50–52; RB, *Theologie des Neuen Testaments*, 597f.

65. UB Tübingen, RB est., RB to E. Teufel, 25. 6. 1906, Mn 2-2393.

66. UB Tübingen, RB est., RB to H. Bultmann, 25. 4. 1903, Mn 2-2740.

67. Cf. UB Tübingen, RB est., RB to E. Teufel, 25. 7. 1906, Mn 2-2393.

68. Cf. T. Haering, *Das christliche Leben*; T. Haering, *Der christliche Glaube*.

69. UB Tübingen, RB est., RB to E. Teufel, 25. 7. 1906, Mn 2-2393.

70. UB Tübingen, RB est., RB to E. Teufel, 25. 3. 1907, Mn 2-2393.

Plate 6: Karl Müller

to Pauline theology.[71] And more than twenty years later, Bultmann harked back to Haering's exposition of the Johannine letters presented in the summer semester of 1904. When he forwarded his *Analyse des ersten Johannesbriefes* [*Analysis of the First Letter of John*] to Haering in 1927, he returned thanks for his old teacher's exegetical efforts.[72]

Among the theologians of Tübingen, the church historian Karl Müller was the one who made the greatest impression on Bultmann. I "enjoy him extraordinarily. He is no great speaker, but everything he says is subtle, spirited, carefully considered, and fascinating."[73] As Bultmann recalled in 1916, Müller made me "enthusiastic about historical scholarship. . . . I owe a great deal to his lectures, as well as to personal contact with him. At that time, during my first Tübingen semesters, I and my friends Noltenius and Lahusen were very adventurous, and Müller once told me later that the three semesters during which we and the other students visited in his house surely marked the finest fellowship he ever enjoyed with students.[74]

During the era of historicism, when Protestant church historiography was at its height, Karl Müller was counted among the leading representatives of his discipline. In Tübingen he carried forward the important tradition that arose from Ferdinand Christian Baur and Carl Heinrich Weizsäcker. To be sure, Müller distanced himself from approaches that sought to understand church history in terms of evolutionary development taken from the

71. Cf. Bultmann's note in UB Tübingen, RB Est.: "Letter to the Romans, Theodor Haering. Tübingen, winter semester 1903–04," Mn 2-3093; also K. de Valerio, *Altes Testament*, 98–100.

72. Cf. RB to Theodor Haering, n.d. (1927), in H. Haering, *Theodor Haering*, 400f; also RB, "Analyse des Ersten Johannesbriefes (1927)," in RB, *Exegetica*, 105–23.

73. UB Tübingen, RB est., RB to H. Bultmann, 25. 4. 1903, Mn 2-2740.

74. UB Tübingen, RB est., RB to H. Feldmann, 24. 8. 1916, Mn 2-3447.

history of ideas or the norms of dogmatics. He understood church history as a part of history in general, and recognized the particular dynamics of historical epochs. Accordingly in his works he ascribed considerable weight to the phenomena of church history, institutions, law, and organizational structure. Bultmann became acquainted with what were then these new and pioneering holistic perspectives, for while in Tübingen he attended Müller's course of lectures on church history over three semesters and took part in his seminar.

Also in his lecture course entitled "Creeds," Müller took pains to make his students familiar not only with the doctrines but also with the constitution, the worship, and the religious character of the different Christian confessions. Bultmann, who up until then had scarcely any contact with the Catholic Church, here acquired his first instruction in matters of Catholic popular piety, for Müller produced Catholic literature, both devotional and formational books by Jesuits, and quoted from them. "The other day he also brought rosaries, medals and scapulars with him and passed them around. I had not had the remotest idea what paganism existed in the Catholic Church, what idolatry, what superstition, what foolish magic. . . . This calls itself Christianity! It is simply hair-raising."[75] The superiority of Protestant Christianity to the Catholic Church that in his debate with Johann Adam Möhler Ferdinand Christian Baur had sought to demonstrate eighty years earlier in the same place, and in a similar manner using the resources of the Hegelian philosophy of history, Müller now grounded in a comparative analysis of the constitution, law, worship, and popular piety characteristic of the great Christian confessions. He evidently shared the opinion widespread in liberal Protestantism that because of its largely conservative, partly pre-Enlightenment orientation, Catholic confessional culture was by nature unsuited to the modern world.

Bultmann hoped—in vain, as it turned out—that the second part of the second volume of Karl Müller's *Kirchengeschichte* [*History of the Church*] would appear in time for him to use it in preparing for his exams.[76] Already in his student days, as his recommendation to his friend Walther Fischer attests, he had clearly and correctly judged the importance of his Tübingen teacher's major work: "If sometime you have the opportunity, take a look at the history of the Reformation in Müller's *Kirchengeschichte*, which is masterful; one cannot help but notice how much he regrets that he cannot

75. UB Tübingen, RB est., RB to (his sister) H. Bultmann, 7. 7. 1904, Mn 2-2747; also in A. Bultmann Lemke, "Unveröffentliche Nachlass," 15f.

76. Cf. UB Tübingen, RB est., RB to E. Teufel, 25. 7. 1906, Mn 2-2393.

convey even more; his mastery of the material is really amazing."[77] When Bultmann left Tübingen following the summer semester of 1904, he was grateful that there in the seminary lecture hall he had encountered teachers who "had implanted in him for the first time the understanding of and the true love for theology.[78]

Bultmann continued his studies in Berlin, but life in the big city did not agree with him at all. During his first semester there he suffered from headaches, fatigue, and nervousness; indeed, some days he could not work at all. To keep up his spirits he spent as much time as possible traveling to Grunewald or to the Wannsee, for his gloomy rear apartment at 11 Albrecht St. was far from cheerful. He thought longingly of the pubs in the *Igel* in Tübingen, where he would have been glad to sit and sing college songs to himself in his lonely hours.[79] When he spent Christmas of 1904 at home, he had a "desire to feel a good, fresh wind blowing in from the sea, for in Berlin one gets absolutely no trace of nature or anything primitive."[80] Following the winter semester of 1904–05, he went immediately back to Oldenburg—uttering a sigh of relief that he "had left Berlin. Ah, to have escaped everything artificial, hackneyed, and hollow!"[81]

But the anonymity of the big city forced Bultmann to be productive. No one in Berlin seemed to value the kind of personal exchange between professors and students he had experienced in Tübingen. At least, however, he enjoyed the city's rich offerings in the visual and performing arts.[82] Frequent trips to the Lessing and German Theatres allowed him to attend performances of Wagner's operas *Lohengrin* and *Die Meistersinger*, as well as Shakespeare's *Merchant of Venice*, *Macbeth* (with Adalbert Matkowski, whom Bultmann admired, in the title role), and *A Midsummer Night's Dream*. The twenty-year-old student of theology could also regularly be seen in the city's museums, and after Ascension Day, 1905, he allowed himself a visit of several days to Dresden. There he spent his time almost exclusively in art galleries, where Raphael's "Sistine Madonna" and Dutch paintings, above all those of Rembrandt, left deep impressions on him.[83] He had a high regard for Rembrandt, who not only saw things as they were but also saw

77. UB Tübingen, RB est., RB to W. Fischer, 3. 9. 1906, Mn 2-2198; cf. K Müller, *Kirchengeschichte*.

78. UB Tübingen, RB est., RB to E. Teufel, 25. 6. 1906, Mn 2-2393.

79. UB Tübingen, RB est., RB to W. Fischer, 8. 12. 1904, Mn 2-2198.

80. UB Tübingen, RB est., RB to W. Fischer, 31. 12. 1904, Mn 2-2198.

81. UB Tübingen, RB est., RB to W. Fischer, 2. 4. 1905, Mn 2-2198.

82. Cf. T. Kucharz, *Theologen und ihre Dichter*, 169–74.

83. Cf. UB Tübingen, RB est., RB to W. Fischer, 5. 6. 1905, Mn 2-2198.

the world from a higher vantage point and did not lose himself in its physical attributes. "Rembrandt's 'Hundred Guilder Note' is nearly my favorite painting; its Christ is my favorite of anything ever painted."[84] Nonetheless, such contemporary painters as Heinrich Vogeler of Worpswede also fascinated Bultmann.[85]

During his time in Berlin, Charles Dickens' *David Copperfield* became his favorite reading material, with Gottfried Keller's *Grüner Heinrich* close behind.[86] Selma Lagerlöf's *Gutsgeschichte* and *Gösta Berling* also appeared on his extensive reading list;[87] and when in 1905 *Hilligenlei*, the bestselling novel of the Dithmar rural pastor Gustav Frenssen, appeared, Bultmann joined other enthusiastic readers of this saga of people who were searching for a holy land called "Hilligenlei." Did his approval of this novel turn out to be so emphatic because the twenty-one-year-old was himself in search of a "holy land" and thus open to perspectives capable of expressing his theological attitudes? Surely he was attracted by the beauty of Frenssen's characters and settings, and by a sense that the author had drawn a picture of Jesus and his eschatological ethical-religious message that rendered in appropriate literary style the insights of recent critical theology.[88]

The Berlin semesters of study turned out to be fruitful for Bultmann, inasmuch as he was able further to clarify his ideas about the task of theology relative to the future of the church. In his characterizations of the Berlin professors whose courses he attended, he repeatedly included reflections about both the content and shortcomings of current studies in theology. In the case of the systematician Julius Kaftan, these suggestions had an exceedingly negative flavor. At first, Bultmann praised the richness of the professor's thought and precision,[89] yet Kaftan increasingly seemed "a terrible sophist and scholastic."[90] Since at this time Bultmann was finding dogmatics his greatest irritation, the problem was surely related to Kaftan's course in dogmatics; but it was more widely rooted in Bultmann's general aversion to theological traditionalism. How stubbornly people held onto received tradi-

84. UB Tübingen, RB est., RB to W. Fischer, 30. 1. 1906, Mn 2-2198.

85. Cf. UB Tübingen, RB est., RB to W. Fischer, 7. 7. 1905, Mn 2-2198.

86. Cf. UB Tübingen, RB est., RB to W. Fischer, 2. 4. 1905, Mn 2-2198.

87. Cf. UB Tübingen, RB est., RB to W. Fischer, 8. 10. 1905, Mn 2-2198.

88. Cf. UB Tübingen, RB est., RB to W. Fischer, 30. 1. 1906, Mn 2-2198; on the differences between Bultmann's judgment and the self-understanding of the popular author G. Frenssen, cf. T. Kucharz, *Theologen und ihre Dichter*, 173.

89. Cf. UB Tübingen, RB est., RB to E. Teufel, 28. 10. 1904, Mn 2-2393.

90. UB Tübingen, RB est., RB to W. Fischer, 7. 7. 1905, Mn 2-2198.

tions was an inescapable reality, even in the case of his own family, and chiefly in the person of his mother. For this reason, reform was urgently required to free dogmatics from its superfluous ballast! "What a bunch of nonsense is retained about 'revelation,' 'Trinity,' 'miracle,' 'divine attributes'—it is frightful!"[91] In Bultmann's view, Kaftan was not the person from whom one could expect a constructive contribution to the renewal of dogmatic theology. More than thirty years later, Bultmann recalled hearing with sharp dissatisfaction Kaftan's decree that "If the kingdom of God is something eschatological, then it is a concept of no use to dogmatics."[92]

How were things to proceed for theology and the church now that the grand and solid doctrinal edifice of the old orthodoxy had collapsed? Bultmann could perceive in the present or the foreseeable future no viable conceptuality that might replace what had become the untenable normative commitments of traditional Christianity.[93] He was fully aware of the enormous achievements that the historical disciplines had brought to modern theology, but he had also developed a strong sense of the problems of the very historicism that had undermined the received doctrinal system. What was lacking, as Bultmann forecast the overall theological weather in 1905, was "a spirit that took hold of the achievements of historical theology and turned them to account systematically, one that would create a theology that was really new from the bottom up."[94]

In the church historian Adolf Harnack, Bultmann encountered the leading representative of liberal Protestantism in the Wilhelmian era. To his regret, he could not yet attend Harnack's seminar as a full participant, yet the "hours of intense and fruitful work" in this course remained vivid in his memory.[95] Bultmann also attended two of Harnack's lecture courses: "The History of Dogma" in the winter semester of 1904–05 and "History of (Nineteenth-Century) Protestantism" in the summer semester of 1905. First of all, Harnack's delivery made an extraordinary impression on Bultmann. "He speaks *completely* extemporaneously, calmly, without emotion and without sham ornamentation, slowly but impressively. Each sentence is

91. UB Tübingen, RB est., RB to W. Fischer, 5. 6. 1905, Mn 2-2198.

92. RB, "Johannes Weiss zum Gedächtnis," 242–46; cf. RB, "Jesus Christus und die Mythologie," *GuV*, vol. 4, 142. However, Bultmann acknowledges here that Kaftan himself later revised this view.

93. Cf. UB Tübingen, RB est., RB to W. Fischer, 31. 12. 1904, Mn 2-2198.

94. UB Tübingen, RB est., RB to W. Fischer, 5. 6. 1905, Mn 2-2198; also in A. Bultmann Lemke, "Unveröffentliche Nachlass," 18.

95. RB, review of A. von Harnack, *Einführung in die alte Kirchengeschichte*, 1929 (1930), in RB, *Theologie als Kritik*, 241.

Plate 7: Adolf von Harnack

thought out precisely before it is uttered, and the listener is compelled by the impression his words make to think along with him. . . . I believe one can call Harnack the ideal lecturer."[96] To be sure, the longer Bultmann listened to the doctrinal historian, the more a degree of qualification blends with his continuing admiration. By the end of 1904, Bultmann perceived that if he had not studied with Karl Müller in Tübingen, Harnack might have become a dangerous influence.[97] "Harnack lets his own spirit shine a bit too readily, whereas Müller in Tübingen was always earnest and always solid."[98] Such nuanced observations at last brought Bultmann to conclude that Harnack was "too very learned" and therefore not suited to lead a fundamental renewal of theology and its responsibility to the church.[99] But despite these limitations, the great liberal theologian retained his preeminent place in Bultmann's regard.[100]

During his theological studies in Berlin, Bultmann focused intensively on the study of the Old Testament. This had much to do with the unusual teaching ability of Hermann Gunkel, a gift that earned the Adjunct Professor of Old Testament a greater influence among students than that of the tenured professors in his field.[101] Bultmann, who attended four series of his lectures of eleven hours a week, was equally enthusiastic: "Gunkel is young, lively, fiery. He is extremely interesting, polemical, but is always subtle and distinguished."[102] Under the guidance of Gunkel, the co-founder of

96. UB Tübingen, RB est., RB to E. Teufel, 28. 10. 1904, Mn 2-2393.
97. Cf. UB Tübingen, RB est., RB to E. Teufel, 31. 12. 1904, Mn 2-2393.
98. UB Tübingen, RB est., RB to W. Fischer, 7. 7. 1905, Mn 2-2198.
99. UB Tübingen, RB est., RB to W. Fischer, 5. 6. 1905, Mn 2-2198.
100. Cf. M. Evang, *Frühzeit*, 15f.
101. Cf. R. Smend, "Hermann Gunkel: 1862–1932," in R. Smend, *Deutsche Alttestamentler*, 166.
102. RB to E. Teufel, 28. 10. 1904, Mn 2-2393.

the history-of-religions school, Bultmann devoted himself ever more closely to the scholarly study of the Hebrew Bible, and thereafter continued to be powerfully influenced by Gunkel's literary and history-of-religions perspective.[103]

Plate 8: Hermann Gunkel

To be sure, their close personal contact began not during the time in Berlin, but on Wangeroog in the summer of 1908. Still, what Bultmann learned as a student in Berlin and thereafter from the trail-blazer in Old Testament form-criticism, always remained with him.[104] What Gunkel conveyed in the lecture hall in Berlin, Bultmann recorded in two sets of notes. According to these, Gunkel used the same organizational pattern in his course on "Theology of the Old Testament," which summarized the history of Old Testament religion, and his lecture, "The Formation of the Old Testament," in which he offered the history of the literature of Israel. In the latter case, after an introduction he treated in the first main section the popular religion of Israel, namely its folk poetry. The second main section consisted of a presentation of the prophetic movement: the great authors, the prophets and psalmists. A concise concluding section was devoted to Judaism—that is, to Jewish literature.[105]

Bultmann further occupied himself with the Old Testament apart from Gunkel's courses of lectures. He read it together with his Jewish friend, Leonhard Frank, who was continuing the study of jurisprudence he had begun in Leipzig. "It is a grand book indeed! Parts of it achieve the heights of the Greek epics"—so reads Bultmann's summation, evidently informed by

103. RB to W. Fischer, 11. 9. 1904, Mn 2-2303. "So, I am busy with a so-called Introduction to the Old Testament, that is to say, the history of how the O.T. came to be. It is most interesting, on account of the issues in the history of religions."

104. Cf. RB, *Die Geschichte der synoptischen Tradition*, 1921, iv.

105. Cf. the analysis of the lecture-notes in K. de Valerio, *Altes Testament*, 50–96.

Gunkel's aesthetic way of looking at things.[106] To be sure, he put to himself the question of whether the ancient sagas of Genesis or the tales of Saul and David were proper material for the religious education of children. He took the Old Testament stories to be indispensable if one were unable to replace them with something of equal value; but he observed that in the long run it would be fatal "to tell stories which, in the ancient times in question were taken to be true . . . , but which later, upon being explained, would have to be declared to be untrue."[107]

But although the two semesters in Berlin brought Bultmann profound intellectual stimulation, he could not really acquire a taste for the city. The two sentiments merged into one as he assessed his time as a student in Berlin: "It was great, despite everything."[108] In Marburg, on the other hand, the final phase of his studies went very smoothly. A decade later he recalled coming to the Hessian university town in the autumn of 1905 with great expectations. Marburg "had been from the first semester onwards the goal of my longing, and in the sixth, I was allowed to go there for the first time. I well remember how I enjoyed my student days at Marburg, where I focused my life entirely on the lectures and study."[109] Undisturbed by any distractions, Bultmann threw himself completely into his work,[110] and completed the enormous total of thirteen lecture courses of twenty-seven hours a week in the winter semester of 1905–06, and another eight courses and seminars of seventeen hours a week in the summer semester of 1906.

In choosing courses, Bultmann was guided by their usefulness in preparing for the approaching exam and by his preference for certain lecturers. He also attended courses because their topics awakened his interest. To these belonged Friedrich Wiegand's lectures on creeds and Carl Mirbt's on the modern history of Christian denominations. Mirbt, who among contemporary Protestant theologians knew most about Roman Catholicism, was especially effective in his specialty.[111] Bultmann also devoted his time in Marburg to what was new in philosophy. He found himself less influenced by Martin Rade's introduction to Kant's philosophy of religion than by the four-hour-long lecture course on logic by Paul Natorp, who along with Hermann

106. UB Tübingen, RB est., RB to W. Fischer, 8. 12. 1904, Mn 2-2198.

107. UB Tübingen, RB est., RB to W. Fischer, 31. 12. 1904, Mn 2-2198; cf. RB to E. Teufel, 31. 12. 1904, Mn 2-2393.

108. UB Tübingen, RB est., RB to W. Fischer, 8. 10. 1905, Mn 2-2198.

109. UB Tübingen, RB est., RB to H. Feldmann, 25. 9. 1916, Mn 2-3447.

110. UB Tübingen, RB est., RB to W. Fischer, 9. 11. 1905, Mn 2-2198: "My . . . life is my studies."

111. Cf. UB Tübingen, RB est., RB to E. Teufel, 25. 6. 1906, Mn 2-2393.

Plate 9: Adolf Jülicher

Cohen was the most authoritative representative of Marburg Neo-Kantianism. Natorp "is a superb Kant scholar, and for this reason the course is particularly worthwhile."[112] Finally, Bultmann was able to follow his aesthetic inclinations through two shorter courses by the practical theologian Johannes Bauer on the religious lyric poetry of the nineteenth century and the history of Protestant architecture.

Among the classical theological disciplines, Bultmann had so extensively studied the Old Testament with Hermann Gunkel in Berlin that he hardly bothered with the offerings of the Marburg Old Testament scholar Karl Budde;[113] instead he concentrated on the New Testament, which in Marburg was brilliantly expounded by Adolf Jülicher and Johannes Weiss. Bultmann repeatedly placed Jülicher at the very top rung in his evaluation of professors at Marburg. "He is my favorite teacher here—of absolute truthfulness, self-denial, and conscientiousness; and besides this, full of warmth and ardor for his work. He has helped me personally several times with his counsel."[114] Although Bultmann attended only two of Jülicher's lecture-courses,[115] he retained an unreserved respect for the New Testament scholar from that time on. He especially appreciated Jülicher's rigorous efforts at a purely historical interpretation of earliest Christianity, finding Jülicher's presentation of the religion of Jesus in "Present-Day Culture" to be excellent.[116] In his 1906 lectures Wilhelm Herrmann called

112. UB Tübingen, RB est., RB to E. Teufel, 25. 6. 1906, Mn 2-2393.

113. Cf. Bultmann's autobiographical notes from the early summer of 1969, in B. Jaspert, *Barth-Bultmann Briefwechsel* (2d ed.), 311.

114. UB Tübingen, RB est., RB to E. Teufel, 25. 6. 1906, Mn 2-2393; cf. also RB to W. Fischer, 9. 11. 1905, Mn 2-2198.

115. All the same, in WS 1905–06, he wrote an assignment in Jülicher's church history seminar on Gnosticism: "The Theology of Heracleon according to the Remnants of his Commentary on John 4."

116. Cf. UB Tübingen, RB est., RB to W. Fischer, 3. 9. 1906, Mn 2-2198; cf. A. Jülicher, "Die Religion Jesu und die Anfänge des Christentums bis zum Nicaenum (325)."

the pictures of Jesus by Jülicher and Julius Wellhausen "the two best we were likely to have" but also complained that neither had consistently followed the principle, *Christum cognoscere, hoc est: beneficia eius cognoscere* [To know Christ is to recognize his gifts]. Bultmann could not assent to this judgment, since for him the superior quality of Jülicher's picture of Christ consisted precisely in its capacity to employ exclusively historical evidence in rendering transparent the *beneficia Christi.*[117]

Plate 10: Johannes Weiss

The bulk of the New Testament courses attended by Bultmann were two lecture courses and two seminars given by Johannes Weiss, the New Testament scholar who, like Hermann Gunkel, represented the history-of-religions school. Weiss is "always interesting" and impresses "through his ability to perceive things."[118] To this impression of 1906 Bultmann added in 1939 a memorial for his teacher, in which he included reminiscences from his time as a student in Marburg. In this article Weiss was portrayed as the ideal embodiment of the conjunction of researcher and teacher. "He gave his lectures with great fervor and joy. His delivery was flowing and lively, and clearly organized and crafted. He depended very little on lecture-notes, and in fact sometimes (as when explaining the Letters to the Corinthians) he spoke completely extemporaneously and had only the text of the New Testament as the basis of his presentation." In his academic teaching Weiss followed the maxim "to awaken in his listeners a desire for independent work and the capacity for independent judgment."[119]

The two semesters at Marburg were the happiest time of his student years—not so much because of the theological stimuli that he received in the lecture hall as due to the atmosphere that was created by and characteristic of the liberal faculty. Unlike the situation in Berlin, profes-

117. UB Tübingen, RB est., RB to E. Teufel, 25. 7. 1906, Mn 2-2393; cf. P. Melanchthon.
118. UB Tübingen, RB est., RB to E. Teufel, 25. 6. 1906, Mn 2-2393.
119. RB, "Johannes Weiss zum Gedächtnis," 244f.

Plate 11: Wilhelm Herrmann

sors and students here cultivated personal contacts, and largely on that account Bultmann found Marburg "ideal for theology."[120] He accepted gladly the invitations of the professors to open evenings, to sociable exchange on art and literature, and to shared music-making. He was an especially frequent guest in the house of Martin Rade, the publisher of *Die Christliche Welt*. Rade took a real interest in Bultmann, though his theological influence on the young "friend of *Die Christliche Welt*" had clear boundaries. In his personal relationship with Rade, Bultmann experienced from the outset a distinct standoffishness on Rade's part, a trait that he later acknowledged would sometimes manifest itself in cool rejection. Regardless of this distance, Bultmann and Rade maintained a strong mutual regard.[121]

Among the professors of theology at Marburg, the systematic theologian Wilhelm Herrmann was probably the only one with whom Bultmann could not develop a personal relationship.[122] In the summer semester of 1906, he took part in Herrmann's course "Dogmatics I" and in his seminar. To be sure, the work of this most important systematician of the school of Albrecht Ritschl affected Bultmann's theological thinking in a lasting way, but only in the long term. At the time, he had ambivalent feelings about Herrmann *as a lecturer*: "With respect to *conceptualizing* the problems clearly, he does not satisfy me, and the way he poses questions often obscures the issue. But one cannot escape the impact of his powerful religious and moral personality. Nearly every session is like a worship service; a peculiarly solemn voice ever holds sway, and one always goes out with the feeling that one can and must become a better person."[123] The reservation concerning the effectiveness of Herrmann's argumentation, woven as it is into this description of the

120. UB Tübingen, RB est., RB to W. Fischer, 30. 1. 1906, Mn 2-2198.
121. Cf. UB Tübingen, RB est., RB to H. Feldmann, 4./5. 10. 1916, Mn 2-3447.
122. Cf. UB Tübingen, RB est., RB to H. Feldmann, 4./5. 10. 1916, Mn 2-3447.
123. UB Tübingen, RB est., RB to E. Teufel, 25. 6. 1906, Mn 2-2393.

professor's religious aura, is typical of the process of generating stimulating questions that Bultmann later made the central task of theology.

The study of practical theology traditionally presupposed knowledge and competence in the exegetical disciplines, in the history of both the church and theology, and in systematic theology. In Marburg, then, Bultmann attended his first intensive courses in practical theology. In these, he was less interested in catechetics—to which he was introduced by means of a course on Luther's catechisms by Ernst Christian Achelis—than in homiletics. He took part in two homiletical practicums that had been felicitously designed by the practical theologian Johannes Bauer. "Bauer has a subtle understanding of the difficulties that we experience in thinking about the practical office—he is so clear, so fresh and certain of victory in this regard."[124]

During his time as a student, Bultmann had often concerned himself with the problems of the pastoral office that arose from the relation between preaching and the traditional language of worship, especially in the matter of the task of theology *vis-à-vis* ecclesial praxis. He spoke of these difficulties in April, 1906, in the course of criticizing a highly controversial Good Friday sermon about the two thieves crucified with Jesus. Bultmann took offense that the sermon had done violence to the biblical text. It displeased him even more that the preacher satisfied himself with employing the "comfortable old formulas." The truth of Christianity, which it is the duty of the sermon to set forth, could be appropriately expounded only if it were expressed in terms of the thought-world and life-world of the hearers. This fundamental hermeneutical task could hardly be acknowledged, let alone fulfilled, if a preacher merely presented his subject-matter "by means of the old dogmatic formulas."[125]

As successful examples of a modern form of preaching, the "village sermons" of Gustav Frenssen filled the bill for the young Bultmann. "I have reread several of these only recently and find them just about ideal. He knows how to translate the old stories into North German and to make them useful, without trying for some subtle manner. Such sermons are really a model, and their only equals are those of Dörries and (perhaps) in part the prayers of Naumann."[126] In the first two decades following 1900, the "village sermons" of the Dithmar pastor and novelist went on to become the most successful collection of sermons in the German language. They owed

124. UB Tübingen, RB est., RB to E. Teufel, 25. 6. 1906, Mn 2-2393.

125. UB Tübingen, RB est., RB to W. Fischer, 19. 4. 1906, Mn 2-2198; cf. on what follows M. Evang, *Frühzeit*, 136–48.

126. UB Tübingen, RB est., RB to W. Fischer, 2. 4. 1905, Mn 2-2198; cf. G. Frenssen, *Dorfpredigten*.

their widespread reception especially in liberal Protestantism to the fact that they seemed intuitively to meet the fundamental demands of the early twentieth-century movement for homiletical reform. Frenssen did not use typical pulpit jargon, but expressed himself in unpretentious, understandable language. He translated the gospel into the present, into the life- and thought-worlds of his hearers and readers, whether they were country folk or those of the academy. In precisely the sense intended by liberal theology, Frenssen reduced the complex content of the ecclesiastical tradition into a simple, non-dogmatic Christianity.[127]

What seemed exemplary to Bultmann in Frenssen's "Village Sermons"—relinquishing antiquated language, renouncing dogmatics, and employing the insights of modern theology—belonged solidly to the canon of liberal homiletics. After all, Bultmann's teacher, Johannes Bauer, was a proponent of "modern preaching." Under this programmatic slogan, preachers who in the early 1900s championed the form sought to exploit the multi-faceted modernizing and revolutionary processes in the Wilhelmian Empire in order to make clear in a new way the relation of church proclamation to the evidently changed reality in the lives of those who heard it. At the same time, following the homiletic tradition of Schleiermacher, Johannes Bauer came to see preaching as a performative activity, a part of worship through which the preacher makes clear his own faith and that of his hearers for the sake of building up the community. However, since Bauer saw that the religious experience of both the community and the preacher depended on the evidential testimony of scripture, the preacher had to explicate his own faith "in strict connection to the pure conceptual content of a text."[128]

It was from the practicums of Bauer that Bultmann appropriated the understanding of preaching briefly sketched above, and while it served to guide him at the outset of what would soon become his own practice of preaching,[129] he was already well aware of "how difficult it is to preach a sermon that really makes sense, and from which the hearers can take something away!"[130] As his studies neared their end, he hoped "soon to be able to do practical work," to preach and to take part in the task "of bringing our

127. Cf. in addition to M. Evang, *Frühzeit*, 136–38, especially A. Crystall, *Gustav Frenssen*, 116–50.

128. J. Bauer, *Predigten über Worte Jesu*; for Bauer's justification for tying the sermon to the text, cf. M. Evang, *Frühzeit*, 139–42.

129. Whether during his studies Bultmann had already adopted Ernst Christian Achelis' principle, "Preach not *yourself*, but rather *from* yourself," which stands in a certain tension to J. Bauer's definition of preaching, cannot be determined from the sources. On this problem and on Bultmann's later references to Achelis' principle, cf. M. Evang, *Frühzeit*, 141f. Cf. E. Achelis, *Lehrbuch der Praktischen Theologie*, vol. 1, 145.

130. UB Tübingen, RB est., RB to W. Fischer, 31. 12. 1904, Mn 2-2198.

modern Christianity to the community."[131] But before this, he had to take the theological examination in Oldenburg for his initial degree.

4. Examinations and Teaching Activity in Oldenburg

> *I am now a little farther along with the examination, since I finished the set part fourteen days ago. . . . The topics were very easy and the whole thing terribly dull. . . . In the New Testament part I had the Areopagus speech of Paul from the Acts of the Apostles; unfortunately, there is in truth nothing to be done but to praise its beginning and to find fault with its ending. In church history I had the quite interesting Pope Nicholas I (858–67) and the quite thankless Wycliffe. Regarding the latter, I followed Müller and Harnack in repudiating his value as a "proto-reformer." So you see that I expressed myself in rather heretical fashion, and I would certainly like to know the feelings of my examiners as they read my incontestable heresies!*[132]

In April, 1906, Bultmann shared with his friend Walther Fischer the news that he had reported to the church assembly in Oldenburg at the beginning of the month for his examination and that he was waiting each day for the topics for his "take-homes": "Naturally, I have plenty to do now, and I sit all day long in the splendid weather on the veranda with my books. I am working on theology in really perfect contentment."[133] The theological examination was now to take stock of this work for the first time. The three written examinations—a paper on 1 Cor 2:6–16, a plan for catechizing based on Matt 13:31–33, as well as a sermon on Phil 2:12f—were submitted in timely fashion on June 18, 1906.[134]

In the take-home paper on 1 Cor 2:6–16, Bultmann begins by offering both an exegesis of the text and an excursus in which he discusses the provenance of the Old Testament citation in 1 Cor 2:9 and, as to the legitimacy of the allegorical use of scripture that arises from this, asserts that the Protestant understanding of scripture calls for the rejection of allegorizing.[135] Then—as is characteristic of his marked interest in the basic ways of

131. UB Tübingen, RB est., RB to W. Fischer, 19. 4. 1906, Mn 2-2198.
132. UB Tübingen, RB est., RB to W. Fischer, 22. 12. 1906, Mn 2-2198.
133. UB Tübingen, RB est., RB to W. Fischer, 19. 4. 1906, Mn 2-2198.
134. Cf. on what follows Niedersächsisches StA Oldenburg, the examination file and the personnel file on Rudolf Karl Bultmann.
135. Cf. RB, "Treatment of 1 Cor 2:6–16," in StAOldenburg, *Prüfungsakte*, 72.

formulating theological problems—he makes of the text and its topic an occasion to discuss in detail in a second excursus the relation between faith and knowledge.[136] Bultmann sees the point of the sharp contrast between divine and human wisdom in 1 Corinthians 1 and 2 reflected in Paul's rejection of a philosophy which, in the delusion that it "can resolve the ultimate questions of life," transgresses the limits placed upon human knowledge. Indeed, in the history of theology and philosophy, first Kant's critical philosophy and then Schleiermacher's definition of religion as a "matter of the feeling, willing subject, had described with precision the limits of theoretical and religious knowing." Faith—as Bultmann defines it with reference to Wilhelm Herrmann—is certainly "not the making of truth-claims about objects that are in principle differentiated from those of the spirit that perceives them; rather, it is personal conviction, derived from the experience of contact with an unconditioned power."

Indeed, Bultmann does not leave off with a merely antithetical dialectic of faith and knowledge, especially because he believes above all that the perceptual modality involved in scientific knowledge "is, religiously speaking, completely irrelevant." For the uniting of both ways of perceiving "in one human spiritual life" leads to recognizing that religion and science are not only related to one another but also function in terms of their different spheres of knowledge. Of course, the form of perception relevant to science performs an indispensable service, since understanding the phenomena of nature and history furthers personal religious life in the world. For us, that is, the kingdom of God can be experienced and actualized only if we have sufficient knowledge of this world. Bultmann therefore emphasizes the sharp differentiation of faith and intellectual knowledge, their interdependent relationship, and the primacy of religious knowledge that rests on revelation.

The principal evaluator of Bultmann's performance on his examination, Pastor Heinrich J. Iben (of Vechta), praised both the way the original exegesis had been put together ("an utterly splendid train of thought") and particularly Bultmann's excursus on the relation of "scientific and religious knowing" as "first-rate in its brevity and clarity."[137] The assessment of the examination sermon was less positive. The principal reader, the privy church councillor Theodor H. E. Hansen (of Oldenburg), thought that Bultmann had "thought through the text seriously in his own way," but nonetheless "his homiletical treatment of the text" was "not to be graded higher than

136. Cf. RB, "Treatment of 1 Cor 2:6–16," 73–80, reprinted in W. Zager, *Liberale Exegese*, 163–68 (from which were taken the citations that follow). M. Evang offers a detailed analysis of this excursus in *Frühzeit*, 253–56.

137. RB, "Treatment of 1 Cor 2:6–16," 80.

'quite good.'" Hansen judged the arrangement to be "logically incontestable, but homiletically unsuitable." The language of the sermon was "suitable, but in part too doctrinaire." In the second evaluation, Pastor Iben disputed even the suitability of the sermon to the text. Its author had not sufficiently brought out Paul's "summons to earnest work, to holy wakefulness, to showing courage" or the soteriological content of the text.[138]

Bultmann had already given his examination sermon on June 17, 1906, in two villages near Marburg—possibly Gossfelden and Sarnau[139]—"without getting stuck."[140] His exposition of Phil 2:12f treats the theme, "Our earnest striving toward holiness—how it has its basis in God's work on us."[141] Here Bultmann introduces a theme that will run through his preaching in the coming years like a *cantus firmus*—the contrast of work and gift. In this first sermon, the major accent still lies on one's own "serious striving toward holiness,"[142] for which religion, the experience of God's grace working on and in us, provides both strength and obligation. Reflecting his Lutheran work ethic, Bultmann argues that this is how religion confers its worth and deeper meaning on all human work, and he accordingly assigns to the proclamation of the gospel a function subordinate to that of the preaching of the law.

After Bultmann had written examination papers on the Old Testament (1 Sam 15:13–23) and the New Testament (Acts 17:22–31) on December 8, 1906, followed by one on church history (Pope Nicholas I and Wycliffe) two days later,[143] he gave the first part of his examination sermon at the opening of his public examination on January 31, 1907, in the chancel of the renovated St. Lambert's Church in Oldenburg. His examiners—alongside Hansen and Iben sat church councillor Georg A. L. Püschelberger (of Bad Zwischenahn)—were extraordinarily satisfied with Bultmann's performances in his examinations, but noted one qualification stated in the report of the church assembly of January 31, 1907 to the Grand Duke: "If his practical work and preaching in particular still leave something to be desired, his whole scholarly formation in the various disciplines nonetheless so far surpasses the average accomplishments of a candidate that the examination-commission considered it to be imperative to award him Grade Ib 'with

138. Cf. Niedersächsisches StA Oldenburg, examination file; the opinions of the evaluators are reproduced in part in RB, *VW*, xf (Introduction).

139. Cf. the details in RB, *VW*, 324n1.

140. UB Tübingen, RB est., RB to W. Fischer, 3. 9. 1906, Mn 2-2198.

141. The sermon is reprinted in RB, *VW*, 1–7; cf. the interpretation of it in K. de Valerio, *Altes Testament*, 107–16.

142. RB, *VW*, 1; cf. RB, *VW*, 5–7.

143. UB Tübingen, RB est., RB to W. Fischer, 22. 12. 1906, Mn 2-2198.

distinction.'"[144] Bultmann responded to the excellent grade with an allusion to the tradition of his family as "doubly gratifying . . . , since I am the first one in it since the examination of my father."[145] On February 9, 1907, the government ministry acted positively on the motion of the church assembly that it provisionally accept the candidate Bultmann into the service of the church.[146]

The examination process dragged on for over three-quarters of a year, all too long a time to suit the candidate. So as not to be "lying about with his parents," Bultmann got himself engaged during the exam period in September, 1906, as a tutor at the home of Count Beissel in Flensburg. "The Count and Countess are splendid, very cultured people; I am treated in exceedingly kindly fashion." Bultmann had "nothing to do except to supervise their son's schoolwork from 5–7:30 p.m. and occasionally to go walking with him from 3:00–4:00 p.m. For my troubles I receive eighty marks and free room and board!"[147] When on a later occasion he was giving private lessons in the house of the Count in Darmstadt, this was no longer enough for him, for, in the meantime, he had "tasted the joy . . . of standing before a class and of gratifying the crowd of interested faces."[148] This was the case from October, 1906, until September, 1907, when Bultmann taught as "head substitute teacher" at the academy in Oldenburg.[149] His teaching load in the winter term of 1906–07 consisted of eighteen hours divided among classes in German, history, and geography; in the summer of 1907, it amounted to twenty-three hours, and this time four hours of religious instruction were included. Bultmann was assigned to classes from the first to the fifth grades of secondary school.

Through his teaching activities Bultmann was becoming part of his family's pedagogical heritage, and this clearly gave him great joy. But teaching history in the upper grades presented him with problems, because he had to read through a "vast amount . . . in order to get command of the material and to select from it." Geography was also difficult, for "there, too, I lack adequate knowledge." Instruction in German, however, went easily: "Reading

144. Copy of the report of the church assembly to the Grand Duke on Bultmann's examination of 31. 1. 1907, in Niedersächsisches StaOldenburg, personnel file.

145. UB Tübingen, RB est., RB to E. Teufel, 25. 3. 1907, Mn 2-2393.

146. Cf. M. Evang, *Frühzeit,* 28.

147. UB Tübingen, RB est., RB to W. Fischer, 3. 9. 1906, Mn 2-2198.

148. UB Tübingen, RB est., RB to E. Teufel, 17. 7. 1907, Mn 2-2393.

149. What follows, including quotations, is from RB to W. Fischer, 22. 12. 1906, Mn 2-2198, in UB Tübingen, RB est.; reproduced in part in R. Rittner, *Rudolf Bultmann und Oldenburg,* 11.

poems and working through essays is always a joy for me, and I always take note of the interest of the students." In order to create the necessary climate of discipline, Bultmann chose the currently accepted method: partly "by punishment, partly by kindness. But on the whole, one achieves more by being strict—I mean one has to start off being strict and let the young people know that one is not going to put up with anything; one can always become more good-natured later on. Among punishments, caning—though forbidden—is by far the most effective, and this is about all I use."

Bultmann used his innovative talents elsewhere. It had "in the past often been painful" for him to see that "some teachers saw their task as only cramming in the material" and took "no personal concern for students." "For this reason," he "always showed a personal interest in the young people." And because he knew from experience the perennial pedagogical mistake—"that we were explicitly motivated to be insincere, partly through too many homework assignments, and partly through negligence on the part of teachers"—he tried "to the best of my ability to produce an enthusiasm for the truth." As part of his teaching activity in Oldenburg, Bultmann was able not only to garner practical experience from teaching but also to broaden his understanding of people. Particularly among his colleagues at the staff table he learned to know a diverse group of interesting people." Moreover, the very ones that he had "thought less well of as students," he now experienced "completely differently" from the perspective of having them as colleagues.

In the courses on religious instruction to which he was assigned for the two quarters of the summer session of 1907, Bultmann treated not only the prescribed stories from the Old Testament and the parables and miracles from the New Testament, the latter of which caused him considerable difficulties, but also the Apostles' Creed according to Luther's *Kleiner Katechismus* [*Small Catechism*].[150] As his letters to Eberhard Teufel and Walther Fischer verify, Bultmann the self-taught pedagogue engaged in his teaching activity vigorously and with enjoyment. During this period of professional transition, he wrote from Oldenburg to discuss with his friends religious questions and things that had appeared recently in theology, such as Gunkel's *Elias* [*Elijah*], Jülicher's "Die Religion Jesu und die Anfänge des Christentums bis zum Nicaenum (325)" ["The Religion of Jesus and the Beginnings of Christianity up to Nicaea (325)"], and Wellhausen's newly published *Israelitische und jüdische Geschichte* [*Israelite and Jewish*

150. Cf. UB Tübingen, RB est., RB to E. Teufel, 25. 3. 1907, Mn 2-2393; RB to W. Fischer, 26. 3. 1907, Mn 2-2198.

History].[151] Emil Balla, his student friend from Berlin, kept Bultmann abreast of new publications on the Old Testament, and especially through Balla's academic contacts, of Gunkel's publishing plans in progress.[152] Thus, although in Oldenburg, Bultmann was not completely cut off from the academic and scholarly discourse that was extremely important to him. The possibility that he might be able to return to the world of university theology after having passed his exams had, incidentally, already arisen prior to his stay in Oldenburg.

151. Cf. UB Tübingen, RB est., RB to W. Fischer, 3. 9. 1906 and 26. 3. 1907, Mn 2-2198. Cf. H. Gunkel, *Elias: Jahve und Baal*; A. Jülicher, "Die Religion Jesu,“ J.Wellhausen, *Israelitische und jüdische Geschichte.*

152. Cf. K. de Valerio, *Altes Testament*, 39f.

II. On the Path to Academic Teaching (1907–1916)

1. Tutor in Marburg

Activity at the academy finishes at the end of September, and I travel to Marburg. I mean to stay the next few years. That is to say—and this is the greatest news I have to share with you—I have received a "call" to go there as tutor at the Residence for Scholarship Students.[1]

In July 1907 the Marburg theological faculty invited Bultmann to apply for the position of second tutor at the Hessian Residence for Scholarship Students in Marburg, which was to become free in the autumn. Johannes Weiss in particular stood behind entrusting him with this position, in order to increase Bultmann's opportunities to pursue his own scholarly work.[2] In accordance with the regulations established in 1849, the theological faculty and the administration of the Residence had to submit a joint motion, according to which the trustees of the university would then engage a new tutor for two years at a time.[3] On July 27, 1907, after Bultmann had presented his application, Wilhelm Herrmann, as Director of the Residence and Acting Dean, requested the Royal Registrar of the university to confer on "the *cand. theol* Rudolf Bultmann . . . the position of second tutor at the *Seminarium Philippinum* for two years. We know Mr. Bultmann from his time as a student here as a highly gifted, earnest, and diligent person."[4] The registrar granted this request. Bultmann took up the position of tutor as the successor to the New Testament scholar Walter Bauer on October 1, 1907.

Bultmann came to an academic institution that was nearly as old as the *Philippina* itself, the oldest Protestant university in the world. In the comprehensive educational program that Franz Lambert of Avignon had developed for the *reformatio ecclesiarum Hessiae* in 1526, the Residence for Scholarship Students represented an important building block.[5] Landgraf Philip of Hesse ("the Magnanimous") implemented this plan in the process of gradually introducing the Reformation into his own territory. In order to

1. UB Tübingen, RB est., RB to W. Fischer, 30. 7. 1907, Mn 2-2198.
2. Cf. UB Tübingen, RB est., RB to E. Teufel, 29. 12. 1907, Mn 2-2393; J. Weiss to RB, 9. 6. 1908, Mn 2-2020; on what follows, cf. M. Evang, *Frühzeit*, 30–35.
3. Cf. Regulations for the Residence for Scholarship Students, 7 (sec. 14).
4. W. Herrmann to the Royal University Registrar, 27. 7. 1907, in M. Evang, *Frühzeit*, 31.
5. Cf. W. Heinemeyer, *Studium*.

make sure that the training of the ecclesiastical and civil servants of Hesse took place in the spirit of the Reformation and of humanism, he had the proceeds from the treasuries of the church in the cities of Hesse invested through the cities for financing scholarships and for promoting suitable candidates. The Marburg Residence served as a pattern for the seminary that was established in Tübingen in 1534 and later became even more famous. The initial concept for a residential community for students affiliated with the Marburg Residence was permanently realized in 1546, when the secularized *Kugelhaus* [ball-shaped house], the fraternity house of the Brethren of the Common Life, became the living-quarters for scholarship students. In contrast to the seminary in Tübingen, the Marburg Residence lost its character as a seminary for scholarship students; for due to both the dilapidated state of the *Kugelhaus* and student opposition to regimentation, the requirement for scholarship students to live communally came to an end in 1812. It was only after the Second World War that the Hessian residence managed to get restored as a normal seminary in the former royal stable buildings of the Marburg castle.

In any case, when Bultmann took up his position in 1907 the status of the Residence was clearly diminished from that of its origins. Accordingly, the list of the new tutor's duties was clearly limited. "In fact," as Bultmann reported on the conditions at Marburg to Eberhard Teufel at the end of December 1907, "there is no seminary there like the one in Tübingen, but rather just twenty to thirty students who have scholarships. They have complete freedom in where they live, where they take their meals, etc., and they have only to attend the Old Testament and New Testament college courses given by the two tutors in their first semesters and to do the written work in the later semesters, the correcting of which falls to the tutors. When I now add that I have to preach the second service on Christmas, Easter, and Pentecost, I have enumerated the duties of my position. I am the tutor for the New Testament college courses, in which, by the way, other students may participate, and I do the correcting of the assignments in New Testament and church history."[6]

One month later, Bultmann had corrected the first assignments of the scholarship students. The subject of these assignments was the elucidation of the sayings about the Son of Man in the Gospel of John. The tutor's criticism of the assignments that had been handed in was annihilating: "Such a load of ignorance, inability to think, and laziness I would have thought impossible . . . absolute unreliability in citations. A train of thought? Out

6. UB Tübingen, RB est., RB to E. Teufel, 29. 12. 1907, Mn 2-2393.

of the question! On every page, the opposite of what was said on the last is asserted at least three times. So, all in all, a torture! Such are the Hessian theologians!" The severe tutor announced that these disgraceful shortcomings would soon have serious consequences. In his classes, he would "take them soundly to task, so that they would not produce such absurd pieces of work in the following semesters."[7]

In addition to the exegetical college courses for scholarship students and correcting their end-of-semester assignments, the duties included preaching. The tutors preached sermons in the Reformed city and university churches on the second day of the celebration of the two great feasts. In accordance with the prescribed regulations, Bultmann performed this preaching assignment from 1907 until 1910, alternating with his Old Testament colleague, Pastor *extr.* Paul Behnke. Naturally, both tutors increasingly regarded it as unfortunate that their preaching duties often prevented them from celebrating the holidays or visiting their friends.[8] Therefore in January of 1911 they asked to be allowed to fulfill their obligations at worship services on Sundays during the semester instead of on the two holidays.[9] Adolf Jülicher, who had succeeded Wilhelm Herrmann as Director of the residence at the end of 1910, passed on Behnke's and Bultmann's wish, along with a petition to the same effect, to the royal consistory in Kassel. As an additional basis for the proposal, Jülicher pointed out that while the sermons by the tutors were originally intended to serve as homiletical models for students, they could not fulfill this purpose at the times assigned to them, since the scholarship students would not even be present in Marburg on the holidays. The consistory was persuaded by this line of argument. On November 24, 1910, it stated its agreement that the two tutors could in the future give their sermons during two worship services during the winter semester and in one during the summer semester.

For his activity as tutor, Bultmann received a nominal annual salary of 975 deutschemarks, which was regularly supplemented by 200–300 deutschemarks from the discretionary budget of the residence. Even with this latter addition, since the salary had been fixed in a bygone time, it was considerably less than the 1500 deutschemarks that Marburg Assistants had received since April 1908 and since 1910 the administration of the residence had repeatedly attempted to induce the Prussian Minister for Cultural, Educational, and Medical Affairs to increase the tutors' income. The commission also made

7. UB Tübingen, RB est., RB to W. Fischer 24. 1. 1908, Mn 2-2198.
8. Cf. UB Tübingen, RB est., RB to W. Fischer, 17. 7. 1908, Mn 2-2198.
9. On what follows, cf. M. Evang, *Frühzeit*, 33f.

reference in this regard to an assurance given to the Director to bring the pay of the tutors into line with that of the Assistants. Not only were these efforts unsuccessful, but the appropriate ministerial authority was for decades unable to obtain a salary increase for the tutors.[10]

Despite the modest compensation of the post, Bultmann considered his new teaching appointment a stroke of good luck. With the examination and teaching activity in Oldenburg behind him, he was able to return to the academic milieu. Collegial interaction with former teachers like Wilhelm Herrmann, Adolf Jülicher, Martin Rade, and Johannes Weiss meant a great deal to him both as a person and as a scholar.[11] Moreover, the position as tutor offered him all the conditions he needed to concentrate on completing the work for his licentiate, and the path towards an academic teaching position offered a second professional possibility to that of the pastorate. At the end of July in 1907 he hinted laconically at the many uncertainties of his present situation: "What the future holds will have to sort itself out."[12]

2. Graduation as a Doctor [of Theology] and Qualification for Teaching

> *JOH. WEISS pointed, above all in his Commentary on 1 Corinthians, to the elements of Cynic and Stoic popular philosophy that are found particularly in the paranesis of Paul. At his suggestion, I have sought to show that the style of many passages in the Pauline letters is influenced by the style of the Cynic-Stoic diatribe.*[13]

Before Bultmann left Marburg in the summer of 1906 to do his examinations in Oldenburg, Johannes Weiss had already designated "the relation of the theology of Paul to the Stoa" as the special focus of Bultmann's dissertation. This head-start induced Bultmann to occupy himself at once with Stoic philosophy.[14] To be sure, reading Epictetus in the spring of 1907 gave him little joy. "On the whole I am disappointed. The 'freedom' of a person is essentially only a negative ideal for the Stoics, and little can be detected of the πάντα μοι ἔξεστιν [All things are lawful to me, 1 Cor 6:12]."[15] During his early years as a tutor, from 1907–10, Bultmann composed his disserta-

10. Cf. M. Evang, *Frühzeit*, 32f.
11. Cf. UB Tübingen, RB est., RB to E. Teufel, 29. 12. 1907, Mn 2-2393.
12. UB Tübingen, RB est., RB to W. Fischer, 30. 7. 1907, Mn 2-2198.
13. RB, "Zur Geschichte," 45.
14. UB Tübingen, RB est., RB to W. Fischer, 3. 12. 1906, Mn 2-2198. On what follows, cf. M. Evang, *Frühzeit*, 35–37.
15. UB Tübingen, RB est., RB to W. Fischer, 26. 3. 1907, Mn 2-2198.

Plate 12: Wilhelm Heitmüller

tion. Its precise theme crystallized towards the end of 1908: "The Style of Paul in Relation to the Stoic-Cynic Diatribe."[16] Bultmann's original hope of finishing the work in the year 1909[17] went unfulfilled, for the topic proved too wide-ranging. And when Johannes Weiss left Marburg for Heidelberg, his students lost a brilliant partner in conversation, a deprivation that had the further effect of hindering the progress of Bultmann's work.[18]

On March 14, 1910, Bultmann handed in his dissertation, with the "request for conferral of the Licentiate in Theology" at the Marburg theological faculty.[19] Wilhelm Heitmüller, who served as first examiner, paid tribute to Bultmann's inquiry—without prejudice to several objections—"as a *meritorious, noteworthy* contribution to the investigation of the Pauline letters."[20] Adolf Jülicher emphasized in his accompanying report that the candidate for the doctorate had, in his useful analysis, carefully delineated the connections between Paul and Greek culture.[21] After the faculty voted to accept the work on July 22, 1910, in consideration of his performance in the public examination, it conferred on Bultmann the overall grade *cum laude* on July 30. The conferee himself considered his public examination "not very splendid." Granted, he was thoroughly at home in New Testament studies, but he had had "mostly tough luck in the other subjects.[22] Thanks to the efforts of Heitmüller, Bultmann was able to publish his dissertation in the autumn of 1910 in the Forschungen zur Religion

16. UB Tübingen, RB est., RB to W. Fischer, 21. 12. 1908, Mn 2-2198.
17. Cf. UB Tübingen, RB est., RB to W. Fischer, 17. 1. 1909, Mn 2-2198.
18. Cf. UB Tübingen, RB est., RB to A. K. Bultmann, 9. 11. 1908, Mn 2-2735; RB to W. Fischer, 17. 7. 1908 and 17. 1. 1909, Mn 2-2198.
19. Cf. UA Marburg, the PhD thesis file for RB.
20. Cf. StA Oldenburg, examination report of W. Heitmüller (9. 7. 1910), 7.
21. Cf. StA Oldenburg, examination report of A. Jülicher (12. 7. 1910).
22. UB Tübingen, RB est., RB to A. K. Bultmann, 31. 11. 1910, Mn 2-2735.

und Literatur des Alten und Neuen Testaments [Studies on the Religion and Literature of the Old and New Testament].

"The Style of the Pauline Preaching and the Cynic-Stoic Diatribe"—the title of the work allows one to recognize the method the author applies to his subject. Along the lines of the history-of-religions school, Bultmann undertakes a stylistic comparison of Hellenistic diatribe and passages from the Pauline letters. As in comparative religion generally, the method consists in stylistic analysis, that is, in comparing the genres of a number of texts in order to separate alien elements from an author's own work and so to determine first and foremost his individuality as an author. To do this, Bultmann refers in philological matters to Eduard Norden, Paul Wendland, and Ulrich von Wilamowitz-Moellendorf, and in New Testament studies to the groundwork on his subject done by Georg Heinrici and Johannes Weiss. To be sure, he does not seek to derive Paul's style of argumentation exclusively from Hellenistic literature. The "correct picture of the literary personality of Paul" is drawn when the Old Testament and Jewish influences on his manner of preaching and his rhetoric are both considered. At that time, however, this was not yet possible, on account of the unsatisfactory state of literary-historical investigation of the Old Testament and Jewish texts. Concentrating, therefore, on Paul's Hellenistic context, Bultmann inquires whether one can demonstrate a relationship between the forms of expression found in the preaching of Paul and those of popular Cynic-Stoic homiletics.[23] The comparison of stylistics and genres that he employs to this end focuses on dialogical and rhetorical elements, the ordering of ideas, methods of argumentation, and matters of tone and mood in both bodies of texts.

Bultmann comes to the conclusion that Paul employed forms of expression that show similarities to those of popular Cynic and Stoic teachers. Historically speaking, these similarities of form could well have facilitated the acceptance of Paul's missionary preaching in Corinth. Despite all the formal echoes in the diatribe, Paul has nonetheless preserved his literary originality: ". . . [T]he cloak of the Greek orator is indeed draped around the shoulders of Paul, but Paul has no feeling for how the folds should fall correctly, and outlines of the alien shape show through everywhere."[24] To go beyond that, to answer the further question of whether in addition to the confirmed stylistic similarities a kinship of spirit also links Paul and the diatribe, requires more than an analysis of style alone. Whether besides certain literary forms Paul also adopted concepts and other intellectual content from Cynic and

23. RB, *Stil*, 1–4.
24. RB, *Stil*, 108.

Stoic philosophy can be demonstrated only by an approach that takes account of both material and formal aspects.[25]

Just as his critical analysis of style shows Bultmann to be a true pupil of the history-of-religions school, and in particular of Hermann Gunkel and Johannes Weiss,[26] this is likewise true of his interpretation of the literary originality of Paul. In this exegesis, the personal essence of the apostle finds expression, and he reveals himself as the subject of his own religious life and literary creativity. Paul "has too little of the artist, the poet. He is everywhere much too passionately invested to be capable of delighting in the words apart from the content."[27] At the deepest level, the literary difference between Paul and Hellenistic diatribe depends, as does more generally his religious certitude, on "his innermost experience, not on philosophical propositions."[28] The apostle comes by "his propositions not in an intellectual way, but rather through experience and intuition."[29] Precisely for this reason he is able when necessary to borrow freely from the preaching of the Cynic beggar-philosophers. Indeed, this might occasionally have helped him validate his religious experience as his own spiritual possession.[30] Thus, using the liberal categories of the religious personality, Bultmann develops the difference between the ideas of Paul—which can be traced back to his own experience—and the varying ways these thoughts take shape in form and style.

The scholars in his field accorded a highly positive reception to Bultmann's first academic work; reviewers offered his dissertation a full measure of appreciation.[31] He received "friendly communications" from Johannes Bauer and Karl Müller, who had read the book with approval.[32] Most of all, one suspects, Bultmann must have been pleased by the praise offered by those New Testament scholars who were most conversant with the subject-matter of his work: C. F. Georg Heinrici, Hans Lietzmann, and Johannes Weiss. Heinrici and Lietzmann declared themselves fully in agreement with Bultmann's investigation and even stressed in particular that Bultmann had rightly accented the distinctiveness of Paul in comparison with Hellenism.[33]

25. Cf. RB, *Stil*, 109.

26. Cf. H. Gunkel, "Ziele"; J. Weiss, *Aufgaben*.

27. RB, *Stil*, 94.

28. RB, *Stil*, 101.

29. RB, *Stil*, 68.

30. Cf. RB, *Stil*, 85, 109.

31. Cf. the review of A. Steinmann, 217; E. Vischer, 259f; W. Wilbrand, 273f.

32. UB Tübingen, RB est., RB to W. Fischer, 29. 11. 1910, Mn 2-2198; cf. J. Bauer to RB, 7. 11. 1910; Mn 2-414; K. Müller to RB, 10. 11. 1910, Mn 2-1430.

33. UB Tübingen, RB est., C. F. G. Heinrici to RB, 27. 11. 1910, Mn 2-959; H. Lietzmann to RB, 16. 12. 1910, Mn 2-1292 (not reprinted in K. Aland, *Glanz und Niedergang*).

Johannes Weiss, too, took note "with great pleasure" of the "splendid" style-critical study of his student. To be sure, along with such appreciation, Weiss also registered certain differences between his and Bultmann's view: "Sometimes you emphasize the distinction more strongly and more deliberately than I would."[34]

Whereas in the decades to come Bultmann's licentiate dissertation of 1910 came to occupy a noteworthy place in form-critical study of the Pauline letters,[35] his *Habilitationsschrift* [second doctoral dissertation], first published posthumously, has remained completely without impact. For even while working on this thesis, Bultmann had already given consideration to "qualifying for university teaching in the history of the ancient church, which at present is more advantageous."[36] Adolf Jülicher proposed to him that, in his *Habilitationsschrift*, he treat "the exegesis of the Antiochene school, especially that of Theodore of Mopsuestia."[37] In May 1912 Bultmann submitted to the Marburg theological faculty the completed study with his "petition for the granting of *venia legendi* [permission for lecturing] for the department of New Testament theology.[38] Jülicher, who made out the first examiner's report, found that the work could just as well have been submitted for the department of church history. Nevertheless, he argued, while investigating the history of interpretation of Theodore's commentaries, Bultmann paid close attention to the letters of Paul; and for this reason, granting the *venia legendi* for New Testament exegesis was justified.[39]

Not so much when it praises and affirmatively underscores Bultmann's work as in its critical statements does Jülicher's report inform us about its author and his estimation of the newly qualified teacher. The examiner, concerned about philological precision, was quite annoyed by Bultmann's orthographic errors, particularly by instances of carelessness in the accenting of Greek words. "He has evidently not gone to much trouble anywhere

34. UB Tübingen, RB est., J. Weiss to RB, 14. 12. 1910, Mn 2-2020.

35. Bultmann's conclusions were first qualified by S. K. Stowers, *Diatribe*. According to Stowers, the diatribe does not reproduce Cynic-Stoic popular preaching. Rather, diatribes are didactically calculated, fictive texts used for teaching by the philosophical schools. The diatribe also did not stamp the missionary preaching of Paul, although it did his doctrinal instruction of already existing congregations.

36. UB Tübingen, RB est., RB to W. Fischer, 21. 12. 1908; Mn 2-2198; on what follows, cf. M. Evang, *Frühzeit*, 37–39; RB, *Exegese*, 13–16 (Introduction by the editors); B. Dieckmann, "Entmythologisierung," 89–94.

37. UB Tübingen, RB est., RB to W. Fischer, 29. 11. 1910, Mn 2-2198.

38. Cf. UA Marburg, qualifying records for RB.

39. Cf. StA Oldenburg, examination report of A. Jülicher (1. 6. 1912), 4; excerpts reprinted in B. Dieckmann, "Entmythologisierung," 91–93.

in matters of form."[40] Jülicher also had clear problems with Bultmann's attempt to forge a constructive connection between history and theology. To be sure, he saw one of Bultmann's strengths in the fact that "he is not a mere New Testament scholar," but this presumptive merit could sometimes leave a negative aftertaste. In summarizing his study, Bultmann formulated the theological perspective of Theodore's exegesis in this way: rather than an object to be explained by the history of interpretation, scripture becomes the real subject that does the explaining. Jülicher supplied a large question mark in the margin to this thesis of Bultmann's.[41] Despite such questions, on July 19, 1912, the theological faculty of Marburg accepted Bultmann's *Habilitationsschrift* on the basis of the evaluations of both Jülicher and Heitmüller.[42]

Bultmann himself did not publish his *Habilitationsschrift*. Various conjectures have been made regarding the reasons for this. After Louis Pirot's monograph on Theodore of Mopsuestia appeared in 1913, he may have regarded his "own work as in part superseded."[43] Perhaps the difficult conditions of publishing during the First World War hindered timely publication.[44] But the decisive factor was that Jülicher's assessment rendered the publication of Bultmann's *Habilitationsschrift* uncertain from the outset,[45] and over the course of time its author increasingly lost interest in bringing it to press.

Theodore of Mopsuestia (ca. 352–428) was probably the most important interpreter of scripture of the Antiochene School. His influential standing in the ancient church of the empire enlarged and maintained its distinctive theological profile as opposed to that of its Alexandrian rivals. In his *Habilitationsschrift*, Bultmann focuses on the Bishop of Mopsuestia's exegesis without providing its precise location within the broad stream of biblical interpretation within the ancient church.[46] At the same time, through the medium of this historical paradigm of exegesis, the twenty-eight-year-old

40. StA Oldenburg, examination report of A. Jülicher, 3.

41. Cf. RB, *Exegese*, 127; further examples in B. Dieckmann, "Entmythologisierung," 91–93.

42. Cf. examination report of W. Heitmüller (10. 7. 1912) in UA Marburg, qualifying records, 94.

43. H. Feld and K. H. Schelkle, in RB, *Exegese*, 14; cf. RB, review of L. Pirot, *L'Oeuvre,* 134f.

44. Thus, M. Evang, *Frühzeit*, 38.

45. Cf. Jülicher's examination report (1. 6. 1912), 3, in Dieckmann, "Entmythologisierung," 92.

46. Cf. RB, *Exegese*, 17f. Detailed analyses of Bultmann's *Habilitationsschrift* are offered by M. Evang, *Frühzeit*, 178f, 208–10, 221f, 224–26, and K. de Valerio, *Altes Testament*, 202–29.

now reveals his own hermeneutical principles in the course of reviewing Theodore's interpretation of scripture. For this reason, the parts of the work in which Bultmann presents such historical findings as the arrangement of Theodore's commentaries, his explanation of formal and linguistic characteristics in the Bible, or the literary-critical competencies of the Antiochene exegete, fail to produce much material of biographical interest.[47] On the other hand, Bultmann allows his own theological reflections to leave their mark wherever his study of Theodore dwells on the theme of "the grasp of the inner life of the [biblical] writings."[48]

Bultmann introduces this section of his *Habilitationsschrift* with a hermeneutical explanation of basic principles for the task of biblical exegesis. If an interpreter such as Theodore of Mopsuestia shows himself to be competent in his ability "to grasp the unity and structure of a writing," he inevitably also poses the question of "the inner life of a writing." The "most profound art" of the exegete consists "in allowing the writing to say from within itself where the center of its life lies, whence it appears as a living whole; in uncovering the point of crystallization, through the grasping of which the lines of the inner structure make themselves visible."[49] Here, as the vocabulary he employs indicates, Bultmann is moving into the conceptual realm of Schleiermacher's hermeneutic, and perhaps also that of Wilhelm Dilthey.[50] The literature created by intuitive genius can be appropriated only through an act of generative understanding that arises from its inner structural principle.

In order to infer the "inner life" of a text, Bultmann argues, two tasks are to be distinguished. One is to discern the "*basic ideas*" of the writing. The other is to consider "*what is individual in the shaping of this idea*"—and to this belongs "the historical context of the writing," but in particular the "*personality of the author.*"[51] Even when thorough consideration is accorded both these tasks in the effort to understand the text, the problem for portraying the exegesis of Theodore is to determine which of the two steps to undertake first. Bultmann takes it to be possible in principle to follow the normal approach in exegesis from the individual instance to the basic religious idea that underlies it. But following the exegetical option of his teacher Johannes Weiss, he here chooses the opposite approach. For, he reasons,

47. RB, *Exegese*, 28–43, 44–68, 69–82.
48. RB, *Exegese*, 83–125.
49. RB, *Exegese*, 83.
50. Cf. the balanced view on this point in M. Evang, *Frühzeit*, 230–32.
51. RB, *Exegese*, 83.

"the ultimate goal of exegesis" consists not in "getting to know the basic ideas, but in understanding the individual instance, the individual writing, the individual sentence."[52]

Under the heading "Theodore's relation to the religious life of the scriptures," Bultmann treats four groups of basic religious ideas. First of all, Theodore is not really able to relate to the religiosity of the Old Testament. He has continual difficulties in harmonizing the anthropomorphic features of the Old Testament picture of God with his own understanding of the Deity. Second, the concept of the divine activity as educative in history proves to be central for Theodore. But in Bultmann's view he has merely appropriated this idea from the Hebrew Bible; it has not actually "grown out of his own religious life."[53] Third, Theodore's interpretation of New Testament religion illustrates the tension between the naturalistic concepts of Greek philosophy and the historical concepts of the Bible. On the one hand, Theodore makes what is new in the New Testament—redemption from the Old Testament—understandable by means of historical concepts. He quite correctly grasps individual New Testament notions—for instance, the spirit as "the power of life for the future" or the new Christian life in its moral orientation.[54] On the other hand, he remains circumscribed by naturalistic philosophical categories, with the result that he misses the sense of the Pauline teaching on law and sin, and generally fails to make clear the connection of redemption with the person of Jesus Christ. Fourth, Theodore develops the concept of "religion as the godly life growing in us in history." He even recognizes "the paradox of the Christian conception of history," which sees the religious life as radically determined by its historical context, but which at the same time "demands a break in history, the transition to something in principle new for each individual as well as for the whole."[55]

Thus, Bultmann emphatically praises the exegete of the ancient church for properly grasping the historical context of scripture, for discerning the reciprocal relation between individual instances and their overall historical connection. In the end, Bultmann says, he means "to understand scripture with a consciousness that is purely historical."[56] Theodore is also able to put himself in a psychologically empathetic way "in the historical and personal

52. RB, *Exegese*, 83f; cf. M. Evang, *Frühzeit*, 221f; J. Weiss, *Aufgaben*, 22–25. On Weiss, cf. also RB, "Johannes Weiss," 244.
53. RB, *Exegese*, 87.
54. RB, *Exegese*, 90.
55. RB, *Exegese*, 93.
56. RB, *Exegese*, 99.

situation of the authors,"[57] and is thus aware not only of the content and the line of argument, but also of "the voice of a passage or a letter."[58]

In short, Bultmann sees Theodore as representing a kind of exegesis that attempts to understand the biblical texts historically: ". . . [N]ot only his approach, but also his results often appear completely modern."[59] In the conclusion of his *Habilitationsschrift*, Bultmann even emphasizes the way the theologian of the ancient church relates the interpretation of scripture to the present. For him, the exegetical work of Theodore is determined not by dogmatic or practical motives, but rather solely by "the desire to understand scripture." As one encounters it in Theodore, the emergence of the historical interpretation of the Bible is to be explained in large part by the internal logic "that arises out of the essence of Christianity as a historical religion."[60] Whether in the past or the present, genuine spiritual conversation with the New Testament as the originating document of the Christian religion must necessarily be conducted only in historical-critical contact with the texts. In this manner alone is it possible to rescue the charter documents from being overwhelmed by alien dogmatic and practical concerns. It is precisely by recognizing this that historical exegesis excludes "all external subjugation of scripture" and serves the spirit of the Bible.[61]

On July 19, 1912, the Marburg theological faculty had Bultmann submit three topics, from which one would be selected for his trial-lecture:

1. What does the sayings-source give us to understand of the original community?
2. The chronology of Paul
3. The ethics of Paul

The faculty decided on the first topic, on which Bultmann lectured on July 27th. In his lecture, he followed the strategy of tracing the sayings-source Q back to the earliest level of Christianity, the original community in Jerusalem. In the printed text of the lecture, Bultmann followed Julius Wellhausen in describing the earliest community—much as he does in his dictionary article that appeared in 1913[62]—as a Jewish sect that has grown out of Old Testament–Jewish roots and that is to be recognized by a peculiar combination of eschatological and ethical ideas. To be sure, the original community

57. RB, *Exegese,* 110.
58. RB, *Exegese,* 119.
59. RB, *Exegese,* 102.
60. RB, *Exegese,* 126.
61. RB, *Exegese,* 127.
62. Cf. RB, "Urgemeinde christliche"; see also 375–77.

Plate 13: The University of Marburg–Assembly Hall and University Church

had not yet attained the insight that at its core Christianity constitutes an ethical religion of redemption. This Bultmann thinks he is able to demonstrate by the original community's ambivalent treatment of the law. On the one hand, it held fast to the Old Testament and the Jewish laws regarding cult and ritual, while on the other hand, as the controversy found in Markan dialogues make clear, it carried on the struggle against contemporary Jewish practice of the law. Thus, the original community was not yet able to grasp the universal and religious-ethical character of Christianity later displayed to advantage by Paul. All the same, by protecting the gospel handed down by Jesus and by transmitting it to gentile Christians, the community was almost from the first moment able to assert and realize freedom from the law.[63] Following his trial-lecture, Bultmann had to "speak to Heitmüller for perhaps half an hour about material with which Heitmüller was not satisfied. The other professors either refrained from comment or satisfied themselves with a few remarks. It was all finished by half past twelve."[64] After the

63. Cf. RB, "Was lässt . . . ," 35–37, 41–44.
64. UB Tübingen, RB est., RB to A. K. and H. Bultmann, 3. 8. 1912, Mn 2-2735.

Plate 14: A Favorite Vacation Spot of Bultmann's (Dammühle near Marburg)

Plate 15: Rudolf Bultmann as Tutor in Marburg, ca. 1912

colloquium, Heitmüller, as Dean, issued Bultmann the *venia legendi* [permission to lecture] for New Testament studies. Bultmann gave his inaugural lecture on July 31, 1912, on the topic "the significance of eschatology for earliest Christianity."[65] "It was nice that the auditorium was full; there was even an overflow audience."[66]

To recover from the protracted struggle to qualify for teaching, Bultmann and Rudolf Günther went in August 1912 to an art exhibition in Frankfurt. Afterwards, he visited the great Special Exhibition in Cologne with works "of the most modern French painters [!] . . . , as one will hardly ever—at least in

65. Bultmann again took up the topic—in severely altered fashion, however—in 1917 in "Bedeutung," 76–87; cf. also M. Evang, *Frühzeit*, 274–76.

66. UB Tübingen, RB est., RB to A. K. and H. Bultmann, 3. 8. 1912, Mn 2-2735.

Plate 16: "As in the picture, this is where I have to give my examination-sermon next Sunday evening . . ." Drawing of Bultmann's for his Niece, Elisabeth Pleus, July 22, 1912

Germany—see them again."[67] The pleasure of reveling in the paintings of Paul Cezanne, Vincent van Gogh, Edvard Munch, Georges Braques, Pablo Picasso, and other representatives of the avant-garde was followed by the joy of vacation. During this time, Bultmann the tutor, newly appointed as lecturer, had to prepare his first course of lectures for the winter semester 1912/13: "Introduction to the Apocrypha and Pseudepigrapha of the Old Testament."[68]

3. Teaching and Research Activities

I still know well . . . [:] How it seemed to me the goal most worth striving for to be a lecturer one day in Marburg.[69]

Having acquired the *venia legendi*, Bultmann found that his list of duties had expanded. Alongside the New Testament practica, which it was incumbent on him as tutor to teach, he took over courses in Greek for beginners, as was

67. UB Tübingen, RB est., RB to A. K. and H. Bultmann, 3. 8. 1912, Mn 2-2375.
68. UB Tübingen, RB est., RB to A. K. and H. Bultmann, 3. 8. 1912, Mn 2-2375. This assertion deals with the desideratum pointed to by M. Evang in *Frühzeit*, 39n40.
69. UB Tübingen, RB est., RB to H. Feldmann, 26. 9. 1916, Mn 2-3447.

standard procedure. Above all, he was as lecturer obliged to present lecture courses. It benefited his teaching activity that Walter Bauer, who had been a Marburg lecturer in New Testament since 1903, accepted a call to Breslau in the summer semester of 1913. This offered Bultmann a broader choice of seminar topics.[70] He made his debut in the winter semester of 1912–13, with a course entitled "Introduction to the Apocrypha and Pseudepigrapha of the Old Testament."[71] During his four years as lecturer, Bultmann presented "The Apostolic Age of the Christian Church" twice more, as well as "The Literature and Religion of Judaism in New Testament Times." In the exegetical seminars, he treated the Pastoral Epistles and Revelation. Whereas his lecture courses as a rule carried two hours of credit, in the winter semester of 1914–15 he gave a four-credit series entitled "Introduction to the New Testament."[72]

Bultmann could not complain of a lack of following. In the summer semester of 1913, he counted eight attendees in his lecture-course and forty-two participants in the practica.[73] In the winter semester of 1913–14, the attendance in his courses rose again: "28 in the seminar on the Pastoral Epistles (moreover in competition with Rade at the same time) and 61 in the practica are a most gratifying fact."[74] To be sure, with the increasing duration of the War, the rows of male students in his lecture hall dwindled. In their place, women gradually formed the primary contingent of his audience. "The few men who sit among them mostly wear the ribbon of the iron cross in their buttonhole."[75] Bultmann was not yet sure whether the admission of women would prove beneficial to scholarship, but in any event it would raise the level of women's education and of culture overall; indeed, female students were already having a favorable impact on the academic atmosphere.[76]

In Bultmann's own scholarly work, reviews of foreign books had a special importance from the outset. Writing book reviews and reports on research, an activity expected of him primarily to make a mark for himself as a compe-

70. Cf. UB Tübingen, RB est., RB to W. Fischer, 7. 4. 1913, Mn 2-2198.

71. Cf. UB Tübingen, RB est., RB to A. K. and H. Bultmann, 3. 8. 1912, Mn 2-2735.

72. Cf. M. Evang, *Frühzeit*, 39. Additional manuscripts of Bultmann's work on Acts and 1 Thessalonians 1–4 from 1912–16 have been preserved. Cf. O. Merk, "Die Apostelgeschichte . . . ," in B. Jaspert, *Werk und Wirkung*, 303–15; O. Merk, "Zu Rudolf Bultmanns Auslegung . . . " in O. Merk, *Wissenschaftsgeschichte*, 350–59. To be sure, these manuscripts formed the basis not of Bultmann's lectures but of his practicums of the years 1912 and following. Cf. M. Evang, *Frühzeit*, 40.

73. Cf. UB Tübingen, RB est., RB to W. Fischer, 4. 5. 1913, Mn 2-2198.

74. UB Tübingen, RB est., RB to W. Fischer, 2. 11. 1913, Mn 2-2198.

75. UB Tübingen, RB est., RB to W. Fischer, 3. 2. 1916, Mn 2-2198.

76. Cf. UB Tübingen, RB est., RB to W. Fischer, 21. 10. 1915, Mn 2-2198.

tent, up-and-coming academic, he found anything but a burdensome duty. When in 1907 Martin Rade entrusted him with reviewing newly published works on the New Testament for *Die Christliche Welt*, the barely twenty-three-year-old tutor was overjoyed. In the course of expressing his joy, Bultmann indicated the central motive that was to direct him in his future activity as a reviewer: "Naturally, it is most agreeable to me to take a small part in theological life in this way."[77]

Beginning in 1908 Bultmann's reviews appeared regularly in *Die Christliche Welt*, and from 1908 until 1912 he published five reviews of individual books and reports on research in the *Monatsschrift für Pastoraltheologie* [*Monthly Journal for Pastoral Theology*]. This periodical's co-publisher and editor, Rudolf Günther, who was lecturer and later associate professor in the history of Christian art in Marburg, welcomed the young doctoral student and co-worker as a friend. And having become qualified for teaching, Bultmann found himself after 1914 contributing to the renamed *Theologische Literaturzeitung* [*Theological Review of Literature*], as well as *Theologische Rundschau* [*Theological Overview*] until the War caused their discontinuation in 1917. During his time as tutor and lecturer in Marburg, he was the author of thirty-nine book reviews and research reports—a number that grew during the course of his life to two hundred and forty. In all, Bultmann reviewed many more than six hundred books. His intense devotion to reviewing contributed greatly to the expansion of his own research library. "A nice side-benefit is that the copies of the books reviewed remain my property."[78]

The thematic breadth of research interests that would come to distinguish his work was already apparent in Bultmann's early book reviews. In view of the popular audience of *Die Christliche Welt,* he reported not only on New Testament literature and the history of the ancient church, but also reviewed writings on biblical topics of general interest. Over and above this, the young devotee of fiction introduced the readers of the liberal culture periodical *Protestantism* to the novels of Claude Tillier, William Makepeace Thackeray, Fyodor Dostoevsky, Peter Rosegger, and Camille Lemonnier in his 1912 and 1913 recommendations for Christmas reading.[79] Far from feeling restricted

77. UB Tübingen, RB est., RB to A. K. and H. Bultmann, 10. 11. 1907, Mn 2-2735; also in RB, *Theologie als Kritik*, 514.

78. UB Tübingen, RB est., RB to A. K. Bultmann and H. Bultmann, 10. 11. 1907, Mn 2-2735.

79. RB, *Theologie als Kritik*, offers a selection of Bultmann's reviews and reports on research; there also can be found both an alphabetical index of the books reviewed by him (523–72) and a chronological index of his reviews and reports on research (573–77).

to his own field of specialization, Bultmann dealt in his reviews not only with New Testament scholarship, but also with the philosophical and historical contexts of the ancient cultures in which nascent Christianity unfolded and asserted itself as a wholly original entity. In time, the reviewer developed his own style,[80] geared his reviews to the presuppositions his readers brought to them, gave an objective description of subjects and conclusions of the research collected in the books, and after a cautious adjudication, rendered his own unambiguous judgment. Not only did he treat with respect the positions of those authors whose position he was not able to share, but in addition to his criticism, especially to the more stimulating authors, he often expressed thanks for the instruction he had gained from reading their works.

"The reader finds more than he expects."[81] So begins Bultmann's first book review—dedicated to a form-critical study by Georg Heinrici. One who reads Bultmann's book reviews and research reports today finds in them more than just material of scholarly interest on the works reviewed and on how they were received. Above all, these writings, undertaken for the workaday scholarly grind, provide important clues for Bultmann's theological biography, both for the formation of certain positions and for the contexts of discourse in which his thought moved and took shape.[82] Writing in 1908–09, for example, he indicated the context of discourse in which he located his report on "New Testament Research of 1905–07" by referring to a "picture of the sea on the day following a storm."[83] He alluded to the storm caused by the history-of-religions school, with its programmatic writings.

Bultmann looks into the waves produced by that storm in his first long report on research.[84] In this, as would become typical for his further activity as a reviewer, he views the individual books from a perspective that is firmly shaped by the previous discussion of a given issue. To begin with, Bultmann explains, Julius Wellhausen has presented the most important work on the synoptic question during the period of time being treated.[85] Along with Jülicher, however, he rejects Wellhausen's assumption of a priority of the Gospel of Mark over against the sayings-source Q. On the other hand, he

80. Cf. U. H. J. Körtner, rev. of *Theologie als Kritik*, 228–32; F. W. Graf, "Individualismus," 48.

81. RB, rev. of C. F. G. Heinrici, in RB, *Theologie als Kritik*, 3.

82. Cf. M. Dreher, *Rudolf Bultmann als Kritiker*.

83. RB, "Die neutestamentliche Forschung 1905–1907," in RB, *Theologie als Kritik*, 7.

84. Cf. RB, *Theologie als Kritik*, 7–26; as well as M. Dreher, *Rudolf Bultmann als Kritiker*, 25–53.

85. Cf. J. Wellhausen, *Einleitung*.

responds positively to Wellhausen's comment on the significance of the preliterary tradition in the gospels. On the relation between the New Testament and the general history of religion and culture, he then discusses the works of Wilhelm Bousset, Hans Schmidt, and Paul Wendland. In passing, and yet at the same time programmatically, Bultmann assigns to comparative religion studies the task of "discerning the generally valid laws of the inner development of a religion and of what is distinctive of it."[86] He characterizes the newly published commentaries of Theodor Zahn, Erich Klostermann, and Hans Lietzmann as real exegesis, with their respective merits and problems; and as one would expect he praises the collected volume on the New Testament produced by the history-of-religions school. He proposes that while this document is accessible to educated lay people, it is so replete with lively exegesis and sensitive to the spirit of the biblical authors that it should also greatly profit specialists in the field.[87]

In dismissing the possibility of depicting the life of Jesus, Bultmann knows himself to be at one with Albert Schweitzer, whose reason for this, namely a "thoroughgoing" eschatology, he nevertheless rejects. Among the contemporary presentations of Jesus, he finds that of Jülicher the best. Recurring to the Enlightenment terminology employed ever since Johann Salomo Semler, Bultmann emphasizes that Jülicher has brought clearly into view both the husk and kernel of the figure of Jesus, "what is Jewish and what transcends what is Jewish," the Jewishness of Jesus and his certitude of victory.[88] At the same time, he criticizes William Wrede's book on Paul on the grounds that it portrays the apostle as a dogmatic zealot who purportedly spoiled the simple religion of Jesus. Because Wrede has not given sufficient credit to Paul's religious experience, he is unable to understand either Paul's theology or the relation of his religion to that of Jesus.[89] With regard to the Gospel of John, Bultmann restricts himself to identifying questions unclarified at present, especially in the literary-critical works of Wilhelm Heitmüller, Julius Wellhausen, and Eduard Schwartz.

Bultmann offers a comprehensive though provisional appraisal of scholarly work in the realm of New Testament up until 1911 in his review of recent "Presentations of the Theology of the New Testament." As a follower of the history-of-religions school, he here shows himself less concerned with

86. RB, *Theologie als Kritik*, 12.
87. Cf. RB, *Theologie als Kritik*, 17; J. Weiss, *Die Schriften*.
88. RB, *Theologie als Kritik*, 20; cf. A. Jülicher, "Die Religion Jesu."
89. Cf. RB, *Theologie als Kritik*, 22f; W. Wrede, *Paulus*.

detailed issues of history and theology than with general reflections on the possibility of creating a theology of the New Testament and on how one should approach this task. To this end he develops his thoughts in the context of a review of the *Lehrbuch der neutestamentlichen Theologie* [*Handbook of New Testament Theology*] by Heinrich Julius Holtzmann, which he acknowledges to be in many respects a "masterwork." To be sure, Bultmann raises a grave objection against Holtzmann's presentation by means of an explicit appropriation of William Wrede's programmatic work, *Über Aufgabe und Methode der sogenannten Neutestamentlichen Theologie* [*On the Task and Method of So-Called New Testament Theology*].[90] Bultmann's objection is that Holtzmann's procedure of reconstructing New Testament theology in terms of doctrines derived from dogmatics deals only with the intellectual aspects of the texts, and thus fails to recognize the vital religio-moral strengths that the "unity of history" concept showed to be central to New Testament religion.[91]

For this reason, Bultmann claims, a presentation of New Testament religion must understand the particular historical phenomena, that is, the religion of such authoritative New Testament personalities as Jesus, Paul, and John, from the comprehensive standpoint of "what is characteristic of the new religion," for this is precisely what manifests itself in the new religious experience of the human person as he discovers his new relation to God.[92] This is the central concept that directs Bultmann's presentation as he assesses the New Testament theology of Heinrich Weinel, Paul Feine, and Adolf Schlatter. Bultmann also shows deep appreciation for Weinel's enterprise of expounding the theology of the New Testament in terms of the history of earliest Christian communities. By contrast, he finds the historical understanding of Feine, a representative of the "positive theology," still too restricted by dogmatic assumptions. And although Schlatter is judged to have been sensitive to the religious content of the New Testament, Bultmann finds him deficient in his understanding of the contemporary historical circumstances of New Testament ideas.[93]

Two years later, it once again fell to Bultmann to review a work of Paul Feine's. In the course of doing so, his sharp eye revealed that the Halle New

90. Cf. W. Wrede, *Über Aufgabe und Methode.*

91. RB, "Vier neue Darstellungen," in RB, *Theologie als Kritik*, 43f; cf. M. Evang, *Frühzeit*, 211f; M. Dreher, *Rudolf Bultmann als Kritiker*, 64–69.

92. RB, *Theologie als Kritik*, 45f.

93. Cf. RB, *Theologie als Kritik*, 46–52; as well as H. Weinel, *Biblische Theologie*; P. Feine, *Theologie*, and A. Schlatter, *Die Theologie.*

Testament scholar had taken long sections of his "Introduction" word for word from Jülicher. Heitmüller, as co-editor of the *Theologische Rundschau* in which the review was to appear, joined Jülicher in persuading Bultmann to consider his future prospects and tone down certain portions of his text. As a result, the review of Feine only implied the charge of plagiarism and muted the extensive evidentiary material. That issue aside, Bultmann noted with evident irony that although a proponent of "positive theology," Feine was beginning to acknowledge the value of historical-critical scholarship.[94] Thereupon, Feine sought to refute the implication of plagiarism by claiming that he had once included the passages in question in his lecture notes and later transferred them to the manuscript of his book, having forgotten where they came from.[95] Bultmann took this dubious explanation as valid cause to issue a charge of "the verbatim dependence of Feine on Jülicher."[96] That Feine's scarcely convincing self-justification was the immediate cause of Bultmann's "Reply" gave further reason for supposing that Feine's unyielding behavior might indicate academic politics as a motive. For in exposing the university professor from Halle, Bultmann was able to show scholarly malfeasance on the part of someone of the "first magnitude among the so-called modern positive school (Seeberg, etc.)"—a theological movement that, he was convinced, had come to be favored over the liberal party by the Prussian regime in appointments to academic chairs.[97]

Between the time of his trial-lecture[98] and the end of his service as a lecturer, Bultmann published in essay form an investigation into the relation of the ethics of Epictetus to the New Testament, as well as a talk on the relevance of scholarly theology to the praxis of the church. The theme of the religious element of Epictetus' approach to ethics had emerged from the time and in the context of his dissertation on Paul and the Cynic-Stoic diatribe. Bultmann arranged it for publication as an alternative framework to that of Adolf Bonhöffer's book, *Epiktet und das Neue Testamen* [*Epictetus and the New Testament*], which had appeared in the meantime.[99] Bultmann

94. Cf. RB, "Einleitung," in RB, *Theologie als Kritik*, 56–60; as well as M. Evang, *Frühzeit*, 48–51.

95. Cf. P. Feine, "Erwiderung," in RB, *Theologie als Kritik*, 514–17.

96. RB, "Antwort," in RB, *Theologie als Kritik*, 67.

97. UB Tübingen, RB est., RB to A. K. Bultmann, 19. 10. 1913, Mn 2-2735; also in RB, *Theologie als Kritik*, 517. For background information, cf. A. Jülicher, *Die Entmündigung*.

98. Cf. RB, "Was lässt . . . ," 35–37, 41–44; see also 53f.

99. Cf. RB, "Das religiöse Moment," 97–110, 177–91; A. Bonhöffer, *Epiktet*. On what follows, cf. M. Evang, *Frühzeit*, 43f; M. Dreher, *Rudolf Bultmann als Kritiker*, 68n2.

sharply distanced himself from Bonhöffer and sought to dismiss his work on Epictetus and Stoicism, claiming that despite its comprehensive erudition, Bonhöffer's opus was "flawed in its statement, as well as its grasp of the problem."[100] This understandably produced consternation on the part of Bonhöffer, who in his rejoinder to Bultmann's essay defended the Stoic philosophy against the criticism of the Christian theologian, though with regard to the vital point of recognizing the overall difference between Christian and Stoic religiousness, he found himself in broad agreement with Bultmann.[101]

In his comparison of the philosophy of Epictetus and the religion of the New Testament, Bultmann employed the distinction between two broad categories: on the one hand he grouped religious ideas, theoretical representations, and concepts; on the other was the religious life as it expressed itself in various objective phenomena. Unlike Stoic philosophy, he argued, earliest Christianity does not find expression in a consistent set of concepts, and therefore the decisive difference between the two spiritual traditions cannot be ascertained from the different complexes of ideas, but can be understood only through the process of opening oneself to the religious life in which each is grounded. In this way, one is able ultimately to trace back to their distinctive concepts of personhood the differences between the two faith traditions with regard to human understanding and the obligation placed upon it as well as the notion of personal relationship with God and providence. Epictetus conceives of the individual primarily in intellectual fashion—as a being endowed with reason and able through its correct exercise to actualize the moral ideal. The New Testament sees the individual as one who can be awakened to his own true life through the power of a living religion and of personal relation to God.[102]

Bultmann's early teaching and research activity took place along the lines marked out by the history-of-religions school. In his exegesis of biblical texts he showed himself to be committed to the methodical principles that characterized liberal theology, specifically those governing historical research and basic hermeneutics employed by Hermann Gunkel, Johannes Weiss, and Wiliam Wrede in the task of biblical interpretation. In the opinion of those who subscribed to the history-of-religions school, biblical exegesis could not

100. RB, "Das religiöse Moment," 97.
101. Cf. A. Bonhöffer, "Epiktet und das Neue Testament," 281–92.
102. Cf. RB, "Das religiöse Moment," 97f, 182–91; as well as M. Evang, *Frühzeit*, 199–203.

be satisfied with a mere historical positivism.[103] On September 29, 1913, Bultmann presented before the "free association" of the Oldenburg General Association of Preachers a seminar paper in which he laid out in detail the relation between a theological scholarship devoted only to truth and the praxis of the church.[104]

In this presentation, Bultmann pleads for a historical scholarship—one form of which is biblical exegesis—that with a view to its potential results works completely without presuppositions. But historical scholarship understood in this way sees its ultimate task not in the mere reconstruction of so-called facts, but rather in fulfilling the goals of the idealistic tradition by discovering the eternal forces that reveal themselves in the temporal events of history. Correspondingly, exegesis aims not at extracting from New Testament texts dogmas or doctrines that are then to be accepted as true. Rather, the historical-critical interpretation of the Bible has to penetrate the surface of the text and track down the representations it employs to promote the religious life that is manifested in all of its individual facets.[105] In doing this, of course, historical Bible scholars must recall a fundamental caveat: "The person who does not stand in a living relation to an historical text cannot write history."[106] Without existential participation, without religious experience on the part of the exegete, the religious life hiding in the New Testament under historically conditioned formulations cannot be grasped.

Apart from the fact that historical study knows "no absolute results, but only relative ones," the knowledge ascertained by it—as Bultmann emphasizes along with Wilhelm Herrmann—can never substantiate faith. All the same, by separating whatever in scripture is accidental and of its own time from the central insights of faith, historical-critical exegesis can eliminate false stumbling-blocks to the Christian message of salvation. The essence of evangelical faith, however, comes to the fore not in the purity of its knowledge, but in the sensitivity of its conscience to "the voice of God." Our "own experience is the only surety we have," and with it the sole "great fact" of evangelical faith, namely revelation, shares itself: "the saving grace of God becoming evident in Jesus in scripture."[107]

103. Cf. H. Gunkel, "Ziele," 521–40; J. Weiss, *Aufgaben*; W. Wrede, *Über Aufgabe und Methode*. Cf. M. Evang, *Frühzeit*, 236–48.

104. Cf. RB, "Theologische Wissenschaft," 123–27, 133–35; as well as M. Evang, *Frühzeit*, 191–98; C. Landmesser, "Rudolf Bultmann: Religion, Kultur und Existenz," 125f.

105. Cf. RB, "Theologische Wissenschaft," 126, 135.

106. RB, "Theologische Wissenschaft," 125f.

107. RB, "Theologische Wissenschaft," 135.

4. Modern Christianity and Preaching

> *As Schleiermacher generally polemicizes against the obsession with conversion, preachers ought to say to themselves that their preaching is not to convert and to teach its hearers, but rather only to bring to expression what is available to all, in one consciously, in another unconsciously. That has always seemed to me the ideal for the sermon: to put myself so far as possible in the heart of the hearers and to awake in it and to bring to clarity what is available there, so that the hearer experiences the sermon as liberation, as it were, as what he would give voice to himself.*[108]

During his studies, Bultmann had distanced himself from forms of piety that had been handed down to him and from an orthodox theology, in order to stand up for a modern Christianity that was in accord with both the nature of faith and the demands of the present. Opposition to established forms of traditional churchliness that have become outdated does not involve challenging the church's role as the institutionalized manifestation of Christianity. In his criticism Bultmann is guided rather by the constructive motive of liberating church praxis from the Procrustean bed of a thoughtless traditionalism and thus enabling it to assure its future by deploying suitable reforms. Even in 1907, when after leaving the Oldenburg academy he decided against a pastoral career to embark on a less secure university career, he never swerved from the task that he formulated towards the end of his studies: "to bring our modern Christianity to the congregations."[109]

Bultmann's plea for a modern Christianity included various facets.[110] The up-and-coming scholar was on solid ground with his recommendation that theology ought to intensify its discourse with interested circles of lay people in the church and society. In Oldenburg during the winter of 1906–07, Bultmann presented to the Friends of *Die Christliche Welt* a report on baptism and the meaning of the death of Jesus,[111] and at the end of 1913 he gave a series of talks on Judaism and the emergence of Christianity[112] before the Oldenburg conference for teachers of religion. He set great hopes on these elementary school teachers, who after his presentations in Oldenburg

108. UB Tübingen, RB est., RB to H. Feldmann, 2.–3. 11. 1916, Mn 2-3447.
109. UB Tübingen, RB est., RB to W. Fischer, 19. 4. 1906, Mn 2-2198.
110. Cf. also M. Evang, *Frühzeit*, 101–33.
111. Cf. UB Tübingen, RB est., RB to E. Teufel, 25. 3. 1907, Mn 2-2393.
112. Cf. UB Tübingen, RB est., RB to W. Fischer, 11. 1. 1914, Mn 2-2198.

became less critical of religion and the church, and even showed a positive religious interest.[113] If cultured and religiously interested lay people were to play an active role in the envisaged modernizing process, it was necessary to acquaint them with the work and the conclusions of theological scholars, and especially those in the field of historical research. During Wilhelm's reign Protestant theology had come under the influence of the Anglo-Saxon sphere of "popular science." It was therefore understandable that efforts by the history-of-religions school to publicize historical-critical theology were highly agreeable to Bultmann, and his popular presentations helped acquaint broad sections of the public with modern views of religion, of Christianity, and of the church.

Bultmann noted several successful examples of this theological popularizing. One was *Religionsgeschichtliche Volksbücher für die deutsche christliche Gegenwart* [*Popular Works in the History of Religions for Christians of Present-Day Germany*],[114] issued by Friedrich Michael Schiele of Mohr Siebeck Press (Tübingen); another was the series of commentaries on the New Testament produced under the aegis of Johannes Weiss,[115] and a third (also brought out by Mohr Siebeck) was the *Handwörterbuch in gemeinverständlicher Darstellung* [*Concise Dictionary in Popular Presentation*], which became the compendium of the history-of-religions research program under the title *Religion in Geschichte und Gegenwart* [*Religion Past and Present*].[116] All of these publicizing efforts shared the intention of serving contemporary religious life, in particular that of an educated middle-class audience, by offering a clear and thorough account of the historical background of Christianity. For precisely this reason, Bultmann cheered the appearance in 1904 of the first *Religionsgeschichtliche Volksbücher*. "Our church has withheld a good deal of criticism and scholarship from the laity and must rapidly make up for what has been missed, if it does not want to atone for this in a painful way. Only through education can the Catholic Church be overcome. Anything else will be of little use."[117] He admitted that the popularization of scholarship might occasionally give rise to mere smatterings of knowledge, but he considered ignorance a greater evil than limited knowledge—which surely no one seeks to attain. By presenting its knowledge in understandable fashion, theology had to strengthen the confidence of lay people in the validity of the

113. Cf. UB Tübingen, RB est., RB to E. Teufel, 17. 7. 1907, Mn 2-2393.

114. Cf. also G. Hübinger, *Kulturprotestantismus*, 204f, 214–19.

115. Cf. J. Weiss, *Schriften*.

116. Cf. also G. Hübinger, *Kulturprotestantismus*, 198–203.

117. UB Tübingen, RB est., RB to W. Fischer, 8. 12. 1904, Mn 2-2198; cf. also W. D. Dennison, "Rudolf Bultmann: Pastor?" 179–87.

scholarly approach to Christianity as a deeply historical religion. "Since we have the Bible as the permanent historical document of the Christian religion and as the basis of liturgy and worship, it will not do in any way to avoid sharing the judgments of scholarship with the people."[118]

How Christianity was to enter in print into the social problems of the imperial era and how it was to react to the alienation of industrial workers from the church were among the questions that barely occupied Bultmann prior to his time in Breslau. Having grown up in the rural milieu of the administrative district of Oldenburg, he had not yet had direct contact with the constellation of social problems that were present in the industrial centers of Germany during the imperial era. Moreover, his personal interest in sociopolitical matters was limited, for he notes that as a student in Berlin he had visited the *Reichstag* in the autumn of 1904 "and listened to several interesting speeches. Actually, the whole parliament made very little impression on me. *Substantive* matters were seldom discussed. The Social Democrats showed very bad manners."[119] Together with his friend Leonhard Frank, whose mind was rather more receptive to "social and political questions," Bultmann pursued "studies of life in Berlin" in 1904–05.[120] During one of these reconnaissance expeditions, he got a close look at the kind of people "one despairingly describes as 'the fallen.'" In the later reflection of one who had seen the light, the twenty-year-old student of theology ruminated on suitable measures for preventing the decline in moral standards in the big cities. He thought that in addition to the work of the Salvation Army and the city mission, the theater—though surely not by means of its classical repertoire—contributes to "the raising of morality and cultural formation."[121] Bultmann therefore outlined an approach to politics grounded in ideals, a program aimed not directly at the political removal of social ills, but that instead recognized the long-term effects of education directed at moral and cultural formation as the conditions for social justice. To be sure, the First World War and the Revolution were to contribute to a noticeable broadening of Bultmann's competence in political and social matters.[122]

Other than that, his ideas about the kind of modern Christianity worth striving for did not look to an unfocused spiritual search by single individuals but rather envisioned a renewed form of *churchly* Christianity. Bultmann

118. UB Tübingen, RB est., RB to W. Fischer, 30. 7. 1907, Mn 2-2198.
119. UB Tübingen, RB est., RB to W. Fischer, 8. 12. 1904, Mn 2-2198.
120. UB Tübingen, RB est., RB to H. Feldmann, 12. 7. 1917, Mn 2-3445.
121. RB to E. Teufel, 28. 10. 1904, Mn 2-2393.
122. See below, 94–104.

hoped for a cautious reform of the church that would as far as possible avoid "destroying the old ecclesiastical forms." He was conscious of the necessity for Christianity, as an innately communal religion, to have a corresponding institutional expression. "Every religion requires and ultimately forms a church; it would therefore be best if a modernizing [ethos] joins itself to the inherited forms of the outward organization."[123]

Bultmann evidently viewed the organization of the Friends of *Die Christliche Welt* as the nucleus of modern Christianity, and on October 6, 1908, he took part in their annual meeting in Eisenach. There the district court judge of Guben, Constantin von Zastrow, gave a much-heralded lecture that unleashed excited debates among the "Friends."[124] In his paper, von Zastrow took issue with the "theology of *Die Christliche Welt*" by championing a rationalist and intellectualist conception of religion. The "Friends" brand of theology, he alleged, too closely resembles the kind of ecclesiastical traditionalism that has become untenable. It is also theologically inconsistent insofar as it has not yet bid a long overdue farewell to those cultic and sacramental practices that inhibit a more spiritual form of religion. Von Zastrow challenged the "Friends" to break with the church of the distant past and to promote the emergence of pantheism as the (presumably) modern embodiment of free Christianity. What von Zastrow had omitted allowed Bultmann to clarify his own conception of the relation of modern Christianity not only to the existing church, but also to competing worldviews.

Bultmann rejected von Zastrow's reproach that the "Friends" were behaving insincerely by retaining traditional forms of worship. To be sure, the use of the old liturgies and preaching on preordained texts presented certain problems, but these were not to be solved by a radical revision of orders of worship. "So the only thing that remains to us is, if possible, to bring the old forms to life. For a person who has an historical sensibility, that is not so difficult."[125] More important than the adjustment of liturgical formulas, Bultmann argues, is the clarification of theological issues. It is a matter of urgent necessity that both lay people and theologians affiliated with *Die Christliche Welt* should be clear and persuasive witnesses to the essential Christian message. Cheerful confidence in victory and clarity of thought were to be seen as mutually sustaining conditions. For Bultmann, "each look at a newspaper, at a handbill, into a bookshop window, every conversation in

123. UB Tübingen, RB est., RB to W. Fischer, 19. 4. 1906, Mn 2-2198.

124. Cf. C. von Zastrow, "Die Theologie der Christlichen Welt," 257–70; see also J. Rathje, *Die Welt*, 221f; M. Evang, *Frühzeit*, 122.

125. UB Tübingen, RB est., RB to W. Fischer, 25. 10. 1908, Mn 2-2198.

the railway coach on a journey with complete strangers" provided evidence that engaging the church in a deepened understanding of the Christian religion would create a positive resonance.[126]

In addition, von Zastrow had reproached the "Friends" with inconsistently compromising religious belief. Insofar as the judge from Guben had thereby held theologians and preachers responsible for the clarity of the worldview they espoused, Bultmann could agree with him without reservation. But Bultmann saw in von Zastrow's encouragement of the "Friends" to adopt monism and pantheism his failure to understand both the conception of religion held in the circle of the "Friends" and "the essence of religious life" overall.[127] Mind you, the theologians at the gathering in Eisenach—among them Adolf Harnack and Wilhelm Bousset—might have failed to make transparent what is distinctive about religion, so adamantly opposed were they to a concept of reality defined in strictly empirical terms. Bultmann, on the other hand, observed that Wilhelm Herrmann had on another occasion "quite splendidly set out the dualism in which the religious person simply *must* find himself."[128] The insight into this dualism between the personal, ultimately irrational experience of the reality of God and the rationally conceived world of appearance allowed Bultmann to reject the anti-ecclesiastical liberalism and syncretistic worldview of von Zastrow as utterly unacceptable. "Religious conviction bears its certitude in itself, and [one] can neither derive it from the experienced world nor, in general, reconcile it thereto."[129]

What did this all mean for the task of the pastor? Bultmann went into this question when on September 29, 1913, he addressed the Oldenburg "free association" on the relation between theological scholarship and church praxis. In his lecture he urgently stressed the necessity of academic education for church office, a need that springs directly from the constitutive significance of Holy Scripture for the church. "If the church has need for Scripture, so it also has need for the work which seeks systematically to understand what is in Scripture; and that is precisely historical biblical scholarship."[130] The more intensively a theologian has pursued academic study, the less he will as pastor succumb to the danger of confusing the pulpit with the podium and thus belabor the community with every novel finding of scholarship. For

126. RB, untitled letter [no. 18], 299.
127. RB, untitled letter [no. 18], 298.
128. UB Tübingen, RB est., RB to W. Fischer, 25. 10. 1908, Mn 2-2198; cf. W. Herrmann, "Der Christ und das Wunder."
129. UB Tübingen, RB est., RB to W. Fischer, 25. 10. 1908, Mn 2-2198.
130. RB, "Theologische Wissenschaft," 125.

his task consists less in criticism "than in the positive proclamation of the one great fact, with the result that his hearers will themselves become responsible for distinguishing what is central from what is peripheral."[131] To this end, historical biblical scholarship provides an indispensable service by sharpening his eye for the difference between the central notions of faith and the merely accidental, contemporary forms of Christianity in the New Testament. Besides, it is not part of the pastor's preaching office "to trot out the assertions of Scripture as teachings that his hearers are to accept, . . . but rather to show what life-giving powers are alive in Scripture, how they are able to grasp us, to give us life as a gift, and to become active in our own present."[132]

Once he had passed his first theological examination and had earned the *licentia concionandi* [license to preach], Bultmann participated in this task himself. Between 1906 and the end of his time in Marburg as a tutor and lecturer in 1916, he gave forty-four sermons.[133] In Marburg he preached predominantly in the Reformed church as part of his duties as tutor in the Hessian Residence for Scholarship Students, but occasionally in special student worship services and, during the First World War, in the local hospital for reserves. Above and beyond this, Bultmann frequently preached at services in his home in Oldenburg. In the summer of 1907, when he was an instructor at the Oldenburg academy, he helped fill vacancies in Athens, Ofen, and Rastede, each time probably in response to a special request by the Evangelical church assembly. Otherwise, the majority of the worship services he conducted in Oldenburg were undertaken as a replacement for his father or pastors who were Bultmann and Ramsauer family relatives. In Hammelwarden alone, he substituted for his uncle Johannes August Bultmann seventeen times. That he both gladly and often entered the pulpit in this village on the Lower Weser may well have been due to the special atmosphere of the Hammelwarden parsonage, which had held an extraordinary attraction for Bultmann during his childhood and student days.[134]

As a general rule, Bultmann followed the analytical method of preaching—though surely not in the narrow sense of serially parsing the verses of the biblical text and showing their application. Rather, he permitted the theme and in large measure the arrangement of the sermon to emerge from the text, developing his homiletic theme in the process of interpreting the text. Up until 1916, he gave only two regular sermons that did not relate

131. RB, "Theologische Wissenschaft," 127.

132. RB, "Theologische Wissenschaft," 126.

133. Cf. the tabular survey in RB, *VW*, 316–25; see also M. Evang, *Frühzeit*, 148–52.

134. Cf. UB Tübingen, RB est., RB to W. Fischer, 2. 4. 1905, Mn 2-2198; reprinted in part in R. Rittner, *Rudolf Bultmann und Oldenburg*, 6.

to a specific text, and both of these exceptions to his usual practice reflected their particular settings. Both "Life and Experience" and "This-worldly and Other-worldly Religion" were given in Marburg during worship for students, in keeping with whose desires the services consisted of religious talks and short hymn-sings.[135] In the sermons he delivered at regular worship services, Bultmann used the prescribed texts only in 1907, while in the following two decades he increasingly made his own choice of sermon texts. In the beginning, he read the sermon-texts for the listening congregation not from Luther's Bible, but rather from contemporary translations. This seemed to him to correspond to the ideal of contemporary proclamation: "The people should hear the Bible in the language that they speak! If we do not bring religion home to them in the language that is familiar to them, that they speak every day, we do them the worst service imaginable."[136] However, he followed this principle only for a short while. In the long-term, the incomparable linguistic power and succinctness of Luther's Bible asserted itself in his preaching.

The theme that the young Bultmann returned to again and again in his sermons was the religious significance of reality, and the central importance of the concepts "work" and "gift."[137] The reciprocal relation of these two motifs in the experience of reality—the religious view of life as gift and the specifically modern notion of fulfilling one's relation to reality in work—was thus fully and clearly expounded. On December 10, 1911, for example, Bultmann preached in Marburg, taking as his text 1 Cor 7:29–31. He first described to the congregation the phenomenon of work in its significance for daily life, culture, and morality, as well as for the institutions of the family and the state. In contrast to this, he pointed out, the sermon text emphasized the eschatological distance that manifests itself in the individual Christian's inward alienation from the world. He tried to reconcile the two ideas by proposing that work is to be done "not for our sake, but rather for the sake of an everlasting future that we have experienced as a godly task."[138] To be sure, he partially retracted this solution to the problem in the latter part of the sermon; for he went on to say that to define religion as experiencing life as a gift and having faith in an undeserved future is to raise the possibility

135. Cf. the sermons, "Leben und Erleben" (23. 6. 1912) and "Diesseits und Jenseitsreligion" (12. 7. 1914), in RB, *VW*, 86–95, 104–14; on the student worship services, cf. E. Simons, "Prediger=Professoren?" 308.

136. UB Tübingen, RB est., RB to E. Teufel, 17. 7. 1907, Mn 2-2393.

137. For more details, cf. also E. Hauschildt, *Rudolf Bultmanns Predigten*, 20–59.

138. RB, *VW*, 71.

of moving beyond faith in one's work and opening oneself to a view of the future as the deed and the work of God. In this sermon, Bultmann still understood religion entirely in the context of the moral world-order dominated by work. If the experience of the gift won out over that of work, religion was nonetheless functionally related to morality, and the gospel found expression within the horizon of the law.

Two and a half years later, Bultmann once again assessed the relation between work and gift. In the sermon, "This-worldly and Other-worldly Religion," which he presented on July 12, 1914, at a student worship service in Marburg, work and gift appear as opposites. Bultmann again emphasized the character of genuine religious life as gift. But, he told his student audience, religion is profoundly different from work of any kind. "From the world of religion, all work, all doing, everything fabricated, is banished. What is relevant here is only being open, being quiet, allowing everything to resolve itself, to fill itself up, letting everything happen of its own accord. It is a world of being given unto, of grace. The forms it takes are not sought by the spirit, not found, and not created: they reveal themselves."[139] Contingent religious experience no longer had to legitimate itself by its functional relation to the moral system of values constituted by work and by the restraint of law. Rather, Bultmann now understood work as a preliminary stage, which at best could lead up to the religion of revelation and gift. "That person alone is capable of reaching religion's other world who has really abandoned this world, who operates in that world of the spirit."[140]

In January 1905 Bultmann had come to recognize that Protestantism could be existentially legitimated by the fact "that it did not represent the Christian religion as morality. A church should not give its members morality, but religion. . . . Morality in itself can never be a motive; I must, as it were, dissolve it in religion."[141] The postulate put forward in 1905 was gradually put to good account in his preaching as he employed the pulpit to carry on a critical dialectic concerning Wilhelm Herrmann's view of the relation between morality and religion with respect to both their connections and their differences. By beginning to reduce religion's integrative role in the overarching context of ethics, and by granting the gospel a sphere of its own not dominated by law, he gradually broke with the conception of

139. RB, *VW*, 110.

140. RB, *VW*, 113; on Bultmann's sermon, "Diesseits und Jenseitsreligion," for more detail, cf. also M. Evang, *Frühzeit*, 257–62; E. Hauschildt, *Rudolf Bultmanns Predigten*, 36–42.

141. UB Tübingen, RB est., RB to W. Fischer, 27. 1. 1905, Mn 2-2198.

religion as a part of culture—at least, as this had been represented in the previous generation of teachers.[142] To this extent, Bultmann's early sermons confirm his later assessment, expressed in 1928, that the experience of war was less decisive for the genesis of his theology than "the internal debate with the theology of our teachers."[143]

Bultmann did not see his preaching as that of a religious virtuoso whose job was to contribute the riches of his personal experience to the congregation. He felt himself to a considerable degree still a seeker, albeit one who was certain of the purpose for which he was entering the pulpit. In the meantime he sought to compensate for the discrepancy between his perception of himself and the expectation of the congregation by means of the optimistic hope "that one will grow oneself through serving the cause; and if one gives the appearance of already being farther along than one is, that too is also only a self-deception for the sake of the cause, one that has to be."[144] Preaching did not become a burden for Bultmann because he presented himself in the pulpit as representing a modern theology. But for this same reason he took pains to be tactful and avoid unnecessary conflicts with tradition-oriented congregations.[145] He struggled with the problem of finding language capable of providing the message of the sermon with a form of expression appropriate to the times. "It is terribly difficult to escape the traditional *language* of preaching; much more difficult than traditional *ideas*. . . . [A] sermon must also not sound too modern; otherwise it will shock the congregation unnecessarily."[146]

Those issues aside, however, Bultmann felt that his main weakness as a preacher lay in the fact that his sermons seldom seemed to satisfy the high ideal of worshipful speech inculcated by his teacher of homiletics, Johannes Bauer. In the sermon, Bauer had insisted, the faith of the preacher was supposed to communicate itself to the congregation. But, as Bultmann realized, "It is so fearfully difficult to speak about religion—or better put, *from* religion."[147] This problem might lead to inward insecurity during sermon preparation: might a thought that had been written down "with true feeling" seem upon review "like a self-deception"? The conflict between the requirement that the sermon be spoken from religious experience and the need for

142. This is the case despite the fact that Bultmann holds fast to certain of W. Herrmann's ways of posing questions and insights. Cf. for example the sermon of 1 April 1907 on Luke 24:13–32, "Wie kommt es," treated in detail by M. Evang, *Frühzeit*, 152–70.

143. RB to E. Foerster (?), 1928, in W. Schmithals, "Ein Brief," 74.

144. UB Tübingen, RB est., RB to W. Fischer, 23. 4. 1908, Mn 2-2198.

145. UB Tübingen, RB est., RB to W. Fischer, 23. 4. 1908, Mn 2-2198.

146. UB Tübingen, RB est., RB to W. Fischer, 1. 1. 1910, Mn 2-2198.

147. UB Tübingen, RB est., RB to W. Fischer, 22. 12. 1907, Mn 2-2198.

adequate preparation before presenting it became clear to Bultmann. "In the sermon, one ought to speak extemporaneously, as it comes from the heart; and yet one must prepare oneself with care and think everything through. I believe that the preacher simply must bear this conflict for the sake of the cause for which one is doing it. And yet for this very reason, it requires a great deal of self-criticism not to undertake to say anything that one cannot inwardly actually stand behind fully."[148]

5. Community Lived and Community Sought

> *In 1908, my teacher Johannes Weiss was called to Heidelberg. I already had a friendly relationship with his successor, Wilhelm Heitmüller, and I feel particularly indebted to him. During these years, I spent a great part of my time in the home of Martin Rade. I was an avid reader of the periodical* Die Christliche Welt, *of which he was the editor, and I was also a member of the organization of Friends of* Die Christliche Welt *and, as my father did regularly for his whole life, attended their annual meetings.*[149] *—At the end of my time in Marburg, both before the War began and at the beginning of the War, I experienced with joy the new spiritual life that arose in the student body and played a part in creating its own highly enjoyable forms of self-expression. I have always felt a connection with this, and I continue to set hopes on it.*[150]

In the decades following the Prussian annexation of Kurhessen in 1866, the University of Marburg underwent astonishing growth both qualitatively and quantitatively. Acting in accordance with its higher education policies, the Prussian state provided Marburg and the new Prussian universities with nearly every imaginable support. Following the establishment of the German Empire in 1871, the college (which since 1885 had officially borne the name "The Royal Prussian University of Marburg") was therefore able to develop in concert with the Prussian Universities a considerable reputation. And significant changes in the cityscape of Marburg mirrored the growth of the university during the Prussian era. Existing hospitals were expanded and new

148. UB Tübingen, RB est., RB to H. Feldmann, 21.-22.-23. 5. 1917, Mn 2-3447.

149. "Autobiographische Bemerkungen," in B. Jaspert, *Barth-Bultmann Briefwechsel* (2d ed.), 304.

150. UB Tübingen, RB est., RB to W. Fischer, 8. 9. 1919, Mn 2-2198.

ones built, the natural sciences received their own buildings in the form of institutes, and a new auditorium building—today's "Old University"—lent an appropriate splendor to the prospering college from 1878 on.

The Marburg theological faculty participated in this university-wide expansion. Through their important achievements in teaching and scholarship, its members saw to it that Marburg became an increasingly attractive place for theology students, whose numbers saw steady growth from seventy-seven in 1866 to 309 in the summer semester of 1914. Marburg was counted among the leading theological faculties of the Empire. Yet despite the expansion, which after 1871 had greatly transformed the university as a whole, the contemporary judgment of Adolf Harnack that the German university system had become a scholarly industry in the Kaiser's Empire was not entirely true of the situation in Marburg. For the *Philippina* became a college of only medium size, and the city of Marburg constituted a comfortably compact community. To be sure, its number of inhabitants increased rapidly from 7,718 to 22,200 between 1866 and 1914, and yet the student body realized even greater rates of growth during this period. Their number shot up from 257 to 2,464, and their share of the population rose from 3.3 to 11.1 percent.[151] Before the First World War local politicians pursued an anti-urban form of politics, and largely opposed bringing in industry in order to give Marburg the look of a college town that remained close to the world of nature. Thus, the university had a lasting influence on public life in the city. What the regional writer Ernst Koch had in 1888 discerned as a characteristic of Marburg under different circumstances still held true at the beginning of the twentieth century: Other cities such as Göttingen might *have* a university; Marburg *was* a university.[152]

To be sure, persons who came from a large urban environment to this small university city in Hesse might have been alienated by the provinciality that they imagined they found here; but others prized Marburg precisely because they could work in quiet here and, to whatever extent they wished, enter into the social and cultural life of the city. Rudolf Bultmann belonged among these. During his time as a tutor in Marburg, he lived first at 29 Wilhelm Street, after April 26, 1909, at 8 Renthof Street, and from August 1910 until moving to Breslau in 1916 he lodged in 2 House Barfussertor. All of these residences were within easy reach of the auditorium building and the homes of the theology professors near the castle or in the southern quarter. Bultmann did not bury himself in his books, but sought out social contacts

151. Cf. B. vom Brocke, "Marburg im Kaiserreich 1866–1918," 377.
152. Cf. E. Koch, *Prinz Rosa=Stramin*, 81.

and fellowship. Four main strands comprised the network of relationships within which his life unfolded from 1907 to 1916. Bultmann maintained close ties to his family in Oldenburg, to his school friend Leonhard Frank, and to his student friends, especially Walther Fischer. In addition to these, new relationships now opened up as a result of his scholarly activity. He made closer contacts, some of them true friendships, with individual professors of theology and up-and-coming scholars from other faculties. Furthermore, he joined in the efforts of the youth movement to develop new forms of community and cultural life among the student body.

The relationship between Bultmann and his parents was sustained by a great mutual trust; indeed, the large collection of preserved letters that the son and his parents wrote to each other gives no hint of dissonance. Bultmann frequently went home to Oldenburg during summer vacations, and he reported by mail regularly and in detail on what he was doing in Marburg. In this way, he allowed his family to share in both his personal life and his career. Because of his father's scholarly interests, Bultmann took pains to include him in conversations regarding developments in theology, recent books, and the many issues on which he was working. When his father decided for reasons of health to take an early pension, the son wrote him a letter so sensitive that it all but seemed an epistle of pastoral care. He assured his father that the decision, which had hardly been taken lightly, would lead to an important turning point in his life. "I am now also sorry that I am not married and cannot invite you at once."[153]

In 1906 Bultmann's sister Helene married the Oldenburg pastor August Pleus, and two years later, Bultmann became the godfather of their first daughter, Elisabeth. When his goddaughter was five years old, he began to write regularly to her and to her sister Marianne, who was born in 1910. What he had to tell his nieces he illustrated on the backs of his postcards with his own drawings: "That is the train I took to Marburg. . . . A long whistle and a short whistle. . . . This is how it looks in the morning here in Baden. . . . This is how Uncle Arthur came here yesterday as a hiker. . . . Here is Uncle Rudolf taking his afternoon nap on his sofa and reading the lovely book that your mommy gave him as a present. . . . Now the semester is over and soon a spider can spin its web in front of my desk. . . . You will have to open the door for Uncle Rudolf next Sunday!"[154]

Just as Bultmann devoted himself with evident joy to his little nieces, he also sought to maintain longer-standing connections. For instance, during

153. UB Tübingen, RB est., RB to A. K. Bultmann, 19. 10. 1913, Mn 2-2735.
154. UB Tübingen, RB est., RB to E. Pleus, 18. 1.–29. 11. 1913, Mn 2-3455.

the week after Pentecost in 1909 he took a trip to southern Germany to pay a number of visits. In the Black Forest he called in on relatives, and in Tübingen he visited Theodor Haering, Karl Müller, and Hermann von Fischer, the father of his friend. Naturally, he also spent a few "lovely hours" in the *Igel*. In Tübingen, he reported, not without nostalgia, "it is too beautiful with all its greenery along the river opposite the magnificent plane trees. If only I could study for a couple more first semesters again!"[155] On the return trip he stopped for a day with Johannes Weiss in Heidelberg and enjoyed a long and pleasant exchange with his former teacher.

Whenever semester vacations found Bultmann unable to meet from time to time with his school friend Leonhard Frank and his student friend from Tübingen, Walther Fischer, he employed correspondence to maintain a close relationship with them. While his letters to Frank have unfortunately not been preserved,[156] the exchange of letters with Fischer provides us with important biographical insights into Bultmann's enormous interest in the arts, particularly in literature.[157] In the summer of 1908, he read Karl Philipp Moritz' psychological novel, *Anton Reiser*, "an artistic masterwork," in which Bultmann rediscovered "infinitely much of myself." The novel made him curious about the period of the Enlightenment and led him to suspect that the present could learn an extraordinary amount from its writers about what initiated "the fusing of religion with modern cultural forms."[158] Bultmann observed to himself that every now and then he seemed to be surrounded by characters like those in the novels he had read, especially those of Charles Dickens. "The reading of Dickens has the distinctive effect of making one begin to see through Dickens' eyes. Whether one is sitting in the coach on a train journey or in a corner in an inn with a glass of beer, one observes the people one sees around oneself as if one were reading a Dickens portrait of them. Each person becomes an original, and yet one rediscovers particular types. It is strange and amusing."[159]

More often than not, Bultmann linked his impressions from reading with evaluations of the authors, whom he then ranked from the point of view of aesthetics and content. For example, he judged Dostoevsky's *Crime and Punishment* and many other works primarily from a psychological perspective: "I have never found the art of psychological analysis anywhere else with *this* degree of perfection. To be sure, reading it is not always pleasant, but

155. UB Tübingen, RB est., RB to A. K. Bultmann, 13. 6. 1909, Mn 2-2735.
156. Cf. K. Hammann, "Rudolf Bultmanns Begegnung," 41n23.
157. Cf. T. Kucharz, *Theologen und ihre Dichter*, 168–84.
158. UB Tübingen, RB est., RB to W. Fischer, 31. 8. 1908, Mn 2-2198.
159. UB Tübingen, RB est., RB to W. Fischer, 2. 4. 1909, Mn 2-2198.

sometimes it grabs you in direct fashion."[160] Bultmann read a wide variety of authors, but nineteenth-century novels and dramas as well as new works stood at the top of his comprehensive list of literature, although lyric poetry was of scarcely any interest. The literary subjects that particularly spoke to him were portrayals of nature—the sea, for example—and psychologically sensitive presentations of a simple life at one with nature in a rural setting. It was no accident that authors such as Selma Lagerlöf, Wilhelm Raabe, Bernhard Kellerman, Jeremias Gotthelf and Gottfried Keller found particular favor with him, though he also read through Dickens, Dostoevsky, Frank Wedekind and Franz Werfel to provide insight into the problems of urban civilization.

Music held a status like that of literature in the life of the Marburg tutor. Bultmann not only attended concerts regularly as well as an occasional opera—the latter mostly in Kassel—and he took an active part in the music-making of social circles he organized in Marburg. Besides scholarship, it was this love of literature and music that led to his connection with Johannes Weiss. In a 1939 article memorializing his teacher, Bultmann recalled that Weiss and his wife, Auguste, a daughter of Albrecht Ritschl, fostered a high level of social life in their home. For Weiss, making music together with Bultmann and other guests was a natural part of domestic cultural life. In the field of music the budding New Testament scholar prized Bach and Brahms above all. At the beginning of his acquaintance with Bultmann, Weiss made it clear whom his student was to regard as the measure of all music: "As long as Bach is not your daily bread, you're still nothing musically." Before his move to Heidelberg, Weiss said goodbye to Bultmann by performing for him the "Serious Songs" of Brahms.[161]

Bultmann felt Weiss' departure especially deeply because his successor, Wilhelm Heitmüller, was for his first several months in Marburg not yet in a position to develop the scholarly exchange Bultmann had hoped for; during this period Heitmüller was preoccupied with his own work and making preparations for his upcoming wedding.[162] But this situation was to change over the course of time. Bultmann was already making music on a weekly basis with Heitmüller's wife, Else, in the autumn of 1908,[163] and his relationship with the new couple soon developed into an intense friendship

160. UB Tübingen, RB est., RB to W. Fischer, 21. 11. 1910, Mn 2-2198; cf. also RB, rev. of F. M. Dostoyevsky, 1206.

161. RB, "Johannes Weiss," 245f.

162. Cf. UB Tübingen, RB est., RB to W. Fischer, 17. 7. 1908 and 17. 1. 1909, Mn 2-2198.

163. Cf. UB Tübingen, RB est., RB to A. K. Bultmann, 29. 11. 1908, Mn 2-2735.

that up to 1916 belonged among the happiest experiences of his years in Marburg.[164] One expression of this close relationship was that Bultmann became godfather to the Heitmüllers' son, Hanfried, in 1911; another was that after the death of the elder Heitmüller on January 29, 1926, Bultmann wrote a literary memorial to his deceased friend for *Die Christliche Welt.* He praised him as a scholar, academic teacher, and human being, who had been a truly free person in the sense of John 8:32, and who in his theological work had been led by the radical pursuit of truth.[165] Thus, Bultmann saw Wilhelm Heitmüller as exemplifying that same part of the inheritance of liberal theology to which he himself dedicated his whole life.

As a reviewer for *Die Christliche Welt*, Bultmann was also regularly a guest at the home of Martin Rade.[166] However, despite a high personal regard for him, Bultmann kept himself at a certain distance from the head of the Friends of *Die Christliche Welt*, being unable to find him theologically helpful. In 1916, looking back on his second stint in Marburg, Bultmann felt Rade's ambitious nature, somewhat dictatorial style, and constant eagerness to exert his influence as powerful hindrances to the formation of a still closer relationship.[167] Nevertheless, at Rade's home Bultmann became acquainted with Karl Barth, a Swiss theologian two years younger than he, who in 1908–09 was active as an editorial assistant for *Die Christliche Welt.* The oldest preserved letter of Bultmann to Barth, dated June 11, 1911, contains the Marburg tutor's wishes for happiness on the occasion of Barth's engagement to Nelly Hoffmann in Geneva.[168]

During a vacation stay on the island of Wangeroog in the summer of 1908, Bultmann had a chance to become better acquainted with the Old Testament scholar Hermann Gunkel, whose seminar he had attended in both of his semesters of study in Berlin. In the years to follow, he was able to intensify a personal and scholarly exchange with Gunkel, who at that time was teaching in Giessen. As he reported to Walther Fischer on January 17, 1909, he was delighted by his visit with the Old Testament scholar: "How refreshing it was . . . this afternoon with Gunkel! I learned more that I otherwise could have in weeks!"[169]

164. Cf. UB Tübingen, RB est., RB to H. Feldmann, 4.–5. 10. 1916, Mn 2-3447; cf. also n. 149 above.

165. Cf. RB, "Wilhelm Heitmüller," 211–13.

166. "Autobiographische Bemerkungen," in B. Jaspert, *Barth-Bultmann Briefwechsel* (2d ed.), 304.

167. Cf. UB Tübingen, RB est., RB to H. Feldmann, 4.–5. 10. 1916; see also M. Evang, *Frühzeit*, 24f.

168. Cf. RB to K. Barth, 11. 6. 1911, in B. Jaspert, *Barth-Bultmann Briefwechsel* (2d ed.), 3.

169. UB Tübingen, RB est., RB to W. Fischer, 17. 1. 1909, Mn 2-2198.

While Bultmann maintained social contacts chiefly with these Marburg professors of theology and their families, his first years as a tutor found him spending extended periods of time on his dissertation; his desire to qualify for teaching was now strengthened by a collegial relationship with several up-and-coming scholars of about his own age. The circle of young scholars from different faculties that gathered at a common lunch table enriched Bultmann's world both personally and as a scholar. Bultmann's friendships with the philosopher Nicolai Hartmann and the classical philologists Christian Jensen and Friedrich Pfister proved beneficial for Bultmann's own work.[170] Other participants in the luncheon group further enabled him to look beyond the horizon of New Testament exegesis and thus gain insights into fields of study that were foreign to him. It is also worth passing mention that in this academic community Bultmann had friendly dealings with three Jewish lecturers: the mathematician Ernst Hellinger, the scholar of Indo-Germanic languages Hermann Jacobsohn, and the classical archaeologist Paul Jacobsthal. Later additions to the circle included two Old Testament scholars—Bultmann's old school-chum Emil Balla, who was active as a lecturer in Marburg in 1914–15, and the Swiss scholar Walther Baumgartner—the latter having made Bultmann's acquaintance two years earlier "through some sort of invitation at the house of Jülicher or Heitmüller." Their relationship deepened when this former student of Gunkel taught Hebrew in Marburg from the summer of 1915. But beyond their common reading of Gnostic texts, a mutual interest in "how to deal with folklore," and "joy in the colorful world of folktales" bound Baumgartner and Bultmann together. Both these topics, of course, found roles in the writing of the *Geschichte der synoptischen Tradition* [*History of the Synoptic Tradition*].[171]

In his old age Bultmann described the atmosphere among the lecturers of the luncheon group: "partly humorous, partly critical conversations livened it up . . . , with the result that we also gained a reputation as a bunch of blasphemers."[172] One might suspect that every now and again the lecturers licked each other's wounds with sarcasm when appointments to academic chairs had not materialized. Bultmann long regarded the chances for him to receive an appointment as slim. To the lecturer who was disposed to liberalism and oriented towards historical criticism, it was clear that debates between the liberal and orthodox-positive elements in the Prussian state

170. Cf. Bultmann's observations from the early summer of 1969 in B. Jaspert, *Barth-Bultmann Briefwechsel* (2d ed.), 312.

171. W. Baumgartner, "Rudolf Bultmann," 1f.

172. Notes of Bultmann's from the early summer of 1969 in B. Jaspert, *Barth-Bultmann Briefwechsel* (2d ed.), 312.

church were becoming increasingly a matter of church politics; and right-wing influence on the politics of ecclesiastical and scholarly appointment in Prussia was at the very least holding up the careers of up-and-coming liberal theologians.[173] In a 1913 phillipic, Adolf Jülicher had just fiercely denounced the discrimination against critical theologians exercised by biased officials in the Prussian Ministry of Education and the Arts. Under the circumstances prevalent in these days, it was the unfortunate duty of all responsible professors "to warn 'free' theologians away from the teaching profession—not for lack of openings, but as *closed to them* on account of the danger of epidemic."[174] Jülicher's criticism of the Prussian educational bureaucracy caused a public sensation. His attack was quickly caught up in the whirlpool of church politics, and even came before the Prussian parliament on April 5, 1913.

To be sure, the way the right wing of the church reacted to Jülicher's justified accusations could only strengthen Bultmann's uncertainties about his own prospects. "One can only keep doing one's work and in the meantime not lose hope," he declared at the beginning of 1914.[175]

When Bultmann accepted the call to an associate professorship in Breslau two and a half years later, it turned out that he himself had done a great deal for the circle of colleagues around the lunch table.[176] "I do know that they were fond of me and sad to see me go, particularly by the garland they gave me," he reported upon his departure from Marburg early in October 1916.[177] The academic round table represented something like a *universitas litterarum in nuce*. His fond memory of this collegial company included valuable interchanges outside the boundaries of his own discipline as much as it did informal fellowship with other young scholars. This example of cultivated collegiality formed for him an indispensable component of personal development.

What Bultmann found in this coterie of lecturers he saw as being largely lost elsewhere in the business of scholarship in the university which, he lamented, "has become a mere sum of individual jobs, which for the most part has lost the feeling of mutuality and just carries on the work of a trade, rather than that of a vocation." For this reason, it was in no way capable of

173. Cf. UB Tübingen, RB est., RB to W. Fischer, 2. 11. 1913, Mn 2-2198; on what follows, cf. also M. Evang, *Frühzeit*, 54–56.

174. A. Jülicher, *Entmündigung*, 36.

175. UB Tübingen, RB est., RB to W. Fischer, 11. 1. 1914, Mn 2-2198.

176. Cf. already C. Jensen to RB, 11. 5. 1912, Mn 2-1069; W. Baumgartner to RB, 11. 5. 1917, Mn 2-420; cf. also W. Heitmüller to RB, 7. 11. 1916, Mn 2-964.

177. UB Tübingen, RB est., RB to H. Feldmann, 4.–5. 10. 1916, Mn 2-3447.

fulfilling one of its most noble tasks, "the methodical reflection upon scholarship *as such*, which supports all scholarly work, and also reflection upon its connection with life."[178] All the more enthusiastically, then, did Bultmann greet the efforts of the youth movement to develop new forms of spiritual and communal life among the student body. In Marburg, he participated from the summer of 1914 onwards in the calendar of events of the Academic Union, which in the autumn of 1913 had played a decisive role in the formation of the various groups and associations initiated by young people at the meeting of Free German Youth at the High Meissner at Eschwege. On the one hand, what he experienced at the celebrations and during the evening discussions of the Academic Union reminded him of his time in the *Igel* in Tübingen; on the other, he sensed that new ideas and forces were taking shape all around him. In a letter he wrote to Walther Fischer on June 4, 1914, Bultmann shared his uncertain feelings. He was still unsure of how to evaluate the "hustle and bustle" of the Academic Union. The group might not yet have the right kind of comradeship, the right sort of foolishness and "high spirits," but the high cultural level of the members, their interest in interdisciplinary scholarly work and the arts, and particularly the "splendid, noble type of sociability" that occurred here gave him hope for the future.[179]

Bultmann understood the emergence of the youth movement as an alternative to the world of work, which threatened to suffocate true life. And in his Breslau sermon of July 1, 1917, as he looked back on his own experiences in Marburg, he saw that young people rightly sought out "life in and with nature," discovered anew "the joy of play . . . of simply being, without goals" and gave the festival celebration its true meaning—namely that of enabling the self-expression of the individual, freed from the compulsions of the culture of work.[180] Bultmann had thus adopted the conceptuality he had been using since about 1912 to describe the search for this sort of life.[181] It reflected the philosophy of life he encountered for instance in the texts of Wilhelm Dilthey.[182] This philosophical understanding of life for its own sake—a life constantly in movement and flux, always having to decide anew between opposing powers, between nature and spirit—enabled him to keep

178. RB, untitled article in *Akademische Vereinigung*, 15.

179. UB Tübingen, RB est., RB to W. Fischer, 4. 6. 1914, Mn 2-2198; reprinted in M. Evang, *Frühzeit*, 59.

180. Sermon on Mark 10:13–16, 1. 7. 1917, *VW*, 159; similarly RB, untitled article in *Akademische Vereinigung*, 16.

181. Cf. the sermon of 23 June 1912 on the theme of "Life and Experience" given by Bultmann at a student worship service, *VW*, 86–95.

182. Cf. G. Sinn, *Christologie und Existenz*, 142–46.

the door open for the actual impressions of lived community, and above all for dealing with the religious question about the source, content, and goal of true life. The "will for shared experience"[183] served for him as the inalienable presupposition for shaping outward communal life, as well as for the experience of religion, of the revelation of life that is transparent to itself.[184]

When Bultmann went to Breslau at the beginning of October 1916 he felt the end of participating in and with the Marburg Academic Union as "especially painful. . . . A beginning of working with students had been made there, and after the War, how gladly would I have raised my hand right there to help carry on with what the War had interrupted."[185] He wrote these lines to Helene Feldmann, to whom he had become engaged in August 1916. Now, in joining his life with hers, Bultmann found a very special form of companionship, one that his friendships and social contacts up to that time had not been able to offer.

183. RB, untitled article in *Akademische Vereinigung*, 16.
184. Sermon, 23. 6. 1912, *VW*, 92.
185. UB Tübingen, RB est., RB to H. Feldmann, 4.–5. 10. 1916, Mn 2-3447.

III. Professor in Breslau and Giessen (1916–1921)

1. Marriage to Helene Feldmann

When I sit at my desk in the evening, I am no longer overcome by the feeling of not having a home, the feeling that, even given all the love and kindness that I experience from others, I am still always only a guest and will again have to travel alone. Rather, a feeling of security happily envelops me, that I can feel at rest with you and that you can feel at rest with me. And even if we do want to keep going off on trips, it is a completely different kind of traveling than before.[1]

In March 1915, Helene Feldmann, a student from Essen, wrote to Bultmann asking for advice. Was the program in Latin and Greek that she had completed up to the seventh year at the lyceum sufficient for her to continue her course of studies to become a teacher?[2] The young woman had attended Bultmann's Greek language course in the winter semester of 1914–15, and now he encouraged her to arrange her course of study according to her own personal inclinations—which clearly favored the natural sciences—but not to view her "guest appearance" in the humanities as wasted time.[3] Following this brief correspondence, Bultmann and Helene Feldmann became closer in the summer of 1915, when both took part in the social and cultural events of the Academic Union. The lecturer and the student soon took a fancy to each other, and arranged to meet at concerts, for rowing parties on the Lahn, for walks on the castle hill. They did all this covertly for fear that being too public might somehow sever the delicate bonds that had formed between them. In any case, their personal situations were not yet in a state of equilibrium. As Bultmann reported to "Miss Feldmann" in August 1915, things were with him "as you write they are with you: I have not yet found my way. I do not wish to hang on to the memories of the Marburg summer, but must first draw a veil over it, so that later they can shine more purely and beautifully for me. And so I am, as it were, suspended in emptiness."[4]

Bultmann wrote these lines six days before his thirty-first birthday. He had no intention of settling down into a permanent bachelorhood, for he

1. UB Tübingen, RB est., RB to H. Feldmann, 12. 10. 1916, Mn 2-3447.
2. Cf. UB Tübingen, RB est., H. Feldmann to RB, 13. 3. 1915, Mn 2-2681.
3. Cf. UB Tübingen, RB est., RB to H. Feldmann, 21. 3. 1915, Mn 2-2739.
4. UB Tübingen, RB est., RB to H. Feldmann, 14. 8. 1915, Mn 2-2739.

felt himself drawn by the austere charm of Helene Feldmann. And the student, who had once wanted to become a concert singer—a vocational choice vetoed by her mother—shared his special love of literature and music. But Luise Feldmann was of the opinion that Helene's choice of profession would not enable her to make her own way in the world. Given their deep common interests, however, minor atmospheric disturbances were unable to endanger what was going on between Bultmann and Helene Feldmann. Once, when they had a misunderstanding, the practical-minded Helene wrote a card to "Dear Mr. Bultmann" that contained merely the following: "How would Isaiah 30:15 find you? 'Were you to turn around and be still, you would be helped; by being still and hoping, you would become strong!'"[5] Being still and hoping would prove useful in sustaining Bultmann's relationship with Helene Feldmann in the long term.

For the moment, particularly during semester vacations, things remained at the level of writing letters, which Bultmann wanted to be understood not as "tokens of self-admiration," but rather as "a substitute for person-to-person exchange." For he was long past "that lyrical and pathetic age" when one wrote letters for the sake of inward reflection, rather than to foster real communication. All the same, Bultmann found communication with his partner in letter-writing not entirely free from obstacles. "As you yourself occasionally say, you have set up a wall that has still not been completely torn down even now."[6] Did the wall behind which Helene Feldmann sought protection have to do with the shadows that had oppressed her since the seventh year of her life? Her father, the architect Heinrich Feldmann, had been ruined by a bank failure, and desperate over the resulting annihilation of his professional existence, he committed suicide. Since that time, Helene's mother had had to provide for the family of four on her own.

Bultmann chose an unusual way to induce the young woman to give up her inner reserve; he wrote her a fairy tale that he enclosed with his letter of April 5, 1916. His "story of Lumpy-Dumpy, who fell down the stairs and still got the princess," is a take-off on Hans Christian Andersen's fairytale "The Christmas Tree"; but he revises Andersen's plot line and adds new details to tell how the social differences between the princess and the simple young Lumpy-Dumpy cannot prevent the two lovers from coming together in the end.[7]

5. UB Tübingen, RB est., H. Feldmann to RB, 9. 1. 1916, Mn 2-2681; cf. also RB to H. Feldmann, 16. 1. 1916, Mn 2-2739, and H. Feldmann to RB, 17. 1. 1916, Mn 2-2681.

6. UB Tübingen, RB est., RB to H. Feldmann, 21. 4. 1916, Mn 2-3447.

7. Cf. RB, *Wachen und Träumen*, 13-20.

Plates 17 and 18: The Engaged Couple Helene Feldmann and Rudolf Bultmann, 1916

On June 19, 1916, Helene Feldmann sent Bultmann a card with the iconic picture of a "waving cornfield" by Hans von Volkmann "as preparation for the cornfields at Rauschenberg."[8] In this place, not far from Marburg on the southern edge of the castle forest, the two met on the last day of June, to walk back to the city. That evening, the two professed their love for each other.[9] From now on, everything was completely changed in their relationship. She: "Darling! Do you know why I am writing to you? Really, only just to write the one word [darling]!"[10] He to his "dear lass": "But there is something else you should know—that when I'm working, it is not as if I just steal a glance at your picture every once in a while, but rather that you are always there like the wonderful sound of a distant violin—warm and happy."[11]

Because Helene and Rudolf had kept their courtship private, many of their friends were taken by surprise when the two became engaged in Marburg at the beginning of August 1916.[12] Nicolai Hartmann asked with perhaps feigned concern whether Bultmann had deserted his principles . . . for

8. UB Tübingen, RB est., H. Feldmann to RB, 19. 6. 1916, Mn 2-2681.

9. Cf. UB Tübingen, RB est., RB to H. Feldmann, 30. 6. 1917, Mn 2-2739 (looking back a year later).

10. UB Tübingen, RB est., H. Feldmann to RB, 3. 7. 1916, Mn 2-2681.

11. UB Tübingen, RB est., RB to H. Feldmann, 30. 6. 1916, Mn 2-2739.

12. Cf. the engagement announcement of Helene Feldmann and Rudolf Bultmann, 655; as well as L. Frank's message of congratulations to RB, 15. 7. 1916, Mn 2-765, and that of H. Gunkel to RB, 5. 8. 1916, Mn 2-883, in UB Tübingen, RB est.

clearly his bride was not from Oldenburg![13] If the families and friends of the betrothed shared in the joy of their happiness,[14] Bultmann went them one better in his belief that the bond with Helene would benefit his other friendships in a healthy and stimulating way.[15] Both Rudolf and Helene were overwhelmed by the mystery of love and the miracle of an unexpected closeness that enabled them "to see each other ever more clearly."[16] And Bultmann saw his old, familiar surroundings in a wholly new way, altered as if by a magic spell: "I have grasped the feeling of the wonder of our love so newly and deeply, that it is as if I were dreaming."[17] In another fairy tale for Helene, he allowed his feelings to pour out into a poem:[18]

Waking and dreaming!
Betwixt the twain,
Dreaming and waking,
How to ascertain?

If dreaming should fool you
And like waking seem,—
Waking while dreaming
Will serve for a dream.

What from your waking
In dreaming was lost
Do you from dreaming
As waking accost.

Should you twine from your waking
A garland of dreams,
From dreaming the splendor
Of waking e'er streams.

However, if devils
Are dancing in line,
Your waking in dreaming
Will once more entwine.

And then if your dreaming
Should swirl you awake,
A bewitching chorus
Upon you will break—

13. Cf. UB Tübingen, RB est., N. Hartmann to RB, 15. 8. 1916, Mn 2-936.
14. Cf. UB Tübingen, RB est., RB to H. Feldmann, 14. 8. 1916, Mn 2-2739.
15. Cf. UB Tübingen, RB est., RB to H. Feldmann, 14. 10. 1916, Mn 2-3447.
16. UB Tübingen, RB est., H. Feldmann to RB, 20. 6. 1917, Mn 2-2681.
17. UB Tübingen, RB est., RB to H. Feldmann, 13. 8. 1916, Mn 2-2739.
18. RB, *Wachen und Träumen*, 43.

Waking that's dreaming—
Who is to say?
Dreaming that's waking—
Which the surer way?

Between the end of August 1916 and the beginning of February 1917, Bultmann thought up three further tales for his betrothed. As befits their genre, the settings are almost completely devoid of local coloring, though in the "Tale of Laughter" the dyke-dam near Wehrshausen provides the scenes. The common theme of these various fairy tales, the relationship between the sexes, allows aspects of the real-life love story of the author and his beloved reader to shine through. This is particularly the case in the tales that tell how one of the two lovers is held captive in an invisible prison and must be freed by the loving partner. In the "Tale of Laughter," the miller lad Hans accomplishes this with his distinctive gift of childlike confidence, giving his melancholy sweetheart Lisbeth back the laughter she had lost.[19] In the "Dream Tale," it is the princess who was able through her devotion so to move the prince that he gradually learns to tell waking apart from dreaming on the road of self-discovery. Above all, as the moon in "Dream Tale" makes clear, it is ultimately true love alone that can save the partner: [20]

I cannot give it!
Nor you it find!
From yourself take what
Alone can bind!

Bultmann sent the two last poems to his betrothed from Breslau, where he had already taken up his position as Associate Professor of New Testament. In the "Tale of the Golden Fleece," a thousand-mile long veil, spun from the purest gold and gleaming miraculously, symbolizes a love that binds two human souls fast to each other despite great difficulties.[21] With hundreds of letters and cards Helene Feldmann and Bultmann bridged the physical distance that separated them. True outpourings of the heart flowed forth and back along the postal route between Breslau and Essen.

But the relationship that somehow fulfilled itself in a realm of private happiness could not be hermetically sealed off from the outside world. Wartime saw to it that the harshness of reality caught up with the couple. The tribute of human life that the War demanded from among the acquaintances and friends of Helene Feldmann and Bultmann raised the question of the

19. Cf. RB, *Wachen und Träumen*, 21–38.

20. RB, *Wachen und Träumen*, 50.

21. Cf. RB, *Wachen und Träumen*, 55–78; see also UB Tübingen, RB est., H. Feldmann to RB, 9. 1. 1917, Mn 2-2681.

meaning of this horror. Death is "to every natural feeling for life . . . something appalling," declared Bultmann in 1916. But he added "that by making it into a living deed one is able to take it into one's life, the reality that many are experiencing out there on the killing fields." To be sure, Bultmann admitted that it remains "ever a matter of grief and a riddle that what has begun to be created is snapped off through death, and that companionship, full of promise, is torn apart." Even if this riddle were never to be solved, one would have to include suffering and death together in the final assessment of life. Only if one accepts suffering and grief is a hope beyond death possible, a hope that no ecclesiastical dogma can give.[22]

In the months and weeks before their wedding, the especially upsetting news reached Bultmann and his betrothed that Helene's brother Hanns and Bultmann's youngest brother Arthur fell in the spring of 1917. And at the front, Bultmann's boyhood friend Leonhard Frank had a fatal accident on July 8, 1917. At the request of one of Frank's aunts, Bultmann wrote for the local paper in Westerstede an obituary in which he paid tribute to the friend's life and his character.[23] To his betrothed he vividly portrayed his grief over the loss of Leonhard Frank and the significance of this friendship for his own becoming who he was.[24] Bultmann felt the deaths of both his brother and Leonhard Frank as a decisive caesura. He became conscious of an existential separation from his Oldenburg home and past life.[25] What most moved him in these days of sadness he recognized once more in the first stanza of Eduard Mörike's poem "Rückkehr" ["Return"]:[26]

> At every turn on your life's journey,
> Even if things turn out auspiciously
> And you suffer loss in order to gain something greater:
> —Touched, you stand suddenly still,
> Fixing your gaze in gratitude on what is past;
> Melancholy leans on your shoulder
> And repeats to you in your soul
> How lovely it all was; and with that,
> It is now forever gone, forever!

At the same time, Bultmann naturally looked forward to the future to be shared with Helene. In July 1917 he wrote to her that things were getting

22. UB Tübingen, RB est., RB to H. Feldmann, 21. 4. 1916, Mn 2-3447.
23. Cf. RB, obituary for Dr. Leonhard Frank (untitled), 3.
24. Cf. UB Tübingen, RB est., RB to H. Feldmann, 12. 7. 1917, Mn 2-3447.
25. Cf. UB Tübingen, RB est., RB to H. Feldmann, 6. 7. and 12. 7. 1917, Mn 2-3447.
26. UB Tübingen, RB est., RB to H. Feldmann, 6. 7. 1917, Mn 2-3447.

worse and worse for him. First, he had left his backpack in the streetcar, then a book and the manuscript of a lecture ended up at the lost and found, and finally, he lost his sugar ration card for August—and had forgotten to hand in his food ration card on time. "Lass, it is high time you came!"[27] But before she came to Breslau, he traveled to Essen, where they were married on August 6, 1917. Pastor Rudolf Becker performed the ceremony at the Feldmanns' residence at 17 Gutenberg Street.[28] Out of consideration for the loss of their youngest son Arthur, Bultmann's parents did not join in the celebration. On the day of the ceremony, the newlyweds left for their honeymoon in the Black Forest, at the Mountain House Wiener Eck in the Münster Valley.

At the end of August 1917 the Bultmanns moved to their first home together, at 33 Auen Street, Breslau, near the university hospitals. They rightly anticipated difficult living conditions in the Silesian metropolis, for the "rutabaga winter" of 1916–17 was to be followed by the even harsher cold spell of 1917–18. Supplies of provisions in the city were catastrophically short. In 1917, residents of Munich had access to a daily ration of 1,750 calories per person, while those in Breslau had to get by on 1,132. Cold and illnesses such as tuberculosis claimed 8,000 victims among the civilian population during the War years. The population of the Silesian capital decreased from 544,000 in 1914 to 472,000 at the end of the War.[29] It was under these difficult circumstances that Rudolf and Helene Bultmann began their married life.

2. Teaching and Lecturing in Breslau

> *In the autumn of 1916 I was called to Breslau as associate professor, where I worked until 1920. . . . In the hard times of the final years of the War and the period following the War, under all sorts of privations, we saw a great deal of want and misery. . . . But we also experienced a great deal of friendship and help.*[30]

On September 8, 1916, Bultmann received the call to the associate professorship of New Testament in the Protestant theological faculty of the Silesian Friedrich-Wilhelms University at Breslau. He accepted the appointment for the winter semester of 1916–17, after arranging on short notice to be relieved

27. UB Tübingen, RB est., RB to H. Feldmann, 19. 7. 1917, Mn 2-2739.

28. Cf. Archive of the Evangelical Church Parish Essen-Altstadt, marriage register, 1917, no. 168.

29. Cf. N. Davies and R. Moorhouse, *Die Blume Europas*, 348.

30. RB, autobiographical remarks, in B. Jaspert, *Barth-Bultmann Briefwechsel* (2d ed.), 304.

of his duties as tutor at the Marburg Residence for Scholarship Students.[31] Bultmann straightaway moved to Breslau, where he took two rooms in the house of a woman named Marga Koztowska at 15 Hobrechtufer in the neighborhood of the hospital. The move from tranquil Marburg to the large Silesian city necessitated adjustments in the arrangements of everyday life, for even with the streetcar system the greater distances to be traveled meant that many errands and especially visits now took up greater amounts of time.

The impressions Bultmann gained on his first explorations of Breslau proved ambivalent. He liked such buildings as the simple, brick gothic Maria Magdalena Church, the similarly styled old town hall on the ring road, the Baroque university buildings—formerly a Jesuit seminary—and the unified group of buildings of the cathedral island that featured many patricians' and merchants' homes with their Renaissance and Baroque gables. But he was put off by the modern office blocks dating from the early industrial days because their architectural bad taste detracted from the city's appearance. "So, one takes joy from particulars; the impression of the city as a whole is, I find, unpleasant. This impression is only strengthened by the fact that the city has a rather thin coat of paint on it. Berlin is imposing due to the truly grand scale of its commercial streets, but here everything merely makes the pretense of being grand."[32]

During the years of the Wilhelmian Empire, Breslau had developed into a cosmopolitan commercial and industrial city with an enormous attraction for immigrants from rural areas in Silesia, Poland, and Austria-Hungary. One result of this rapid growth was that the city became a melting-pot of ethnicities, nationalities, and religions that was out of tune with the German-Protestant identity of the majority of its population.[33] Bultmann gained his first impressions of what was to him an alien world as he explored Breslau. He went to the "Ohlen," the old alleys of the city, and the residential ghettos in which the "Little Jews"—mostly Eastern European Jewish migrants from Upper Silesia, Austria-Hungary, and the province of Posen—eked out their miserable existence.[34] This was where, in *Soll und Haben* [*Debt and Credit*], the Silesian author Gustav Freytag had set Veitel Itzig and the or-

31. Cf. M. Evang, *Frühzeit*, 34f; U. Hutter-Wolandt, "Rudolf Bultmanns Berufung."

32. UB Tübingen, RB est., RB to H. Feldmann, 15. 10. 1916, Mn 2-3447.

33. Cf. N. Davies and R. Moorhouse, *Die Blume Europas*, 375–83.

34. During his years in Breslau, RB restricted himself to personal contacts with Jews who were academics. Thus, in 1918, Edith Stein, who had not yet converted to Catholicism, took part in his *Graeca* (alongside the philosopher of religion Heinrich Scholz, the philosopher Julius Stenzel, and the classical philologist Konrat Ziegler). Cf. RB, *Chronik 1917–1945*, Mn 2-224, 5.

thodox Ashkenazi Jew Schmeie Tinkeles, the two main characters portrayed in strongly anti-Jewish stereotypes in his widely read social novel of the nineteenth century.

Despite the warning of his printed guide to the city, Bultmann undertook a careful survey of the slum dwellings of Breslau not far from the ring road, and the result depressed him. Even the people he had met in October of 1916 while taking a Sunday walk on the dike on the Oder River were unable to brighten his mood. Bultmann "did not get very much beyond noticing that there is a boring conformist society everywhere in the world"; but then had to "scold [himself] for this, since one ought to be glad that people who sit all week long amidst gray and crumbling walls, in dull shops, dusty typists' offices, and dark rooms of cellars, can find this joy on Sunday." At any rate, on the way back Bultmann himself was able to enjoy the marshes of the Oder and the quietly flowing river with the outlines of the mighty willows and the imposing silhouette of Breslau against the blood-red streaks of the evening sky.[35]

Still, a strong homesickness for Marburg seized Bultmann during his first weeks in Breslau. He dealt with this by turning "again and again" to the *Annuaria "Hessen-Kunst"* [*"Art of Hesse"*], edited by the Giessen art historian Christian Rauch. Gazing fondly at the illustrations by Carl Bantzer, Hermann Kätelhön, Wilhelm Thielmann, Otto Ubbelohde, Walter Waentig, and other contemporary artists, he could at least return in his thoughts to the landscapes of Hesse and his beloved Marburg. Reading Walter Sohm's *Habilitationsschrift, Territorium und Reformation in der hessischen Geschichte 1526–1555* [*Territory and Reformation in Hessian History: 1526–1555*] also called to mind numerous associations with the events and places portrayed in that historical presentation.[36] Still, he would probably not have agreed with the nationalistic economist Lujo Brentano, who was appointed to Breslau in 1872 and who viewed this city on the eastern periphery of the German empire as his place of exile.[37]

As an associate professor in Breslau, Bultmann had to present "New Testament Practica for Beginners" on a regular basis,[38] and in addition to these, he twice offered "New Testament Theology" and "Introduction to

35. UB Tübingen, RB est., RB to H. Feldmann, 16. 10. 1916, Mn 2-3447.

36. UB Tübingen, RB est., RB to H. Feldmann, 16. 10. 1916, Mn 2-3447. Cf. W. Sohm, *Territorium*. Walter Sohm, a son of the Leipzig jurist Rudolph Sohm, had a fatal accident on the way to the front before he was able to finish qualifying for teaching at Marburg.

37. Cf. N. Davies and R. Moorhouse, *Die Blume Europas*, 359.

38. On what follows, cf. the list of courses taught by Bultmann from WS 1916–17 to SS 1920 in M. Evang, *Frühzeit*, 63f.

the New Testament." Also, he gave overview courses on the Gospel of John and the Pauline letters in the departmental exegetical seminar—In the case of the latter, twice on Galatians and once on Romans. To such lectures, which came to comprise the bulk of his teaching activity after his time in Breslau, he added seminars on "The History of the Apostolic and Post-Apostolic Age" and "An Introduction to the General History of Religion." In "An Analysis of the Synoptic Gospels," offered only once, in the summer semester of 1918, he was able to work on the rough draft of *The History of the Synoptic Tradition*, which was essentially completed in 1919 and published in 1921. Bultmann was also in the habit of making extracurricular contact with his students. They were always happy to accept his invitation "to smoke a cigar at my home every other Tuesday evening."[39] Due to the "tight financial situation of the scholarship students," Bultmann had avoided discussing certain subjects with the Silesian students, but he found the better-off students in Breslau to be "more skillful and livelier" than those in Hesse.[40]

The Breslau Protestant theological faculty that Bultmann joined in 1916 served as a way-station for ambitious young scholars, but in spite of the above-average fluctuation in personnel that resulted, the continuing presence of strong teachers made for a healthy continuity in the faculty.[41] Bultmann was determined to establish a closer relationship with his colleagues. He envisioned a more sociable and scholarly exchange among the faculty, like that he had known at Marburg. His initial visits with the Old Testament scholar Carl Steuernagel, his New Testament colleague Gustav Hoennicke, the church historian Carl Franklin Arnold, and the practical theologian Johannes Steinbeck indicated that the faculty would accord him a friendly reception.[42] To his considerable disappointment, however, it soon appeared that most of his Breslau colleagues did not share his marked interest in the kind of intensive scholarly collaboration that went beyond formal contact.[43]

Only with Rudolf Otto did there arise a closer relationship that Bultmann found to enrich his world of thought.[44] When he visited the philosopher of religion for the first time, he saw himself brought into "a colorful world, in which one finds oneself in the room of an original oddball as in Dickens or Raabe." Otto, who had just recovered from a bout of malaria, had filled

39. UB Tübingen, RB est., RB to H. Feldmann, 21. 11. 1916, Mn 2-2739.
40. UB Tübingen, RB est., RB to H. Feldmann, 22.–24. 11. 1916, Mn 2-3447.
41. Cf. D. Meyer, "Zur Geschichte," 149–74.
42. Cf. UB Tübingen, RB est., RB to H. Feldmann, 9.–12. 10. 1916, Mn 2-3447.
43. Cf. UB Marburg, A. Jülicher est., RB to A. Jülicher, 18. 12. 1916, Ms. 695/294.
44. Cf. UB Marburg, M. Rade est., RB to M. Rade, 3. 6. 1917, Ms. 839.

his residence chock-full of souvenirs from his foreign travels. There were Chinese carpets, Turkish weapons, Renaissance madonnas, Mongolian water bottles, Asiatic horse whips, Buddha statues, "a piece of ceiling paneling from the Chinese imperial palace (really!)" that later was to form part of the collection of religious regalia that Otto established in Marburg—all these seemed to Bultmann in the Breslau of 1916 the conglomeration of a curiosity shop.[45] He found conversation with Otto to be "always extraordinarily interesting," if also "remarkably disjointed."[46] In one such conversation during a walk along the Oder, Otto confided to his young colleague the basic ideas of his new book, *Das Heilige* [*The Idea of the Holy*], then in press.[47] The work was to become a theological bestseller. That its author left Breslau following the summer semester of 1917 to take the place of Wilhelm Herrmann was a cause of regret to Bultmann,[48] for apart from Otto the Breslau faculty seemed to him "to have no really significant personality" to show for itself.[49]

With Heinrich Scholz, who took over Otto's chair in Breslau, Bultmann was able to develop no closer contacts[50] than with Erich Schaeder, the representative of a theocentric theology who was called to Breslau in 1918. Bultmann welcomed the fact that Schaeder created a fresh breeze in the faculty with his personally winning style,[51] but he regarded it as disastrous that Schaeder's success among the students was accompanied by his stern rejection of an historical theology, and particularly one oriented to the history of religions.[52] Even if Bultmann's initial hope for working closely with his Breslau colleagues was largely unfulfilled, a definite change in what had been an unsatisfying situation occurred when in 1918 Hans von Soden became Associate Professor of Church History in the faculty. This student of Harnack combined a solid historical education with a readiness to take part in what had become necessary especially with the end of the First World War: the reconstruction of the Protestant Church.[53] The friendship between

45. UB Tübingen, RB est., RB to H. Feldmann, 9.–12. 10. 1916, Mn 2-3447.

46. UB Tübingen, RB est., RB to H. Feldmann, 9.–12. 10. 1916, Mn 2-3447.

47. UB Tübingen, RB est., RB to H. Feldmann, 14. 10. 1916, Mn 2-3447; cf. R. Otto, *Das Heilige*.

48. Cf. UB Marburg, M. Rade est., RB to M. Rade, 2. 12. 1917, Ms. 839.

49. UB Tübingen, RB est., RB to H. Feldmann, 9.–12. 10. 1916, Mn 2-3447. On the tensions between Bultmann and Otto, see below, 134f and 167–69.

50. Cf. UB Marburg, M. Rade est., RB to M. Rade, 2. 12. 1917, 7. 7. and 1. 9. 1918, Ms. 839; however, see also n. 34 above.

51. Cf. UB Marburg, M. Rade est., RB to M. Rade, 7. 7. 1918, Ms. 839.

52. Cf. UB Marburg, M. Rade est., RB to M. Rade, 16. 1. 1920, Ms. 839.

53. Cf. UB Marburg, M. Rade est., RB to M. Rade, 7. 7. 1918 and 19. 3. 1919, Ms. 839.

Bultmann and von Soden that began in Breslau was to continue and to prove its worth in Marburg.

Bultmann also maintained friendly relationships in Breslau with the pastors Wilhelm Gottschick and Ernst Moering.[54] He had been friends with his fraternity brother Gottschick since the year they spent together as students in Tübingen, and both pastors belonged, as did Bultmann, to the Breslau group of the Friends of *Die Christliche Welt.* Moering in particular became a stimulating conversation partner. This student of Ernst Troeltsch had done a doctoral degree with Johannes Weiss with a thesis in form criticism. In his publications on popular mission, Moering advocated for the view that the church needed to become increasingly aware of people's actual life situations, particularly where in moving to the cities they had moved away from the church. Only in this way could the church's proclamation overcome the many obstacles that stood in the way of faith and religion taking hold. Moering's apologetic interest in church work that was directly related to the people it addressed resonated with Bultmann's intent to demonstrate the value of a Christianity that was both true to the church and contemporary in character. Bultmann especially esteemed his friend as a preacher,[55] for as two printed volumes of sermons confirm, Moering was an orator who believed the preaching office demanded both a seriousness derived from Søren Kierkegaard's understanding of Christianity and great homiletic skill.[56] Upon reading Moering's sermons, Rudolf Otto is said to have exclaimed that if he could preach *like that*, he would give up his professorship and go around as a preacher.[57] Moering's involvement in society and in church politics, his stand for social justice, and his insistence that the church must make clear the social implications of the Christian message may have deepened Bultmann's attitudes to these questions. At any rate, the Breslau pastor moved Bultmann to speak to such pressing issues in lectures that he gave throughout the university.[58]

Bultmann presented these talks to a variety of audiences.[59] For example, he addressed such subjects as "The Ethical Problem of Earliest Christianity" or "Troeltsch's Conception of the Earliest Church in his *Social Teachings*"

54. Cf. A. Bultmann Lemke, "Unveröffentliche Nachlass," 19; M. Evang, *Frühzeit*, 67–70.

55. C. UB Tübingen, RB est., RB to H. Feldmann, 1. 12. 1916, Mn 2-3447; see also M. Evang, *Frühzeit*, 69; UB Tübingen, RB est., RB to H. von Soden, 20. 4. 1922, Mn 2-2385.

56. Cf. E. Moering, *In ungemessene Weiten*.

57. UB Tübingen, RB est., RB to H. von Soden, 20. 4. 1922, Mn 2-2385.

58. Cf. A. Bultmann Lemke, "Unveröffentliche Nachlass," 19.

59. Cf. the list (with citations) in M. Evang, *Frühzeit*, 74f.

when speaking to a church-related group like the Friends of *Die Christliche Welt* or the Breslau Theological Union. Later, following the outbreak of the Revolution in November 1918, he allowed himself to venture into the local educational scene and address more secular topics. As a member of both the Council of Spiritual Workers (1918), the Cultural-Political Working Group (1919) that emerged from it, and the Humboldt Union for Popular Education, he lectured on topics in education, religion, and worldview. Beginning early in 1919, he and Wilhelm Gottschick led the Section for Issues of Religion and Ideology in the youth organization of the German Democratic Party. Here he gave his lecture "Religion and Culture"[60] and a series of lectures on "The Ideology of the Enlightenment" that were followed by readings from Schleiermacher's *Reden* [*Speeches*]. Bultmann explained that he found it necessary to take on these additional responsibilities because they enabled him to supplement his modest income as an associate professor. To be sure, he came to understand the drawback of his lecturing activity only too well: "But the lovely time and strength for work—which it always costs!"[61]

Bultmann preached rather seldom in Breslau. He probably gave all three of his preserved sermons from this time to the congregations of his friends Gottschick and Moering.[62] On Pentecost in 1917 he presented a sermon on 1 Cor 2:9–12 in the Queen Luisa Memorial Church, "On the Mysterious and the Revealed God," and on the recommendation of Rudolf Otto, who had been in the congregation, allowed it to be printed in *Die Christliche Welt*.[63]

In this Pentecost sermon, Bultmann sounds pensive notes in discussing the religious significance of the present. In view of the pitiful condition of the wounded in the sick bays, the distress of the soldiers at the front, and the awful fate of the fallen, Pentecost can no longer be celebrated in the pre-war manner—as a happy, bright festival of joy. The experience of war is nevertheless fundamentally open to the experience of the mystery of God in humility and reverence. In this regard, one must protect oneself from an all too quick, simplistic, and historicizing connection of the War with God's rule in the world. War is not to be understood directly as the judgment of God, nor to be taken as an occasion for sermons calling to repentance. On the other hand, neither is one to deny that God has nothing whatever to do with the

60. See below, 124–26.

61. UB Tübingen, RB est., RB to W. Fischer, 8. 9. 1919, Mn 2-2198.

62. Cf. M. Evang, *Frühzeit*, 151f. The three Breslau sermons are reprinted in *VW*, 135–47, 148–62, 163–72.

63. Cf. RB, "Vom geheimnisvollen," 572–79; also in *VW*, 135–47.

War and its horrors. With the War, God has laid a burden on humanity as never before. If it can be seen that our duty is to assure "that something as appalling as this War does not come upon the world again," then the War has "revealed divine strengths in humanity" and generated "a sense of sacrifice and a heroism" that has not been possible in peacetime.[64] Ultimately, only in the figure of the crucified Christ does the light of promise shine forth, a light that is able to drive out the dark, demonic powers in human beings that have been revealed in the War. One can regard Bultmann's sermon "On the Mysterious and Revealed God" as a snapshot of his theological diagnosis of the times in the decisive year of 1917. His Breslau years extended from the middle of the War into the early postwar period, and thus witnessed powerful social and political changes. How did he experience the upheaval of the times, and how did he react to it?

3. In Times of Upheaval

> *Like nearly all Germans, I was convinced of our cause and believed in our victory at the start of the War; but from 1916–17 on [I believed] in neither. I had spoken out earlier in favor of negotiations, and as early as 1917 I foresaw the necessity of ceding Alsace-Lorraine. More and more, the corruption of the official culture and the middle class in Germany has also become clear to me, and now I stand on the side of the radicals—that is, ultimately, of the "independents." In my opinion, these have again, even now in the question of peace, taken the only possible point of view.*[65]

During the Pentecost vacation of 1913, Bultmann and his friend Rudolf Günther had made a tour to the as yet unfinished Edertal dam near Hemfurth; he found the nearly completed dam, a large-scale engineering project to supply electricity and water to large portions of the Wilhelmian Empire, imposing. He was strangely moved on the journey through the valley of the Eder by the partly evacuated villages of Asel, Berich, and Bringhausen, which would soon be covered by Lake Stau. Most inhabitants had already abandoned their houses, and "[l]oaded furniture vans stood in the courtyards; many people want to take their dead with them and have fetched the coffins from the churchyard. It was rather touching to see that the few who still lived in the old houses had adorned their homes with Pentecost censers

64. RB, *VW*, 142, 144.
65. UB Tübingen, RB est., RB to W. Fischer, 23. 6. 1919, Mn 2-2198.

in the midst of this world that was soon to be submerged."[66] Was this impression an unconscious portent of the world that was soon to be submerged by the tidal wave of the First World War?

Bultmann shared the collective enthusiasm that gripped the majority of Germans at the outbreak of the First World War in August of 1914.[67] It weighed on him that due to his hip trouble he was unable to perform any type of military service, and was assigned only to temporary guard duty on a bridge over the Lahn near Marburg.[68] "[W]hat was greater—service by bearing arms—was closed" to him,[69] and he sought to find partial justification in the consideration that "there also have to be those who live through this time at home. One has one's task here as well: to try hard to live through this in a way that is pure and without a sour note."[70] Bultmann admonished those who heard his sermons that such thoughts of solidarity "for those who are braving the elements" were the moral duty of all who remain at home.[71] He behaved in accord with this maxim with regard to his brother Arthur, his friends, and the colleagues from the Marburg luncheon group who had been called up for service in the War. He redoubled his correspondence with Leonhard Frank, Emil Balla, Nicolai Hartmann, Hermann Jacobsohn, and Friedrich Pfister, and even sent scholarly literature, the *Biblia Hebraica*, the *Novum Testamentum Graece*, cognac, and cigars to friends at the front.[72] In November 1914 Leonhard Frank expressed his thanks for the Bible Bultmann had sent: "This is what one needs now."[73]

In his wartime sermons, Bultmann at first showed himself fully convinced "that our cause is God's cause."[74] On September 20, 1914, speaking in Hammelwarden on "God's Providence in the War," he appropriated the clichés typical of sermons on war. The War is just and necessary; it frees the individual and the people from egoism and hedonism; in it God's work of educating is carried out among the German people; "God awakens a sense

66. UB Tübingen, RB est., RB to A. K. and H. Bultmann, 18. 5. 1913, Mn 2-2735.

67. UB Tübingen, RB est., RB to W. Fischer, 23. 6. 1919, Mn 2-2198.

68. Cf. A. Bultmann Lemke, "Unveröffentliche Nachlass," 18.

69. UB Tübingen, RB est., RB to W. Fischer 3. 2. 1916, Mn 2-2198. Referring to his hip problem, the Berlin war ministry denied an (additional?) application of Bultmann's for military service in the air corps in the summer of 1916. Cf. UB Tübingen, RB est., war ministry to RB, 25. 7. 1916, Mn 2-3049.

70. UB Tübingen, RB est., RB to W. Fischer, 21. 4. 1915, Mn 2-2198.

71. Cf. his sermon on Gal 6:2, "Our Duties to Those in the Field," delivered several times in August and September of 1914, RB, *VW*, 128.

72. Cf. in detail K. de Valerio, *Altes Testament*, 132f; A. Bultmann Lemke, "Unveröffentliche Nachlass," 18.

73. UB Tübingen, RB est., L. Frank to RB, 22. 11. 1914, Mn 2-765.

74. RB, *VW*, 121.

of sacrifice and courage, a sense of community and a sense of eternity in each one of us."[75] As the war dragged on, to be sure, melancholy tones increasingly eclipsed the patriotic certitude expressed at its beginning in 1914. On Pentecost of 1917 he preached in Breslau on 1 Cor 2:9–12, and the talk was no longer of war's moral task and power. Bultmann now explicitly warned of "fitting the war and its misery into God's rule in the world." It is the duty of humanity to see to it "that something as appalling as this War does not come upon the world again." The preacher now attributed a religious meaning to war only in that it had smashed false images of God. The experience of war had in this way made "everything become so alien to us" that God "is to be confronted only with our naked self."[76]

In February of 1917, Bultmann's younger brother Arthur fell, and five months later, his boyhood friend Leonhard Frank had a fatal accident on the front. And that same year it became apparent that the German empire would not be able to realize its original war aims. The public debate over German war policy came to a head over whether the country was to carry on with a "peace through victory" policy of expansive annexation, or whether it ought to strive for "negotiated peace" with the European community of nations. Bultmann pleaded for negotiation,[77] an option that such leading representatives of liberal Protestantism as Adolf von Harnack and Ernst Troeltsch also publicly endorsed that year. In the middle of 1918, Bultmann joined the "People's Alliance for Freedom and Fatherland," which had been founded by Troeltsch and other liberal Protestants in December of 1917. Above all else, this group opposed the annexationist German Party of the Fatherland and supported a foreign policy of negotiated peace and a domestic policy focused on a moderate program of democratic reform. Bultmann offered a rather modest assessment of the Alliance's political future: "I do not expect much of it."[78]

It was from the distance of Breslau that Bultmann experienced the November Revolution of 1918, the ensuing fierce debates in state and church politics, and finally the inauguration of the Weimar Republic. As his correspondence of this period makes clear (and especially that with Martin Rade), he spoke out for an overall reordering of the relationship of state and church, he welcomed—initially, at any rate—the revolutionary upheaval, and he approved the establishment of a democratic state.[79] Minor differ-

75. RB, *VW*, 123. The text for the sermon was Matt 10:28–31.

76. RB, *VW*, 141f; cf. also 96 above.

77. UB Tübingen, RB est., RB to W. Fischer, 23. 6. 1919, Mn 2-2198.

78. UB Marburg, M. Rade est., RB to M. Rade, 7. 7. 1918, Ms. 839.

79. On what follows, cf. also M. Evang, *Frühzeit*, 75–84; H. Oelke, "Bultmann und Weimar," 90–100.

ences aside, Bultmann's call for a new beginning in church and politics in Germany was in keeping with the left-liberal line espoused by Martin Rade, the elected representative of the German Democratic Party in the Prussian Provincial Assembly and mover-and-shaker in church politics.[80] When Rade and the Chemnitz pastor Hermann B. Gay called for the nationwide establishment of people's church councils in order to release the church from its state connection and to replace the consistorial structures of church leadership with people's councils, Bultmann declared himself ready to support this initiative.[81] Although he did add principled reservations to this support, as well as to his cooperation in establishing a local branch of the Alliance for a Free People's Church in Breslau, he considered the concept of a "people's church" aimed at restructuring the entire ecclesiastical institution to be as yet not clearly enough defined.[82] Bultmann did not think much of the work of the first German Protestant church congress, which was intended to prepare for the establishment of the German Evangelical Church Union at the beginning of September 1919—and which was dominated by a conservative majority. "What we are experiencing in the church is absolutely pitiful. What a bunch of second-raters got together at the church congress!"[83]

During his last two years in Breslau, Bultmann was not active in politics or in church politics, though he did support particular initiatives in these areas. "Joining in on political actions—I'm not the man for it; but what I do take to be the main thing I can help out with and wholeheartedly, so that something good for the Fatherland can still come out of the great κρίσις [crisis]. And the main thing is spiritual renewal."[84] These priorities led Bultmann to engage in political education efforts of various committees and groups; for instance, he let his two Breslau pastor friends, Wilhelm Gottschick and Ernst Moering, persuade him to give lectures and reading courses on topics in religion and ideology in the local youth section of the liberal German Democratic Party.[85] However, the engagement in political education for the sake of the party youth did not include Bultmann's membership in or party work for the DDP [German Democratic Party] in any way at all. That he was to have become a member of the SPD [Social Democratic Party] in Breslau[86] can be neither verified nor completely excluded. It is not probable, even if later on in Marburg he could be identified as a Social Democrat—for which,

80. Cf. A. C. Nagel, *Martin Rade*, 161–232.
81. Cf. UB Marburg, M. Rade est., RB to M. Rade, 27. 1. 1919, Mn 839.
82. Cf. UB Marburg, M. Rade est., RB to M. Rade, 6. 3. 1919, Ms. 839.
83. UB Tübingen, RB est., RB to W. Fischer, 8. 9. 1919, Mn 2-2198.
84. UB Tübingen, RB est., RB to W. Fischer, 23. 6. 1919, Mn 2-2198.
85. See 95 above.
86. Thus (without evidence), W. Schmithals, "Das wissentschaftliche Werk," 26.

incidentally, there is an equal lack of evidence.[87] In any event, rather than activity in a political party Bultmann preferred cooperating in popular educational work for the sake of a comprehensive spiritual renewal, because for him this spiritual reorientation was the indispensable foundation for building a new social and political order after the collapse of the Wilhelmian Empire.

When after several years in Shanghai Walther Fischer returned to Germany in the summer of 1919, Bultmann drew his friend a picture of the political situation in two letters. Looking back on the wartime situation, he said that "the corruption of the official culture in Germany and of the middle class had become clear."[88] Bultmann sympathized with the Independent Socialists, who had split from the SPD in 1916–17 over irreconcilable differences on war policy. To be sure, he set his hopes less on the policy of the independents than "on the spiritual currents that are alive in their circles,"[89] and as for the radical left, he liked its uncompromising support for the Treaty of Versailles. This corresponded to his position on the question of peace. Bultmann distanced himself from the representatives of an ideological nationalism, who were intent on preventing the signing of the treaty through their polemical protests. "I hope that the world of Bismarck—which I have never admired—has finally foundered, the world of Realpolitik, of subservience, and of the cult of 'officialdom.'"[90] He found it disillusioning to note that even after the Revolution, the administration of the state was controlled by the old ministerial bureaucracy, and the national assembly by the old party bosses. It seemed to him highly suspicious that the "settlement commission" formed in Silesia consisted entirely of high-ranking aristocrats and large

87. On the problem, cf. M. Evang, *Frühzeit*, 77f; H. Oelke, "Bultmann und Weimar," 99. It is no longer possible to verify Bultmann's membership in the SPD, since its membership cards from the period before 1933 were destroyed during the Third Reich. Bultmann's having already joined the SPD in Breslau is utterly improbable, since he was working with the youth section of the DDP during the upheavals of 1918–19 and developed clear sympathies with the SPD. Against Bultmann's joining the SPD during the Marburg years following 1921 speaks not only the lack of evidence to that effect, but also the circumstance that Bultmann did not, in any case, get into difficulties in 1933 due to such a possible membership. Evang and Oelke want to draw a reference to Bultmann's having belonged to the SPD around 1925 from a speech that Bultmann gave in Marburg on 1 March 1925 in memory of those killed in the First World War. In this speech, Bultmann declares his support for the Weimar Republic and democracy. He includes Reichspräsident Friedrich Ebert, who had died only a few days before, in his memorial to the war dead. It is clear that he pays tribute here to Ebert not as a member of the SPD, but rather as the representative head of the Weimar democracy, "who stood at the head of our beloved republic" (RB, "Gedenken," *VW*, 219).

88. UB Tübingen, RB est., RB to W. Fischer, 23. 6. 1919, Mn 2-2198.

89. UB Tübingen, RB est., RB to W. Fischer, 8. 9. 1919, Mn 2-2198.

90. UB Tübingen, RB est., RB to W. Fischer, 8. 9. 1919, Mn 2-2198.

landowners—and so no improvements in providing for nutrition, electricity transmission, and housing were to be expected. "In short, if yet a second, and this time a real revolution doesn't come, everything will remain as it was or even get much worse."[91]

Bultmann raised the point that in the wake of the Revolution political renewal was progressing only slowly or not at all under Lenin's influence, particularly in his "State and Revolution."[92] Bultmann saw in Lenin's description of developments following the February "Revolution" of 1917 in Russia a mirror image of the circumstances in post-revolutionary Germany. Bultmann developed a degree of sympathy for Lenin, because already in 1917 the Russian revolutionary had accurately described reaction and restoration as direct results of the bourgeois revolution, and one could observe these dynamics at play in the Germany of 1919. "Since reading Lenin, I've become enthusiastic about his personality. My only fear is that we have no Lenin."[93] Bultmann even held that before a new government could be established a "period of 'dictatorship'" was unavoidable. "One does not need to carry on the shootings to the extent that occurred in Russia (and this will not, in fact, happen with us . . .), but if one could get rid of a sufficient number of big shots and petit bourgeois philistines both inside and outside of the university, that would certainly be a good thing."

Mind you, however enthusiastically he was reading Lenin in 1919, he was never a Marxist. He did not adopt Lenin's communistic theory of society or the notion of world revolution that was part of it. And in further contrast to Lenin, Bultmann never spoke of a dictatorship of the proletariat or of the proletariat first crushing the machinery of the state by force and replacing the exploitative capitalistic system with a truly egalitarian communist society. He was deeply convinced that the social, governmental, and economic tribulations of post-revolutionary Germany could be ameliorated only on the basis of a spiritual reorientation.[94]

As a member of the educated class, Bultmann dreamed of a better form of modernity, one whose victory over the washed-out "old world of Realpolitik, of economic interests, of materialism, of expediency, bourgeois values, and philistinism" he predicted. He saw harbingers of this new time in both the ideals of the youth movement and avant-garde currents in art and literature. Ever since the 1912 Cologne Special Exhibition of the works of Cezanne and

91. UB Tübingen, RB est., RB to W. Fischer, 8. 9. 1919, Mn 2-2198.

92. On what follows, cf. the details in M. Evang, *Frühzeit*, 80–84; cf. W. I. Lenin, *Staat*, 393–507.

93. UB Tübingen, RB est., RB to W. Fischer, 8. 9. 1919, Mn 2-2198.

94. Cf. also RB, "Religion und Socializmus," 424–47.

van Gogh had opened his eyes to modern painting, he had followed "with growing joy" the expressionist art of Oskar Kokoschka, Emil Nolde, and Max Pechstein. He showed himself similarly taken with recent poetry, whose representatives—like Rainer Maria Rilke, Georg Trakl, Frank Wedekind and Franz Werfel—were for him "marvelous epiphanies." Bultmann saw in expressionism, the youth movement, and *Lebensphilosophie* [philosophy of life] new forces at work that would culminate in a radical break with the now obsolete bourgeois world of the prewar period. He proposed an expressionistic interpretation of the development of modern art: "Nietzsche's best thoughts are full of life, this experience of the irrational, a sense of the value of existence apart from being goal-driven, and the capacity for self-expression, [for forging] a relation [between] the elemental forces of nature and the human soul."[95] The spiritual dynamic that began to unfold here would ultimately lead to changes in society—this was Bultmann's conviction. It was on this account that he understood his own political task to be the fostering of political education in the period of upheaval during and after the Revolution.

With his liberal political attitude developed and deepened during the Breslau years, Bultmann discovered an affirmative relationship to Weimar democracy. Among Protestant theologians in the university and German Protestantism in general, he belonged to the minority of liberal republican intellectuals who, unlike the antidemocratic majority in the Protestant milieu, remained loyal to the fragile democratic government.[96] When on March 1, 1925, Bultmann delivered in Marburg a commemoration address for the dead of the First World War, he appealed to his listeners to commit themselves energetically to the "Germany of the future, . . . in which law and justice rule. . . . Our primary political duty is to stand courageously for our convictions, for the Republic, and for democracy."[97]

His experiences in Breslau, his increased awareness of social problems in the urban context, and also his reflections on the radical political upheaval following the end of the Wilhelmian Era doubtless contributed to enlarging Bultmann's social and political insight. To be sure, the basic political conviction that he had shared with Helene in his letters of 1916 remained unaffected by the development of his assessment of concrete political circumstances. To remedy social ills required concerted effort aimed at alleviating cases of individual need. All the same, an equally important task was that of "meeting the root ills and seeking to bring about ideal conditions."

95. UB Tübingen, RB est., RB to W. Fischer, 8. 9. 1919, Mn 2-2198.
96. Cf. K. Nowak, *Evangelische Kirche*; K. Nowak, *Geschichte*, 222–30.
97. RB, *VW*, 218f.

For example, the introduction of universal public education for children of the upper strata *and* the proletariat would result in many of the educated elite coming face to face with burning social problems and promoting even stronger engagement in this area. And measures that promised an improvement in the field of education would surely promote a political climate in which "'clean government' and ideas of justice would be the basis of legislative action," and thus reduce the power of social elites and special interests.[98] Understanding politics as a moral community's means of self-expression would enhance the moral spirit and civic responsibility of the members of this community.

If Bultmann set the state within the realm of autonomous morality, the distinction of state and church in this ideal political theory directly followed suit. The religion of grace, whose meaning Luther had proclaimed, implied the experience "that the eternal is not the world that we discover, but rather a world that reveals itself to us," as Bultmann explained in his sermon of July 1, 1917.[99] This axiom meant that a political mandate for the church was excluded. The fourth Speech of Schleiermacher's *Über die Religion* [*On Religion*], and particularly its criticism of merging church and state, seemed to Bultmann as if "it was written from the heart." Schleiermacher rightly emphasized, he said, "that religion is not to involve itself with the educational functions of the state," for such a fusion would lead to the corrupting of both religion and morality. The church may not deprive the state of its social obligation; rather, it must awaken vigorous support for the state and "for all of the duties that grow out of being a governing community."[100]

Bultmann argued the strict distinction of state and church by using an analogy to the difference between culture and religion. The Christian must endure the tensions between the respective realms of life and establish a balance between them. "Each person has to find for himself the way between his inner participation in shaping the world and his inner freedom from the world."[101] This is not a task that can be dealt with once and for all, but must always be tackled anew. At the Philipps-University of Marburg on January 18, 1928, Bultmann delivered the address at the celebration of the founding of the German Empire. In the course of reconstructing historically the relation between earliest Christianity and the state, he described the double challenge that arises from the ambivalent relationship of the Christian to the

98. UB Tübingen, RB est., RB to H. Feldmann, 19. 3. 1916, Mn 2-3447.
99. RB, *VW*, 158f.
100. UB Tübingen, RB est., RB to H. Feldmann, 2.–3. 1916, Mn 2-3447.
101. RB, "Religion und Sozialismus," 447.

world and the state. The realms that belong to the emperor and to God are indeed "radically separated," and yet the human being is under obligation to both. Jesus' saying in Matt 22:21 can therefore be thus paraphrased for the present: "Give to the Republic what belongs to the Republic, . . . and to God, what belongs to God." However, the intent of Jesus' critical demand can be fulfilled only by political action that understands itself as service of love.[102]

Since Bultmann understands the state as an autonomous element of culture separate from the unmediated realm of religion, the ideas he expressed around 1920 on the ethics of citizenship coincide partially with the negation of culture and of the world represented in early dialectical theology by Friedrich Gogarten with uncompromising strictness, and later by Karl Barth in a gentler tone. Nonetheless, Bultmann accorded a greater weight to the Christian's role in shaping the world than did Gogarten and Barth.[103] As much as religion transcends the world in its relation to the eternal realm, so little does its relationship to the secular world exhaust itself in the mere negation of worldly matters. Rather, it is precisely religion's function as critic of culture that enables its constructive turning to the world. "The person who . . . understands religious freedom from the world not as an outward thing but rather as inward freedom, cannot use religion as a pretext to evade his duty to shape the world."[104]

4. The History of the Synoptic Tradition [Die Geschichte der synoptischen Tradition]

> *I must work in an orderly way; and I hope to finish a book in this semester and the coming vacation. To be sure, the time hardly seems suited to writing books, especially when it is a form-critical investigation of earliest Christian literature. However, completely apart from the fact that it has ripened gradually as the fruit of my labors, and that in spite of present conditions I am bound in a lively way to my work with an eye to the future, it is necessary that I once again publish something, even if the future is very uncertain, indeed.*[105]

Bultmann had begun to occupy himself more closely with his scholarly work on the synoptic tradition soon after he qualified as a teacher. In a discussion

102. RB, "Urchristentum und Staat," 4.
103. Cf. also H. Oelke, "Bultmann und Weimar," 111–17.
104. RB, "Religion und Sozialismus," 446.
105. UB Tübingen, RB est., RB to W. Fischer, 23. 6. 1919, Mn 2-2198.

of Johannes Weiss's and Paul Wendland's literary-critical works on the New Testament, he had by 1914 already developed rather precisely the basic plan of his own program for work on the literary- and form-critical reconstruction of the material handed down in the synoptic gospels.[106] However, his teaching obligations, his activity as a lecturer in Breslau, and last but not least, the difficult working conditions and poor nutritional situation during and after the War made it difficult to complete the book project any time soon.[107] Thus, not until December 1919 was Bultmann able to finish the manuscript of his *History of the Synoptic Tradition*—considerably later than he had hoped.[108] At first he intended to include a word in memory of David Friedrich Strauss at the beginning of the book, but Wilhelm Heitmüller managed to dissuade him. To be sure, such a dedication to David Friedrich Strauss would be appropriate to the subject matter, but it could also be taken as a provocation. So long as Bultmann was not yet in the budget as a full professor, his own best interests might be imperiled by such a dedication.[109] The associate professor followed this advice, and dedicated the book to the Marburg theological faculty as well as to its members Wilhelm Heitmüller and Eduard Simons.[110]

Then problems arose over getting the work printed. Wilhelm Bousset had recommended to the publisher, Vandenhoeck & Ruprecht, that it include Bultmann's investigation in its series, Forschungen zur Religion und Literatur des Alten und Neuen Testaments [Studies on the Religion and Literature of the Old and New Testament],[111] but the publisher rejected the manuscript.[112] Only after Bousset died on March 8, 1920, and on Hermann Gunkel's recommendation Bultmann succeeded him as co-editor of the *Research* series, did the Göttingen publishing house declare itself "glad now to take on" Bultmann's book.[113] It finally appeared at the beginning of April 1921. Even before its appearance in printed form, *The History of the Synoptic*

106. Cf. RB, "Einleitung," *Theologie als Kritik*, 56–71, esp. 61–63; see also UB Tübingen, RB est., RB to W. Fischer, 21. 6. 1914, Mn 2-2198.

107. Cf. UB Tübingen, RB est., RB to W. Fischer, 23. 6. 1919 and 8. 9. 1919, Mn 2-2198. On what follows, cf. M. Evang, *Frühzeit*, 70–72; K. Hammann, "Das abscheuliche Wort 'Apophthegma.'"

108. Cf. UB Tübingen, RB est., RB to W. Bousset, 1. 2. 1920, Mn 2-2149.

109. Cf. UB Tübingen, RB est., W. Heitmüller to RB, 30. 4. 1920, Mn 2-964.

110. Cf. RB, *Geschichte*, 1st ed. (1921), iii; from the 2d ed. (1931) onwards, the book was dedicated "To the Memory of Wilhelm Heitmüller."

111. Cf. UB Tübingen, RB est., W. Bousset to RB, 12. 2. and 27.–29. 2. 1920, Mn 2-518.

112. Cf. UB Tübingen, RB est., H. Gunkel to RB, 31. 3. 1920, Mn 2-883.

113. Cf. UB Tübingen, RB est., H. Gunkel to RB, 19. 7. 1920, Mn 2-883.

Tradition was decisive for Bultmann's appointments to Giessen in 1920 and to Marburg in 1921.[114]

With his book, Bultmann became a leading voice in the then innovative field of study called form-criticism that found great favor among New Testament scholars following the First World War. To be sure, the roots of form-critical examination of the New Testament, especially of the synoptic gospels, reached back to the eighteenth century work of Johann Gottfried Herder. Bultmann himself described how discoveries about the transmission process in the gospels and their form-critical context had emerged.[115] The older research in the second half of the nineteenth century, strengthened by the two-source theory, had still assumed that one could lift the basic facts of the life of Jesus and his proclamation out of the Gospel of Mark and the sayings-source Q. William Wrede had undermined this assumption by showing that Mark, the oldest gospel, does not present an account of Jesus' life that is usable as a biographical source. Rather, Mark has put the traditions available to him into a biographical context that reflects the theological perspectives of his particular community. Thus, statements about the development of Jesus' messianic consciousness are based solely on the evangelist's theological beliefs.[116] Scholars like Johannes Weiss and Emil Wendling continued the work begun by Wrede's insights by differentiating between old traditions in the synoptic gospels and identifying redactional work on them. Even if these two were not yet aware of the complexity of the layering of tradition and redaction that developed within the Gospel of Mark, Bultmann's teacher Johannes Weiss in particular made important progress in shaping New Testament form-criticism.[117]

Bultmann considered the contributions of Julius Wellhausen to synoptic research to be even more forward-looking. For Wellhausen recognized that pre-literary traditions, individual stories, and groups of narratives found in the three synoptic gospels had been woven into literary unities by the redactive hands of the gospel-writers. To be sure, Bultmann thought that Wellhausen had not yet achieved "a definitive conclusion that sifted through and combined the results. . . . He understood the complexity of the problem and stopped at the recognition that, 'in the case of a redaction, one is not yet dealing simply with orally transmitted materials. . . . However, the most important thing is the realization that it is chiefly secondary materials

114. Cf. also 117f and 131f below.

115. Cf. on what follows RB, *Geschichte*, iv (Foreword), 1–3; RB, *Erforschung*, 2d ed. (1930), 5–16.

116. Cf. W. Wrede, *Messiasgeheimnis*.

117. Cf. W. Schmithals, "Johannes Weiss," 389–410; see also M. Evang, *Frühzeit*, 52–54.

that come to the fore in the tradition.'"[118] The form-critical analysis of the synoptic process of transmission was also a useful complement to the work of Hermann Gunkel and his students on the Old Testament. Gunkel had reconstructed the literary and pre-literary traditions in Genesis—legends, myths, sagas, and other genres of popular ancient Israelite literature—and had sought to understand them on the basis of their contemporary *Sitz im Leben* [setting in life]. Of course, literary elements had different appearances in the New Testament than they did in the Old, and therefore the theological implications of New Testament form-criticism would differ greatly from those that Gunkel's genre-criticism had defined.

Three works that emerged independently soon after the First World War marked the advent of the form-critical approach to synoptic exegesis: those of Martin Dibelius, Karl Ludwig Schmidt, and Rudolf Bultmann. In his investigation of 1919, which he wished to be understood explicitly as literary-criticism, Karl Ludwig Schmidt showed that apart from the passion story the oldest tradition about Jesus consisted primarily of short individual units, and therefore could be termed "pericope-transmission." The gospel narratives into which these individual units were inserted were created by the gospel writers, who in doing so provided such sketchy stage-directions that the story of Jesus contained neither a complete chronological ordering nor a coherent itinerary. Schmidt had thus for the first time distinguished between tradition and redaction in the Gospel of Mark; he had not yet subjected the individual pericopes to a more precise form-critical analysis.[119]

This was undertaken by Martin Dibelius, like Schmidt a student of Adolf Deissmann, in *Die Formgeschichte des Evangeliums* [*From Tradition to Gospel*]. Dibelius classified the synoptic gospels as ancient popular literature that lacked any definite aesthetic or literary pretensions, but simply assimilated the largely anonymous, popular tradition of a community. As a result, the gospel writers were not so much authors as collectors and redactors of this transmitted material. Since the forms of those small units of tradition had already assumed their final form before being incorporated into the gospels, "form-criticism of the gospel" had to penetrate the literary surface of the gospels and ascertain the laws governing the emergence and history of those pericopes. To accomplish this Dibelius applied a "constructive method" by starting from specific crises and themes that defined the life of the community, and working backward from these to see how and according

118. RB, *Geschichte*, 2; cf. also R. Smend, *Julius Wellhausen*, 36–40.

119. Cf. K. L. Schmidt, *Rahmen*; see also Bultmann's rev. of K. L. Schmidt, in RB, *Theologie als Kritik*, 104–11.

to what laws the synoptic transmission developed and which forms it had initiated in so doing.[120]

Bultmann regarded Dibelius' procedure as problematic; defining the two genres of the synoptic tradition that Dibelius had characterized as "novellas" and "paradigms" seemed to him more a hindrance than a help.[121] Instead of the constructive method, he favored an analytical approach. He first investigated the individual pieces of tradition in order to obtain a reliable picture of the earliest Christian community based on both the history of the literary forms they had produced and shaped, and the way these forms reflected their communal life. In the second edition of *The History of the Synoptic Tradition*, Bultmann qualified the difference between his approach and that of Dibelius. The two procedures supplemented and corrected each other, as he explained with reference to the hermeneutical circle of historical knowledge, a concept that applied equally to work in form-criticism. Just as Bultmann naturally had in mind a "picture, [even if] provisional, of the earliest Christian community and its history," the exact contours of which could be ascertained only by the *analysis* of individual units, so Dibelius, starting from his understanding of the community and its cultic exigencies, had made use of observations regarding the *forms* of the units of literary transmission.[122] And even in 1931, when after more than a decade of form-critical work on the synoptic gospels Bultmann took pains to underline his fundamental consensus with Dibelius, this nonetheless recognizable difference of approach between the two main representatives of New Testament form-criticism retained more than just a marginal significance.

The analytical form of access to the synoptic tradition corresponds to Bultmann's basic intention, namely, "to write an actual *history* of the individual pieces of tradition (in their various genres) . . . and [to trace] the laws of the transmission."[123] He does not mean to confine himself to a purely form-critical and stylistically oriented description of the genres. Rather, his priority is to grasp both the many-layered process of transmission revealed in the history of the forms and the modifications within the individual forms. In short, Bultmann would prefer to deal with the problem of the emergence and development of the synoptic tradition from the point of view of the

120. Cf. M. Dibelius, *Formgeschichte*; as well as Bultmann's rev. of Dibelius, in RB, *Theologie als Kritik*, 92–94.

121. Cf. Bultmann's rev. of Dibelius, in RB, *Theologie als Kritik*, 93.

122. RB, *Geschichte*, 5f; cf. Dibelius' somewhat more reserved view of the consensus claimed by RB in M. Dibelius, rev. of *Geschichte* (2d ed.), 1105–11.

123. UB Tübingen, RB est., RB to W. Bousset, 1. 2. 1920, Mn 2-2149; on what follows cf. also E. Baasland, *Theologie*, 163–303.

history of transmission, while at the same time illuminating the history of earliest Christianity. In doing so, he achieves a more differentiated picture of the diverse layers of the tradition than does Dibelius. His special focus is on assigning individual pieces of tradition to the authentic proclamation of Jesus, or to such other layers of transmission as the Jewish, Jewish-Christian, Palestinian, Hellenistic Jewish-Christian, or Hellenistic Gentile-Christian. To this end, Bultmann brings to bear as a working hypothesis the view of primitive Christian history pioneered by Wilhelm Heitmüller and developed by Wilhelm Bousset. In this connection it seems to him imperative to determine more closely the relationship between the original community in Palestine and earliest Hellenistic Christianity in order to further clarify "the central problem in the history of earliest Christianity."[124] He grants, of course, that now and then individual pieces of tradition cannot be assigned to the layers of transmission that have been postulated, but asserts that such cases call for developing the most plausible hypotheses possible and supplementing the analysis of genre and style by arguments regarding content. In this way, Bultmann does not allow himself to be undermined by the objection raised by Dibelius: namely, that, "for the purpose of making critical judgments about history, he has made use of observations about form, the significance of which is questionable from the point of view of content," and to that degree "has entered a field that lies outside the work of form-criticism."[125] For on the contrary, Bultmann insists that since the literary forms reflect the life and history of earliest Christianity, such considerations of content are absolutely necessary.[126]

In general, the approach of tradition-criticism opens up the possibility of tying the form-critical analysis of the synoptic transmission process into other methods that also have a useful role. This is why Bultmann is able to make the literary-critical investigations of Julius Wellhausen quite fruitful for his *History of the Synoptic Tradition*.[127] Furthermore, Bultmann relies much more strongly than does Dibelius on folkloristic parallels—anecdotes, tales, sagas, and folk songs—especially since these analogues show many of the same characteristics found in the synoptic tradition. In doing so, however, Bultmann does not reflect the Romantic notion that "the people"—in this case the earliest Christian community—comprises a sort of collective

124. RB, *Geschichte*, 6.

125. M. Dibelius, "Zur Formgeschichte," 214; cf. M. Dibelius, rev. of *Geschichte* (1st ed.), 130, 132f.

126. RB, *Geschichte*, 6.

127. Cf. E. Baasland, *Theologie*, 167–71, 300–303. For more details on what follows, cf. K. Hammann, "Das abscheuliche Wort 'Apophthegma,'" 203.

voice that gave birth to the gospel tradition. Rather, he envisions elements of the tradition as having been created by individual members of the early Christian community who were teachers, prophets, apostles, and scribes. Then, when the community passed on the tradition, this process was consummated according to the universal patterns for conveying popular sayings and narratives.

Like Dibelius, Bultmann classifies the synoptic gospels as ancient popular literature. The form-critical principle of taking the narrow view of things promotes the goal of "discerning the original form of a piece of narrative, a dominical saying, a parable."[128] As a rule, Bultmann holds, the pure, simple text, not yet elaborated or embellished, represents the original form. Although he shares this premise of Dibelius' form-critical analysis, his own primary interest is to reconstruct the history of the synoptic tradition. For this reason, despite his shared conviction that the oldest tradition is to be regarded as oral, he can nonetheless declare that whether material originated in oral or written form is not particularly important: "There is no difference in kind between the oral and the written tradition. And thus Bultmann maintains the consistency of his perspective on the history of the process of transmission."[129]

From here Bultmann constructs a formal classification that is substantially more differentiated and more complete than that of Dibelius.[130] He first subdivides the material into the overarching rubrics of sayings- and narrative tradition. It is clear from the way he characterizes genres, that in addition to formal criteria that emerge from considerations of style, Bultmann also considers the content or substance of a given tradition in determining the genre. Thus, within the sayings-tradition he distinguishes apophthegms—such as examples of controversy, scholastic dialogues, and biographical aphorisms—from dominical sayings, which include wisdom-sayings, apocalyptic and prophetic utterances, legal formulas, community rules, "I"-sayings, parables, and related forms. Under the narrative tradition Bultmann subsumes the miracle stories—healings and nature miracles—as well as the historical narratives and legends dealing with the period between the baptism of Jesus and his entry into Jerusalem. Other elements of this group include the passion

128. RB, *Geschichte*, 7.

129. RB, *Geschichte*, 347, along with 50, 58, 64.

130. K. L. Schmidt, rev. of *Geschichte* (1st ed.), 397: "With regard to completeness in executing the material and to clarity of critical standards, what is presented here is, apart from Jülicher's great work on the parables of Jesus, unequalled." Cf. also M. Dibelius, rev. of *Geschichte* (1st ed.), 133, on Bultmann's assigning the rubrics of dominical sayings and narrative material besides those of the apophthegms and miracle-stories.

narrative, the Easter reports, the pre-histories, and therefore the birth narratives as well. Bultmann is evidently desirous of classifying the material of the synoptic tradition as unambiguously and as comprehensively as possible. This is why in exceptional cases he also deals with such mixed forms as the stories of the Syro-Phoenician woman (Mark 7:24–31) and the centurion in Capernaum (Matt 8:5–13), and why he discusses them in an addendum to the apophthegms.[131]

Bultmann's way of dealing with the history of the transmitted material comes to the fore with particular clarity in his analysis of the apophthegms.[132] As a rule, these are pieces of tradition in which a logion is fitted into a narrative context by way of a particular theological motif. To be sure, Bultmann less often employs standard form-critical criteria than he does matters of content to assign sometimes disparate material to the apophthegms. Despite the great variety in detail to be observed even within this genre, he particularly addresses to the material the question of how the apophthegms emerged and were transmitted. He concluded that as soon as the community forgot or no longer understood the situation in which a saying of Jesus originated, a new "ideal" scene or situation would be generated in an attempt to illustrate the logion anew against the background of the newly created situation. Bultmann ascribes to the apophthegms a "generating power," which arises as a matter of course from the process of appropriating and passing on a saying of Jesus that lacks its originating context.[133] But Dibelius, predictably enough, criticized both his generalizing assumption that "the sayings would have produced a situation, not the other way around,"[134] and his overall program that proceeds by analyzing the transmission of the apophthegms, as "overstepping the boundaries of purely form-critical method."[135]

For classical form-criticism, the original form of a piece of tradition has an inalienable connection to its "setting in life." It is striking that this central concept does not occur with any particular frequency in the early pioneering works of New Testament form-criticism.[136] Dibelius and Schmidt do not use the expression at all, but Bultmann employs it in 1919 to describe the

131. Cf. RB, *Geschichte*, 1921 (1st ed.), 19f; 1931 (2d ed.), 38f.

132. Cf. RB, *Geschichte*, 1931 (2d ed.), 8–73; also E. Baasland, *Theologie*, 250–53, 276–80.

133. Cf. RB, *Geschichte*, 53, 58, 65. For discussion led by Bultmann and H. Gunkel on the term, "Apophthegma," cf. K. Hammann, "Das abscheuliche Wort 'Apophthegma'," 204f.

134. RB, *Geschichte*, 20, 49.

135. M. Dibelius, rev. of *Geschichte* (1st ed.), 132; cf. K. L. Schmidt, rev. of *Geschichte* (1st ed.), 397. In further research, however, the ways in which Bultmann specified genres largely prevailed over those of Dibelius, with modifications, as the case may be. Cf. G. Theissen, epilogue in RB, *Geschichte*, 1995 (10th ed.), 415–17.

136. On what follows, cf. W. Schmithals, "Kritik," 164–70; E. Baasland, *Theologie*, 192–96.

procedure adopted by Dibelius and again in 1921 with a less specific application.[137] He first assigns a constitutive significance to the technical term *Sitz im Leben*, that is, "setting in life," in the second edition of *The History of the Synoptic Tradition*.[138] Dibelius and Bultmann concur in seeing the subject matter denoted by this concept as the facts of a case when understood not in an aesthetic, but rather in a sociological fashion. Dibelius, to be sure, seeks first and foremost to discern the situation that gave rise to material representing the standard forms of the synoptic tradition. He finds this in the preaching of the earliest Christian community, whether directed to the congregation or outsiders, but which in any case furnished the immediate institutional point of adhesion for the parables and the passion narrative. Bultmann, in contrast, is not primarily interested in how the institutions of the earliest Christian community reflect its religious phenomenology, but rather in locating where the individual pieces of tradition "arose and functioned in the community."[139] Bultmann really conceives of a text's *Sitz im Leben* in history-of-religions fashion—that is, as the concrete historical location of its emergence and transmission. Thus, it is crucial to the reconstruction of a text that one recognize the priorities and motives of the community that the text reflects. Starting there, Bultmann was able to accept a multitude of settings in life for the synoptic tradition. He regards as short-sighted Dibelius' proposal that the church's preaching was the only context that shaped how things were transmitted in the synoptic tradition. "Apologetic and polemic as well as community-formation and discipline must be taken into account, and also the work of scribes."[140] By Bultmann's own admission, to be sure, one comes up against limits in determining the setting in life of the individual elements of tradition. For,

> . . . as surely as the miracle stories, for instance, must have been used for apologetic and propagandistic proofs of the Messiah, so it is difficult to regard one special interest as a dominating factor; and likewise it is wrong to inquire *only* after purpose and priority, for matters of the spirit also objectify themselves without any special purposes in mind.[141]

To a number of the early reviewers, *The History of the Synoptic Tradition* seemed above all a hypercritical book. A few of them expressed their disap-

137. Cf. RB, rev. of M. Dibelius, in *Theologie als Kritik*, 92; RB, *Geschichte*, 1921 (1st ed.), 4.
138. Cf. RB, *Geschichte*, 1931 (2d ed.), 5, 8.
139. RB, *Geschichte*, 1931 (2d ed.), 8.
140. RB, *Geschichte*, 1931 (2d ed.), 64, also 393.
141. RB, *Geschichte*, 1931 (2d ed.), 393.

proval of what they saw as Bultmann's exaggerated historical skepticism.[142] Others specifically praised his radical and effective undermining of all attempts to reconstruct a life of Jesus from the synoptic gospels.[143] Indeed, Bultmann regarded comparatively few pieces of tradition as genuine and direct reflections of the proclamations and actions of Jesus. In contrast to the liberal quest for Jesus, he did not urgently seek to lift authentic Jesus material out of the synoptic texts. Nevertheless, his interest in the history of the synoptic tradition did give thorough consideration to the question of authenticity.

Bultmann understands that whether a text goes back to Jesus himself or is to be seen as a post-Easter formation by the community, is sometimes either uncertain or only hypothetical. He does, however, employ a number of criteria that allow him to make a reasonably firm judgment on the authenticity or the secondary nature of many texts. First of all, he applies as a material criterion his specific understanding of Jesus—namely, his concept of Jesus as an eschatological prophet. On this basis, logia may be more certainly identified as coined by Jesus, "the more their content has a personal note, the more characteristic [they appear] of Jesus as the preacher of repentance and the coming reign of God, as the one who demands truthfulness."[144] Then he approaches the parables with the criterion of double difference, an approach later extended to the entire gospel tradition by Ernst Käsemann. "The greater the contrast to the morality and piety of Judaism, the clearer Jesus' characteristically eschatological voice, and the more notable an absence of specifically Christian features, the more likely one is to possess a genuine parable of Jesus."[145] In addition, Bultmann occasionally makes use of the criterion of coherence, now and then derives the authenticity of a text from the genre, and occasionally includes formal and linguistic criteria in making a judgment.

Viewing the synoptic tradition critically leads to the conclusion that the main part of the authentic Jesus material is allotted to the sayings-tradition. The narrative tradition, on the other hand, includes little genuine material, though most of what it does contain has developed out of historical kernels. Among the genres of the sayings-tradition, the parables display the most genuine sayings of Jesus, followed by the apocalyptic-prophetic

142. Cf. K. L. Schmidt, rev. of *Geschichte* (1st ed.), 398; M. Werner, "Zwei Schriften," 33f; as well as RB, *Geschichte*, 1931 (2d ed.), 6n2 (with reference to M. Kähler).

143. Cf. G. Bertram, "Geschichte," 13; M. Dibelius, rev. of *Geschichte* (1st ed.), 132.

144. RB, *Geschichte*, 1931 (2d ed.), 106; on what follows cf. E. Baasland, *Theologie*, 230–61.

145. RB, *Geschichte*, 1931 (2d ed.), 222.

and wisdom sayings. And while a few legal sayings and I-sayings can be shown to be genuine, none of the rules for the community can raise a claim to authenticity. Still, although a critical study of the history of transmission indicates that only a very small portion of the apophthegms is to be regarded as genuine, Bultmann takes much of the information reported in the apophthegms—for instance Jesus' breaking of the Sabbath, his dealings with the tax-collectors, his teaching activity as a rabbi, his connection to his relatives, and the cleansing of the Temple—to be historically credible. In addition, he ascribes genuineness to quite a few of the logia handed down in the context of the apophthegms, though the narrative tradition itself, like the greater stock of apophthegms, is to be viewed as secondary. This does not, however, rule out the reliability of individual elements of tradition. Thus, the passion narrative consists of "a brief report of historical reminiscence of Jesus' arrest, trial and conviction" that has been considerably expanded.[146] Even the miracle-stories, all of which Bultmann understands as having been formed by the community, preserve historically accurate reminiscences of Jesus the miracle-worker, who performed healings and drove out demons.[147] Overall, the findings show, authentic Jesus-material is most likely to be found in the Palestinian tradition, while the Hellenistic tradition evinces a certain detachment from Jesus. To this extent, the analysis of the synoptic tradition confirms for Bultmann the historical assumption that Christian faith first assumed a distinctive form recognizably different from Judaism in the context of earliest Hellenistic Christianity, rather than in the original Palestinian community.

Bultmann concluded that continuous redactional work on the synoptic tradition had already begun well before the evangelists undertook their final redactions of the tradition. At an early stage, this was a matter of individual pieces of tradition being written down and given a framework, although this did not happen for all genres to the same degree and with the same intensity. The redactional working-over of the material also combined individual logia, bound narratives into larger complexes, and inserted later pieces of the sayings-tradition into the connected narratives. By means of this collecting and ordering, evangelists were able to augment the basic material transmitted in the earliest Palestinian community. The gospel genre created by Mark first grew in the soil of earliest Hellenistic Christianity. This presupposes not only that the Hellenistic community took over the Palestinian tradition,

146. RB, *Geschichte*, 1931 (2d ed.), 298.

147. Cf. RB, *Geschichte*, 1931 (2d ed.), 234, 244. To be sure, Bultmann only deals in detail with the apophthegmatic miracle-stories in early Palestinian Christianity; he sees all of the remaining miracle-stories as stamped by Hellenistic motifs of the genre.

but also that the gospel genre of necessity produced new motifs in earliest Hellenistic Christianity. For the gospel genre was to serve as "a completion and an illustration . . . *of the Christian kerygma*." Since together with the rest of the history-of-religions school Bultmann conceives the earliest Christian proclamation of Christ as "cult legend," he can characterize the gospels as "*expanded cult legends*."[148] Having grown "out of the Christ-cult and -mythos of Hellenistic Christianity," the gospel represents more nearly "*an original Christian creation*."[149] And as Bultmann and other representatives of classical form-criticism emphasize, because of its kerygmatic intent it cannot be analogically derived from ancient biography or other folkloric traditions.

Together with the works of Dibelius and Schmidt, Bultmann's *History of the Synoptic Tradition* stimulated considerable further inquiry into New Testament form-criticism during the 1920s. Not only German-language scholars, but English and Scandinavian academics as well took part in an ongoing and highly controversial debate on the possibilities and limits of the form-critical approach.[150] Up to 1931, Bultmann reviewed various new form-critical works on the synoptic gospels and also published several essays of his own on the subject.[151] In the second edition of the *History of the Synoptic Tradition*, he included research since 1921 to which he felt the need to respond, whether by way of agreement or rejection. A foreign observer described the strategy of Bultmann this way: "Bultmann's method of answering objections consists in repeating his initial thesis. It is simply as if he were to say, 'But have you heard what I said at all? Let me say it again!'"[152] As a result of these expansions and minor modifications as well as an enlarged printing format, the original 232-page book grew to 408 pages.[153] The 1931 edition became a twentieth-century classic of New Testament scholarship, and produced lasting effects on research.[154] In the second half of the

148. RB, *Geschichte*, 1931 (2d ed.), 396.

149. RB, *Geschichte*, 1931 (2d ed.), 399f.

150. Cf. F. Hahn, "Formgeschichte," 454–62.

151. Cf., among others, RB, "New Approach," 337–62; RB, "Urchristliche Religion," 117f (on W. Bussmann), 120 (on M. Albertz), 121 (on E. Fascher), 130 (on A. Fridrichsen), 132 (on L. Brun); RB, rev. of E. Fascher, in RB, *Theologie als Kritik*, 140–46; RB, rev. of L. Köhler, 578–80; RB, *Erforschung*.

152. V. Taylor, "Formung," 375.

153. If the book appeared only with paper covers and cramped printing on poor, post-war paper in 1921 for reasons of cost, the publisher brought it out in the second edition in 1931 on good paper, with clearly better type and bound in cloth.

154. Cf. G. Theissen, epilogue, in RB, *Geschichte*, 451. Up to 1995, the book had appeared in ten editions.

twentieth century, very few doctoral programs in New Testament were offered in which this now standard work on the synoptic gospels played no role.

The History of the Synoptic Tradition also helped create the basic axioms of what came to be called dialectical theology, a development that over time further contributed to the great influence of the book. For while Wilhelm Herrmann had already made clear that Christian faith could not be justified by relying only on so-called historical facts, Bultmann now showed through the medium of historical criticism that only the basic features of the proclamation of Jesus could be drawn from the synoptic gospels—and that they provide no valid reports about the life and activity of the historical Jesus. For he concluded from his analysis of the forms and their transmission in the gospels that the gospel message consisted solely of the proclamation of Jesus as the crucified and risen Kyrios, the Son of God who had become a human being.

The affinity between the form-critical work on the synoptic Jesus-tradition and a theology oriented to the event of the word of God[155] is reflected in a significant way in Bultmann's use of the concept of kerygma in *The History of the Synoptic Tradition*. Bultmann evidently took the term from Martin Dibelius and first used it in 1919 to characterize the genuinely Christian proclamation that originated within earliest Hellenistic Christianity and through the Christ myth made explicit the significance of the death and resurrection of Jesus.[156] He also used the concept of kerygma, and in the same context, in the first edition of *The History of the Synoptic Tradition*.[157] Ten years later, the second edition had doubled the number of places in which Bultmann spoke of the kerygma of the earliest Christian community.[158] Above and beyond that, and not only from the point of view of the history of religion, he had now begun to regard the specific content of "*the Christian kerygma*" as a theological criterion for the emergence of the synoptic gospels. As intrinsic elements of the kerygma of the Hellenistic community, these proclaim not the historical Jesus, but rather "the Christ of faith and cult." As a matter of theological necessity, however, the gospels depict

155. Cf. also (on the example of M. Dibelius) G. Theissen, "Formgeschichte," 143–48.

156. Cf. RB, rev. of M. Dibelius, in RB, *Theologie als Kritik*, 93; RB, rev. of K. L. Schmidt, in RB, *Theologie als Kritik*, 109. However, Bultmann may also have taken the kerygma-concept over from M. Kähler.

157. Cf. RB, *Geschichte*, 1921 (1st ed.), 167, 211f, 214; as well as, to be sure, the provisional observations on the history of the concepts in G. Ebeling, *Theologie*, esp. 112–14.

158. Where there are six references in the first edition, there are fourteen in the second. At the same time, the newly added references take on an even greater significance. Cf. RB, *Geschichte*, 1931 (2d ed.), 297f, 362, 372, 374, 376, 396f, 399. M. Dibelius, rev. of *Geschichte* (2d ed.), 1105f, judged Bultmann's emphasis on the kerygmatic aspect as an index for the correctness he himself had attached to early Christian preaching.

the tradition as a unity, "so that in it, both the one who speaks and the one who is spoken of is he who, as God's son, has lived on earth, has suffered, died, risen, and been raised to heavenly glory."[159]

5. Professor in Giessen

> *The work here gives me ever more joy. Seminar papers and debates show high academic attainment; I have become part of a most pleasant tradition. The relationship to colleagues inside and outside the faculty is very agreeable, the intercourse informal and pleasant.*[160]

In March 1920 Bultmann received mail from Giessen. Hermann Gunkel asked him for his manuscript of *The History of the Synoptic Tradition.*[161] Bultmann had offered this investigation a few weeks before to Wilhelm Bousset for publication in the series Research on Religion and Literature of the Old and New Testament.[162] But, as noted earlier, on March 8, 1920, Bousset had died. Besides Erwin Preuschen and Hans Windisch, Gunkel had for some while had his eye on Bultmann to succeed Bousset as Professor of New Testament at Giessen, and, should such an opportunity present itself, that would solidify the work in the history of religions already established by Gunkel and Bousset in the theological faculty at Giessen.[163] A recent report on research in which Bultmann offered a glowing acknowledgement of the contributions of the history-of-religions school to New Testament scholarship rendered Gunkel's hope and expectation more than justified. Furthermore, in that overview of recent research Bultmann had explicitly affirmed Gunkel's understanding of earliest Christianity as a syncretistic religion and declared that the Palestinian-Hellenistic distinction, pioneered by Heitmüller and effectively promoted by Bousset as the actual beginning of the Christian religion, was the most significant insight of both contemporary New Testament scholarship and recent theology in general.[164]

For Gunkel, who already respected Bultmann on the basis of a personal acquaintance that went back years,[165] the manuscript of *The History of the*

159. RB, *Geschichte*, 1931 (2d ed.), 396, also 362.

160. UB Tübingen, RB est., RB to H. von Soden, 23. 12. 1920, Mn 2-2385.

161. Cf. H. Gunkel to RB, 13. 3. 1920; cf. also H. Gunkel to RB, 24.–25. 3. 1920, Mn 2-883, in UB Tübingen, RB est.

162. Cf. UB Tübingen, RB est., RB to W. Bousset, 1. 2. 1920, Mn 2-2149; on the details, see above 106.

163. This was all the more so, as Gunkel accepted a call to Halle in June 1920.

164. Cf. RB, "Neutestamentliche Forschung," in RB, *Theologie als Kritik*, esp. 101–4; see also below 395–98.

165. Cf. W. Klatt, *Hermann Gunkel*, 168n14; as well as UB Tübingen, RB est., H. Gunkel to RB, 11. 12. 1909, 27. 1. and 28. 1. 1914, 5. 8. 1916, 30. 10. 1916, Mn 2-883.

Synoptic Tradition was the decisive factor in putting Bultmann first on the list for appointment and in expediting his appointment to Giessen.[166] However, the proposal that Gunkel had drawn up for the Giessen theological faculty put Bultmann in third place, behind Erwin Preuschen and Hans Windisch. While those two had already in 1915 been considered for the professorship that Bousset subsequently assumed, Gunkel championed Bultmann as an especially promising young scholar. He also praised Bultmann's as yet unpublished work on the earliest synoptic tradition as an innovative contribution that would help the form-critical approach produce a significant breakthrough in New Testament studies.[167] When Erwin Preuschen died on March 24, 1920, and Hans Windisch turned down the appointment to Giessen, the way was open for Bultmann, and it surely did no harm that Wilhelm Heitmüller had given sustained encouragement from Marburg to this personnel shift.[168] Thus, Bultmann finally received the call to the New Testament professorship in Giessen,[169] where he and his family moved in September. There the Bultmanns took up residence in the house of the widow of the systematic theologian Samuel Eck at Loberstrasse 20, in the immediate vicinity of the university.[170] Ernst Lohmeyer, a student of Adolf Deissmann and Martin Dibelius, became Bultmann's successor as associate professor in Breslau. Immediately after being appointed, Lohmeyer contacted Bultmann, who was able to arrange for a guest-house for his successor,[171] and thus began a relationship of many years—one that, despite the differences of opinion between the two New Testament scholars, was to develop into a strong friendship.

Hermann Gunkel keenly regretted that his move to Halle meant that he could not fulfill his hope of teaching in the same faculty as Bultmann. Nevertheless, he tried to make Bultmann's new place of work seem appeal-

166. Cf. UB Tübingen, RB est., H. Gunkel to RB, 31. 3. 1920, 10. 5. and 11. 5. 1920, Mn 2-883.

167. Cf. H. Gunkel's report of 29. 3. 1920, received on 8. 4. 1920 by the Giessen theological faculty, in UA Giessen, file regarding replacement hire, 17f. See also K. Hammann, "Das abscheuliche Wort 'Apophthegma,'" 205f.

168. Cf. UB Tübingen, RB est., E. and W. Heitmüller to RB, 18. 4., 27. 4., 30. 4., and 22. 6. 1920, Mn 2-962; Mn 2-964.

169. Cf. UB Tübingen, RB est., Hessian Office of Education to RB, 23. 6. 1920, Mn 2-3037; cf. UA Giessen, RB to Dean of the Giessen Theological Faculty (3. 7. 1920), 11: "As pleased as I am over the call to be allowed to work amidst the esteemed Theological Faculty of the University of Giessen, it is just as painful to me that the position there has been made vacant by the premature death of D. W. Bousset. And I am filled with a feeling of diffidence in face of the task of continuing on the work of this master of our discipline."

170. Cf. RB, *Chronik 1917–1945*, Mn 2-224.

171. Cf. E. Lohmeyer to RB, 10. 10. and 5. 12. 1920, in U. Hutter, "Theologie," 154f.

ing. Giessen would have "many great advantages: a nice location, agreeable relationships within the university, friendly intercourse among the faculty, no factions, soil that has been well-tilled under those who are studying."[172] The theological faculty at the *Ludovicina* had in fact been on a steady upswing since its thorough organizational renewal under the Old Testament scholar Bernhard Stade in 1878. The high academic standing of a faculty dominated by liberal theologians had also resulted in a continuing increase in enrollment.

Bultmann felt at home in Giessen right from the start. Even in his old age he looked back on his two semesters in Giessen "with particular joy, because the friendly intellectual exchange with colleagues—and, indeed, not only within the theological faculty—was extraordinarily lively."[173] In the Giessen theological faculty "collegiality and matter-of-factness" made for a good working atmosphere. Bultmann soon established a close personal relationship with the church historian Gustav Krüger, "whom I am learning to esteem more and more; his intellectual elasticity is admirable and the nobility of his character is always agreeable." With the Old Testament scholar Gustav Hölscher, who had come to Giessen as Gunkel's successor, Bultmann established a friendly as well as scholarly exchange. Hölscher's "absolute lack of interest concerning questions of principle" might indeed prove inhibiting, but his intellectual alertness and personal probity compensated for this deficiency, Bultmann found. And he developed a similarly reserved judgment on the scholarly abilities of the systematician Emil Walter Mayer and the practical theologian Martin Schian, though he wrote that he had kind and personable dealings with both of them, as well as with their students.[174]

Bultmann felt especially grateful for the enthusiasm of his students in Giessen and for their readiness to work. He attributed their seriousness and joy in pursuing their scholarly preparation for the pastoral vocation to the fact that most of them had participated in the War. One sensed "how the War had served to shape their character,—an observation that is unfortunately not that widespread and [thus] all the more gratifying." Bultmann was pleased to note the marked interest in matters of theological principle on the part of the students, particularly as it did not inhibit their readiness to deal

172. H. Gunkel to RB, 28. 6. 1920; cf. also UB Tübingen, RB est., H. Gunkel to RB, 19. 7. 1920, Mn 2-883.

173. Bultmann's autobiographical notes in B. Jaspert, *Barth-Bultmann Briefwechsel* (2d ed.), 304; cf. UB Tübingen, RB est., RB to H. von Soden, 23. 12. 1920, Mn 2-2385.

174. UB Tübingen, RB est., RB to H. von Soden, 3. 4. 1921, Mn 2-2385; on Hölscher, cf. also Bultmann's autobiographical remarks in B. Jaspert, *Barth-Bultmann Briefwechsel* (2d ed.), 306.

with historical issues. This fit in with his own intention "that we not allow ourselves to get lost in the philological side of historical investigations, but rather be able to do history in the full sense, not separate from its connection with systematics."[175]

Bultmann was also taken with the intense communal life that the theological students in Giessen promoted through weekly evenings of reading, as well as Christmas and end-of-semester celebrations.[176] Academic worship, which had been given new life in 1917 under difficult circumstances, was part of this.[177] Since the university did not have its own church, academic worship took place for the most part in the assembly hall. As Bultmann noted approvingly, university worship in Giessen, with its own liturgy and a sermon directed to its academic audience, had reached the point that "students and teaching staff of all faculties took part in large numbers, and there was a really lively feeling in the congregation, the like of which I cannot recall in any other experiences in connection with university congregational worship."[178]

Bultmann gave two sermons in the university worship service in Giessen. On Convocation Sunday of 1921, in expounding on 2 Cor 4:5–7, 16, under the title "The Way to Oneself," he developed thoughts on human self-realization. In discussing the sense of self that comes from the experience of alienation from the self, Bultmann begins by naming criteria for the liveliness of the self: the capacities for play, for community, and for solitariness. However, a threshold experience of profound solitariness not only awakens longing for the true self, but also leads to self-reproach arising from a sense of conflict between willing and doing like that described in Rom 7:15. Out of this conflict, only the self that becomes aware of itself as gift, as a thought of God, is able to achieve true selfhood.[179] In both his choice of subject and his insightful examination of the self and self-discovery, Bultmann echoed Hermann Hesse's novel *Demian*,[180] though unlike Hesse, he saw self-discovery as initially made possible and mediated through the revelation of God. In 1922, in his review of the second edition of Karl Barth's *Römerbrief* [*Epistle to the Romans*], he explicitly invoked something Hesse had said in *Demian*: "The life of each person is a way back to himself. . . ."[181] In this

175. UB Tübingen, RB est., RB to H. von Soden, 3. 4. 1921, Mn 2-2385.
176. Cf. UB Tübingen, RB est., RB to H. von Soden, 3. 4. and 1. 8. 1921, Mn 2-2385.
177. Cf. K. Hammann, "Giessener Universitätsdienst," 99–123.
178. UB Tübingen, RB est., RB to H. von Soden, 21. 12. 1921, Mn 2-2385.
179. Cf. RB, *VW*, 173–81.
180. Cf. RB, *VW*, 173, 178f, 331; as well as H. Hesse, *Demian*; also the interpretation of T. Kucharz, *Theologen und ihre Dichter*, 190–95. Cf. also in general S. Jones and J. Gareth, "The Play," 96–111.
181. RB, "Karl Barth's 'Römerbrief' in zweiter Auflage," 129f.

way Bultmann meant to illustrate Barth's idea that faith is not a possession, and that we can only believe that we believe. But Barth soon gave Bultmann to understand that he did not take gladly to being mentioned in the same breath with Hesse.[182] Bultmann did not comply with the request that Barth thus made explicit—namely that he delete the passage with the citation from *Demian*—but he thereafter indicated differences in their assessment of the relation between anthropology and theology in less pointed ways.

On June 5, 1929, Bultmann's second sermon in Giessen treated prayer in connection with Rom 8:26f. He intensified the proverb "Want teaches prayer" by applying Paul's implication that the inability to pray as one knows one ought reflects one's falling silent for fear of dying separated from God. The person who, contrary to all appearances, senses the power before which he bows in prayer to be the reality of God, will become free in the humbling effect of accepting the gift of grace and finding security in the power of God. For that person, then, the true nature of prayer is revealed, and with it a new understanding of the world and its duties.[183]

Following the summer semester of 1921, Bultmann was able to look back "with great joy and thankfulness on the year in Giessen." What the beginnings promised, the end fulfilled; it was an ideal situation of working together with colleagues and students. He "experienced a great deal of trust on the part of the students."[184] As Bultmann reported these impressions to his friend von Soden, it had already been settled that, albeit with a heavy heart, he would take his leave of Giessen.

6. Religion as the Subject-Matter of Theology

> *. . . [I always still see] as the task of systematic theology what Schleiermacher and Herrmann took it to be: the re-presentation of the religious consciousness.*[185]

In January 1917 the German booksellers were able to present to their customers a new release that was soon to prove to be a big seller, Rudolf Otto's *The Idea of the Holy.* In this book the author took up a central issue of liberal theology reminiscent of Schleiermacher: How is one properly to define what is distinctive and essential to religion? Otto traced religion as a

182. Cf. K. Barth to RB, 14. 4. 1922, in B. Jaspert, *Barth-Bultmann Briefwechsel* (2d ed.), 8.
183. Cf. RB, *VW*, 182–89; as well as E. Hauschildt, "Rudolf Bultmanns Predigten," 55f.
184. UB Tübingen, RB est., RB to H. von Soden, 1. 8. 1921, Mn 2-2385; cf. also RB to H. Gunkel, 21. 5. 1922, in K. Hammann, "Das abscheuliche Wort 'Apophthegma,'" 219f.
185. UB Tübingen, RB est., RB to H. von Soden, 19. 3. 1922, Mn 2-2385.

solitary phenomenon back to the organizing structure of the human spirit that is an *a priori* datum, a given. He saw this religious *a priori* supported by Jacob Friedrich Fries' transcendental hypothesis that the feeling of truth can only be experienced, not proven. In order to understand the religious feeling more closely, Otto took the concept of the holy as the basis for his phenomenological analysis of religion. As the central category of religion, the holy could no longer remain located in ethical or rational contexts of explanation; rather, Otto assigned to the holy a meaning that discloses itself solely through religious experience. He asserted the absolute singularity of the holy by means of the concept of the numinous. The numinous "Wholly Other" shows itself on the one hand in the *mysterium tremendum* and, on the other, in the *mysterium fascinosum.* To be sure, the qualities for the "Wholly Other" that make one shudder with fear and cause fascinated wonder form a unity rich in tension. Otto finds the evidence for this understanding of religion both in non-Christian religion and in the Bible. Still, he directs his primary attention not to the history of religion, but rather to its intrinsic quality, the religious experience of the wholly other.[186]

Otto had already told Bultmann about his project in the autumn of 1916, on one of their walks together in Breslau.[187] Bultmann read the book immediately after its appearance and then several more times. He had previously devoted intensive study to Schleiermacher's *Speeches.*[188] Against this background, Otto's work had a stimulating effect on Bultmann's own reflections on the essence of religion. On April 6, 1918, he posted to the author a number of questions concerning his understanding of religion and his interpretation of Schleiermacher.[189] Through the discussion with Otto, Bultmann desired primarily "to clarify in my own mind the thoughts that arise out of my reading."[190] But he did not explain in this letter—which, by the way, remained unanswered—what stage his own efforts at an adequate concept of religion had reached in the spring of 1918.

First, Bultmann complains that Otto has passed off merely psychic phenomena as presumably genuine religious states of feeling, but that in so doing has clearly not grasped the essence of religion. Over against such a psychological misunderstanding of religion, it must be insisted that religion consists in an inward and personal experience that knows itself constituted through

186. Cf. R. Otto, *Das Heilige.*
187. Cf. UB Tübingen, RB est., RB to H. Feldmann, 14. 10. 1916, Mn 2-3447.
188. Cf. UB Tübingen, RB est., RB to H. Feldmann, 2.–3. 11. 1916, Mn 2-3447.
189. Cf. RB to R. Otto, 6. 4. 1918, in H.-W. Schütte, *Religion*, 130–39; also M. Evang, "Rudolf Bultmanns Berufung," in B. Jaspert, *Werk und Wirkung*, 5–13.
190. RB to R. Otto, 6. 4. 1918, in H.-W. Schütte, *Religion*, 130.

the relation "to an otherworldly reality of life." The religious individual experiences this reality, as Bultmann formulates it following Schleiermacher, "in the feeling of absolute dependence." However, this feeling does not, as Otto believes, correspond to a psychic state, nor does it denote "the faculty of judgment of the aesthetic reason." It is rather to be characterized, following Schleiermacher, as a form of self-consciousness.[191] Bultmann locates Otto's understanding of religion in the area of Paul Natorp's neo-Kantian philosophy of religion. But Natorp's idea of religion as "a registering of an otherworldly world," a concept that strongly affected Otto, represents a projection of psychic states, and therefore Bultmann must needs reject it as a denial of the transcendental reference of religion.[192] Contrary to such a dissolving of religion into illusion, Bultmann's interpretation of the feeling of absolute dependence leads him to assert the validity of its "objective relation" to otherworldly reality. To be sure, it may not be possible to comprehend this relation to its object rationally; but viewed from the opposite direction, the otherworldly reality may *reveal* itself as *mysterium*—mystery in a positive sense, inasmuch as such a revelation opens up an ever-increasing appreciation of existence. Accordingly, what Otto sees as the psychic states in which a person's sense of being rises to a feeling of self-realization would not be significant for the understanding of religion. What remains decisive is the dual orientation of the religious self-consciousness. On the one side, it "consists in relations to the this-worldly world and in the participation in formulating the material of experience through the faculties of reason." On the other, it is experienced precisely *in* this relation to this same world, so that "into one's individual life" there pours a content that grants one the certitude of a life grounded in the transcendent.[193]

Despite his fundamental criticism of Otto's understanding of religion, Bultmann agreed with the author of *The Idea of the Holy* that one must strictly differentiate the "Wholly Other" from the idea of the good, for the heterogeneity of religion and morality show themselves in the different modes in which the two entities are to be grasped: with religion the issue is *experiencing* an otherworldly reality, whereas the idea of the good identifies an act of moral *cognition*.[194] In viewing things this way, Bultmann shares Wilhelm Herrman's understanding of religion in a common effort to avoid

191. RB to R. Otto, 6. 4. 1918, in H.-W. Schütte, *Religion*, 137.

192. RB to R. Otto, 6. 4. 1918, in H.-W. Schütte, *Religion*, 134; cf. M. Evang, "Rudolf Bultmanns Berufung," in B. Jaspert, *Werk und Wirkung*, 7–11.

193. RB to R. Otto, 6. 4. 1918, in H.-W. Schütte, *Religion*, 138f.

194. Cf. UB Tübingen, RB est., RB to H. von Soden, 3. 4. 1921, Mn 2-2385; reprinted in M. Evang, *Frühzeit*, 329n144.

a complete separation of religion and culture. Between 1917 and 1920 Bultmann made several attempts to describe more closely the tension-filled relation between religion and the three realms of culture constituted by reason—art, morality, and scholarship.

In his contribution to the Festschrift for Wilhelm Herrmann that appeared in 1917, Bultmann examines the question of the essence of religion by working outwards from the "Significance of Eschatology for the Religion of the New Testament." In doing so he takes up his early exegetical works and premises from hermeneutics and the philosophy of history that he used there.[195] Bultmann regards the eschatological consciousness of earliest Christianity merely as a historically necessary yet time-conditioned expression of the psychic state of the primitive community; and therefore it is not essential to New Testament religion itself. The essence of religion, that is, "the relation of the human being to the transcendent, to a divine world, to God," is granted to the human being only through experiences that he interprets as revelation and in which he is aware of himself as "absolutely dependent."[196] An account of the history of earliest Christianity therefore enables one to visualize how a culturally conditioned primitive community learned to express its faith, but not to comprehend the essential character of religion. As a phenomenon *sui generis* constituted by revelation, religion can have no history. Nevertheless, the analysis of its mediated, historically conditioned expressions—and in paradigmatic fashion, of the eschatological consciousness of earliest Christianity—makes it possible to explain the relations of individual religious subjects to transcendent reality.

It was probably in the spring of 1919 that Bultmann gave a lecture to the youth organization of the DDP in Breslau on the topic of "Religion and Culture." In correspondence with Martin Rade that preceded the printing of the lecture in *Die Christliche Welt*, Bultmann insisted that the citations of Schleiermacher that he had included in his text absolutely had to be printed with it. He obviously regarded it a matter of principle that the central importance of his appeal to Schleiermacher in the essay be recognized. Clearly, more was at stake than merely an obligatory obeisance on the hundred and fiftieth birthday of the most famous son of the city of Breslau, to whom the university of the Silesian metropolis had recently paid tribute on November 21, 1918, with a Schleiermacher celebration.[197] In a time of political up-

195. Cf. esp. RB, "Urgemeinde, christliche"; as well as M. Evang, *Frühzeit*, 264–76.
196. RB, "Bedeutung," 81.
197. On the origin of the lecture and Bultmann's treatment of it under the same name, cf. M. Evang, "Rudolf Bultmanns Berufung," in B. Jaspert, *Werk und Wirkung*, 14f.

heaval, with a pressing need for clarification of the relation between church and state—an issue then in the process of being negotiated—Bultmann was asking fundamental questions about the significance of religion for culture.

A look at history yields an ambivalent picture. At first glance, there is much to be said for acknowledging religion as a factor of culture. For the culture that embraces scholarship, art, and morality has grown from religious roots. To be sure, a second glance makes it clear that culture has emancipated itself from its initial connection with religion; for this development of autonomy, often hindered by religion, is a typical stage of cultural evolution. Three elements are characteristic of it. Culture is an activity of the human spirit. It proceeds in a strictly methodical way in accordance with a definite pattern, and in its objective forms it aims at common rather than individual goals. By nature, religion stands in contrast to culture conceived in the neo-Kantian sense, for it is characterized by the passive activity of allowing oneself to be given unto. Religion has no universally applicable apparatus at its disposal, nor does it express itself in objective forms, "*but rather in becoming actualized, that is, in what happens on the part of the individual.*"[198] In religion, which, along with Schleiermacher, Bultmann defines more specifically as a consciousness of absolute dependence, the self submits itself "in free self-abandon" to a power that frees it for the first time.[199]

Certain consequences result from this strict demarcation of religion from culture. For one, religion recognizes the autonomy of culture, since it behaves towards it in a neutral way. For another, on account of the individualistic nature of religious experience, there is "*no history of religion,*"[200] for that term refers merely to the objectifications of religion in their mutual connections that can be described within the framework of cultural history. This is how Bultmann reaches the provisional conclusion that religion represents no historically powerful element in culture. However, one may not therefore overlook the positive connection between religion and culture, for this arises from a human being's participation equally in culture and nature. Because of this participation, each individual experiences himself as a living self that yearns for meaning, for a power that will release his fate from blind nature. Neither culture nor nature drives this yearning to find fulfillment. For this, the experience of a culture and nature is needed, one which freely grants the riches of a life fulfilled with meaning. This experience of absolute dependence, "of free self-abandon, is the hour when *religion* is

198. RB, "Religion und Kultur"; on what follows cf. M. Evang, "Rudolf Bultmanns Berufung," 16–20; M. Evang, *Frühzeit*, 278–80; D. Korsch, "Religion," 123–25.
199. RB, "Religion und Kultur," 18.
200. RB, "Religion und Kultur," 22.

born."[201] Religion mediates to the seeking self an awareness, a certitude of one's innermost self in that moment of experience.

From there, Bultmann sees that "it is not that religion is justified by culture, but rather that *culture is justified through religion.*" Since only religion is in the position to make "the person into a human being," one can yet view it as an element in culture, even if as a most peculiar one.[202] For religion both makes it possible to work out the meaning of culture while at the same time limiting culture's claim to validity. In Bultmann's estimation, not only modern writers such as Dostoevsky and Franz Werfel, but in its own way communism, have registered a protest against the divinizing and absolutizing of culture. Such protest counts for Bultmann as "the strongest expression of the yearning for a religious rebirth." However, communism especially promotes the dangerous opinion that culture or the state is responsible for the realization of true individual life. And yet this cannot be seen as the purpose of culture or the state, because the individual recognizes something higher than culture—namely, his life, his fortune, which even if deserved is not worked for, but rather received as a gift. "Higher than creating stands experiencing."[203]

With his essay "Religion and Culture," Bultmann moved even further toward Wilhelm Herrmann's conception of religion. If here and there he may have struck different notes—for instance in the strict separation of morals and religion—he still remained indebted to his Marburg teacher both for what was fundamental to the understanding of religion and for the interpretation of Schleiermacher.[204] A while later this was to change significantly on *one* point, the assessment of the significance of the historical Jesus for contemporary religion. During the celebration of the anniversary of the Friends of *Die Christliche Welt* on September 9, 1920, Bultmann gave the first major address, entitled "Ethical and Mystical Religion in Earliest Christianity."[205] A day later, in the second major address, Friedrich Gogarten affirmed "The

201. RB, "Religion und Kultur," 25.

202. RB, "Religion und Kultur," 27f.

203. RB, "Religion und Kultur," 28f; cf. also the analogies to this passage in RB, "Religion und Sozialismus," 442–47.

204. Bultmann later repeatedly pointed to Herrmann's significance for his working out of an existentialist theology. Herrmann had grasped, if only in approach and in inadequate terms, the problem of history and of the historicity of human existence. Cf. RB to W. de Boor, 22. 3. 1926, in W. Schmithals, "Ein unveröffentlicher Brief," 212–14; RB to G. W. Ittel, 13. 5. 1955, in G. W. Ittel, "Einfluss," 92f; RB to F. W. Sticht, 11. 3. 1964, in F. W. Sticht, *Bedeutung*, 35n116.

205. Cf. RB, "Ethische und mystische Religion," 29–47; as well as, in detail, M. Evang, *Frühzeit*, 290–332.

Crisis of Culture."[206] Both addresses drew a considerable and largely critical response from among the "Friends." The criticism of Bultmann was ignited by his statements regarding the historical Jesus and his significance for the Christian religion.

In the first part of his lecture, Bultmann declared no longer tenable the picture that had prevailed since Ferdinand Christian Baur, one that presented the history of early Christian religion as an organic development from Jesus to Paul and John, and as an account dominated by ethical motifs. For, he argued, research in the history of religions has shown that Hellenism had strongly influenced the history of early Christianity before Paul. Bultmann therefore agreed with the new view of history developed by Wilhelm Heitmüller and Wilhelm Bousset, according to which the earliest Hellenistic community put a decisive stamp on the Christian religion between the time of the earliest Palestinian community and that of Paul.[207] And whereas the earliest Palestinian community had understood Jesus as eschatological preacher of repentance, prophet, and teacher of wisdom, the earliest Hellenistic community formulated the Christ-myth and Kyrios-cult. While earliest Palestinian Christianity stood for an ethical religion, earliest Hellenistic Christianity represented religion of a mystical-cultic type. Using this sociological differentiation, Bultmann turns to Ernst Troeltsch's description of the specific nature of the Christian community. Yet he does not follow Troeltsch in seeing a purely religious community and a specifically religious ethic fully realized in Jesus and the earliest Palestinian community; rather it first appears in earliest Hellenistic Christianity.[208]

On the basis of his ethical message, says Bultmann, "Jesus belongs to the history of Judaism as its conclusion and fulfillment."[209] By means of this thesis, Bultmann further emphasizes Julius Wellhausen's assertion that Jesus was not a Christian, but a Jew.[210] For, concurring with Hermann Cohen's view that the ethically based system of the Old Testament prophets did not yet constitute religion in the real sense,[211] Bultmann sees that the primary characteristic of Jesus' ethical proclamation is his having formed for the first time the concept of God "through the consciousness of the moral

206. Cf. F. Gogarten, "Krisis." On the origin and the title of the lecture, incorrectly given in the first printing, cf. H. G. Göckeritz, *Bultmann-Gogarten Briefwechsel*, 4n3.

207. Cf. also 395–98 below.

208. Cf. RB, "Ethische und mystische Religion," 34–36; E. Troeltsch, *Soziallehren*, 16–58. Cf. also M. Evang, *Frühzeit*, 293, 297f.

209. RB, "Ethische und mystische Religion," 35.

210. Cf. J. Wellhausen, *Einleitung*, 113.

211. Cf. H. Cohen, *Begriff*, 100; as well as M. Evang, *Frühzeit*, 299–303.

demand."[212] Yet this also means that while in the Jewish context Jesus no doubt represents a religious system of ethics, he does not yet represent religion in the full sense. What does this now mean for the relation between piety and history, not to mention for Christian religion in the present?

First of all, liberal theology, of which Bultmann considers himself part and parcel, is wrong in having thought it could provide a basis for piety through historical-critical work. Still, the function of historical-critical theology is to initiate critical self-reflection on "the spiritual balance in human consciousness,"[213] and thus liberal theology is further blameworthy for making the religion of the historical Jesus into the normative basis of Christianity. For "a limited historical person," even Jesus—who after all, from the perspective of history does not yet represent Christianity—cannot possibly provide a basis for religion.[214] Although Bultmann offers considerations of principle for abandoning any historical norms for religion, in the special case of the religion of Jesus he makes reference to the very uncertain picture established by research. Insofar as the sources permit a judgment,[215] Jesus is to be conceived as at most a religious moralist. So long as "liberal theology" orients itself to *this* Jesus, it merely speaks out in favor of religious moralism. True religion, in contrast, directs the person away from action to the existence that is a gift, away from striving to the experience derived from divine grace.[216]

Paul Wernle reacted to the publication of Bultmann's Eisenach lecture in the *Die Christliche Welt* with the sharpest possible protest. The Swiss liberal theologian was indignant that Martin Rade's periodical had printed "the Bultmannian rubbish."[217] The way Bultmann simply assumes the hypotheses of Bousset and Heitmüller without grounds "as finished dogmas" and especially the way he portrays Jesus as a good Jew "with a few moral sayings & a bit of faith in providence, but really not any actually deep religion," signifies "a nadir of critical research running off the tracks."[218] To Rade, who had made Wernle's criticism available to him, Bultmann once again explained

212. RB, "Ethische und mystische Religion," 35.

213. RB, "Ethische und mystische Religion," 41.

214. RB, "Ethische und mystische Religion," 42.

215. Cf. RB, "Ethische und mystische Religion," 32; as well as RB to M. Rade, 19. 12. 1920, in B. Jaspert, "Rudolf Bultmanns Wende," *Werk und Wirkung*, 30–33, esp. 31: "It came to this . . . that we know hardly anything about the religion of the historical Jesus. I had to regard the Jesus-piety of 'liberal theology' as a self-delusion. . . . One has to free piety from what is, in my view, an utterly untenable connection to history, to which the 'liberal theology' meant to tie it."

216. Cf. RB, "Ethische und mystische Religion," 44f.

217. P. Wernle to M. Rade, 6. 12. 1920, in B. Jaspert, *Werk und Wirkung*, 29.

218. P. Wernle to M. Rade, 13. 2. 1921, in B. Jaspert, *Werk und Wirkung*, 34.

the motives for his distancing of himself from the liberal picture of Jesus. He regretted that in view of his own assumptions, Wernle had been unable to summon up any understanding of "critical self-reflection" such as that proposed in the lecture at the Wartburg.[219] He was even more pained by Wernle's lack of feeling for "how through Gogarten religion spoke with the most tremendous and shattering power."[220]

In addition to Bultmann, other participants in the meeting at the Wartburg had grasped the suggestive force of Gogarten's lecture, "The Crisis of Culture."[221] In his lecture "Ethical and Mystical Religion in the New Testament," Bultmann took on board the ideas that Gogarten had developed in his "wonderful little book *Religion weither* [*Religion from Afar*]" in order to clarify his own view of the relationship between religion and history. Gogarten had rightly emphasized the historicity of religious experience and excluded historical norms for religion.[222] Consequently, Bultmann found in Gogarten's opus an expression of what Wilhelm Herrmann had sought in vain.[223] Yet in his Wartburg lecture he left open the question of where the reality of God was to be experienced—that is, wherein does God reveal himself to us if that revelation cannot be discerned in the religion of Jesus?[224] Bultmann confessed to von Soden that this was indeed a problem. In his essay "Religion and Culture" and in the Eisenach lecture, he had struggled to indicate the "content of the experience of the 'Wholly Other,' . . . without meaning to claim that I had yet succeeded."[225] Bultmann saw that taking up this issue in a definitive way would be a central task of his theological work in the future. And with this recognition in mind, he pursued ever further and diligently the trains of thought he had discussed with his theological teachers. This scholarly path led to his active involvement in that movement characterized by others as "dialectical theology," a school of thought that would ere long produce "an important reversal in the history of theology."[226]

219. Cf. RB to M. Rade 19. 12. 1920 and 24. 3. 1921, in B. Jaspert, *Werk und Wirkung*, 30.

220. RB to M. Rade, 19. 12. 1920, in B. Jaspert, *Werk und Wirkung*, 32.

221. Cf. RB, "Ethische und mystische Religion," 45n7; as well as the late recollection of the first meeting with Gogarten in RB to F. Gogarten, 10. 1. 1957, in H. Göckeritz, *Bultmann-Gogarten Briefwechsel*, 254; with details in M. Kroeger, *Friedrich Gogarten*, vol. 1, 221–28, 280–85, 315f.

222. RB, "Ethische und mystische Religion," 45n7, also 40f; F. Gogarten, *Religion weither*, 59–74; as well as M. Evang, *Frühzeit*, 308–10.

223. RB to M. Rade, 19. 12. 1920, in B. Jaspert, *Werk und Wirkung*, 30.

224. Cf. RB, "Ethische und mystische Religion," 43f.

225. UB Tübingen, RB est., RB to H. von Soden, 3. 4. 1921, Mn 2-2385.

226. Bultmann's autobiographical remarks in B. Jaspert, *Barth-Bultmann Briefwechsel* (2d ed.), 308.

IV. Setting Off on a Theological Career (1921–1933)

1. Beginnings: Teaching in Marburg

In Marburg, one senses very strongly the current of modern mysticism and the aversion to history, a trend that is understandable under the influence of Otto and Heiler. I am regarded as the radical critic and philological historian, and will have a good deal of resistance to overcome.[1]

When Wilhelm Heitmüller accepted a call to Bonn in the winter semester of 1920–21, the Marburg theological faculty first tried to secure Heinrich Weinel and Hans Lietzmann for the New Testament professorship thus made vacant, but both preferred to remain in Jena.[2] The faculty was able to resolve the problems caused by their refusals by drawing up a new list at the end of 1920. At that point the faculty proposed consideration of three candidates for the appointment: as first choice, Walter Bauer (Göttingen); of equal standing, Rudolf Bultmann (Giessen); and third, Erich Klostermann (Münster).

In the negotiations that had preceded the adoption of the list, Heitmüller had sent from Bonn his strong support for Bultmann.[3] The reason for this was that Adolf Jülicher and Rudolf Otto at first opposed Bultmann's appointment because of his Eisenach lecture, "Ethical and Mystical Religion in Earliest Christianity." Within the faculty, Heinrich Hermelink spoke up for Bultmann, having seen in Giessen the printed sheets of the *History of the Synoptic Tradition*, and his advocacy eventually won over Jülicher to a level of conviction that resulted in Bultmann's becoming the faculty's candidate of choice.[4] The faculty included reasons for this preference in presenting their new appointment list. Both Bauer and Bultmann were "well-known as capable scholars," but while the faculty expressed a rather *pro forma* appreciation of Bauer's accomplishments, it was more concrete in Bultmann's case. "He has just published a comprehensive work on the history of the synoptic tradition. It has been examined by us. It is a work of far-reaching, independent research, exhibits fundamental erudition, astuteness and precision in

1. UB Tübingen, RB est., RB to H. von Soden, 1. 8. 1921, Mn 2-2385.
2. Cf. H. Weinel to the Marburg theological faculty, 5. 11. 1920; H. Lietzmann to the Marburg theological faculty, 4. 12. 1920, for the time being in UA Marburg, hiring files.
3. Cf. UB Tübingen, RB est., W. Heitmüller to RB, 7. 1. 1921, Mn 2-964.
4. Cf. UB Tübingen, RB est., RB to H. von Soden, 20. 2. 1921, Mn 2-2385.

method, and it will occupy an important place in the field of New Testament studies and will make a name for its author." Bultmann "would, of all current New Testament scholars, certainly be most in keeping with his predecessor in orientation and method."[5]

As had been expected by the Marburg faculty, Bauer turned down the nomination, and on February 15, 1921, Bultmann accepted the call extended to him "to Marburg as a great honor."[6] Besides New Testament theology and exegesis, his teaching responsibilities included theological encyclopedia, which well suited his ambitions in systematic theology.[7] To be sure, it was "infinitely hard" on Bultmann to leave Giessen. He had "been received there with confidence by colleagues and students," and in his short time at Giessen "had opened up so wide a circle of projects and such agreeable ways of working together" that the decision for Marburg was not at all an easy one. In the end a decisive factor was the feeling that "the greater duty" lay in Marburg, and that in comparison with his work in Giessen, he had "greater projects" in Marburg to which he could dedicate all his strength in the future.[8] Out of consideration for his former faculty, however, Bultmann still saw to his teaching duties in Giessen during the summer semester of 1921 and kept his teaching schedule in Marburg to two days a week.[9]

At that time, Bultmann's old teacher Adolf Jülicher was still teaching on the Marburg faculty as Professor of New Testament and ancient church history (remaining there until 1923), along with church historian Heinrich Hermelink, and Martin Rade and Rudolf Otto, who both held chairs in systematic theology. Karl Bornhäuser taught practical theology, as did Friedrich Niebergall, who was called to Marburg in 1922, and, like Bultmann, with whom he "had formed a cordial friendship during the time together in Giessen,"[10] Old Testament scholar Gustav Hölscher joined the faculty in 1921. In addition, there was Friedrich Heiler, whose work was in the history and psychology of religion. Serving as associate professors were Walter Baumgartner (Old Testament), Rudolf Günther (history of Christian art),

5. Theological faculty of Marburg to the Minister for Scholarship, Art, and Popular Education, 30. 12. 1920, in UA Marburg, hiring files.

6. RB to the Marburg theological faculty, 17. 2. 1921, in UA Marburg, hiring files.

7. Board of Trustees to the theological faculty of Marburg, 8. 4. 1921, in UA Marburg, hiring files.

8. RB to A. Jülicher, 18. 2. 1921; cf. UB Tübingen, RB est., RB to H. von Soden, 20. 2. 1921, Mn 2-2385; as well as Bultmann's autobiographical remarks of 1956, in B. Jaspert, *Barth-Bultmann Briefwechsel*, 304.

9. University trustees to the theological faculty of Marburg, 8. 4. 1921, in UA Marburg, hiring files.

10. Bultmann's notes of 1969, in B. Jaspert, *Barth-Bultmann Briefwechsel*, 312.

and Horst Stephan, who was "personal" (i.e. automatically reappointed) professor of systematic theology.

Bultmann's hope that a lively exchange would come along in the faculty was fulfilled only to a very limited degree during his first semesters in Marburg. Neither Jülicher—who had approached him "with friendliness and trust" but had "become old and stiff in many things"[11]—nor Otto had any particular interest in the personal encounters Bultmann wished for. Such fellowship he found primarily with the younger scholars who participated in both the faculty meetings, which following the summer semester of 1922 offered the opportunity for closer contacts, and in sporadic gatherings with the Giessen theology students.[12] At the beginning of his time at Marburg, Bultmann was still quite uncertain in his assessments of two of his colleagues, Heiler and Niebergall, as his letters to Hans von Soden verify.[13]

In contrast, his first impressions of Hermelink and Otto were more or less definite. As Bultmann reports to Breslau in September, "I was most often together with Hermelink, who attended my lectures on New Testament theology. We are in essence rather different, but my respect for his human and scholarly qualities has risen. His efforts at always trying to mediate and to avoid conflicts don't suit me at all, but I see that these efforts spring from an inner need in him. He has a very strong feeling for the church, and the traditions of pietism have a very strong effect on him. I have heard two splendid sermons from him. Unfortunately, he has a great need always to be doing something about things and to be making arrangements; he holds innumerable offices and little posts. As a result, his scholarly activity suffers, just as it does from a certain lack of discipline in his manner of working. . . . But he is full of ideas, versatile, and has great capacity for work. A conversation with him is always fruitful, and he is one of the most stimulating, best elements in our little historical-philological circle."[14] If Bultmann was still able in 1922 to cherish the hope that Hermelink might participate actively in the redirecting of theological studies that began to emerge with progress in dialectical theology, he was forced to note more soberly during the course of the following years that Hermelink was too deeply rooted in liberal cultural Protestantism to be capable of fulfilling that expectation.[15]

11. UB Tübingen, RB est., RB to H. von Soden 1. 8. 1921, Mn 2-2385.

12. UB Tübingen, RB est., RB to H. von Soden 8. 9. 1921, Mn 2-2385.

13. Cf. UB Tübingen, RB est., RB to H. von Soden, 1. 8. 1921, 19. 3. and 8. 9. 1922 (to Heiler); 30. 4. and 8. 9. 1922 (to Niebergall), Mn 2-2385.

14. UB Tübingen, RB est., RB to H. von Soden, 8. 9. 1922, Mn 2-2385.

15. Cf. K. Hammann, "Heinrich Hermelink," 85–106.

The relationship with Rudolf Otto took shape with far greater difficulty. In his old age, Bultmann still remembered the tensions in his relations with this colleague: "Even though we had once been friends in Breslau, we had become so alienated from each other that even our students sensed the conflict between his and my work."[16] What disturbed Bultmann in 1922 was not that Otto positioned himself theologically against him, but rather the uncollegial way in which he did this.

> Otto has become so infuriated over my book, as over my lectures, because they allegedly "undermine the bases of his dogmatics," that he structured his series of lectures on dogmatics entirely into one on the life of Jesus and engaged in polemics against me all through the semester. In my lectures, I have deliberately made no reference to this, but simply developed my subject matter, which in the long run proved the right thing to do. . . . It is remarkable how strong Otto's conservative tendencies are becoming. For the life of Jesus of the synoptics everything has to be "genuine"; even the story of Jesus the twelve-year-old and of the stilling of the storm that he defends as historical (the latter is based according to him on the one hand on the spirit-filled nature of Jesus the pneumatic, to which power over the forces of nature is ascribed, and, on the other hand, on the accident of the storm's passing in a moment!). He draws Jesus as one filled by the spirit; his life would have to correspond to the biological laws of the *vita religiosa*. To such laws belongs among others the law of the "caliphate," that is, the pneumatic founded a church with a line of succession, *therefore* Jesus' saying to Peter "the rock" about the power of the keys is historical! He pronounces such things in his dazzling style with great certitude and illustrates with such a wealth of material from the history of religion that he naturally makes an impression on a good many. To be sure, this is in itself not troublesome to me or even unwelcome, since these conflicts between him and me are actually most instructive and allow for discussions of method and for an energetic thinking things through.[17]

In contrast, Bultmann found "most unpleasant . . . Otto's personal conduct in this; not only the style of his polemics in the lectures, but above all the fact that he has not said a word to me personally about it." Moreover, Otto avoided the numerous opportunities for discussion offered him, something that Bultmann considered uncollegial and that led him to break off

16. Bultmann's observations of 1969, B. Jaspert, *Barth-Bultmann Briefwechsel*, 312; cf. also 306; as well as M. Lattke, "Rudolf Bultmann on Rudolf Otto," 353–60.
17. UB Tübingen, RB est., RB to H. von Soden, 8. 9. 1922, Mn 2-2385.

"personal-collegial contacts" with Otto. Bultmann regretted this development greatly, since Otto was not harming him, but only himself, and reducing his own effectiveness.[18] Fifteen years later Bultmann finally delineated his continuing opposition to Otto's interpretation of Jesus in his comprehensive discussion of Otto's 1934 opus, *Reich Gottes und Menschensohn* [*The Kingdom of God and the Son of Man*].[19]

If Bultmann's contacts with his Marburg colleagues were initially limited—though he found in Baumgartner, Günther, Hermelink, Hölscher, and Rade congenial conversation partners—he partly compensated for this perceived deficiency through extracurricular personal exchange and companionship with his students. "We often had students over in the evening, and these evenings were as a rule more interesting than those—very few, by the way—when one was together with colleagues."[20] As much as Bultmann valued the "additional visits of people who share their problems or also develop their ideas" as "a gratifying indication of interest on the part of the listeners," still he found "heavy demands on his personal time . . . were sometimes stressful."[21] This did not happen by accident, for Bultmann involved himself gladly and frequently with students who, in the tumultuous period after the War and especially under the influence of the completely new theological problems posed by Karl Barth and Friedrich Gogarten, had a great need to identify and to examine their existential and religious questions in conversation.

Incidentally, this marked interest on the part of the student body corresponded to Bultmann's own idea that academic theological work must fulfill itself and prove its worth first and foremost in conversation, in frank discussion between teachers and students. In those first years of teaching in Marburg, Bultmann created numerous occasions for this to happen by putting himself at others' disposal as a conversation partner. Thus, at the request of his students who had been confused by Otto's polemic against "the rationalist,"[22] he scheduled during the summer semester of 1922 an evening session to clarify the questions of method and substance that had arisen from his opposition to Otto's mysticism.[23] And Bultmann's own examination of

18. UB Tübingen, RB est., RB to H. von Soden, 8. 9. 1922, Mn 2-2385.

19. Cf. RB, "Reich Gottes" (1937), *Theologie als Kritik,* 328–53; as well as Lattke, "Rudolf Bultmann on Rudolf Otto," 359f.

20. UB Tübingen, RB est., RB to H. von Soden, 19. 3. 1922, Mn 2-2385.

21. UB Tübingen, RB est., RB to H. von Soden, 23. 12. 1922, Mn 2-2385.

22. According to the recollections of Hermann Mörchen, Otto is not supposed to have mentioned Bultmann by name in his lectures, but rather always to have referred to him by the title of "the rationalist." Cf. H. Mörchen, "Heidegger," 75.

23. Cf. UB Tübingen, RB est., RB to H. von Soden, 8. 9. 1922, Mn 2-2385.

phenomenology harked back to the stimulus of students who sought him out "individually . . . or in groups in the evening" with their questions regarding the phenomenological conceptions represented in the Marburg theological faculty and especially by Wilhelm Mundle.[24] Besides the stimuli occasioned by "Otto's and Heiler's mystical contemplations" and those arising from phenomenology, Bultmann saw himself challenged by "the biblicist tendencies that hold sway in the DCSV [German Christian Student Association]," issues that resulted in his adding several discussion sessions to his lectures on "Introduction to the New Testament" in the winter semester of 1921–22.[25]

The need for discussions of this sort increased even further as Barth's and Gogarten's publications began to have an impact among the Marburg theology students.

> The books most read among the theology students here are probably Gogarten's *Religiöse Entscheidung* [*Religious Decision*] (in my opinion an excellent essay on mysticism and revelation) and Barth's *Epistle to the Romans* (second edition). . . . I mean . . . here to say only that the second edition has made a very strong impression on me and is a great improvement on the first edition. Also, Barth made a personally agreeable impression during a Saturday and Sunday visit here. He was invited by a student group that had read his book and wished to have a discussion with him. The student body had asked me to give a talk on the book, which I did. A discussion ensued; anyway, I made use of the last fourteen days of my lecture course on Romans (after I was finished with the exegesis of the letter), to conduct a discussion of Barth's *Epistle to the Romans* with these students. Gogarten, too, was here in February [1922], having been asked by the student body, and he gave a lecture, "Time and Revelation." . . . The problem was dealt with in depth, and the first half of the lecture was stirring.[26]

Bultmann also supported the activities of Marburg theological students in other ways.

> The theology students frequently arrange evenings, and so [we spent] two evenings on curriculum revision, which I had to introduce with a paper;[27]

24. UB Tübingen, RB est., RB to H. von Soden, 21. 12. 1921, Mn 2-2385.

25. UB Tübingen, RB est., RB to H. von Soden, 21. 12. 1921, Mn 2-2385.

26. UB Tübingen, RB est., RB to H. von Soden, 19. 3. 1922, Mn 2-2385. Cf. F. Gogarten, *Die religiöse Entscheidung*, 1921; K. Barth, *Der Römerbrief*, 1922 (2d ed.); F. Gogarten, "Offenbarung und Zeit," 20–40.

27. Cf. as a later product of this paper RB, "Zur Frage der Reform," *GuV*, vol. 2, 1968 (5th ed.), 294–300.

> one evening, K. L. Schmidt was here from Giessen to talk about eschatology and mysticism in early Christianity.[28] . . . In January [1923], Gogarten and K. Barth want to come. You see, it's all pretty lively.[29]

With all the liveliness of the theological discussion, Bultmann from the outset emphasized the importance of not allowing historical problems to be postponed in favor of the pressing contemporary issues raised by systematic theology. But as he noted during the summer semester of 1921, this intention met with great resistance—and of all places, in liberal Marburg:

> In Marburg, one senses very strongly the current of modern mysticism and the aversion to history, which is understandable given the influence of Otto and Heiler. I am regarded as the radical critic and philological historian and will have much resistance to overcome. All the same, I did have a group of people who evidently have placed their trust in me, particularly some Swabians who in this case turned up as partisans on the side of history.[30]

Nonetheless, Bultmann's scholarly work soon enabled him to break through the "distaste for history and criticism";[31] for on March 19, 1922, he happily reported to his friend von Soden that the students were participating with surprising diligence in his seminar and lecture courses. The "students in 'Introduction' wanted yet extra sessions on March 2 and 3. I am especially happy about the fact that overall I've had the good fortune to get my students interested in and working on historical problems, and thus have been able to overcome a lot of mistrust and aversion."[32] In the following semesters, Bultmann was able to keep this historical interest alive among his students, even outside the regularly scheduled courses. In the winter semester of 1922–23, a working group that grew out of his lecture course on the Gospel of John read Richard Reitzenstein's *Poimandres* together.[33] And during the following summer semester this same group, now joined by Gustav Hölscher, dealt with the *Odes of Solomon*.[34] The reading of both of these texts was of direct benefit to Bultmann's own research interests, as he was occupied intensely at that time with reassessing the Fourth Gospel's place in the history of religion.[35]

28. Cf. K. L. Schmidt, "Eschatologie," 277–91.
29. UB Tübingen, RB est., RB to H. von Soden, 23. 12. 1922, Mn 2-2385.
30. UB Tübingen, RB est., RB to H. von Soden, 1. 8. 1921, Mn 2-2385.
31. UB Tübingen, RB est., RB to H. von Soden 21. 12. 1921, Mn 2-2385.
32. UB Tübingen, RB est., RB to H. von Soden, 19. 3. 1922, Mn 2-2385.
33. Cf. UB Tübingen, RB est., RB to H. von Soden, 23. 12. 1922, Mn 2-2385; cf. R. Reitzenstein, *Poimandres*.
34. Cf. UB Tübingen, RB est., RB to H. von Soden, 11. 6. 1923, Mn 2-2385.
35. See also below 311f.

In 1956, thankful for having begun his teaching career at Marburg in the 1920s, Bultmann reminisced: "Working with students who were still infused with the 'youth movement' from the beginning of the century was most gratifying."[36] Also gratifying for him was the increasing popularity of his course offerings. Between the summer semester of 1921 and the winter semester of 1923–24, the number of students in his lectures and participants in his seminars rose steadily. Of approximately 200–250 theology students in Marburg, seventy attended his lecture-course on the synoptics, eighty joined his seminar on New Testament theology, and more than a hundred showed up for his lecture course on the life of Jesus. To these figures one might add the more than a hundred students in his lectures on the synoptics and nearly a hundred in the seminar on the Corinthian correspondence during the summer semester of 1923. He regularly had to limit the number of participants in his seminars.[37]

Bultmann's enormous popularity might even have exceeded somewhat that attained by Karl Barth during the same period in Göttingen.[38] Bultmann himself attributed the attraction of his courses to the fact that he "emphasized strongly the significance of being educated in history for systematic problems," and that he "was glad to get into the systematic questions, above all in personal get-togethers."[39] In any case, his students rewarded him for this readiness to enter into discussions of the theological questions that concerned them—and clearly interested him as well. And clearly they were ready to accept the idea that the true meaning of theology could be grasped only by correctly combining its systematic and historical dimensions. For Bultmann, an unintentional but not unwelcome consequence of his popularity as a teacher was that students fled from his New Testament colleague Jülicher. While Jülicher lectured on Romans in front of twelve students, over a hundred attended Bultmann's seminar on the Gospel of John.[40] Evidently taken aback by this less-than-flattering development, Jülicher submitted in the summer of 1923 an unexpectedly early petition for emeritus status. This in turn cleared the way for calling Hans von Soden to Marburg, as Bultmann had long wished, and as he later noted, "meant the greatest gain not only for the theological faculty, but indeed for the entire university."[41]

36. Bultmann's autobiographical notes of 1956, in B. Jaspert, *Barth-Bultmann Briefwechsel*, 305.

37. Cf. the overview of Bultmann's letters to H. von Soden put together by M. Evang, *Frühzeit*, 94f.

38. Cf. E. Busch, *Karl Barth's Lebenslauf* (3d ed.), 144.

39. UB Tübingen, RB est., RB to H. von Soden, 19. 3. 1922, Mn 2-2385.

40. Cf. UB Tübingen, RB est., RB to H. von Soden, 30. 3. 1923, Mn 2-2385.

41. Bultmann's notes of 1969, in B. Jaspert, *Barth-Bultmann Briefwechsel*, 312f.

2. Dialectical Theology

> *Karl Barth,* Der Römerbrief (The Epistle to the Romans *[new ed. 1922]). From this book it became decisively clear to me (1) that the essence of Christian faith does not consist in an attitude of the soul, but in its relation to its object, God's revelation; and (2) that the interpretation of a text presupposes a personal relation to the matter of which the text speaks.*[42]

In Bern at the beginning of 1919 there appeared a new interpretation of Romans, the author of which ascribed to Paul a "message from *God*" to be proclaimed in place of a human religious teaching and "objective knowledge" to be offered in place of "experiences, searchings, and feelings."[43] With these claims a young Swiss pastor named Karl Barth categorically distanced himself from the theological tradition derived from Schleiermacher that had left a lasting mark on German Protestantism prior to the First World War. Soon after its appearance, Barth's *Epistle to the Romans* became the founding document of a theological movement that burst forth in the thickening crisis of modernity caused by the First World War. In the midst of the rubble of what had previously been taken to give order and worth to life, this new dispensation sought to provide security and orientation through a new understanding of the biblical message. In "Ethical and Mystical Religion in Earliest Christianity," the lecture that he gave on September 29, 1920, at the Wartburg, Bultmann took up a position on the periphery of Barth's first Epistle to the Romans. He affirmed Barth's religious criticism of culture, but the most he could discover in the best sections of the book was "an arbitrary propping up of Paul's Christ-myth."[44] Bultmann complained in particular that Barth's interpretation paid insufficient attention to the religious significance of historical-critical studies.[45]

On September 25, 1919, Bultmann attended the religious-social meeting in Tambach at which Barth presented his lecture, "The Christian in Society,"[46] but how he received Barth's remarks is not known. Barth and Friedrich Gogarten entered into a heated exchange at Tambach, but

42. RB, *Milestones in Books.* IV, ET 70 (1958–59), 125; also in RB, *Theologie als Kritik*, 513 (from Bultmann's list of the books to which he ascribed a decisive significance for his theological work).

43. K. Barth, *Römerbrief*, 1919 (1st ed.), 1f.

44. RB, "Ethische und mystische Religion," 43.

45. Cf. UB Tübingen, RB est., RB to H. von Soden, 30. 3. 1923, Mn 2-2385.

46. Cf. RB, *Chronik 1917–1945*, Mn 2-224, 5.

Bultmann and Gogarten had not yet met personally. At any rate, despite the theological objections of the Stelzendorf pastor, Bultmann gained entry into the group just then being formed, which under the banner of "dialectical theology" that others hung on them in 1922 purposely sought to bring about a radical upheaval in Protestant theology.[47] In September 1922 Bultmann and Gogarten got to know each other better during the meeting of the Friends of *Die Christliche Welt* at the Wartburg. There Bultmann showed that he had been greatly influenced by Gogarten's religious diagnosis of the "Crisis of Culture." In his own lecture, "Ethical and Mystical Religion in Earliest Christianity," he spoke approvingly of the understanding of the historicity of religious experience that Gogarten had developed in his little book, *Religion from Afar*.[48] After 1922 Bultmann moved closer theologically to the group around Barth under the influence of Gogarten's thinking about history. Bultmann had, after all, created the possibility of beginning a constructive discussion with Barth and Gogarten by means of his exposition of how religion was understood by liberal theology. On the other hand, he attached to the wartime experience no significance for the way his theological thinking developed.

> To be sure, for many the impact of the War has been the occasion for revising how they understand existence; I confess to you that this does not apply to me, . . . for the War was no shattering experience for me. Of course, many specific events [affected me], but not the War as such. . . . I am of the opinion that when people seek for the genesis of our theology, personal acquaintance with the theology of our teachers will have played an incomparably greater role than the impact of the War or of reading Dostoevsky.[49]

The completely revised second edition of Barth's *Epistle to the Romans* appeared at the beginning of 1922. Barth, who in the meantime had been teaching in Göttingen, came to Marburg on February 18, 1922, to discuss his book with the student body. Besides presenting the introductory paper for the session, Bultmann used the last two weeks of his own lecture course on Romans to go through Barth's interpretation with the students. Better

47. To be sure, the characterization by outsiders of a "dialectical theology" refers to the usage of language by K. Barth and E. Thurneysen. Cf. M. Kroeger, *Friedrich Gogarten*, vol. 1, 315. On the beginnings of the relation between Bultmann and F. Gogarten, cf. Kroeger, *Friedrich Gogarten*, vol. 1, 315–17 and n78.

48. See above, 140.

49. RB to E. Foerster, (?) 1928, in W. Schmithals, "Ein Brief," in B. Jaspert, *Werk und Wirkung*, 72–74. Bultmann's letters and writings from the period 1914–20 bear out this later assessment of 1928.

yet, the two theologians enjoyed each other's company during this meeting in Marburg.[50] Bultmann paid tribute to Barth's latest understanding of Paul's theological concern in a review that turned out—in keeping with the significance of the work under review—to be so extensive that Martin Rade had to spread it out over four issues of *Die Christliche Welt.*[51] The review revealed Bultmann's essential agreement with Barth's second edition of *Epistle to the Romans*, though within the framework of this fundamental consensus, Bultmann expressed several reservations that arose from important matters of principle.[52]

With regard to the intention of proving "the independence and absoluteness of religion," one can set Barth's *Epistle to the Romans* obliquely alongside Schleiermacher's *Speeches* and Rudolf Otto's *The Idea of the Holy*—for each is an attempt at a sympathetic understanding of Paul's aim to make clear the integrity of religion.[53] Bultmann views as justified Barth's struggle against the widespread psychologizing and historicizing of religion to be found in both liberal theology and other theological and spiritual currents in contemporary life. To the degree that Barth distances himself from such "cults of experience" and from the understanding of religion as a phenomenon of culture, he reflects the Pauline radicalism that is quite clear in its own mind about the nature of grace and faith, yet in doing so he adopts the modern polemic against "historicism" and "psychologism" that Bultmann had already discerned all too clearly in Wilhelm Herrmann.[54]

And Barth is above all original in the clear and forceful conceptuality by means of which he describes "*the great paradox of faith: the confrontation of the visible with the invisible self*, of the unredeemed human being with the justified."[55] In this way, Barth overcomes the confused conception of Wilhelm Herrmann, that faith can be made understandable psychologically as "experience."[56] Rather, Barth accurately characterizes faith as "obedience," "miracle," "risk," a "leap into emptiness" or "an impossible possibility."[57] To be sure, he seems to have put too much strain on the paradox of faith when

50. Cf. UB Tübingen, RB est., RB to H. von Soden, 19. 3. 1922, Mn 2-2385; as well as E. Busch, *Karl Barths Lebenslauf*, 149.

51. Cf. H. Thyen, "Rudolf Bultmann," in B. Jaspert, *Werk und Wirkung*, 44f.

52. Cf. RB, "Karl Barths *Römerbrief* in zweiter Auflage"; as well as B. Jaspert, "Sachkritik," 163–68; M. Dreher, *Rudolf Bultmann*, 151–86.

53. RB, "Karl Barths *Römerbrief* in zweiter Auflage," 119.

54. Cf. RB, "Karl Barths *Römerbrief* in zweiter Auflage," 120–24.

55. RB, "Karl Barths *Römerbrief* in zweiter Auflage," 130.

56. Cf. RB, "Karl Barths *Römerbrief* in zweiter Auflage," 135. Cf. also, however, Bultmann's defense of the theology of W. Herrmann on 121n1.

57. Cf. RB, "Karl Barths *Römerbrief* in zweiter Auflage," 127–30.

he makes the point that we can only believe "that we *believe.*" Such a "faith on the other side of consciousness," Bultmann regards as "in *that* respect an absurdity."[58] For faith is "an entirely distinctive specification of the content of our consciousness,"[59] and in order to grasp the meaning of this point, it is necessary to make clear the relation between faith and *logos.*

Bultmann asserts the need for further clarification in the matter of Barth's relation to the biblical text. He concurs in Jülicher's criticism of Barth's historical-philological exegesis and his substantive understanding of Romans.[60] In Bultmann's eyes, Barth does violence to Romans and to the Pauline riches it communicates, for behind his exegesis there appears to stand a "modern dogma of inspiration" that serves as an obstacle to arriving at a consistent understanding of the substance of Romans.[61] However it is occasionally necessary to practice content-criticism on the text, for Paul does not always speak "only out of his subject-matter," and spirits other than that of Christ also speak through his words.[62]

To Bultmann's review, which Martin Rade had placed at Barth's disposal ahead of time, Barth reacted in a letter by return mail and later in detail in the Preface to the third edition of *Epistle to the Romans.* He felt himself to have been "in a general sense *understood* by Bultmann . . . and yet on one ultimately decisive point *not* understood."[63] In Barth's view, the content-criticism of Paul that Bultmann called for is *eine Stilwidrigkeit*, "a function of adversarial style."[64] For one cannot find the spirit of Christ only in specific texts; indeed, it's the other way round: those other spirits come to expression constantly in the human words of Paul. On account of this, Barth regards content-criticism as meaningless. It is rather a matter of conceiving the spirit of Christ as "the crisis, in which the *whole* consists. *Everything* is literal," everything is meant to be understood as expressing the substance "as the voice of the spirit of Christ."[65] Barth recognizes that the perpetual task of the exegete is to discover and to point out in what ways those other spirits "are in fact somehow in service to the *pneuma Christi.*" The interpreter then has

58. RB, "Karl Barths *Römerbrief* in zweiter Auflage," 131.

59. RB, "Karl Barths *Römerbrief* in zweiter Auflage," 132.

60. Cf. RB, "Karl Barths *Römerbrief* in zweiter Auflage ," 141n4; as well as RB to K. Barth, 25. 5. 1922, B. Jaspert, *Barth-Bultmann Briefwechsel*, 10. Cf. A Jülicher, "Ein moderner Paulus-Ausleger," 87–98.

61. RB, "Karl Barths *Römerbrief* in zweiter Auflage,“ 141.

62. RB, "Karl Barths *Römerbrief* in zweiter Auflage,“ 142.

63. K. Barth to RB, 14. 4. 1922, in B. Jaspert, *Barth-Bultmann Briefwechsel*, 5.

64. K. Barth to RB, 14. 4. 1922, in B. Jaspert, *Barth-Bultmann Briefwechsel*, 7.

65. K. Barth, *Der Römerbrief. Vorwort zum dritten Auflage.* Cf. also E. Jüngel, "Die theologischen Anfänge," 96–98.

to decide whether he is willing "to place himself in a relation of *loyalty* to his author" and to write his commentary *with* Paul or rather merely *about* him.[66]

Plate 19: Professor in Marburg, ca. 1912

In his reply, Bultmann declared himself to be in fundamental agreement with Barth's recommendation that the interpreter put himself in a relationship of loyalty to the author. However, he did not see why this ought to exclude applying critical understanding to biblical texts, whatever the consequences. For him, the recognition "that the spirit of Christ is not to be placed alongside other spirits, but is rather the crisis of the whole" does not in the least make

66. Barth, *Der Römerbrief. Vorwort zum dritten Auflage*, 149. Cf. as a further reaction to Bultmann's review, F. Gogarten to RB, 30. 6. 1922, H. G. Göckeritz, *Bultmann-Gogarten Briefwechsel*, 10–15.

Plate 20: Dialectical Theology: Friedrich Gogarten, Eduard Thurneysen, and Karl Barth at the *Bergli* in the summer of 1922

content-criticism superfluous.[67] It is beyond question that the common ground occupied by Barth and Bultmann defined the theological orientation towards biblical exegesis in 1922; it is equally clear that they differed in the hermeneutical implications of their interpretation of scripture. In subsequent years, to be sure, the two theologians occasionally strove to reach mutual understanding. On February 6, 1924, Barth and twelve students from Göttingen traveled *incognito* to Marburg to hear a lecture of Bultmann's. He was extremely pleased that in this lecture, "the *former* Marburg theology came away pretty badly, and the good cause rather well." The next day they participated in the theological seminar and "sat 'up there' like two rabbis *smoking their pipes* in solitary dignity," thus confirming the impression of far-reaching theological agreement. Barth reported to Switzerland: "Marburg has once more become one of the points on the map of central Europe on which one can cast an eye with satisfaction."[68]

"Liberal Theology and the Latest Theological Movement," the essay that grew out of Bultmann's February 6th lecture, documents Bultmann's partisanship for dialectical theology, but it also contains undertones that make clear his divergences from Barth's theological approach. Bultmann first issues a sharp criticism of liberal theology. "The object of theology is God, and the reproach to liberal theology is that it has dealt not with God, but with human beings. God signifies the radical negation and cancellation of the human being; theology whose object is God, can on this account have only the λόγος τοῦ σταυροῦ [message of the cross] as its content; but this is a σκάνδαλον [stumbling-block] for the human being. Accordingly, the accusation against liberal theology is that it has sought to evade this σκάνδαλον [stumbling-block] or to soften it."[69]

Bultmann develops this criticism in more detail by deprecating the attempt of liberal theology to make Christianity a phenomenon of the history of religion, to portray Jesus as a founder-figure of genius, and to explain faith as a psychic experience. This undertaking inevitably failed because it did not recognize that "God's transcendence means the cancellation of the whole person, of his whole history."[70] To provide faith with a generalizing justification contradicts its essence. Since God is the total negation of the

67. RB to K. Barth, 31. 12. 1922, in B. Jaspert, *Barth-Bultmann Briefwechsel*), 17.

68. K. Barth to E. Thurneysen, 4. 3. 1924, in E. Thurneysen, *Barth-Thurneysen Briefwechsel*, vol. 2, 231; cf. K. Barth to RB, 15. 4. 1924, in B. Jaspert, *Barth-Bultmann Briefwechsel*, 31f.

69. RB, "Die liberale Theologie," *GuV*, vol. 1, 2.

70. RB, "Die liberale Theologie," *GuV*, vol. 1, 13.

human being, the individual cannot in and of himself establish any relation to God. Only in faith, which as response to the word of God recognizes the cancellation of the human being by God, does this relation paradoxically fulfill itself. As he does in the review of Barth's second edition of the *Epistle to the Romans*, Bultmann draws a sharp line between faith and any religion focused on experience and piety. Reversing the stand he took in 1922, he now declares that faith is not a state of consciousness.[71] Since it is something God creates in the human being, faith is neither brought about nor illustrated in the natural life of the individual. The faithful person is never the natural person, but rather always "the person killed and brought back to life by God."[72] The identity of the person who by faith is made new and otherworldly is utterly different from that of the old, this-worldly person. For this reason, Bultmann is now able—in distinction from the position he represented in 1922—to approve of Barth's revival of Luther's paradoxical expression that we could "only *believe* that we believe."[73]

Granted that in 1924 Bultmann joins forces with dialectical theology in the course of a critical discussion of basic assumptions of liberal theology, he remains indebted to the legacy of the latter, particularly insofar as it embraces "education for criticism" and "the seriousness of radical truthfulness."[74] Moreover, at the end of his essay he at least partially recants his initial criticism that liberal theology has spoken of human beings instead of God. For according to his view, theology is to speak of God as its object, "by speaking of the human being as he is placed before God, [and] therefore from faith."[75] With this last sentence, however, Bultmann makes one of liberal theology's concerns his own. It still remained to be seen whether and to what extent his understanding of theology as explication of faith and Barth's understanding of theology oriented to the word of God were compatible.

From the outset, the protagonists of dialectical theology showed a strong interest in including their students in theological discourse. They were therefore glad to invite to their lectures any theological faculties whose members were ready for open debate on current issues. Emil Brunner presented a review of "The Question of Humanity in Humanism and Protestantism" in Marburg on January 23, 1925. As he later admitted, the Swiss systematician had a bad day of it. Bultmann found Brunner's appearance an aggravation

71. RB, "Die liberale Theologie," 22. In contrast, see above, n. 58.
72. RB, "Die liberale Theologie," 20.
73. RB, "Die liberale Theologie," 24. In contrast, see above, n. 58.
74. RB, "Die liberale Theologie," 2.
75. RB, "Die liberale Theologie," 25.

and his performance extremely "weak, almost shameful."[76] And although it had not gone quite so badly for Paul Althaus a few days earlier, [77] the critical opinions of Martin Heidegger and Paul Tillich were especially likely to make things difficult for out-of-town speakers. Bultmann again picked up the thread of his discussion with Barth when he lectured at Göttingen on February 6, 1925. Because of his difficult position in the Göttingen theological faculty, Barth was determined that he and Bultmann should present a united front in the "gladiatorial battle" that was expected in the Göttingen "arena" after the lecture. Especially since Emmanuel Hirsch would be present, he wanted for them to clarify their differences not in public, but rather in private discussions.[78] For his part, Bultmann gave Barth to understand that he could not and would not bring up anything already completely worked out in "The Problem of a Theological Exegesis of the New Testament," but would merely present preliminary thoughts for discussion.[79]

In his Göttingen lecture, Bultmann tries to clarify a problem that had been posed with new urgency by the dialectical theology: that of the relation between theology and historical interpretation of the Bible. He argues that instead of ascertaining what a text says from an objective and supposedly neutral standpoint, one must confront the claim raised by the text, hear its *word*, and in the very act of understanding allow it to become an *event*. This implies that the interpreter has to be at the mercy of the *content* of the text and that the interpretation must be led by the question of truth. To be sure, the exegesis of the New Testament must uphold general methodological standards for scholarly interpretation, but since it is *theological* exegesis, it becomes a meaningful undertaking only insofar as it presupposes faith. In this regard it corresponds to "*theology in general*," which presupposes faith even though this presupposition may not be at the exegete's own disposal.[80] Since genuine historical exegesis leads to an existential encounter with history in terms of the content intended in the text, then "theology and exegesis, or systematic and historical theology, basically collapse into each other."[81]

76. RB to K. Barth, 24. 1. 1925, in B. Jaspert, *Barth-Bultmann Briefwechsel*, 40. The basic ideas of Brunner's lecture, along with a subsequent answer to the critical opinions are reproduced in E. Brunner, "Gesetz und Offenbarung," 290–98; cf. J. Fehle, *Emil Brunner*, 238f.

77. Cf. RB to F. Gogarten, 10. 3. 1925, in H. G. Göckeritz, *Bultmann-Gogarten Briefwechsel*, 73.

78. Cf. K. Barth to RB, 26. 1. 1925, in B. Jaspert, *Barth-Bultmann Briefwechsel*, 41–43.

79. Cf. RB to K. Barth, 24. 1. and 3. 2. 1925, in B. Jaspert, *Barth-Bultmann Briefwechsel*, 39f, 44f.

80. RB, "Das Problem einer theologischen Exegese," *Neues Testament und christliche Existenz*, 33.

81. RB, "Das Problem einer theologischen Exegese," 34; cf. also 38.

Barth found Bultmann's remarks on theological exegesis excellent and was glad that Hirsch's attempt to do battle proved a manifest failure. As they had agreed, Barth and Bultmann had a public discussion in front of about thirty to forty students who had traveled to Göttingen in Bultmann's entourage. When they later discussed their differences in detail and in private, Barth accused Bultmann of thinking "in too anthropological-Kierkegaardian-Luther-ish (and Gogarten-ish) fashion" and of "not yet" having rid himself of "the historical eggshells." In return, Bultmann reproached Barth for failing to base his theology on a clear conceptuality.[82] In the last year of his life, Barth still recalled as one of "the most unforgettable individual memories" of his earthly existence, that during his 1925 visit to Göttingen Bultmann had read aloud

> over coffee and streusel cake for hours from the lectures of Martin Heidegger he had heard in Marburg and transcribed. Purpose of the exercise: we would employ this modality (existentialist, of course) in striving to understand the gospel documented in the New Testament as we would all works of the spirit.[83]

Thus, despite the contrasts highlighted during that get-together in Göttingen, the meeting had made it possible "to continue to talk with profit."[84]

A few months later, Barth and Bultmann were once again theologically shoulder to shoulder, as the Bonn New Testament and patristics scholar Erik Peterson sounded the general attack on dialectical theology with his work, "What is Theology?" Peterson was enraged over Bultmann's essay, "What Sense Does it Make to Speak of God?" but also attacked Barth's Elgersburg lecture, "The Word of God as Task of Theology"—since in his view both texts pointed up inconsistencies in dialectical theology.[85] Both Barth and Bultmann immediately recognized Peterson as an opponent who was to be taken seriously. "Up until now, nobody has gotten onto us *like this*," declared Bultmann in *Die Christliche Welt*.[86] In Peterson, an adversary

82. K. Barth to E. Thurneysen, 15. 2. 1925, in E. Thurneysen, *Barth-Thurneysen Briefwechsel*, vol. 2, 306f.

83. K. Barth, "Nachwort," in H. Bolli, *Schleiermacher-Auswahl*, 299. On Barth's mistake in dating (1922 instead of 1925) cf. Busch, *Karl Barths Lebenslauf*, 170 and 527n160.

84. K. Barth to E. Thurneysen, 15. 2. 1925, in E. Thurneysen, *Barth-Thurneysen Briefwechsel*, vol. 2, 307.

85. Cf. RB, "Welchen Sinn," *GuV*, vol. 1, 26–37; on this essay, see below, 230–33. K. Barth, "Das Wort Gottes," 197–218. On what follows, cf. E. Jüngel, "Von der Dialektik"; B. Nichtweiss, *Erik Peterson*, 512–17.

86. RB, rev. of G. Krüger, *Der Historisismus*, and E. Peterson, "Was ist Theologie?," in RB, *Theologie als Kritik*, 140.

had finally taken the field "with whom it is worth having a discussion!"[87] Barth showed himself similarly engaged and challenged: "It's a long time since I've read anything that so incited and angered me as these brilliant and in every respect outrageous pamphlets, by which we have all been backed into *one* corner with Herrmann."[88] A joint reply to Peterson's criticism that Barth and Bultmann had at first envisioned did not get written due solely to a misunderstanding.[89] Their "Petersoniads," conceived independently of each other, appeared "very nicely alongside each other" in 1926 in the same issue of *Zwischen den Zeiten* [*Between the Times*], the journal of dialectical theology.[90] Since the two works supplemented each other, they were, as Barth opined, well-suited for cross-examining Peterson, the "friend with the violet stockings."[91] [Cf. "Seated Woman with Violet Stockings," the title of a somewhat risqué painting by Egon Schiele.]

In his radical criticism of dialectical theology, Peterson maintained in opposition to Bultmann that the Son of God—and he alone—could make the claim that when he spoke of God he was at the same time speaking of himself.[92] For Peterson, only Christianity possessed a true theology, and assertion rested on the premise that the Logos become flesh had previously spoken of God. Theology completes itself as the continuation in argument of the revelation of the Logos, leaving its stamp on the dogma of the church.[93] Bultmann based his dissent to Peterson on the latter's catholicizing thesis that the dogma of the church represents the unbroken extension of the revelation of Christ, and that a non-dialectical continuity therefore exists between the event of revelation and church history.[94] In Bultmann's view, however, dogmas can refer only indirectly to the revelation of God attested in scripture. Since the revelation of God forms the sole object of theology, and since the revelation-occurrence is attested in scripture, theology must, given the form it takes, fulfill itself as interpretation of scripture. As regards

87. RB to K. Barth, 19. 7. 1925, in B. Jaspert, *Barth-Bultmann Briefwechsel*, 50.

88. K. Barth to RB, 25. 9. 1925, in B. Jaspert, *Barth-Bultmann Briefwechsel*, 56. On the writings of Peterson meant by Barth, cf. in B. Jaspert, *Barth-Bultmann Briefwechsel*, 56n3.

89. Cf. RB to K. Barth, 23. 9. and 19. 10. 1925, in B. Jaspert, *Barth-Bultmann Briefwechsel*, 55, 57f.

90. K. Barth to RB 3. 12. 1925, in B. Jaspert, *Barth-Bultmann Briefwechsel*, 61.

91. K. Barth to RB, 26. 10. 1925, in B. Jaspert, *Barth-Bultmann Briefwechsel*, 59. Cf. K. Barth, "Kirche und Theologie," 302–28.

92. Cf. E. Peterson, "Was ist Theologie?" 15f. On what follows, cf. J. Rohls, "Rudolf Bultmanns frühe Marburger Theologie," 72f; as well as E. Peterson to RB, 22. 6. 1925 in E. Peterson, *Theologie und Theologen*, 220.

93. Cf. Peterson, "Was ist Theologie?" 18–25.

94. Cf. RB, "Die Frage der 'dialektischen' Theologie," 79f.

content, theology must speak of revelation in light of the biblical evidence, and so make conceptually explicit human existence as determined by God.[95]

Another of Peterson's objections to dialectical theology concerned its employment of dialectical forms of thought. Peterson reproached Barth in particular for proffering in the guise of dialectic a knowledge that was incapable of giving to God the honor due to him. For such dialectical speaking does not take God seriously; indeed, the seriousness of God consists precisely in the fact "that he is visible concretely and that he is there in an utterly non-dialectical way."[96] By becoming human in Jesus Christ, God has revealed himself and given himself to be recognized. It is precisely this state of affairs that makes theology possible in the first place. Bultmann engages this criticism by allowing that it may be misleading to speak of a "dialectical" theology. However, the meaning of theological dialectics can be reconstructed from the Socratic διαλέγεσθαι [to reason]. The revelation-occurrence as the presupposition of theology is utterly non-dialectical, and hence it is appropriate to speak of it only in the manner of proclamation.[97] Correspondingly non-dialectical is the obedience of faith in receiving the word.[98] To be sure, insofar as theology is done with a consciousness of the difference between its own speaking and God's speaking, it has to understand itself as "dialectical," for thus it recognizes "that all talk of God, however so serious it be . . . stands under the reservation" of the seriousness of God that manifests itself at the last judgment.[99] Furthermore, Bultmann follows Kierkegaard in taking dialectic to be unavoidable because as "the *actual* person at any given moment" does not have himself at his own disposal, he can truly comprehend himself only from the perspective of the justifying God.[100] Dialectical speaking of human existence is therefore carried out on the basis of faith and as its expression.

Peterson's attack made Karl Barth more determined than ever to push ahead energetically with reconstructing his theology, which he had already recognized as a task before him. The longer Barth marched forward on the journey from a dialectical to a dogmatic theology of the word of God, from dialectic to analogy, the more he saw Bultmann's efforts at tying together theology and anthropology to be the decisive point at which disagreement inevitably had to break out. Bultmann, in contrast, regarded the different

95. Cf. RB, "Die Frage der 'dialektischen' Theologie," 89–92.
96. Peterson, "Was ist Theologie?" 7.
97. Cf. RB, "Die Frage der 'dialektischen' Theologie," 77f,
98. Cf. RB, "Die Frage der 'dialektischen' Theologie,", 81f.
99. RB, "Die Frage der 'dialektischen' Theologie," 79.
100. RB, "Die Frage der 'dialektischen' Theologie," 75.

weights they placed on history as the defining reason for his differences with Barth. On the basis of the two interpretations of Romans, it seemed to him that Barth's concept of history was deficient.[101] Typically enough, however, Bultmann saw it as his task "specifically as a historian to give a critical explanation of how history has heretofore been practiced in theology," and not primarily on the basis of the crisis of the bourgeois world of culture, but rather on that of the critical self-reflection of theology as it grows out of history itself.[102] He shared the axiom of dialectical theology that Christian faith cannot be justified by history. However, in distinction from Barth, he considered it an irrevocable responsibility of theology to define the relation of faith and history so clearly that, while yet recognizing faith to be grounded in revelation, one could make plausible the extent to which faith that arises from the word of proclamation represents in a paradoxical way a miracle, the creation of God, and at the same time a human act of obedience.[103]

In Friedrich Gogarten, Bultmann found within dialectical theology the conversation partner with whom he was able to think through the questions surrounding the problem of history.[104] This conversation was maintained by visits back and forth between Marburg, Stelzendorf, and Dorndorf, as well as through correspondence. To be sure, Gogarten proved to be one of the decisive partisans of the "anti-historical revolution." He was one of those who had sought to surmount the crisis of legitimation over historicism—which after 1918 had become the leading scholarly paradigm in bourgeois culture—by setting in motion a radical de-historicizing process in the scholarly study of culture in general and in Protestant theology in particular.[105] As Gogarten told Bultmann on November 3, 1924, he almost ventured "to claim . . . that ultimately history is something that happens only *in the present.*" Theology has to free the concept of history completely "from the sense of observing history, of knowledge of history, of the philosophy of history, and of all these concepts of history that come out of the notion of the knowing and comprehending and therefore isolated self completely perched

101. See above nn. 45 and 60; cf. RB to K. Barth, 24. 1. 1925, in B. Jaspert, *Barth-Bultmann Briefwechsel,* 40; RB to F. Gogarten, 22. 12. 1923, in H. G. Göckeritz, *Bultmann-Gogarten Briefwechsel,* 51–56.

102. RB to F. Gogarten, 11. 6. 1923, in H. G. Göckeritz, *Bultmann-Gogarten Briefwechsel,* 32.

103. Cf. RB to F. Gogarten, 31. 12. 1922, in H. G. Göckeritz, *Bultmann-Gogarten Briefwechsel,* 17–21.

104. On Bultmann's relationship with Gogarten, see also above 129, 136, 159–61, 165–67, 280f.

105. Cf. K Nowak, "Die 'antihistorische Revolution'," 133–71; F. W. Graf, "Die 'antihistorische Revolution," 377–405; F. W. Graf, "Geschichte," 217–44.

upon itself."[106] Although Bultmann's reply to this letter is not preserved, he clarified his position with regard to the question that Gogarten had posed a little later in the course of reviewing a book by his colleague Martin Dibelius and in a report on current scholarly work in theology in the *Frankfurter Zeitung*—at least for the time being.

In 1926 Bultmann wrote for *Zwischen den Zeiten* an article in which he subjected Dibelius' pamphlet, "Historical and Suprahistorical Religion in Christianity" to an analysis that was as extensive as it was critical. It should be said that this review failed to do justice to Dibelius' aims in his pamphlet,[107] for in it Dibelius argued for a differentiated, by-and-large affirmative relationship of Protestantism to modern cultural life. He saw the autonomy of culture with respect to every religious denomination as a historical effect of the Protestant relation to the world, and one to be regarded as thoroughly legitimate. Bultmann found serious fault with the conceptuality employed by Dibelius, which from the perspective of dialectical theology appeared anachronistic to him.[108] Above all, however, he rejected as a naïve misunderstanding of the essence of Christian faith Dibelius' attempt to enrich the historical reality of Christendom by means of an irrational, suprahistorical consummation in a new way of being and ethical values. For Christian faith is not to be to be treated simply as a phenomenon of religion that is equivalent to other cultural phenomena.[109] Rather, faith is the obedient deed of a human individual who thus becomes aware of his or her concrete historical existence as determined by God and God's future.[110]

Along the same lines, in the evening editions of the *Frankfurter Zeitung* in September and October of 1926, Bultmann declared the conversation with modern historicism to be the central concern of current work in theology. Erik Peterson had rightly raised anew the question of what theology actually is. The representatives of the older generation—theologians Adolf von Harnack and Ernst Troeltsch as well as biblical scholars Hermann Gunkel and Wilhelm Bousset—conceived of "Christianity as a phenomenon of the

106. F. Gogarten to RB, 3. 11. 1924, in H. G. Göckeritz, *Bultmann-Gogarten Briefwechsel*, 64.

107. Cf. also RB to F. Gogarten, 29. 7. 1925, in H. G. Göckeritz, *Bultmann-Gogarten Briefwechsel*, 87. For the rest, Bultmann was of the opinion that "most of the reviewers are much too nervous and lenient" (RB to F. Gogarten, 12. 7. 1927, in H. G. Göckeritz, *Bultmann-Gogarten Briefwechsel*, 112).

108. Cf. RB, Geschichtliche und übergeschichtliche," *GuV*, vol. 1, 68–70. Cf. M. Dibelius, *Geschichtliche und übergeschichtliche*. How Dibelius reacted to Bultmann's criticism is shown in S. Geiser, *Verantwortung*, 60–62, nn. 61 and 63.

109. Cf. RB, "Geschichtliche und übergeschichtliche," *GuV*, vol. 1, 75–79, 84.

110. Cf. RB, "Geschichtliche und übergeschichtliche," *GuV*, vol. 1, 80f.

history of culture and religion as a whole," and accordingly understood theology as a branch of the historical study of culture. The result of this was a form of relativism, under the influence of which dogmatics as the central theological discipline dissolved into cultural philosophy.[111] But Bultmann held that theology cannot satisfy itself with exhibiting faith phenomenologically, whether in the human psyche or the history of culture and religion. If theology deals with faith, it must "of necessity also deal with the object of faith"; and "as the study of faith [it must] be at the same time the study of God"—and the other way round.[112] Bultmann proposes that in one way or another all theological currents of the postwar period seek to overcome historicism, but dialectical theology does this in the most effective manner. Following the second edition of Barth's *Epistle to the Romans*, which has revolutionized theology, the group around Barth and Gogarten has reconceived faith as the eschatological occurrence grounded in Jesus through the revelation of God. Along with this, dialectical theology rejects every idealistic view of culture and especially the understanding of Jesus as a heroic religious personality. Gogarten has taken the lead in the debate with idealistic historicism over basic principles and, as a student of Troeltsch, seeks to overcome the inconsistencies of historicism that he has most insightfully recognized.

To be sure, in that report in the *Frankfurter Zeitung*, Bultmann allows that dialectical theology is "far removed from presenting a theological system." Rather, it stands "at the beginning of theological work."[113] To the extent that this assertion reflected the fundamental openness of theological discourse, it certainly did not have any enigmatic meaning, but Bultmann's statement emphatically pointed up the wide-open state of the discussion within dialectical theology in 1926. Not least, this remark obliquely alludes to Bultmann's ongoing attempt to focus the positive potential of dialectical theology on deepening the religious criticism of culture[114] and to join forces with historicism in order to prevent the total de-historicizing of theology. Sooner or later, following this path would lead Bultmann into controversy with Barth *and* Gogarten, but it also created an urgent need for him to

111. RB, "Die evangelische-theologische Wissenschaft," *Theologie als Kritik*, 156f.

112. RB, "Die evangelische-theologische Wissenschaft," *Theologie als Kritik,* 158.

113. RB, "Die evangelische-theologische Wissenschaft," *Theologie als Kritik,* 162. In reply to a corresponding question from Gunkel, Bultmann declared in the same fashion that the work of the dialectical theology seemed to him not yet to be "of such a character as to be capable of being presented in a lexicon article" (ULB Sachsen-Anhalt, H. Gunkel est. RB to H. Gunkel, 24. 5. 1925); on the background, cf. K. Hammann, "Das abscheuliche Wort," 209f.

114. Cf. RB, "Die evangelische-theologische Wissenschaft," *Theologie als Kritik,* 162.

clarify his relation to the theological tradition from which he came—a tradition represented by Martin Rade's *Die Christliche Welt* even after 1918.

3. The Critical Friend of Die Christliche Welt

> *But while I have the feeling that what our times need has been worked through from the philosophical side by men like Gogarten and Bultmann, and while I grant that the whole so-called dialectical theology gives an answer—though not a final answer, mind you—to the generation that is growing up in such a way that we cannot do this, I am not in a position to say to them, "Yes, you occupy a position inside the gospel, and we are on the outside!" And that is what they really want. That is, they want our conversion. This is where their fine passion comes from.*[115]

After the First World War the flagship publication of the liberal Protestant culture, *Die Christliche Welt*, had increasingly come to lurch from side to side. The political activity of Martin Rade in the DDP [German Democratic Party] led to such dissension among the members of the Friends of *Die Christliche Welt* that some of them cancelled their subscriptions to the periodical.[116] Hans von Soden's criticism of the direction being taken by *Die Christliche Welt* thrust the question of its future to the forefront. Regardless of its readers' widely divergent positions in national and church politics, the paper had once again to turn to critical theology as the bond that unified its supporters. Nor could *Die Christliche Welt*, in view of current pressing problems of church and religion, keep religious liberalism at a distance but rather had to connect it more closely to the church. Von Soden underlined his demands with the comment, "Our friend Bultmann . . . sees many things differently from me, and in politics he is often of a different opinion; but he shares my regret that *Die Christliche Welt* has become so non-theological, and he is of one mind with me that this must cease if it is to continue to exist and to grow."[117]

In accord with this basic line of argument, Bultmann, Wilhelm Gottschick, and von Soden opposed the merger of the Friends of *Die Christliche Welt*

115. M. Rade, "Eine ungehaltene Diskussionsrede," 1099. In the original, the print of the word 'conversion' is spaced out.

116. Cf. J. Rathje, *Die Welt*, 273–75; M. Evang, *Frühzeit*, 85–89.

117. H. von Soden to M. Rade, July 1920, in Rathje, *Die Welt*, 291–93.

with various regional groupings of liberal Protestants to form a League for Contemporary Christianity, an aim that had been pursued since the spring of 1920. The idea was to bring the new umbrella organization of free Protestantism together with the German Protestant Union for the purpose of unifying church politics. The group from Breslau opposed these plans. They argued that *Die Christliche Welt* and its circle of friends should preserve its theological stamp. Whoever wanted to be active in church politics could do so in the Protestant Union. Despite such misgivings, the general meeting of the Friends of *Die Christliche Welt* in Eisenach on October 1, 1920, resolved to form the League for Contemporary Christianity. Unfortunately, it was soon to become clear that the new organization would be unable to make a long-lasting contribution to the solution of the internal philosophical problems of the Friends of *Die Christliche Welt.*

When in 1921 the publishing arm of *Die Christliche Welt*, located in Marburg, had to be given up for economic reasons, the question arose whether and if so, how the periodical was to be kept going. Bultmann took part in these discussions,[118] but his ideas about the course *Die Christliche Welt* should take were not listened to. First of all, he took it to be "a bad omen for our cause that we cannot name anyone who would be the right person" to edit *Die Christliche Welt*, either in place of Rade or together with him. He took even greater exception to an agenda formulated by Rade and Rudolf Otto that called for a new era for the periodical. Bultmann presented his critical objections to Rade and Otto, complaining that their agenda was much too general and unclear; above all, it did not make any concrete statements of "what new was to be done that was different from what had been done before." To overcome this deficiency, Bultmann worked out an alternative to the ideas proposed by Rade and Otto.[119]

In his programmatic outline of 1921 for continuing the crisis-ridden *Christliche Welt*, Bultmann develops thoughts on four sets of topics, the theological exploration of which he regards as pressing tasks for the present: history and scholarship, culture, mysticism, and worship. He formulates two theses in each of these areas, the first of which in each case sets out a new view in relation to the cause that is at stake—new not for Bultmann, but for the publishers and readers of *Die Christliche Welt*—and the second of which expounds this with a view to preserving the periodical.

118. Cf. Ratje, *Die Welt*, 287–90.

119. UB Tübingen, RB est., RB to H. von Soden, 30. 10. 1921, Mn 2-2385; cf. Evang, *Frühzeit*, 86.

With respect to the relationship to *history*, Bultmann demands "going beyond the historicism of the past generation" and grasping the suprahistorical working of God. Scholarship, especially historical scholarship, has no right at all to provide grounds for faith, but must be retained as permanently necessary in the realm of religion. The reason is that it trains one in truthfulness and contributes to the clarification of the strengths and motives of the inner religious life. The relation of theology to *culture*, Bultmann admonishes, is not to be taken uncritically as having to do with the kingdom of God. "God's world transcends the work we have to do." Furthermore, it is necessary to establish a connection between life in God and the life of practical activity in this world, for the tension between the task of culture and that of religion, which is directed to the transcendent, enriches the inner life.

Bultmann affirms *mysticism* insofar as it includes and makes transparent life as gifted by God. Nevertheless, mysticism is still to be rejected if it is practiced as a religious method with the goal "of grasping the divine by means of one's own striving and guiding the soul." If Bultmann takes his orientation towards mysticism from the criterion of the Reformation doctrine of justification by faith, in like manner the Reformation's high respect for the word affects how he determines the task of *worship*. The service of worship has no pedagogical function, but "rather [consists] in the celebration of the congregation bound together in God before the eyes of the eternal." Now as ever, the "word" is the center of worship. Here Bultmann follows Schleiermacher in emphasizing that in worship, proclamation—and indeed the entire worship service—must both grow out of inner religious life and lead on to a new inner religious life.[120]

Bultmann's programmatic outline did not play a direct role in the further discussions and decisions about the future of *Die Christliche Welt*.[121] A new publisher for the periodical was finally found after intensive negotiations. Beginning in July of 1922, *Die Christliche Welt* appeared from the house of Friedrich Perthes in Gotha/Stuttgart, with Rade remaining as editor and the philosopher Hinrich Knittermeyer assuming the associate editorship.[122] In the end, Bultmann played an authorial role, for he wrote several lead

120. UB Tübingen, RB est., RB to H. von Soden, 30. 10. 1921, Mn 2-2385; the text is reprinted in M. Evang, *Frühzeit*, 87. Cf. also the paraphrase in M. Evang, *Frühzeit*, 338f.

121. We know nothing more of H. von Soden's reaction to Bultmann's program, since what he wrote in reply to Bultmann's letter of 30. 10. 1921 has not been preserved.

122. Cf. Rathje, *Die Welt*, 288f. Following the removal of Leopold Klotz from Perthes in 1925, *Die Christliche Welt* was published by Leopold Klotz Press in Gotha until its prohibition in 1941.

commentaries of a meditative character for the first issues that appeared after the change of publishers: "God in Nature," "Restlessness and Rest," "On Praying," and "On Destiny."[123] Additionally his reviews continued to appear in *Die Christliche Welt* up until 1930. To be sure, Rade's periodical did not remain the only medium through which Bultmann acquainted a broader reading public with problems and discussions in theological scholarship. From 1921 on he preferred to publish his book reviews and research reports designed for the general reader in the liberal *Frankfurter Zeitung*, which belonged to the small number of democratic daily newspapers of the Weimar era. The feature section of the *Frankfurter Zeitung*, headed by Rudolf Geck until 1924 and after that by Benno Reifenberg, was for Bultmann and numerous other great minds of the period a forum they gladly used to share ideas with the wider public up until 1933.

Despite his criticism of the lack of a discernible agenda on the part of *Die Christliche Welt*, Bultmann at first harbored the hope that this organ of free Protestantism and the group of "Friends" might be able to open themselves to the newer theological developments of the 1920s and to engage in constructive discourse with their common tradition of liberal theology and the dialectical theology that was then in the process of formation. In the beginning of October 1923, the Friends of *Die Christliche Welt* held their annual meeting in the midst of a conference of the League for Contemporary Christianity. Bultmann did not take part in the event, but he used the opportunity to share his ideas on reform with Hans von Soden, who was to represent both groups in Weimar.[124] Bultmann made the case for the Friends of *Die Christliche Welt* no longer joining in conferences with the League for Contemporary Christianity, and above all for a resolute and concentrated focus on theology when they did come together. Naturally, such theological discussion also involved the examination of questions of church politics. The problem was that *Die Christliche Welt* had to avoid the chimera of thinking it could be "an organ for Protestantism as a whole or for the spiritual culture of modern Protestantism (more or less an analogy to the *Hochland* [a German Roman Catholic magazine published in Munich from 1903–41 and again from 1946–71])."[125]

123. Cf. RB, "Gott in der Natur," "Unruhe und Ruhe," "Vom Beten," "Vom Schicksal."

124. Cf. RB to F. Gogarten, 31. 8. 1923, in H. G. Göckeritz, *Bultmann-Gogarten Briefwechsel*, 43.

125. UB Tübingen, RB est., RB to H. von Soden, 29. 9. 1923, Mn 2-2385; cf. also the report on the Weimar meeting in F. Gogarten to RB, 9. 10. 1923, in H. G. Göckeritz, *Bultmann-Gogarten Briefwechsel*, 44f.

A year later, Bultmann renewed his initiative for changing the profile of the gatherings of the "Friends". Even if more at the urging of his wife than as a matter of his own wishes, he participated in the meeting of the League for Contemporary Christianity and the Friends of *Die Christliche Welt* that took place from October 6 through 8 in Frankfurt. The gathering impressed him as having been a poor mixture of lectures of varied quality, miserable discussions, and a completely unsuccessful supporting program. Full of sarcasm, Bultmann described to Gogarten what he had experienced in Frankfurt, and he announced that if things were to continue this way, he was not prepared to stand it any longer.[126] After all, he had earlier shared his thoughts on how the gathering ought to have been run and had made proposals for structuring future gatherings of the Friends of *Die Christliche Welt* on the basis of a unified conceptuality.[127]

What ought to stand at the center of the gatherings was doing theology together. This would mean concentrating on *a single* topic that would be examined in a substantive way.[128] The circle of participants needed to bear in mind the fact that theological debate "requires *thinking*, and that it is *difficult* and not for everybody." Bultmann recommended a rigorous elimination from the agenda of all cultural and devotional collateral functions, and as for content, he called for focusing theology on the contemporary theological situation. His experiences at the Frankfurt gathering had made clear to him that he "was diametrically opposed" to the view purported by pastors Johannes Herz and Paul Luther to be that shared among the group of "Friends." It was shattering to Bultmann that a large number of the "Friends" were in no position to understand the aims and intentions of the newer theological movement and the theological problems it posed.[129] Bultmann's diagnosis of the central problem facing these gatherings—naturally enough, one related to the issue of specific topics—was that the only beneficial activity would be the debate between the older liberals and the dialectical theologians over the generational struggle—that is to say, the struggle over the direction of theology.[130] Bultmann's proposal did not elicit any reactions worth mentioning

126. Cf. RB to F. Gogarten, 19. 10. 1924, in H. G. Göckeritz, *Bultmann-Gogarten Briefwechsel*, 61.

127. On what follows, cf. RB, "Zur Frankfurter Tagung."

128. Cf. RB to F. Gogarten, 19. 10. 1924, in H. G. Göckeritz, *Bultmann-Gogarten Briefwechsel*, 60f: ". . . if a theme such as Kant and Protestantism is dealt with, two hours are not enough for the discussion, but two days at least."

129. RB, "Zur Frankfurter Tagung," 854.

130. Cf. RB to F. Gogarten, 19. 10. 1924, in H. G. Göckeritz, *Bultmann-Gogarten Briefwechsel*, 61.

from the "Friends." Only Martin Rade tried to take up Bultmann's proposal as a stimulus for discussion, but he did not get any response.[131]

In the end Bultmann's various initiatives to open up *Die Christliche Welt* and its circle of "Friends" to theological dialogue came to nothing—especially disappointing was the failure to confront dialectical theology—and he saw no point in further activities in this matter. This was especially true because, since 1927, the yearly gatherings of the "old Marburgers" had become the very forum for doing theology that Bultmann had been trying to create from the "Friends" get-togethers since 1924. In addition, Bultmann and Hans von Soden had created another journal similar to *Die Christliche Welt*, at least for its scholarly readers, by reviving the *Theologische Rundschau*, which had been discontinued during the First World War. The decisive planning meeting for reestablishing the *Theologische Rundschau* took place in Marburg on January 28, 1928. Taking part were Dr. Oskar Siebeck and Dr. Oskar Ruhle, the editors of Mohr Siebeck Publishers in Tübingen, together with editors-in-chief Bultmann (New Testament) and von Soden (church history), and as consultants representing various disciplines, Walter Baumgartner (Old Testament), Friedrich Gogarten (systematic theology), Hermann Faber (practical theology), and Martin Heidegger (philosophy).

The publishers and consultants agreed that the *Theologische Rundschau* should for the most part be open to colleagues of differing theological orientations; indeed, Bultmann was especially determined not to create the false impression that the journal was to function as an instrument of dialectical theology.[132] He was nevertheless insistent that "*one* theological group be excluded from the collaboration, because it lacks upstandingness and honesty in the way it does theology: the positivistic right, typically embodied, for instance, in Reinhold Seeberg and Althaus."[133] The *Theologische Rundschau* was not to be an organ for reviews, but was rather to provide a comprehensive view of the problems and results of research in all areas of theology. Besides the representatives of academic theology, the initiators envisioned pastors, teachers of religion, and theologically interested laypersons as part of their target group. Bultmann and von Soden sympathized with what had been the aim of the *Theologische Rundschau* since its first appear-

131. Cf. M. Rade, untitled article, 854.

132. RB to F. Gogarten, 5. 8. 1928, in H. G. Göckeritz, *Bultmann-Gogarten Briefwechsel*, 133f. Characteristically, Gogarten saw a danger in putting together the list of disciplinary representatives too early in the process, lest the *Theologische Rundschau* appear as an undertaking of liberals. Cf. F. Gogarten to RB, in H. G. Göckeritz, *Bultmann-Gogarten Briefwechsel*, 135.

133. UB Tübingen, RB est., minutes of the consultation, 28. 1. 1928, Mn 2-2484.

ance in 1897—that of mediating between scholarly theology and vocational praxis in churches and schools. In this way, the editors of the "new series" of the journal that first appeared in 1929 emphasized that Christian faith did not represent an isolated sphere of life, but rather claimed whole persons in everything they did in life. Therefore, theological scholarship had to pursue theology in such a way as to assure that the faith and life of the church would neither waste away nor be completely swamped by alien interests.[134]

Karl Barth took it as an implicit rejection of his theology that Bultmann "sat down publicly at the same table with Hans von Soden at the reestablishment of the *Theologische Rundschau*."[135] When he passed this judgment, Barth was so convinced of the irreconcilable differences among dialectical theologians that he could only view the revival of the *Theologische Rundschau* as an unequivocal return to liberal positions.[136] An indication of his alienation from Bultmann and Gogarten was that two years earlier he had cancelled his participation in the 1929 autumn meeting of the League for Contemporary Christianity in Eisenach. Barth reacted to Rade's invitation to this meeting[137] by informing him laconically that he "would rather let *Bultmann* and *Gogarten* represent their cause alone" in Eisenach, for he was already busy enough with answering for what he was doing himself.[138]

Rade had great expectations for the meeting in Eisenach, which was intended to bring about a dialogue between the liberal Protestants organized in the League for Contemporary Christianity and leading representatives of dialectical theology—something that had not occurred in previous years. Organizing the meeting was difficult: Bultmann insisted on a unified theme and a unified list of speakers for the meeting, but Rade had trouble getting the board of the League to agree to this proposal.[139] For his part, Bultmann had trouble convincing Gogarten to give a lecture as his part in the meeting,[140] for not only had Gogarten long ago renounced liberal theology, but

134. Cf. A. Lindemann, "Zur Geschichte," 1–3; as well as the circular letter to the future collaborators of the *Theologische Rundschau* in H. G. Göckeritz, *Bultmann-Gogarten Briefwechsel*, 289–91.

135. K. Barth to RB, 20. 6. 1931, in B. Jaspert, *Barth-Bultmann Briefwechsel*, 126.

136. See also below 233–38.

137. Cf. M. Rade to K. Barth, 18. 7. 1929, in C. Schwöbel, *Barth-Rade Briefwechsel*, 244–46.

138. K. Barth to M. Rade 24. 7. 1929, in C. Schwöbel, *Barth-Rade Briefwechsel*, 246.

139. Cf. M. Rade, Eisenach 1929, *AdF* 92, 15 March 1929, 1059f; as well as RB to F. Gogarten, 17. 2., 24. 2. and 20. 3. 1929, in H. G. Göckeritz, *Bultmann-Gogarten Briefwechsel*, 155, 156, 162–64.

140. Cf. n. 139, Bultmann's letters to F. Gogarten.

he also felt little inclination to pursue what he saw as a pointless discussion with the "the gullible culturites,"[141] as he contemptuously characterized the liberal Protestants. Only Bultmann's lobbying and the prospect of bringing about "a clarification of our relationship with the *CW* [*Die Christliche Welt*], or rather of the *CW* with us" persuaded Gogarten to relent.[142]

On October 2, 1929, Bultmann and Gogarten gave their lectures in Eisenach on the theme "Truth and Certitude."[143] The following day a debate ensued, during which 192 participants offered detailed contributions.[144] Rade, concerned about a balance between the theological movements, perceived a harmonious mood in the debate. But something he failed to see for a long time was what Bultmann and Gogarten mercilessly made public in their closing remarks—namely, the utter failure of the attempt to achieve a theological understanding between the older "liberals" and the younger "dialecticals." In his concluding remarks Bultmann revealed his disappointment in the way the discussion had gone, for only Ernst Bizer and Rudolf Paulus had gotten involved in what mattered to him and Gogarten. "A depressing situation has emerged from this mess, like a Babel of languages."[145] At best, he thought, it might still be worthwhile for the two parties to discuss the word of God with each other. Gogarten declared that it made no sense at all to pursue conversation in this company. Rade blamed the disaster not on the two speakers, but rather on those liberals who either stayed away from the meeting or had remained silent. Disappointed that the League for Contemporary Christianity had failed as a forum for theological discussion, Rade resigned the chairmanship, but he did not leave Eisenach with the impression that Bultmann and Gogarten "had broken with us older folks." For this reason, Rade left as a legacy to his successors in the leadership of the League an opportunity to continue the dialogue with dialectical theology.[146]

141. F. Gogarten to RB, 16. 8. 1923, in H. G. Göckeritz, *Bultmann-Gogarten Briefwechsel*, 39.

142. F. Gogarten to RB, 26. 2. 1929, in H. G. Göckeritz, *Bultmann-Gogarten Briefwechsel*, 157; cf. also F. Gogarten to RB, 11. 5. 1929, in H. G. Göckeritz, *Bultmann-Gogarten Briefwechsel*, 168f.

143. Cf. RB, "Wahrheit und Gewissheit," *Theologische Enzyklopädie*; F. Gogarten, "Wahrheit und Gewissheit," 96–119. Pastor Karl Aé (Dresden) had been slated as a third speaker. Since Aé dropped out due to illness, Pastor Karl Fischer (Lauenstein in Saxony) took up the task of orienting the theme of the meeting to life in the church.

144. Cf. E. Stier, "Bund"; R. Paulus, "Wahrheit und Gewissheit"; J. Rathje, "Die Welt," 375f.

145. Bultmann's concluding remarks in E. Stier, "Bund," 1097; cf. also RB to K. Barth, 14. 11. 1929, in B. Jaspert, *Barth-Bultmann Briefwechsel*, 95

146. M. Rade, "Zur Orientierung," 1100.

Bultmann's readiness to conduct theological debate with the older liberals in the Friends of *Die Christliche Welt* was finally exhausted following the failure of the meeting at Eisenach in 1929, at the latest. The fact that in October of 1929 Rade contradicted his public statements on Bultmann's and Gogarten's lectures by warning Karl Barth that Gogarten was of unsound mind is indicative of the atmospheric disturbances that made it even more difficult for Bultmann to entertain any further expectations of forging a relation to Rade and his circle.[147] Still, he blamed his gradual alienation from Rade and the Friends of *Die Christliche Welt* primarily on their inability to engage in constructive discussion with initiatives coming out of the newer theological movement.[148]

4. Faculty Matters

> *The star of Marburg is Rudolf Bultmann (N. T.), a scholar as diligent as he is well-read. . . . Bultmann's lecture courses and seminars are the fruit of admirable meticulousness and astuteness. His historical-critical work often leads to exegetical results that on occasion certainly seem daring to a down-to-earth Dutchman.*[149]

The above characterization of Bultmann's teaching activity comes from the pen of the Dutch theology student Jonkheer Willem van Lennep, who recorded his impressions of two semesters abroad in Marburg in 1933. His report praising the Marburg Philipps-University and its theological faculty appeared a year later in a Dutch newspaper. Like the author's intention of inspiring his Dutch fellow-students to study abroad in Marburg, the newspaper article was intended as a kind of recruiting document. Still, van Lennep's observations, impressions, and concise analyses furnish instructive insights into Marburg's curriculum and environment at the time, what it was like to teach in the theological faculty, and the foci of research of individual theology professors. This foreign observer understood quite correctly that although the faculty was unanimously committed to a scholarly ethos strictly oriented to historical criticism, the faculty at that time gave no appearance of

147. Cf. F. Gogarten to RB, 21. 10. 1929, in H. G. Göckeritz, *Bultmann-Gogarten Briefwechsel*, 175; RB to K. Barth, 25. 11. 1919, in B. Jaspert, *Barth-Bultmann Briefwechsel*, 97.

148. Cf. RB to K. Barth, 9. 12. 1928, in B. Jaspert, *Barth-Bultmann Briefwechsel*, 93; RB to F. Gogarten, 11. 12. 1928, in H. G. Göckeritz, *Bultmann-Gogarten Briefwechsel*, 149f.

149. H. Schneider, *Marburg, das irdische Paradies*, 29.

homogeneity. Also, due to the theological diversity that he encountered here and simply as a congenial place to study, Marburg seemed to van Lennep "above all in the summer . . . the earthly paradise of the theologians."[150]

If one examines the scene from the vantage point of history, a perspective not available to the contemporary visitor from abroad, it is clear that even the Marburg theological faculty had to do its work on the other side of Eden. At any rate, once he had joined the faculty Bultmann was not inclined to restrict himself to work in the Department of New Testament and let everything else move along as it would. Rather, from the beginning he strove to involve the entire Marburg theological faculty in the dialectical movement he characterized as the reconstruction of theology. Accordingly, he developed little interest in academic committee work, though he did not shirk the duties it entailed. He could summon up even less interest in how individual colleagues—the church historian Hermelink or Martin Rade, for example—busied themselves in various offices in the areas of university business or politics. Such involvements seemed to Bultmann a waste of the powers that were urgently required for concentrated work in the cause of theology, and in the decade following 1921, he pursued a different path toward shaping the future of his faculty.

During the winter semester of 1921–22 Bultmann was occupied with the business of placing Marburg's academic worship on a new conceptual footing.[151] He considered sermons of the two university preachers, Karl Bornhäuser and Friedrich Niebergall, to be unsatisfying. Worse yet, he found it objectionable that university worship in Marburg was celebrated in the same traditional way as that of the Reformed churches of the city and the university. Bultmann aspired to a basic structural reform—the establishment of an independent university worship service, completely freed from entanglement with the local parish. As in Giessen, for instance, this worship service could, through liturgies and sermons appropriate to its audience, invigorate the sense of community of the teachers and students of all faculties. And all professors of theology—not only the two university preachers—should share in the preaching.

Getting such a model adopted in Marburg proved difficult. The university preachers, Bornhäuser and Niebergall, showed little inclination to give up their hereditary rights for the sake of the rest of the faculty. To establish a new set of regulations in spite of this, Bultmann proceeded along two tracks.

150. H. Schneider, *Marburg, das irdische Paradies*, 25.

151. Cf. RB to H. von Soden, 21. 12. 1921, Mn 2-2385; details on what follows in K. Hammann, "Rudolf Bultmann und der Universitätsgottesdienst."

With the support of Hermelink and Rade, who felt as he did in this matter, he first promoted a resolution of the theological faculty to arrange for twelve academic worship services per year over and above those conducted by the university preachers. These additional services, for which the theological faculty and student body would be jointly responsible, could be held after Pentecost of 1923 in the *Michelchen* [Little Michael Chapel] on the hillside across from the Michael Chapel of the Elizabeth Church.

Besides that, Bultmann was occupied with a basic clarification of the legal state of affairs involving university worship and the university preaching office, and on May 14, 1923, the theological faculty undertook an examination of the legal situation of university worship. To this end it commissioned Marburg law professor J. V. Bredt, who excelled as a referee in cases involving church law.[152] Bredt's opinion, presented on July 28th, traced the history of the legal structure of the relationship between university worship and the Reformed congregation back to an agreement in the year 1676. On the basis of canon law and the historical evidence, Bredt came to the conclusion that despite the special role of the university preaching office in the relation between state and church, the arrangement of 1676 formed the basis in law for academic worship from that time forward. This was the case irrespective of later developments in the relation between state and church after the abolition of the Sovereign Ministry of Oversight through the Constitution of the German Empire of August 11, 1919.[153]

Although Bredt's opinion resulted in the recommendation that the *status quo* be maintained for university worship, Bultmann did not relax his efforts at reform. In this, he felt strengthened by considerations that Hans von Soden had put forward regarding the relative status of university worship and the preaching office as set forth in the law governing the relation of state and church. In contrast to the opinion of Bredt, von Soden understood the end of the state church as a profound caesura that could not remain without consequences for the institution as a whole. He argued that university worship should be transferred completely to the responsibility of the theological faculties. On the basis of liturgical and religious freedom in general, academic freedom of instruction included the right of the theological faculties to carry out spiritual functions in university worship.[154] Supported by von Soden's

152. J. V. Bredt (1879–1940) taught law at Marburg from 1910 onward. He wrote, among other things, a multi-volume work on Protestant church law for Prussia. As of March 31, 1930, Bredt served as the Reich Minister of Justice.

153. Cf. J. V. Bredt, *Das Amt*; as well as K. Hammann, "Rudolf Bultmann und der Universitätsgottesdienst," 100–108.

154. Cf. H. von Soden, rev. of U. Stutz, *Das Bonner*, 262–64.

judgment regarding the legal situation, Bultmann once more seized the initiative in this matter when he occupied the deanship of the theological faculty in the winter semester of 1924–25. He instituted an inquiry among the German Protestant theological faculties regarding the actual situation regarding university worship, its legal and financial circumstances, and possible changes consequent to the reorganization of the relation between state and church.[155] Doubtless, Bultmann hoped for results from the inquiry that might prove useful for the planned reform in Marburg, but this was not to be. Both institutional and personal reasons revealed by a survey of fifteen faculties showed such disagreement concerning university worship that no clear case could be made for Bultmann's plan to reform the relations between the theological faculty and the Marburg university church.

But eight years later, at the instigation of Bultmann and von Soden, the theological faculty managed to agree that until further notice all duly qualified members of the faculty should conduct services of university worship. Owing to Friedrich Niebergall's death in 1932 and Karl Bornhäuser's accepting emeritus status in 1933, academic worship services that had until then been conducted by the university preachers became orphans. The faculty, dominated by Bultmann and von Soden, thereupon came to an agreement with the Reformed congregation that university worship services would be assigned to professors of theology. Although in Bredt's opinion the faculty had no right to this, the "discovered" pragmatic arrangement paved the way for university worship in Marburg to become an important forum for Bultmann and von Soden to conduct a spiritual and theological dialogue with National Socialism from 1933 to 1945.[156]

In the delicate area of filling academic openings, Bultmann intervened especially where he thought the professorship's stake would significantly shape the profile of the Marburg theological faculty. As a member of the department and thus directly affected, he had an obvious interest in selecting Adolf Jülicher's successor, and particularly because of systematic theology's special role among the theological sub-disciplines, he regarded it vital to make sure that this chair was adequately filled.

Soon after his arrival at Marburg, Bultmann had conceived the idea of getting his friend Hans von Soden to fill Jülicher's professorship, which would become free in the foreseeable future.[157] As the time for Jülicher to accept emeritus status neared and for the faculty to make proposals for filling his

155. Cf. the text of Bultmann's inquiry of 3. 2. 1925 in K. Hammann, "Rudolf Bultmann und der Universitätsgottesdienst," 110f.

156. See below, 270f, 285–87.

157. Cf. UB Tübingen, RB est., RB to H. von Soden, 30. 10. 1921, Mn 2-2385.

chair, Bultmann easily succeeded in placing von Soden at the head of the faculty's list. Even Jülicher agreed that this student of Harnack should become his successor.[158] In arguing on behalf of its appointment list, the faculty emphasized that von Soden was among the few scholars who had made excellent, original contributions to knowledge through his own research in both New Testament and church history. And on the basis of his numerous field studies, he was best suited for strengthening the field of Christian archaeology, which was connected with the position. Above all, however—and here the wording reflects the vital interest that Bultmann had in having his friend called—von Soden would "participate as a decidedly theological personality in the ecclesial and religious problems of our time with calm judgment, with a historian's knowledge of his subject, and with sureness and steadiness of character."[159] Von Soden accepted the call to Marburg in 1924,[160] and by his effectiveness would more than justify the expectations that Bultmann placed in him.

Bultmann's efforts to bring Gogarten to Marburg were without success. At the end of 1921, when Horst Stephan's position became vacant through his departure for Halle, Bultmann initially contemplated the Stelzendorf pastor as a candidate for an adjunct professorship in systematic theology. Therefore, he sent a confidential inquiry to Gogarten, asking whether he could accommodate himself to the strongly historical-critical orientation of the Marburg faculty. He perceived a great similarity between Gogarten's attempt "to get beyond the old 'liberal' theology" and his own theological work. And with an inner conviction about Gogarten's being able to join in, he asked how much weight he would assign to the positive legacy of historical theology for dealing with the future tasks of theology.[161] Bultmann's need for clarification in this matter was understandable if he meant to bring into an academic teaching post a pastor who had unequivocally announced his presence in the most recent theological debates, but who lacked the formal qualifications for an academic career. As it turned out, Bultmann's

158. Cf. UB Tübingen, RB est., RB to H. von Soden 30. 3. 1923, Mn 2-2385.

159. UA Marburg, hiring files of the theological faculty at Marburg. The faculty placed H. Windisch in second position and W. Sattler and E. Peterson in later positions on the list. It announced that it was not agreeable to an appointment of the formerly Catholic liturgical scholar L. Fendt, who had been proposed by F. Heiler, as, with Heiler, one convert was already on the faculty.

160. Von Soden's teaching responsibilities included New Testament and church history, together with Christian archaeology and canon law.

161. RB to F. Gogarten, 19. 12. 1921, in H. G. Göckeritz, *Bultmann-Gogarten Briefwechsel*, 2; cf. Gogarten's answer to RB of 23. 12. 1921, in H. G. Göckeritz, *Bultmann-Gogarten Briefwechsel*, 3–6.

initiative soon proved to be irrelevant, since it was decided that the adjunct professorship for which Gogarten was to be considered would no longer be filled by a systematic theologian.[162] Despite this, Bultmann's personal contact with Gogarten marked the beginning of a friendship that lasted for many years, and was one in which the question that Bultmann raised at the end of 1921 about the relation of theology and historical study, of faith and historical existence, would remain the central topic.

In 1929 Bultmann undertook a second attempt to find a place for Gogarten in Marburg. When the professorship in systematic theology was once again to be filled, the faculty proposed on February 4, 1929, to put Heinrich Frick first on its list, Paul Tillich second, and Theodor Siegfried and Georg Wünsch jointly in third place. But even before the proceedings began the Prussian Ministry of Culture had already committed itself to Frick as Rudolf Otto's successor. Frick was a student and friend of Otto, who had gotten the Ministry to assure him that his position would not be filled without his consent.[163] Bultmann decided to submit a separate opinion, although it was clear to him that as things stood it would not accomplish anything.

In his special opinion of January 27, 1929, Bultmann began by dissociating himself from the faculty's proposed list. Heinrich Frick might well be a capable theologian and talented historian of religion, but he was not a productive scholar. The work of Theodor Siegfried might be distinguished by its erudition, but surely it displayed no theological impulse. Georg Wünsch might have served the cause of social ethics, but this was not enough to qualify him for the systematics professorship, and Paul Tillich was more of a speculative philosopher of religion than a systematic theologian. It also spoke against him that not only was his relation to the tradition in dogmatics unclear, but he was also insufficiently knowledgeable. Tillich's inclination for constructing a system purely on aesthetic grounds also appeared problematic.[164] Bultmann thereupon presented his own candidates of choice: Friedrich Gogarten, Karl Barth, and Friedrich Karl Schumann. Although he recognized the excellent theological work that Barth had carried out "with

162. Cf. RB to F. Gogarten, 29. 1. 1922, in H. G. Göckeritz, *Bultmann-Gogarten Briefwechsel*, 6f.

163. Cf. RB to F. Gogarten, 4. 11. 1928, in H. G. Göckeritz, *Bultmann-Gogarten Briefwechsel*, 145; as well as L. Vogel, "Die Sondervoten," 127–50. Cf. also Bultmann's reports to M. Heidegger, 16. 12. 1928 and 8. 1. 1929, in A. Grossmann and C. Landmesser, *Bultmann-Heidegger Briefwechsel*, 83f, 89–91. Bultmann was annoyed over the way the business went. "It is pitiful that they have not a little means of throwing rubbish in front of you" (84). On the proceedings, cf. also A. Christophersen, *Kairos*, 146–50.

164. Cf. RB, "Sondervotum," in H. G. Göckeritz, *Bultmann-Gogarten Briefwechsel*, 291–93; cf. also E. Sturm, "Rudolf Bultmann über Paul Tillich," 175–81.

dazzling intuition," he could only place him second behind Gogarten. For in Barth's case, scholarly interest trailed behind orienting theology to the church.[165] Gogarten, in contrast, had to an unmatched degree energetically taken hold of the "real theological task" and, following Luther, had so posed "the question in a basic way" as to have enabled it to spring solely "from faith's own reflection upon Christian existence." Gogarten had shunned phenomenology *per se* but had taken paths that run parallel to the more recent philosophical attempts in phenomenology or those of Jaspers. In so doing, he was seeking to legitimate a position not with the philosophers but with the theological tradition, and especially with Luther.[166] Even with this outspoken endorsement of Gogarten, Bultmann was not able to alter the course of events, and in February of 1929 the Prussian Minister of Culture called Heinrich Frick to be the Professor of Systematic Theology in Marburg.

Bultmann had already taken various stands in opposition to the faculty majority before the appointment proceedings of 1929. In 1923 the entire faculty except Bultmann had acceded to the decision of the university senate to transfer the Christian archaeological collection to the house of the landgrave in order to create more room in the old university for the department of art history. Bultmann lodged a protest with the Rector of the university against this measure, since he felt that the Christian archeological collection and the department of theology were dependent on each other and their libraries should be accommodated on the same premises. He also thought it irresponsible to impair the conditions for working with the Christian archaeological collection just when its future head was about to come on board.[167] In such cases, he confined himself to "the most essential contradiction, but even that will be held against me," Bultmann said of the reaction among the faculty.[168]

In view of his strained relationship to Martin Rade and Rudolf Otto, Bultmann did not at first wish to expand on why he rejected the proposal Otto had made for celebrating the four-hundredth anniversary of the Marburg Colloquy in 1529. However, since he regarded the plans of Otto

165. RB, "Sondervotum," in H. G. Göckeritz, *Bultmann-Gogarten Briefwechsel,* 296.

166. RB, "Sondervotum," in H. G. Göckeritz, *Bultmann-Gogarten Briefwechsel,* 294f. On Bultmann's opinion on F. K. Schumann, cf. "Sondervotum," 296f.

167. Cf. UB Tübingen, RB est., RB to the Rector of the University of Marburg, 3. 8. 1923, Mn 2-2385.

168. UB Tübingen, RB est., RB to H. von Soden, 22. 7. 1923, Mn 2-2385. In 1926, under the aegis of H. von Soden, the collection in Christian archaeology found a permanent location in the *Jubiläumsbau*, today's Ernst von Hülsen House.

and Hermelink for the format of the celebration as "nonsense,"[169] he finally decided to give the faculty a full explanation of his position on the matter. Otto and Hermelink had succeeded in getting a resolution by the majority of the faculty on October 31, 1925, according to which the celebration of 1929 was to set forth the essence and unity of Protestantism, as well as its tasks for the future. In view of the ecumenical movement's insistence that the planned events also contribute to a visible strengthening of international Protestantism, Otto and Hermelink pursued this goal.[170]

From the outset, however, Bultmann regarded it an illusion to think that the anniversary celebration would be able to strengthen feelings of Protestant unity, inasmuch as no sign of such a feeling was currently to be seen in the popular church. If one took seriously how far things had gone with people leaving the churches, German Protestantism represented "at best an army of officers without troops."[171] Bultmann made the further criticism that Otto's and Hermelink's project made the "distinctiveness of German Lutheranism" stand out, and the use of the aesthetic notion of distinctiveness caused one to miss how things actually happened historically, since one then viewed the distinctiveness of a person or a group as an intrinsic quality and thereby eliminated oneself from the purview of history. But at issue was "a historical activity" that "could grow only by capturing the decisive character of the moment."[172] Finally, Bultmann opposed using the anniversary celebration to promote "the historical significance of world-Protestantism."[173] Indeed, the concept of "world-Protestantism," a term derived from analogy to the worldwide Roman Catholic Church, should be rejected as a terminological error irreconcilable with the Protestant understanding of the church. As regards content, Protestantism is not about something with worldly standing, but is concerned exclusively with the message it brings to the world. Serious theological work is served only by attending to this central task, not by a social get-together with some sort of diffuse program like the one Otto and Hermelink were planning.

Otto and Hermelink did not let Bultmann's harsh critique hinder them in any way from pushing their project forward and eventually realizing it.[174]

169. RB to F. Gogarten, 3. 11. 1925, in H. G. Göckeritz, *Bultmann-Gogarten Briefwechsel*, 95.
170. Cf. K. Hammann, "Heinrich Hermelink," 104f.
171. F. Wolff, "Das Zirkular," 55.
172. F. Wolff, "Das Zirkular," 56f.
173. F. Wolff, "Das Zirkular," 57.
174. To be sure, the chair of the German Protestant Commission, Hermann Kapler, also distanced himself from the arrangements. Cf. F. Wolff, "Das Zirkular," 50f. The anniversary celebration of 1929 in Marburg did not lead to the concrete results intended by the plans for forming an international Protestantism.

The course of events made Bultmann even more conscious of his separation from the majority of the faculty. "Relations in the faculty are not pleasant. Otto's presumptuous behavior and his eagerness nowadays to enter into intrigues are unbearable. Most of the colleagues are weak. To be sure, v. Soden, the only one with any real character, is absolutely reliable and objective, bound to me by friendship as well, but not by theology. Apart from him, the atmosphere is one of jealousy and mistrust, even if outwardly we get along well. So far as real dialogue goes, except for v. Soden, I have only Heidegger and the classical philologist Friedländer. So the work with students is all the more gratifying."[175] The historian of religion Friedrich Heiler frequently caused irritations and controversies within the faculty. He characterized his theological approach as Protestant-Catholic and made much of belonging to the Protestant Church without having left the Roman Catholic Church. Bultmann and von Soden regarded this as a self-deluding obfuscation of Heiler's position, which they judged to be Catholic and which they rejected.[176]

At the end of 1929, there arose a possibility that Bultmann might be able to leave behind him the sometimes disagreeable relationships in Marburg. The University of Leipzig was planning to establish a second chair in New Testament as a way of compensating for existing deficiencies in the teaching of the subject.[177] A list of candidates submitted by a majority of the Leipzig theological faculty to the Ministry of Public Education of Saxony on December 10, 1929, placed Rudolf Bultmann, Martin Dibelius, and Hans Windisch on the same level. The New Testament scholar Johannes Leipoldt, not exactly a shining light in his department, distanced himself from this slate by casting a special vote, and took this opportunity to record his strong reservations—in particular with regard to calling Bultmann, whose "hypercritical theology" would offer no prospect at all of working together in a beneficial way.[178] Unimpressed by this postulation, the President of the

175. RB to F. Gogarten, 29. 7. 1925, in H. G. Göckeritz, *Bultmann-Gogarten Briefwechsel,* 85.

176. Cf. UB Marburg, Rade est., RB and H. von Soden to F. Heiler, 25. 7. 1932. The occasion of this letter was Heiler's protest against E. Foerster, "Kirche wider Kirche" ["Church against Church"], a rev. of F. Heiler, *Im Ringen um die Kirche.* Bultmann and von Soden rejected Heiler's demand to publish a retort in the *ThR* to Foerster's review, because they did not see Roerster's criticism to be refuted by Heiler's "corrections." Cf. also UB Tübingen, RB est., RB and H. von Soden to F. Heiler, 16. 8. 1932 (fragment), Mn 2-2241. Heiler had to publish his retort elsewhere. Cf. F. Heiler, "Wider grobliche Verkennung," 343–49.

177. On what follows, cf. G. Wartenberg, "Verpasste Chance," 285–301.

178. Special report of J. Leipoldt of 6. 12. 1929, cited by G. Wartenberg, "Verpasste Chance," 290.

Ministry of Public Education, Wilhelm Bunger, decided to extend the offer to Bultmann and to undertake negotiations with him.

Bultmann traveled to Dresden on January 6, 1929, to negotiate with the appropriate official, Robert Ulrich. The conversation proceeded satisfactorily for both sides. Bultmann's salary was to be about 21,000 Reichsmarks per year, a slight increase over that in Marburg.[179] The issue of where he was to live was also agreed upon, and Bultmann was able to secure the promise of a research assistant. When he communicated with his prospective colleague Leipoldt about the arrangements for administering the New Testament seminar, everything seemed in order for him to accept the call to Leipzig. At this point, Bultmann called on the Bishop of Saxony, Ludwig Ihmels, to confer with him. The bishop, obviously taken by surprise, made it clear to Bultmann that the consistory disapproved of his call and, should the occasion arise, would not admit him to the ecclesiastical examining board—and incidentally, as regards the government, Ihmels would assert his right to have a part in the calling of professors of theology. Bultmann thereupon gave Ihmels to understand that the matter would not be helped if the Saxon consistory were to tie the general matter of ecclesiastical involvement in the calling of professors of theology to the specific business of his or another person's call. Yet even if he was not inclined to base his decision on the stance of the Saxon church leadership,[180] Bultmann had to take into consideration the mistrust directed at him by the consistory.

The situation was made more difficult by the fact that Bultmann "[had] not had the feeling of a common purpose" on the part of the Leipzig theological faculty "apart from Mr. Rückert."[181] In fact, the church historian Hanns Rückert made a special effort to get Bultmann for Leipzig in order to work with him in renewing the theological direction of the State Church in Saxony. This student of Karl Holl hoped that as one of the leading representatives of dialectical theology, Bultmann would help to end the theological isolation of the Saxon State Church.[182] But Rückert had no success with his personal venture, for Bultmann declined the call to Leipzig on January 18,

179. The sum of 21,000 Reichsmarks comprised a basic salary of 17,100 Reichsmarks and lecture fees and child and residence expenses of 3,900 Reichsmarks.

180. Cf. RB to the ministerial councillor R. Ulich, 13. 1. 1930, in G. Wartenberg, "Verpasste Chance," 293.

181. RB to the ministerial councillor R. Ulich, 18. 1. 1930, in G. Wartenberg, "Verpasste Chance," 298.

182. Cf. UB Tübingen, RB est., H Rückert to RB, 14. 1. 1930, Mn 2-1659, reprinted in G. Wartenberg, "Verpasste Chance," 295–97.

1930. He based his decision less on the Saxon church's mistrust of him than on the prospect of giving up his productive teaching activity in Marburg for the considerable uncertainty of being effective in Leipzig.[183]

Following his negative reply to Leipzig, Bultmann soon found a new sense of community with his Marburg colleagues in dealing with an article in the contract of the Prussian church pertaining to faculty. After assuming his post in the spring of 1930, the new Prussian Minister of Education, Adolf Grimme, pushed for completion of stalled negotiations over a contract between the free state of Prussia and the Protestant State Church of Prussia. According to article 11, paragraph 2 of the draft contract that had been worked out by the Bonn canon lawyer Johannes Heckel, the appropriate ecclesiastical authority had the right to present an expert opinion before a professor of theology was called to a Protestant theological faculty. A comparable procedure had been in force in the calling of professors of theology in the Old Prussian faculties since 1855, in accordance with an order of the cabinet of King Frederick William IV.[184] This arrangement was now to be adopted by the New Prussian State Churches for the theological faculties of Göttingen, Kiel, and Marburg.

The Old Prussian faculties approved of standardizing the procedure called for by the Old Prussian general synod of 1929, and given what was at stake, the New Prussian State Churches also favored cooperation in appointing professors of theology. But the New Prussian faculties, led by the Marburg contingent, raised strenuous objections to this. In a statement of November 16, 1930, Hans von Soden, Heinrich Frick, and Heinrich Hermelink pointed out the serious consequences this plan would have for church governance in Nassau and Hessen-Kassel. If, as a discussion of November 7, 1930, suggested, the Hessian churches were to ignore dogmatic considerations and accept this article of the Prussian church contract merely for the sake of solidarity with the rest of the State Churches in Prussia, they would be attempting "to deal with a question of conscience on the basis of considerations that had to do purely with church politics." Were the Hessian churches to allow "the violation of the second largest theological faculty of Prussia," they—the undersigned professors—would have to resign from

183. Cf. RB to ministerial councillor R. Ulich, 18. 1. 1930, in Wartenberg, "Verpasste Chance." In his continuing negotiations in Berlin with the Director of the Ministry in Prussia, Dr. Werner Richter, Bultmann secured the right to apply for stipends to further the studies of doctoral and post-doctoral students.

184. However, according to the cabinet order of 1855, the Ministry of Education was not bound by the vote of the Protestant Church Council.

their theological teaching posts and to leave their State Church "which had become un-Protestant."[185] Bultmann and Emil Balla endorsed this position on December 22, 1930.[186]

The protest of the Marburg theological faculty against the new protocol triggered an intense debate. Burdened as it was by many misunderstandings, the dispute over the clause on faculty appointments took an unfortunate course, not least because the discussion was conducted on the most disparate levels. Not only did journalistic exchanges *pro* and *contra* appear in both *Die Christliche Welt* and *Theological Papers*, but individual theological faculties undertook negotiations with their State Churches as well as with the Prussian Ministry of Education. The leading lights in the dispute also unleashed a flood of correspondence in attempts to secure agreement with the positions they supported.[187]

Unfortunately, the fact that emeritus professor Martin Rade represented a view opposed to that of Bultmann, von Soden, and the other Marburg professors led to a fatal misunderstanding of the Marburg faculty's position with respect to the contested article. Rade presupposed that a theological faculty constituted an organ of the church in the same way as did the highest ecclesiastical authority. On this basis, it made no sense for the ecclesiastical authority to deal with whether a prospective theological professor subscribed to the confession of the church or with the content of what he taught; this task fell within the area of competence of the theological faculty.[188] But the Bonn New Testament scholar Karl Ludwig Schmidt promptly rejected Rade's opinion as absolutely untenable, and in this regard pointed to the governmental supervision under which the theological faculties stood in the Weimar Republic. Above all, he emphasized the close connection between church leadership and church doctrine, which when viewed from a biblical and historical perspective might very well justify ecclesiastical influence on the formation of state-governed theological faculties.[189]

One result of this dispute, much of which was carried on through correspondence, was that Schmidt was misled into thinking that Rade's posi-

185. H. von Soden to the governing body of the Protestant State Church in Nassau, 16. 11. 1930, in B. Jaspert, *Barth-Bultmann Briefwechsel*, 242.

186. Cf. B. Jaspert, *Barth-Bultmann Briefwechsel*, 242f.

187. Cf. RB to F. Gogarten, 24. 1. 1931, in H. G. Göckeritz, *Bultmann-Gogarten Briefwechsel*, 190–97; as well as the exchange of letters between H. von Soden and H. Lietzmann in K. Aland, *Glanz und Niedergang*, 628–30.

188. Cf. M. Rade, "Missio canonica," 170f; as well as H. Liebing, "Die Marburger Theologische Fakultät," 272f.

189. Cf. K. L. Schmidt, "Evangelisch," 235–40; as well as A. Mühling, *Karl Ludwig Schmidt*, 118–21.

tion reflected that of the remaining Marburg theologians. And Karl Barth, whose only information on the matter had come through Schmidt, similarly judged the Marburg opposition to the faculty article to be "evidently a liberal affair."[190] Despite repeated attempts, Bultmann was unable to correct this misjudgment.[191] In January 1931, a Marburg special faculty meeting was called at short notice for the discussion of the questions in dispute, but it failed to take place. The Old Prussian faculties declined the invitation of the Marburgers. Karl Ludwig Schmidt, who was in the dubious company of Erich Seeberg, played a major part in foiling the Marburgers' request.[192] And their threatened resignation and withdrawal from the State Church if the faculty paragraphs were adopted was widely felt to be an unreasonable challenge that did not allow for an impartial discussion of the questions in dispute.[193] And all the while, submerged in the hectic bustle of the conflict, the fact remained that Bultmann and von Soden were not expressing a political threat by their announcement, but simply wished to underscore the existential seriousness of their view.[194]

Feelings of resentment towards the church played no role in Bultmann's opposition to the faculty article; rather, he was motivated by the local memory of the church assembly's veto that had nearly prevented the calling of Adolf Harnack from Marburg to Berlin in 1888, and his experience of ecclesiastical complaints against the teaching of Paul Tillich and Rudolf Otto. Still, these played as little role in his argumentation as did the more recent experience of the full-press attempt of the Saxon consistory to block his call to Leipzig. It troubled him that the church authorities and the state were negotiating the faculty article without including the faculties in the discussions. It angered him that the concomitant question of the churches had been needlessly and indeed improperly reduced to serving as an instrument of power politics. What he had in mind was strengthening still further not only the responsibility that the faculties bore to the churches, but also their

190. K. Barth to RB, 20. 6. 1931, in B. Jaspert, *Barth-Bultmann Briefwechsel,* 126.

191. Cf. RB to K. Barth, 14. 6. 1931, in B. Jaspert, *Barth-Bultmann Briefwechsel,* 121–23; RB to F. Gogarten, 24. 1. 1931, in H. G. Göckeritz, *Bultmann-Gogarten Briefwechsel,* 197.

192. Cf. the parts of letters reprinted in B. Jaspert, *Barth-Bultmann Briefwechsel,* 248–57, and A. Mühling, *Karl Ludwig Schmidt,* 123–30.

193. Cf. as an illustration K. Barth to RB 27. 5. 1931, in B. Jaspert, *Barth-Bultmann Briefwechsel,* 116f.

194. Cf. RB to F. Gogarten, 24. 1. 1931, H. G. Göckeritz, *Bultmann-Gogarten Briefwechsel,* 196. Bultmann considered in the *ultima ratio* qualifying to teach in the philosophical faculty of a non-Prussian university (such as Freiburg) and then further pursuing academic theology as an honorary professor. Cf. RB to M. Heidegger 21. and 26. 1. 1931, in A. Grossmann and C. Landmesser, *Bultmann-Heidegger Briefwechsel,* 150, 155f.

cooperative relations with the church authorities, both of which had been intended in the Prussian church contract.[195]

Bultmann gave his view of things in a memorandum put on record on January 18, 1931. Presupposing the functional assignment of theology to the church, he here grants legitimate motives to the claim of the leadership of the church to control theological scholarship, for church doctrine, which the theological faculties engage to preserve in their work of education, must be distinguished from heresy, and the church must forever work out this distinction anew. Nevertheless, the authority to distinguish right doctrine from heresy does not belong to church leadership, which Bultmann evidently understands to be merely an arm of administration. Rather, it arises from the common relation of church doctrine and theology to their one purpose, the revelation of God, so that in the Protestant Church only theology can exercise the doctrinal office. To be sure, theology is subject to control through the life of the church; however, it is not the ecclesiastical authorities but only theology itself—and only as it relates to its purpose—that is able to exercise this control.[196]

Even if Bultmann's explanations were strictly intended to check the neutralizing of theology in the institutional church, Barth believed that its assignment of administrative and teaching functions to church government and to the faculties was too "mechanical."[197] With all their activities and their various votes,[198] the Marburg theologians did not ultimately achieve the fundamental revision of the faculty article they sought. But of course they could not more explicitly come to grips with the new regulation, since the final protocol on the faculty article guaranteed that the opinion issued by the church had a merely consultative character and could therefore apply only in exceptional cases of dissent between faculty and church leadership.[199] Also, declarations by the synods of Nassau and Hessen-Kassel promising not to attempt to infringe on the freedom of teaching and research of the Marburg theological faculty made it easier for the Marburg professors to consent to the final version of the faculty article.[200]

195. Most important of all, RB to F. Gogarten, 24. 1. 1931, in H. G. Göckeritz, *Bultmann-Gogarten Briefwechsel,* 192–95.

196. Cf. RB, memorandum (18. 1. 1931), in B. Jaspert, *Barth-Bultmann Briefwechsel,* 243–48; W. Härle and H. Leipold, *Lehrfreiheit,* 145–47.

197. K. Barth to RB, 20. 6. 1931, in B. Jaspert, *Barth-Bultmann Briefwechsel,* 126.

198. Cf. also the memoranda of H. von Soden of 1929 and H. Frick of 1930, in W. Härle and H. Leipold, *Lehrfreiheit,* 139–43 and 143f.

199. Cf. H. Liebing, "Die Marburger Theologische Fakultät," 273f.

200. Cf. W. Härle and H. Leipold, *Lehrfreiheit,* 138f.

During the decisive phase of the dispute over the faculty article, Hans Lietzmann, one of the opponents of the Marburg position, offered the opinion that the situation for church and theology was "terribly serious." In view of the uncertain future of the state, the "time of theorizing" was over, and now "every word in the matter is a decisive deed."[201] Two years later, church and theology were no longer dealing with a state that was neutral in its worldview, but rather with one that was totalitarian. Despite their differences during the discussion of 1930–31, Karl Barth and Karl Ludwig Schmidt on the one side, and Bultmann and Hans von Soden on the other, knew equally well what theology would have to do in order to fulfill its responsibility to the church.

5. Paul as Interpreter of the Christian Understanding of Existence

I think that, the more one makes clear the existential character of Pauline thinking, the more one will again see that the significance of Paul for world history lies nowhere else than in his having been a theologian.[202]

In 1929, in the first issue of the newly founded *Theologische Rundschau*, Bultmann published an essay on the history of research into Pauline theology. In this article, he refrained from referring extensively to specific recent publications, for his intention was to make clear in programmatic fashion the state and the task of current efforts to understand Paul in the light of a critical history of research. This undertaking was to have great significance in a number of respects. From the very outset of historical-critical consciousness, the more-or-less definite outlines of the figure of the apostle from Tarsus had formed a natural starting point for all attempts to construct a historical picture of early Christianity. The way one interpreted the theology of Paul and situated him in the context of the history of ancient religion always bore a reciprocal relation to one's overall historical and theological view of the New Testament.[203] And therefore, whoever was prepared—and Bultmann

201. H. Lietzmann to his (Göttingen?) colleagues, 19. 1. 1931, in K. Aland, *Glanz und Niedergang*, 631.

202. RB "Zur Geschichte," 59.

203. Cf. RB, "Zur Geschichte," 27–29. The text grew out of the seminar on "The Recent Study of Paul" that Bultmann gave in WS 1927–28. Cf. also B. Jaspert, *Sachgemässe Exegese*, 48–53.

was prepared[204]—to expose his own interpretation of Paul to an evaluation in terms of the hermeneutical and theological issues that distinguished Luther's exegesis would also have to expound on the status and meaning of the apostle's doctrine of justification.

In Bultmann's view, Ferdinand Christian Baur, William Wrede, Adolf Schlatter, and Karl Barth had set up the decisive milestones along the road of Pauline scholarship from the beginning of the nineteenth century onwards. Because he allowed himself to be directed by a specific understanding of human existence in his interpretation of Pauline theology, Ferdinand Christian Baur was able to draw an imposingly unified portrait of Paul. This is fundamentally to his credit, even if one must be critical both of Bauer's understanding of existence—that he took over from Hegel—and his interpretation of the Pauline concept of spirit as it bears on Christian self-consciousness. Within the history-of-religions school, William Wrede again showed the validity of treating religion and theology as a unity in Paul, and by a series of accurate interpretations of specific points he partially anticipated the understanding of Paul by Karl Barth and dialectical theology. However, the way he marginalized Paul's teaching of justification clearly demonstrates his lack of insight into Paul's understanding of existence and the distinctive conceptuality that grew out of it. In contrast, an understanding of the historicity of human existence lies at the very base of Adolf Schlatter's interpretation of Paul, for Schlatter was able to set out the theology of the apostle as a unified expression of the act of thinking and living—though to be sure, his intuitive interpretation suffers from the shortcoming of not having subjected the basic concepts of Pauline thought to any systematic analysis. Finally, even if Karl Barth did not develop his understanding of Paul as a contribution to scholarly research, his work benefitted scholarly exegesis indirectly. For although the Pauline concepts having to do with existence would not play a role in Barth, in repudiating the liberal tradition of interpretation, he correctly emphasized central motives and intentions in Paul's theology of Paul that were becoming increasingly important in critical analyses.[205]

In his overview of the history of research, Bultmann made little mention of his own works: besides a brief reference to his dissertation, only—and likewise in passing—his essay on the ethics of Paul "as [my] first attempt . . . to

204. In the decisive phase of working out his own understanding of Paul, Bultmann gave a seminar on "Luther's Interpretation of Galatians" in SS 1927 (cf. B. Jaspert, *Sachgemässe Exegese*, 46–48) and a seminar on "Luther's Exposition of Romans" in SS 1930 (cf. B. Jaspert, *Sachgemässe Exegese*, 654–67).

205. Cf. RB, "Zur Geschichte," 29–33, 46–49, 52–54.

push forward in capturing the Pauline understanding of existence."[206] This reserve obscured the fact that by 1929 Bultmann had already developed the outlines of a new comprehensive interpretation of Pauline theology, a unified interpretation that he was then to present in its nearly complete form in 1930, in his *RGG* [*Die Religion in Geschichte und Gegenwart*] article, "Paul." He had worked out his new interpretation of Paul during the decade between 1923 and 1932, a period that also marks the setting in which Bultmann developed his discourse for understanding Paul as the interpreter of Christian existence. The poles of this force field were the critical rejection of the picture of Paul developed by the history-of-religions school—one that Bultmann had largely shared until about 1920[207]—and the critical adaptation of the impulse that came out of Karl Barth's commentaries on the various Pauline letters. Along the same line was the conversation with philosopher Martin Heidegger, in whose ontology of existence Bultmann found the right hermeneutical key for working out the meaning of the conceptual world of Paul. In addition, Bultmann sought to test his conception against other interpretations of Paul—especially those of Ernst Lohmeyer and Albert Schweitzer, both of which reflected conceptual underpinnings.

Against the background of his conversation with Barth's *Epistle to the Romans*,[208] Bultmann held a seminar on the ethics of Paul in the winter semester of 1923–24 in which he was joined by Heidegger, who had just been called to Marburg.[209] In the essay that came out of the work of the seminar, "The Problem of Ethics in Paul," Bultmann's intention is to demonstrate that what such exegetes as Paul Wernle and Hans Windisch construe as a contradiction between indicative and imperative in Paul is "a genuine antinomy."[210] Indicative and imperative in themselves state contradictory things; nevertheless they refer to a unified state of affairs. Paul grounds ethics in justification. He understands the otherworldly salvation of justification

206. RB, "Zur Geschichte," 58.

207. Cf. G. Sinn, *Christologie und Existenz*, 37–117, 118–28; G. Sinn, "Existenz," 27–31. On what follows, cf. also W. G. Kümmel, "Rudolf Bultmann als Paulusforscher," in B. Jaspert, *Werk und Wirkung*, 174–93.

208. UB Tübingen, RB est., RB to H. von Soden, 23. 12. 1923, Mn 2-2385: Barth's "*Epistle to the Romans* is certainly an extraordinary book, and as much as his exegesis is often artificial or allegorizing, the way he formulates the issues is also just as fruitful for interpretation. This is being borne out for me in the seminar."

209. Cf. B. Jaspert, *Sachgemässe Exegese*, 26–33. See below, 203–6.

210. RB, "Problem," *Exegetica*, 36. Bultmann was the first to coin the pair of concepts "indicative and imperative" to characterize the ethics of Paul. On the enormous influence of this formulation of Bultmann's, see U. Schnelle, "Begründung," 109–31; R. Zimmermann, "Jenseits," 259–64.

as an event that is grounded in the judgment of God and that has been completed in God's act of salvation in the Christ-event. Accordingly, the indicative of justification or sinlessness denotes not some natural, empirically demonstrable "alteration of the moral quality of the human being." Rather, the justification consisting in the judgment of God can become available only in faith.[211]

Similarly, sin is not primarily something in the human being that is accessible to sense perception; indeed, it is discernible only in the light of faith—which is to say, only where it is forgiven (cf. Rom 7:7–25). For this reason, the identity of the empirical person who is declared just is ultimately visible only to faith. Thus in justification God grants a new manner of existence and likewise effects obedience through the spirit so that the one who is freed from sin seeks to comply with the demand for holiness in his life. Because of this, the paradox of indicative and imperative is perfectly clear to faith: εἰ ζῶμεν πνεύματι, πνεύματι καὶ στοιχῶμεν [If we live by the Spirit, let us also be guided by the Spirit] (Gal 5:25). Over against this conception of Bultmann's, Hans Windisch raised the objection that for Paul, the new existence of the one who is justified finds fulfillment in a form that is also fully open to sense perception.[212] In Bultmann's judgment, of course, this criticism did not touch the core of his thesis of the invisibility of faith in principle and of the ethical praxis of the one who is redeemed.[213]

Bultmann first pursued this topic with Barth in a lecture he gave in Göttingen on February 6, 1925: "The Problem of a Theological Exegesis of the New Testament."[214] In this, he strengthened and made more explicit his call for a type of criticism directed at the content of New Testament texts, one that gauges what is said in the texts by deciding what they mean. Bultmann put that view of theological exegesis to the test on a text from Paul when he explicitly engaged Barth's commentary on 1 Corinthians in 1926. He agreed with Barth that eschatology is the basic and decisive theme for this letter in which Paul sees the structure of the believer's existence as characterized by hope in the eschatological future of God. According to 1 Cor 7:29–31, therefore, the Christian's eschatological existence takes place

211. RB, "Problem," 49.

212. Cf. H. Windisch, "Problem," 265–81.

213. Cf. RB to F. Gogarten, 10. 4. 1927, in H. G. Göckeritz, *Bultmann-Gogarten Briefwechsel*, 106f. It can at least be asked whether Bultmann comes closer to the position of H. Windisch in his *Theologie des Neuen Testaments*, 332–35.

214. Cf. RB, "Problem," *Neues Testament und christliche Existenz*, 13–38; as well as RB to K. Barth, 24. 1. and 3. 2. 1925, in B. Jaspert, *Barth-Bultmann Briefwechsel*, 39f, 44f. See above, 146f.

"in a peculiarly broken relation to the world": in the world, to be sure, but essentially adrift from the future of God.[215] Thus the basic eschatological theme of 1 Corinthians also serves as a critical standard for individual statements of Paul on the subject.

While Barth regards chapter 15 as the high point of this Pauline letter, Bultmann views chapters 12–14 as the real crux of Paul's argumentation, and chapter 13 in particular as its climax, inasmuch as the eschatological occurrence realizes itself in ἀγάπη [love] (1 Cor 13:4–8).[216] In 1 Corinthians 15, however, Paul partly remains obscured behind his claim that our resurrection, being grounded in the resurrection of Christ, is a transparent reality of our existence (cf. 1 Cor 15:20–22). For in 1 Cor 15:1–11, Bultmann contends, Paul undertakes the inappropriate apologetic task of proving the historicity of Christ's resurrection. The apostle creates "a contradiction with himself" (cf. 1 Cor 15:20–22).[217] The problem is that all of the statements in the penultimate chapter of the letter that fail to express Christ's resurrection as undergirding the possibility of the eschatological existence of the Christian have to be tested against this main point. To be sure, insofar as he replaces the cosmological eschatology of Paul with the *futurum aeternum* [eternal future], Barth also offers a basically critical interpretation of the apostle; however such a theological exegesis, since it includes within itself criticism of content, must be much more strongly supported by historical investigations into context and precise conceptual analysis than Barth does.[218]

Bultmann did not find the various studies of Paul by Wilhelm Mundle at all convincing, but they did help him achieve greater clarity in his own interpretation of Paul. Mundle, who was Bultmann's successor as tutor at the Hessian Residence for Scholarship Students in Marburg and the last student of Adolf Jülicher, sought in 1923 to understand Paul's religious life not from the perspective of the history of his time, but rather in accord with its inner structural laws. Bultmann argued that in doing this Mundle was proceeding not phenomenologically, as he claimed, but rather merely psychologistically, by deriving Paul's piety from his conversion.[219] Bultmann was particularly severe in his criticism of Mundle's opposition to his concept of the relation

215. RB, "Karl Barth," *GvV* I, 46; cf. K. Barth, *Die Auferstehung der Toten*.

216. Cf. RB, "Karl Barth," 49–51.

217. RB, "Karl Barth," 54f.

218. Cf. RB, "Karl Barth," 63.

219. Cf. W. Mundle, *Das religiöse Leben*; as well as RB, "Urchristliche Religion," 141f; RB, "Zur Geschichte," 57. Cf. also UB Tübingen, RB est., RB to H. von Soden, 29. 1. 1922, Mn 2-2385, cited in M. Evang, *Frühzeit*, 98n73. Bultmann offers an explicit criticism to W. Mundle in 21. 11. 1925, in AEKR Boppard, W. Mundle est., no. 874.

between indicative and imperative.[220] In Bultmann's opinion, Mundle's talk of "religious faith" overlooked the intentionality of faith; for by "faith" Paul specifically rejected the idea that "religion" was a form of human behavior or a phenomenon of culture. When in opposition to Bultmann, Mundle stressed that πίστις as ὑπακοή [faith as obedience] was to be understood as a something one did, Bultmann reminded him that he had long understood it in this way himself.[221] Mundle's problem was that he did not grasp the problem of ethics in Paul when he discussed it against the background of the relation "of the *consciousness* of salvation and the imperative." In fact, it had to do with the relation of "*being saved* and the imperative," and so also with the status of the doctrine of justification in Paul's theology.[222]

By 1924, Bultmann had already distanced himself from William Wrede's thesis that the doctrine of justification was a subsidiary "combative doctrine" that Paul held merely as a strategy for mission, one used to demonstrate the superiority of the Christian religion of salvation over Judaism and Jewish Christianity.[223] Lecturing in 1930 at Uppsala and Oslo on "The Christology of the New Testament," Bultmann focused on the central role of the doctrine of justification in Pauline theology. First he examines the theory of his teacher, Johannes Weiss, who proposed that Paul had already conceived of a mythological "christology" before his conversion to Christianity, and that the charisma of Jesus made so powerful an impression on him that he could express it only in mythological images. And this Weiss saw as christology in the proper sense.[224]

In contrast to such a construct, which is a product of imagination, Bultmann asserts the inner connection between christology and Paul's teaching on justification. As a form of direct address, christology is the proclamation of the eschatological deed of God that occurred in Jesus Christ, while as a form of indirect speech, christology makes explicit the new self-understanding of the believer that is made possible through the salvation-event. Thus, justification proves to be the explication of christology, just

220. Cf. W. Mundle, "Religion," 456–82; as well as M. Dreher, "Rudolf Bultmann als Kritiker," 383. However, Dreher does not take account of Bultmann's letter to Mundle of 13. 11. 1927, in AEKR Boppard, W. Mundle est., no. 874.

221. Cf. RB, "Zur Frage," *GuV*, vol. 1, 101f.

222. AEKR Boppard, W. Mundle est., RB to W. Mundle, 13. 11. 1927, no. 874. Mundle later joined the evangelical circles of Bultmann's detractors. Cf. AEKR Boppard, W. Mundle est., RB to W. Mundle, 10. 11. 1963; UB Tübingen, RB est., W. Mundle to RB, 6. 12. 1964, Mn 2-1443.

223. Cf. RB, "Problem," 53n11; as well as W. Wrede, *Paulus*, 72–74; cf. O. Merk, "Adolf Jülicher als Paulusforscher," 159f.

224. Cf. RB, "Christologie," *GuV*, vol. 1, 246–52.

as talk of Christ is conversely to be understood as implied by the event of justification. Since Paul emphatically unfolds christology after the manner of a doctrine of justification, he makes clear that an understanding appropriation of the Christ-occurrence "is a matter not of speculation, but rather of self-reflection, a thinking-through of one's new existence."[225]

From this point of view, Bultmann can gain a *particula veri* [an element of truth] from Wrede's conception of the doctrine of justification as a combative doctrine—though to be sure one contrary to Wrede's own intention. For the fact that the doctrine of justification is of central importance to Paul is shown by the way he employs its basic ideas to combat not only Judaism, but also Gnosticism in Corinth. In the cross of Christ, divine judgment is issued "on all human boasting, . . . be it on the ἔργα νόμου [works of the law] or on human σοφία [wisdom]." Through this judgment, which "shatters all human self-assurance, the human being is freed from himself and precisely therein does the justifying grace of God take effect."[226]

In his discussion with Johannes Weiss, Bultmann also touched on the question of "Jesus and Paul." Under this heading lay a concealed problem for the history-of-religions school that in view of its premises it was quite unable to solve. It had worked out the differences between the proclamation of Jesus and the preaching of the apostle to the gentiles as an issue in the history of religion, but historians of religion found it difficult to evaluate these findings. For the most part they fell back on the idea that the simple folk-religion of Jesus was replaced by the highly reflective theologizing of Paul; and in the context of that distinction, the religion of Jesus was given preference over the theology of Paul—who had only to serve as "the second founder of Christianity."[227] For Bultmann, the subject of "Jesus and Paul" was part of *the* problem "of New Testament theology in general"—that of how to understand "that Jesus the proclaimer becomes the proclaimed Jesus Christ."[228] In the autumn of 1928, Bultmann gave a lecture on "The Meaning of the Historical Jesus for the Theology of Paul," in which he elucidated his view of this matter.[229]

In essence—as the exegetical findings show—the proclamation of Jesus has no significance for the theological views of Paul. The evident similarities

225. RB, "Christologie," 262.

226. RB, "Christologie," 261f.

227. Wrede, *Paulus*, 104.

228. RB to K. Barth, 10. 12. 1926, in B. Jaspert, *Barth-Bultmann Briefwechsel*, 65.

229. Cf. RB, "Bedeutung," *GuV*, vol. 1, 188–213. Bultmann presented this lecture on 23 August 1928 in Carlshof (East Prussia) and at the second meeting of the "old Marburgers," which took place in Marburg from the 22nd to the 24th of October 1928.

and differences between the preaching of Jesus and the theology of Paul with regard to the law and eschatology cannot be explained in terms of the history of ideas—that is, as if one had developed out of the other. Rather, the decisive difference consists in the fact that "Paul regards as present what for Jesus is future—which is to say, as something in the past breaking into the present."[230] Bultmann now views two stages as significant for the emergence of christology. Jesus understood himself as bearer of the word of God in the end times. His call to decision in the face of his person implied a christology. Thereupon, with its confession of the crucified Jesus as the Messiah, the earliest community understood the cross as the eschatological deed of God and understood itself anew on this basis. What was implicit in the kerygma of the earliest community, Paul made explicit in his *theologia crucis*, namely, the meaning of the cross as the decisive fact of salvation for the self-understanding of the believer. But since Jesus Christ encounters a person solely in the proclaimed word, one may "not go back behind the kerygma . . . in order to reconstruct a 'historical Jesus.'" This is precisely what Paul thought through theologically: "It is not the historical Jesus, but rather Jesus Christ, the one who is preached, who is the Lord."[231] In his theology, therefore, Paul interprets the new self-understanding of those who believe in the Christ present in the kerygma as Lord over their existence.

But to be more specific, how does Paul go on to explain the Christian understanding of existence? Bultmann discussed this question further in the setting of the lecture that he gave before a large audience[232] in October 1927 at the first meeting of German Protestant theologians in Eisenach. Here, following the analysis presented by Martin Heidegger in *Sein und Zeit* [*Being and Time*], he interpreted potentiality-for-being—that quality through which "the individual does not choose *something for himself*, but rather *chooses himself as his possibility*"—as an expression of the historicity of human existence.[233] This Bultmann illustrated by means of Paul's set of concepts. Thus, by σῶμα [body], Paul denotes not a "what" in the human being, for a human being does not *have* a body, but rather *is* body. Consequently, σῶμα stands as a cipher for historical existence, with its alternative possibilities "of being determined through God or through sin. The 'how' of the σῶμα determined through sin is called σάρξ [flesh], while the 'how' of the new person is the πνεῦμα [spirit]."[234]

230. RB, "Bedeutung," 201.
231. RB, "Bedeutung," 208.
232. Cf. A. Titius, "Deutsche Theologie," 97f.
233. RB, "Die Bedeutung der 'dialektischen Theologie,'" *GuV*, vol. 1, 118. See also below, 207f.
234. RB, "Die Bedeutung der 'dialektischen Theologie,'" 130f.

The exegesis of Rom 7:7–25 formed the main focus of the advanced[235] seminar on Pauline anthropology that Bultmann offered in the winter semester of 1925–26. Stimulated by this seminar and by Bultmann's insights that came out of it,[236] Werner Georg Kümmel rendered plausible a new understanding of Romans 7 in his dissertation done under the supervision of Martin Dibelius. The "I" speaking in this passage is not to be taken to refer in autobiographical fashion to Paul himself. It denotes rather the situation of existence prior to faith under the law, as this situation has become re-envisioned in light of the event of revelation in Christ.[237] Taking up this interpretation in his contribution to the Festschrift for Gustav Krüger in 1932, Bultmann discussed in detail the question of wherein the conflict of existence under the law represented in Rom 7:14–25 consists. Paul sees the human being here "not at all primarily as the conscious subject," but rather as a being that finds itself under the lordship either of σάρξ or πνεῦμα [flesh or spirit]. These "powers" do, in truth, represent "the two possibilities of historical existence."[238] Therefore, the human being *is* that conflict, because he does really want to achieve authentic life; but in what he does, he in fact misses it. It is therefore possible for the individual to be himself only in eschatological existence—that is, when he abandons himself completely in the obedience of faith to the claim of God.[239]

Thus, Bultmann saw the historicity of human existence, with its possibility of deciding between authenticity and inauthenticity on the basis of the kerygma, expressed *par excellence* in Romans 7. For this reason, it was from this text that he gained the hermeneutical access to his account of the theology of Paul, which he presented in 1930. To be sure, during that period other New Testament scholars developed alternatives to his interpretation of Paul, the most significant of which came from Ernst Lohmeyer and Albert Schweitzer. Bultmann engaged in critical discussion of both Lohmeyer's and Schweitzer's comprehensive interpretations of Pauline theology.

In his detailed discussion of Lohmeyer's book, *Grundlagen paulinischer Theologie* [*Principles of Pauline Theology*], Bultmann is at special pains—in view of the both symbolistic and occasionally tortured style of its author—

235. Participants included, among others, Hannah Arendt, Ernst Bizer, George Boobyer, Günter Jacob, Hans Jonas, Ernst Käsemann, Gerhard Krüger, Werner Georg Kümmel, Hermann Mörchen, Martin Rang, Martin Schmidt, Martin Stallmann, and Wilhelm Weischedel. Cf. B. Jaspert, *Sachgemässe Exegese*, 39–42.

236. Cf. RB, "Die Bedeutung der 'dialektischen' Theologie," 131f.

237. Cf. W. G. Kümmel, *Römer 7.*

238. RB, "Römer 7," *Exegetica*, 201.

239. Cf. RB, "Römer 7," *Exegetica,* 208f.

to do justice to the content and intentions of the work under review.[240] Bultmann praises Lohmeyer's effort to understand Paul's theology in a critical manner instead of simply reproducing it in a historical or psychological fashion, and to take it on board "by way of a modern conceptuality." However, Bultmann rejects all the more decisively "the overall presentation . . . as completely turning Pauline theology into transcendental philosophy." In Bultmann's view Lohmeyer has utterly misrepresented the thought of Paul along the lines of Ferdinand Christian Baur's idealistic understanding of history. By reframing the contrast between God and the world as one of idea and appearance or spirit and nature, Lohmeyer fails to recognize the existential character of Pauline theology. "According to Paul, it is not that faith transcends the sphere of the historical, but rather that in faith as a historical act of obedience, the 'I' transcends itself," by opening itself to the forgiving word of God and, thereby, "to the possibility of a new historical existence in obedience."[241]

Bultmann acknowledges Schweitzer's *Die Mystik des Apostels Paulus* [*The Mysticism of the Apostle Paul*] as a great conceptual achievement that seeks to come to terms with Paul as a thinker.[242] To begin with, Bultmann regrets that in contrast to the history-of-religions school, Schweitzer does not see Paul's theology as coming out of the Hellenistic mystery religions but rather understands it as a continuation of Jewish eschatological views. But Schweitzer has rightly presented Pauline theology as an eschatological mysticism.[243] With his mysticism Paul intends above all to make clear the existential point "that in the resurrection of Jesus the decisive cosmological-eschatological event with which the end-time begins has occurred, but that its consummation must wait until Jesus has returned."[244] Nonetheless, Bultmann find unsatisfactory Schweitzer's claim that here Paul is falling back on existing apocalyptic motifs; his objection is that because Paul conceives human existence as historical, he interprets the eschatological occurrence not

240. Cf. RB, rev. of E. Lohmeyer, in RB, *Theologie als Kritik*, 244–51; as well as E. Lohmeyer, *Grundlagen*. On Lohmeyer's interpretation of Paul, cf. A. Kühn, *Der Neutestamentler*, 254–59; D. Kühn, *Metaphysik*, 95–120.

241. RB, rev. of E. Lohmeyer, in RB, *Theologie als Kritik*, 250f; cf. also RB, rev. of E. Lohmeyer, *Der Brief*, and RB, rev. of Lohmeyer, *Kyrios Jesus*, in RB, *Theologie als Kritik*, 252–59.

242. Cf. RB, rev. of A. Schweitzer, *Die Mystik*, in RB, *Theologie als Kritik*, 263–66; A. Schweitzer, *Die Mystik*. Cf. also RB to A. Schweitzer, 28. 8. 1930, in W. Zager, *Albert Schweitzer*, 180–82.

243. It is only that the word "mysticism" is to be replaced by the more appropriate concept "gnosis."

244. RB, rev. of A. Schweitzer, *Die Mystik*, in RB, *Theologie als Kritik*, 264.

with cosmic or naturalistic images of apocalypticism but rather by means of a conceptuality drawn from eschatological Gnosticism.[245]

In the second edition of the *RGG* (1930), Bultmann offered a systematic presentation of his understanding of Paul. He composed this comprehensive article of at least twenty-seven double-columned lexicon pages on "Paul," an essay that amounted to a summation of his previous statements on the subject, during a fourteen-day stay in April 1930 at the "Black Buck," a spa in Wiesbaden.[246] In this presentation he devotes more space to the theology of Paul than to such biographical data as the apostle's background, education, conversion and activities.[247] Bultmann categorically refuses to derive Pauline theology from the conversion *experience* or the personality of the apostle, as was *en vogue* in the history-of-religions school. The conversion of Paul, however exceptional in the details of its occurrence, exemplifies in iconic fashion the event of conversion from law to Christ, from an old "I" to a new self-understanding—an event that in one form or another can happen to everyone. To have arrived at precisely this conclusion through an existential process of thinking is what constitutes the apostle's genuine significance, for "as *a theologian* [he] has given to Christian faith the proper understanding of itself."[248] The presuppositions relevant for the theology of Paul are his self-understanding as a Jew under the law, his tying into the proclamation of the earliest community, and—from the history-of-religions viewpoint—the motifs and ideas characteristic of his thinking.[249]

Bultmann derives his plan for presenting the theology of Paul from the fact that Paul understands God, Christ, and the human being as correlates of each other. On this basis the theology of Paul may be unfolded as anthropology that understands human beings to be *coram Deo* [in the presence of God]. However, since the human being has acquired "a new possibility in his position before God," the following distinction suggests itself: "1. the human being prior to the revelation of faith, and 2. the human being under faith."[250] Bultmann first deals with existence prior to faith: the human being

245. Cf. RB, rev. of A. Schweitzer, *Die Mystik,* in RB, *Theologie als Kritik,* 265f. Cf. also Schweitzer's reaction to RB, 11. 10. 1931, in W. Zager, *Albert Schweitzer*, 183f.

246. Cf. RB, *Chronik 1917–1945*, Mn 2-224, 17. Bultmann had taken on the article at a late date (at the request of the publisher), after "complications had arisen at the last moment in the assignment of this article, so important for the new edition [of the *RGG*]" (UB Tübingen, RB est., O. Siebeck to RB, 23. 12. 1929, Mn 2-2485).

247. Cf. RB, "Paulus," 1020–26 ("Life"), 1026–45 ("Theology").

248. RB, "Paulus," 1025f; cf. 1026f.

249. Cf. RB, "Paulus," 1027–31.

250. RB, "Paulus," 1031. This arrangement presupposes, as does Rom 7:7–25, that the understanding of existence that is prior to faith is first recognizable on the basis of faith.

as creature of God, the concepts that always describe the human being as a whole, the historicity of existence, and the sin that comes to expression in the human being's willing to be himself.[251] Following this, Bultmann describes existence under faith: the righteousness given by God as a gift as human "authenticity," God's act of salvation fulfilled in the death and in the resurrection of Jesus Christ, faith as a new human self-understanding, preaching as the eschatological act of salvation occurring ever anew, and the new life determined by the spirit. Whereas the individual existed under the lordship of the law, sin, and death before and outside the revelation in Christ, now under faith he lives in freedom from these powers in order to realize in service to neighbor the love that fulfills the law.[252]

Bultmann's picture of Paul and the outline of his theology presented in the *RGG* article of 1930 was only slightly modified, as it were, in his *Theologie des Neuen Testaments* [*Theology of the New Testament*], though even in 1930 Albert Schweitzer had found Bultmann's article on Paul to be "actually a book" that was distinguished by the extraordinarily clear exposition of its material.[253]

6. The Jesus-Book and the Question of Christology

It would therefore appear that the critic who wants to rescue dogma from the conflagration that his criticism has brought about must undertake something that from his own perspective is untrue in order to accommodate faith as such, which is something he himself takes no stock in.[254]

The historical Jesus . . . does not make any direct demand on us, nor does he condemn us for any deed we have committed against him. . . . I have done him no wrong and there is nothing for which he has to forgive me.[255]

I have never yet felt uncomfortable with my critical radicalism; to the contrary, I have been entirely comfortable. But I often have the impression that my conservative New Testament colleagues feel very

251. Cf. RB, "Paulus," 1031–37.
252. Cf. RB, "Paulus," 1037–43.
253. A. Schweitzer to RB, 15. 10. 1930, in W. Zager, *Albert Schweitzer*, 182.
254. D. F. Strauss, *Leben*, vol. 2, 687.
255. RB, "Zur Frage," *GuV*, vol. 1, 95–97.

> *uncomfortable, for I see them perpetually engaged in salvage operations. I calmly let the fire burn, for I see that what is consumed is only the fanciful portraits found in life-of-Jesus theology, and that is precisely the* Χριστὸς κατὰ σάρκα *[Christ according to the flesh]. But the* Χριστὸς κατὰ σάρκα *is no concern of ours. How things looked in the heart of Jesus I do not know and do not want to know.*[256]

Was 1926 a "Year on the Edge of Time?"[257] No event that took place in this year was to have any extraordinary symbolic importance. A threshold year, one in which one might have been able to illustrate laws that shape far-reaching historical processes—that 1926 was certainly not. But must one view that one limited period of twelve months to destroy the widespread conviction that human beings can learn anything from history? May one not attempt to view 1926 as if it were happening now, just as one might for any other period of time?[258] At any rate, between April and December of 1926, on the edge of civilization—that is, living and working mostly in his hut above Todtnauberg—Martin Heidegger wrote his early, unfinished major work, *Being and Time.* One of the intentions that Heidegger pursued with his fundamental ontology consisted in overcoming the subject-object paradigm that ruled the history of modern philosophy, a *tour de force* he undertook by means of working out the question of being as a question of the meaning of being. Be that as it may, the same year saw the issuance of Bultmann's Jesus-book by the Jewish publisher Wolf Wertheim's German Library Publishing Company. The volume opened a series with the title, "The Immortals: The Spiritual Heroes of Humanity in their Life and Work."[259] In his little book, Bultmann endeavored in his own way to make possible an encounter with history—in this case, with the proclamation of Jesus—that would no longer prejudge the issue according to subject-object thinking, but that instead would embody a hermeneutic of contemporaneity.[260]

Contradictory claims have been made about how Bultmann's Jesus-book came to be, and these have dragged corresponding scholarly controversies behind them. In his old age, Bultmann recalled to Otto Merk that he had written the text in a week's time, although he did not immediately

256. RB, "Zur Frage," *GuV*, vol. 1, 101.
257. Cf. H. U. Gumbrecht, *1926. Ein Jahr am Rand der Zeit*, 445–80.
258. Cf. H. U. Gumbrecht, *1926. Ein Jahr am Rand der Zeit*, 466–70.
259. In this series, volumes on Buddha, Confucius, Friedrich Nietzsche, Giordano Bruno, and Zarathustra followed Bultmann's Jesus-book.
260. Cf. RB, *Jesus*, n.d. [1926]. In what follows, I also use the UTB 1272 edition (1988).

incorporate the extensive biblical references.[261] In June of 1972, in a letter to Hans Hübner, Bultmann described as utterly false the opinion that he wrote the Jesus-book under the influence of the philosophy of Martin Heidegger.

> I wrote it before I knew anything of Heidegger or was aware of his philosophical thoughts. I read aloud the manuscript and the Introduction to Heidegger, and that is how our exchange began. The only thing that comes from him is the term *Wirkungszusammenhang* ["living complex of events"] set in brackets in the Introduction, which he recommended that I insert.[262]

Bultmann explicitly confirmed this statement when Günther Bornkamm approached him on the topic during his last visit in the spring of 1976.[263]

These reports from Bultmann's old age do not at all agree with the relevant contemporary sources. Bultmann first took up the specific topic of the Jesus-book in the summer semester of 1922 with his lectures on "The Life of Jesus" and in his seminar, "Problems in Research on the Life of Jesus."[264] However, there is no evidence for his having begun to compose the Jesus-book directly in connection with these two courses. Heidegger came to Marburg in the fall of 1923 and soon made Bultmann's acquaintance. In the winter semester of 1923–24, Heidegger took part in Bultmann's seminar on "The Ethics of Paul," and in the following months and years, the philosopher and the theologian maintained close contact with each other. The first concrete reference to Bultmann's work on the Jesus-book is contained in a letter written by Karl Barth, with whom Bultmann had spent the night after his lecture in Göttingen on February 6, 1925. "He is writing at a little 'Life of Jesus,' from which I don't actually expect anything of any value, based on what little he's told me about it."[265] Under the terms of the contract, Bultmann was to deliver the manuscript of the Jesus-book in April 1925 and therefore felt considerable time pressure while writing the book. This he let Friedrich Gogarten know at the beginning of March, 1925: "Since I didn't get to it during the semester, I am now under stress, writing nearly from morning to evening, and have substantially completed the third part."[266]

261. Cf. Hammann, private collection, O. Merk to K. Hammann, 2./10. 1. 2006; on what follows, cf. for additional evidence K. Hammann, "Die Entstehung."

262. RB to H. Hübner, 5. 6. 1972, cited by H. Hübner, "Bultmanns," 286.

263. Cf. G. Bornkamm, "*In memoriam*," 239.

264. Cf. B. Jaspert, *Sachgemässe Exegese*, 21–23, 210.

265. K. Barth to E. Thurneysen, 15. 2. 1925, in E. Thurneysen, *Barth-Thurneysen Briefwechsel*, vol. 2, 307.

266. RB to F. Gogarten, 10. 3. 1925, in H. G. Göckeritz, *Bultmann-Gogarten Briefwechsel*, 72.

Although Bultmann was still not finished with the manuscript at the beginning of April 1925,[267] he succeeded in bringing the work to a close by the end of the month and in submitting the manuscript to the press on time.[268] In other words, Bultmann began writing his Jesus-book in the winter semester of 1924–25, but produced most of the manuscript during February and April of 1925.[269] Contrary to his much later recollection,[270] he must have written the book at a time when he was already engaged in intense discussions with Heidegger.[271]

Given this context, Bultmann's comment that Heidegger had advised him (merely) to insert the term *Wirkungszusammenhang* ["living complex of events"] into the Introduction might preserve accurately his recollection of the significance of Wilhelm Dilthey's philosophy of history and Søren Kierkegaard's existential dialectic for both the conversation with Heidegger in the years 1923 through 1926 and the hermeneutical conception of the Jesus-book.[272] The statement of the aged Bultmann contains a further *particula veri*, inasmuch as the Jesus-book evinces no specific borrowing from Heidegger's distinctive set of concepts.[273] This bit of verbal circumstantial

267. Cf. RB to F. Gogarten, 9. 4. 1925, in H. G. Göckeritz, *Bultmann-Gogarten Briefwechsel*, 77.

268. Cf. RB to F. Gogarten, 6. 5. 1925, in H. G. Göckeritz, *Bultmann-Gogarten Briefwechsel*, 79; UB Tübingen, RB est., RB to H. Roth, 16. 6. 1925, Mn 2-2349.

269. Cf. W. Schmithals, "Jesus," 394f.

270. Cf. Hammann, private collection, O. Merk to K. Hammann, 2./10. 1. 2006; RB to H. Hübner, 5. 6. 1972, cited by H. Hübner, "Bultmanns," 286; Cf. G. Bornkamm, "*In memoriam*," 239.

271. It is not necessary to explain away the memory lapse of Bultmann's old age by the hypothesis that he wrote an original version of the Jesus-book before the autumn of 1923 and worked this over during the course of time (such as H. Hübner, "Bultmanns," 278f, taken over uncritically by C. Bartels, *Kierkegaard*, 254–56n771). Practically everything speaks against this hypothesis. There is not a single piece of contemporary evidence for the Jesus-book having been composed before 1925 (or even before WS 1923–24). Looking back in 1928 on his first meeting with Bultmann in the autumn of 1923, Heidegger has nothing to say about the Jesus-book (cf. M. Heidegger to RB, 2. 4. 1928, in A. Grossmann and C. Landmesser, *Bultmann-Heidegger Briefwechsel*, 55f). Bultmann does not mention the Jesus-book in his correspondence with H. von Soden from 1920–24. This has weight inasmuch as Bultmann otherwise told his friend about everything he was working on and his plans for publishing. Finally, the wording of the sources from the time (cf. above, nn. 265–68) makes clear that Bultmann was not *working over* a text that was already in front of him in 1925, but that he was *writing* the Jesus-book for the first time; for more details, cf. K. Hammann, "Die Entstehung," 192–99.

272. Cf. also W. Schmithals, "Jesus," 400–404; H. Hübner, "Bultmanns." 288–300; C. Bartels, *Kierkegaard*, 269–313.

273. Cf. also (in my view, somewhat too apodictically) W. Schmithals, "Jesus," 393; reminiscences of Heidegger's conceptuality are not completely lacking in the Jesus-book, as is shown by the statement cited in n. 295 below.

evidence supports Bultmann's comment—contained in different variants—that before he knew of Heidegger's analysis of *Dasein* [human existence] in *Being and Time*, he had derived his insight into the historicity of human existence from Wilhelm Herrmann—though to be sure only the first indications of the concept had been developed by Herrmann.[274] Therefore it is clear that Bultmann wrote his Jesus-book during a period when he was examining with Heidegger the issue that had long perplexed him. He had, of course, been aware of the historicity and temporality of human existence, but he had not yet been introduced to this new and fuller elaboration of the ontology of human existence.[275]

This is also indicated by the lecture on "The Problem of a Theological Exegesis of the New Testament," which Bultmann presented in Göttingen on February 6, 1925, at a time when he was otherwise occupied with putting his Jesus-book down on paper. In that lecture, he promoted the view that the critical interpretation of the New Testament must fully and meaningfully deal with the way human beings interpret themselves. This self-interpretation can capture the human being as a historical individual only if it recognizes itself as interpretation of history.[276] From the outset, *philosophical* exegesis questions history with regard to the possibilities of human existence. This it does presupposing "that the human being as such can pose the question of existence and has the possibility of acting freely, by virtue of which it acquires its existence." In contrast to this, *theological* exegesis must assert the claim of the New Testament that "the human being does not, in fact, have his existence at his own disposal, since he is unable to pose the question of existence and lacks the possibility of acting freely."[277]

This train of thought, not yet brought to a conclusion in the Göttingen lecture,[278] reaches its provisional goal in the Introduction of the Jesus-book. Here Bultmann develops the basic outlines of the hermeneutical program

274. Cf. with evidence W. Schmithals, "Jesus," 400–402; see also above, 126, n. 204.

275. It was only after he had finished the manuscript of the Jesus-book that Bultmann heard Heidegger's lecture, "A History of the Concept of Time," in SS 1925. In any case, *Being and Time* appeared after Bultmann's Jesus-book. Bultmann had, however, heard Heidegger's lecture, "The Concept of Time," on 25. 7. 1924; see below, 206f. For the particulars, see also K. Hammann, "Die Entstehung," 207–11.

276. Cf. RB, "Das Problem einer theologischen Exegese," *Neues Testament und christliche Existenz*, 34; see also above, 146.

277. RB, "Das Problem einer theologischen Exegese," *Neues Testament und christliche Existenz*, 32.

278. Bultmann himself regarded his Göttingen lecture as "always quite open to question," that is, what he had said in it marked "a stage of the discussion." (RB to K. Barth, 19. 7. 1925, in B. Jaspert, *Barth-Bultmann Briefwechsel*, 49)

that was to enter into the history of theology in the twentieth century under the term "existentialist interpretation of the New Testament." Taking up ideas of Wilhelm Dilthey,[279] Bultmann first clarifies the difference between how the human being perceives his relationship to history and how he perceives his relation to nature. While by observation the individual knows nature as something present-at-hand outside himself,[280] in turning to history, he cannot simply view it as something that is similarly present-at-hand, for his very being is involved in history, in its "living complex of events." For this reason, whenever the individual says anything substantive about history, in a way he also says something about himself. Whoever would now grasp the essence of a historical phenomenon, therefore, can do so only in continual dialogue, in an actual encounter with history. In this way, the one who writes history must place his own subjectivity utterly in question, must be prepared to question history radically, and to hear its answer as authoritative.

Only in such a dialogue with history does one's own being disclose itself to oneself, and this consists in making "the possibilities of one's existence" transparent to the human being.[281] An understanding of Jesus' world of ideas can therefore be nothing else "than the interpretation of one's own existence in the midst of change, uncertainty, and the decisions of life as we find it; [it can be seen only] as the expression of a possibility for comprehending this existence; as the attempt to become clear about the possibilities and necessities of one's own existence."[282] Since Bultmann is therefore concerned to "avoid what is beyond history and to find a place within history,"[283] his presentation cannot orient itself to the life of Jesus or to his personality. Clearly distancing himself from the title of the series in which the Jesus-book appears (The Spiritual Heroes of Humanity), Bultmann means to exclude beforehand any echo of valorizing descriptions of Jesus as a great man, a religious genius, or a hero. For an encounter with Jesus that allows itself to be guided by the question of human existence, only what Jesus intended can be relevant. Since Jesus did what he did through the word, what he intended can ultimately be comprehended only through an intuitive internalization of his teaching. And the teaching of Jesus is not to be misunderstood as a system of universally valid doctrines; rather, what is needed is to hear the proclamation of Jesus as a question, just as we must in order to apprehend our own existence.

279. Cf. H. Hübner, "Bultmanns," 288–90; C. Bartels, *Kierkegaard,* 271–82.
280. RB, *Jesus* (1988), 7, still (in 1926!) presupposes the world picture of classical physics.
281. RB, *Jesus* (1988), 9.
282. RB, *Jesus* (1988), 12.
283. RB, *Jesus* (1988), 10.

While we know but little about the life and personality of Jesus, what we do know of his proclamation is sufficient to give us a picture of him that hangs together. In saying this, Bultmann presupposes that historical-critical research has shown that the proclamation of Jesus can be ascertained "with a high degree of probability" from the oldest layer of tradition of the synoptic gospels. Were Jesus not shown to be the bearer of the thoughts handed down in that oldest layer, as the tradition indicates he was, this would still not change anything in presenting the proclamation of Jesus. And so, each reader is at liberty to put "Jesus" in quotation marks and to allow this to serve "merely as shorthand for the historical phenomenon" that forms the object of this Jesus-book.[284] It was in this regard that Bultmann explained in September of 1928 to Pastor Hans Roth of Ahlhorn that he had not presented a "Jesus Christ" according to the synoptics or the Gospel of John. "I have given a description of a 'historical Jesus,' not, to be sure (at least not deliberately), in the sense of historicism, which takes Jesus to be a phenomenon of the past, but rather as he speaks to the historical understanding that intends to let itself be addressed by history, and that therefore does not locate itself outside of history 'by way of observing.'"[285]

The plan of the Jesus-book derives from the way Adolf Harnack presents Jesus' proclamation in his *What Is Christianity?*. Bultmann deviates from Harnack only in the order of the topics: the coming of the reign of God, the will of God, and Jesus' proclamation of God.[286] These topics form three concentric circles. "In each circle, what is dealt with is ultimately the same thing and the whole."[287] The method by which Bultmann lays out the message of Jesus likewise corresponds to that chosen by Harnack in *What Is Christianity?* and is the procedure typical of liberal presentations of Jesus in general. Bultmann lifts the proclamation from its Jewish context and works out its contours by means of comparison with the Jewish environment. To be sure, before pacing along the three concentric circles, he stakes out the "contemporary framework of Jesus' appearance" with a few remarks. Here he gives a picture of the Jewish religion at the turn of the age by means of a few central concepts such as law and obedience, promise and hope; then he touches briefly on the diverse messianic movements that were stirring among the Jewish people during the period of Roman rule, and concludes

284. RB, *Jesus* (1988), 14.

285. UB Tübingen, RB est., RB to H. Roth, 25. 9. 1928, Mn 2-2349.

286. In A. von Harnack, *Wesen*, 40, the message of the kingdom of God follows Jesus' understanding of God, and then comes the ethic of Jesus. F. Wittekind treats the relation of Bultmann's Jesus-book to Harnack's presentation of Jesus in "Gott," 587–600.

287. RB, *Jesus* (1988), 14.

by sketching the character and outward course of the messianic movements instigated by John the baptizer and Jesus. Bultmann winnows a great deal of the material found in traditional presentations of the "life of Jesus" down to the relatively secure data regarding Jesus' person and appearance. The brief compass of this introduction to the period makes conspicuous the consequences of what Bultmann drew from the breakdown of liberal research on the life of Jesus.[288]

In the outer circle, Bultmann deals with eschatology, Jesus' message of the coming reign of God. Since eschatological salvation comes with God's reign, the individual is "placed before the great either-or: whether or not he means to decide for the reign of God and then to sacrifice everything for it."[289] Jesus does not conceive the reign of God after the manner of a condition. Neither is it the highest good, as ethics understands this, nor is it a state of affairs that actualizes itself in the history of humanity. Jesus does not relate the reign of God to a situation of the end-time glory on which contemporaneous Jewish hopes are focused, either. Likewise, universalist or individualist images are foreign to him, since for Jesus such humanistic concepts would have raised a claim on God—an impossible notion for Jesus. The utter transcendence and miraculousness of the reign of God discloses itself to the person who, faced with its proclamation, acknowledges that it consists in the future acting of God and is therefore also the power that completely determines the present. Since it constitutes "what is coming towards the person," the reign of God confronts him with the necessity of decision. It shows him that "his very being" consists precisely in this deciding.[290] For the human being this means (negatively) understanding the present situation of one's life as alien territory, and (positively) fashioning this same present in accord with the will of God.[291]

In the middle circle Bultmann treats Jesus' proclamation of the will of God. He emphasizes Jesus' activity as a Jewish rabbi for whom the authority of the law is self-evident. In accordance with the Jewish tradition, Jesus' ethic is oriented towards obedience in the face of God's demand. In this it differs fundamentally "from the Greek ideal of humanity and from a modern rational ethics of autonomy or a contemporary ethics of value." As opposed to the Jewish ethical system, which refers obedience to a formal authority,

288. Cf. E. Lohmeyer, rev. of RB, *Jesus*, n.d. [1926], 434.

289. RB, *Jesus* (1988), 25; cf. also 28; as well J. Hess, "Jesus," 413f.

290. RB, *Jesus* (1988), 39.

291. Cf. RB, *Jesus* (1988), 41. On the eschatology in Bultmann's Jesus-book, cf. also F. Wittekind, "Eschatologie," 78–84.

Jesus has "radically thought through the idea of obedience."[292] He sees the whole person as confronting decision, for it is not *something* that is claimed of the human being, but rather *he himself* is claimed in his *being*, and he exists in obedience, inasmuch as "all he is is in what he does."[293] For this reason, neither does Jesus appeal to the external authority of the law. Rather, he believes that the human being is capable of recognizing what the will of God is. Over and above ethical theories that are oriented to either the individual or the community, and that elevate the individual to become the standard for what is to be done, Jesus sees "the human being and his existence . . . as absolutely insecure in facing what encounters him." Thus, since a human being "stands, as it were in empty space," he must take seriously the fact that the claim of the good is actually that of the transcendent God.[294]

Faced with the will of God, the individual must actualize this obedience now, taking personal responsibility for what he does and what he allows to be done. In so doing, he chooses in this fundamental existential situation "not something for himself; rather it is himself that he decides with each choice, in a fundamental way choosing his own possibility."[295] This is exemplified in the double command of love. For Jesus, love is neither a virtue nor an ethical principle. Rather, love presents the claim to obedience and at the same time shows how obedience can and should acquire its form in the concrete encounter with other people. This is just what the double command of love also makes clear with its dialectical specification of the relation between love of God and love of neighbor. Love is understood by Jesus as "a specific stance of the will."[296] In this context his saying, "You are to be perfect, as your heavenly Father is perfect" (Matt 5:48), epitomizes the situation of a defining decision into which the human being is thrust *coram Deo* [in the presence of God]. This situation lays bare the future of the reign of God, in which the human being gains "his existence in the now." In encountering a genuine decision between the possibilities opened up for him by God, the human being becomes "either sinner or righteous."[297]

However, whether a genuine future can really be in store for human beings—since the future is not under one's control—is something that the interpretation of Jesus' thought about God must clarify. In the inner circle Bultmann therefore takes up the paradoxical Jewish image of God as be-

292. RB, *Jesus* (1988), 53.
293. RB, *Jesus* (1988), 56.
294. RB, *Jesus* (1988), 61.
295. RB, *Jesus* (1988), 63.
296. RB, *Jesus* (1988), 82. On Bultmann's reference to S. Kierkegaard's interpretation of the double command of love (*Jesus* [1988], 81), cf. C. Bartels, *Kierkegaard*, 302–6.
297. RB, *Jesus* (1988), 91.

ing distant and near at hand in order to address the question of the extent to which the God of the future is as such also the God of the present. For Jesus speaks of God only by speaking of God's dealings with human beings. This Jesus does—and here Bultmann recalls once more the outer and middle circle—by showing the individual "that he stands at the final hour, in decision, that he is claimed in his willing by God."[298] It is characteristic of Jesus' proclamation that it stresses the utter and indissoluble unity between the future and the present of God. For particular features of the message of Jesus—such as faith in providence and theodicy, faith in miracles and in prayer—also provide ample expression of the paradox of faith in the future and present, God as distant and near at hand.

The meaning of the paradox of the God who is distant and yet at the same time near at hand can especially be grasped in Jesus' understanding of sin and forgiveness. Jesus understands sin against the backdrop of God directing his claim to the whole person, and therefore the individual stands "before God as a sinner, which is to say that his sin has not a relative, but an absolute character."[299] Forgiveness is conceived just as radically as sin. Precisely in accepting forgiveness, the human being submits to the judgment of God, yet forgiveness means that God grants to the individual the possibility of becoming a new person. "God is the God of the present for the sinner, precisely through casting him away from God, and he is at the same time the God of the future, because he maintains his claim on the sinner and for new obedience opens a new future for him in his forgiveness."[300] In this, Jesus is not pointing to publicly perceptible events that might make one certain of forgiveness. Rather, he *proclaims* forgiveness, and it occurs in his word to the extent that this grips the hearer. Jesus does not seek to prove the truth of this word by way of one sort of guarantee or another; Jesus is, however, the bearer of this word sent by God. Because he brings forgiveness only in the word, the hearer faces the decision of whether to take Jesus' word as truth, whether to believe in Jesus as sent by God. Therefore, the situation is as Jesus' word has it: "*Blessed is the person who takes no offense at me*" (Matt 11:6).[301]

Bultmann's Jesus-book called forth a critical response from academic theology.[302] Karl Barth said to Edmund Haake, the pastor at Varel, that

298. RB, *Jesus* (1988), 105.
299. RB, *Jesus* (1988), 135.
300. RB, *Jesus* (1988), 143.
301. RB, *Jesus* (1988), 148.
302. The major share of the 41 discussions of the book that Bultmann preserved (cf. UB Tübingen, RB est., Mn 2-3120) did, in fact, occur in ecclesial and congregational publications.

he did not understand what Bultmann was trying to show with his presentation.[303] Barth complained, "In the book there is still too much of a quest for the historical Jesus," and offered the subtly ironic suggestion that Bultmann's Jesus "was evidently already a dialectical theologian."[304] Ernst Lohmeyer judged that in Bultmann's interpretation of the proclamation of Jesus, "what finds expression is nothing other . . . than the apologia for his own religious attitude." The strength of this Jesus-book, which as if with a primitive religiosity discloses the meaning of faith in the personal encounter with history, proves to be a weakness from the critical point of view. The book is a document of religious apologetics; however, it neither intends nor is able to offer findings of a historical kind.[305] In similar fashion, though on the basis of different premises, the liberal Frankfurt theologian Erich Foerster expressed doubt that Bultmann had based the message of Jesus on the simplest possible reconstruction of the oldest layer of tradition in the synoptic gospels. Rather, the book "was written under the powerful influence of the so-called Barthian theology," or better, under the philosophical-theological impulse that has come from the more modern philosophies of culture and life, such as those of Kierkegaard, Tolstoy, Nietzsche, and others. On the whole, it is the work not of a New Testament scholar, but of a systematic theologian.[306] In view of the way the Jesus-book had been received, Bultmann summarized the situation as follows: "That the systematic theologian has violated the New Testament scholar is an accusation that is constantly repeated."[307]

Bultmann responded to this accusation by seeking to explain to Barth as well as Foerster the nature of the theological problem that he had posed in the Jesus-book. In his view the central problem of New Testament theology was "how we are to understand (and I do not mean 'causally account for!') the fact that out of the proclaimer Jesus there comes to be the proclaimed Jesus Christ."[308] Thus, with his Jesus-book, Bultmann meant to make a contribution to *grasping* in precise fashion how the point of the message of

303. Cf. RB to K. Barth, 10. 12. 1926, in B. Jaspert, *Barth-Bultmann Briefwechsel,* 64.

304. K. Barth's communication to Bultmann, via H. Roth to RB, 12. 9. 1928, in UB Tübingen, RB est., Mn 2-1650.

305. E. Lohmeyer, rev. of RB, *Jesus,* n.d. [1926], 437, also 439; as well as D. Lührmann, "Ernst Lohmeyers," 73–79.

306. E. Forester, "Rudolf Bultmanns Jesusbuch," 29.

307. RB to E. Foerster, n.d. [1928], in B. Jaspert, *Werk und Wirkung,* 71.

308. RB to K. Barth, 10. 12. 1926, in B. Jaspert, *Barth-Bultmann Briefwechsel,* 65; RB to E. Foerster, in B. Jaspert, *Werk und Wirkung,* 74f. Cf. on what follows, W. Schmithals, "Jesus," 404–10, 417f (with important suggestions on the difference between the position represented by Bultmann in 1925–26 and his view of things in the Wartburg lecture of 1920, "Ethical and Mystical Religion in Earliest Christianity").

Jesus was related to that of the earliest Christian preaching of Jesus Christ. But he had purposefully not posed this problem explicitly in the Jesus-book, in order to allow it to come out in all its urgency. Because of this, many readers had come away with the false impression that Jesus' proclamation already contained the gospel in the sense of Christian preaching. This was certainly not the case, however, as Bultmann explained with reference to the history-of-religions school. It is the earliest Christian proclamation that presents the gospel in the proper sense for the first time,[309] and therefore the basic problem of New Testament theology can be clearly grasped only if one looks first at the proclamation of the historical Jesus. Against Barth and Foerster Bultmann tentatively insisted that in the context of the difference between law and gospel, his Jesus-book sought to bring "the reader, as it were, into the situation before the death and resurrection of Jesus . . . as into the situation of law and promise."[310]

If the Jesus-book was intended primarily to announce the theological problem thus sketched out, it already contained an implicit indication of the line of thought that could have led from the proclamation of Jesus to the Christ-kerygma of the earliest community. At the end of the book, Bultmann had pointed to the authority that accrued to Jesus as the bearer of the word of forgiveness, a claim to authority he saw epitomized in Jesus' self-assertion in Matt 11:6.[311] A little later, Bultmann developed the concept of "implicit christology" for the point at issue. He presented this view again in 1929, in connection with Matt 11:6 and Luke 12:8: Jesus' "call to decision in the presence of his person *implies a christology*,"[312] which as the earliest community's confession of Jesus Christ can be nothing other than the explication of obedience in the face of Jesus' word and, thereby, in the face of the decision for Jesus. To be sure, this connection made at the conclusion of the Jesus-book was more implicit than explicit, and accordingly the criticism that Bultmann had ignored the question of the person of Jesus especially caught fire among the first reviewers. In this context, Ernst Lohmeyer contributed the lapidary quip that Bultmann had written "a book on Jesus without Jesus."[313] Emmanuel Hirsch was particularly emphatic in posing the question during his discussion with Bultmann on the meaning of the person of Jesus for christology.

309. Cf. RB to E. Foerster, in B. Jaspert, *Werk und Wirkung*, 75.

310. RB to E. Foerster, in B. Jaspert, *Werk und Wirkung*; cf. RB to K. Barth, 10. 12. 1926, in B. Jaspert, *Werk und Wirkung*, 66.

311. Cf. RB, *Jesus* (1988), 148.

312. RB, "Bedeutung," *GuV*, vol. 1, 204.

313. E. Lohmeyer, rev. of RB, *Jesus*, n.d. [1926], 433.

In his review of Bultmann's Jesus-book, Hirsch dispenses with a discussion of the methodological premises that might have led to Bultmann's critical radicalism and historical skepticism.[314] He acknowledges Bultmann for having understood the teaching of Jesus as a message in the present that speaks to a person in his situation. "Bultmann does the most important thing that a theologian can do: For his readers he makes their own relation to God into a question of decision."[315] Nevertheless, in the way he defines the relation of sin and grace in Jesus' message, he has not made it sufficiently clear that the will of God demands obedience and grants forgiveness *at the same time*, that ultimately God's word of grace effects the decision demanded by Jesus. Indeed, the inner unity of Jesus' proclamation of sin and forgiveness is grounded in Jesus' God-consciousness. This Bultmann fails to recognize, as his exposition of Jesus as the bearer of the word shows. If the word is to lead to a personal relationship with God, everything depends on "its not having fallen as a printed book from heaven, but rather on its being spoken by a living person." It is as bearer of the word that Jesus distinguishes himself from any old dockworker who bears a sack of whatever from A to B. It is only from Jesus' heart that faith discloses itself, that his call to decision issues forth to us from God.[316]

Hirsch's review put Bultmann in an uncomfortable situation: "Despite its being full of critical complaints, it is most charmingly done, so that my discussion of his Jesus-book has put me in a fatal situation."[317] This referred to Hirsch's book, *Jesus Christus der Herr* [*Jesus Christ the Lord*], which Bultmann was scheduled to review in *Zwischen den Zeiten*.[318] Bultmann made the decision not to review the work of his opposing colleague from Göttingen on its own grounds, but rather, to take Hirsch's review of his Jesus-book as the point of departure for a discussion of the starting-point and the basis of christology. By doing this, Bultmann specifically brought into the discussion his teacher, Wilhelm Herrmann, since Hirsch seemed to Bultmann to carry on the liberal tradition that Herrmann represented.[319] More precisely, Bultmann believed that pietism and rationalism had become siblings in Hirsch's christology.[320]

314. Cf. E. Hirsch, "Bultmanns Jesus," 309.
315. E. Hirsch, "Bultmanns Jesus," 311.
316. E. Hirsch, "Bultmanns Jesus," 312; cf. U. Barth, *Christologie*, 76–78.
317. UB Tübingen, RB est., RB to H. von Soden, 24. 8. 1926, Mn 2-2385; cf. similarly GStA PK Berlin, RB to E. Lohmeyer, 23. 8. 1926, no. 5/260.
318. Cf. E. Hirsch, *Jesus Christus der Herr*, vol. 1.
319. Cf. RB, "Zur Frage," *GuV*, vol. 1, 101.
320. Cf RB, "Zur Frage," *GuV*, vol. 1, 95, 98.

Bultmann grants to his adversary that he intends to speak theologically of Jesus Christ, but argues that in developing christology out of the person Jesus and his picture of God he has fallen back into the now badly discredited life-of-Jesus theology.[321] The Jesus that Hirsch draws by means of psychological analysis is at best the Χριστὸς κατὰ σάρκα [Christ from a human point of view] of 2 Cor 5:16 (NRSV). This historical Jesus cannot, as a matter of principle, confront the believer in a personal way. In the picture of the soul of the *past* Jesus that Hirsch has endowed with idealistic features, "the Jesus Christ who has the power *to forgive sins* is not to be seen."[322] The idea that inner experience can function to ground faith is one that Bultmann rejects as theologically illegitimate.[323] Seeing as analogous the I-thou relation between people and a relation of trust in Jesus is excluded by the fact that, "for us, as a 'thou' in the sense of an actual contemporary, [Jesus] has passed away."[324] Instead of attempting to ground faith (with Hirsch) on the inner experience of the one who believes, and on Jesus as an individual, or (with Herrmann) on the "inner life" of Jesus, one must take Rom 10:17 seriously: "Faith is referred to the word and to the proclamation it authorizes. Therefore, no other legitimation is to be demanded for the word and no basis is to be created for it other than what it is itself."[325]

321. Cf. RB, "Zur Frage," *GuV*, vol. 1, 98.
322. RB, "Zur Frage," *GuV*, vol. 1, 97.
323. Cf. RB, "Zur Frage," *GuV*, vol. 1, 93f, 105f.
324. RB, "Zur Frage," *GuV*, vol. 1, 106.
325. RB, "Zur Frage," *GuV*, vol. 1, 107. U. Barth, *Christologie*, 150, thinks that 2 Cor 5:16 has taken on "the role of a theological key argument" for "opposing the dogmatic legitimacy of a christology [such as that of Hirsch's] grounded in historical observation." Bultmann did, indeed, cite 2 Cor 5:16 in order thereby to identify Hirsch's formulation as inadequate. To be sure, in his dispute with Hirsch, he did not touch on any exegetical details (as also U. Barth, *Christologie*, 149). Hirsch's claim that in 2 Cor 5:16 the prepositional phrase κατὰ σάρκα is to be construed as referring not to Χριστόν, but rather to ἐγνώκαμεν, was also unable to shake Bultmann's historical and theological argument against a christology fixed on the earthly Jesus. Cf. E. Hirsch, "Randglosse," 58–60; E. Hirsch, "Antwort," 645f, as well as U. Barth, *Christologie,* 156; G. Lüdemann, "Emanuel Hirsch," 24f. Cf. RB, "Bedeutung," *GuV*, vol. 1, 206f; RB, *Theologie*, 239. What Bultmann in fact brought to bear against Hirsch as a "key argument" is that the synoptic gospels in no way give to be understood "what it looked like in Jesus' heart" (see n. 256). The intentional referent of faith must be conceived as the word that creates it. For this reason, faith does not subject itself to, as it were, a supernatural authority, but rather orients itself "to something that *encounters* me, that is, that does not lie within the possibilities for life of which I can dispose" (RB, "Zur Frage," 111). On the controversy between Bultmann and Hirsch cf. finally C. Bartels, *Kierkegaard*, 353–89. E. Hirsch swore the theological oath of revelation on his christology for the last time in 1939, when he not only pretended to know "what it looked like in Jesus' heart," but also believed he was able to set out the "proof" for how it will have been with regard to Jesus' "race": ". . . [A]ccording to every rule of scholarly probability, Jesus was of non-Jewish blood" (E. Hirsch, *Wesen*, 161; cf. 158–65, "Appendix to Lecture Three. The Descent of Jesus").

Bultmann took hold of the theological problem that he had kept constantly in view in the writing of the Jesus-book and of which he had also sent a reminder to Erich Foerster, Emmanuel Hirsch, and Ernst Lohmeyer, each in his own way in 1929, in his essay on "The Significance of the Historical Jesus for the Theology of Paul," and he took it up again in his 1936 study, "Paul and Jesus."[326] The Jesus-book remained authoritative for his further theological work, for he was convinced that despite the complex problematic of the transmission of materials, he had in large measure adequately reconstructed the proclamation of Jesus in 1926.[327] The chapter dealing with Jesus in his small book on early Christianity (1948), and its parallel in the *Theologie des Neuen Testaments* of 1948–53, also offered, with some abridgments and slight modifications, substantially the same picture as that of the presentation of 1926. And as ambivalent as the reception of the Jesus-book remained among academic theologians,[328] Bultmann's sudden success, above all among the younger generation of academics, was just as sweeping.[329] Obviously, Bultmann encountered widespread resistance from anti-bourgeois voices in the 1920s, when he declared psychologizing or historicizing ways of viewing the proclamation of Jesus obsolete, and in general rigorously distanced himself from any interest in the "personality" of Jesus. The way Bultmann spoke of the insecurity of human existence and, using an astonishingly small vocabulary, lucidly described the obedience of faith as the way of becoming oneself that is made possible for human existence solely by God, commended his interpretation of the message of Jesus to many contemporaries.[330] As evidenced by the sixty-two thousand copies of

326. Cf. RB, "Bedeutung"; RB, "Paulus und Jesus," 68–90.

327. Cf. W. Schmithals, "Jesus verkündigt das Evangelium," 406, over against E. Käsemann, "Das Problem," *Exegetische*, vol. 1, 188. The surprising state of affairs that, in his Jesus-book, Bultmann made allowance for several sayings as belonging to Jesus on which he had still made an adverse judgment in the *Geschichte der synoptischen Tradition*, J. Schniewind regarded as quite justified: "The Jesus-tradition rather constitutes a distinctive complex of sayings that, in its total character, is presupposed in what the community proclaims. This fact is completely independent of being able to demonstrate the 'genuineness' of any individual saying or story" ("Zur Synoptiker-Exegese," 173). Bultmann read Schniewind's report on research "with the most lively interest and in what is essential with joyful agreement" (RB to J. Schniewind, 13. 3. 1930, in ULB Sachsen-Anhalt in Halle/Saale, J.Schniewind est., 12).

328. Cf. as examples besides the critical reviews cited above, see K. Barth, *Die christliche Dogmatik*, vol. 1, 236; H. J. Iwand, *Theologiegeschichte*, 391–400.

329. Cf. as an example the euphoric opinion of the Danish student Aage Benjamin Kilch: ". . . [I]f there were immortality under the sun, then in my opinion your book would be worthy of it" (A. B. Kinch to RB, 9. 12. 1928, in UB Tübingen, RB est., Mn 2-1127). On the early history of the printing, cf. W. Schmithals, "Jesus verkündigt das Evangelium," 388–92.

330. Cf. also E. Schulz, "Die frühe," 25.

the German version printed between 1926 and 1988 and sold by 2008, in addition to ten translations,[331] his Jesus-book remained, as did hardly any other of this genre, lasting and available in a large number of printings on the twentieth-century book market.

7. Theology and Philosophy—Martin Heidegger

It is a terrible pity, how utterly disoriented Protestant theology is in its basics. Bultmann is the only one here from whom I can still learn—an Oldenburger, acute and cautious, he means at all costs to work out of the history-of-religions theology in which he grew up.[332]

It is splendid outside, no problems in the university, sleepy, as average as possible, no stimulation. The only real person: the theologian Bultmann, with whom I get together every week. Not a bit grumpy.[333]

In the opening weeks of the winter semester of 1923–24, recently appointed to an associate professorship yet with the rights of a full professor, the philosopher Martin Heidegger[334] went up to the *Villa Sibiria* to pay his initial call on Bultmann. Up to that moment, the student of the Freiburg phenomenologist Edmund Husserl knew nothing of the relations among the Marburg theological faculty. He knew of Bultmann only what one could find out about his research and teaching from a colleague from somewhere else,[335] but many further discussions were to follow from this first encounter between the theologian and the philosopher. Bultmann would soon report delightedly to Hans von Soden in his Christmas letter of 1923 that Heidegger was participating in his seminar: "He comes out of Catholicism, but is completely Protestant, which he proved recently in the debate on an essay of Hermelink's on Luther and the Middle Ages. He has not only a superb knowledge of scholasticism, but of Luther as well, and he rather

331. Bultmann's Jesus-book appeared in eight foreign language editions: Swedish (1928), Danish (1930), Japanese (1933), English (1934), Japanese again (1963), French (1968), Norwegian (1968), and Italian (1972).

332. M. Heidegger to J. Ebbinghaus, 4. 1. 1924, in JEA Wuppertal, J. Ebbinghaus est.; also cited in O. Pöggeler, "Heideggers Weg," 177.

333. M. Heidegger to K. Jaspers, 18. 6. 1924, in W. Biemel and H. Saner, *Heidegger-Jaspers Briefwechsel*, 49.

334. Cf. B. Martin, "Heidegger," 107–22.

335. Cf. (in retrospect), M. Heidegger to RB 2. 4. 1928, A. Grossmann and C. Landmesser, *Bultmann-Heidegger Briefwechsel*, 55f. The *Villa Sibiria* was the house—difficult to heat—on Hainweg 6 in which the Bultmann family lived from 1921–24.

embarrassed Hermelink—he had obviously grasped the issue more profoundly than had Hermelink. It was interesting to me that Heidegger—who is also otherwise familiar with modern theology and particularly an admirer of Herrmann—also knows Gogarten and Barth, and especially in the case of the former has an opinion similar to mine."[336]

In the small world of Marburg, Heidegger's arrival excited notice from the outset.[337] It was not that he intended to break with academic convention, but that he stage-managed himself and his thought in a way that many experienced as unusual. Outwardly, the son of a verger from the Alemannic-Baden Catholic Church certainly stood out from his distinguished, mostly Protestant professorial colleagues in Marburg. He was in the habit of wearing a suit designed by the Gossfeld artist Otto Ubbelohde. This garb that his students called the "existential suit" was a novel type of men's clothing adapted from a Hessian peasant's costume; the philosopher presented himself in the husbandman's Sunday best. In the winter, he might also—to the great consternation of his elegantly appointed colleague Nicolai Hartmann—come to his lectures in skiing apparel in order to give a report there on the skiing. When the University of Marburg observed its four-hundredth anniversary in 1927 (for indeed, it represented the first university founded by Protestants)[338] and the majority of the academic staff celebrated the commemorative worship service in the Reformed Church of the city and the university, Heidegger was seen going with a dark countenance and in an unaccustomed black suit to the Catholic Church that he otherwise never visited.[339]

But then, the philosopher did not place any particular value on regular exchange with the professors in other disciplines and faculties. Under Rudolf Otto's aegis, a "Society of the Sciences" had been established, a sort of Marburg Academy of the Sciences. From the beginning Bultmann regarded the project as a farce, but to avoid any unpleasantness he at first accepted election as a full member. But when he tried to secure Heidegger's membership in the new academic institution, he managed to get him elected only

336. UB Tübingen, RB est., RB to H. von Soden, 23. 12. 1923, Mn 2-2385; cf. RB to F. Gogarten, 22. 12. 1923, in H. G. Göckeritz, *Bultmann-Gogarten Briefwechsel*, 52f.

337. Cf. A. von Buggenhagen, *Philosophische*, 133–40; W. Weischedel, untitled article, 320f; H.-G. Gadamer, "Einzug," 109–13; H.-G. Gadamer, *Philosophische Lehrjahre*, 214–18; K. Löwith, *Mein Leben*, 29–32; R. Safranski, *Meister*, 154–66; B. Martin, "Heidegger," 112–15.

338. The true first Protestant university in the world was founded in 1526 in Liegnitz. However, it did not last long.

339. Cf. H. Mörchen, "Heidegger," 74.

as an associate member. The proceedings in the early meetings persuaded Bultmann to announce his resignation from the Society of the Sciences on March 25, 1927. Heidegger categorically rejected the idea that he and Bultmann should work on the kind of "rubbish" the Society considered to be "positive tasks for the future."[340]

Heidegger's forceful manner of teaching went down well with the students—and this, even though in the early semesters he began his lectures at seven in the morning. Soon, one hundred and fifty students were attending his lecture courses. Heidegger's extraordinary teaching success also resulted in a diminished audience for his colleague and rival, Nicolai Hartmann. Under the pressure of this development, Hartmann gladly accepted a call to Köln in 1925. Heidegger did not really lecture *on* something—whether a philosophical system, a book, or a problem. Basically, he did not conduct organized courses in the conventional style, since he was not intent on transmitting a set of ideas or mere knowledge to his hearers. He wanted to make them think. He communicated the passion of his thinking and questioning to his assembled audience in what might be called an unemotional style. Time and again he searched the entire tradition for the original meaning of a word or an expression, and examined in depth whatever this probing uncovered. It was a process that many found fascinating. Looking back, Ernst Fuchs observed that "it seemed as if a new Plato had come along."[341] As Gerhard Krüger described his first impressions in November 1923, Heidegger had "a real relationship to the subject-matter."

> [He] did not speak at all "objectively," with Hartmann's sort of smiling distance, but aggressively addressed his audience. He was very concerned to challenge their notions of the "accomplishments" of science, and particularly of natural science; in his view, one was meant to learn to see things themselves without theoretical distortion, as they appear or "show themselves" (φαίνεσθαι), and as they "address" (λόγος) one in *existential* intercommunication.[342]

In his first semester in Marburg, Heidegger was already taking part in Bultmann's seminar on the ethics of Paul, before which he presented papers on February 14th and 21st, 1923, addressing Luther's understanding

340. M. Heidegger to RB, 14. 3. 1927, A. Grossmann and C. Landmesser, *Bultmann-Heidegger Briefwechsel,* 20; cf. RB to M. Heidegger, 13. and 27. 3. 1927, A. Grossmann and C. Landmesser, *Bultmann-Heidegger Briefwechsel,* 5–18, 23.

341. E. Fuchs, "Aus der Marburger Zeit," *Wagnis,* 73.

342. G. Krüger to F. Gogarten, 14. 11. 1923, in H. G. Göckeritz, *Bultmann-Gogarten Briefwechsel,* 275f.

of sin. Appealing to Luther's early disputations of 1516–18, the Catholic philosopher presented the connection between sin (*peccatum*) and original righteousness (*iustitia originalis*) that Luther had worked out in critically disassociating his view from that of medieval scholasticism; his aim was to connect them with the late lectures on Genesis of 1535–45 in order to reflect on Luther's interpretation of the story of the fall in Gen 3:1–15. As a mode of fundamental opposition to faith, sin directs itself against God and his word, just as the sin of Adam and Eve is to be seen in their granting obedience to the word of the serpent, which is precisely not the word of God.[343] Human beings forfeit their original "in-God's-presence" existence (*esse coram Deo*) whenever they get into a *disputatio* over God's will. But God proves himself to be even more merciful after the fall, for he does not remain silent, but rather speaks. The being of God takes place as *verbum* [word]; the relation of the human being to God fulfills itself as *audire* [hearing].[344]

The scholarly comradeship of Bultmann and Heidegger mutated into a comradeship in arms when guests from elsewhere gave lectures in Marburg. At these "theological bloodbaths," as Hans-Georg Gadamer has called them,[345] the New Testament scholar and the philosopher always formed a common front so that should the situation arise they could drive the guest speakers into a corner, uncover the inconsistencies in their remarks, and emphasize the existential orientation of theology.[346] The sense of mission that Bultmann and Heidegger exhibited on such occasions often irritated the rest of the Marburg theology professors, who sometimes felt demoted to the status of second-class graduate assistants.[347] But even at the beginning of their relationship, Bultmann and Heidegger hardly saw it as the role of the "great Marburg union of theology and philosophy" (as Hans Jonas called it to mind in 1929[348]) to join the two in interdisciplinary conversation and thereby provide critical grounding for theology.[349] According to Gadamer,

343. Gen 3:5b: ". . . and you will be like God and know what is good and what evil."

344. Cf. the record of Heidegger's presentation produced by an unnamed seminar participant and H. Schlier in B. Jaspert, *Sachgemässe Exegese*, 28–33; as well as O. Pöggeler, *Neue Wege*, 467; A. Grossmann, "Reformatorische Impulse," *Heidegger-Lektüren*, 22–24.

345. Cf. H.-G.Gadamer, *Philosophische Lehrjahre*, 37.

346. RB to K. Barth, 24. 1. 1925, in B. Jaspert, *Barth-Bultmann Briefwechsel*, 40: "Heidegger gave it to him, [that is, E. Brunner] something terrible." Critical of this Marburg "interrogation": K. Barth to RB, 20. 6. 1931, in B. Jaspert, *Barth-Bultmann Briefwechsel*, 124–26.

347. Cf. M. Heidegger to E. Heidegger, 30. 6. 1925, in G. Heidegger, "Mein liebes Seelchen!" 141.

348. UB Tübingen, G. Krüger est., H. Jonas to G. Krüger, 23. 5. 1929.

349. Cf. E. Jüngel, "Gott entsprechendes Schweigen?" 37–42.

during the discussion of a lecture by Eduard Thurneysen, Heidegger called theology to its unique task, which he said consisted solely in seeking and in finding that word which is able to call to faith and to preserve it.[350]

Bultmann and Heidegger soon intensified their contacts with each other. After October of 1924, they met each Saturday afternoon to read the Gospel of John together.[351] Having attended a course of lectures by Nicolai Hartmann, Bultmann now went to two of Heidegger's lecture series, "Prolegomena to the History of the Concept of Time" in the summer semester of 1925[352] and "Logic" in the winter semester of 1925–26.[353] In August 1926 Bultmann spent the summer vacation in Todtnauberg with his family, during which time he and his wife read what was to him philosophically and theologically the highly instructive correspondence between Wilhelm Dilthey and Count Yorck.[354] Heidegger reworked his manuscript of *Being and Time* during that same summer and gave it the finishing touches before publication,[355] while at their meetings up in the hut he and Bultmann concerned themselves with Kierkegaard's *Philosophical Fragments*.[356] Bultmann had already made numerous efforts in 1924 and 1925 to involve Heidegger in what then was still a frank discussion within dialectical theology,[357] but just then no encounter between them took place, because at first neither had the time for it. And in the long run Barth was not really interested in discussions with Heidegger, since he thought that philosophy as such—and so not just Heidegger's—"had nothing to say to theology and in theology."[358] Bultmann, on the other hand, considered this position of Barth's unhelpful to the cause of theology. The disagreement between the two theologians that had remained latent since 1922,

350. Cf. H.-G. Gadamer, *Philosophische Lehrjahre*, 37.

351. Cf. RB to F. Gogarten 19. 10. 1924, in H. G. Göckeritz, *Bultmann-Gogarten Briefwechsel*, 62.

352. Cf. RB to F. Gogarten, 6. 5. 1925, in H. G. Göckeritz, *Bultmann-Gogarten Briefwechsel*, 81; M. Heidegger, *Prolegomena*.

353. Cf. RB to F. Gogarten, 21. 11. 1925, in H. G. Göckeritz, *Bultmann-Gogarten Briefwechsel*, 97; M. Heidegger, *Logik*.

354. Cf. UB Tübingen, RB est., RB to H. von Soden, 24. 8. 1926, Mn 2-2385; S. von der Schulenburg, *Briefwechsel zwischen Wilhelm Dilthey und dem Grafen Paul Yorck von Wartenburg 1877–1897*.

355. Cf. M. Heidegger to RB, 13. 10. 1926, A. Grossmann and C. Landmesser, *Bultmann-Heidegger Briefwechsel*, 4f, as well as T. Kisiel, *Genesis*, 484.

356. Cf. UB Tübingen, RB est., RB to H. von Soden, 24. 8. 1926, Mn 2-2385.

357. Cf. RB to K. Barth, 4. and 18. 7. 1924; 24. 1., 3. 2., and 19. 7. 1925, in B. Jaspert, *Barth-Bultmann Briefwechsel*, 35f, 36f, 45, 50; RB to F. Gogarten, in H. G. Göckeritz, *Bultmann-Gogarten Briefwechsel*, 63.

358. K. Barth to RB, 20. 6. 1931, in B. Jaspert, *Barth-Bultmann Briefwechsel*, 127.

almost inevitably became stronger in the face of this grave difference of opinion.[359]

At Bultmann's invitation, Heidegger presented his lecture "The Concept of Time" to the Marburg theological community on July 25, 1924. In it, speaking as a philosopher to the theologians, he anticipated the thoughts that he would soon develop in *Being and Time*. The true meaning of time can be grasped only from eternity, from the direction of God. For this reason, the task of theology consists precisely in interpreting human existence in its relation to eternity and to time as qualified in the first instance by the coming of the Son of God (cf. Gal 4:4; Mark 1:15). To the philosopher, however, for whom faith does not exist, this access to time from the direction of the eternity of God is closed off. The philosopher has "to understand time on the basis of time."[360] The fundamental structures of human existence—being in-the-world, being with-one-another, the self-interpretation of human existence in speaking, one's very own existence and one's existence as oneself at any particular time—are completely determined by the temporality of human existence. This temporality gives itself to be understood as "indeterminate certitude of one's unique possibility of Being-at-an-end."[361] As my own mineness, human existence knows about its death. "It is an anticipation on the part of human existence of its being over and done with as its own utmost possibility standing before it in certitude and complete indeterminateness."[362] With these thoughts, Heidegger distances himself from the overriding tradition of metaphysics that conceived of God as the *summum ens* [highest being], relieved of time, and of the human being on the basis of its relation to God and to eternity.

It was precisely this philosophy of the temporality and historicity[363] of human existence that seemed to Bultmann to open up ways of escape from the inconsistencies of both a theology that continued in unbroken fashion the old metaphysics, and the relativism of historicism. In his discussion of Ernst Lohmeyer's little book *Vom Begriff der religiösen Gemeinschaft* [*On the Concept of the Religious Community*], Bultmann indicated this in programmatic fashion in 1927. Theology can scarcely allow itself to continue to treat its object and its way of dealing with it by means of a philosophy that professes to be a system of all truth. Nevertheless, theology does well to

359. See below, 233–38.

360. M. Heidegger, *Der Begriff der Zeit*, 6; cf. Safranski, *Meister*, 164f; K. Hammann, "Die Entstehung," 207–11.

361. M. Heidegger, *Der Begriff der Zeit*, 16.

362. M. Heidegger, *Der Begriff der Zeit*, 17.

363. Cf. also M. Heidegger, *Der Begriff der Zeit*, 24–26.

refer to "philosophy as a critical form of knowledge of *being*" and to expose its own concepts of being to examination by philosophy so understood.[364] Both at the time and in later comments Bultmann was always aware of the connection between his conversations with Heidegger and the problem of history and the historicity of human existence that had forced itself on him from his time with Wilhelm Herrmann. Kierkegaard's dialectic of existence and Wilhelm Dilthey's understanding of history were also important for the exchange with Heidegger.[365] For his part, Heidegger was generally reluctant to identify other authors as having influenced either his thinking or particular motives for it. Still, as early as September 15, 1925, he wrote to his student Gerhard Krüger that it was no wonder that Krüger should find "cognates" to his analysis of human existence in Wilhelm Herrmann—though to be sure, Herrmann showed as little insight as Dilthey into the historicity of human existence.[366] In the 1928 *RGG* article on "Heidegger, Martin"—which appeared under Bultmann's name though in fact it was drafted largely by Heidegger himself—Augustine, Luther, and Kierkegaard are listed as thinkers to be referred to for the philosopher's understanding of human existence, Dilthey for his understanding of history, and Aristotle and the scholastics for his grasp of how certain ontological questions are posed.[367]

That article ends with the observation that Heidegger's philosophy treats neither theology nor worldview, but that it nevertheless offers approaches that might be of assistance to theology for corroborating its ontological implications.[368] These were Bultmann's premises as he read *Being and Time*, his friend's foremost early work, when it appeared in 1927. As he did so, the book gripped him so powerfully that each time he had finished reading a

364. RB, rev. of E. Lohmeyer, "Vom Begriff," in RB, *Theologie als Kritik*, 199.
365. See above, 126, n. 204, along with 189f.
366. UB Tübingen, G. Krüger est., M. Heidegger to G. Krüger, 15. 9. 1925.
367. Cf. RB, "Heidegger, Martin," 1688. Georg Wünsch was originally to have written the lexicon article on Heidegger. Wünsch turned to Bultmann in this regard, who in turn asked Heidegger for information about the sources of his philosophy. Heidegger's draft, "an enumeration of sources, out of which one is equally put together," Bultmann then took over nearly verbatim into the article. Cf. RB to M. Heidegger, 29. 12. 1927 and 7. 1. 1928, as well as M. Heidegger to RB, 31. 12. 1927, in A. Grossmann and C. Landmesser, *Bultmann-Heidegger Briefwechsel*, 43–47, 50f, 47–49. In view of this origin and derivation of the article, the doubts raised by H. Hübner ("Bultmanns 'existentiale Interpretation,'" 300) regarding the adequacy of the reproduction of Heidegger's intentions are invalid. Incomprehensible as well is the criticism by B. Martin ("Heidegger," 118f) of the contribution Heidegger has made to the history of Marburg philosophy since 1866. That "Heidegger treated his predecessors as simple predecessors of himself" (B. Martin, "Heidegger," 118) is incorrect. Cf. M. Heidegger, "Zur Geschichte," 681–87.
368. RB, "Heidegger, Martin," 1688.

section, he felt "physically worn out," but "not so much from the exertion of following it as because it is so uncannily 'concrete.'"[369] The way Heidegger spoke here of the insecurity of human existence and its temporality, of being-towards-death and of care, of the flight of the human being into inauthenticity and of the available potentiality-for-being—all this seemed to Bultmann to comprise a masterful understanding of the existentialist conceptualization of human existence. For the theologian, whose goal was to interpret the texts of the New Testament in their relevance for the present, the evidence for this analysis of existence now lay at hand.

If Bultmann had already taken into account particular elements of the Heideggerian analysis of human existence in his lectures and essays since 1925, after the appearance of *Being and Time* he was able further to work out the significance of the existentialist hermeneutic for theology. On the occasion of the first meeting of German Protestant theologians in Eisenach, on October 19, 1927, Bultmann gave his well-received lecture, "The Significance of the 'Dialectical Theology' for New Testament Scholarship." He now saw the catchword "dialectical theology" to betoken the historicity of human existence and mankind's potentiality-for-being. Existence is no longer at the individual's disposal, but is every moment at issue in those concrete situations of decision "in which one is never *choosing something for oneself, but rather choosing oneself as one's possibility.*"[370] For New Testament exegesis, this means that it makes use of the texts not as sources for reconstructing the past of specific events, but rather that it interprets them as witnesses of another person's understanding of existence that now opens up to me the possibility of gaining a new understanding of myself. To do this, such an understanding of the text necessarily presupposes an already existing understanding of the matters with which the text deals. At the same time, since it is always directed towards my own possibility, this understanding leads to decision, whether by affirming or by denying that possibility for existence.[371]

Bultmann also made good use of Heidegger's existentialist analysis of human existence in the case of technical exegesis, and particularly for the interpretation of Pauline[372] and Johannine theology. Thus, in 1928, he used Heidegger's account of the original sense of the word ἀλήθεια as "not be-

369. RB to M. Heidegger, 14. 9. 1927, in A. Grossmann and C. Landmesser, *Bultmann-Heidegger Briefwechsel*, 39.

370. RB, "Die Bedeutung der 'dialektischen Theologie'," *GuV*, vol. 1, 118.

371. Cf. RB, "Die Bedeutung der 'dialektischen Theologie'," *GuV*, vol. 1, 117–28; as well as J. Rohls, "Rudolf Bultmanns," 76f.

372. Also, see above 182f.

ing hidden" or as "having been disclosed"[373] in an etymological examination of ἀλήθεια in the realm of Greek literature; and in the same year he began with Heidegger's interpretation of "being-out-of-the-world" as the abandonment of the self to "the 'they,'" and, using the concept of revelation, defined human fallenness into the world theologically—as sin.[374] That is, the revelation-occurrence actualizes two possibilities for existence, which as such are disclosed through the coming of Jesus as the revealer. The human being either reduces himself to his worldly being—and, in so doing, to death—or he grasps the opportunity of potentiality-for-being that has been opened up through revelation and in doing so grasps life. With the stance that one adopts towards the sending of the revealer—in faith or in unfaith—the eschatological crisis occurs; or, more precisely, it happens in the moment that is characterized by the proclamation of Jesus' having come.[375]

And Heidegger? "We honor theology by remaining silent about it," he occasionally announced in seminar.[376] To be sure, until at least 1928 he did not hold himself to this condition of an eloquent silence in his intensive dialogue with Bultmann. In his lecture, "Phenomenology and Theology," given in Tübingen on March 9, 1927, and in Marburg on February 14, 1928, Heidegger addressed the relation between philosophy and theology, and the character of theology as a form of critical study.[377] The lecture exhibits partial verbal agreement with the manuscript of Bultmann's lectures on theological encyclopedia. Taking into account the various versions in which Bultmann delivered his lectures on the theological encyclopedia before and after Heidegger's lecture, it is scarcely possible today to know "which thoughts which of the two thinkers thought first."[378] Be that as it may, in both their numerous agreements and their no less significant differences, both texts document what Bultmann and Heidegger had cultivated between 1923 and 1928: an intellectual exchange unique to German philosophy and theology of the twentieth century.[379]

373. Cf. RB, "Untersuchungen zum Johannesevangelium. A. Ἀλήθεια," *Exegetica*, 144–61; as well as M. Heidegger, *Sein und Zeit*, 212–30.

374. Cf. RB, "Die Eschatologie des Johannesevangelium," *GuV*, vol. 1, 135–39; as well as M. Heidegger, *Sein und Zeit*, 126–30. Cf. also A. Christophersen, *Kairos*, 133f, 139–41.

375. Cf. RB, "Die Eschatologie des Johannesevangelium," 139–45.

376. Safranski, *Meister*, 162.

377. Heidegger presented a draft of the lecture (probably already in 1926) to a small circle of Marburg professors.

378. E. Jüngel, "Glauben und Verstehen," 34.

379. Cf. M. Heidegger, *Phänomenologie*; RB, *Theologische Enzyklopädie*. On what follows, cf. E. Jüngel, "Glauben und Verstehen," 31–36; A. Grossmann, "Zwischen Phänomenologie und Theologie," 42–54; M. Jung, "Heidegger," 475f.

Neither Heidegger nor Bultmann shows any thought of easing the tension between theology and philosophy by means of a type of Christian philosophy, for that would amount to "wooden iron."[380] For among other reasons, since each is a positive or ontic form of critical study, theology is absolutely distinct from philosophy because the latter, as *the* ontological form of study, is concerned with being. Yet in agreement with Bultmann (but in opposition to Schleiermacher) Heidegger explains that it is not the historical phenomenon of Christianity, but rather faith—as a "mode of human existence" generated through what is believed in and therefore "*not out of* human existence, *nor through* it out of free-floating items"—that presents the reality to which theology has access. And what is believed in "is for Christian faith Christ, the crucified God."[381] Formally speaking, faith as a relation of existence to the crucified is a manner of historical existence "in a history that first unveils itself in faith and only for faith." For this reason, theology is to be defined as a historical [*historische*] form of study that constitutes a historical [*geschichtliche*] form of study *sui generis*, corresponding to the unique historicity of the revelation-event that is given with faith.[382] At the same time, its systematic character does not consist in constructing a doctrinal system but rather manifests itself in its endeavor to bring to conceptual expression "the Christian occurrence as such, *in the way that it attests itself in faith to the believer.*"[383] Grounded solely in faith, theology therefore "does not need to borrow from other forms of study" in order to validate its object or "to add to the evidence of faith."[384]

Nevertheless, theology does well to open itself to philosophical-ontological reflection. For, inasmuch as Christian faith is the "existential overcoming of pre-Christian existence, the structure of pre-Christian existence that has been overcome remains existentially-ontologically contained within believing existence."[385] In this connection, philosophy is able to serve theology "*as a corrective with regard to the ontic, and to the pre-Christian content of the basic theological concepts.*"[386] However, by functioning in this way, philosophy in no way assumes command of theology and its unique conceptuality that has grown out of faith. Certainly, philosophy does not need theology, for as "unfettered questioning of existence positing itself," philosophy stands in an

380. M. Heidegger, *Phänomenologie*, 23.
381. M. Heidegger, *Phänomenologie*, 18.
382. M. Heidegger, *Phänomenologie*, 21f.
383. M. Heidegger, *Phänomenologie*, 23.
384. M. Heidegger, *Phänomenologie*, 26.
385. M. Heidegger, *Phänomenologie*, 29.
386. M. Heidegger, *Phänomenologie*, 30.

antagonistic relation to faith, which grounds itself in revelation.[387] What is more—and this claim of Heidegger's enraged the students at his lecture[388]—*faith* remains "in its inmost kernel as a specific possibility for existence, [and thus] the mortal enemy of the utterly variable *form of existence* that belongs essentially to *philosophy*." According to Heidegger, this existential opposition must be upheld in all its severity in order to maintain proper communication between theology and philosophy.[389]

Heidegger's remark about faith and the philosophical approach to life being mortal enemies can scarcely have startled Bultmann as it did the students in 1928. On the contrary, he had arrived at a similar assessment, though from premises different from those of Heidegger. For Bultmann, the question of truth controls all forms of critical study, including theology and especially philosophy.[390] Philosophy knows—just as faith does—about the limitedness of human existence and asks about the authenticity of actual existence. Nonetheless, faith disputes the idea that the individual can simply by means of his own decision achieve authenticity. "Faith can judge the choice of philosophical existence only to be an act grounding itself in human freedom, a commitment that denies one's being bound to God."[391]

On February 25, 1928, just a few days after Heidegger had given his lecture "Phenomenology and Theology" in Marburg, he received a call to Freiburg, his old university, where he accepted the appointment to Husserl's chair. He explained in person to Karl Jaspers that except for contact with the theologians, he couldn't cite one thing that spoke in Marburg's favor. "I haven't felt at home for a single hour."[392] It was only the personal relationship with Bultmann, as Heidegger informed Jaspers, that had made the decision to go to Freiburg difficult for him.[393] In his later memories, however, he repeatedly recalled the Marburg years as the happiest phase of his life.[394] If this reminiscence could contain transfiguring moments, it also preserved the experience of the intensive dialogue and the personal companionship

387. M. Heidegger, *Phähomenologie*, 31.

388. Cf. H. Mörchen, "Heidegger," 76.

389. M. Heidegger, *Phänomenologie*, 32.

390. Cf. RB, *Theologische Enzyklopädie*, 49.

391. RB, *Theologische Enzyklopädie*, 89. It is in *this* judgment that Bultmann's political decision in 1933, different from Heidegger's, was based. See below 269f.

392. M. Heidegger to K. Jaspers, 13. 5. 1928, in W. Biemel and H. Saner, *Heidegger-Jaspers Briefwechsel*, 96.

393. M. Heidegger to RB, 2. 4. 1928, in A. Grossman and C. Landmesser, *Bultmann-Heidegger Briefwechsel*, 55.

394. Cf. H. Mörchen, "Heidegger," 75f, as well as H. Ott, *Martin Heidegger*, 123f. See also below 514.

with Bultmann. When Heidegger returned to Freiburg, the friends adopted the familiar "Du."

Heidegger, however, was unable to follow Bultmann's suggestion to publish his friend's study, "The Concept of Revelation in the New Testament"[395] and his own "Phenomenology and Theology" together as a way of documenting the time they shared in Marburg. In justifying this decision, Heidegger partially rescinded the starting point of his essay that was too circumscribed by its occasion—namely, the rather practical clarification of the relation of theology and phenomenology. A revised treatment of the subject would have to work out the *specific* character of theology that "gives it in a certain, formal way, parity of treatment with philosophy, inasmuch as it is concerned with the whole, but in ontic fashion."[396] Heidegger expressed his reservations more clearly and in more decisive fashion in a letter of August 8, 1928, to Elisabeth Blochmann. He feared that publication of the essay might give the fatal impression that he was offering an apologia for Christian theology. As "a document of the time *in Marburg*"—that is, concerning the exchange with Bultmann—the essay was focused on the support that philosophy could provide to theology. The fundamental problem of whether theology really is a form of critical study and "what critical study itself is," he had not yet touched on.[397] Still holding something back, on December 18, 1928, Heidegger indicated to Bultmann that theology differs from the other positive forms of critical study in its positivity, and stands "outside of them in a completely different way from the way philosophy does."[398] To his distancing of himself from his essay, Heidegger joined his wish to be removed from the circle of editors of the *Theologische Rundschau*. His involvement in a theological periodical would ultimately promote the widespread tendency to confuse theology and philosophy, and so for the good of the cause it would be "cleaner and more honest, if philosophy were to remain silent for the time being."[399]

Although Bultmann regretted Heidegger's withdrawal from the conversation between theology and philosophy,[400] and in time also perceived

395. Cf. RB, "Der Begriff der Offenbarung im Neuen Testament," *GuV*, vol. 3, 1–34.

396. M. Heidegger to RB, 23. 10. 1928, in A. Grossmann and C. Landmesser, *Bultmann-Heidegger Briefwechsel*, 62; cf. on what follows, A. Grossmann, "Zwischen Phänomenologie und Theologie," 54–57.

397. M. Heidegger to E. Blochmann, 8. 8. 1928, in J. W. Storck, *Heidegger-Blochmann Briefwechsel*, 25f.

398. M. Heidegger to RB, 18. 12. 1928, A. Grossmann and C. Landmesser, *Bultmann-Heidegger Briefwechsel*, 87.

399. M. Heidegger to RB, 23. 10. 1928, A. Grossmann and C. Landmesser, *Bultmann-Heidegger Briefwechsel*, 64.

400. Cf. RB to M. Heidegger, 29. 10. 1928, in A. Grossmann and C. Landmesser, *Bultmann-Heidegger Briefwechsel*, 69–78.

that their paths had separated farther "than was to be foreseen during the time in Marburg,"[401] the two maintained a friendly professional relationship.[402] Their personal relationship also remained largely cordial until 1933, particularly since Heidegger more than once expressed his appreciation for Bultmann's theological work. He saw in Bultmann the only theologian who understood that theology had to pursue the same kind of work that philosophical reflection did, but on its own and for its own sake.[403] A theology that was oriented exclusively to faith and that sought to invigorate it could best fulfill its task "by means of Barth's indifference *to* philosophy, but also by means of an understanding *of* it"—an understanding that Bultmann had worked out for himself.[404]

It was hardly accidental that Heidegger withdrew from the dialogue about the relation of theology and philosophy during the period in which he was preparing for and executing the "turn" from considering the ontology of human existence to pondering the historicity of being. Heidegger left behind "any existential meaning . . . of the talk about the authenticity of human existence and, with this, the concept of authenticity itself"[405] when he set out on the intellectual path that ultimately led him into language as the dwelling-place of being. By doing so, he dropped out as a philosophical conversation partner for the theologian Bultmann, who interpreted the New Testament kerygma as a call to faith, as a call into the authenticity of a new existence that was not to be constituted from what was at one's disposal, but rather from what was granted by the coming of God. Because of this basic orientation of his theological work, Bultmann was not prepared to follow Heidegger along his new path.[406] It was likewise a consequence of Bultmann's insistence on safeguarding the independence of theology from philosophy that he understood and employed *Being and Time* not as the fundamental ontology that Heidegger had intended but rather as a fundamental anthropology.[407] Even though Bultmann consistently followed *Being*

401. RB to M. Heidegger, 11. and 14. 12. 1932, in A. Grossmann and C. Landmesser, *Bultmann-Heidegger Briefwechsel*, 184.

402. M. Heidegger to RB, 16. 12. 1932, in A. Grossmann and C. Landmesser, *Bultmann-Heidegger Briefwechsel*, 189f: "Fortunately, our friendship does not depend on how one specifies the relation between theology and philosophy."

403. M. Heidegger to RB, 16. 12. 1932, in A. Grossmann and C. Landmesser, *Bultmann-Heidegger Briefwechsel*, 189f.

404. M. Heidegger to RB 14. 11. 1931, A. Grossmann and C. Landmesser, *Bultmann-Heidegger Briefwechsel*, 172.

405. H.-G. Gadamer, "Martin Heidegger und die Marburger Theologie," in E. Dinkler, *Zeit und Geschichte*, 487.

406. Cf. however as a qualification of this *opinio communis* of the research, H. Hübner, "Wahrheit und Wort," 159–61.

407. Cf. E. Jüngel, "Glauben und Verstehen," 44.

and Time in expressing the difference between "ontological" and "ontic," as well as that between "existential" and "existentialist,"[408] he ultimately ignored Heidegger's concentration on being as the exclusive subject-matter of philosophy.

In 1928 the Jena philosopher Eberhard Grisebach claimed that a supposedly critical theology could scarcely adopt as its premise Heidegger's allegedly uninterpretable philosophy of human existence.[409] Soon afterwards, in 1928, his student Gerhardt Kuhlmann assumed a critical position towards Bultmann. He agreed with Bultmann's having made the concept of human existence the point of departure for his theological approach but raised doubts about the neutrality of a philosophical method. Rather, when it became subservient to a philosophical method, theology unnecessarily and improperly abandoned its object to the foreign influence of philosophy. This was especially true, he proposed, in the case of Bultmann's adaptation of Heidegger's philosophy. For Heidegger's ontology of human existence could hardly be accepted by theology, since it did not represent a critical analysis of being, but from the outset aimed at revealing its own interpretation of human existence as the only one possible. Thus Heidegger's philosophy was in essence a metaphysics. "Since the analysis of existence has as its field of vision the complete 'horizon' of human existence, it cannot tolerate theology's discovery of a new possibility for being as its own object—or that such a conceptuality should 'reveal' itself."[410] From this perspective, Bultmann could at best lend a supplementary mythological form to the dialectical relation between inauthentic and authentic existence. However, theology retains the task of working out how each person's existence is circumscribed by the alien being of God acting through the paradoxical revelation-occurrence.

Kuhlmann's critical challenges caused some degree of trouble for Bultmann.[411] During the Pentecost vacation of 1929 he mulled over the problems Kuhlmann and Heidegger had raised in Freiburg. In the course of responding to his critics, he had second thoughts.[412] Bultmann hoped he had not misunderstood Heidegger "in the respect that what is at issue in the ontology of human existence is the working out of the structure of human existence in general; . . . however, regarding the rootedness of ontology in ontic existence and therefore regarding the ultimate intention of philoso-

408. Cf. H. Hübner, "'Existentiale' Interpretation," 562–65.

409. Cf. E. Grisebach, *Gegenwart*, 511f, n. 1.

410. G. Kuhlmann, "Zum theologischen Problem," 50.

411. Cf. RB to M. Heidegger, 15. 7. 1929, in A. Grossmann and C. Landmesser, *Bultmann-Heidegger Briefwechsel*, 112.

412. Cf. RB to M. Heidegger, 19. 1. 1930, in A. Grossmann and C. Landmesser, *Bultmann-Heidegger Briefwechsel*, 126.

phy, I don't yet clearly see my way through."[413] In his reply to Kuhlmann, Bultmann discusses in detail the relation of theology and philosophy with regard to their basic intentions. Both forms of study deal with the same object, human existence, but they certainly do this in different ways. Philosophy deals with the concrete existence of each person, and therefore focuses on the "that" of the "how" of human existence. Philosophy works from within the formal-ontological structures of human existence. In contrast to this, theology speaks of a particular "how" of human existence: that is, of concrete human existence "inasmuch as it believes (or does not believe—which for it is not something negative, but rather something positive)—inasmuch as its 'how' is characterized by being affected or by the prospect of being affected by a particular proclamation."[414]

For Bultmann, then, theology can take over Heidegger's ontology of human existence, since unlike a systematic philosophy it does not presuppose a particular idea of being, but rather as a phenomenology it merely "means to bring the phenomena themselves to self-disclosure."[415] It is precisely in its neutral orientation towards the structures of human existence that philosophy is able to perform an indispensable service to theology. For, if theology understands itself as a critical form of study—and not only as preaching—it will resort to the philosophical analysis of existence in order to demonstrate the ontological-existential possibility of such realities of existing in faith as revelation and life, grace and forgiveness. Insofar as theology focuses on existing in faith, it must refer to the philosophical analysis of existence, for existence in faith is still existence, and theological concepts such as sin and forgiveness cannot be understood in their proper sense apart from their formal-ontological reference. Naturally, this does not mean that theology must be grounded in a philosophical analysis of human existence or a theory of knowledge. Rather, as "a movement of faith itself," theology cannot be externally derived but has its basis exclusively in existence in faith.[416]

413. RB to M. Heidegger, 24. 8. 1930, in A. Grossmann and C. Landmesser, *Bultmann-Heidegger Briefwechsel*, 133.

414. RB, "Die Geschichtlichkeit des Daseins und der Glaube: Antwort an Gerhardt Kühlmann (1930)," *Neues Testament und christliche Existenz*, 62; cf. also J. Rohls, "Rudolf Bultmanns,“ 78f.

415. RB, "Die Geschichtlichkeit des Daseins," *Neues Testament und christliche Existenz*, 64.

416. RB, "Die Geschichtlichkeit des Daseins," *Neues Testament und christliche Existenz*, 67. Cf. also the reply of G. Kuhlmann, "Krisis der Theologie?"; as well as M. Heidegger to RB, 22. 5. 1931, in A. Grossmann and C. Landmesser, *Bultmann-Heidegger Briefwechsel*, 160: "The gentlemen need only show for once what an actual theology without any philosophy looks like. Then we will see, and it's not hard to predict this—that what they are working with is a pretty messy workaday philosophy that comes out of what they know from their more or less adequate education."

In his discussion with Kuhlmann, Bultmann confirmed his view that the ontology of human existence has to do with a neutral, merely formal access to human existence. It is just this premise that Karl Löwith challenged in 1930, in two interrelated essays.[417] He saw presupposed in Heidegger's ontology an ontic ideal for existence that determined this ontology. The existential structures worked out in Heidegger by no means dealt with basic and thus presumably neutral ontological categories but rather with concepts from the theological tradition that had been secularized. Obviously, the reason why theology can assert

> the determination of human existence by "death," "anxiety," "guilt," "conscience," and "care" is not that these existential structures give expression to a strictly natural constitution of human existence, but rather that they give expression to the sort of philosophical understanding of human existence *which*, in the ambiguous Hegelian sense, *has "canceled and preserved" in itself the Christian interpretation of human existence*—that is to say, has at once saved and disposed of it.[418]

Heidegger's critical application of a specifically Protestant understanding of human existence and, above all, of Kierkegaard's conception of human existence, makes it understandable why Bultmann attaches to this analysis of human existence such a high degree of importance for the ontological self-validation of theology.

While Bultmann engaged in detailed discussion with Kuhlmann, he dealt only comparatively briefly with the critical inquiries of Löwith.[419] In his reply, he insisted that Heidegger's concept of authenticity arose not from a particular ideal of human existence, but rather that it expressed the historicity of human existence as a basic phenomenon that is always an inherent element of human existence.[420] However, he could not persuade Karl Barth to accept this view of things that he had presented in the debate with Kuhlmann.[421] And thus it became certain that the relation between theology and philosophy remained a topic that would be interpreted and discussed in increasingly controversial fashion by dialectical theology.[422]

417. Cf. K. Löwith, "Grundzüge" and "Phänomenologische Ontologie."

418. K. Löwith, "Phänomenologische Ontologie," 366.

419. Bultmann saw his own theological work called into question less by Löwith than Heidegger's existentialist interpretation of human existence as such.

420. Cf. RB, "Die Geschichtlichkeit des Daseins," 65n8.

421. Cf. K. Barth to RB, 5. 2. 1930 and 27. 5. 1931, in B. Jaspert, *Barth-Bultmann Briefwechsel*, 99, 117.

422. See also below 233–38.

8. The Theological Encyclopedia

For the word of proclamation . . . one is to claim no other legitimation and to create no other basis than itself. . . . Cf. Luther: ". . . Let us completely disavow any anxiety. The gospel does not need our help, it is strong enough on its own for it was authorized and ordered by God himself. . . . I have consigned it to the dear Lord; it is his own word, and he is man enough to champion and protect it."[423]

In the summer semester of 1926, Bultmann gave the two-hour lecture course "Introduction to Theological Study" for the first time. He repeated this course in 1928, 1930, 1933, and 1936, in a repeatedly expanded and reworked form under the title "Theological Encyclopedia." Lectures of such encyclopedic character were part of the traditional offerings of theological faculties. Before Bultmann, Martin Rade had last lectured in Marburg on "Introduction to the Study of Theology" in the summer semester of 1925. Beginning in 1926 Bultmann took over this standard course as part of his teaching duties, which in addition to New Testament exegesis and theology included the Theological Encyclopedia.[424] To teach "Theological Encyclopedia" was, beyond being of general interest, an integral part of the different concept of the task of New Testament exegesis that Bultmann represented. For him, exegetical work could never exhaust itself in historical positivism. Rather, it had to think through the systematic-theological implications not only of the questions that drove it but also of the answers it derived from the biblical texts—and the new questions those answers might raise. What the New Testament scholar was always trying to explain to his students in the exegetical courses within his discipline, he was now able to lay out on a broad canvas in the course on encyclopedia, since it was structured to address specifically systematic-theological issues concerning the close correlation between the interpretation of the New Testament and the dogmatic self-understanding of theology as a form of critical study.

Bultmann originally meant to work these lectures into a book that would inaugurate a series, Neue theologische Grundrisse [New Outlines for Theology], that he himself edited for J.C.B. Mohr (Paul Siebeck).[425]

423. RB, *Theologische Enzyklopädie*, 152; cf. M. Luther, "Sermon zu St. Michael," 18–24, 354.

424. Cf. UA Marburg, hiring files, 8. 4. 1921.

425. On what follows cf. the Foreword of the editors in RB, *Theologische Enzyklopädie*, ix; E. Jüngel, "Glauben und Verstehen," 19–21.

Bultmann fully intended to comply with his publisher's wish, which he received on February 11, 1930, to have the *Theologische Enzyklopädie* [*Theological Encyclopedia*] ready for publication soon. This is evidenced by his reply to Oskar Siebeck of February 12th, as well as by his communication by letter to Martin Heidegger on August 24, 1930, that he believed he "would once more make a bit of progress on his encyclopedia."[426] But the publication of the planned volume never took place. As he told Oskar Siebeck in person at the beginning of 1936, Bultmann had decided "to put the *Encyclopedia* aside for as long as it takes for the theological situation to become somewhat more clarified."[427]

With this explanation, Bultmann was evidently alluding to developments related to the seizure of power by the National Socialists, an occurrence that must certainly have seemed to throw "the theological situation" into disarray in 1936. In 1933, the shared work and struggle of dialectical theology had collapsed. Karl Barth and Bultmann had once again discerned commonalities in their theological intentions in the Confessing Church, and had made use of these in the struggle against the church politics of National Socialism, whereas in that same year Friedrich Gogarten had at times sided with the "German Christians" in 1933. His belief that the "law of the people" could express the law of God called forth Bultmann's vehement opposition. It was also with the gravest reservations that Bultmann took note of Martin Heidegger's address as university Vice-chancellor in 1933, and as a result he distanced himself from both Gogarten and Heidegger in the period that followed. His primarily favorable references to texts of both Barth and Gogarten in the encyclopedia lectures coupled with an appropriation of Heidegger's work in pursuing the dialogue between philosophy and theology would, in the years following 1933, have caused publication of the lecture manuscripts to evoke unwelcome misunderstandings.

After 1945, other publishing ventures on Bultmann's part and claims on his time arising from the demythologizing debate made it difficult to publish the *Theological Encyclopedia*. In his old age, he entrusted Erich Dinkler with the task of preparing the manuscript for publication. Although Dinkler's death made this plan impossible, Eberhard Jüngel and Klaus W. Müller produced an exemplary edition of the *Theological Encyclopedia* in 1984 to

426. Cf. O. Siebeck to RB, 11. 2. 1930, in RB, *Theologische Enzyklopädie*, ixn20; RB to O. Siebeck, 12. 2. 1930, in RB, *Theologische Enzyklopädie*, ixn21; RB to M. Heidegger, 24. 8. 1920, in A. Grossmann and C. Landmesser, *Bultmann-Heidegger Briefwechsel*, 133.

427. O. Siebeck to RB, 18. 2. 1936, in RB, *Theologische Enzyklopädie*, ixn22.

mark the one-hundredth anniversary of Bultmann's birth. The editors took their direction from the final manuscript text of 1936, but whenever possible indicated the various levels of the text's evolution. Thus, this edition makes it possible to follow and verify the developments in Bultmann's thinking through the several manuscript versions from 1926 to 1936, as well as the criticism of the worldview of National Socialism that he worked into the text in the summer semester of 1933.[428]

In his lectures on the encyclopedia, Bultmann did not pursue the intention of presenting a "Realencyclopedia" of the specialized content of theological knowledge.[429] Nor was it his interest to clarify the relations among the theological disciplines and to the subject matter of theology as a whole, though to be sure, his understanding of the subject contained enough points of connection to enable those questions to be worked out as the case arose. In 1941 Bultmann essayed just such an expansion, when in addition to his lecture on "New Testament and Mythology" before the general meeting of the Society for Protestant Theology in Alpirsbach, he gave a seminar paper entitled "Theology as a Form of Critical Study." In this latter lecture he not only presented an abridged edition of his encyclopedia lectures, but also offered explicit comments on the critical tasks of the individual theological disciplines, as well as on their relation to each other and to theology as a whole.[430]

In the *Theological Encyclopedia*, Bultmann starts out from Hegel's concept of the formal encyclopedia and therefore focuses on the principles and basic understandings of the special fields of critical study. The classic outline of a Protestant theological encyclopedia, Schleiermacher's *Kurze Darstellung* [*Brief Outline on the Study of Theology*] is also oriented to this conception of encyclopedia. Schleiermacher defines theology as a positive form of critical study, and in so doing derives the positive character of theology not from its object but rather from its function. It is only with reference to the practical purpose of theology, that is, the leadership of the church, that critical forms of knowledge in general can become theological forms of knowledge. Christian theology is therefore "the assemblage of those critical forms of knowledge and professional rules, without the possession and application of which a united leadership of the church . . . is not possible."[431]

428. Cf. RB, *Theologische Enzyklopädie,* 7f, 40f, 63–65.
429. Cf. RB, *Theologische Enzyklopädie*, 1.
430. Cf. RB, "Theologie also Wissenschaft"; as well as K. W. Müller, "Zu Rudolf Bultmanns Alpirsbacher Vortrag," 470f.
431. F. Schleiermacher, *Kurze Darstellung*, 2 (para. 5).

Bultmann likewise declares that theology is a positive form of critical study,[432] but he differs fundamentally from Schleiermacher in the way he understands this definition. Bultmann criticizes Schleiermacher for having derived theology not from what distinguishes its particular object, but rather from what philosophy has historically understood as ethics. Be that as it may, since theology is a positive form of critical study, it cannot allow its object to be handed over to philosophy.[433] Besides, what is to be considered as its object is "not Christianity as it is empirically given in history," but rather "that very thing which first makes Christianity into Christianity and so constitutes Christianity and theology itself."[434] On the basis of this line of thinking, developed in the exchange with Heidegger,[435] Bultmann concludes that the task of theological encyclopedia consists in theology's own reflection upon the object that constitutes it.

This object was to be conceived provisionally as doctrinal correctness. Theology would then be the form of critical study of right doctrine, of that which the church, and specifically preaching, is to proclaim. Therefore, the *fides quae creditur* [content of faith] forms the object of theology. If, in contrast, one is determined to understand theology as a doctrine of faith, and thereby as a form of critical study of faith in the sense of the *fides qua creditur* [faith that enables belief], one has already missed its actual object. For instance, Schleiermacher, whom Bultmann criticizes as clearly a representative of such an approach, wrongly judged that faith can be rightly understood only on the basis of an intentional relation to its object, "so that faith can be spoken of only if one speaks at the same time about God."[436] The fact is, however, that the essence of theology cannot be understood on the basis of another form of critical study, but only in theology's performing its own reflection on the object that constitutes it; and thus a circular structure of knowledge is implied, one that Bultmann holds to be unavoidable and implicit in the subject-matter itself.[437]

In order to answer the question of what theology is, Bultmann first distances himself from both the liberal theology of the nineteenth century and Protestant orthodoxy. Against liberal theology he objects that it conceives faith merely as *fides qua creditur* [that which enables belief]. By concentrating completely on the act of faith, interpreted by means of the concept of

432. RB, *Theologische Enzyklopädie*, 10.
433. RB, *Theologische Enzyklopädie*, 5–7.
434. RB, *Theologische Enzyklopädie*, 12.
435. Cf. esp. E. Jüngel, "Glauben und Verstehen," 31–36.
436. RB, *Theologische Enzyklopädie*, 21.
437. RB, *Theologische Enzyklopädie*, 28; cf. W. Härle, rev. of RB, *Theologische Enzyklopädie*, 163.

religion, it loses sight of the *fides quae creditur* [content of faith] as theology's object. In so doing, however, liberal theology has excused itself from the truth-question. For whoever focuses on the *fides qua creditur* [faith as belief] without taking account of its relation to the object that constitutes it, must ultimately misunderstand that *fides qua creditur* as a human attitude and thus overlook the fact that faith can rightly be conceived of "only as a concrete, historical relation to a determinate object."[438]

Bultmann concedes that Protestant orthodoxy, as distinguished from liberal theology, is consistently interested in the truth of the *fides quae creditur* [content of faith] and in the intentional relation of faith to its object, the saving activity of God. Nevertheless, by dissecting the concept of faith into the elements of *notitia* (knowledge), *assensus* (assent), and *fiducia* (confidence), orthodoxy has surrendered its presumed advantage. For by accepting the acknowledgment of particular saving facts to be an interim stage necessary to faith proper, it misunderstands the *fides quae creditur* [content of faith] to be mere agreement with right doctrine. Orthodoxy thus confuses the kerygma and theoretical reflection upon it, the event of the word of God and the human doctrine that interprets this event.[439] In order to avoid the errors of liberalism and orthodoxy, the *fides qua creditur* and the *fides quae creditur* must be distinguished and understood in their reciprocal relation to each other. From this there arises for Bultmann,

> the task of specifying the nature of theology on the basis of its object along the only lines possible for it—that is, on the basis of the *fides quae creditur* and *qua creditur*. What God is cannot be understood if what faith is is not understood, and vice versa. Theology is therefore the critical study of God because it is the critical study of faith, and vice versa.[440]

As do all other forms of critical study, theology represents reflective knowledge, which is always at work when one is dealing with the objects that are determinative for life. Knowledge originates in the care for oneself that impels human existence, and out of which grows the question of the "whither" of human existence. For Bultmann, this understanding of knowledge as a feature of human existence, a concept he adopted from Heidegger, excludes both the idealistic derivation of critical forms of study from reason and the neo-Kantian conception of a critical form of study as an end in itself.

438. RB, *Theologische Enzyklopädie*, 31.

439. RB, *Theologische Enzyklopädie*, 31n7: "*Fides quae creditur=quod deus dixit!* Theology=what the human being says."

440. RB, *Theologische Enzyklopädie*, 34.

It is especially in the latter case that when critical forms of study are so understood, they fail to come to grips not only with their life-relation to their object, but also with the object itself. "Genuine knowing is therefore not something additional that supervenes upon life, but rather a piece of life itself. A critical form of study is . . . only human existence in general operating with a special purpose."[441] Therefore, genuine knowing cannot be expected to represent an acquisition of knowledge apart from the life-relation to its object, but can take place only by opening itself to this object and presupposing its claim.

If genuine knowing is made determinate by its object, then as Bultmann emphasizes (again following Heidegger), truth means "the disclosedness of the object."[442] Truth therefore marks the epitome and the measure of that recognition which perceives its object in the way in which the object gives itself to be recognized. The quest for truth is inherent in human existence. For human existence needs to understand itself, wants to be itself and achieve its authenticity. Moreover, since human existence always means acting, I must seek truth in order to recognize what I am to do at any given time. Nevertheless, Bultmann is convinced that the question of truth cannot be given an adequate answer in terms of idealistic Greek thought, since in this tradition one supposes that truth can be found not in the realm of "the finite and temporal," but exclusively "in the sphere of the eternal, of the timeless, of the idea."[443] But human existence is historically constituted, and at the core human existence is a potentiality-for-being, as Bultmann and Heidegger emphasize in repudiating "the ontological primacy of actuality over possibility maintained in the Aristotelian tradition."[444] To seek after truth can therefore only mean that I seek the truth of my moment whenever I perceive my existence as time constituted by deciding. But where theology involves itself in the quest for truth, the quest for God announces itself as word. For, "if he is to be thought of at all," God "is to be regarded as the power ruling the now."[445]

To be sure, this raises the problem that the almighty God cannot be a possible object of knowledge for a positive form of critical study. For as utterly transcendent to human existence, "*God cannot be made into the object of our dealings.*"[446] The unavailability of God results from the human being's

441. RB, *Theologische Enzyklopädie,* 43.
442. RB, *Theologische Enzyklopädie,* 35, 42, 45; cf. M. Heidegger, *Sein und Zeit,* 212–30.
443. RB, *Theologische Enzyklopädie,* 49.
444. E. Jüngel, "Glauben und Verstehen," 57; cf. RB, *Theologische Enzyklopädie,* 50, 199.
445. RB, *Theologische Enzyklopädie,* 50.
446. RB, *Theologische Enzyklopädie,* 55.

inability to dispose of his own existence. In order to be able to think of God, we would have to be able to dispose of our existence. Only then could we actually think of God as that which determines our existence and "*speak* of him as the '*how*' *of our existence*."[447] This, however, does not lie within the realm of human possibilities. Since a human being exists only from moment to moment, his ability to recognize God, and in the act of so doing achieve authenticity, must be due to the self-disclosure of God, which by its very nature can be experienced only through faith.

The discussion of these two central themes, the idea of revelation and the concept of faith, dominates the rest of the course of Bultmann's encyclopedia lectures. From a formal point of view this is evident in the carefully structured layout of the relevant fourth and fifth chapters.[448] Paragraph 11, which treats "revelation as historical event," corresponds to paragraph 14, in which an account is given of "faith as historical act." Bultmann critically precedes each of these treatments with the characterization and rejection of the traditional ecclesiastical concepts of revelation and faith in paragraphs 10 and 12. And although paragraph 13, with its theme of "Mysticism and Faith," seems to interrupt the strict systematization of Bultmann's train of thought as an inorganic insertion into the whole, one must note that Bultmann had not yet finished developing paragraphs 12–14.[449]

Bultmann develops his understanding of revelation and faith by means of a series of critical distinctions that challenge church tradition. In his view, both medieval scholasticism and Protestant orthodoxy dismiss the biblical specification of the connection between revelation and faith, since for them "faith signifies a way of knowing, and revelation the mediation of what is known."[450] Thus they misjudge the character of revelation as an occurrence in the present. And romanticism, which identifies the act of revelation with religious experience, in the opposite way loses sight of the fact "that in the act of revelation something is revealed."[451] But in the biblical understanding revelation is a historical event: it is the word of God coming to the moment of human existence, "which makes the truth of the moment visible and, thereby, makes God visible."[452] Revelation takes place more specifically as God's address, which as the word of forgiveness interrupts the history of the human being that is determined by sin. The word of the forgiving love of

447. RB, *Theologische Enzyklopädie*, 63.
448. See also Härle, rev. of RB, *Theologische Enzyklopädie*, 163.
449. Cf. the Foreword of the editors, in RB, *Theologische Enzyklopädie*, vii.
450. RB, *Theologische Enzyklopädie*, 69; cf. in corresponding fashion to orthodoxy, 71f.
451. RB, *Theologische Enzyklopädie*, 81.
452. RB, *Theologische Enzyklopädie*, 88.

God specifically calls the individual out of the past determined by his own doing, and into decision by enabling him to grasp the "now" of his existence—the new possibility of authentic existence now coming towards him from the future of God. In this connection, Bultmann explicitly denies "that, prepared for death, the human being can win his authenticity through his own resolve."[453] Faith must raise this objection against philosophy generally, an assertion here evidently aimed at Heidegger in particular. If faith means to safeguard its autonomy *vis-à-vis* philosophy, it cannot debate this with philosophy even for a moment. It "can only judge the choice of philosophical existence as a self-justifying act on the part of the human being who denies his being bound to God."[454]

The possibility of salvation—that of understanding oneself anew in faith in the word of God addressed to him—is grounded in the historical event of revelation that presents Jesus Christ as the word of God. Faith is primarily the obedient acceptance of the kerygma of Jesus Christ, though surely not "as gullibly assuming an empirical-historical report." Rather, faith implies an understanding that to the believer becomes increasingly certain, for indeed faith consists in this "certitude that through the historical [*historische*] fact of Jesus Christ, history [*Geschichte*] is shown to be a history of salvation." For the believer relies utterly on the word spoken to him of the forgiveness of sins. In this way, "as one justified in my 'now,' . . . as one having been loved and loving, I come to understand the question of the moment and to discover the 'what' of my doing."[455] In this way, the new self-understanding that comes to the believer with his believing can never be reduced to a condition of *splendid isolation* in order to cut one off from others. "A faith that stays within itself is no more faith than a love that stays within itself is love."[456]

Bultmann now emphasizes the character of faith as gift. In faith, the human being receives the forgiveness of sins and the new life in Christ. He *becomes* justified by God, and so as object of the divine activity, the believer is passive. But in the same breath, Bultmann insists that faith fulfills itself as historic [*geschichtliche*] deed, and by stressing the deed-character of faith, he explicitly opposes a misunderstanding that he thinks is often present in mysticism: the passive nature of faith. Mysticism seeks, by various methods—

453. RB, *Theologische Enzyklopädie,* 89.
454. RB, *Theologische Enzyklopädie,* 89. See also above 210f.
455. RB, *Theologische Enzyklopädie,* 130.
456. RB, *Theologische Enzyklopädie,* 157.

silence, for instance—to bring "the human being to pure passivity," but in so doing, overlooks the obvious fact that the practice of such a method is itself a form of activity.[457] To be sure, specifying faith as historic deed has a still more fundamental basis. The very size of paragraph 14 indicates this, as Bultmann—quite purposely citing numerous points of agreement and conflict with Wilhelm Herrmann—presents his view of faith as historic deed.

Bultmann shares the view represented in contemporary philosophy by Heidegger and Max Scheler and by Karl Barth in theology, that whereas human existence continuously fulfills itself in acting, it is "in his doing" that the human being is himself.[458] With this assumption as a backdrop, Bultmann examines—as previously in the essay, "What Sense Does It Make to Speak of God?"—the distinction between deed and work in order to elucidate faith as a historic deed and to protect against misinterpretations. This distinction, which is to be understood along the lines of a specific analogy to the Aristotelian differentiation of πρᾶξις and ποίησις [*action and creation*], implies that work, as at most the result of doing, describes "something that is then 'present-at-hand,'" while the deed "is only there in the doing" and, to this extent is "never 'present-at-hand.'"[459] If, then, the individual understands his being on the basis of his works, he binds himself to the reality of something present-at-hand. In doing so, however, he forfeits the possibility of free potentiality-for-being, for he can lay hold of this possibility only in the deed. Only in concretely enacting his being as a person can he attain authenticity of existence. Indeed, his bondage to work, to what he finds at hand, only stands in his way. The kerygma frees the individual from this non-freedom by granting him ever anew the possibility of enacting his potentiality-for-being in openness to the future of God, and in so doing, of discovering himself anew in the truth of the moment. On the one hand, the human being passively receives what the word of God promises him. On the other hand, it is precisely in the passivity of this receiving that he enacts the deed of decision to perceive himself as what the word of God confronts him as being. He no longer has to accept his existence as something determined by his past. Rather, the free deed of obedience to the kerygma enables him to understand himself anew as a creature loved by God and freed for love.

457. RB, *Theologische Enzyklopädie,* 120.

458. RB, *Theologische Enzyklopädie,* 134; cf. on what follows E. Jüngel, "Glauben und Verstehen," 59–61, as well as the critical objections brought to bear against Bultmann there (72f); see also K. Hammann, "Der Glaube als freie Tat des Gehorsams."

459. RB, *Theologische Enzyklopädie,* 134.

The concluding paragraph 15 takes up once more the central question of the Theological Encyclopedia, "What is theology?" Despite the question of whether Bultmann meant to add it to chapter 5 of the lectures or to view it as a free-standing final chapter, a question we can no longer hope to answer, this paragraph forms "both the counterpart to the first chapter and the unfolding of its theme."[460] In it, Bultmann summarizes his exposition. The character of theology cannot be deduced from the concepts of other positive forms of critical study or from that of philosophy. It finds its own appropriate motif only in faith. As "a conceptual explication of believing existence," theology therefore presupposes that "*it is imposed on faith on the basis of faith and for the sake of faith.*"[461] Since the object of theology is not objectifiable, not to be disposed of, and by nature accessible to faith alone, the claim of Christian doctrine to truth cannot be subject to control by a general form of critical study. Rather, the assertions of theology are "true only if it pleases God to make them true."[462] It follows from this that theology must draw the criterion of its validity "from proclamation heard as proclamation."[463] For this reason, the substance of theological study is the critical examination of the received texts of scripture, of dogma, and of the history of theology—in each case with regard to whether it is a genuine or false proclamation.

Thus scripture has exclusive authoritative significance for the study of theology, for scripture not only presents the original evidence for the Christian proclamation, it is also characterized by a way of speaking in which human existence is constituted as determined by God and through the historic occurrence of revelation. Theology must therefore reflect an unswerving commitment to an existentialist interpretation of scripture. And accordingly, "there is no longer any systematic theology besides this which might portray a system of Christian doctrine according to its own principles."[464] Within this framework, as Bultmann himself perceives in exemplary fashion in his *Theological Encyclopedia*, the task of systematic theology must be the critical "self-understanding of the historical work of exegesis itself."[465]

Bultmann laid out his lectures on encyclopedia as a fundamental theological treatment focused exclusively on the question of the essence of theology.

460. Foreword of the editors in RB, *Theologische Enzyklopädie*, xiin12; cf. RB, *Theologische Enzyklopädie*, 12.

461. RB, *Theologische Enzyklopädie*, 163. For the corresponding view of M. Heidegger, see above 209.

462. RB, *Theologische Enzyklopädie*, 166.

463. RB, *Theologische Enzyklopädie*, 168.

464. RB, *Theologische Enzyklopädie*, 170.

465. RB, *Theologische Enzyklopädie*, 170.

By resolutely concentrating the encyclopedic thematic on the task of theology, the New Testament scholar presented himself as a systematician to the audience of his lectures on encyclopedia. To the extent that they had carefully read his already published texts, his listeners would have discovered few trains of thought that Bultmann had not already presented and developed in other connections. This is especially true for the essay published in 1925, "What Sense Does It Make to Speak of God?" as well as other essays that make systematic-theological claims. These texts, which reflected more or less a decade of his theological work, became once again accessible in the form of a volume of essays in 1933, and thus Bultmann offered a sort of provisional substitute for the *Theological Encyclopedia* that had not been published.

The lectures on encyclopedia certainly had a powerful, immediate effect on Bultmann's hearers. The young Gerhard Ebeling attended this series of lectures during his first semester of study in the summer of 1930, even though Bultmann had given his audience the admonition that they were designed for advanced students only.[466] As he had done for others with his exegetical lectures, his *Theological Encyclopedia* awakened in Ebeling "the sensibility for the hermeneutical task."[467] In the summer semester of 1936, when Walter Schulz heard Bultmann's lectures on encyclopedia, they made such a lasting impact on this student of Hans-Georg Gadamer that he was impelled to think through on his own the relation between theology and philosophy when he was later teaching in Tübingen. Thus, for the young Schulz, "the impression *of Bultmann*—his methodical rigor and his unpretentious engagement—was overwhelming, and it grew even stronger through *Bultmann's* commitment in the struggle between church and state."[468]

466. Cf. UB Tübingen, RB est., G. Ebeling to RB, 14. 11. 1933, Mn 2-669; on what follows, cf. A. Beutel, *Gerhard Ebeling*, 12–15.

467. G. Ebeling, *Evangelische Evangelienauslegung*, 549 (Afterword); cf. Ebeling, "Mein theologischer Weg," 7. Thirty years later, when Bultmann gave up the plan to work through and rework his lectures in the encyclopedia due to old age and other responsibilities, he offered G. Ebeling the task of taking over the *Theologische Enzyklopädie* along with the "Dogmatics" and "Ethics" in the *Neuen Theologischen Grundrissen*. Cf. UB Tübingen, RB est., RB to G. Ebeling, 15. 11. 1960, Mn 2-2189. Various works on fundamental theology strengthened Bultmann in the hope that Ebeling would write the *Theologische Enzyklopädie*. Cf. RB to G. Ebeling, 5. 9. 1965, 1. 3. 1971, 31. 1. 1972, in UA Tübingen, G. Ebeling est., 633/616. Cf. G. Ebeling, *Studium der Theologie. Eine enzyklopädische Orientierung*; as well as A. Beutel, *Gerhard Ebeling*, 400f.

468. W. Schulz, untitled article, 274; cf. also UB Tübingen, RB est., W. Schulz to RB 4. 10. 1958 and 14. 7. 1964, Mn 2-1794.

9. Faith and Understanding [Glauben und Verstehen]

Most of these essays have already appeared in journals. However, what we have here is not a random collection, but rather the most basic essays of a thinker who does not rest until his thoughts have found the clearest and, through their simplicity, often surprising form.[469]

When, in the spring of 1932, Bultmann recommended to Oskar Siebeck the publication of his student Ernst Käsemann's dissertation in the Beiträge zur historischen Theologie [Contributions to Historical Theology] series, his Tübingen publisher sent him a negative reply on April 9. He had not generally accepted dissertations recently for the series in question, as one could expect only an extremely limited sale for manuscripts of this type, and despite Bultmann's judgment of its extraordinary quality, he would have to turn down Käsemann's work as a matter of principle.[470] The publisher did, indeed, have to make some hard calculations, especially because of the increasing economic crisis that year, but also in view of the situation of the theological branch of his publishing house. For that same year the second edition of the renowned dictionary *Die Religion in Geschichte und Gegenwart* [*Religion Past and Present*] was due to be finished, and it was above all textbooks, not the dissertations of younger scholars, that produced high sales figures and thereby ensured the long-term health of the theological publishing program.

Oskar Siebeck had been wondering since 1925 how he might be able to expand the theological program of the press, which had traditionally focused on liberal Protestant theology: he was interested in moving into new areas, and in particular that of dialectical theology.[471] In the business of planning the further development of the theological branch of Siebeck's publishing house, Bultmann and later Emil Brunner came to play central roles. Bultmann was the initiator and co-editor of the new series of the *Theologische Rundschau*. As editor and as one of the authors of the Neuen theologischen Grundrisse [New Theological Outline] series, he assumed a large measure of responsibility for a project that promised to bring the press

469. H. Herrigel, "Ein protestantischer Theologe."

470. UB Tübingen, RB est., O. Siebeck to RB, 9. 4. 1932, Mn 2-2488. To be sure, Bultmann was able in the long term to bring his influence to bear with the publisher in the matter of printing Käsemann's work. Cf. E. Käsemann, *Leib*.

471. On what follows cf. S. Knappenberger-Jans, *Verlagspolitik*, 200–224, esp. 214–23.

great prestige and economic success. This series, which was to take the place of the old compilation Grundriss der theologischen Wissenschaften [Outline of the Theological Sciences] that was committed largely to liberal theology, gave unmistakable notice of the new accents in the theological program of the press.[472] Not only did Bultmann represent historical-critical theology, the cultivation of which had always been a primary matter of concern to the press, but in the theological debates that had broken out since the end of the First World War, he had gained a hearing as one of the spokespersons for dialectical theology by producing contributions that were as weighty as they were distinctive.

All this makes it understandable that Oskar Siebeck was enthusiastic about the prospect of a volume of essays by the Marburg New Testament scholar. Once he had signaled his interest in this project to Bultmann in the above mentioned letter of April 9, 1932,[473] the author and publisher were able to reach agreement over publishing arrangements. The contract, dated October 29, 1932, provided that the collection should appear in the same large format used for the *Collected Writings* of Ernst Troeltsch and would contain twenty-five folded sheets of paper. The size of the first and any further editions was fixed at two thousand copies each. Bultmann was to receive a flat-rate payment of three hundred Reichsmarks per edition, as well as ten percent of the retail price of each paperback copy sold.[474]

The title was not specified in the contract,[475] but after lengthy consultations with Hans von Soden, Bultmann proposed the title *Glauben und Verstehen* [*Faith and Understanding*] to Siebeck in December of 1932. "We did not find any other formulation that would express succinctly that the essays dealt, on the one hand, with what the meaning of Christian faith is to be determined to be, and, on the other hand, with the question of how the texts in which this faith finds expression, and therefore, above all, the New Testament, is to be understood."[476] In the Introduction to the book, Bultmann clarified the programmatic claim formulated in the title, *Faith and Understanding:* the essays in the volume "all basically concern the problem

472. Moreover, Karl Müller, the editor of the old *Grundrissen der theologischen Wissenschaften*, had suggested to Siebeck that he entrust Bultmann with the editorship of the *Neuen theologischen Grundrisse.* Cf. UB Tübingen, RB est., O. Siebeck to RB, 22. 5. 1928, Mn 2-2484.

473. UB Tübingen, RB est., O. Siebeck to RB, 9. 4. 1932, Mn 2-2488.

474. Cf. the contract with the press of 29. 10. 1932, in UB Tübingen, RB est., Mn 2-2488.

475. Cf. UB Tübingen, RB est., RB to O. Siebeck, 27. 10. 1932, Mn 2-2609.

476. UB Tübingen, RB est., RB to O. Siebeck, 13. 12. 1932, Mn 2-2609.

of what understanding is intrinsic to Christian faith. First of all, that involves the question of how the kerygma, which grounds faith, is to be understood, but it also involves the question of how the human being who is subject to the kerygma is to understand himself as one who believes."[477]

Beginning on November 5, 1932, Bultmann sent the press for typesetting those copies of the essays that had already appeared in the *Theologische Blätter* [*Theological Papers*] or in *Zwischen den Zeiten*, followed by the manuscripts of studies that had not yet been published. Off to Tübingen on December 22, 1932 went the final essay, "The Significance of the Old Testament for Christian Faith," a text in which Bultmann had already defended against the "German Christians" the importance of the Old Testament as an inalienable component of the historical tradition of Christianity.[478] In accordance with the author's wish, the press set the collection of essays in Roman type, and in February of 1933, the booksellers were able to display the work, bound in distinguished indigo blue, in their shop windows.

Faith and Understanding can be variously encountered. Since the order of the texts is chronological, it is easy for the reader to follow the path of Bultmann's thought between 1924 and 1932. But it is also possible to visit individual essays in the contexts from which they arose, and this makes a biographical understanding plausible.[479] There is also the question of whether one particular contribution represents something like the climax of the entire collection—whether in light of it and on its basis one can more fully comprehend the intention as well as the content of the remaining essays. As the first reviewers of *Faith and Understanding* recognized,[480] the 1925 essay "What Sense Does It Make to Speak of God" doubtless fills this key role.

This text goes back to a lecture that Bultmann gave to a group of pastoral candidates in Oldenburg on March 25, 1925 at the invitation of his student Hans Roth.[481] In an exchange of letters in 1923 and 1924 after completing his studies, Roth formulated a series of questions that had grown out of his preoccupation with early dialectical theology, and especially with what seemed to him incomprehensibly paradoxical expressions on Barth's part.

477. Introduction, *Glauben und Verstehen*, RB to O. Siebeck, 16. 12. 1932, in UB Tübingen, RB est., Mn 2-2609.

478. Cf. RB, "Bedeutung," *GuV*, vol. 1, 324n1; see below 304–6.

479. This procedure has therefore been followed extensively in our presentation. For individual essays, see chapters IV, sec. 2, sec. 5–7 and V, sec. 2–5.

480. Cf. H. Herrigel; "Ein protestantischer Theologe," W. Kamlah, *Zur christlichen Glaubenslehre, . . .* ; R. Winkler, rev. of RB, *Glauben und Verstehen*," 164; similarly, H. Stephan, rev. of Rudolf Bultmann, *Glauben und Verstehen*, 282f.

481. On what follows, cf. R. Rittner, "Hans Roth und Rudolf Bultmann," 137–59.

On August 12, 1924, Bultmann wrote to his former student that it had been helpful for him to be able to talk through the problems that concerned both Roth and himself with his philosophical colleague Heidegger. In the same letter, Bultmann indicated the direction he was thinking of adopting for working on the questions that had been addressed to him: "Speaking of God theologically is necessarily a way of revealing how my own existence is determined, and it is true only if this speaking is itself an event of my existence that is being determined by God. Therefore, it can never take place in universally valid propositions, general truths; otherwise, the existential situation is abandoned."[482] In the spring of 1925, Roth asked to discuss with Bultmann his understanding of the human being in the Bible and in modern times, for one could not help noting a great uncertainty among the academics of Oldenburg with regard to how "faith" was to be conceived.[483] What Roth reported renewed Bultmann's inclination "to choose the topic, 'What does it mean to speak of God,'" for the lecture on March 25, 1925.[484]

In this lecture, Bultmann begins by defining the concept of God as, in effect, "the almighty, i.e., the reality that determines everything."[485] This idea excludes speaking *about* God. For such speaking presupposes that I occupy a neutral standpoint apart from that about which I speak. But there cannot be such a standpoint with respect to God, because God is the reality that determines everything. By speaking *about* God, the human being would be making God into an object, rather as if he were asserting critically valid universal truths about God. Such objectifying talk of God would be inappropriate; it would mistake the reality of God as well as that of the individual. As the reality that determines everything, God is the reality that also determines my own existence, and therefore the individual can speak of God only by speaking at the same time of himself, of his very own concrete existence.

Bultmann now includes in his considerations Rudolf Otto's idea that had a marked effect on early dialectical theology: that of "God as the wholly other."[486] In contradistinction to Otto, Bultmann does not take this to mean that God as the wholly other is a metaphysical quantity or an external supranatural quality to which I might be able to attain by escaping my concrete existence. Rather, Bultmann insists on the double definition of God as the

482. UB Tübingen, RB est., RB to H. Roth, 12. 8. 1924, Mn 2-2349; cf. R. Rittner, "Hans Roth und Rudolf Bultmann," 150.

483. UB Tübingen, RB est., H. Roth to RB, 22. 2. 1925, Mn 2-1650.

484. UB Tübingen, RB est., RB to H. Roth, 25. 2. 1925, Mn 2-2349, and the facsimile thereof in R. Ritter, "Hans Roth und Rudolf Bultmann," 152.

485. RB, "Welchen Sinn," *GuV*, vol. 1, 26.

486. RB, *GuV*, vol. 1, 30.

reality that determines my existence and as the wholly other—for only this formulation captures the meaning of God "standing over against me the sinner as *this* wholly other."[487] Therefore, it is necessary to recognize that man's sinful nature makes it impossible to speak correctly of God and of one's own existence, for only thus can the concept of God as the wholly other have its true meaning.

And as with God, so also with our existence: we cannot speak *about* it. This is the case especially from the perspective of the modern worldview, by virtue of which the human being distinguishes himself as subject from other objects, thus observes himself from the outside as object, and so is effectively unable to grasp his own true nature. Accurate speaking of God, however, would always have to be speaking at once of our existence as one that is grounded in God and vice versa. It is for just this reason that Bultmann here agrees with the proposition of his teacher Wilhelm Herrmann, one that he also approvingly cites in other contexts, "Of God we can say only what he does to us."[488] Bultmann gives to this statement his characteristic interpretation that renders the action of God one with the word of God. "The clear sense of this word of God, this doing of God to us, is that by giving us existence God changes us from being sinners to being justified; by forgiving sin, he justifies us."[489] Faith, as the free deed of obedience,[490] affirms the doing, the word of God to us. Thus, "faith becomes the Archimedean point" from which vantage the individual can forever speak anew of the justifying God and at the same time of his sinful and grace-filled existence.[491]

The essay "What Does It Mean to Speak of God?" became a classic in the history of twentieth-century theology.[492] In this text, Bultmann outlined for the first time the basic plan of his existentialist theology, which he followed consistently after 1925, soon afterwards adapting it to include Heidegger's conceptuality. In this respect, the essays printed in *Faith and Understanding* document the path that Bultmann first took as a proponent of dialectical theology and the course he later followed in developing his existentialist program of the reciprocal interpretation of God's reality and

487. RB, *GuV*, vol. 1, 30.
488. RB, *GuV*, vol. 1, 36; cf. W. Herrmann, *Die Wirklichkeit Gottes*, 42.
489. RB, *GuV*, vol. 1, 36.
490. Also, see above 256.
491. RB, *GuV*, vol. 1, 37.
492. Cf. G. Ebeling, "Zum Verständnis"; W. Pannenberg, *Problemgeschichte*, 205–32; F. Wittekind, "Gott." Bultmann, moreover, declared himself to be in unconditional agreement with Ebeling's interpretation of his essay (made available to him before it was printed by E. Fuchs) and also with his criticism. Cf. UA Tübingen, G. Ebeling est., RB to G. Ebeling, 13. 9. 1967, 633/616; as well as A. Beutel, *Gerhard Ebeling*, 269f.

human existence. The resulting and increasing alienation between Barth and Bultmann is likewise reflected in *Faith and Understanding.* To an outside observer, it must have seemed an accident that the book appeared in the year when dialectical theology as a working group engaged in a common struggle finally fell apart. To be sure, this situation is highly symbolic of the end of a movement, the eventual end of which had become apparent long before 1933. The latent disagreement between Barth and Bultmann that had been present since 1922 often came to light in the latter half of that decade, revealing differences related to various complexes of topics—the relation between philosophy and theology, for instance, and above all in the case of Barth, to the problem of natural theology. In essence, it was a question of how theological reflection should deal with the issue of the real significance of human beings in relation to the word of God—a topic that was also part of Barth's discussion with Emil Brunner and Friedrich Gogarten. Did the understanding of truth in modernity fall within the subject-area of theology? Or, given the context of the contingent self-revelation of God, was it a topic to be disregarded?

In June, 1928, Bultmann greeted Barth's *Christliche Dogmatik in Entwurf* [*Christian Dogmatics in Outline*] as "a start to genuine dogmatic work," but criticized the way it was carried through. In particular, he disapproved of Barth's failure to engage in discussion with modern philosophy—in particular with phenomenology—while uncritically adopting the superseded ontology of early church and scholastic dogmatics. Still, theology could not allow itself to ignore philosophy: "For since faith is the faith of *one who has faith*, which is to say of an existing human being (I may also say, 'since the one who is justified is the *sinner*'), dogmatics can speak only in existentialist-ontological concepts. But these are worked out by philosophy (having originated from an original understanding of existence)."[493] Precisely in order to protect theology from a philosophy that claims to be a system, Bultmann recommended enlisting philosophy as *ancilla theologiae* [the maid-servant of theology] for the purpose of forming concepts. In contrast, Barth's answer confessed to a "deep abhorrence [of such an enlistment] . . . in view of the spectacle of how theology has time and again intended only to accommodate the philosophy of its time and has then disregarded its own subject-matter." Earlier in the *Epistle to the Romans*, and now again in the *Christian Dogmatics*, he made use of concepts that he "most certainly found and found to be most suitable, without thinking about the problem of a pre-established

493. RB to K. Barth, 8. 6. 1928, in B. Jaspert, *Barth-Bultmann Briefwechsel*, 81f; cf. K. Barth, *Die christliche Dogmatik*, vol. 1. On what follows cf. B. Jaspert "Sachkritik," 172–76.

harmony between the subject-matter and these *particular* concepts, since I had both hands [full] in trying to *say* something quite particular."[494] All the same, as Barth admitted, Bultmann had exposed the boundaries that he could not possibly cross over. To be sure, Barth showed only slight inclination to involve himself actively in discussions like that of the relation between theology and philosophy.[495]

When on January 20, 1930, Barth lectured to theology students in Marburg on "Theological and Philosophical Ethics," he took the opportunity to visit Bultmann, who read aloud to him his rejoinder to Gerhardt Kuhlmann's criticism of his approach of an existentialist theology.[496] This essay of Bultmann's, the conversations with Barth, and the discussion after Barth's lecture caused Barth to return home "right worried by Marburg." Barth now saw Bultmann as one of a group including Brunner, Gogarten, and Friedrich Karl Schumann that was engaged in "something like a splendid return to the fleshpots of Egypt." They were all "in collusion in attempting to understand faith afresh—certainly in a very new and very different way from that of the theology of the nineteenth century—as a human possibility or . . . as grounded in a human possibility, and thereby once again to deliver theology into the hands of philosophy." As Barth saw it, Bultmann would be playing "with the possibility of a natural theology" if he were to drive "theology into the framework of a pre-understanding that had been won untheologically."[497] Such an undertaking Barth judged to be a falling away from the original goal that had once motivated dialectical theology to line up against theological liberalism. From then on, the catchword "natural theology" formed the interpretive key for Barth's view of Bultmann's theological work and for his growing disapproval of it. His accusation was that in conceiving the relation between anthropology and theology as he had, Bultmann had ultimately "accepted the old, shameless dictate of modern philosophy under the new Heideggerian key-signature." On this basis Barth felt himself justified in judging "that the new Marburg is only too akin to the old."[498]

Bultmann studied Barth's critique of February 5, 1930, in the hope that it might be "the start of a serious conversation that, up to now, has sadly been avoided." He insisted on the necessity of making faith understandable as an ontological possibility, and concerning other matters viewed the differences

494. K Barth to RB, 12. 6. 1928, in B. Jaspert, *Barth-Bultmann Briefwechsel,* 85f.

495. Cf. K Barth to RB, 24. 7. 1928, in B. Jaspert, *Barth-Bultmann Briefwechsel,* 90–92.

496. Cf. G. Kuhlmann, "Zum theologischen Problem," 28–57; RB, "Die Geschichtlichkeit des Daseins," *Neues Testament und christliche Existenz,* 59–83. See above, 214–16.

497. K. Barth to RB, 5. 2. 1930, in B. Jaspert, *Barth-Bultmann Briefwechsel,* 99f.

498. K. Barth to RB, 27. 5. 1931, in B. Jaspert, *Barth-Bultmann Briefwechsel,* 117.

between his work and that of Barth differently than Barth did.[499] When Barth complained that his conception of the word of God might not have been a real matter of concern to Bultmann,[500] Bultmann responded that this issue was at least implicit in his reference to the "concept of the word of God in the New Testament" at the third meeting of German theologians in Breslau on October 6, 1930.

In this lecture, Bultmann first analyzed the way the language of "word" and "word of God" is used in the religious environment of the New Testament. In the Old Testament, in ancient Judaism, and in the proclamation of Jesus, the word of God applies not to the intellect, but rather to the will. It is not something to be seen, but to be heard, and for this reason cannot be responded to by means of critical study but only by obedience. In Greek-Hellenistic usage the term lacks the "here-and-now" characteristic of address, so that it is likewise not conceived as a temporal event in a concrete, historical situation. The New Testament picks up on the Old Testament-Jewish use of language and now emphasizes the importance of understanding the word of God as address, "spoken to a person."[501] As address, then, the word of God demands to be acknowledged, neither needing nor being capable of any other neutral human legitimation. In the New Testament, the content of the word of God is Jesus Christ alone, more specifically his cross and his resurrection. As the word of God *per se*, the Christ-event means "*the end of the old aeon*," and Christ "is the final word that God has spoken and speaks."[502]

Therefore the individual can encounter Christ as the word of God only where this word becomes event. This occurs in the preaching of the church, which makes present the past history of Jesus as the word of God, "in whom judgment and forgiveness, death and life become event."[503] These explanations might still have conformed to Barth's understanding of the word of God, but the difference from Barth becomes apparent from the fact that Bultmann refers to the Pauline and Johannine witness to elucidate faith as a mode of understanding. Just as the word of God totally renounces every form of legitimation, so it also resists all demands for blind obedience, for as address it implies the necessity of being understood. More precisely, the word of God opens to the person the possibility of understanding himself—and specifically in the way that the word expects of him. In this case,

499. RB to K. Barth, 16. 2. 1930, in B. Jaspert, *Barth-Bultmann Briefwechsel*, 102.
500. K. Barth to RB, 5. 2. 1930, in B. Jaspert, *Barth-Bultmann Briefwechsel*, 101.
501. RB, "Der Begriff des Wortes Gottes," *GuV*, vol. 1, 280.
502. RB, "Der Begriff des Wortes Gottes," *GuV*, vol. 1, 293.
503. RB, "Der Begriff des Wortes Gottes," *GuV*, vol. 1, 292.

however, it is necessary to elucidate the meaning of faith as an ontological possibility for human existence. "The possibility of the word's being understood is inseparable from the possibility of the human being's understanding himself."[504]

In February of 1930 Bultmann launched an initiative to bring Barth, Thurneysen, Gogarten, Brunner, and himself together for a discussion to clarify the differences that had arisen in the camp of dialectical theology.[505] Notification was sent of a meeting set for the autumn of 1930 in Marburg that would have the character of a meeting of the "old Marburgers" on the question of natural theology. The encounter did not take place. To begin with, Brunner and Gogarten declined for reasons having to do with schedules. Thereupon, and at short notice, Barth also withdrew his agreement to speak about the problem of natural theology before the "old Marburgers." Barth also suspected that Gogarten declined the invitation to come to come to Marburg because his chief adversary would not be there, and thus the main reason for his taking part in the meeting no longer held.[506] Bultmann took Barth's cancellation as an affront to theology at Marburg and was accordingly annoyed, but he had to reckon with the likelihood that Barth was unwilling really to engage in conversation concerning the theological work of the Marburgers and the philosophy of Heidegger. Barth's refusal resulted in a definite worsening of the climate for discussion. Between October 1931 and July 1933 the exchange of letters between Barth and Bultmann came to a complete standstill.

When in the following year the "old Marburgers" reconvened the meeting that had been canceled in 1930, Bultmann himself assumed the task originally intended for Barth—that of presenting a lecture on the "Problem of Natural Theology." In this lecture, Bultmann categorically excludes "natural theology" in its usual sense of a basic foundation for Christian dogmatics. On the one hand, the Catholic concept of natural knowledge of God fails to deal with God, who gives himself to be discerned only through his revelation and only to faith. On the other hand, the effort of philosophies of religion to exhibit a religious *a priori* makes the mistake of taking faith to be a human attitude and therefore does not take God seriously as a transcendent counterpart to the human being. Nevertheless, the catchphrase "natural theology"—which Bultmann usually places in quotation marks—

504. RB, "Der Begriff des Wortes Gottes," *GuV*, vol. 1, 284.

505. On what follows, cf. the correspondence of Barth and RB from 16. 2. 1930 to 14. 6. 1931, in B. Jaspert, *Barth-Bultmann Briefwechsel,* 102–22, and of RB and F. Gogarten from 6. 3. to 6. 9. 1930, in H. G. Göckeritz, *Bultmann-Gogarten Briefwechsel,* 178–90.

506. K. Barth to RB, 30. 9. 1930, in B. Jaspert, *Barth-Bultmann Briefwechsel,* 110.

does make reference to three topics that constitute a task yet to be dealt with by Protestant theology.

First, as the individual's new self-understanding that is made possible by revelation, faith implies a constitutive reference to the pre-understanding of faith—a category that must not be misunderstood as a sort of point of connection for revelation. Rather, in the light of revelation the role of a "natural theology" is to show "the extent to which unfaithful existence and its self-understanding is ruled and motivated by its own dubiousness, which, as such, has first become visible to the faithful [person's] understanding of existence."[507] In this fashion, even if faith unmasks it as idolatry, or along the lines of Feuerbach's criticism of religion as illusion, each religion hides an unknowing suspicion if not of the true God, then of the dubiousness of unfaithful existence itself. Of course, when faith uncovers religion as unfaith, and hence as sin, it does not thereby make contact with an assumed human propensity for God. However, faith here approaches "natural theology" to the extent that on the basis of revelation, it formulates and answers the question of unfaith as such for the first time.[508] Finally, theology and philosophy do not treat faithful and unfaithful existence as two completely separate sets of topics; for theology in particular cannot operate with two sets of concepts for describing reality. And this is the reason it must and can take over the formal analysis of existence in philosophical ontology. To be sure, it realizes that the freedom attributed to existence by philosophy is, from the perspective of faith, unfaith; and that unfaith characterizes "the basic constitution of human existence in general."[509] Indeed, for Bultmann the ontology of unfaith is marvelously suited to playing a part in the conceptual explication of the event of justification. For this is how the secret of justifying faith allows itself to be kept: namely, that this is "*no phenomenon of existence*," but rather the eschatological event that cannot be affirmed in worldly terms.[510]

With his Marburg lecture on the "Problem of Natural Theology," Bultmann took up a completely solitary position with respect to the controversy then going on among Barth, Brunner, and Gogarten. He pleaded for a theology that would accept the primacy of and remain within the framework of revelation and faith, and would take account of the modern person's

507. RB, "Das Problem der 'natürlichen Theologie,'" *GuV*, vol. 1, 298.

508. Cf. RB, "Das Problem der 'natürlichen Theologie,'" *GuV*, vol. 1, 304; as well as C. Gestrich, *Neuzeitliches*, 360–63.

509. RB, "Das Problem der 'natürlichen Theologie,'" *GuV*, vol. 1, 309; see also C. Gestrich, *Neuzeitliches*, 368f, 370–80, for reflections on locating Bultmann's position in the controversy of the time among Barth, Brunner, and Gogarten.

510. Cf. RB, "Das Problem der 'natürlichen Theologie,'" *GuV*, vol. 1, 311.

experience of reality. When the text of Bultmann's essay appeared in *Faith and Understanding* at the beginning of 1933, the one for whom it was really intended, Karl Barth,[511] was already too fixated on the discussion with Brunner and Gogarten to perceive the specific ways in which Bultmann's argumentation clearly differed from the views of both these theologians. If by his departure from *Zwischen den Zeiten* in the autumn of 1933 Barth had wanted explicitly to distance himself from Brunner and Gogarten,[512] so in the spring of 1933 he felt that he had to accuse Bultmann with the rest of having actively contributed by their "shocking statements" over the recent years to "the utter darkening of the theological situation."[513] Given his theological premises, Barth was in no position in that time of partings to comment on what mattered to Bultmann except with such sweeping and therefore misleading accusations. For his part, Bultmann allowed himself to express his disappointment by saying *privatim* in December of 1932, "I have not been able to learn anything more from Barth's work in recent years. He is becoming ever more obstinate and more jittery in refusing to enter into discussion with other people."[514]

As a humanist, Paul Friedländer dissented from many of the specific positions taken in *Faith and Understanding*, but he accorded Bultmann "admiration for the acuteness and energy of your thought, the seriousness of your thoroughgoing treatment, the richness of scholarship in substance and intellect." Friedländer read *Faith and Understanding* with the awareness that "these are essays written by a friend."[515] Bultmann dedicated the book to Martin Heidegger "in grateful friendship"[516] in order to express that the contributions printed in the volume were "in large part the fruit of the companionship" of the philosopher.[517] Heidegger was delighted with the

511. Cf. the debate with Thurneysen in RB, "Das Problem der 'natürlichen Theologie,'" *GuV*, vol. 1, 305; correspondingly, RB to K. Barth, 25. 5. 1931, in B. Jaspert, *Barth-Bultmann Briefwechsel*, 134.

512. Cf. K. Barth, "Abschied."

513. K. Barth, "Das Erste Gebot," 313.

514. RB to M. Heidegger, 14. 12. 1932, in A. Grossmann and C. Landmesser, *Bultmann-Heidegger Briefwechsel*, 187.

515. UB Tübingen, RB est., P. Friedländer to RB, 18. 2. 1933, Mn 2-787.

516. RB, *GuV*, vol. 1, vol. 3; cf. UB Tübingen, RB est., RB to O. Siebeck, 22. 12. 1932, Mn 2-2609.

517. RB to M. Heidegger, 14. 12. 1932, in A. Grossmann and C. Landmesser, *Bultmann-Heidegger Briefwechsel*, 185. In the copy that Bultmann dedicated to Heidegger, he wrote the inscription, "To Martin Heidegger, with kind regards! πλὴν εἰς ὃ ἐφθάσαμεν, τῷ αὐτῷ στοιχεῖν (Phil 3:16)." Cf. A. Grossmann and C. Landmesser, *Bultmann-Heidegger Briefwechsel*, 190n2.

dedication,[518] and following the end of the Third Reich, Bultmann placed in the first volume of the 1954 edition of *Faith and Understanding* a new and heartfelt dedication: "To MARTIN HEIDEGGER this book remains dedicated in grateful memory of the time together in Marburg."[519]

Following the Second World War, three more volumes, all of which gained wide circulation, took their places alongside the collection of essays published in 1933.[520] Admittedly, the first volume of *Faith and Understanding* went through the most editions—nine, at present—thereby placing it first among all twentieth-century volumes of essays in Protestant theology—still ahead of the seven volumes of Karl Holl's Luther book that appeared in seven editions between 1921 and 1948. Surely this stands as a ringing endorsement of the continuing significance of Bultmann's essays in *Faith and Understanding*.

10. The Teacher in Exchange with Students and Colleagues

> *When, in about 1930, the scholar of Romance languages and literature Leo Spitzer accepted a call from Marburg to Cologne and held a farewell celebration on this occasion, he gave a talk on the question, "What is Marburg?" I remember well how he named a list of institutions and names and said of them, "All of this is not Marburg"—whereupon some were offended—and that the first name of which he said, "This is Marburg" was that of Rudolf Bultmann.*[521]

In July of 1925 a nineteen-year-old theology student from Bonn named Ernst Käsemann petitioned Bultmann to accept him as a member of his seminar for the winter semester of 1925–26. Bultmann informed the petitioner that in recent semesters he had been granting such acceptances only as exceptions, but in this case he might be willing to make such an exception. Before giving his definitive consent, he would like Käsemann to

518. M. Heidegger to RB, 16. 12. 1932, in A. Grossmann and C. Landmesser, *Bultmann-Heidegger Briefwechsel*, 190: "I am so particularly delighted with your dedication; it must not document something in the past, but rather indicate a challenge, the fulfillment of which is certainly not tied up with allegiance to my work. However, that I have at the same time above all been favored by this expression of your consciousness of friendship and am thankful for it doesn't need any long-winded confirmation."

519. RB, *GuV*, vol. 1, vol. 3.

520. Cf. E. Herms, "Glauben und Verstehen," 346–48.

521. H.-G. Gadamer, *Philosophische Lehrjahre*, 14.

submit to him a short piece of work of not more than thirty pages. The first of the four outlined topics proposed by Bultmann, all of them demanding, was "The Significance of Romans 7 in Connection with the Epistle to the Romans (and the Consequences in Detail of this Position for Exegesis)."[522] During the Pentecost vacation of 1941, theology students Gustav Hammann and Jochen Niemöller wished to participate in the "theological week" in Alpirsbach and to attend Bultmann's lecture "New Testament and Mythology" there. Since for financial reasons they could get to Alpirsbach only by bicycle, they would have had to miss the following session of the New Testament seminar, but of this Bultmann did not approve: "That is out of the question. You will both be in class!" Hammann and Niemöller went to Alpirsbach and appeared on time for the first session of the seminar following the vacation. In 1946, after theology student Helmut Koester had attended his first-year New Testament course, the lecturer Ernst Fuchs sent him to Bultmann. Fuchs gave Koester a list of more than a dozen books that he was to read in preparation for the oral entrance examination to Bultmann's seminar. Bultmann then opened with the question, "Now, Mr. Koester, have you read Wrede's *Messiasgeheimnis* [*Messianic Secret*]?" After half an hour, Koester was accepted into the seminar. Two years later, he became Bultmann's last doctoral student.

If entry into Bultmann's New Testament seminar was subject to such strict prerequisites, the work of the seminar placed even greater demands on those enrolled in it. Bultmann was an exceedingly demanding teacher. Not only must the participants in his seminar demonstrate extensive previous knowledge of the topic of the course, but the discussion and the results of each session were to be recorded in a set of minutes that was then subjected to brief critical scrutiny in the following session.[523] And only at the end of each session did Bultmann specify who was to write up the minutes, a procedure that ensured the undivided attention of the seminar participants.[524] It was necessary not simply to translate correctly the New Testament and other ancient texts under discussion, but also to read them fluently in the original language. If, in doing this, a student made a mistake, Bultmann took his pipe out of his mouth and dispassionately issued a reprimand: "Well, your Greek does not seem to be particularly good."[525] Even if Helmut Thielicke's recol-

522. UB Tübingen, RB est., RB to E. Käsemann, 20. 7. 1925, Mn 2-2251; cf. also E. Käsemann, "70 Jahre," 95.

523. Cf. B. Jaspert, *Sachgemässe Exegese.*

524. Cf. H. Urner-Astholz, "Erinnerungen," 207; H. Ramsauer, "Rudolf Bultmann," 13.

525. Cf. D. Trautwein, *Komm Herr*, 104; P. Biehl and P. Schulz, *Autobiographische*, 51.

lection of studying with Bultmann is not precisely accurate, it may well contain a strong element of truth. "In the seminar, we all trembled before him, at least if we were not perfectly prepared."[526] In his own work Bultmann considered the meticulous, detailed work of philology dealing with the wording and meaning of the text to be essential to grasping the point a text was making, and he expected of his students this same effort at formulating exact exegesis and locating the testimonies of New Testament and ancient literature in the history of religion.

During Bultmann's lifetime, the master's pedagogical charisma was acknowledged in writing by Erich Dinkler, and after his death by Hans-Georg Gadamer, Otto Kaiser, and Eduard Schweizer. For Wilhelm Weischedel, Bultmann became "the theological teacher *katexochen* [most outstanding, *par excellence*]. The absolute honesty of his research, the passionate involvement in his subject-matter, the impression of the deepest conviction, the care for his students, perceptible through all the reserve of the Oldenburger, made him seem to me the model of an academic teacher."[527] Hans Jonas has no doubt most impressively traced Bultmann's extraordinary capacity as a teacher to the way that aim and method converged in his academic instruction. "The freedom of Protestantism held true in relation to his teaching. He insisted on understanding, but not on agreement. It was painstaking, but never once apodictic. In discussion, his style was to consider, not to assert. An *ex cathedra* manner was utterly foreign to him, and he strove to create a sense of equality in his discussion partner as if this went without saying—a quality made possible only by great inward security and practiced only in conjunction with humility. Feeling thus honored by his humane bearing and tranquility, students avoided the kind of rash talk for which they might later feel ashamed. And no disputatious fireworks were tolerated. This is how one learned to interpret the New Testament—as a risk-taking experiment in the course of which learnedness earned approval but not necessarily success. This was an unforgettable school of inquiring thinking."[528]

The word soon got out in the early 1920s among theology students even outside of Marburg that it was worth going to this school. Bultmann's

526. H. Thielicke, *Zu Gast,* 172. Thielicke's report, *Zu Gast,* 173, may in part be subject to challenge, for he tells of Bultmann's insistence that the members of his seminar were to use his conceptuality (that was taken over from Heidegger); and this detail, at least, is inconsistent with virtually all the other recollections of Bultmann's style in his seminars.

527. W. Weischedel, untitled article, 318; cf. E. Dinkler, "Rudolf Bultmann," 423f; H.-G. Gadamer, "Gedenkworte," 132; E. Schweizer, *Jesus,* 11–13; O. Kaiser, "Worte," 41f. Cf. also the contemporary impressions of M. Stallmann, in E. Stallmann, *Martin Stallmann,* 42–49.

528. H. Jonas, "Im Kampf," 42.

success as a teacher showed in the numbers of students who frequented his courses.[529] Among those who attended his lectures and who took part in his seminars between 1921 and 1951 were over seventy students who later went on to become professors of theology themselves.[530] Just as theology students in Marburg attended Heidegger's courses, students of the philosopher made use of Bultmann's offerings in theology during that time of intensive dialogue between theology and philosophy: among them were Wilhelm Anz, Hannah Arendt, Hans Jonas, Wilhelm Kamlah, Gerhard Krüger, and Wilhelm Weischedel. Gerhard Krüger, a young philosopher versed in theology, was over the course of time to become Bultmann's congenial discussion partner and friend. After coming to Marburg in 1921, he followed with great interest the beginnings of dialectical theology—on which he offered journalistic comments from a philosophical point of view—as well as on Bultmann's journey to the existentialist interpretation of Christian faith. Krüger's own efforts were aimed at constructively determining the relation between thinking and believing, philosophy and Christian theology, and especially in critically delimiting the claims that modern subjectivity makes for itself in asserting itself to be autonomous. He was especially determined to discover within the Western religious tradition the possibility of a philosophically supportable faith.[531]

Along with Hans-Georg Gadamer, Günther Bornkamm, and Heinrich Schlier, and later, Erich Dinkler, Krüger belonged to Bultmann's *Graeca*. For about fifteen years this group met at Bultmann's home every Thursday evening to read the classics of Greek antiquity with him. One member of the group read a German translation aloud, and the others followed along in the Greek original. In his *Graeca* as in his classes, Bultmann strictly insisted that his rules be followed. The group's reading began punctually at 8:15 p.m. and ended at 11:00 o'clock. When on occasion a reading ignited a discussion, Bultmann admonished his young colleagues to return to reading the text. Smoking was permitted during the reading—but only Brazilian cigars or a pipe. Cigarettes were prohibited: "They stink." Following the reading, the social part of the evening began at 11:00pm, when over a glass of wine, the company delighted in the latest academic gossip and jokes. "Just as the former was allowed to be very malicious, the latter was allowed to be very

529. Cf. the statements on the numbers of participants in B. Jaspert, *Sachgemässe Exegese*, *passim*. The attendance at Bultmann's seminars fell only during the Second World War.

530. Cf. B. Jaspert, *Sachgemässe Exegese*, 6f.

531. Cf. F. Lilie, "Bultmann-Krüger Briefwechsel," *ZNThG* 4, 282–86.

Plate 21: Rudolf Bultmann and Günther Bornkamm in Conversation

Plate 22: Erich Dinkler

ribald, and Günther Bornkamm above all scored real triumphs with his gift for story-telling. Bultmann jotted down the jokes that he deemed worthy of recording, and in later years, being the model of a true scholar in this point as well, went back with a smile to the supply accumulated long ago."[532] Even his collection of jokes he organized in precise fashion by catchwords, from "doctor" [*Arzt*] to "joke" [*Witz*].[533] Despite the joy that the shared reading of the Greeks and the social exchange gave Bultmann and his friends, his *Graeca* represented something completely different from cultivating the hobby of going to a museum, for it formed a part of his persistent interest in understanding the distinctiveness of the Christian kerygma by means of contrasting it with non-Christian antiquity.[534] And incidentally, Bultmann invited Hans-Georg Gadamer into his *Graeca* at a time when deep doubts had overtaken that student of Heidegger as to whether he was suited to scholarship and philosophy. As he wrote to Bultmann five decades later, that invitation was what led Gadamer to become a scholar.[535]

Since Bultmann understood his academic position as service to the church and its proclamation, he saw the main task of his teaching activity to be the exegetical-theological education of future pastors and teachers of religion. He was not satisfied with supplying his numerous students with knowledge acquired at school that would be relevant only to their exams, but involved them in a demanding and supportive way in theological research. This included encouraging particularly gifted students in their own scholarly work and accompanying them on their way to becoming qualified for the teaching office. Bultmann demanded of them what he knew to be binding on himself: truthfulness in theological thinking, sound historical-critical work, freedom to undertake criticism, and personal accountability for what one had done.

One of Bultmann's first students for the doctorate was Heinrich Schlier.[536] Strongly influenced by Karl Barth's interpretations in *The Epistle to the Romans*, Schlier was powerfully motivated in his Marburg studies by his theology teacher Bultmann and by the early Martin Heidegger. Once he had passed his first theological examination, Schlier began work on his dissertation, a history-of-religions study on the Ignatian epistles. For this

532. H.-G. Gadamer, *Philosophische Lehrjahre*, 38f, cf. 225f. Alongside Bultmann's *Graeca* there was yet a second *Graeca*, to which only professors belonged: R. Bultmann, P. Friedländer, M. Heidegger, P. Jacobsthal, and H. von Soden, as well as later E. Frank.

533. Cf. RB, joke collection, Mn 2-3053.

534. Cf. G. Bornkamm, "*In memoriam*," 240.

535. Cf. UB Tübingen, RB est., H.-G. Gadamer to RB, 16. 8. 1974, Mn 2-2082; as well as J. Grondin, *Hans-Georg Gadamer*, 141.

536. Cf. R. von Bendemann, *Heinrich Schlier*, 1995; R. Schwerendt, "Heinrich Schlier," 263–86.

project, which was suggested by Bultmann, he received his degree from Marburg in 1926.[537] Following this, he completed the practical training for the pastorate in the State Church of Thüringia, and went on to pastoral service in Casekirchen. In 1928, he qualified as a university lecturer in Jena with an investigation supervised by Karl Ludwig Schmidt on the relation between christology and ecclesiology in Ephesians.[538] Upon receiving an offer from Bultmann, Schlier returned to Marburg in 1930, where he served for several years teaching biblical Greek and the history of the New Testament period. Aided by extensive theological agreement, the teacher-student relation between Bultmann and Schlier had by 1926 developed into a genuine friendship. On November 30, 1927, Bultmann officiated at the wedding of Heinrich and Erna Schlier, née Haas, in Elberfeld.[539]

The scholarly gifts of the theological student Günther Bornkamm had equally attracted the attention of Bultmann and Hans Lietzmann in Berlin. Lietzmann would gladly have overseen Bornkamm's qualification as a university lecturer, but he made it clear that he was in agreement with Bultmann's standing offer to Bornkamm to see this through in Marburg.[540] Bultmann recommended to his student a topic that he himself was also interested in—the interrelationship of early Christianity, Gnosticism, and Manichaeism.[541] So it was that in 1931 Bornkamm earned the *Lic. Theol.* from Marburg with a thesis on the apocryphal Acts of Thomas,[542] for which not only his two referees Bultmann and von Soden but also Lietzmann found most appreciative words.[543] Bornkamm then qualified as a university lecturer in 1931 with an investigation of the confession of faith in earliest Christianity, an effort completed not under Lietzmann but rather under Julius Schniewind in Königsberg.[544] In his case as well, a lasting friendship with Bultmann developed from having been his student.[545]

537. Cf. H. Schlier, *Religionsgeschichtliche.*

538. Cf. H. Schlier, *Christus.*

539. Cf. Bultmann's wedding sermon on 1 Cor 7:29–31, in UB Tübingen, RB est., Mn 2-3435. Like her husband, Erna Haas had studied with Bultmann. She was among the women whose initiative led to the founding of the Association of Women Protestant Theologians of Germany. In 1930, Bultmann became the godfather of Christoph Schlier.

540. Cf. RB to H. Lietzmann, 21. 2. 1930, in K. Aland, *Glanz und Niedergang*, 601; H. Lietzmann to E. Brunner, 8. 5. 1931, in K. Aland, *Glanz und Niedergang,* 657.

541. Cf. UB Tübingen, RB est., RB to G. Bornkamm, 20. 5. 1928, Mn 2-2147.

542. Cf. G. Bornkamm, *Mythos und Legende.*

543. Cf. H. Lietzmann to G. Bornkamm 6. 3. 1933, in K. Aland, *Glanz und Niedergang,* 729f.

544. Cf. D. Lührmann, "Günther Bornkamm"; G. Theissen, "Theologie und Exegese." See also H. Lietzmann to G. Bornkamm, 6. 3. 1933, in K. Aland, *Glanz und Niedergang.*

545. RB was the godfather of Bornkamm's daughter Anna Elisabeth. Cf. UB Tübingen, RB est., RB to G. Bornkamm, 28. 3. 1940, Mn 2-2147.

Plate 23: Ernst Fuchs, Bonn 1931

Ernst Fuchs came to Marburg in 1924 from the seminary in Tübingen where, impressed by a course of lectures by Adolf Schlatter, he had given up the study of law and turned to theology. The semesters away from home in Marburg, and especially the encounter with Bultmann and Heidegger, were to determine the future for this Swabian with an original turn of mind.[546] With Bultmann, besides the hermeneutical approach to the New Testament, he learned above all that one "cannot believe properly if one overlooks oneself."[547] Following his exam, Fuchs entered into the educational service of the Württemburg State Church. In his first published writing, he emphasized the significance for theology of the understanding of being and of the temporality and the historicity of human existence that Heidegger had worked out in *Being and Time.*[548]

The church leadership of Württemburg made it possible for Fuchs to return to Marburg in 1928–29, where he earned the doctoral degree *Lic. Theol.* in 1930 with an investigation of "The Relation of Faith to Deed in the Shepherd of Hermas." Although his doctoral advisor regarded this as "a capable piece of work," he was not willing to include it in the series Investigations into the Religion and Literature of the Old and New Testament, for it suffered from its author having depended too heavily in language and style on Heidegger's existentialist analysis. Nonetheless, Bultmann believed that "Fuchs, a highly gifted Swabian somewhat given to ruminating, deserves every encouragement," and therefore inquired of Hans Lietzmann whether a chapter of Fuchs' work might not appear in the *Zeitschrift fur die neutestamentliche Wissenschaft* [*Journal of New Testament Studies*].[549] Lietzmann refused on the grounds that he would not publish an

546. Cf. E. Fuchs, "Aus der Marburger Zeit," *Wagnis,* 73–75.
547. E. Fuchs, "Am Ostersonntag," *Wagnis,* 165.
548. Cf. E. Fuchs, "Sein und Zeit," in C. Möller, *Freude an Gott,* 285–89.
549. RB to H. Lietzmann, 24. 5. 1931, K. Aland, *Glanz und Niedergang,* 666f; cf. also Bultmann's criticism of Fuchs' dissertation in RB to M. Heidegger, 15. 7. 1929, in A. Grossmann and C. Landmesser, *Bultmann-Heidegger Briefwechsel,* 113f.

Plate 24: Ernst Käsemann, Jugenheim 1958

essay that he could not understand himself.[550] Fuchs then published extracts of his dissertation as separate units[551] and, not long after becoming Karl Ludwig Schmidt's assistant, qualified in 1932 for a teaching position at Bonn.[552]

Unlike the case with Bornkamm, Fuchs, and Schlier, the issue of the relation between theology and philosophy was not of pressing interest to Ernst Käsemann during his time as a student. The Westphalian came to Marburg after a semester in Bonn—where Erik Peterson's interpretation of Romans had held an extraordinary fascination for him—in order to pursue New Testament exegesis with Bultmann and von Soden.[553] Continuing his studies with Adolf Schlatter in Tübingen, he passed the first theological exam in 1929, and afterwards took up a curacy, from whence he maintained contact with Bultmann. Even as a young theological student, he had been sufficiently bold to pose critical questions to his Marburg teacher, who by that time had long been famous. Did the relation between the proclamation of Jesus and the earliest Christian message of Christ not have to be explained otherwise than as "a mere sudden change?" Should one not concede that utterly "real events"—the cross and resurrection of Jesus—were the basis of the Christian proclamation?[554] And what about "the meaning of the forgiveness of sins in Christian preaching?"[555] Bultmann did not evade Käsemann's questions but instead enjoyed discussion with him. "For it is not my view that I have said anything that brings things to a close, but rather feel each time in a discussion of that sort, how much we are getting

550. Cf. H. Lietzmann to RB 29. 5. 1931, in K. Aland, *Glanz und Niedergang,* 667.

551. Cf. E. Fuchs, *Glaube und Tat.*

552. Cf. E. Fuchs, *Christus.*

553. Cf. E. Käsemann, "Aspekte der Kirche," *Kirchliche Konflikte*, vol. 1, 8f; Käsemann, "70 Jahre," 95.

554. UB Tübingen, RB est., E. Käsemann to RB, 23. 3. 1927, Mn 2-1083.

555. UB Tübingen, RB est., E. Käsemann to RB 7. 9. 1927, Mn 2-1083.

back to the basics of doing theology."[556] And when Käsemann proposed his own project and topic for his dissertation, Bultmann agreed.[557] From the very beginning he was most independent of all Bultmann's students, and in 1931 he graduated with a *Lic. Theol.* awarded for his dissertation, *Leib und Leib Christi* [*The Body and the Body of Christ*]. Already in his first work, Käsemann clearly struck new and different notes in interpreting the New Testament concept of σῶμα [body] and distinguishing its use by Paul from that of Bultmann. He was later surprised that despite their obvious differences his teacher gave the dissertation high praise.[558] Could this have been related to Bultmann's having assigned himself the role of a Socratic midwife in caring for his graduate?

Finally, to the narrower circle of Bultmann's earliest students belonged Hans Jonas, a Jewish philosophy student who was in Bultmann's seminar in the summer semester of 1925 and presented a report on "Gnosis in the Gospel of John."[559] Bultmann found the presentation so convincing that he asked Jonas to pursue the topic in a dissertation, and persuaded Heidegger to serve as mentor for the doctoral process.[560] Jonas earned the doctorate in philosophy in 1928, with his thesis on "The Concept of Gnosis," and Bultmann accepted the investigation for the Investigations into the Religion and Literature of the Old and New Testament series that he edited.[561] The National Socialists' seizure of power prevented Jonas from gaining qualification as a university lecturer, but despite strong opposition, Bultmann arranged for the publication of the postdoctoral thesis that constituted the first part of Jonas' great work on Gnosticism.[562] Shortly before his death, Bultmann still remembered with gratitude the friendship and the scholarly exchange with Jonas, without whose research he could not have written his commentaries on the Gospel of John and the Johannine epistles.[563] Still, just as Jonas' qualification continued to be denied on the grounds of his Jewish origin, Bultmann's New Testament students were barred from all regular

556. UB Tübingen, RB est., RB to E. Käsemann, 15. 4. 1927, Mn 2-2251.

557. Cf. UB Tübingen, RB est., E. Käsemann to RB, 8. 10. 1929, Mn 2-1083; RB to E. Käsemann, 13. 7. 1930, Mn 2-2251; as well as E. Käsemann, "Aspekte der Kirche," *Kirchliche Konflikte*, vol. 1, 8–12.

558. Cf. E. Käsemann, *Leib und Leib Christi*; as well as E. Käsemann, "Aspekte der Kirche," *Kirchliche Konflikte*, 8–12.

559. Cf. B. Jaspert, *Sachgemässe Exegese*, 39.

560. Cf. H. Jonas, *Erinnerungen*, 117–20.

561. Cf. H. Jonas, *Der Begriff der Gnosis.*

562. See below 197f.

563. Cf. RB to H. Jonas (1976) in B. Aland, *Gnosis*, 13.

academic chairs in the state-run theological faculties during the Third Reich because of their affiliation with the Confessing Church. This would not change until after the Second World War.

In the Weimar era, the Academic Union that had evolved from an earlier youth movement developed numerous activities in Marburg. "An elite among theological and philosophical youth," this group met[564] in order to discuss current scholarly questions in a sort of *studium generale* [common search for knowledge] and to cultivate social intercourse on a high plane. Bultmann and his wife had themselves been active in the Academic Union before the First World War, and now supported these efforts to create a serious community life for students—one that would be far different from the existing student fraternities. And soon Bultmann's students set the tone of the Academic Union. Gerhard Krüger served as the philosophical advisor, and Heinrich Schlier took over the corresponding theological role. From 1927 on, the theological discussions of current topics in Bultmann's student circle grew into a well-organized tradition: the annual meetings of the "old and new Marburgers."[565]

In every detail these gatherings followed Bultmann's ideas of how theology should be done. In his view, theological knowledge was to be preserved through dialogue that was open to whatever results followed from it; indeed, the thrust and parry of lively discussion was an indispensable element of theological discourse. The theological community called the "old Marburgers" had begun to take shape—at first with few rules or patterns—when in October 1926 the students from the previous year who had passed the faculty exams met with Bultmann in the café of the castle. On this occasion they decided to hold the first regular meeting on October 24–26, 1927, at the quarters of the Academic Union on 6 Nicholas Street, near the Lutheran parish church. At first the old Marburgers were drawn from among Bultmann's students and from among those of his fellow-travelers in philosophy: Gerhard Krüger, Hans-Georg Gadamer, and Karl Löwith. In addition to in-house worthies like Bultmann, Krüger, and Schlier, they invited such outside lecturers as Karl Barth, Friedrich Gogarten, Günter Jacob, Heinrich Vogel, and Ernst Wolf. Until 1934[566] the topics chosen for meetings

564. H.-G. Gadamer, *Philosophische Lehrjahre*, 225, also 37. On the Academic Union, cf. in detail E. Stallmann, *Martin Stallmann*, 35–41; Urner-Astholz, "Erinnerungen," 207.

565. RB to F. Gogarten, 26. 6. 1927, in H. G. Göckeritz, *Bultmann-Gogarten Briefwechsel*, 111; cf. on what follows W. von Rohden, *Geschichte* (manuscript).

566. The meeting of 1930 was not able to take place due to the cancellations of K. Barth and F. Gogarten. See above 236.

Plate 25: Meeting of the "Old Marburgers," October 26–28, 1931 in Marburg: Heinrich Schlier and Rudolf Bultmann in Conversation, Friedrich Gogarten in the Background

reflected the pulse of the times: on the one hand, dialectical theology and, up until 1933, political developments; on the other[567]—Theology or History of Ideas? (1927), Jesus and Paul (1928), Christology (1929), The Question of Natural Theology (1931), The Sovereignty of the State and the Right to Revolution (1932), Political Religion and the Theological Understanding of the Law (1933), State and Church (1934). The old Marburgers recognized no sacrosanct theological positions, though this was not to everyone's taste. As Karl Barth complained in May 1931, "the peculiar Marburger self-consciousness" that Bultmann's students exhibited from the meeting's outset unduly restricted other theological views from being laid out.[568] Since it was clear that Barth chiefly meant his own views, Bultmann sent the shaft back at him, calling the charge unjustified. The joy of debate and criticism in his Marburg group rested solely on its being "conscious of its openness and of doing theology in a critical fashion."[569]

567. The topics are given only incompletely in von Rohden, *Geschichte*; on what follows cf. also H. G. Göckeritz, *Bultmann-Gogarten Briefwechsel*, *passim*.

568. K. Barth to RB, 27. 5. 1931, in B. Jaspert, *Barth-Bultmann Briefwechsel*, 117; cf. also G. Göckeritz, *Bultmann-Gogarten Briefwechsel*, 124–26.

569. RB to K. Barth, 14. 6. 1931, in B. Jaspert, *Barth-Bultmann Briefwechsel*, 121.

Plate 26: Leisure Time for the Marburg Theologians, February 6–7, 1937 in Kirchvers: Gerhard Krüger and Rudolf Bultmann

Plate 27: Hans von Soden

Such readiness for theological dialogue gained only limited favor among Bultmann's colleagues. He was certainly good friends with the Old Testament scholar Gustav Hölscher and his departmental colleague in New Testament, Hans von Soden. Hölscher entered into historical discussions with Bultmann, since in the area of gospel criticism, for instance, the two were largely in agreement; but by his own admission he lacked "the organ" to be able to understand some of Bultmann's essays dealing with systematic theology.[570] And as much as the close relationship between Bultmann and von Soden included scholarly exchanges, the two were well aware of their theological differences.[571] In view

570. Cf. G. Hölscher, *Aus meinem Leben*, pt. 2 (manuscript), 270f.

571. Cf. RB to F. Gogarten, 29. 7. 1925, in H. G. Göckeritz, *Bultmann-Gogarten Briefwechsel*, 85; on Bultmann's relation to his faculty, see also above 161–75.

Plate 28: Paul Friedländer

Plate 29: Martin Heidegger, 1927

of the restricted possibilities for interdisciplinary discussion with colleagues on his own faculty, it was all the more enjoyable for Bultmann to maintain outside his own department such intense personal and intellectually stimulating relationships as those he enjoyed with Heidegger and the classical philologist Paul Friedländer.[572]

Friedländer taught at Marburg from 1920 to 1932, and this period was one of the most fruitful of his life as a scholar.[573] In the academic culture of Marburg of the twenties, the classical philologist found a hearing for his distinctive voice in the circle of scholars who, like him, were counted among the outstanding representatives of their disciplines. Friedländer sought out and enjoyed dialogue with Bultmann, Heidegger, the archaeologist Paul Jacobsthal, and romance language scholars Ernst Robert Curtius and Leo Spitzer. His pioneering works on Greek tragedy were written in Marburg, where he also achieved great success with his two-volume work on Plato,

572. RB, autobiographical comments, in B. Jaspert, *Barth-Bultmann Briefwechsel,* 307: "In particular, I have to mention my friendship with the classical philologist Paul Friedländer, who was teaching in Marburg at that time and to whom I feel very much indebted." Cf. also Bultmann's autobiographical sketch from the early summer of 1969 in B. Jaspert, *Barth-Bultmann Briefwechsel,* 313; as well as P. Friedländer, *Platon*, vol. 1, viii.

573. Cf. W. Bühler, "Paul Friedländer"; A. Lesky, rev. of P. Friedländer, *Studien*; RB, "Paul Friedländer (1882–1968)."

which was recognized as occupying a special position in post-World War I Platonic studies and for decades remained a standard work in the field.[574] His interpretations did not so much attempt to objectify the Platonic dialogues and other ancient literature and art by means of a historical reconstruction, but rather sought to show the relevance of the Platonic world of thought and that of ancient culture in general for present-day understanding—an appreciation that depended on recognizing the unity of its spiritual content and aesthetic and literary form as both the criterion and the goal. To accomplish this, Friedländer remained thoroughly committed to the standards that had been set for historical-philological analysis, and in particular those of his teacher, Ulrich von Wilamowitz-Moellendorff. However, his work was aimed at overcoming the crisis caused by historicism, which had sucked classical philology into its vortex. This explains why Friedländer became a stimulating conversation partner for Bultmann, who recognized a comparable crisis in his own field and similarly met it with a single-minded understanding of history that sprang from an insight into the historicity of human existence.[575] If one were to assay the large number of Bultmann's friendships according to their lifelong significance for him, that of Friedländer would stand at the very top.

Plate 30: Ernst Lohmeyer

Between 1915 and 1930 Bultmann reviewed not fewer than nine of Ernst Lohmeyer's books and other writings.[576] For his part, Adolf Deissmann's student took part in the critical discussion of Bultmann's Jesus-book and

574. Cf. P. Friedländer, *Platon*, vols. 1 and 2; as well as H.-G. Gadamer, "Die neue Platoforschung," 221–27. M. Heidegger expressed himself critically on the first volume of Friedländer's work: "I have appreciated a great deal of it, but the philosophy of this circle around Stefan George gets on my nerves and eventually becomes sterile—and above all, much of what it has produced loses its precision and significance." (M. Heidegger to RB, 27. 1. 1929, in A. Grossmann and C. Landmesser, *Bultmann-Heidegger Briefwechsel*, 96). Cf. also later the appreciative remarks by Bultmann on Friedländer's presentation of Plato in "Zum Thema," 218f; RB "Christentum und Antike," 16.

575. Cf. RB, "Paul Friedländer," 92.

576. Cf. the overview in RB, *Theologie als Kritik*, 548f.

his demythologizing lecture.[577] Neither reviewer gave the other any special treatment.[578] Their disagreement was not over particular points of exegesis, but rather over the fundamental understanding of the relation between faith and history. Lohmeyer saw the principal mistake of Bultmann's Jesus-book as the fact that it elevated "points of view arising from faith" into "invariant elements of scholarly research."[579] In 1925 Bultmann had raised the objection against Lohmeyer that despite many excellent individual observations in his little book, *On the Concept of the Religious Community*, he had ultimately distorted earliest Christian theology into an idealistic philosophy of history and thus made theology an *ancilla philosophiae* [slave of philosophy].[580] To be sure, Bultmann did explain at the end of his extraordinarily comprehensive discussion that "a deep, common interest" in the "task of exegesis" united him with Lohmeyer, who had recognized that it would not suffice to explain religious phenomena and concepts merely on the basis of their historical context. Rather, they are properly to be understood only "on the basis of their origin in grasping the meaning of human existence itself."[581]

But Lohmeyer accomplished this task by recourse to the philosophical authority of Richard Hönigswald, a strategy that Bultmann regarded as deeply flawed. Still, he esteemed his successor in Breslau as he did no other German-speaking New Testament scholar of his generation, specifically because his astonishingly productive work had broken the stranglehold of historical positivism that exegesis had too long accepted, and had kept in view the systematic-theological implications of scholarly interpretation of biblical texts.[582] At the end of 1931, Lohmeyer endured an intense struggle with Hans Lietzmann, who had turned down a manuscript Lohmeyer had submitted to the *Zeitschrift für die neutestamentliche Wissenschaft* [*Journal of New Testament Studies*]. Contrary to Lietzmann's belief, the problem did not primarily concern matters of historical method or the language of scholarship, but the collision of opposing positions on theological objectives of New Testament exegesis.[583] Lohmeyer asked Bultmann as well as

577. See also above 197–200 and below 335f.

578. Cf. D. Lührmann, "Ernst Lohmeyers exegetische Erbe," 72–85; A. Köhn, *Der Neutestamentler Ernst Lohmeyer*; D. Kuhn, *Metaphysik.*

579. E. Lohmeyer, rev. of R. Bultmann, *Jesus*, 439.

580. Cf. RB, "Vom Begriff der religiösen Gemeinschaft," *Theologie als Kritik*, 195.

581. RB, "Vom Begriff der religiösen Gemeinschaft," *Theologie als Kritik*, 200.

582. Cf. (as reflexes) E. Lohmeyer to RB, 10. 12. 1935; 7. 8. 1937; 2. 3. 1939, in UB Tübingen, RB est., Mn 2-1315. Bultmann's letters to Lohmeyer from the period following 1931 are, apart from a few exceptions (cf. Mn 2-2287), not preserved.

583. Cf. as well in detail Lührmann. "Ernst Lohmeyers exegetische Erbe," 60–69; Köhn, *Der Neutestamentler Ernst Lohmeyer*, 224–38.

Martin Dibelius and Richard Hönigswald for advice on how he should react to Lietzmann's rejection of his essay.[584] Although Bultmann was unable to comprehend Lietzmann's decision, he regretted that Lohmeyer had taken the "legitimate matter of concern" in the essay in question "to the extreme" and therefore advised Lohmeyer to publish the study in another journal, and by way of avoiding a useless escalation of the conflict to refrain from making the details of the controversy public.[585]

During the Third Reich, Bultmann's connections with Paul Friedländer as well as with Ernst Lohmeyer deepened, and his interest in intensifying discussions between German and foreign scholars bound him to his professional colleagues. Bultmann and Lohmeyer found a conversation partner in Anton Fridrichsen, who pursued goals similar to theirs.[586] The Norwegian exegete, who taught first in Oslo and then in Uppsala from 1928 until his death, had completed part of his theological study in Germany. Since that time, he had held German New Testament scholarship in high regard. He considered the exegetical work carried on in Marburg to be exemplary. Jülicher's *Gleichnisreden Jesu* [*Parables of Jesus*] and Bultmann's *History of the Synoptic Tradition* were for him representative of its high standards.[587] Fridrichsen recognized the significance of the form-critical method early on, and transmitted the new approach to researchers in Scandinavia.[588] He himself provided a noteworthy contribution to the form-critical study of the New Testament with an investigation of the earliest Christian miracle stories.[589] In the second edition of the *History of the Synoptic Tradition*, Bultmann made frequent reference to this study—mostly by way of agreement.[590]

The Marburg theological faculty bestowed the honorary doctorate in theology on Anton Fridrichsen at the four-hundredth anniversary celebration

584. Cf. E. Lohmeyer to RB, 13. 12. 1931, in U. Hutter, "Theologie als Wissenschaft," 156.

585. Cf. RB to E. Lohmeyer, 18. 12. 1931, in GStA PK Berlin, E. Lohmeyer est., no. 5/405. Bultmann also held out prospects in this letter of making a case to H. Lietzmann regarding the matter in dispute after consulting with H. von Soden. From the sources that are preserved it is not clear whether it came to this.

586. Cf. W. Bauer, "Zur Erinnerung"; B. Gerhardsson, "Anton Fridrichsen."

587. Cf. UB Tübingen, RB est., A. Fridrichsen to RB, 17. 8. 1927, Mn 2-783. Unfortunately, Fridrichsen did not save the letters directed to him by Bultmann. Only one draft of a letter of Bultmann's is preserved (cf. Mn 2-3478).

588. Cf. UB Tübingen, RB est., A. Fridrichsen to RB, 20. 1. 1924, Mn 2-783.

589. Cf. A. Fridrichsen, *Le problemme du miracle.*

590. Cf. UB Tübingen, RB est., A. Fridrichsen's letter of thanks to RB, 28. 12. 1931, Mn 2-783.

of the Philipps-University in 1927.[591] Bultmann had taken the initiative in awarding this honor. In his recommendation of February 22, 1927, he argued for the proposal to grant Fridrichsen the *D. theol.* not only for the Norwegian's scholarly achievements in the areas of New Testament form-criticism and the history of the literature of early Christianity, but also for his tireless commitment to consolidating German and Scandinavian theological studies.[592] Fridrichsen later developed the idea of forming a German-Swedish *Societas Neotestamentica*, for the German members of which he had in mind Walter Bauer, Rudolf Bultmann, Martin Dibelius, Joachim Jeremias, and Ernst Lohmeyer.[593] Twice, in 1930 and 1947, he invited Bultmann to Uppsala for lecture and research visits. The two scholars also agreed in their deprecatory attitude towards National Socialism. Numerous times during the inflationary period following the Second World War, Fridrichsen sent parcels of foodstuffs to Marburg, and in return Bultmann supplied the colleague in Uppsala with whom he had become friends with periodicals and scholarly literature.[594] In 1952, Bultmann dedicated the second volume of *Glauben und Verstehen* to Anton Fridrichsen, "true friend in good and evil days."[595]

Along with and in addition to its professional and personal side, scholarly exchange across borders also had a political significance for Bultmann. In 1929–30, in an urgent exchange concerning the relation between German and French theologians, he made this clear. German theologians had occasionally contributed essays to the *Revue d'Histoire et de Philosophie religieuses* [*Review of Religious History and Philosophy*], which had been published since 1921 by the Protestant theological faculty at Strassburg. Their collaboration on a French journal appearing in what was at that time the German "border zone" of Alsace immediately received harsh criticism from German professors at Strassburg, who saw alleged German interests being compromised

591. Bultmann allowed himself to endure the celebrations on the occasion of the anniversary "alternating between irritation, indignation, and amusement. The best gift of the anniversary is doubtless the coffee at the castle, on the terrace of which one can have a lovely sit and, partaking of good delights for the body (there is excellent beer), enjoy the view out over the valley of the Lahn." (RB to M. Heidegger, 14. 9. 1927, in A. Grossmann and C. Landmesser, *Bultmann-Heidegger Briefwechsel*, 36f)

592. Cf. Bultmann's recommendation of 22. 2. 1927, in UA Marburg, honorary doctorates.

593. Cf. B. Gerhardsson, "Anton Fridrichsen," 665f; as well as UB Tübingen, RB est., A. Fridrichsen to RB, 20. 5. 1948, Mn 2-783. The founding of the *Studiorum Novi Testamenti Societas* in 1947 rendered this plan of Fridrichsen's superfluous.

594. Cf. UB Tübingen, RB est., A. Fridrichsen to RB, 18. 10. 1923; 13. 6. 1946; 24. 10. 1948, Mn 2-783.

595. Cf. RB, *GuV*, vol. 2, vol. 3.

in favor of those of France through cooperation with the Strassburg *Revue*. When Bultmann became convinced of the groundlessness of the reproaches launched against the journal, he came out publicly in a short piece in the *Theologischen Blättern* in favor of maintaining the research that was being shared with foreign scholars. "So you mean to say that we German theologians are to leave it only to the Dutch and Swiss, the Scandinavians and Anglo-Saxons, to keep up scholarly exchange, and are we on both sides to be deprived of the fruits that such exchange can bring?" It is precisely in view of the strained relation between Germans and French that the Strassburg journal in the historical tradition of French Protestantism manages to make an important contribution "to maintaining the common purpose of those who are *bonae voluntatis* [of good will] above and beyond borders."[596]

Bultmann underscored the importance of readiness for a dialogue that also serves understanding between peoples when he published an essay in French in the next edition of the Strassburg *Revue*. To be sure, he did not mention the events that formed the immediate occasion for the essay, but he did make unmistakable reference to the issue in the title of his contribution: "The Christian Commandment of Love of Neighbor." Christian love, Bultmann explained, no longer knows anyone "according to the flesh" (2 Cor 5:16). Only insofar as it affirms the love of God that has been revealed in the Christ-event and reflects this in the love of neighbor is it in a position to overcome mistrust and hatred between persons and peoples.[597]

11. Family Life

> *To put it in a few words, true human community occurs between person and person; that is to say, it is that community in which the person comes to himself by giving himself away to the other. True human community exists between persons who reveal themselves to each other and who themselves exist for and from each other.*[598]

In Breslau, two daughters were born to Rudolf and Helene Bultmann, Antje on July 27, 1918, and Gesine on July 1, 1920. The girls were baptized

596. RB, "Mitarbeit," 252. From a National Socialist point of view, Pastor Paul Diesner contended against Bultmann that, for the time being, Alsace was "not an appropriate place for German-French agreement" (P. Diesner, "Noch einmal," 360). Cf. as well RB, response to P. Diesner, 360–62. The Protestant theological faculty at Strassburg explicitly thanked Bultmann for his involvement. Cf. UB Tübingen, RB est., R. Will to RB, 11. 9. and 21. 12. 1930, Mn 2-2060.

597. RB, "Das christliche Gebot," *GuV*, vol. 1, 244; for the context of the study, cf. also K. Stock, "Das Ethos," 79n34.

598. RB, "Formen menschlicher Gemeinschaft," *GuV*, vol. 2, 263.

by friends in Breslau: Antje by Wilhelm Gottschick, and Gesine by Ernst Moering. Heilke, the third of the band of Bultmann daughters, caught sight of daylight in Marburg on February 21, 1924. At the wish of her parents, Hans von Soden performed the baptism "of the youngest, who, thriving happily," lay "in her pram with her little red cheeks, alternating between sleep and contented prattling."[599] The godparents of the three girls came from the parents' families and the circle of family friends. In Antje's case, these were Helene Pleus, her father's sister, as well as Anne Haun and Benny Henke, two of her mother's friends. Gesine took on four godparents at the same time: her two grandmothers Helene Bultmann and Luise Feldmann, Elise Heitmüller, Wilhelm Heitmüller's wife, and Hans von Soden. In Heilke's case, her parents conferred the role of godparent on their friends Walther Fischer, Paul Friedländer, and Nicolai Hartmann.

During the first years in Marburg, Bultmann gave explicit and regular reports to Hans von Soden on how the two older daughters were developing. Antje "is remarkably thoughtful and does less asking about causes and origins than she does forming hypotheses about them; she evidently has an imagination. She has a great love for her little sister. For the rest, the mixture of stubbornness and tenderness in her makeup already makes life not always easy for her, and bringing her up is often difficult. Gesine seems to be a simpler creature, always full of amusement and laughter, but she can also get quite furious. Physically, she has a strong constitution and is developing well, repeats herself a lot, and in general has a great drive to imitate."[600] Over the long run, as the father observed, the maturation processes of the girls were certainly subject to fluctuations: ". . . both are very bright and are making good progress. Antje is proving in the long term to be easier to raise than Gesine, whose qualities of egoism and vanity are much more pronounced than is the case with Antje, who has a basically tender disposition. Both seem to be endowed with good minds; Gesine is superior in gracefulness."[601] Such perceptions were snapshots that caught only a stage of development and that underwent appropriate modifications over the course of time.

As was the case in other middle-class families, the year was structured in the Bultmann house by birthdays and the Christian holidays.

> "St. Nicholas," who made his appearance on December 6, [1921], gave the children great joy—unfortunately, he (one of my students) let

599. RB to F. Gogarten, 19. 10. 1924, in H. G. Göckeritz, *Bultmann-Gogarten Briefwechsel*, 58. All dates in this section are according to RB, *Chronik 1917–1945*, Mn 2-224.
600. UB Tübingen, RB est., RB to H. von Soden, 1. 8. 1921, Mn 2-2385.
601. UB Tübingen, RB est., RB to H. von Soden, 8. 9. 1922, Mn 2-2385.

> the *Tremendum* [trembling, fearfulness] come in a poor second to the *Fascinosum* [bewitching, fascination], and the next day the only warnings Antje claimed to have heard were the ones to Gesine.[602]

In the Bultmann family culture, Christmas took on great importance for the sake of the children. The head of the family kept a close watch on how preparations were done, on the keeping of secrets, on all the joy and companionship of the period. "If one does not let the family joy of Christmas be diminished by all the poverty of the times, one can still always set his mind on what the celebration is really about and be gladdened by the fact that even in these bleak times, one may possess a world of light."[603]

It was not that Bultmann family life formed some kind of romantic idyll, for the adversities of life in the years following the First World War forbade this. The obligatory childhood diseases that Antje, Gesine, and Heilke had to get over proved drastic from time to time, not only because of the overall strictures on life's necessities, but also because of the family's special problems with their first living quarters in Marburg. 6 Hainweg, a half-timbered house located on the northern side of the castle mount, made a good first impression:

> The house stands quite alone and by itself in a large yard right up close to the castle, except for which it is probably the tallest house in Marburg. . . . The fog does not reach us, and it is splendid to see how, in the morning, it rolls like a white river through the valley of the Lahn, and the summits of the chain of mountains opposite look out over it, and the towers of the Elizabeth Church jut out from the midst of the fog. The view is magnificent in all directions, but especially towards the castle.[604]

But the good view was soon eclipsed by a sobering perception of the reality of the situation. The thin-walled, half-timbered house could not be adequately heated. During the winter months, icy temperatures created problems in the *Villa Sibiria*, as the Bultmanns took to naming their inhospitable domicile on account of its endless capacity for causing chronic illnesses for Helene Bultmann and the children. The problems with the unloved dwelling also led almost inevitably to conflicts with its owners, who steadfastly refused to improve the precarious living conditions of their renters. Dealings with the office of housing over getting assigned a new residence continued for a long

602. UB Tübingen, RB est., RB to H. von Soden, 21. 12. 1921, Mn 2-2385.
603. UB Tübingen, RB est., RB to H. von Soden, 23. 12. 1923, Mn 2-2385.
604. UB Tübingen, RB est., RB to H. von Soden, 30. 10. 1921, Mn 2-2385.

time without the desired result. Given this situation, Bultmann tried exerting pressure by threatening to switch to an Oldenburg pastorate if they could not find better housing. In this regard, "the path to the pastorate" would have been for him "not only a commandment of necessity," but he would have taken it upon himself "with rejoicing."[605] However, it did not come to this. In November 1924 the Bultmanns were finally able to move to a new home in the southern quarter of Marburg, at 1 Friedrich Street. When the daughters were older, they moved on March 1, 1930, to a roomier house at nearby 7 Bismarck Street.

In the highly stratified makeup of German society during the Weimar era,[606] the Bultmann family belonged to the upper social stratum. As was customary in the households of professors, Helene Bultmann had "help"—usually an unmarried young woman from the rural area around Marburg—to lend a hand with the shopping and household duties. Still, the Bultmanns had to live modestly. The period in Breslau, full of privations as it was and during which they had gratefully relied on parcels of foodstuffs from the Oldenburg family of Leonhard Frank and others, continued to have a marked impact.[607] The parents experienced "the consequences of the years of war and hunger in Breslau" long afterwards in Antje's case, "and she should have spent time at the seaside, but this didn't happen on account of the costs involved."[608] Whenever the occasion presented itself, then, they sent the eldest daughter, who suffered from rickets, on a bus for children to Pany, in the canton of Graubünden in Switzerland in 1923. The eight-week stay in the strange surroundings caused the five-year-old to suffer terrible homesickness, especially since she did not understand Schwyzerdeutsch, and severe separation anxiety in the parents.[609]

During the first half of the twenties, longer vacation trips for the whole family were out of the question for financial reasons.[610] Therefore, Bultmann and his wife made do with such temporary solutions as his going

605. UB Tübingen, RB est., RB to H. von Soden, 22. 7. 1923, Mn 2-2385; also RB to himself, 27. 1. 1924: "It was grimly cold here, twenty-nine on the coldest morning; no water in the house, only *one* room can be heated (at least usually)!"

606. Cf. also H. A. Winkler, *Weimar 1918–1933*, 285–305.

607. Cf. RB, *Chronik 1917–1945*, Mn 2-224, 5. UB Tübingen, RB est., H. Frank to RB, 18. 11. 1918, Mn 2-762; J. Lewy, née Frank to RB, 30. 8. 1917; 18. 3., 25. 4. and 27. 11. 1918, Mn 2-1280.

608. UB Tübingen, RB est., RB to H. von Soden, 1. 8. 1921, Mn 2-2385.

609. RB to F. Gogarten, 31. 8. 1923, in H. G. Göckeritz, *Bultmann-Gogarten Briefwechsel*, 43.

610. Cf. RB to F. Gogarten, 17. 7. 1923, in H. G. Göckeritz, *Bultmann-Gogarten Briefwechsel*, 37.

alone with Antje to visit his mother in Oldenburg, or he and his wife relaxing at the pastorate of his university fraternity brother Hermann Noltenius in Rinteln in 1921, or at the pastorate in Langwarden, between the marsh and the shoals of the Weser River. After the stabilization of the economic situation from about 1925 onwards, the Bultmanns were able to take their children for summer vacations on the island of Langeoog in 1925, and to Todtnauberg in the Black Forest in 1926. When Leni Bultmann went to Langeoog on a seaside vacation with the children in 1927 and 1928, the father of the family was enabled to spend a few weeks working in peace and quiet at home.

From October 1, 1922, on, Bultmann's mother-in-law was also part of the household. Luise Feldmann had lost everything she owned during the period of inflation. When she had to give up her dry goods shop in Essen, her daughter and son-in-law took her in, not without initial misgivings in view of the additional financial burden on the household.[611] The loss of independence was not easy for Leni's mother to deal with,[612] but in time, she accepted her situation. As she developed a sensitivity for knowing when Rudolf and Leni wanted to spend intimate time together, they began to get along more harmoniously. On the other hand, the presence of grandma meant a great deal to the granddaughters, and it was also of inestimable value that she willingly babysat when her daughter and son-in-law went on trips without the children. Heinrich and Erna Schlier also helped out in this regard and took the Bultmann daughters to the parsonage in Casekirchen for a few weeks in 1929.[613]

Rudolf and Helene Bultmann took breaks from their many and varied professional and family duties at regular intervals. During these periods of "R and R," the couple could revel in one another alone. "The two were infatuated with each other," reported Gustav Hölscher, who had taken up residence with the Bultmanns at the *Villa Sibiria* in the winter of 1921–22 while he looked for housing. Hölscher and his (first) wife Borghild, a Norwegian by birth, went to a dancing lesson with Leni Bultmann "in order to learn modern dances." Rudolf was unable to dance with them on account of his hip trouble, but was glad to sit back and watch his wife.[614] A great interest

611. Cf. Bultmann's announcement to H. von Soden, 8. 9. 1922, in UB Tübingen, RB est., Mn 2-2385.

612. Cf. UB Tübingen, RB est., RB to H. von Soden, 23. 12. 1922, Mn 2-2385.

613. Antje and Gesine had already spent the summer of 1924 with Erna Haas, the future wife of H. Schlier, in the Harz.

614. G. Hölscher, *Aus meinem Leben*, pt. 2 (manuscript), 300f.

in art, literature, and music bound the two. Helene Bultmann, who had a fine contralto voice, loved to sing, and every now and then let herself be persuaded to perform as a soloist in church concerts and Advent and Christmas celebrations.[615] Occasionally the couple also attended talks together, as when in the winter semester of 1922–23 they heard "a splendid lecture" of Nicolai Hartmann's on the history of ancient philosophy.[616]

In time, strong habits formed out of the things they undertook together. During Pentecost vacations, Rudolf and Leni Bultmann set off on short trips, mostly of a cultural sort. The destinations were Büdingen and Gelnhausen (1922), the Main (1924), Basel, Lucerne, and Zürich (1926), the Bodensee (1927), Jena and Casekirchen (1928), Freiburg with a visit to Heidegger (1929), as well as the Lahn and Rhine valleys (1931), which they explored together with their daughters, who had gotten older in the meantime. As a rule, the couple traveled together to the meetings of the Friends of *Die Christliche Welt*, and whenever possible, Leni accompanied her husband to his out-of-town lectures. It was only for spa treatments, which he took in Wiesbaden nearly every spring from 1926 on, that Bultmann went on his own. The cultural experiences they enjoyed during a trip to Italy in April of 1929 remained memorable: Lago Maggiore, Lago di Como, Lecco, Bergamo, Brescia, Riva del Garda, and Verona were among the places that left lasting impressions of the harmonious unity of art, landscape, and music.

Rudolf and Helene Bultmann invested a great deal in providing their children with an appropriate humanistic education. In time, Antje, Gesine, and Heilke took music lessons, and when still young they could take part in music-making at home. Their father also familiarized them early on with *belles lettres*. When the daughters were small, he told them stories and tales, some of which he made up himself. Later on, there were regular evening reading sessions, in which Bultmann shared with his daughters the works of Charles Dickens, Fritz Reuter, and Adalbert Stifter. In doing so, as his daughters remembered, their father could enter into the world of the readings with the sort of emotion that, from time to time, would bring tears to his eyes.[617] For him, the passing on of literary culture was in essence guidance in understanding oneself and in the free development of the individual.

Naturally, an education of this sort pursued in a framework of humanistic sensibility could not remain without effect. Antje, the eldest of the Bultmann daughters, was fascinated by Albert Schweitzer and his work in

615. UB Tübingen, RB est., RB to H. von Soden, 23. 12. 1922, Mn 2-2385.
616. UB Tübingen, RB est., RB to H. von Soden, 23. 12. 1922, Mn 2-2385.
617. Cf. E. Hauschildt, *Rudolf Bultmanns Predigten*, 270.

Lambarene. One day she informed her parents that she wanted to study medicine and then go to help the famous jungle doctor in the Congo. Her father reported this to Albert Schweitzer and added to it—presumably not without a gentle smile—that "it might take a while" to realize this plan, since Antje was only twelve.[618] Schweitzer understood. He promptly sent his young admirer a postcard with a photo of "distributing food rations" in the hospital at Lambarene. On it, the great humanitarian wrote the following lines to "Dear Miss Bultmann": "All these blacks send you kind regards! They wish you good health for your medical studies. But you must enjoy your youth. And don't forget to learn to be a good cook. Much love. Yours, Albert Schweitzer."[619]

In accordance with their father's principle of freedom, the religious socialization of the Bultmann daughters took place without external pressure. The religious practices of the family were free from theatrics. Prayers before bed with the children and grace at table were standard. A prayer like "Come, Lord Jesus, be our guest" did not come from Bultmann's lips, since for him supplication and thanksgiving for the necessities of life went without saying. He preferred graces that expressed praise of the Creator. On Sunday morning, he took some time to read his daughters stories from the Old Testament, for rather that forcing religious convictions on them he thought it better to share the content of faith with them indirectly, as the opportunity presented itself—for instance, by explaining the point of the Christmas chorales they sang together. Bultmann was vehemently opposed to having his daughters come under the religious influence of outsiders. When in kindergarten Antje became acquainted with "all sorts of indigestible ideas about the dear God and salvation," her father reacted angrily, "that this is how one is exposed to the uncontrollable influences of others precisely in an area where circumspection is most necessary. In any case, I mean to keep the children away from religious instruction during their early years at school."[620]

Even if Bultmann did not fully succeed in this intention, he did remain critical of understanding the task of religious instruction in schools in too fulsome a manner. When the era of the state church ended and discussions arose concerning constitutional prescriptions for church-state relations and the future form of religious instruction, Bultmann's father took the occasion to enter the debate in Oldenburg. In an article that appeared in 1919

618. RB to A. Schweitzer, 28. 8. 1930, in W. Zager, *A. Schweitzer*, 182.

619. A. Schweitzer to A. Bultmann, 11. 10. 1931, in W. Zager, *A. Schweitzer*, 185.

620. UB Tübingen, RB est., RB to H. von Soden, 23. 12. 1922, Mn 2-2385; printed in E. Hauschildt, *Rudolf Bultmanns Predigten*, 270n5.

in the periodical of the critical teaching staff of Oldenburg, Arthur Kennedy Bultmann spoke up for the complete separation of church and state and for waiving all previous ecclesiastical privileges. Only state-run religious instruction, not an ecclesiastical and confessional one, could accomplish the goal of allowing each citizen to choose his or her own religion. Such a form of instruction would convey knowledge about religion and would especially afford insights into "actual religion" from the pictures of the lives of men and women of all lands and times, confessions and religions.[621] Rudolf Bultmann might have been in broad agreement with these remarks of his father, stamped as they evidently were by liberal ideas.[622]

The pedagogical heritage of his family, the sense of responsibility for education on the part of his own father, and the insight into the hermeneutical task of theology saw to it that Bultmann would likewise move beyond the boundaries of his own discipline and take an active part in the discussion about religious education in his own time. Invited as a representative of the recent theological movement around Barth and Gogarten, he spoke to the fiftieth anniversary gathering of Protestant teachers of religion at the institutions of higher education of the Rhine province held at Düsseldorf on June 11, 1925. In his talk, "The Christian Meaning of Faith, Love, and Hope," Bultmann emphasized the basic theological features of the topic more than those that bore on religious education.

In this presentation he was constantly concerned to safeguard the Pauline triad of faith, love, and hope against an idealistic misunderstanding. Faith represents neither a worldview, nor a generalized trust in God, nor a mystical connection of the soul to God; it is rather "the stance of one who sees oneself face to face with the claim of God in the concrete situation of one's here and now." Love is not to be understood in humanistic-idealistic fashion as moral virtue, generalized love of humanity, or as the principle of an ethics, for it consists in the "stance of the person obedient to the demand of God in the face of the other person," in the "stance of the I to the Thou in the concrete situation of the here and now" that is ultimately possible only to faith. Finally, hope does not ground itself in the idea of the immortality of the soul, but rather directs itself utterly "to a future given miraculously by God," which at once signifies the end "of all things worldly and human."[623]

621. Cf. A. K. Bultmann, *Staat—Kirche—Religion[—]Schule.*

622. Infortunately, Bultmann's letters to his parents from the year 1919 are not preserved. Cf., however, A. Bultmann Lemke, "Theology for Freedom and Responsibility," 4.

623. RB, "Der christliche Sinn," 197.

Fifty years later at the hundredth anniversary event of the same group, the Duisburg principal, *Lic. Dr.* Friedrich Karl Feigel, disagreed with Bultmann. He saw in more recent theological movements an attempt to depart from modern Protestantism and thereby from German idealism—an attempt condemned to failure from the outset. Bultmann assured Feigel in writing that he had therein represented "'the *deus in nobis* [God within us] with moving and naïve enthusiasm"[624] and that the rest of the program of presentations and discussions had been interesting. At the time, Bultmann's existentialist approach to the task of religious education was not widely hailed in Düsseldorf, but in the long term his theological thinking proved exceedingly fruitful for the teaching of religion.[625]

624. RB to F. Gogarten, 29. 7. 1925, in H. G. Göckeritz, *Bultmann-Gogarten Briefwechsel*, 86f.

625. Here I can only refer in summary fashion to a few representatives of a variety of approaches to the teaching of religion who paid attention to Bultmann, were his students, or who allowed themselves to be inspired by his theology: Martin Rang, Gerhard Bohne, Martin Stallmann, Hans Stock, Klaus Wegenast, Peter Biehl and Marie Veit.

V. Time of Testing (1933–1945)

1. The Clash with National Socialism

Do we no longer recognize the verdict of conscience, which confronts us with the ultimate solitariness? . . . [or] its judgment, *which* condemns *us? It would be a sad sign for the moral strength of the nationalist movement if individual mistakes, cruelties, and injustices are indeed acknowledged, but in its collective wisdom pardoned, so that an about-face of this kind does not incur any negative consequences. When you chop wood, you make chips. Certainly, that is what the victim must say to comfort himself, and history can also pronounce this judgment, but not the person himself who is responsible for his actions. This wisdom does not pardon him before God. Do we no longer know the meaning of guilt and sin?*[1]

In 1933, "the year of Germany's fate," Rudolf Bultmann inaugurated his course of lectures for the summer semester on May 2nd with a statement on "The Task of Theology in the Present Situation." He explicitly intended that the stand he was taking should not be understood as a political statement, but in view of political events and the immense "*possibilities* for the future" inherent in them, he felt it necessary to ask "what is the responsibility we *as theologians*" have in this situation.[2] Bultmann develops his thoughts on this responsibility by taking up the Lutheran doctrine of the two kingdoms or rules, in light of the way Paul speaks of ὡς μὴ—the "as if not" (1 Cor 7:29–31)—and by bringing its critical potential to bear in the face of an all too joyous affirmation of the National Socialist seizure of power. It is not that faith has a negative relation to the world, however inherently critical its relation to the world and the world's "ordinances" may be. For faith refers to God, who as creator is likewise the judge of the world; and from this, there arises a structural ambiguity in the ordinances given us by which we are to shape our lives. "They are *God's* ordinances, but only insofar as they call us to service in our concrete tasks. In their mere 'givenness,' they are ordinances of *sin*."[3]

1. RB, "Gott ruft uns" ["God Calls Us"], sermon at the academic worship service in Marburg on 2. 7. 1933, in RB, *VW*, 257f.

2. RB, "Aufgabe," in RB, *Neues Testament und christliche Existenz*, 172.

3. RB, "Aufgabe," in RB, *Neues Testament und christliche Existenz*, 175.

In the present, Christian faith has to test its critical strength through reflection upon the possibilities and temptations that are distinctive of the ordinances of the state and the nation. Particularly in view of the fact that the nation is increasingly understood as an ordinance of creation, reflection on the ambiguity of this ordinance must remain just as vigorous as the question, "what is, and what is not the genuine demand of the nation?"[4] In his service to the state and the people, the Christian has to orient himself exclusively to the command of love. In this regard, Bultmann views theologians as having the particular duty of working together for the future of Germany by bearing witness to the truth. He illustrates this demand with three examples: the hasty renaming of streets in Marburg, the denunciation and the defamation of those who think differently, and especially that of German Jews.[5] In all of this, Bultmann warns his student audience, the only decision must be "whether Christian faith is to be valid for us or not. . . . The issue is either/or!" Furthermore, this decision—and not only in view of the "falsifications of the faith by national religiosity"—will have to be answered over and over again in the future.[6]

As did Karl Barth in his widely disseminated *Theological Existence Today!*,[7] Bultmann in his lecture course recommended continuing to do serious theology under the changed political circumstances of the "Year of the Revolution" of 1933. It was precisely therein that he saw the indispensable critical contribution of theology to the political reordering of Germany. His observation of political developments following the seizure of power by the National Socialists soon led him to the critical judgment of the "national uprising" that he addressed to the lecture audience on May 2, 1933, and also made public in the *Theologische Blätter* in June.[8] In terms of the spectrum of the numerous stands taken by Protestant church representatives and professors of theology on the political events of 1933 (a majority of which were euphoric),[9] Bultmann represented a remarkably clear and solitary position of

4. RB, "Aufgabe," in RB, *Neues Testament und christliche Existenz*, 176.

5. Cf. RB, "Aufgabe," in RB, *Neues Testament und christliche Existenz*, 178f; on the passage in which Bultmann objects to the injustice perpetrated on the German Jews, see below 289f.

6. RB, "Aufgabe," in RB, *Neues Testament und christliche Existenz*, 180.

7. Cf. K. Barth, *Theologische Existenz heute!* (2d ed.)

8. Bultmann had his statement printed, not because he regarded it "to have come off particularly well," but because to him "it was intolerable that not a single theologian had spoken out publicly on behalf of the critical task of theology in the present situation" (RB to M. Heidegger, 18. 6. 1933, in A. Grossmann and C. Landmesser, *Bultmann-Heidegger Briefwechsel*, 196.)

9. Cf. A. Lindemann, "Neutestamentler," 26f; K. Nowak, "Protestantische Universitätstheologie," 89–112.

skeptical dissent relative to that of many who saw "great possibilities" opening up in 1933.[10]

On the basis of first impressions he had gained "of magnificent National Socialist students," Bultmann had a year earlier "placed great hope in the movement," but this hope vanished immediately. Freed of his illusions, he had seen as early as 1932 that the National Socialist movement as a *party* was no different from any other, since where they took over power—as in his home city of Oldenburg—corruption set in and the self-aggrandizement of party politics gained the upper hand.[11] On May 27, 1933, on the occasion of his assuming the office of Chancellor of the University of Freiburg, Martin Heidegger gave his address, "The Self-Assertion of the German University." Unlike the numerous voices that extolled Heidegger's inaugural address as Chancellor—it would be remembered especially for the praise that Karl Jaspers accorded it[12]—Bultmann reacted with disgust to the speech, the content of which he first learned only from the Freiburg press. As he let Heidegger know, he saw fully "the *positive possibilities* of the present." He was also ready to work together towards them. Unlike Heidegger, however, he would draw the "courage to risk everything" not from radical political change but rather from the historic spiritual awakening that had already begun with the thought of Kierkegaard and Nietzsche. Bultmann particularly balked at Heidegger's claim—based on an admittedly unconventional translation of Plato to the effect that all great things stand firm in a storm—that his philosophy and the German university were in accord with the national rallying cry, "We shall will ourselves!" Such a willing seemed to Bultmann to be blind, for he saw "how this willing stands in danger every moment of misplacing itself." In any case, Bultmann could not summon up "the same clear courage for the present" as Heidegger did, precisely because he saw "that an atmosphere of ὕβρις [arrogance] and concealed anxiety is spreading in oppressive fashion."[13]

Bultmann distanced himself from Heidegger's embrace of National Socialism from the outset, and a noticeable estrangement occurred between

10. Cf. E. Jüngel, "Redlich von Gott reden," 476. Cf. also, to be sure, the statement by H. von Soden in his lecture of 4 May 1933, in E. Dinkler and E. Dinkler-von Schubert, *Theologie und Kirche*, 37–43.

11. RB to M. Heidegger, 11./14. 12. 1932, in A. Grossmann and C. Landmesser, *Bultmann-Heidegger Briefwechsel*, 188.

12. Cf. K. Jaspers to M. Heidegger, 23. 8. 1933, W. Biemel and H. Saner, *Heidegger-Jaspers Briefwechsel*, 155; as well as R. Safranski, *Meister*, 291–93.

13. RB to M. Heidegger, 18. 6. 1933, in A. Grossmann and C. Landmesser, *Bultmann-Heidegger Briefwechsel*, 194f. Cf. M. Heidegger, *Die Selbstbehauptung*, 19.

the theologian and the philosopher. The former vigorous exchange of ideas was now a rarity, and personal correspondence all but ended during the Third Reich. After the collapse of his chancellorship, Heidegger visited Marburg from March 8–11, 1935, in order to discuss "the unresolved questions" with Bultmann "in complete calm."[14] At an evening conversation, in which Heinrich Schlier also took part, the principal topic was the Third Reich. According to Schlier's recollection, Heidegger received harsh criticism "for his conduct in 1933"—though he was unable to admit his political error at that time.[15]

On July 2, 1933, two weeks after his reaction by letter to Heidegger's address as Chancellor, Bultmann preached on 1 John 4:7–12 at the university worship service in Marburg. He directed his audience's attention to the widespread sense of "having experienced a decisive turning point in history."[16] The judgment that had emerged from this experience, namely, that the era of individualism had run its course and had finally been overcome by the present demand for national solidarity, Bultmann declared to be both too sweeping and unfair to the aspirations of previous generations. Overall, he warned the congregation not to give way to the euphoria of the national uprising, not to forget that in the context of "the discovery of national solidarity," egoistic individualism can be overcome only by the person who has faced himself and recognized his responsibility to the community. That represented the *one* central question that Bultmann posed to the National Socialist movement: Was it ready to acknowledge that individualism "without which no socialism, not even that of the people, has substance and strength?" Would it recognize that the Christian proclamation insists on individualism that values and promotes the self-realization of human beings? For understanding "that the human being exists on his own means that he stands before God, and when such a proclamation calls the human being to himself, it calls him before God."[17] Bultmann did just this by addressing the injustice that had taken place in the previous months and by indicting those responsible with their guilt before God.[18]

14. M. Heidegger to RB, 15. 2. 1935, in A. Grossmann and C. Landmesser, *Bultmann-Heidegger Briefwechsel*, 199.

15. H. Schlier, "Denken," in G. Neske, *Erinnerung*, 221; cf. O. Pöggeler, *Neue Wege*, 89f, 323f. On Schlier's error in dating cf. A. Grossmann and C. Landmesser, *Bultmann-Heidegger Briefwechsel*, 199f, n. 4. In UB Tübingen, RB est., guestbook, vol. 1 (1917–54), Mn 2-3041, p. 32, Heidegger recorded his "lovely, memorable stop" in March of 1933 below Hölderlin's saying, "But what is lasting is set by the poets."

16. RB, "Gott ruft uns," 247.

17. RB, "Gott ruft uns," 255.

18. See above, n. 1.

It took courage to express in public speech and writings such criticism of the illegal and pseudo-legal violence and injustice of the National Socialist dictatorship in the first half of 1933.[19] During the beginnings of the dictatorship, Bultmann probably had no more than a minimal understanding of the political and social dimensions of the radical change from the Weimar Republic to the Third Reich.[20] The capacity for theological judgment derived from his schooling in biblical scholarship was a primary factor in enabling him to keep a cool head during the heady enthusiasm of the "national uprising" of 1933 and to measure political developments by the standard of Christian faith, humanity, and the rule of law. In the years that followed, Bultmann found himself provoked to argument with National Socialism in a variety of institutional contexts and on a variety of topics. The common denominator of these disagreements was the claim of the National Socialist regime to have authority over all aspects of German life.

Forcing the University of Marburg to conform to National Socialist doctrines generated a politicizing pressure that was primarily felt by the teaching staff. Bultmann tried to avoid this pressure and did his best to minimize their negative effects on research and teaching. On July 22, 1933, together with Hans von Soden, he urged the university Senate—in vain—to postpone the political and paramilitary training that had been recently ordered for students during their vacation time—an additional obligation that he knew would increase the already considerable strain of academic work.[21] When the Chancellor of the university required the faculty to take part in the carnival procession organized by the NSDAP [National Socialist German Workers Party] for May 1, 1934, the day of "work for the nation," Bultmann begged off on account of his hip trouble.[22] And in 1938 he and von Soden were the only professors on the theological faculty to ignore strong urgings to enroll in the National Socialist welfare program, a refusal they justified mainly on the grounds that the state-run welfare scheme had aggressively sought to displace the charitable work of the Christian church.[23]

State interventions in the development and support of young scholars were a constant source of conflict. On November 30, 1933, the Prussian Minister for Science, Art, and National Education informed Bultmann and von Soden that he was unable to award the stipend they had sought for the

19. Bultmann published the sermon in the periodical "Neuwerk." Cf. RB, *VW*, 337.

20. On this deficiency in theology throughout the German universities, cf. (in retrospect!) K. Nowak, "Protestantische Universitätstheologie," 111f.

21. Cf. A. C. Nagel, *Die Philipps-Universität Marburg*, 164.

22. Cf. A. C. Nagel, *Die Philipps-Universität Marburg*, 189n22.

23. Cf. A. Lippmann, *Marburger Theologie*, 260f.

support of Götz Harbsmeier; but after they refused calls to other universities, both professors were entitled to claim such stipends for the support of doctoral students. Despite their appeal of this decision, the Minister did not rescind his negative decision.[24] When a new process of qualifying for professorships was to be introduced in 1935, Bultmann asked Heidegger to employ either an official memorandum or a personal intervention to dissuade the Ministry of Culture from its plans. For in Bultmann's eyes, the new arrangements would lead "in no time to young academics who would be either bootlickers or troublemakers."[25] In order to counteract a significant decline in the coming generation of academics, the Ministry of Education and the National Socialist League of Lecturers of the Reich founded in 1936 the "Association of Registered Lecturers of the Reich." Following von Soden's lead, Bultmann categorically refused to do the bidding of officialdom and become a member of the "Association." For, he argued, the existing qualifications already restricted to a considerable degree "the freedom of the faculties and especially the free development of the young researchers themselves." Instead of demanding that candidates show their political trustworthiness, they ought once more to be granted the freedom to become qualified for an academic career through their scholarly achievements.[26]

In his own teaching arrangements and with regard to his doctoral students, Bultmann was able to maintain academic freedom during the entire period of the Third Reich. Things were otherwise with ecclesiastical freedom, the considerable loss of which was threatened by National Socialist church politics, and the defense of which required considerable effort. Even before working to form ecclesiastical confession-groups that opposed aligning the Evangelical Church with the National Socialist state, Bultmann and von Soden took various initiatives to forestall the election of the "German Christian" Ludwig Müller—Hitler's 1933 appointee as his representative for church affairs—to be archbishop of the *Reichskirche* then in the process of being formed. On July 13, 1933, at this early stage of the *Kirchenkampf* [struggle of the churches] Bultmann signaled to Karl Barth his full agreement with Barth's *Theological Existence Today!*;[27] and in the months that followed, both theologians rediscovered common theological principles that

24. Cf. E. Dinkler and E. Dinkler-von Schubert, *Theologie und Kirche*, 71f.

25. RB to M. Heidegger, 27. 1. 1935, in A. Grossmann and C. Landmesser, *Bultmann-Heidegger Briefwechsel*, 198.

26. UA Marburg, RB to P. Gieseke, the Prochancellor of the University of Marburg, 4. 10. 1936. Cf. also UA Marburg, H. von Soden to P. Gieseke, the Prochancellor of the University of Marburg; as well as A. C. Nagel, *Die Philipps-Universität Marburg*, 47f.

27. Cf. RB to K. Barth, 13. 7. 1933, in B. Jaspert, *Barth-Bultmann Briefwechsel*, 135.

they asserted in taking responsibility for a church that was under threat of being forced to align itself with the new national state.[28]

Together with all of his colleagues on the Marburg theological faculty, Bultmann joined in the "Marburg Declaration" of June 17, 1933, that favored conferring the archbishopric upon Friedrich von Bodelschwingh, Jr., the leader of the Bethel Institutes and the person favored by most representatives of German church governing bodies.[29] But once the National Synod had finally chosen Ludwig Müller in Wittenberg on September 27, 1933, Bultmann and von Soden intensified their discussion with the "German Christian" church leadership. Together with the lecturer Heinrich Schlier, they discussed the church situation in detail with their Bonn colleagues Karl Barth, Gustav Hölscher, Fritz Lieb, and Ernst Wolf on November 11–12, 1933. This group decided to send the Archbishop an open letter drafted by von Soden in which the Bonn and Marburg theologians charged the "religious movement of German Christians" with "renouncing and damaging the essence of the Protestant Church through its . . . teaching in opposition to scripture and confession." They also repudiated Müller's misrepresentation that opposition to the "German Christians" was based on "purely political grounds," and criticized the pressure that the "German Christians" had brought to bear on pastors and parishioners who could not be considered truly independent.[30]

On the occasion of the Bonn theologians' visit to Marburg, Karl Barth "was impressed by Mr. Von Soden," whom he had previously considered merely a representative of theological liberalism, "to a degree that even [he] found surprising."[31] Moreover, Barth confessed to Bultmann in a nighttime conversation on November 11–12, 1933, that in view of Bultmann's theology he had felt certain that Bultmann would go over to the "German Christians." This confession hit Bultmann hard,[32] for it suggested Barth's

28. Cf. B. Jaspert, "Sachkritik," 169–72.

29. Cf. the text of the Declaration in E. Dinkler and E. Dinkler-von Schubert, *Theologie und Kirche*, 49f, n. 11. E. Hirsch transmitted the Marburg Declaration to the Prussian Minister of Education and Public Worship on 20. 6. 1933, adding as commentary that the "propaganda that has come to light" in it was "intolerable and . . . irreconcilable with the duties of an official of the state" (cited in K. Meier, *Theologische Fakultäten*, 106).

30. E. Dinkler and E. Dinkler-von Schubert, *Theologie und Kirche*, 363f. The Bonn and Marburg theologians withheld publication of this open letter only because, following the "Sport Palace Scandal" of 13. 11. 1933, Müller partially distanced himself from the closing of these institutions by the "German Christians." Cf. H. von Soden to colleagues, 20. 11. 1933, in E. Dinkler and E. Dinkler-von Schubert, *Theologie und Kirche*, 65.

31. K. Barth to RB, 13. 11. 1933, in B. Jaspert, *Barth-Bultmann Briefwechsel*, 136.

32. Cf. RB to K. Barth, 7. 7. 1934, in B. Jaspert, *Barth-Bultmann Briefwechsel*, 149f.

inability to imagine that anyone who held theological views different from his own would combat the heresies of the "German Christians" as resolutely as himself. At any rate, he apologized to Bultmann: "The facts have now clearly shown that I was mistaken in this case, and also that something was therefore amiss in my basic understanding."[33] Following the successful meeting in November of 1933, Bultmann and von Soden proposed to their colleagues a further meeting,[34] which took place in Bonn at the beginning of May 1934. The discussion focused on the question of how to mount an effective opposition to the plans of the "German Christian" leadership of the German Evangelical Church to abolish the legal autonomy of the state churches that did not belong to the Old Prussian Union. The Bonn and Marburg theologians involved adopted a declaration drafted by Hans von Soden that laid claim to the sole sanction of the Holy Scriptures and the Reformation Confessions over questions pertaining to church order and belief, and further rejected as contrary to scripture the "Führer-principle" that the "German Christians" in the Evangelical church had introduced.[35]

Bultmann and von Soden immediately joined the emergency league of pastors of the Confessing Church that had arisen from this issue in 1933. With their statement repudiating the introduction into the Evangelical church of the so-called Aryan Paragraph demanded by the "German Christians," they made an authoritative contribution to clarifying theologically what did and did not belong to the essence of the Christian church according to the biblical witness and the Reformation Confessions.[36] On August 1, 1934, Hans von Soden assumed the leadership of the State Council of Brethren of the Confessing Church in Kurhessen. A few days later, referring to paragraph 6 of the law of April 7, 1933, that provided for the re-establishment of a professional civil service, the Prussian Minister of Culture forced him into retirement.[37] Since this action was a clear retaliation against von Soden's activity in theology and church politics on behalf of the Confessing Church and lacked any basis whatever in law, Bultmann immediately drew up a petition to the

33. K. Barth to RB, 10. 7. 1934, in B. Jaspert, *Barth-Bultmann Briefwechsel*, 151.

34. Cf. RB to K. Barth, 24. 2. 1934, in B. Jaspert, *Barth-Bultmann Briefwechsel*, 140f.

35. Cf. [H. von Soden,] "Bekenntis und Verfassung," in E. Dinkler and E. Dinkler-von Schubert, *Theologie und Kirche*, 364–68. To the thirty-five signatories of the declaration, published 23. 5. 1934, immediately before the Barmen Confessional Synod, belonged (from Bonn) K. Barth, G. Hölscher, F. Horst, H. E. Weber, and E. Wolf and (from Marburg) K. Bornhäuser, R. Bultmann, R. Günther, A. Jülicher, W. Maurer, H. Schlier,T. Sippell, and H. von Soden.

36. See also below 289–97.

37. Cf. E. Dinkler and E. Dinkler-von Schubert, *Theologie und Kirche*, 101–3.

Prussian Minister of Culture that demanded a review of the decision as well as a hearing for the individual affected. He also reminded the Minister of the duty of Protestant graduate professors to take part in current ecclesiastical discussions.[38] Signed by fifty theology professors, this declaration of solidarity played a decisive role in getting the Prussian Minister of Culture to order von Soden's reinstatement as Professor on October 24, 1934.

The fragile nature of the professors' position in the state-run theological faculties belonging to the Confessing Church was made especially clear by the proceedings relating to the suspension of Karl Barth a month later. From August 20th on, officials of the German Reich had to swear a personal oath to the Führer, Adolf Hitler. Barth declared that he was prepared to take this oath "of unlimited, hence confused content"[39] only if he were allowed to add the restrictive clause, ". . . insofar as I take responsibility for it as a Protestant Christian."[40] He meant thereby to limit the nature of the personal duty owed to the Führer and thus publicly reject the totalitarian claim of the Führer-oath.[41] By means of this personal addition, Barth finally moved the Confessing Church to adopt a similar public disavowal of the absolute duty prescribed by the oath.[42]

As did Hans von Soden, Bultmann feared that Barth's refusal of the oath might bring in its wake increasingly grave consequences for the position of the Confessing Church in relation to the state. Barth's action would make it more difficult to debate the state's claim of exclusivity, an issue that the church would eventually have to take up.[43] The nature of the case was such that Bultmann deemed it out of the question that the state would permit the clause that Barth demanded. Indeed, the state could not do so, for it would thus render its general demands subject to an individual official's Christian duty of obedience to God. "I can only view the matter in such a way that the reservation you demand in fact goes without saying for every Christian,

38. Cf. [RB,] "Eingabe theologischer Hochschullehrer," in E. Dinkler and E. Dinkler-von Schubert, *Theologie und Kirche*, 103–5.

39. Declaration of K. Barth before the Bonn District Court on 27. 11. 1934, in B. Jaspert, *Barth-Bultmann Briefwechsel*, 266.

40. K. Barth to RB, 27. 11. 1934, in B. Jaspert, *Barth-Bultmann Briefwechsel*, 154. On the background of Barth's dismissal from German state service and of the role of E. Hirsch in connection to this, cf. H. Assel, "Barth ist entlassen . . ." 445–75.

41. Cf. K. Barth to H. von Soden, 5. 12. 1934, in B. Jaspert, *Barth-Bultmann Briefwechsel*, 274–76.

42. K. Barth to H. von Soden, 5. 12. 1934, in B. Jaspert, *Barth-Bultmann Briefwechsel*, 278; cf. H. Assel, "Barth ist entlassen . . ." 464f.

43. Cf. RB to K. Barth, 3. 12. 1934, in B. Jaspert, *Barth-Bultmann Briefwechsel*, 155; H. von Soden to K. Barth, 2. 12. 1934, in B. Jaspert, *Barth-Bultmann Briefwechsel*, 271f.

but that the Christian cannot hold the state to it except in the sense that in *the case of a conflict* he must renounce the office he has assumed on condition of this reservation."[44] In accord with von Soden's rigorous argument from canon law, Bultmann ruled out the suggestion that the secular state be made subject to a special Christian privilege. Christians could not abstractly and defensively claim the right to resist the state. Only when the Christian confession ruled out fulfilling a specific demand of the state was it valid to resist and to suffer the consequences of this resistance.[45]

On February 28, 1935, the Minister of Culture of the Reich and of Prussia, Bernhard Rust, prohibited the Protestant theological faculties and the professors of theology from publicly taking a position in the *Kirchenkampf*.[46] On March 11, 1935, Hans von Soden, Rudolf Günther, Heinrich Schlier, and Theodor Sippell protested against this "muzzling decree," and Rudolf Bultmann did so a day later.[47] Referring to theology's direct relationship to the life of the church, Bultmann explained to the Minister that it would be impossible for him to abstain from taking a public position on the controversy over the church. In a calculated tactical thrust Bultmann added that his commitment to a theological scholarship that involved a duty to the life of the church and thus to the life of the people and the state, exhibited a precise correspondence to the connection between the life of all Germans and the scholarship propagated by the National Socialists.[48] When the Minister sharpened his decree even further in the summer of 1935, von Soden once more became a target of the Ministry of Culture's administrative sanctions for taking part in the synod of the Confessing Church in Augsburg in June of 1935. To be sure, von Soden showed himself unimpressed by this: "The nature of the case is such that the good Lord Minister can neither prescribe nor proscribe in accordance with theological decisions, and it is not as if this were a matter of theology finding the boundaries of its own responsibility relative to the governmental jurisdiction of the good Minister, but rather the

44. RB to K. Barth, 3. 12. 1934, in B. Jaspert, *Barth-Bultmann Briefwechsel*, 155; cf. A. Lindemann, "Neutestamentler," 38–40; G. Klein, "Rudolf Bultmann," 198f.

45. On further developments in the case of Barth, cf. E. Busch, *Karl Barths Lebenslauf*, 268–75; H. Assel, "Barth ist entlassen . . ." 465–75.

46. Cf. the decree of the Ministry of 28. 2. 1935, in A. C. Nagel, *Die Philipps-Universität Marburg*, 213–15.

47. Cf. H. von Soden to B. Rust, the Minister of Education and Public Worship, 11. 3. 1935, in E. Dinkler and E. Dinkler-von Schubert, *Theologie und Kirche*, 135–40; as well as A. Lippmann, *Marburger Theologie*, 210–13.

48. Cf. RB to B. Rust, Minister of Education and Public Worship, 12. 3. 1935, A. C. Nagel, *Die Philipps-Universität Marburg*, 215f.

other way around."[49] Such determined opposition contributed appreciably to the Minister's rescinding the "muzzling decree" in 1936.

Following the failure of the attempt to use the "German Christians" to force the Protestant Church's alignment with the National Socialist state, Hitler altered his strategy on church politics. On July 16, 1935, he appointed Hanns Kerrl as Minister without portfolio for national churches. The new minister was to serve as a kind of court of appeals authorized by the State Administration of Last Resort for reconciling the quarreling church parties and restoring the unity of the Protestant Church. To this purpose, Kerrl set up a committee of the German Evangelical Churches, a group that appeared to provide for equal participation of the various church groupings but was ultimately calculated to carry out the interests of the state. Bultmann took part one time—in Berlin on June 29–30, 1936—when he participated in a session of the theological chamber of the committee of the German Evangelical Church. But the proceedings made it clear to him that under the chairmanship of Wilhelm Zoellner, the retired General Superintendent of Westphalia, the committee had no real interest in a theological clarification of ecclesiastical problems. For this reason Bultmann withdrew from the committee on October 2, 1936, whereupon he received a second inquiry, asking whether he was prepared to cooperate with the committee of the German Evangelical Churches. He again issued a refusal to the committee, stating by way of justification his concern that the committee had been formed by the state and in all its proceedings had yet to produce any real evidence of its ecclesiastical legitimation.[50]

While Hans von Soden occupied himself in an unswerving commitment to church and university politics, and assumed the responsibility for leading numerous committees of the Confessing Church,[51] Bultmann focused on speaking out for the cause of the Confessing Church in his teaching, sermons, and publications. To be sure, he also took part in debates on current issues when the situation required. In May of 1937, a group of pastors

49. H. von Soden to B. Rust, Minister of Education and Public Worship, 4. 9. 1935, in E. Dinkler and E. Dinkler-von Schubert, *Theologie und Kirche*, 179. Bultmann achieved the following: "that 70–80 professors of theology have written to the Minister in more or less the same vein" (RB to E. Käsemann, 26. 4. 1936, Mn 2-2251).

50. The ongoing events are reproduced in minute-by-minute fashion in H. G. Göckeritz, *Bultmann-Gogarten Briefwechsel*, 211–13, n. 6; cf. RB, Letter to the Reich's Ecclessiastical Committee, 6.

51. Cf. E. Dinkler and E. Dinkler-von Schubert, *Theologie und Kirche*, along with the three case studies of Hans Lietzmann, Hans von Soden, and Hermann Wolfgang Beyer in W. Kinzig, "Evangelische Patristiker," 559–64.

sought to overcome the differences between the "German Christians" and the Confessing Church by forming a unified Protestant national church founded on the biblical faith and solidarity with the Third Reich. Asked for a statement on this initiative by the leader of the Oldenburg confessional community, Heinz Kloppenburg, Bultmann stressed that the question of the unity of the church had to be decided theologically and in accordance with the truth of the Christian proclamation. In calling for church unity, the pastors' group proposed a merely formal definition of the church, for it was promoting organizational unity less out of concern for the church than with an eye to the political unity of the people and the state. Still, since the unity of the church was inseparably related to the unity of the proclamation and of faith, the church had to be ready to identify false doctrine and to eliminate it. And precisely because certain powers (of course National Socialism was primarily intended) were presently involved in an all-out struggle against Christianity, the church for its part had to combat "the anti-Christian powers inside and outside the church."[52]

The National Socialist state repeatedly attempted to weaken the confessional front formed by Bultmann and von Soden to represent the Marburg theological faculty. But such strategies as calling to Marburg two decidedly "German Christians"—the church historian Ernst Benz and the practical theologian Alfred Uckeley—did not in the long run produce the desired result.[53] The state suffered an even greater defeat when in the summer semester of 1934 students and faculty who belonged to the Confessing Church formed a single group that grew steadily over the following years. Bultmann and von Soden supported the work of the Confessing students by regularly joining in their devotions, academic events, and spare-time activities during vacations.[54] In an internal report of June 2, 1936, the state secret police reported that to their great surprise the Confessing students of the Marburg theological faculty were largely able under Bultmann and von Soden's protection to carry out activities that in many cases were highly critical of the state.[55] The Gestapo had already noted with regret the "significant role" of the two Confessing professors Bultmann and von Soden "and their disastrous influence on the theology students" during the previous year.[56] In October

52. R. Rittner, "Ein Brief Rudolf Bultmanns," 14.

53. Cf. A. Lippmann, *Marburger Theologie*, 219–31.

54. Cf. A. Lippmann, *Marburger Theologie*, 292–322. On the continuation of this work by students during the Second World War, cf. E. Dinkler-von Schubert, *Feldpost*, see also below 361f.

55. Cf. A. Lippmann, *Marburger Theologie*, 312n155.

56. T. Klein, *Lageberichte*, vol. 1, 293.

of 1937, Eugen Mattiat, the intermediary for Emmanuel Hirsch in the Reich and Prussian Ministry of Culture, announced concerning Bultmann and von Soden that, "as the opportunity presents itself, we should call one or both of them away from Marburg or retire them, in order to make room for more constructive personnel."[57] For the time being, however, such an opportunity did not present itself, and the National Socialist state may also have refrained from taking action against Bultmann and von Soden out of consideration for their international scholarly reputations.

Bultmann did not totally rule out that the increasingly aggressive tenor of National Socialist church politics might sooner or later endanger the existence of the theological faculties. As it was, given the conflicts within the church and efforts by the National Socialists to drive the church out of public life, the education of theologians posed a complex problem. Only after prolonged negotiations did Bultmann and von Soden manage to get the theological examinations at Marburg administered by faculty and not, as the "German Christians demanded," given under the supervision of their commissars in church government until the end of 1935.[58]

Once the third synod of the Confessing Church of the Reich in Augsburg had created in June of 1935 the conditions for founding church graduate schools, the establishment of such institutions in Berlin-Dahlem and Wuppertal-Elberfeld offered alternatives to conventional study at the theological faculties. Hans von Soden wanted to avoid a rivalry between the state faculties and the church schools, but in view of the Third Reich's political restrictions for scholars in the new theological schools, he saw possibilities for strengthening the ecclesiastical character of theology as well as for assuring academic freedom in theological scholarship and teaching.[59] Against Ernst Käsemann, Bultmann argued in 1936 that despite state-imposed restrictions, theology ought to remain in the universities for as long as possible, for it was quite conceivable "that in the years to come the state-run theological faculties would completely lose their legitimation as places of teaching for the church." As long as it could be taught unhindered, theology should remain in the universities and where possible sustained by those teachers—in Marburg, for instance, by von Soden and himself—who emphasized the connection of theology with the church. Bultmann likewise spoke in favor of the gradual construction of church-affiliated graduate schools, and did

57. A. Lippmann, *Marburger Theologie*, 188n136.

58. Cf. RB to G. Bornkamm, 2. 9. 1935, Mn 2-2147; on the background in detail, A. Lippmann, *Marburger Theologie*, 217–77.

59. Cf. A. Lippmann, *Marburger Theologie*, 267–69.

not hide the fact that Confessing professors were committed to a bond between the church and scholarly theology, and felt themselves deserted by the churches.[60] When Günther Bornkamm took up a teaching position at the theological school in Bethel, Bultmann welcomed this step. To be sure, he warned his student not to allow himself to be put under excessive obligation to ecclesiastical tasks. "Doing theology is *as such* churchly, and does not become so simply by its participation in matters related to it. . . ."[61]

Bultmann was of two minds in the tug-of-war between one's attitude toward the Third Reich and the theological options and consequences for church politics that were taking effect. This matter had consequences for his personal and scholarly relations to other theologians as well. As early as 1930 Bultmann had given Friedrich Gogarten to understand that he was "at a complete loss" over Gogarten's work *Wider die Ächtung der Autorität* [*Against Outlawing Authority*]. He saw a lack of nuance in Gogarten's distinction between the order of law and the order of love, between the authority of the state as including compulsion and the true authority of human cooperation based on trust. Bultmann opposed Gogarten's opinion that theology and the church could take direct action to solve political difficulties of the present. In particular, he was appalled that the publisher offered Gogarten's treatment "as a political broadsheet" and that the text looked as if Gogarten's theology had been exploited for party politics.[62]

In June 1933 Bultmann declined to sign a memorandum concerning the relation of church and state that Gogarten had drawn up. He fully recognized that the intention of the memorandum was to safeguard "the autonomy of the office of churchly proclamation" even in the new political reality created by "the national uprising."[63] Nevertheless, Bultmann feared that the memorandum would be read exclusively in the sense it would have for those who, like the "German Christians," were misusing the church to aid the purposes of the state. What was necessary just now was a memorandum "that protests the exclusivist claim of a state that means to take charge not only of

60. UB Tübingen, RB est., RB to E. Käsemann, 26. 4. 1936, Mn 2-2251.

61. UB Tübingen, RB est., RB to G. Bornkamm, 19. 5. 1937, Mn 2-2147. To H.-G. Gadamer, Bultmann made the argument that, in the case of the dissolution of the theological faculties by the National Socialist state and the complete shift of theological education over to ecclesiastical instruction, indivual theologians might nevertheless in the future teach in the university—in the philosophy faculty, for instance, in order to pursue the interdisciplinary conversation that was indispensable. Cf. DLA Marbach, RB to H.-G. Gadamer, 19. 11. 1939.

62. RB to F. Gogarten, 6. 9. 1930, in H. G. Göckeritz, *Bultmann-Gogarten Briefwechsel*, 184–87. Cf. F. Gogarten, *Wider der Ächtung*.

63. Cf. F. Gogarten, "Denkschrift," in H. G. Göckeritz, *Bultmann-Gogarten Briefwechsel*, 300, 302.

political life, but also of the life of faith, a manifesto that protests the direct identification of the empirical state with that willed by God."[64] As a consequence of the disagreement in regard to theology and church politics that Bultmann delineated here, his contact with Gogarten broke off in the years following 1933, and the two did not meet again until June of 1936, when they were among a group of expert witnesses on theology.[65] To be sure, Gogarten's stance on church politics did not become any more plausible either at that meeting or through his book *Gericht oder Skepsis* [*Judgment or Skepticism*]. That Gogarten found the law of God grounded in peoplehood, and that he passed off the *nomos* [law] of the people as a form of the divine law, Bultmann found both incomprehensible and theologically impossible.[66]

Despite their theological differences, the relation between Bultmann and Emanuel Hirsch had until 1933 been marked by mutual respect. Bultmann regarded Hirsch as, "for all of his weaknesses, an estimable and unhappy human being . . . who, despite all of his outstanding talent, still suffers, in my opinion, from its being negative and critical, and not productive."[67] When Gogarten and Hirsch got into a violent dispute in 1928, Bultmann came to Hirsch's aid, believing that Gogarten had not developed a sufficient understanding of Hirsch's legitimate theological concern to recognize the reception of revelation as a way of conceptualizing more precisely the hearer's self-understanding of the revealed word.[68] For the sake of clarifying the theological situation, Bultmann took it upon himself to bring about an understanding between the two estranged theologians. Hirsch reacted to this effort with a nine-page letter in which he responded with thanks to Bultmann's initiative.[69] But during the Third Reich, the Göttingen theologian elevated himself in the service of National Socialism—serving as chief ideologue of the "German Christians" and as "Christian tribune of the

64. RB to F. Gogarten, 26. 6. 1933, in H. G. Göckeritz, *Bultmann-Gogarten Briefwechsel*, 210.

65. Cf. also the particulars given in H. G. Göckeritz, *Bultmann-Gogarten Briefwechsel*, 211–13, n. 6.

66. Cf. RB to F. Gogarten, 18. 4. 1937, in H. G. Göckeritz, *Bultmann-Gogarten Briefwechsel*, 211–13. Cf. F. Gogarten, *Gericht oder Skepsis*. On the statements regarding the "nomos of the people," cf. F. Gogarten, *Einheit?* On Gogarten's membership in the "German Christians" from August until November 1933, cf. H. G. Göckeritz, *Bultmann-Gogarten Briefwechsel*, 207n6.

67. RB to F. Gogarten, 25. 3. 1928, in H. G. Göckeritz, *Bultmann-Gogarten Briefwechsel*, 117.

68. Cf. H. G. Göckeritz, *Bultmann-Gogarten Briefwechsel*, 118.

69. Cf. E. Hirsch to RB, 26. 3. 1928, Mn 2-997. Cf. already UB Tübingen, RB est., E. Hirsch to RB, 26. 9. 1927, Mn 2-997: "It's remarkable that I get on well with you and [H.] Knittermeyer, but just not with your common friend Gogarten."

people"[70] —to a greater degree than any other German professor of theology. Bultmann had only one further contact with Hirsch, and that was in April of 1936, when he announced that their relation had ended.[71]

Among those in the closer circle of Bultmann's students, Günther Bornkamm, Ernst Fuchs, and Heinrich Schlier became involved with the Confessing Church. Bultmann engaged in intensive correspondence with them as the *Kirchenkampf* developed, and he obtained important pieces of information from them about the current state of the discussions in Württemberg, East Prussia, and Westphalia.[72] Ernst Käsemann was the only one of his students to join the "German Christians," in 1933. As a pastor in Gelsenkirchen-Rotthausen he was confronted with the daily problems of church work in a working-class congregation in the Ruhr region from February 12, 1933, on,[73] and he hoped to turn the "German Christians'" sense of a popular mission into a way of overcoming the barriers that had arisen between parties and social and economic classes.[74] Once Käsemann had informed his teacher in Marburg that he had gone over to the "German Christians" and had also taken this opportunity to criticize Barth's *Theological Existence Today!* as mistaken in its approach,[75] Bultmann declared himself astonished and pained by his student's step. He made it clear to Käsemann that approving the impulse of "German Christians" for popular mission served only to provide Käsemann with a clear conscience concerning "everything they are doing against the meaning of the church and the gospel."[76] Curiously enough, Käsemann did not turn away from the "German Christians" even after the scandalous Sport Palace rally on November 13, 1933. It was only his vehement protest against the absorption of the Evangelical youth organizations into the Hitler Youth that led to his expulsion from the "faith movement" at the beginning of 1934. Persuaded in large part by Bultmann's stand on the Aryan Paragraph, Käsemann came

70. K. Nowak, "Protestantische Universitätstheologie," 109.

71. This is shown by E. Hirsch to RB, 21 April 1936, Mn 2-997, in UB Tübingen, RB est. What concrete occasion led to this step on Bultmann's part can no longer be discovered, since apparently his letter to Hirsch no longer exists. According to information provided by his heirs, Hirsch seems to have destroyed the correspondence directed to him by the end of the War.

72. Cf. for examples J. Heise and U. Schoenborn, *Kostproben*, 290–322. An edition of the correspondence between Bultmann and G. Bornkamm is in preparation at the present time.

73. Cf. UB Tübingen, RB est., (looking ahead) E. Käsemann to RB, 31. 1. 1933, Mn 2-1083.

74. Cf. R. Walter, "Ernst Käsemanns Wirken," 201f, J. Kampmann, "Engagiert," 30f.

75. Cf. UB Tübingen, RB est., E. Käsemann to RB, 4. 8. 1933, Mn 2-1083.

76. UB Tübingen, RB est., RB to E. Käsemann, 19. 9. 1933, Mn 2-2251.

to recognize that he had "traveled a wrong path."[77] Furthermore, it was only with difficulty that he found his way into the Confessing Church thereafter, for his relationship with it remained full of tension up to his resignation from the Confessional Synod of Westphalia in November 1940.[78] During all those years Bultmann attempted both to dispel Käsemann's reservations concerning individual steps taken by the Confessing Church and to help his former student by keeping an eye out for alternatives.[79]

During the Third Reich, Bultmann made it the duty of his students "to continue doing theology" in the direction shown by Karl Barth in 1933, "as if nothing has happened." Nevertheless, they were also exhorted to carry the word [of the gospel] that they were endeavoring to understand in their studies, "precisely into the struggles of the times."[80] It was not easy for Bultmann to keep to this course, especially following the outbreak of the Second World War, but he tried to move his work forward. ". . . I am certainly convinced that it has never been as important as it is today, when it may seem unimportant; but it always requires a powerful resolve to rouse oneself from the numbness that continually oppresses one."[81] His theological work found expression not only in opposition to the church politics of National Socialism, but also in the ongoing crucial debate with key elements of National Socialist ideology and of its understanding of the state. In this regard, he distanced himself either explicitly or implicitly from such Lutheran theologians as Paul Althaus, Werner Elert, Friedrich Gogarten, and Emanuel Hirsch, who in various ways accorded the priceless gift of theological legitimation to the Third Reich by interpreting the historical and natural realities

77. UB Tübingen, RB est., E. Käsemann to RB, 15. 1. 1934, Mn 2-1083.

78. Cf. also R. Walter, "Ernst Käsemanns Wirken," 204–22; J. Kampmann, "Engagiert," 32–37.

79. Cf. already RB to E. Käsemann, 27. 5. 1934, Mn 2-2251 in UB Tübingen, RB est. When, in the late summer of 1937, Käsemann was imprisoned for three weeks for alleged violation of the Law against Treason (cf. R. Walter, "Ernst Käsemanns Wirken," 213f), Bultmann, dismayed by this, expressed sympathy for him. Cf. UB Tübingen, RB est., RB to (E. Käsemann through) Superintendent E. Kluge, 22. 8. 1937, Mn 2-2267. An edition of the correspondence between Bultmann and Käsemann is in preparation.

80. Thus the report of D. Stoevesandt to K. Barth, 24. 2. 1937, in S. Holtmann and P. Zocher, *Als Laien*, 112; cf. already in a similar vein RB to E. Käsemann, 19. 9. 1933, Mn 2-2251, in UB Tübingen, RB est.

81. DLA Marbach, RB to H.-G. Gadamer, 5. 9. 1939; cf. in a similar vein RB to G. Bornkamm, 27. 1. 1940, Mn 2-2147, in UB Tübingen, RB est. When, during the Second World War, theology students in military service demanded a reduction in the curriculum, Bultmann vehemently opposed this. Systematically reflective, critical interpretation of the biblical texts and, as its presupposition, knowledge of the ancient languages, was indispensable for church praxis. Cf. RB, "Zur Frage der wissenschaftlichen Ausbildung," 34–40.

of human life in an utterly un-Lutheran way—that is, as direct or indirect manifestations of the law of God.

In a 1936 study on the "Meaning of the Christian Faith in Creation," Bultmann reprises thoughts from his May 1933 address in order to demonstrate the ambiguity of what had recently come to be called "ordinances of creation."[82] He begins by criticizing the inflated use of that theological concept so as to demonstrate that the state does not belong to the genuinely original ordinances of creation, but at very best is to be acknowledged "as an ordinance of the sinful creation." In contrast to the Lutheran concept of these ordinances current at that time, Bultmann maintains that "it is impossible to deduce from the natural conditions which determine our immediate situation that unambiguous demands are demands of God."[83] This holds true for nationhood, which as an integral part of history,[84] is always exposed to the possibility of evil, and also for the state, which with its coercive power of law is an agent of God's wrath. To the extent that the ordinances of the state have their ultimate origin in sin, every deification of the state is forbidden—both that of previous times and in particular that of 1936.[85]

In his contribution to the *Festschrift* for Karl Barth in the same year, Bultmann goes a step further. Here, in an interpretation of the *Antigone* of Sophocles that bears as directly as possible on the present situation, he opposes the totalitarian claim of the National Socialist regime. He locates the problem of the *Antigone* in the conflict between the power of the state represented by Creon and the divine norm invoked by Antigone and the god Hades—a principle that governs life in a community. In his rule Creon sees the realization of the will of God and therefore insists that the laws of the polis apply without restriction; in reality, however, his falsely legitimated tyrannical arbitrariness tramples on the honor of the gods. Antigone, on the other hand, breaks Creon's law, but cannot appeal to a code of laws to justify her having done so. She simply acts in accordance with the ancient "knowledge that human existence and in particular the existence of the polis are subject to the otherworldly power of Hades."[86] For Bultmann, Creon manifestly embodies the arbitrary power of National Socialism, while in Antigone he recognizes the person who refuses to obey the totalitarian state

82. RB, "Der Sinn des christlichen Schöpfungsglaubens," 18.

83. RB, "Der Sinn des christlichen Schöpfungsglaubens," 19.

84. Characteristically, Bultmann does not reckon race ("blood") among the natural givens of human life; see RB, "Der Sinn des christlichen Schöpfungsglaubens," 19.

85. Cf. RB, "Der Sinn des christlichen Schöpfungsglaubens," 19f; as well as RB, "Die Bergpredigt Jesu," 100–102.

86. RB, "Polis und Hades," *GuV* (5th ed.), vol. 2, 22.

because she takes the law of love issuing from the divine "beyond" as the exclusive norm of her behavior.[87]

After the Second World War had broken out, Bultmann continued his critique of the National Socialist state by interpreting John 18:28–19:16 ("Jesus before Pilate") in a way that needs no allusion to Antigone but stands as a paradigm of "the intermediate position between God and the world that is peculiar to the state."[88] Pilate is no longer merely a representative of the Roman state of the past, but represents the state itself, which in Bultmann's view receives its authority not from the world, but solely from its relation to God. Pilate knows about the state's accountability before God that this entails and recognizes that, since its dealings rule out personal interests, the state thereby distinguishes itself from the cosmos, which is at enmity with God. To be sure, it can allow itself to be corrupted by the world, as happens in Pilate's case. But even if it pursues subjective or even personal goals, the state that is empowered by worldly concerns certainly does not completely forfeit its authority. For, as John 19:11–16 gives one to understand, Pilate has "no personal interest whatever in the death of Jesus" and, in his unjust verdict, he still preserves at least the outward form and authority of the law.[89] Bultmann compellingly suggests to his readers in 1941 that precisely therein does the state as embodied by Pilate still distinguish itself from the German state of the present day. For since it no longer preserves even the appearance of law, the National Socialist state can in no way claim itself to be what the New Testament intends by that term. This perverted state is nothing but a manifestation of the cosmos at enmity with God. It is institutionalized evil.[90]

Nor did Bultmann's sermons lack for public criticism of the National Socialist worldview. Basing his argument on the Christian faith in creation, he condemned making idols of the forces of nature and the social forces that shape people and the state. Like Paul, Bultmann understood these idolized forces in terms of their relation to the one God who alone gives meaning and purpose to life, and therefore saw them as invalid perversions of the

87. Cf. RB, "Polis und Hades," *GuV* (5th ed.), vol. 2, 29–31; as well as A. Lindemann, "Neutestamentler," 43; O. Pöggeler, *Schicksal*, 169f. It is possible that Bultmann's interpretation of *Antigone* takes up the first part of Alfred Döblin's novel, *November 1918*, written in exile from 1937 to 1943. Cf. also H. Flashar, *Inszenierung der Antike*, 170.

88. RB, *Das Evangelium des Johannes*, 513; cf. D. Lührmann, "Der Staat," 359–75.

89. RB, *Das Evangelium des Johannes*, 359–75.

90. Following the Second World War Bultmann retracted or, more specifically, modified this interpretation of the scene of "Jesus before Pilate," bound to a particular time as it was, and especially his identification of Pilate with the state. Cf. also in detail D. Lührmann, "Der Staat," 370–75.

divine power of creation.[91] In this connection, the National Socialist ideology of race was in particular the target of his sharpest condemnation. For Bultmann, the glorification of blood and soil, the apotheosis of race,[92] could not have derived from a natural or primordial paganism. For as he made clear shortly after the National Socialists enacted the "Nuremberg Race Laws," such a naïve paganism could not possibly exist where Christianity had already proclaimed its message; therefore, making idols of race and nationality must be seen as a desperate rebellion against Christianity. At any rate, the advocates of the National Socialist worldview had realized that because of its dialectical relationship to the world, the Christianity they were fighting was committed to the disruption of a world that sought to understand itself purely on its own terms and that believed in its own self-sufficiency.[93]

During the Third Reich Bultmann used sermons to outline the National Socialist ideology that he more fully articulated later on.[94] In addition to the delusion about race, the basic elements of the National Socialist worldview included a utilitarian conception of human life, a naked striving after economic success patterned on social-Darwinist convictions,[95] the use of technology for the purpose of control, and the destruction of nature.[96] For him this ideology was nothing but a hopeless attempt on the part of humans to establish and maintain for themselves a degree of security that is simply not possible to obtain.[97]

In Bultmann's view, National Socialism required and had dedicated itself to the suppression of the Christian proclamation.[98] For insofar as this message proclaimed God's judgment on all human striving to assert its own power over life and to create its own meaning in terms of the world, it proved to be "*the great disruption* of world history and of worldly life."[99] For this reason, Bultmann entertained no illusions concerning the role of the

91. Cf. RB, "Der Glaube an Gott den Schöpfer," *VW*, 261–73 (sermon on 1 Cor 8:4–6, delivered 1. 7. 1934); RB, *MP*, 26–40 (sermon on Gen 8:22, delivered 9. 5. 1937).

92. Cf. RB, *MP*, 34; RB, "Echtes Bekenntnis," *VW*, 292 (sermon on John 6:60–69, delivered 6. 4. 1935).

93. Cf. RB, "Advents-Bereitschaft," *VW*, 299 (sermon on Rom 13:11f, delivered 1. 12. 1935); as well as B. Jaspert, "Sachkritik," 177f.

94. See also below 371f and 384f.

95. Cf. RB, *MP*, 63f (sermon on Rom 8:18–27, delivered 2. 7. 1938).

96. Cf. RB, *MP*, 6–10 (sermon on Acts 17:22–32, delivered 7. 6. 1936).

97. Cf. RB, *MP*, 6f; RB, *MP*, 67f; RB, *MP*, 121f (sermon on John 3:14–20, delivered 8. 12. 1940).

98. Cf. RB, *MP*, 58f (sermon on John 16:5–15, delivered 15. 5. 1938).

99. RB, "Advents-Bereitschaft," *VW*, 299.

church in a dictatorship: "The very existence of the Christian church in the world is a protest against the world and the world's claim to provide ultimate commitment and obligation, ultimate fulfillment. . . . For this reason, the world perceives the church as a foreign body, and if it does not conform to the power of the world's goals and gifts, the church must expect to feel the world's might in all its wrath."[100]

On June 22, 1941, Hitler's Wehrmacht [armed forces] attacked the Soviet Union. The Spiritual Council of Faith of the German Evangelical Church conveyed to Hitler "once again in these thrilling hours the unwavering loyalty and readiness for action of all of Protestant Christendom of the Reich" and declared the German attack on the Soviet Union to reflect God's will in service of the deliverance of "Western-Christian culture."[101] But in his sermon on the day that Germany began the war against the Soviet Union, Bultmann spoke of the "great trouble that lies on us all today," and he made the National Socialists' drive to eliminate the church from German society the object of his critical reflection: "We all know that Germany today is no longer any kind of Christian country; that religious life is only a remnant, and that many wish and hope that even this remnant will soon vanish."[102]

Bultmann obtained the strength and the motivation for such opposition to the demon of National Socialism from the New Testament message of Christ, which to him imparted first and foremost "the absolute security of life" that was especially necessary under the unfree conditions of the dictatorship.[103] By showing the Christian that he is an alien in the world, the biblical word calls him to that "radical inward honesty" in which alone he can gain himself.[104] And this word proves to be one of grace, since it promises to the individual the possibility of living in terms of God's future.[105] And even in the context of external bondage, this same word frees the Christian by awakening within him a readiness for open opposition, for sacrifice,[106] for suffering[107]—and last but not least, for active solidarity with those who became the victims of the racial delusion of National Socialism.

100. RB, *VW*, 53.

101. Telegram of the Spiritual Council of Faith of the German Evangelical Church to the Führer A. Hitler, 30. 6. 1941, in J. Beckmann, *Kirchliches Jahrbuch*, 458.

102. RB, *MP*, 127, 129 (sermon on Luke 14:16–24, delivered 22. 6. 1941).

103. RB, *MP*, 115 (sermon on Luke 18:9–14, delivered 4. 8. 1940).

104. RB, *VW*, 300.

105. Cf. RB, *VW*, 66–70 (cf. 1 Cor 7:29–31).

106. Cf. RB, *MP*, 24f (sermon on Matt 6:25–33, delivered 15. 11. 1936).

107. Cf. RB, *VW*, 282f; as well as RB to E. Käsemann, 26. 4. 1936, Mn 2-2251.

2. The Persecuted Jews

> *The theologian Bultmann invited us, together with my closest colleagues (Gadamer, Krüger, and Frank), for a farewell on the evening before my departure: this representative of Protestant Christianity was, characteristically, the only host to a Jew who had been thrown out,* [*and was*] *one who in his lectures had presented to theology students the downfall of Christianity!*[108]

Racial anti-Semitism formed a central component of the National Socialist worldview. In 1933, however, only a few Germans recognized the effect that enmity towards Jews was to have on the politics of the new wielders of power. No doubt many theologians and church leaders silently repudiated the anti-Semitic rage that exploded on the streets of German cities in March of 1933 and the "spontaneous" boycott of Jewish businesses and medical and legal practices that Hitler had ordered for April 1, 1933. Indeed, many saw these campaigns as highly regrettable eruptions that accompanied the still-seething transitional phase of the "national revolution," but as excesses that would not be repeated following the consolidation of National Socialist rule.

The April 1, 1933 "Law for the Re-establishment of a Professional Civil Service," which enabled the elimination of civil servants who had fallen out of favor politically, elicited few reactions from church or theology. Paragraph 3 of the law called for the forcible suspension of all civil servants not of Aryan descent, but church leaders felt no compelling reason to take an official position against this provision unless it appeared to touch on matters of ecclesiastical significance. And in 1933 a good many Protestant Christians, theologians, and church representatives regarded moderate action against the Jews as justified. The view that Jews were disproportionately represented in certain occupations and had a detrimental or even "subversive" influence on the body politic was readily apparent in the same Protestant circles that rejected the racial anti-Semitism of National Socialism.

But even before 1933, buttressed by his incorruptible theological judgment and strengthened by his numerous friendships with Jews and with Christians of Jewish background, Bultmann had shown himself opposed to every form of anti-Semitism. During the period of the empire at the beginning of the twentieth century, he had discussed in detail the problem of anti-Semitism.[109]

108. K. Löwith, *Mein Leben*, 81.
109. Cf. K. Hammann, "Rudolf Bultmanns Begegnung," 41f.

Discussion of racial anti-Semitism played a considerable role in Bultmann's correspondence with his friend and scholar of Indo-Germanic languages, Hermann Jacobsohn.[110] Characteristic of Bultmann's attitude was the scene involving Hannah Arendt's application for his New Testament seminar in the winter semester of 1925–26. When the young philosophy student added to her request for admission to the seminar the peremptory declaration that "there had better not be any anti-Semitic remarks," Bultmann calmly reassured her that if anything of that sort were to happen, "the two of us will make short work of the situation."[111]

On April 25, 1933, Hermann Jacobsohn was one of the first professors at the University of Marburg to receive notification that he was to be provisionally suspended from service. Since paragraph 3 of the civil service law could not be construed to apply to Jewish scholars who had entered state service before 1914, his dismissal was made a political matter by citing paragraph 6 of the law and referring to his liberal democratic commitment to the Weimar Republic. In despair, Jacobsohn took his life the day after receiving the news.[112] His fate evoked great consternation in the Bultmann household, and may also have provided the final impetus for Bultmann's making the growing discrimination against Jews a central theme a week later in his lecture at the opening of the summer semester of 1933. Also in April of 1933, Marburg's German Student Association had circulated anti-Semitic slogans at a rally, in response to which Bultmann protested against this "defamation of the Jews," representing a "demonic distortion" and "not borne by the spirit of love. As a Christian, I must deplore the injustice that is done in particular to the German *Jews* by such defamation."[113] Such unequivocal and courageous words were to be heard in few if any German lecture-halls at this time. What scholar except for Bultmann could risk going public with such open criticism? At any rate, during the controversy he pursued in 1933 with the Tübingen New Testament scholar Gerhard Kittel over Kittel's anti-Jewish segregation program, Martin Buber made note of Bultmann's positive example in speaking up for Jews.[114] Scarcely any comparable statements by Christian theologians could have been cited on behalf of Buber's cause.

In a lecture on May 2, 1933, Bultmann again repudiated defamation of the Jews by referring "to a word of Adolf Hitler, . . . that those who thought

110. Cf. K. Hammann, "Rudolf Bultmanns Begegnung," 44f.
111. E. Young-Bruehl, *Hannah Arendt*, 108; cf. H. Jonas, *Erinnerungen*, 111.
112. Cf. H. Maier-Metz, "Hermann Jacobsohn," 71–80.
113. RB, "Aufgabe," in RB, *Neues Testament und christliche Existenz*, 179.
114. Cf. M. Buber, "Offener Brief," 608.

differently were not to be suppressed, but won over."[115] Bultmann evidently did this for tactical reasons, for it is out of the question that despite recent events he was still unaware of the leading role that anti-Semitism was playing in National Socialist politics.[116] He was not one to be this naïve, as he demonstrated in the course of the summer semester of 1933. Bultmann was teaching his accustomed course in theological encyclopedia and was amplifying the text he had earlier presented in 1926, 1928, and 1930 by taking issue with the National Socialist biological-racial ideology of nationality. Nationality, he insisted, is "never something unambiguously given as present-at-hand, but [is] rather . . . always something posited; . . . [it is] not a natural, biological reality, but rather a historical one." In connection with this, Bultmann gave an unmistakable example: "Understood properly, a people is not a biological, but rather a historical phenomenon, and therefore our participation in it is a matter not of descent, but of existence."[117] His condemnation of racial anti-Semitism could not have been more clearly expressed: he had stated his position and made it clear to his audience that with its pronouncement on Aryans, the National Socialist state had initiated its political program of eliminating the Jews.

The civil service decree enacted on May 6, 1933, expressly stipulated that it "does not apply to civil servants with or without tenure [nor] to workers in legally constituted, public religious societies."[118] To this extent, then, the National Socialist state exerted no pressure of any kind on the churches; but individual voices—like that of Gerhard Kittel, for instance—were immediately raised in favor of inserting an Aryan Paragraph that would apply to churches.[119] And following their triumph in the church elections in July of 1933, the "German Christians" exerted their newfound power derived from numerous positions of church leadership by employing laws they had vehemently supported to get rid of any pastors and church officials who were "descended from Jews." On September 6, 1933, the State Churches of Saxony, Braunschweig, Lübeck, Schleswig-Holstein, Thüringia, Mecklenburg, and Hessen-Nassau soon followed the resolution of the General Synod of the Old Prussian Union to this same effect. Fearing that the new and also "German Christian" dominated National Synod of the German Evangelical Church might make the Aryan Paragraph binding everywhere, delegates

115. RB, "Aufgabe," in RB, *Neues Testament und christliche Existenz*, 179.
116. This in A. Lippmann, *Marburger Theologie*, 128.
117. RB, *Theologische Enzyklopädie*, 65.
118. Cited by H. Liebing, *Die Marburger Theologen*, 5.
119. Cf. G. Kittel, *Die Judenfrage.*

from the Kurhessian church representing the three Upper Hessian church circles requested on September 11, 1933, a clarification of the situation from the theological faculties of Marburg and Erlangen.[120]

The Marburg report, drawn up by Hans von Soden and unanimously passed by the faculty on September 19th, established the incompatibility of the Aryan Paragraph "with the essence of the Christian church." For the sake of the independence of its mission, the church could not accept preconceived norms of a political or ecclesiastical nature from external authorities. And should it prove necessary, the church's free pursuit of its spiritual mission also included the right to voice criticism of "events in state and church life." As for the Aryan Paragraph, it contradicted both scripture and confession, since it demoted Christians of non-Aryan origin "to church membership of inferior right and inferior worth"—whereas the message of Jesus Christ was directed equally to all peoples and races, and joined together all believers and all those baptized into the church of Christ. All church members were brothers one of another, and for this reason any inequality in rights among them must be prohibited, and in particular a separate status for Jewish Christians. Inasmuch as both the history of the church and "the civil and canon law of all peoples" regarding this point understand Judaism not as a race but as a religious denomination, it necessarily follows that baptized Jews are no longer Jews in the church's eyes. Even if the state has recently felt obliged to take account of racial considerations, the church, particularly since it has never consented to "restrictions of civil law for baptized Jews," is unable to recognize such considerations in its own realm. For the church may in no way relinquish "the unity of the body of Christ," which realizes itself in the "full unity between Jewish and non-Jewish Christians in the church." It is also "uncontestable, that God has proclaimed his word" in both the Old and New Testament "through Jews and has chosen his son from among the Jews." Attempts to make of Jesus an Aryan would lack any historical basis. Were one to deprive Jewish Christians of their rights, the divine history of salvation would be openly abrogated.[121]

The Erlangen report of September 25, 1933, that was worked out by Paul Althaus and Werner Elert did not achieve nearly the definitive precision of the Marburg statement. To be sure, the Erlangen theologians proceeded from the axiom of the oneness of the community of believers with Christ to

120. Cf. for particulars A. Lippmann, *Marburger Theologie,* 17.

121. "Report of the Theological Faculty of the University of Marburg on the Canon Law regarding the Facts of the Case in the Matter of Religious and Church Officials (1933)," in H. Liebing, *Die Marburger Theologen*, 9–15.

the conclusion that there was "no distinction between Jews and non-Jews" *coram Deo* [in the presence of God], but it then brought matters of biology and nationality into play. With regard to outward church order, the "principle of the solidarity of office holders with their congregation in respect of nationality" had to be heeded. Since the church was to fulfill the task "of being a people's church for the Germans," the filling of its offices with those of Jewish descent "did present a problem in the current situation." The church would "therefore need to demand that offices be withheld from its Jewish Christians," particularly as the German people were experiencing Jews as a foreign nationality more strongly than ever before. To be sure, Althaus and Elert recommended to the church that it permit exceptions to the rule—for instance, to leave tried and tested pastors of Jewish origin in office—but their report amounted to a cautious approval of the Aryan Paragraph in the church.[122]

But the Marburg report proved of decisive help in strengthening opposition within the church to this paragraph of the law. And lest the National Synod set for September 27, 1933, adopt similar legislation for the whole German Evangelical Church, Bultmann deemed it necessary to both sharpen and to broaden the protest against such a development. He therefore drew up a further report, "New Testament and the Question of Race,"[123] that was made public in the *Theologische Blätter* and in the "young church" on September 23rd. Signed by twenty-one New Testament scholars, this report developed an exegetical argument on the basis of the contrast "Jew vs. gentile," which in the New Testament "is not to be understood as a contrast between natural or cultural individualities of a people," inasmuch as the salvation-occurrence in Christ had made this contrast irrelevant. And Paul also declared that the difference between Jews and gentiles had become invalid. The historical "conflict between Jewish and gentile Christianity" had been based not on questions of peoples and races, but rather on the problem of the relevance of the Old Testament ritual law. Paul provided a principled legitimation for rejecting the notion that differences "within the human sphere"—and thus distinctions grounded in racial biology—had any significance in God's eyes.

According to the witness of the New Testament, "the Christian church consists of both 'Jews and gentiles.'" Faith and baptism alone are decisive

122. "Theological Report regarding the Authorization of Christians of Jewish Descent for Offices of the German Evangelical Church," in H. Liebing, *Die Marburger Theologen*, 20–23.

123. On Bultmann's authorship, cf. E. Dinkler, "'Neues Testament und Rassenfrage,'" *Im Zeichen*, 410, 412.

for belonging to the church, and no significance is given to evaluations of a biological or racial nature. Hence Jews and gentiles are equally fit for church offices, eligibility for which is effected by the Holy Spirit. The church calls individual Christians to office-bearing according only to the measure of faith, life experience, and personal suitability.[124]

Hans Lietzmann presented this report of the New Testament scholars to the interim leadership of the German Evangelical Church on September 20th.[125] In a letter to Ludwig Müller only five days earlier, the Swedish archbishop Erling Eiden had threatened to break off relations between the Swedish and German Evangelical Churches if the Aryan Paragraph were introduced throughout the German church. Müller was obviously influenced by the stand of the New Testament scholars and the threat of the Swedish church, and decided against having the Aryan provision accepted into church law by the national synod meeting in Wittenberg on September 27th. Bultmann was not satisfied with this temporary success of his efforts, however, because the tabling of the Aryan legislation was merely a tactical strategy of the newly installed archbishop Müller. In order to lend even greater force to his initiative, on October 16th Bultmann asked his Zürich colleague Werner Georg Kümmel "to obtain the agreement of as many German New Testament scholars as possible outside of Germany" with the New Testament scholars' report.[126] Kümmel and his departmental colleague at Zürich, Gottlob Schrenk, immediately complied with this request and secured the signatures of fifty-six of the seventy German New Testament scholars abroad in Europe and America to whom they wrote seeking support of the declaration, "The New Testament and the Question of Race."[127] To be sure, this action by Kümmel and Schrenk that Bultmann initiated was partially undercut when three of the original signatories, Karl Heim of Tübingen together with Alfred Juncker and Julius Schniewind of Königsberg, withdrew their signatures on October 30th—desiring, they said, to counteract the "appearance . . . of making common cause with the critics of Germany from other countries."[128]

Heim in particular changed his mind in an attempt to steer the German people's alleged interest in German folk tradition away from exegetically

124. [RB,] "Neues Testament und Rassenfrage," in H. Liebing, *Die Marburger Theologen*, 16–19.

125. Cf. H. Lietzmann to H. von Soden, 21. 9. 1933, in K. Aland, *Glanz und Niedergang*, 749f, cf. also 748f, 750f.

126. RB to W. G. Kümmel, 16. 10. 1933, in E. Dinkler, *Im Zeichen*, 411.

127. Cf. E. Dinkler, *Im Zeichen*, 412–14.

128. Cf. H. Liebing, *Die Marburger Theologen*, 46f.

grounded theological recognition of the truth, and back towards the Tübingen faculty's position in support of the Aryan provision that had been initiated by his colleague Gerhard Kittel. Explicitly declaring their support for Kittel's memorandum "Church and Jewish Christians,"[129] the Tübingen theologians opposed the "courting" of agreement from theologians outside the country against the Aryan legislation. The whole affair was not "a question of faith, confession, and the purity of biblical proclamation," they insisted, but rather it concerned the problem of whether Jewish Christians could assume positions "in a church which, due to its own individual character, was becoming conscious of being the distinctive church of a people." Clearly, this matter was merely "a question of the administration of this people's church," and the Tübingen faculty had made clear how this question ought to be decided by recommending that Jewish Christians form their own communities outside the church of the German people."[130]

The Erlangen report, the position taken by Tübingen, and Heim, Juncker, and Schniewind's rejection of the New Testament scholars' report signaled unmistakably that the opposition to the Aryan Paragraph led by Bultmann and von Soden had received less than widespread support. In addition, a further opponent of the Marburg position appeared in the person of the Göttingen psychology of religion professor, Georg Wobbermin. The "German Christian" Wobbermin openly propagandized on behalf of the National Socialist doctrine of race. He complained that both the report of the Marburg faculty and the declaration of the New Testament scholars were inconsistent from the outset, since they totally rejected applying the Aryan Paragraph to the realm of the church, but did not so much as question its validity for the state. Indeed, the Aryan legislation belonged solely to "the human sphere," which displayed a concrete, historical problem: namely, "the appallingly excessive degree of Jewish impact and influence in German cultural life." The Protestant Church, Wobbermin went on, was to blame for this crisis through its baptism of numerous Jews from the nineteenth century onward. The aim of the Aryan Paragraph was simply to help in remedying this affliction. Unfortunately, the Marburg theologians had not sufficiently recognized that the question of the Jews was exclusively a racial problem and that Hitler was the first to render the service of bringing this fact to broader public attention. That the New Testament does not address

129. Cf. G. Kittel, *Die Judenfrage*, 101–13.

130. Cf. the votes of the Protestant Theological Faculty of Tübingen of 9. 11. 1933, as well as attachment 1 thereto, 1. 11. 1933, in H. Liebing, *Die Marburger Theologen*, 47f.

the topic of race at all in no way compels one to ignore the racial aspect of the Jewish question.[131]

Among the Marburg theologians and the German New Testament scholars, it was Bultmann who felt most compelled to issue a rejoinder to what Wobbermin had proposed. His defense of the Marburg position, which appeared in December of 1933, turned out to be as comprehensive as it was incisive. Bultmann also took this opportunity to offer a merciless rebuttal of half-truths and theologically untenable statements in the arguments of Kittel and the Erlangen and the Tübingen theological faculties, and to take full advantage of the manifest aberrations of the Jena New Testament scholar Heinrich Weinel. In particular, Bultmann identified as an unacceptable offense to the Reformation understanding of the church and its offices the strategy of appeasement pursued by the Erlangen and Tübingen theologians as well as by the Archbishop Ludwig Müller. The problem was obvious: these people held that the exclusion of non-Aryan Christians from bearing office in the church had nothing to do with their being Christians. Bultmann's riposte was devastating: "Were I a non-Aryan or a not-purely-Aryan Christian, I would be ashamed to belong to a church in which I was allowed to listen but had to keep silent." He refused to countenance "[pushing] aside the fundamentally different question of whether and how far the legislation of the state may be questioned by the church." In his pointed discussion he once more assailed the application of the Aryan Paragraph to the church as contrary to scripture and Confession. Sharpening the previous Marburg stands, Bultmann further maintained that the ideological thinking standing behind this provision contradicted "the truth of the church of Christ." By this thrust, Bultmann registered his unequivocal opposition to the state's Aryan legislation, regardless of whether the state meant to incorporate this Christian truth into its making of law.

In the course of the controversy with Wobbermin on 1 Cor 14:34f and 1 Cor 7:17–24, the texts to which the advocates for the Aryan Paragraph had appealed, Bultmann offered an exegetical lesson that could not have been more explicit. He asserted that as regards content, the gospel is always issued "*to* the people, not *from* the people," and therefore with respect to the people, the church remains "ever a mission church." As an eschatological entity, the church cannot take over "all the customs and ordinances of a people"; rather it performs its task by standing in permanent tension with

131. G. Wobbermin, "Zwei theologische Gutachten in Sachen des Arier-Paragraphen—kritisch beleuchtet," in H. Liebing, *Die Marburger Theologen*, 28–31.

the popular consciousness of both the people and the state. If (as alleged) this popular consciousness today feels it an offense for descendants of the Jewish spiritual tradition to hold office, then this reflects "the consciousness of an *unchristian* people, which has forgotten that God has set boundaries for it."[132]

The pressure that the "German Christians" exercised in the matter of the Aryan Paragraph had fatal internal consequences for the church. For although the opponents of applying this legislation to the church stoutly supported the rights of Christians of Jewish descent within the Protestant Church, they did not see it as their task similarly to oppose the increasingly common practice of depriving Jews of their civil rights. From the comfortable position of a later generation fully aware of the extent of National Socialist persecution of Jews, it is easy to complain about this deficiency. Consideration certainly has to be given to the fact that the positions enunciated by von Soden and Bultmann constituted a determined condemnation of applying the Aryan Paragraph to the church. To Wobbermin's demand that a German people's church had to accept this legislation for the sake of the state, Bultmann was bound to react by limiting the theological discussion of the problem to the sphere of the church. But by accepting this framework Bultmann also failed to confront the issue of Aryan legislation for the state. He did so explicitly by declaring the idea behind it incompatible with the truth of Christianity, and implicitly by casting his criticism in formulations such as the following: "It may be that legislation for the state remains as it always has been. . . ."[133]

Under the conditions of the dictatorship, all this amounted to a single, unambiguous opposition to National Socialist politics regarding Jews; and besides their clear and uncompromising biblical justification, the cogency of Bultmann's arguments stood out from the other ecclesial and theological views on the subject of applying the Aryan provision to the church. In June of 1933, Karl Barth had issued a warning in his polemic *Theological Existence Today!* The danger, he saw, was the attitude following the National Socialist seizure of power that what matters "afterwards as before, and as if nothing had happened . . . is to do theology and nothing but theology." That in itself was "taking a position . . . even, [if only] indirectly, a political one."[134]

132. RB, "Der Arier-Paragraph," in H. Liebing, *Die Marburger Theologen*, 32–45.
133. RB, "Der Arier-Paragraph," in H. Liebing, *Die Marburger Theologen*, 32; on the whole issue, cf. K. Hammann, "Rudolf Bultmanns Begegnung," 48–50.
134. K. Barth, *Theologische Existenz heute!*, 26.

And with his strict, theologically grounded rejection of the Aryan Paragraph, Bultmann was taking just such a clearly political position.

Through his Jewish friends and students, Bultmann from the outset came face to face with the effects of National Socialist politics regarding Jews. Hans Jonas, one of the first Jews to leave Germany, visited Bultmann one last time in the summer of 1933, just before his departure. During lunch Jonas reported that the German General Society for the Blind had just expelled its non-Aryan members, and incensed by the very thought of this infamous decision, he became more and more enraged until he ". . . stopped short, for my eye fell on Bultmann, and I saw that a deathly pallor had fallen on his face and in his eyes such a pain that the words died in my mouth. I knew at that moment that one could without reservation attribute to Bultmann the very essence of what it means to be human—that here words, explanations, arguments, and above all rhetoric, are completely beside the point."[135]

The following year, Bultmann gave Jonas, who meanwhile had emigrated, a foreword [he had written for] his Jewish student's book on Gnosticism—a manuscript Jonas understandably recognized as especially magnanimous and courageous in view of the circumstances. In it, Bultmann acknowledged that through the work of his student the significance of Gnosticism "for the change in the way the world was understood in the transition from antiquity to Christianity . . . had for the first time been opened up for him in its full scope." The path Jonas followed in employing existentialist analysis to expound on the significance of the historical phenomenon of Gnosticism had brilliantly proven its worth.[136] Bultmann mentioned briefly that his foreword had been occasioned by irritations that had arisen in the preliminary stages of publication. Jonas had already published his first work, a monograph that had grown out of a seminar with Heidegger on Augustine, in *Studies in the Religion and Literature of the Old and New Testament*, a journal that had been edited by Bultmann.[137] The Roman Catholic historian of dogma Hugo Koch subjected Jonas' book on Gnosticism to a devastating review in 1930, although he failed to deal closely with its content; he was outraged by Jonas' "lingo," which noticeably leaned on Heidegger's existentialist way of speaking. Koch deemed it an unreasonable demand to have to discuss such "gross nonsense" and found the work in general an offense "against the Holy

135. H. Jonas, "Im Kampf," 44; cf. Jonas, *Erinnerungen*, 235f.
136. RB, "Vorwort," in H. Jonas, *Gnosis*, pt. 1, v.
137. H. Jonas, *Augustin*.

Spirit of the German language."[138] Frightened by this negative criticism, the publisher Wilhelm Ruprecht told Bultmann that he found it necessary to withdraw his commitment to bring out Jonas' book on Gnosticism as part of the *Studies in the Religion and Literature of the Old and New Testament* series. Bultmann vouched for the quality of his student's work, but said that if Ruprecht lacked confidence in his [Bultmann's] judgment, he would step down as editor of the series. And in order to boost Ruprecht's confidence, Bultmann promised that he would add a foreword to the book. And thus it was that Bultmann redeemed this unusual promise in all respects in 1934.[139]

From those Jewish college and university teachers whom the Reich Ministry of Education had not been able to discharge on the grounds of the civil service law, it removed the *venia legendi* [permission to lecture] on December 31, 1935, when it put into effect the "Nuremberg Race Laws." Those affected from among Bultmann's circle of acquaintances and friends were the scholar of Romance languages and literature Erich Auerbach, the philosopher Erich Frank, the archaeologist Paul Jacobsthal, and the lecturer in philosophy Karl Löwith (all in Marburg), and elsewhere the classical philologists Paul Friedländer (Halle) and Eduard Fraenkel (Göttingen), as well as the mathematician Ernst Hellinger (Frankfurt). To these were added the Marburg pediatrician Ernst Freudenberg and the historian of literature Friedrich Carl Sell, teaching in Kassel, whom the National Socialist state dismissed in 1937 because both were married to Jewish women. Their careers destroyed, they all eventually decided, some with a heavy heart, to leave Germany.

Bultmann remained bound to his Jewish friends with unswerving loyalty after their dismissal from the civil service, and he supported them in whatever ways he could. For Erich Auerbach, who was hampered by poor library facilities in Istanbul, Bultmann repeatedly acquired scholarly literature and gave him bibliographical information.[140] His wife, Helene, made illegal arrangements to send to Ada Löwith, the wife of Karl Löwith, the viola she had to leave behind when she emigrated.[141] In order to get his friend Friedrich

138. H. Koch, rev. of H. Jonas, *Augustin*, 469.

139. Cf. H. Jonas, *Erinnerungen*, 238–40.

140. Cf. E. Auerbach to RB, 26. 12. 1937, 21. 5./26. 11. 1939, Mn 2-379; Auerbach's inquiries pertained to literature in historical theology on questions revolving around iconography. Cf. E. Auerbach, "Figura," 75; as well as M. Vialon, "Erich Auerbach und Rudolf Bultmann," 189.

141. Cf. UB Tübingen, RB est., A. Löwith to H. Bultmann, 21. 12. 1934 and also n. d. Mn 2-2863.

Carl Sell off to an easier start in the United States, Bultmann managed to evade postal censorship to secure financial donations for Sell.[142] He also enabled authors of Jewish descent to continue publishing scholarly reports in the *Theologische Rundschau*, which he and von Soden jointly edited, despite their having been ostracized by the National Socialist state.[143] And he challenged Gerhard Kittel, the editor of the *Theologisches Wörterbuch zum Neuen Testament* [*Theological Dictionary of the New Testament*], to exclude the anti-Semitic New Testament scholar Walter Grundmann from collaborating on that work.[144]

As he had done in the cases of Jonas and Löwith, he invited Erich Frank and the family of the physician Ernst Freudenberg to his home before they left to become émigrés.[145] During the 1930s Bultmann had met weekly for friendly and scholarly conversation with Frank, the former student of Jaspers. Even after he was forced to accept emeritus status in 1935, the philosopher, a charming but somewhat reclusive bachelor, underestimated the danger he was in. At first the Bultmanns and other friends urged him in vain to emigrate. Only when Bultmann's friends Ernst Hellinger and Paul Friedländer were arrested on the night of the national pogrom in 1938 and deported to the concentration camp at Dachau (that is, Sachsenhausen),[146] did Frank realize the seriousness of the situation. Not until relatively late—in April of 1939—did he succeed in leaving the country, and then only after Bultmann had at the last minute obtained the necessary papers and forwarded them to his friend who was waiting to disembark in Amsterdam.[147]

142. Cf. UB Tübingen, RB est., RB to K. Grobel, 23. 3. 1937, Mn 2-2743; as well as K. Grobel to RB, 14. 4. 1937, Mn 2-2700.

143. Among others, E. Frank, K Löwith, the New Testament scholar of "half-Jewish" descent W. G. Kümmel (and F. C. Sell).

144. Cf. UB Tübingen, RB est., RB to G. Kittel, 4. 4. 1937, Mn 2-2264.

145. Entry of the couple Ernst and Ida Freudenberg and their two daughters in Bultmann's guestbook, vol. 1 (1917–54), 10. 6. 1938, "on the way to Basel", Mn 2-3041, in UB Tübingen, RB est.; entry of E. Frank in the same guestbook, 9. 3. 1939, "In remembrance of all the lovely hours spend in this house at the time of our final departure, in sincere gratitude."

146. During the 1930s, Bultmann maintained his friendship with Ernst Hellinger by letter. After Hellinger had been arrested on 9. 11. 1938 and been delivered to the concentration camp at Dachau, he emigrated to the United States in 1939, where he taught mathematics at Northwestern University. Cf. UB Tübingen, RB est., E. Hellinger to RB, esp. 4. 2. 1939, Mn 2-965.

147. Cf. UB Tübingen, RB est., E. Frank to RB, 1. 4, 14. 4., and 24. 4. 1939 (from Amsterdam), Mn 2-760; cf. Bultmann's remark to H.-G. Gadamer, 23. 11. 1938; as well as RB to H.-G. Gadamer, 30. 4. 1939, in DLA Marbach: "You will have heard that Erich has completed his sea passage."

Bultmann also aided such students of Jewish descent as Dr. Klaus Oppenheimer[148] and Friedemann Boschwitz, who as one of the last Jews allowed to receive the doctorate, submitted his dissertation on Julius Wellhausen to the philosophy faculty of Marburg in January 1934. The Old Testament scholar Emil Balla, citing his lack of competence, turned down the position of second referee for this work, which had begun under the aegis of the historian Wilhelm Mommsen. Bultmann assumed the role in place of Balla and later aided Boschwitz, who emigrated to Palestine in 1935, in getting his dissertation printed.[149]

Under pressure from the Nazi policy of eliminating Jews, bands of friendship often strengthened, as was especially the case with Bultmann and Paul Friedländer. When the classical philologist accepted a call to Halle in 1932, he had already made this entry in Bultmann's guestbook:

> Think you not that, in these hours of going,
> The bonds between us even more are growing?[150]

From June of 1933 on, the correspondence between these two friends moved from the formal "*Sie*" to the familiar "*du.*" In August of 1933, at the end of his first visit in Marburg following the National Socialist seizure of power, Friedländer gave eloquent expression to his certainty over his friendship with Bultmann:

> Though time o'er us with violence range,
> Our essence it shall never change.[151]

Friedländer's prognosis was to be borne out completely in the years to follow.

The relationship between the two scholars was sustained by a basic *humanitas christiana,* of which an essential element was their readiness to resolve differing views in matters of scholarly detail. During the Third Reich, Bultmann and Friedländer kept up an especially intensive dialogue, often

148. Cf. UB Tübingen, RB est., K. E. H. Oppenheimer to RB, 3. 7. 1935, Mn 2-1499; M. Sulzbach to RB, 1. 8. and 10. 11. 1933, Mn 2-1893.

149. Cf. UB Tübingen, RB est., F. Boschwitz to RB, 2. 9. 1936, Mn 2-512; as well as F. Boschwitz, *Julius Wellhausen.* Cf. also M. Lemberg, "'. . . eines deutschen akademischen Grades unwürdig,'" 56–59.

150. Entry of P. Friedländer in Bultmann's guestbook, vol. 1 (1917–54), Oct. 1932, Mn 2-3041, in UB Tübingen, RB est.

151. Entry of P. Friedländer in Bultmann's guestbook, vol. 1 (1917–54), 14.–16. 8. 1933, Mn 2-3041, in UB Tübingen, RB est.

maintaining close weekly contact. Of the entire correspondence, 175 letters and 25 cards of Friedländer's to Bultmann are preserved, but with three exceptions Bultmann's letters to Friedländer have disappeared without a trace. Despite this imbalance, what remains affords instructive insights into biographical connections and the history of scholarship—not to mention a high-mindedness that was without pretense and a strength of personal character on the part of both that reflected a shared commitment to truth.

The dialogue between the classical philologist and the Protestant theologian spanned a wide variety of subjects. They discussed personal and family matters, developments in church politics, the Confessing Church's debate over the policy of National Socialism towards the church, and in addition their own publications, problems in the interpretation of New Testament concepts and ancient philosophical authors, or the most recent publications of Barth and Heidegger. Even more important, Friedländer became Bultmann's constant and grateful conversation-partner for philological questions in Johannine exegesis. In view of this exchange, rich in both its human and scholarly qualities, Friedländer's reports to Marburg about the increasing forms of repression to which he and his family were subjected was all the more depressing.[152]

Still, Friedländer was astonished when the catastrophic possibility of being dismissed from his position at the university did not at first occur (June 2, 1933), and was grateful for Bultmann's declaration at the opening of the summer semester of 1933 (July 2, 1933). To the decision of the General Synod of the Old Prussian Union to enforce the Aryan Paragraph in the church, Friedländer reacted by citing, among other texts, Gal 3:28. He suspected that Bultmann would be saddened by this development and asked whether in his case "a line has not been reached, or rather crossed" (September 9, 1933). When Bultmann was invited to receive an honorary doctorate in St. Andrews (Scotland) in 1935, Friedländer asked his friend to sound out whether he, too, might be invited to lecture in the British Isles, since "they want to be rid of 'us' as soon as possible" (May 25, 1935). Soon afterwards, he suspected, "My ousting is apparently imminent, and only the 'how' remains a question. . . . The whole thing is presumably being dealt with" (September 23, 1935). After his dismissal at the end of 1935, there arose the possibility that Friedländer might be offered a new position in

152. What follows according to P. Friedländer's letters to RB, Mn 2-787, in UB Tübingen, RB est.

Berlin as a library employee, but as of December 31, 1935, the school that had been planned for non-Aryan Christian children had not yet been approved. Having already moved to the capital, Friedländer requested the ancient historian Wilhelm Weber, the executive director of 'his' old Institute for the Study of the Ancient World, to permit him to use the institute's library. The National Socialist Weber refused: "'You will understand . . .' I understand completely! A pig remains a pig. That is a biological fact" (November 29, 1936).[153] The *Göttingischen Gelehrten Anzeigen* [*Announcements of Göttingen Scholars*] also informed Friedländer on February 13, 1937 that it would no longer publish his reviews.

The Friedländers were forced to put their daughter, Dorothy, in a Jewish private school in 1937. "The new ghetto looks odd . . . there is Protestant religious instruction in a Jewish school" (n. d. [1937]). From the spring of 1938 on, Friedländer was firm in his resolve to emigrate as soon as possible. He intensified contacts with Leo Spitzer, the scholar of romance languages and literature with whom he had become friends, who had gone to the U.S. on March 2, 1938, but on June 3, 1938 his passport was taken from him. Undeterred, he furthered his knowledge of English and wrote essays in English—hoping for a chance "that may never come" (June 20, 1938). In his reply, Bultmann encouraged Friedländer not to let his future plans be completely obstructed by the "present troubles," and assured his friend that he "sincerely shared in these troubles."[154] As it happens, the three preserved letters of Bultmann to Friedländer from the summer of 1938 are devoted to problems of Johannine exegesis, particularly to the questions of the authenticity of John 4:22 [". . . for salvation is from the Jews"] and the original literary form of chapters 5–8.[155] In any case, Friedländer's personal troubles were the subject of the occasional private conversations the two scholars shared between 1933 and 1939 in Marburg, Halle, and later in Berlin.[156]

On November 6, 1938, Friedländer confidently reported to Marburg, "If my plan succeeds, I will embark on a ship in six weeks (this for your ears only)." But things were to turn out otherwise, for on the night of the national pogrom of November 9–10, 1938, National Socialist thugs burned down synagogues all over Germany and thousands of Jews were arbitrarily arrested. The Marburg synagogue was among those set on fire and de-

153. On W. Weber, cf. K. Christ, *Klios Wandlungen*, 69–73.

154. UCLA collection, RB to P. Friedländer, 11. 7. 1938.

155. UCLA, RB to P. Friedländer, 11. 7., 15. 7., and 19. 8. 1938.

156. According to RB, *Chronik 1917–45*, Mn 2-224, Bultmann and Friedländer visited each other eleven times between 1933 and 1945, partly with their families.

stroyed, and on November 10 Bultmann and von Soden sent their students home: "When synagogues are burning, we cannot give lectures."[157] A little later, Bultmann received a desperate plea from Charlotte Friedländer. Her husband had been arrested during the November pogrom in Berlin and, as it was later learned, had been sent to the Sachshausen concentration camp.[158] Bultmann immediately did everything he could to get his friend released, and when Ernst von Hülsen, the Registrar of the university, "didn't want to deal with the matter," Bultmann enlisted the aid of Hans Lietzmann.[159] Thanks to Lietzmann's good connections with the ministries in Berlin, they finally succeeded in obtaining Friedländer's release. But as a result of his five-week confinement (during which he had among other things read Bultmann's *Jesus* as a book of edification and consolation of a higher order), Friedländer returned at the end of December with a physical injury. In addition, as Bultmann learned on a visit to his friend in Berlin in January of 1939, Friedländer had contracted an illness in the concentration camp.[160] Still, Friedländer was able to emigrate to the U.S.,[161] where he taught first in Baltimore and then in Los Angeles. He found it especially painful that his forced departure from the country due to the National Socialist persecution of Jews also meant separation from Bultmann: "I suppose your [forthcoming work] *John* must now be approaching its conclusion—when do you think this will be? How wonderful it would have been to work together—or, to put it more modestly, for me to take an active part in your work—right up to its conclusion!"[162]

157. Cited according to A. Lippmann, *Marburger Theologie*, 348, with n. 125. According to another oral tradition, on the morning following the burning of the synagogue, Bultmann is to have opened the windows in a lecture hall of the landgrave's house and, in the smell of the fire, to have upheld a lengthy period of silence in place of his lecture. Cf. K. Hammann, "Rudolf Bultmanns Begegnung," 94.

158. Cf. C. Friedländer to RB, 14. 11. and 26. 11. 1938, Mn 2-785.

159. RB to H. Lietzmann, 16. 11. 1938, in K. Aland, *Glanz und Niedergang*, 930; cf. also *Glanz und Niedergang*, 932.

160. Cf. P. Friedländer to RB, n. d. (ca. the end of December 1938), Mn 2-787; in addition, (hedged on account of the censor) Bultmann's communication to A. Bultmann Lemke of 29. 1. 1939 regarding his visit with Friedländer on 22. 1. 1939, Mn 2-3452 in UB Tübingen, RB est.: "We had a few lovely hours together. He has secure prospects of a position [in the U. S.], but he has to recuperate first, because he has returned from his vacation [!] with a severe cold, since his hotel room [!] was not heated. He still had a fever, and I hope that his lungs, which are in delicate condition, have not been affected." On Friedländer's incarceration in the concentration camp, cf. also RB, "Paul Friedländer," 91.

161. DLA Marbach, RB to H.-G. Gadamer, 5. 9. 1939: "You will know that Paul Fr[iedländer] went on a big trip on August 14th."

162. UB Tübingen, RB est., P. Friedländer to RB, 4. 5. 1939, Mn 2-787.

During the Third Reich, Bultmann did more than stand up for the rights of Christians of Jewish descent in the church and support Jewish friends who suffered either open or covert persecution and discrimination. Beyond these efforts he strove to establish at least the beginnings of a theological clarification of the relation between Judaism and Christianity. With his essay, "The Significance of the Old Testament for the Christian Faith," this New Testament scholar (!) was among the first to weigh in on a debate that far from accidentally and with increasing intensity was to occupy Protestant theology during the 1930s. As part of a lecture series by the Marburg faculty during the winter semester of 1931–32, Bultmann had spoken about "The Relation of the Old Testament to the Christian Proclamation." But the new essay redefined and sharpened the topic in such a way as to emphasize its relevance to the current debate regarding the Old Testament.[163]

In this essay Bultmann first rejects as theologically irrelevant the attempt of liberal theology to solve the problem, and insists that viewing it from the history of religions vantage point was the best way to understand Old and New Testament religion "from the outside . . . as historical phenomena"—although not to clarify whether the message of the Old Testament has any significance for one's faith and for the Christian church of the present.[164] Existentialist interpretation, in contrast, turns to the Old Testament with the "posing of the genuinely historical question of what basic possibility for human understanding of existence finds expression there."[165] Bultmann affirms in principle the classical understanding of the Old Testament as derived from Paul and Luther, as an expression of the demanding will of God. For the proclamation of the gospel, which frees the believer from the law, always requires this very law as the necessary presupposition for the ability to accept and understand the new order of being that is the gift of the gospel. Clearly, the cultic and ritual demands of the Old Testament are no longer valid for us, and as Paul shows in Rom 1:32 and 2:14f, neither can its moral demands claim to be the exclusive representation of the law. In consequence, only in a pedagogical context can the Old Testament assume the function of law in the church.[166]

163. Cf. RB, "Bedeutung," *GuV* I, 313–36. Bultmann had sent the manuscript of this essay to Mohr Siebeck Publishers on 22. 12. 1932. To say more than this in what follows is possibly to interpret the text. A. H. J. Gunneweg, "Altes Testament und existentiale Interpretation," in B. Jaspert, *Werk und Wirkung*, 334–40; H. Hübner,"Rudolf Bultmann," 252–63; M. Wolter, "Das Judentum," 19–24; K. de Valerio, *Altes Testament*, 370–77.

164. RB, "Bedeutung," *GuV* (1st ed.), vol. 1, 317.

165. RB, "Bedeutung," *GuV* (1st ed.), vol. 1, 318.

166. Cf. RB, "Bedeutung," *GuV* (1st ed.), vol. 1, 319–22.

Now, however, a weighty consideration ensues. The understanding of existence articulated in the faith in creation and the consciousness of history peculiar to the Old Testament corresponds perfectly to that of the New Testament. In both cases, the human being is seen "in his temporality and historicity." And hence to the person who "has even a minimum of historical sensibility, . . . it makes no sense to think of holding on to Christianity and of discarding the Old Testament. He can be sure that such a Christianity is no longer the real one. It is not a matter of either/or, but of both or neither."[167] With these observations, Bultmann specifically rejects the attempt to understand the Old Testament as "an expression of the spirit of a certain people (the Israelite-Jewish)" and to relativize it.[168] And in this manner he furnishes an early and unambiguously negative reply to the demand of the "German Christians" to banish the Old Testament from the Christian Bible as "foreign."

If the Old Testament understanding of existence is the same as that in the New, that poses the question of what is "new" in the New Testament. Bultmann answers thus: "Insofar as the idea of God is radically examined in Israel and the ideas of sin and grace are understood in a radical way, the faith of the Old Testament is one of hope, and *the faith of the New Testament* stands in relation to it *as the faith that has been fulfilled*."[169] This is so to the extent that Christian faith perceives the eschatological activity of God solely in Christ, through whom God has reconciled the world to himself (2 Cor 5:19). And for this reason, even if one encounters law and gospel in the Old Testament, and even if in its pages the grace of God precedes the law, the Old Testament cannot in an unqualified sense be revelation, cannot be word of God. For the Old Testament binds God's revelation to the empirical history of a specific people, whereas in assenting to but transcending such a limiting of the activity of God, the Christ-event constitutes the true eschatological revelation. On the basis of Christ, then, the Old Testament can be said to be "God's word in a qualified way," and thus as promise of and preparation for the Christian understanding of existence, rightfully deserves consideration in the proclamation of the church.[170]

As Bultmann was thus defending the Old Testament's proper place in the Christian church, he was also discovering the especially urgent task of freeing New Testament exegesis from anti-Jewish themes to be found in

167. RB, "Bedeutung," *GuV* (1st ed.), vol. 1, 324f.
168. RB, "Bedeutung," *GuV* (1st ed.), vol. 1, 325n1.
169. RB, "Bedeutung," *GuV* (1st ed.), vol. 1, 331.
170. RB, "Bedeutung," *GuV* (1st ed.), vol. 1, 335f.

the interpretive tradition. One element of this problem derived from the apostle Paul's dismissal of the Jewish understanding of the law and of salvation. Several weeks after the November pogrom and a day before his visit to Friedländer, who had just been released from the concentration camp, Bultmann spoke on January 21, 1939, at the invitation of the theological faculty in Halle on "Christ the End of the Law." Before the lecture, he found an opportunity for a substantive conversation with the Halle theologians Friedrich Karl Schumann, Ernst Wolf, and Julius Schniewind, in whose "most pleasant home" Bultmann was a guest.[171] To his daughter Antje, Bultmann clarified the hermeneutical intent of his interpretation of the Pauline understanding that Christ is the end of the law (Rom 10:4): it was a matter of "showing that Paul's opposition to the Jewish law was not a specifically Jewish matter, but rather a universally human one. For when Paul opposes the Jewish zeal for the law that focuses on its 'own righteousness,' he is thereby opposing the universal human striving for validation by seeking security through achieving, and therein failing to recognize that the individual cannot find fulfillment through his accomplishments, but only in the grace that is given to human beings as a free gift. The need for validation is once again poisoning human life today, and in a particularly strong way (and, naturally, in a way that displays a particular historical character)."[172]

In his January 21, 1939, lecture, which appeared in print in 1940, Bultmann distances himself equally from several anti-Jewish prejudices of Protestant and particularly Lutheran views of Jewish piety in relation to the law. Since he considers the Torah to be valid in the context of the history of Israel's election as "a proof of the grace of God,"[173] he explicitly agrees with Jewish exegetical demonstrations that Judaism does not experience the law as an onerous burden. The pious Jew rather rejoices in the law as a way of guiding his life. Neither did Paul suffer under the law (cf. Phil 3:4–7), nor did he rule out false obedience to the law on that account.[174] Nor can Paul's opposition to law be explained by psychological considerations employed in Christian theology regarding a consciousness of sin and self-condemnation on the part of the individual at odds with himself—whether this results from imperfect fulfillment of the law, an inner conflict due to willing what is good

171. UB Tübingen, RB est., RB to A. Bultmann Lemke, 29. 1. 1939, Mn 2-3452.

172. UB Tübingen, RB est., RB to A. Bultmann Lemke, 29. 1. 1939, Mn 2-3452.

173. RB, "Bedeutung," *GuV* (1st ed.), vol. 1, 26.

174. RB, "Christus des Gesetzes Ende," *GuV* (5th ed.), vol. 2, 33–35; on what follows, cf. K. Hammann, "Rudolf Bultmanns Begegnung," 60–64.

and doing what is evil, or the putative conflict of flesh and reason.[175] Nor is the apostle's criticism initiated by the content of the law, which as a gift of God is necessarily holy, just, and good (Rom 7:12), and which, as God's binding demand must be fulfilled through corresponding "works of the law."[176]

For Paul, the soteriological ineffectiveness of the law is to be understood in terms of the revelation in Christ, and therefore from the perspective of faith. The real sin consists precisely in defining one's own righteousness according to one's fulfilling of the law, and consequently in measuring one's very existence by one's achievements. According to Bultmann, it is precisely this "madness"—a total obliviousness to the fact that the individual has only the grace of God to thank for his existence and his salvation—in which Paul sees "the Jews imprisoned." For they attempt to find security and assert themselves before God by means of the "works of the law," and seek thus to satisfy their καύχημα [boasting] instead of becoming aware of their own creatureliness and reliance on the grace of God and of honoring God.[177] For this reason, Bultmann observes, "the will to do [is] . . . evil from the outset, since even when in order to live it wills what the law wills—namely, to do what is good—it yet wills what is evil—namely, to establish its own righteousness."[178]

Bultmann did not, as it might seem, derive the religious insufficiency of human existence under the law from the presupposition of a negative picture of Jewish Torah-piety. Quite the opposite, since the will to assert oneself before God is in no way peculiar to the Jews. That need of validation reflects the same universal human striving that characterizes both the gentiles who are blind to the fact of their creatureliness (Rom 1:20f) and the Gnostics in Corinth who boast of their own wisdom (1 Cor 1:18–31). Likewise, what finds expression in the prayer of the Pharisee (Luke 18:11f) is "nothing specifically Jewish, but rather something universally human."[179] Bultmann once again emphasized these ideas on August 4, 1940, when he preached on the parable of the Pharisee and the tax collector (Luke 18:9–14).[180]

175. Cf. RB, "Christus des Gesetzes Ende," *GuV* (5th ed.), vol. 2, 34–36, 43–46 (with reference to P. Althaus, *Paulus und Luther*, cf. also M. Meiser, *Paul Althaus*, 198–205).

176. Cf. RB, "Christus des Gesetzes Ende," *GuV* (5th ed.), vol. 2, 40.

177. RB, "Christus des Gesetzes Ende," *GuV* (5th ed.), vol. 2, 40–43.

178. RB, "Christus des Gesetzes Ende," *GuV* (5th ed.), vol. 2, 45.

179. RB, "Christus des Gesetzes Ende," *GuV* (5th ed.), vol. 2, 39.

180. Cf. RB, *MP*, 110.

Bultmann developed this interpretation of Paul's doctrine of justification and his criticism of the law as a direct alternative to what can be characterized as a specifically modern understanding of existence, according to which the individual acts under a compulsion to constitute and to justify his own being. As a counter to this human self-understanding that precedes πίστις [faith] and leads to bondage, faith opens up the possibility of a new human self-understanding, one that recognizes the sinner's new being to be constituted solely by means of the justifying grace of God and that therefore requires no attempt whatever at self-justification through any sort of work or achievement. Using this approach, Bultmann set justification by faith over against what we might call the "modern" understanding of the person who defines himself on the basis of his activities, his works, his achievements. In doing so, "the Marburg theologian proved to be one of the most significant interpreters of the Reformation doctrine of the justification of the ungodly by faith alone."[181] To be sure, Bultmann's approach applied to a certain rendering of the concept of Jewish observance of Torah as a form of piety directed towards achievement. Nevertheless, in employing this hermeneutical model, he succeeded in freeing the interpretation of the Pauline criticism of the law from its traditional fixation on Judaism, and thereby undermined anti-Jewish proposals on the part of Christian theology. It was not accidental that Bultmann explicitly maintained the impossibility of a pious Jew's agreeing with Paul's recognition in the light of faith in Christ of the insufficiency of existence under the law.[182]

A further painful issue in New Testament exegesis concerned the interpretation of anti-Jewish statements in the Gospel of John. When he began his commentary on John, Bultmann committed himself to an interpretation that such liberal exegetes as Otto Pfleiderer, Heinrich Julius Holtzmann, Wilhelm Heitmüller, and Walter Bauer had mapped out.[183] According to this, "the Jews" in the Fourth Gospel represented the world hostile to God. But whereas Walter Bauer, for instance, assigned these anti-Jewish statements in John to contemporary attitudes, Bultmann created a new hermeneutic possibility by arguing that the evangelist "adopted the hostility of the Jews only as a literary motif."[184]

181. E. Jüngel, "Glaube," 970.

182. Cf. RB, "Christus des Gesetzes Ende," *GuV* (5th ed.), vol. 2, 47.

183. On what follows, cf. for a detailed discussion K. Hammann, "Rudolf Bultmanns Begegnung," 65–72.

184. RB, rev. of W. Bauer, *Das Johannesevangelium*, in RB, *Theologie als Kritik*, 147f; cf. W. Bauer, *Das Johannesevvangelium*, 29.

Bultmann could not help but feel his view of things confirmed by the blatantly anti-Jewish interpretation that Emanuel Hirsch presented in 1936. In his critical discussions of Hirsch's works on the Fourth Gospel, Bultmann first showed the exegetical untenability of the thesis of his Göttingen opponent, for whom "every basic controlling thought of the Gospel" was to be seen in the fact "that between Christianity and Judaism, between faith in the word that frees and that has life, and the Jewish servitude that makes for bondage, there consists an irreconcilable conflict."[185] Bultmann further exposed the arbitrariness of Hirsch's allegorical interpretation of Jesus' discourse on the shepherd in John 10, in which he sees Jesus leading his own "out of the walled-in sheepfold of the Jewish law into the free meadow of the gospel."[186] Further still, he protested against Hirsch's attempt to use the purported "*struggle against Jewish legalism* and Jewish messianism" in the Fourth Gospel as an instrument against the Confessing Church. In contrast to Hirsch's anti-Jewish exegesis, Bultmann made it clear that in John the struggle of revelation was waged not against Jewish legalism, but rather against the worldliness by means of which human beings shut themselves off from faith.[187]

Thus from the start Bultmann set out to undermine any anti-Jewish interpretations of the Fourth Gospel's rhetoric concerning "the Jews." Accordingly, in his commentary on John that appeared from 1937–41 and by consistent use of existentialist theology in his interpretative approach, he explained the theological function of the term οἱ Ἰουδαῖοι [the Jews] at the internal textual level of the Gospel: "The evangelist's characteristic term οἱ Ἰουδαῖοι lumps the Jews together in such a way that from the perspective of Christian faith they are seen as representatives of unbelief (and so . . . of the unbelieving 'world' in general)."[188] Also, in order to make clear in a formal way that the evangelist was not thinking of the historical Jewish people, Bultmann for the most part set the term "the Jews" in quotation marks at key places in the text. Further, the existentialist model of interpretation offered him presuppositions that were suited to excluding an anti-Jewish interpretation of the Gospel of John, for it obviated the need for a close historical contextualization of the evangelist's negative statements about the

185. E. Hirsch, *Das vierte Evangelium*, 78f; cf as well as, critically, RB, "Hirsch's Auslegung," RB, *Theologie als Kritik*, 361, 366f.

186. E. Hirsch, *Das vierte Evangelium*, 254; as well as, critically, RB, "Hirsch's Auslegung," *Theologie als Kritik*, 364, ". . . the interpretation of the sheepfold in relation to the Jewish law is a monstrosity."

187. Cf. RB, "Hirsch's Auslegung," *Theologie als Kritik*, 367.

188. RB, *Das Evangelium des Johannes*, 59; cf. also, "Johannesevangelium," 845.

Jews. And in fact the Christian congregation had long been excluded from the synagogue, so that the evangelist was writing at a considerable distance from Judaism, as Bultmann then pointedly demonstrated.[189] After all, since the Fourth Gospel was a *vita Jesu*, it was necessary that Jews appear in it! Furthermore, Bultmann set all statements about "the Jews" against the background of the Johannine dualism of decision. From that point of view, "the Jews" appeared exclusively as representatives of an unbelieving cosmos that rejects the revealer and thereby decides against God and true life. A problematic consequence of this interpretation was, as later exegesis showed, that Bultmann underestimated the significance of "the Jews," that is, of Israel, for John's history of salvation concept.[190] Nevertheless, especially under the historical circumstances of the Third Reich, his interpretation—which rightly included somewhat more than half of all the Fourth Gospel's references to οἱ Ἰουδαῖοι—offered a far-reaching exegetical basis for rejecting attempts to employ the Gospel of John as an anti-Jewish document.

3. The Gospel of John and Its Commentary[191]

His commentary constitutes the greatest accomplishment of the first half of the [twentieth] century. Rudolf Bultmann's imposing achievement is superb in his blending of dialectical theology, existentialist interpretation, history of religions, source criticism, and redaction history with "fascinating unanimity" in such a sublime unity that scarcely any critic could carry on a discussion with him at this height and in this manner—a dazzling overall solution, . . . which unfortunately doesn't work.[192]

Even the first reviewers had a sure sense that Bultmann had achieved a great success with his commentary on the Gospel of John, with which he had brought to a definitive conclusion previous efforts at a solution of the Johannine question. Moreover, Martin Dibelius, Joachim Jeremias, and a little later Ernst Käsemann gave unanimous notice that with his *magnum opus* and especially in his masterful synthesis of its exegetical, hermeneutical, and systematic-theological aspects, Bultmann had "set Johannine research as a

189. Cf. RB, *Das Evangelium des Johannes*, 59, 428.
190. Cf. also in detail K. Hammann, "Rudolf Bultmanns Begegnung," 68f, 71.
191. E. Haenchen, "Das Johannesevangelium," 881.
192. J. M Robinson, "Vorwort," in E. Haenchen, *Das Johannesevangelium*, v.

whole on a new footing"[193] and had brought about a "breakthrough . . . to a . . . proper and fruitful understanding" of the Fourth Gospel.[194]

Bultmann's explication of the Fourth Gospel displays the result of more than twenty years of research. In 1880 Bernhard Weiss had published a relatively conservative interpretation of the Johannine writings in Meyer's series Critical-Exegetical Commentaries on the New Testament. It was originally planned that his son Johannes Weiss, Bultmann's teacher, would undertake a revision of the commentaries on the Gospel and the letters, but his early death in 1914 intervened. Finally, on the recommendation of Wilhelm Heitmüller, the publisher Vandenhoeck & Ruprecht assigned to Bultmann the task of writing new commentaries on the Johannine writings. The contract dated March 17, 1918, between the publisher and Bultmann provided for the commentary on John to contain thirty printed sheets and for completion in the fall of 1920. But this deadline could not be met, as Bultmann explained to the publisher numerous times during the 1920s, owing to the still-fluid state of the research.[195] The commentary first appeared between August 31, 1937, and March 27, 1941, in seven installments of five printed sheets and at a price of three Reichsmarks each. By the time of the final installment, the first was already out of print, and wartime restrictions were such that an immediate reprint could not be seriously contemplated.

Both the unsettled nature of the research mentioned above and Bultmann's progress toward the more comprehensive view of the evangelist's theology that he offered in the commentary are reflected in Bultmann's correspondence and in his publications on the Johannine corpus from about 1922 on. Before 1920, under the influence of Wilhelm Bousset and Wilhelm Heitmüller, Bultmann had still understood the Fourth Gospel in the context of the Hellenistic mysticism of Alexandria.[196] After 1922, following the history of religions model, he derived the Johannine world of ideas from the Gnostic-syncretistic milieu of a Palestinian-Syrian baptist circle.[197] He also

193. J. Jeremias, rev. of RB, *Das Evangelium des Johannes*, 420.

194. M. Dibelius, "Ein neuer Kommentar," 264; cf. E. Käsemann, rev. of RB, *Das Evangelium des Johannes*, 182–201.

195. Cf. M. Evang, *Frühzeit*, 72f.

196. Cf. RB "Die Bedeutung der Eschatologie," 79; RB, "Biblische Theologie," *Theologie als Kritik*, 88–90.

197. UB Tübingen, RB est., RB to H. von Soden, 23. 12. 1922, Mn 2-2385: ". . . the course on the Gospel of John (an audience of more than ninety) demands much more work, since now I have to work it up for the Meyer commentary. Also, it is in fact the most difficult book in the NT and it is only gradually that the darkness begins to clear. I believe I can show that baptist sources have also been used apart from the prologue, and that baptist ideas

made clear in his lecture course in the winter semester of 1922–23 that he was determined from then on to bid farewell to the idealistic interpretation of the Gospel of John that dominated the nineteenth century from Ferdinand Christian Baur to Albert Schweitzer. His colleague Friedrich Heiler, who attended this course, was "quite appalled" that Bultmann "interpreted away the beloved mysticism."[198] At about the same time as Walter Bauer, and even more forcefully, Bultmann emphasized the significance of the Mandaean texts published by Mark Lidzbarski and other Gnostic sources for classifying the Gospel of John according to the history of religions.[199] In the winter semester of 1924–25, during which Bultmann dealt anew with the Gospel in a lecture course and with the Johannine letters in his seminar, he also read "the Gospel of John with Heidegger one afternoon a week," in the hope "thereby of learning all manner of things."[200]

Although up to 1926 Bultmann's primary interest had been how the history of religions frames questions, in 1927 he developed in a research report the first signs of the existentialist interpretation that he sought to employ in a "history of mythology" interpretation of the Gospel of John.[201] In the following year he outlined the basic features of his eschatological understanding of Johannine theology in a programmatic essay.[202] Then, through research into the history of such concepts as ἀλήθεια [truth], he undertook an investigation into the presuppositions of the relevant concepts that the evangelist had appropriated and was dealing with—for this preparatory work was imperative for understanding Johannine conceptual language.[203] By around

have also exercised a strong influence in a general way. In this respect, what is at issue is in essence the ἄνθρωπος-myth that Bousset and Reitzenstein have demonstrated, which is to say suspected. That both scholars have given the Gospel of John scarcely any consideration is remarkable and can probably be explained only as due to their standing under the spell of the old view that the Gospel of John is influenced by the Alexandrian philosophy of religion, for which the false interpretation of the logos of the prologue is to blame. The more I come to know Philo, the more clearly I see that that was on the wrong track; Philo and John are two completely different worlds." Cf. RB, "Der religionsgeschichtliche Hintergrund," *Exegetica*, 10–35.

198. RB to K. Barth, 16. 7. 1923, in B. Jaspert, *Barth-Bultmann Briefwechsel*, 20.

199. Cf. W. Bauer, *Das Johannesevangelium*; as well as RB, rev. of W. Bauer, *Das Johannesevangelium*, in RB, *Theologie als Kritik*, 146–48; RB, "Die Bedeutung der neuerschlossenen," *Exegetica*, 55–104.

200. RB to F. Gogarten, 19. 10. 1924, in H. G. Göckeritz, *Bultmann-Gogarten Briefwechsel*, 62.

201. RB, "Das Johannesevangelium in der neueren Forschung," *Theologie als Kritik*, 214.

202. Cf. RB, "Die Eschatologie des Johannes-Evangeliums," *GuV* (1st ed.), vol. 1, 134–52.

203. Cf. RB, "Untersuchungen zum Johannesevangelium. Ἀλήθεια," *Exegetica*, 124–73; "B. Θεὸν οὐδεις ἑώρακεν πώποτε (John 1:18)," *Exegetica*, 174–97.

1930, Bultmann had fully worked out the basic contours of his Johannine exegesis—an author-focused, theological interpretation of the text that drew on the existentialist theological conceptuality and focused on explicating Johannine eschatology. During the 1930s, he had needed only to work on the exegesis of individual passages; and that was certainly difficult enough under the pressure of continuing academic responsibilities and provocations in theology and church politics that arose during the National Socialist period.[204] In short, he seems to have found his definitive literary-critical position relatively late, and specifically in the debate over Emanuel Hirsch's interpretation of the Fourth Gospel. Bultmann flatly rejected Hirsch's determined anti-Jewish interpretation, arguing that his opposite number from Göttingen had completely misjudged the basic eschatological character of the Gospel of John, and had furthermore advanced an exegetically untenable thesis by alleging that the evangelist's guiding theme was an attack on "Jewish legalism." And yet, Hirsch's relatively extensive recourse to depicting textual units as ecclesiastical redaction seems to have led Bultmann to make more precise his own conception of the redactional interpolations in the Gospel and to work out the "hypothesis of a mix-up of pages" that is presented in the commentary.[205]

The dedication "to the old Marburg Friends" that prefaced the commentary alluded to the colleagues expelled by the Nazi regime: Erich Frank, Paul Friedländer, and Friedrich Carl Sell. Friedländer was especially aware that this sign of Bultmann's unwavering loyalty was intended for his friends who had been ostracized by the Third Reich,[206] for the classical philologist had been the one scholar during the long gestation of the commentary with whom Bultmann constantly and in detail discussed questions regarding Johannine exegesis—a process that went on verbally during Friedländer's time in Marburg, by way of correspondence after his call to Halle in 1932, and even after he was forced into emeritus status in 1935.[207] At the request of the publisher, Bultmann sent the completed work on its way in 1941 with a separately printed "Epilogue," in which with apparent reluctance he explained his decision not to preface the commentary with an introduction.

204. Cf. Bultmann's earlier complaint to F. Gogarten, 3. 4. 1927, in H. G. Göckeritz, *Bultmann-Gogarten Briefwechsel*, 104f.

205. Cf. RB, "Hirsch's Auslegung," *Theologie als Kritik*, 354–59.

206. UB Tübingen, RB est., P. Friedländer to RB, 24. 4. 1949, Mn 2-787.

207. Unfortunately, from this correspondence, with few exceptions, only Friedländer's letters remain; cf. UB Tübingen, RB est., Mn 2-787. Among the exceptions, see above, n. 155. H.-G. Gadamer supported Bultmann in the proofreading of each delivery of the commentary; cf. DLA Marbach, RB to H.-G. Gadamer, 23. 11. 1938, 30. 4., 4. 10., and 19. 11. 1939.

The reason given is that the problems normally discussed in detail in an introduction, such as the distinctive character of the text relative to the history of literature, literary-critical details, or the Gospel's place in the history of religion, are treated extensively in the commentary itself. And since "the discussion of the author . . . does not affect the exegesis in any way," it belongs "in the realm of 'Introduction to the New Testament,' that is, in that of the history of the ancient church."[208]

With this, Bultmann had unmistakably set aside as without significance for interpretation the question of the author that had been hotly discussed in earlier research, and what had been the closely related issue of the Gospel's authenticity ever since Irenaeus insistently traced it back to John, the son of Zebedee. Besides that, he made it clear in the "Epilogue" that whether integrated into the actual interpretation or treated in the notes or excursus, the questions traditionally dealt with in an Introduction had no independent relevance, but were intended simply to support the text's theological interpretation and to function as indirect historical and literary supplements. To this extent, Bultmann's intention to subordinate the book's historical, literary, and history-of-religions aspects to the strictly theological interpretation of the Fourth Gospel by assigning them an ancillary role, is evident in the distinctive structure of the commentary—not only in its avoidance of an introduction, but especially in its detailed examination of typically "Introduction" questions within the far-ranging and extensive treatments found in small print. Bultmann's overall concept of his commentary on John may perhaps be seen as a semi-conscious parallel to Karl Barth's *Epistle to the Romans* of 1922. In any case, both his nearness to and his distance from Barth's interpretation of Romans had emerged early on, as one sees from Barth's inquiry in the spring of 1924 concerning the progress of Bultmann's work on John: "How will you connect what you are doing to what Walter Bauer and I have done, and in doing so put it to the test?"[209] With this question, Barth was probably alluding to a conversation in which Bultmann must have indicated the desire to connect what he was planning to the Johannine exegesis of Walter Bauer and Barth's *Epistle to the Romans.* The aim, of course, would be to synthesize the historical criticism represented by Bauer with the theological struggle to capture the essence of the text—a struggle that Barth had all too one-sidedly undertaken.

The theological unity of Bultmann's approach in the commentary on John rests on understanding the text as centered on its author. This Bultmann

208. RB, Epilogue, cited according to W. Schmithals, *Johannesevangelium*, 166.
209. K. Barth to RB, 15. 4. 1924, in B. Jaspert, *Barth-Bultmann Briefwechsel,* 32.

seeks to support by means of literary-critical analyses and by illuminating the Fourth Gospel's context in the history of religion. Seen in this perspective, the evangelist appears on the whole to be a creative theologian of considerable stature even if he seems at times to treat his sources somewhat mechanically. And he is completely original in having interpreted the Christ-event in such a convincing and prescient way that it is capable even today of serving as a paradigm for adequately interpreting the eschatological revelation in Christ. To this extent, one might rightly observe that the picture Bultmann has offered of the evangelist is really "a mirror-image of its interpreter."[210]

Thus from the outset Bultmann's literary-critical procedures serve to reconstruct from the canonical text's numerous literary fractures and material tensions an original gospel that is the stylistically and theologically unified work of the evangelist. Whereas older literary criticism—for instance that produced by Julius Wellhausen and Eduard Schwartz of Göttingen—had sought to explain the literary inconsistencies by hypothesizing a core writing often expanded and corrected by a single person, Bultmann rejects such unconvincing hypotheses and sets out on another path. Furnished with a set of widely diverse methods—analytic methods based on style, form, and tradition supplemented by content criteria derived from his own view of the evangelist's theology—Bultmann sets out to demonstrate that the evangelist has taken up various sources and, commenting critically upon them, has integrated them into his own presentation.

To these alleged sources belongs first of all a collection of miracle-stories, the semeia-source, from which the evangelist took over the seven wonder-discourses of his presentation and to which may probably be added the supplementary introduction in John 1:35–50, the concluding passages 12:37f and 20:30, and several smaller textual units. To be sure, the evangelist has critically worked over the semeia-source. In particular, its empirical understanding of wonders as miracles has been corrected by the evangelist; he interprets them symbolically, as "signs" of the underlying wonder of revelation. Furthermore, Bultmann recognizes that the evangelist has before him various written units from the synoptic tradition and uses them to create such passages as John 1:19–34 (call of the disciples), 2:13–22 (cleansing of the Temple), and 12:1–19 (Jesus' entry into Jerusalem), and portions of the passion and Easter accounts. Naturally, because it has been extensively worked over, one can no more reconstruct this material than one can the semeia-source.

210. W. Schmithals, *Johannesevangelium*, 171; cf. also J. Frey, *Die johanneische Eschatologie*, 141–45.

Also of central importance is a Gnostic source of revelation-discourses that Bultmann had earlier cited in his analyses of the prologue in 1923[211] and of the First Letter of John in 1927.[212] This source, which also undergirds the prologue, supplied the major elements of the Gospel's elaborated Jesus-discourses. These passages the author extensively worked over, commented on, and occasionally transformed into dialogues. He also reordered the revelation-discourses of a Gnostic summarization which, like Semitic poetry that employs apodictic statements uttered without argument, is often characterized by antitheses of *Parallelismus membrorum* [grammatical parallelism].[213] Since the evangelist has attributed revelation-discourses derived from Gnostic baptist sects to the historical figure of Jesus, and moreover has based the entire composition of his gospel on them, this Gnostic source and its critical reworking by the evangelist takes on the function of a hermeneutical key for understanding the entire work.

Above and beyond this, Bultmann presupposes that the original gospel was subjected to a redaction and that its present form reflects yet further editing. Seeking to moderate the radical theology of the evangelist and thus bring it into line with the orthodox ideas of the broader church and the synoptic accounts, this ecclesiastical redaction added the epilogue of John 21. Furthermore, all texts that refer to the sacraments (among others, John 3:5; 6:51b–58; 19:34b–35) are to be attributed to this same redaction. Then, in order to square the evangelist's "realized" eschatology with the contemporaneous ecclesiastical expectation of a future apocalyptic end of history, it has appended any eschatological statements of a purely futuristic character to passages containing the work of the evangelist (among others, John 5:27b–29; and in part 6:39, 40, 44–54, and 12:48).

Above all, however, Bultmann sees in the ecclesiastical redaction an attempt to reorder the text, which for unknown reasons—possibly by pages getting mixed up—had already become disordered before being edited, an attempt that he admits did not produce a convincing result. For this reason, Bultmann undertakes himself to restore the original order of the Gospel by rearranging texts. For example, he combines John 8:12, 12:44–50, 8:21–39, 12:34–36, and 10:19–21 into a light-discourse, which he attaches to John 9:1–41. Together with his theory of sources and his redaction hypothesis, Bultmann's bold and sweeping rearrangement of texts constitutes a further important instrument for reconstructing the original composition of the

211. See above, n. 197.
212. Cf. RB, "Analyse des ersten Johannesbriefes," *Exegetica*, 105–23.
213. Cf. RB, *Das Evangelium des Johannes*, 100n2, 117n1, 136n5.

text. And the theological unity of the Gospel revealed by a literary-critical examination in turn makes possible for the first time a coherent interpretation of the Gospel. Stating the case otherwise and in the form of a critique, it has been said that Bultmann understands John as "a gospel that, to a considerable extent, he . . . himself has helped to shape."[214] In doing so, Bultmann follows the underlying theme of the original gospel and likely the narrative structure of the revelation-discourse source: the Gnostic redeemer myth contained in this source. Parallel to this story that Richard Wagner called the drama of the "redeemed redeemer," Bultmann structures the original gospel as follows: "The Encounter with the Revealer," "The Revelation as κρίσις" [decision], "The Revealer's Struggle with the World," "The Revealer's Secret Victory over the World," "The Revealer's Farewell," and "Passion and Easter."[215]

Therefore, the assumption derived from the history of religions that in this work the evangelist appropriated the postulated pre-Christian Gnostic redeemer myth and critically interpreted it by applying it to the historical figure of Jesus takes on the function of a hermeneutical key for Bultmann's interpretation of the Gospel. In his reconstruction of this Gnostic myth of the redeemed redeemer, Bultmann largely agrees with the investigations of Richard Reitzenstein into Manichaean and Mandaean texts and especially with the studies of mythological Gnosis that his student Hans Jonas wrote under the influence of Heidegger's ontology of human existence.[216] To be sure, the evangelist employs the mythological language of the Gnostic material, for the myth is an early expression of how the human being lost in the world is a conundrum to himself, it understands the radical idea of revelation, and it formulates the salvation-drama as an escape from the world. However, the myth can exhibit only the possibility of the salvation-occurrence with respect to the individual, while the writer of the Fourth Gospel, as a Christian theologian of revelation, presents the paradoxical reality of the eschatological redemption-event in the historical sending of Jesus, in the proclamation of his work through the community, and in the existence of the believer. The evangelist therefore employs the Gnostic conceptuality of the redeemer myth—both in order to unfold the new, eschatological understanding of being and self through faith that is made possible through the historical revelation in the earthly Jesus, and with critical reference to the understanding of existence expressed in that myth.

214. E. Haenchen, "Das Johannesevangelium," 886.

215. RB, *Das Evangelium des Johannes*, v–viii.

216. Cf. H. Jonas, *Gnosis*; RB, *Das Evangelium des Johannes*, 41–43; for the context of the historical research, cf. J. Frey, *Die johanneische Eschatologie*, 133–40.

The evangelist's anti-Gnostic interpretation of the Gnostic myth clearly exhibits itself by eliminating such elements of the myth as the pre-existence of the soul and the materiality of both the redeemer and the redeemed. Furthermore, the redemption-occurrence in the Gospel is not conceived cosmically and naturalistically, but rather historically, so that the Gnostic material's cosmological dualism of substances is transformed into a dualism of decision, and the determinism of the Gnostic myth becomes the interpretive basis for the power of sin. Whereas the myth traces the creation of the world to demonic powers opposed to God, the Gospel inculpates the very nature of the cosmos that guiltily rejects the claim of the revealer and so forfeits its divine purpose.

Basically, by historicizing the drama of redemption and understanding it as an occurrence that impinges on human existence by confronting the human being with the decision of faith, the evangelist has in narrative form anticipated Bultmann's program of an existentialist interpretation of the New Testament. The evangelist subjects to this interpretation especially the apocalyptic images of Jewish and Christian eschatology that have come down to him, and completely demythologizes them. Rather than at the end of history, the universal future judgment is a definitive separation that occurs in an existential present through the sending of Jesus and the proclamation of the Christian congregation characterized as an eschatological moment. Since the resurrection is envisioned as completely present to faith in the life-bringing revealer, the hope in a future resurrection has become irrelevant. The same holds for the traditional expectation of Christ's parousia at the end of days, since his advent presently occurs in the form of Christian existence characterized by Easter and in the sending of the paraclete. According to Bultmann, inasmuch as John the evangelist understands the eschatological salvation-occurrence in a way unique to early Christianity—that is, as a matter strictly of the present—and with logical consistency dispenses with any sort of objectification of the content of salvation, then his work can be claimed as the decisive Christian interpretation of the eschatological understanding of being and of self.

In his interpretation of the Gospel of John, Bultmann shows himself to be radically committed to the fundamental insights of dialectical theology. The monolithic unity of his theological interpretation of the Fourth Gospel does not ultimately derive from the existentialist theology that informs his approach and by means of which he can apply the critical clarifications of Heidegger's ontology of human existence to a reformulation of the evangelist's message that will provide it with a new and modern understanding.

Another important factor in the swift and sweeping success of his commentary consisted in Bultmann's bringing to bear the exclusive claim of the revealer as depicted in the Gospel of John, but doing so without overlooking the possibility of being both in and out of the world. The attentive reader of the first edition of this commentary, which appeared from 1937–41, could read between the lines and find indications enough of a vigorous repudiation of the totalitarian claims of a National Socialism that was currently monopolizing how one was to view the world and give meaning to life.

The theology of the Gospel of John fulfills itself as an interpretation of the statement, ὁ λόγος σὰρξ ἐγένετο [the word became flesh] (John 1:14). In the Son of God's becoming flesh occurs the paradoxical revelation that eschatological salvation is present in the concreteness of the historical event of the coming and going of the revealer. The form of the revelation, indemonstrable to the eyes of the world, is mirrored especially in the fact that the revelation of the Johannine Jesus consists not in a teachable content, but rather "in the fact that his glory consists in nothing else than in his being the revealer."[217] In everything he does, Jesus reveals God. He reveals the lordship of God and his name, he accomplishes the works of God, and he speaks his words. It is thus that in his person one encounters God himself in the lowliness and depth of human existence.

It is not as if the outrage this contains—that is, the offence of the incarnation—holds true only for those who cannot be eyewitnesses of Jesus' life; it was equally true at first hand for the disciples. For Jesus first becomes the revealer sent in the wholeness of his being—that is, in the original unity shared by his coming and going—and, as revealer in this sense, he imposes on both his contemporaries and those who succeed them the eschatological κρίσις, that is, the decision whether in faith in the revealer they choose to receive life and salvation from God and recognize God as the source of their existence, or whether they sinfully choose to close themselves off from the word of the revealer and thus incur death and disaster. Since the historicity of his existence always affords the individual the ontological possibility of achieving the authenticity of true life, this possibility is realized by that person who allows himself to be called by the word of the revealer into the authenticity of life that is understood as coming from God and his grace.

As the evangelist John indicates in the prologue to his gospel, the revelation of God has the nature of a word; and this proves that the revelation-occurrence is to be understood as a genuine encounter between the God

217. RB, *Das Evangelium des Johannes*, 47.

who speaks and the creaturely world. Thus this word, contrary to Goethe's concept in *Faust,* does not fade as do "mere sound and smoke," but rather makes present the mighty power of God, who through the word of the revealer proclaims his advent in the world that has become alienated from him and so imparts to it salvation and life. The character of revelation as word safeguards the eschatological salvation-occurrence particularly from the misunderstanding that this event, identified with the person and the sending of Jesus as well as his departure from his own, was simply a fact of the historical past. For as eschatological occurrence it can be rightly understood only if it is perceived as an event that forever recurs anew in the kerygma of the Christian community and when heard in faith becomes the one adequate "answer to the question of the divine love."[218] The true καιρός [right moment], the now of revelation and thus the decision for or against the world, can be grasped only by the person who opens himself to encounter with the revealer.[219]

Eschatological existence realizes itself in faith, which conforms to the word of the revealer ever anew and which, as such, reflects the paradox of the revelation. Because the sending of Jesus represents both the unseen eschatological event and at the same time a historical occurrence, and because in revelation history God's majesty appears in the lowliness of the human being Jesus, then neither is faith an objectifiable possession, but rather a decision to be made ever anew so as to overcome the offensiveness and the outrage of the revelation. But it is precisely thus that faith transforms the person who hears the word of God's coming and opens himself to eschatological existence. Therein the believer decides to understand the source and goal of his existence in the world as coming not from the world, but rather from the grace of God, which is not at his disposal. To that degree, eschatological existence means an existence removed from the world; to that degree, the believer in the world is already free from the world; to that degree, he can in the historical present receive the eschatological saving gift of life—"that authenticity of existence bestowed as the gift of an enlightened and definitive understanding of oneself."[220] In other words, the eschatological existence in faith that comes only through revelation realizes itself when the human being permits himself to return to God the God-given freedom that he has lost through sin. This he does "in order to grasp his authenticity,"[221] thereby

218. RB, *Das Evangelium des Johannes,* 113; cf. also 430–33.

219. Cf. RB, *Das Evangelium des Johannes*m 220f; as well as A. Christophersen, *Kairos,* 143f.

220. RB, *Das Evangelium des Johannes,* 194.

221. RB, *Das Evangelium des Johannes,* 115.

to live in freedom from the world, from the past, from himself, and finally, therefore, in freedom from sin.[222]

To be sure, to the extent that the world is satisfied with what it finds presently available and deludes itself that this is sufficient, it is blind to the light that comes into the world with the coming of God and sheds new light on existence. The blindness of the cosmos, hostile to God as it is, is revealed in the grotesque misunderstandings with which Jesus' hearers react to even the most straightforward things he says. This blindness of those who do not grasp the eschatological possibility of faith but rather "bind themselves to their blindness"[223] is a guilt they bring upon themselves by their decision and in that sense bring upon themselves judgment for the sin that revelation first exposes for what it is.

The early reviewers unanimously praised Bultmann's decidedly theological interpretation of the Gospel of John and found highly plausible his history-of-religions derivation of the Johannine thought-world from mythological Gnosis.[224] To be sure, Martin Dibelius, Joachim Jeremias, and Ernst Käsemann—and later Emanuel Hirsch and Ernst Haenchen—voiced doubts about Bultmann's literary-critical procedures,[225] particularly his extensive textual rearrangements and his hypothesis of a mix-up of pages to explain a presumed disordering of the transmitted text.[226] It might well be Bultmann's resolutely theological approach to understanding the Fourth Gospel that was responsible for the effect of his commentary on John and its dominant role in further research up until about 1970—and this is above and beyond the fact that twelve editions had appeared previously and more than 45,000 copies were in circulation.

In later editions Bultmann added a supplement in which he noted relevant literature that had appeared in the meantime and in which he made minor

222. RB, *Das Evangelium des Johannes*, 336.

223. RB, *Das Evangelium des Johannes*, 259.

224. Cf. M. Dibelius, "Ein neuer Kommentar," 259f, 262f; J. Jeremias, rev. of RB, *Das Evangelium des Johannes*, 418–20; E. Käsemann, rev. of RB, *Das Evangelium des Johannes*, 190–96. Bultmann found Käsemann's critical discussion of his commentary on John, already completed by 1942, so suggestive that he wanted to have it reprinted in the *Theologische Rundschau*. This did not take place only on account of the restrictive measures of the National Socialist state over against ecclesiastical and theological publications. The *Theologische Rundschau* was also affected. Cf. UB Tübingen, RB est., RB to E. Käsemann, 1. 8. 1942, 17. 5. 1943, and 16. 12. 1945, Mn 2-2251.

225. Cf. M. Dibelius, "Ein neuer Kommentar," 260–62; J. Jeremias, rev. of RB, *Das Evangelium des Johannes*, 416–18; E. Käsemann, rev. of RB, *Das Evangelium des Johannes*, 183–88; E. Hirsch, "Stilkritik"; and E. Haenchen, "Das Johannesevangelium," 882–84.

226. Cf. J. Jeremias, "Johanneische Literarkritik," 33–46; E. Haenchen, "Das Johannesevangelium," 885f.

but sometimes important corrections and improvements to his work. Among these, for instance, was the partial revision of his original interpretation of Jesus' appearance before Pilate.[227] The unified picture of Johannine theology that we find in Bultmann's commentary and later in his *Theology of the New Testament* reflected a complex hermeneutical circle. The reciprocal interplay among literary analysis, history-of-religions reconstruction, and theological interpretation was supplemented by tying his own interpretive premises—which were shaped by dialectical theology and guided by Kierkegaard's philosophy and Heidegger's phenomenological analysis of existence—to the exegetical working out of the meaning of the text. This complexity protected his interpretation from both historical criticism of particular points and objections of a systematic nature.[228]

Bultmann's persistence in maintaining the existence of a pre-Christian Gnostic redeemer-myth can serve to illustrate this. After Erik Peterson raised objections to Walter Bauer's placing the Mandaean writings in the pre-Christian period, Hans Lietzmann in particular argued against a Mandaean influence on the development of early Christianity, saying that it was more likely to have been the other way round.[229] Similarly, Carsten Colpe raised the problem that using Manichaean texts to reconstruct a pre-Christian redeemer-myth was historically questionable.[230] And concerning the priority of the Gnostic myth to the New Testament and its having served as a model for the myth's understanding of human existence, Bultmann had followed Hans Jonas, who admittedly had not so much analyzed the Gnostic myth in a detailed history-of-religions fashion as he had interpreted it after the manner of phenomenology of religion. Still, Bultmann always maintained—understandably, in view of his hermeneutical approach—that the pre-Christian existence of that myth was sufficiently verified.[231]

It hardly needs mention that Bultmann wanted it understood that the fundamental inconclusiveness of scholarly knowledge applied to his work on the Gospel of John. He therefore accepted with his characteristic humor even an Englishman's satire on his hypothesis on the mix-up of pages. This told of a secretary "who, standing and taking dictation for the gospel writer John, was surprised by a gust of wind and who was in total despair at the

227. Cf. D. Lührmann, "Der Staat," 359–75.

228. Cf. J. Frey, *Die johanneische Eschatologie,* 154f.

229. Cf. H. Lietzmann, *Ein Beitrag zur Mandäerfrage*; as well as RB's review of 1931 RB, *Theologie als Kritik*, 260–62. B. Nichtweiss deals with Erik Peterson's contributions to the problem of the Mandaeans in *Erik Peterson*, 321–27.

230. C. Colpe, *Die religionsgeschichtliche Schule*, 1961.

231. Cf. Frey, *Die johanneische Eschatologie*, 137–40.

prospect of collecting and reordering the pages that were strewn all over the floor, when suddenly John called off her Sisyphean task with the comment, 'Never mind. There's a guy at Marburg—he will put it in order.'"[232]

Whether the principles guiding Bultmann's theological overview of the Gospel of John can be acknowledged as legitimate irrespective of his literary critical and history-of-religions assumptions remains a matter of dispute in today's exegetical literature.[233] But that his commentary marks a high point in the history of the interpretation of the Fourth Gospel is beyond dispute. And several generations of preachers have garnered a variety of stimuli and useful sermon topics from his scholarly interpretation of the text, because it consistently deals with the hermeneutical question of how to understand oneself today in light of the revelation-occurrence.[234]

4. Alpirsbach, 1941—The Demythologizing Lecture

> *I am sending you the extraordinary lecture of Bultmann's that reveals him, who in personal contact is so infinitely versatile, nimble, humorously patient, of a nearly fearsome seriousness—a seriousness the radicalism of which is exciting and provocative not only for the religiously undecided, but also for many theologians of the strictly observant sort. I do find most of it important and splendid. Naturally, enormous differences arise in our more intimate regular contact, but I am happy to have it and I respect it heartily, and I find it splendid of him that he is willing to spare so much time for me.*[235]

After finishing work on the Johannine commentary, Bultmann turned to a project he had long been contemplating. He wanted to expound in a short work the theological problems resulting from mythological concepts in the New Testament. Wilhelm Kamlah's *Christentum und Selbstbehauptung* [*Christianity and Self-Assertion*], which appeared in 1940, played an important part in seeing to it "that the plan was finally carried out."[236] For Bultmann saw in the work of his student "the either/or: the question of eschatological or political self-understanding posed with great clarity and

232. E. Dinkler, "Rudolf Bultmann," E. Dinkler, *Im Zeichen*, 431.

233. Cf. in this regard in divergent fashion W. Schmithals, *Johannesevangelium*, 173f; E. Haenchen, "Das Johannesevangelium," 210; J. Frey, *Die johanneische Eschatologie*, 142.

234. Cf. as an example H. Braun, "Die Paradoxie," 32f.

235. M. Kommerell to E. Kommerell, 20. 4. 1942, in I. Jens, *Max Kommerell*, 37.

236. PhAU Konstanz, RB to W. Kamlah, 19. 7. 1942. Cf. W. Kamlah, *Christentum*; cf. also UB Tübingen, RB est., RB to G. Bornkamm, 14. 4. 1941, Mn 2-2147.

acuity, and therein the struggle against eschatology waged not only with a real knowledge of the subject as well as extraordinary insight, but also in a truly noble manner." The philosopher Kamlah challenged theology to undertake that critical self-reflection "in which its existence or non-existence" is at stake.[237]

Bultmann understood his lecture *Neues Testament und Mythologie* [*New Testament and Mythology*]—which he gave at a regional meeting in Frankfurt am Main of the Society for Protestant Theology on April 21, 1941, and a second time at the meeting of the organization as a whole in Alpirsbach on June 4, 1941—as his contribution to this demand for self-reflection.[238] The Society for Protestant Theology was formed in Berlin at the beginning of 1940 as a reaction on the part of Confessing Church theologians[239] to the threat posed to Christianity by the aggressive church politics of the National Socialists. Through its work the Society pursued the goal of uniting theological scholarship and church proclamation in order to ward off attacks on Christianity resulting from the worldview of the National Socialist state. Bultmann was likewise convinced of the necessity for theological debate with the National Socialist worldview and the heterodoxy it had caused within the church. It was on this account that he published *New Testament and Mythology* together with his lecture on *Die Frage der natürlichen Offenbarung* [*The Question of Natural Revelation*], presented at Alpirsbach in October 1940.[240] In the latter he discussed in detail the question of whether the exclusive revelation of God in Jesus Christ indicated a similar revelation of God in nature and history. In opposition to the Third Reich's assertion that the will of God reveals itself in the history of the German people, Bultmann pointed to the ambiguity of all phenomena past and present. Thus he declared unequivocally that "the essence of the German people"

237. PhAU Konstanz, RB to W. Kamlah, 2. 4. 1941. Cf. also PhAU Konstanz, RB, "Bemerkungen zu W. Kamlah." This text of at least 35 pages is taken up in part in RB, *Neues Testament und Mythologie*, 42–48. For the context of this treatment see also RB, "Review" of E. Hirsch, *Die Auferstehungsgeschichten*, RB, *Theologie als Kritik*, 389–94, and RB, rev. of W. Nestle, *Vom Mythos*, in RB, *Theologie als Kritik*, 394–97.

238. On what follows, cf. H. Wassmann, "Der 'Fall Bultmann,'" 141–44; W. Schmithals, "Zum Problem der Entmythologisierung," 167–70.

239. Ernst Wolf, Hans von Soden, Martin Fischer, and Joachim Beckmann had been chosen as the directorate of the Society for Protestant Theology on 7.–8. 2. 1940.

240. Cf. RB, *Offenbarung und Heilsgeschehen*. The first essay is also reprinted in *GuV* (5th ed.), vol. 2, 79–104. On the other hand, Bultmann did not publish the the essay, "Theology as a Science," which he also gave on 5. 6. 1941 at the general meeting of the Society for Protestant Theology. Cf. RB, "Theologie als Wissenschaft"; as well as K. W. Müller, "Zu Rudolf Bultmanns Alpirsbach Vortrag," 470f.

cannot be used "as a clear criterion . . . [by] which we may judge the rightness of what we do." Rather, when it comes to dealing with God's demand and God's holiness, history ultimately proves to be characterized by the sin of human beings and therefore to conceal God.[241]

With this eminently political statement, Bultmann in 1940–41 provided an example of theological engagement with current myths. His demythologizing lecture belonged within this political context, but he also directed himself against other tendencies within the Confessing Church: he feared it was overly restricting itself to a mere repristination of the ecclesiastical confessions and so was running the risk of being able to express the Christian faith only in terms of a bygone language and an outmoded worldview. Especially in the context of a debate with the worldview of the present day, was not an understandable and credible proclamation of the Christian message what really mattered? Bultmann gave an indication of the problem in his greeting to the Marburg students at the front in the beginning of January 1941. He had listened to a sermon at Christmas that he considered successful in terms of its dogmatic correctness and its form, but had gone home from the Christmas service "deeply disappointed and depressed" because the preacher had not been able "to translate the gospel into the language of the present" so that the person who heard it could experience it as a message of concern to himself.[242]

This is the background for Bultmann's description of the problem and the task of demythologizing the New Testament kerygma in his lecture at Alpirsbach. Not only the New Testament worldview, but also its presentation of the salvation-occurrence is mythical. The motifs it employs in so doing are taken from the contemporaneous "mythology of Jewish apocalyptic and of the Gnostic myth of redemption."[243] Since the mythological world has become obsolete for people of today, they find the mythological language incredible, and both their empirical worldview and self-understanding preclude them from holding onto the mythological ideas of the New Testament. Among the motifs that Bultmann brusquely declares to be "finished" are the ascension of Christ to heaven, belief in spirits and demons, miracles as actual

241. RB, "Die Frage der natürlichen Offenbarung," *GuV* (5th ed.), vol. 2, 92f; cf. E. Dinkler, "Die christliche Wahrheitsfrage," 29f. From the beginning, the political context of the demythologizing essay went all but unnoticed in the debate it triggered.

242. Cf. Bultmann's New Year's Day word of greeting for January 1941, in E. Dinkler-von Schubert, *Feldpost*, 143, 145; also, already RB to E. Käsemann, 11. 8. 1937, Mn 2-2251, "The increasingly hardening orthodoxy in the B. K. [Confessing Church] seems to me a great danger."

243. RB, *Neues Testament und Mythologie*, 13.

happenings, the mythical eschatology, the idea of a supranatural agency of the Spirit and the sacraments, the conception of death as punishment for sin, the doctrine of satisfaction, and the understanding of the resurrection as a physical occurrence. To the degree that any of these involves miracles, Bultmann sums up his conclusion thus: "We cannot use electric lights and radios and, in the event of illness, avail ourselves of modern medical and clinical means, and at the same time believe in the New Testament's world of spirits and wonders."[244]

In view of the Bible's mythical worldview, the theologian and the preacher owe their listeners intellectual clarity about what one can, and what one cannot accept as true, for in dealing with the mythological representations of the New Testament, the only sensible strategy is to demythologize. In fact, demythologizing is in keeping with the nature of myth—a term that specifically denotes not an objective account of an event or a cosmology, but rather the expression of a particular human self-understanding. Of course it does this by representing the divine as human and the other-worldly as this-worldly, and to that degree blurs or conceals the difference between God and humanity. By means of this rhetorical objectifying, moreover, myth also disguises its real intention. For its intent is to show that the individual is not lord of himself, but that like the world he knows he is dependent on transcendent powers. The basis for critical analysis of a myth's realistic representations is implicit in the discrepancy between its objectifying language and its ultimate intention.

In the case of the New Testament, which reflects at least the beginnings of a critique of myth, the need for demythologizing forces itself upon us because it represents the human person in contradictory ways: "On the one hand the individual is understood as a cosmic being; on the other he is an autonomous person who can gain or lose himself by his own decision."[245] Bultmann then goes on to denounce the procedure employed by nineteenth-century critical theology to demythologize the New Testament proclamation. In applying the analogical distinction of husk and kernel, that now-dated liberal theology not only removed the time-bound mythological representations, but also eliminated the kerygma's special function of proclaiming the person of Jesus Christ as the decisive salvation-occurrence.[246]

244. RB, *Neues Testament und Mythologie*, 16.

245. RB, *Neues Testament und Mythologie*, 24.

246. RB, *Neues Testament und Mythologie*, 26, takes as an example A. Harnack, *Das Wesen des Christentums.*

Quite to the contrary, the purpose of demythologizing is to uncover the truth of myth in general, and that of the New Testament kerygma in particular. Only the existentialist interpretation of New Testament mythological statements is able to achieve this. In Bultmann's view, Hans Jonas' analysis of mythological Gnosticism provides the model for this because it focuses on myth's understanding of existence.[247]

In the second part of the Alpirsbach lecture, Bultmann uses a broad brush to demythologize the New Testament's basic features. First, from a Christian perspective, he contrasts human existence outside of faith with human existence in faith. Outside of faith, the human being lives by what is visible and disposable and therefore transient. By doing so, he becomes subject to death and forfeits his authentic existence. Genuine life, in contrast, receives itself from what is invisible and non-disposable; it finds fulfillment in trust, since that which cannot be surrendered encounters the individual as love, and yields him not death, but rather life and a future. This faith commends one to the grace of God that forgives sins, that frees the human being from his past, from binding himself to what is disposable and dying. In faith he realizes an obedient turning from himself and towards God. Thus, faith also takes the individual out of the world and into eschatological existence. According to 1 Cor 7:29–31, so far as his relation to the world is concerned, the believer exists in the attitude of "as if not" (ὡς μὴ), that is, in the freedom that comes from rejecting the world. Living in this way entirely from God means to be a new creation (2 Cor 5:17). Because the believer's future has already become present and the time of his salvation has already broken in, the Gospel of John has eliminated apocalyptic eschatology and replaced it with a present or "realized" eschatology, while in the case of Paul, Gnostic eschatology has been demythologized.[248]

However, the New Testament both specifically and exclusively understands faith in Christ as the essence of the Christian understanding of existence. Indeed, faith first became possible as a result of the Christ-occurrence. This poses the question of whether this assertion contains a mythological remainder that needs to be demythologized—that is, whether "*the Christian understanding of being can be realized without Christ.*"[249] Both Karl Jaspers' philosophy of existence and Martin Heidegger's existential analysis of being evidently come very close to the New Testament understanding of human

247. Cf. RB, *Neues Testament und Mythologie*, 29; as well as H. Jonas, *Gnosis.*
248. Cf. RB, "Neues Testament und Mythologie," 32–38.
249. RB, "Neues Testament und Mythologie," 39.

existence without reference to the revelation in Christ. To be sure shades of difference may exist between Heidegger and Wilhelm Kamlah. For instance, philosophy agrees that the individual can achieve authenticity by having his nature pointed out to him;[250] nevertheless, from the viewpoint of the New Testament this claim of philosophy has to be disputed, because the New Testament assigns the achievement of genuine existence not to the human being, but to God alone—that is, to God's power and act of salvation. Christian faith fully concedes to philosophy that it can uncover the knowledge of the fallenness and the authenticity of life in the sense of abstract structures of existence, but it disputes philosophy's assumption that human beings are able to achieve authenticity by themselves. For the individual faces death, and in the light of revelation we recognize that his despairing attempt to achieve true being through his own strength is the sure sign of his overweening pride, and therefore of his sin. This indicates that the meaning of the Christ event consists precisely in the fact that through the revelation of his love, God frees the individual from himself and therein makes it possible for the individual to live in the self-abandonment of eschatological existence and in openness to God's future.[251]

If only faith in Christ can free the individual from his fallen state, the question arises as to whether the Christ-occurrence, being the event in which God has revealed his love, does not also exhibit a mythical character. Indeed, history and myth are peculiarly intertwined in the person of Jesus Christ, for the New Testament identifies the pre-existent Son of God with Jesus of Nazareth, a particular historical person. To the extent that by thus portraying things the New Testament commingles what is historical and what is mythical, the suspicion arises that the mythological language might serve to clarify the significance of the historical Jesus as that of the one who brings salvation, and of his history as that of the salvation-occurrence. Bultmann discusses this problem in detail with regard not to a composite of specific motifs that one might suspect of being mythology, but rather to the cross and resurrection as the heart of the kerygma.[252]

The crucifixion of Christ is also conceived throughout the New Testament as a mythical occurrence—as we see, for instance, in its representation of Christ's death as an atoning sacrifice. Surely, this is its way of emphasizing

250. Cf. RB, "Neues Testament und Mythologie," 42–45; also Kamlah, *Christentum und Selbstbehauptung*: "As the true understanding of being, philosophy frees natural devotion for its complete truth."

251. Cf. RB, "Neues Testament und Mythologie," 45–52.

252. Cf. RB, "Neues Testament und Mythologie," 52–54; as well as W. Schmithals, "Zum Problem der Entmythologisierung," 186f, 200f.

the cross' significance for us. In other words, the cross does not represent an objective event having an effect that God would, so to speak, dedicate to us after the fact. Rather, as the decisive eschatological occurrence, the cross is always a matter of the present: ". . . to believe in the cross means to take on the cross of Christ as one's own; it means to allow oneself to be crucified with Christ."[253] Still, the resurrection of Christ cannot somehow miraculously authenticate the meaning of the cross, for it is itself an object of faith. The belief in resurrection is identical with the belief in the cross of Christ as salvation-event, for the crucified and risen Christ encounters us exclusively in the word of the proclamation. The understanding faith awakened by this word is precisely the Easter faith that accepts the word of proclamation as "legitimated word of God."[254] As the cross and the resurrection of Christ together comprise the salvation-occurrence that is present in the proclaimed word, so this word and the church that proclaims it also belong to the eschatological occurrence.

Bultmann's challenge to demythologize the New Testament was resisted from the very beginning. The intense debate that followed his lecture in Alpirsbach, a colloquy joined by Otto Bauernfeind, Ernst Bizer, Günther Bornkamm, Peter Brunner, Friedrich Delekat, Hermann Diem, Erich Foerster, Ernst Fuchs, Gerhard Krüger, Edmund Schlink, Richard Widmann, and Ernst Wolf, soon made clear the explosive nature of the subject.[255] As soon as the demythologizing lecture appeared in Beiträge zur evangelischen Theologie [Contributions to Evangelical Theology], edited by Ernst Wolf, it produced a sharply divided response in the Confessing Church. Bultmann found gratifying the conversation with the Württemberg Society for Church and Theology that took place in Ebersbach during a three-day seminar in April 1941. Although the work of the seminar focused

Plate 31: Rudolf Bultmann in Alpirsbach, June 1941

253. RB, "Neues Testament und Mythologie," 55.
254. RB, "Neues Testament und Mythologie," 61.
255. Cf. E. Fuchs, Minutes of the general meeting of the Society for Protestant Theology in Alpirsbach, 1941; H. Diem, *Ja oder Nein*, 265.

on the exegesis of 1 John, the members of the Society also raised topics from the Alpirsbach lecture in discussing with Bultmann how to put his program of demythologizing into practice. At their request, Bultmann read aloud to them several of his sermons, among which was one on the pericope of Peter's "miraculous draught of fishes" (Luke 5:1–11) that he had preached in Marburg only a few weeks before, on July 13, 1941, by way of an example of how demythologizing is done.[256] To be sure, he failed to gain unanimous agreement from the Society's pastors, but the conversations in Ebersbach struck him as hopeful; after all, he did not somehow imagine that the Alpirsbach lecture "had set out a definitive solution to the problem," but rather understood it as a stimulus to discussion.[257]

In various meetings in 1942, the Berlin-Brandenburg section of the Society for Protestant Theology dealt with Bultmann's concept of demythologizing in precisely the critical and controversial sense in which Bultmann had intended.[258] But other voices were to be heard from Berlin. At a general convention of the Berlin Confessing Church, the student pastor Otto Dilschneider declared that it was highly regrettable that the Confessing Church had wasted paper on Bultmann's publication.[259] Ernst Wolf felt obliged to explain that it was *Bultmann's own* paper that had been used, not that of the Confessing Church.[260] On behalf of the Berlin convention, Hans Asmussen, the chair of the Berlin council of brothers of the Confessing Church, joined Wolf in registering a sharp protest against Bultmann's publication.[261] Asmussen demanded that "Christendom not treat what Bultmann had perpetrated any differently from the errors of the G[erman] C[hristians]." For Asmussen, there was only one kind of church Christianity, and it was in fundamental opposition to the world in general and in particular to the modern ethos characterized by Enlightenment beliefs. In its

256. Cf. RB, *MP*, 137–47.

257. UB Tübingen, RB est., RB to H. H. Schrey, 16. 11. 1941, Mn 2-2376; cf. H. Wassmann, "Der 'Fall Bultmann,'" 144–47. Among others, Hermann Diem, Karl Dieterich, Ernst Fuchs, Friedrich Höltzel, and Richard Widmann took part in the Society's seminar in Ebersbach; H. Diem, *Ja oder Nein*, 265f.

258. Cf. E. Bethge, *Dietrich Bonhoeffer*, 799.

259. On what follows cf. E. Konukiewitz, *Hans Asmussen*, 234–38, 275. A few items of the correspondence between H. Asmussen and E. Wolf exist as carbon copies in Wolf's correspondence with Bultmann, as well, in UB Tübingen, RB est., Mn 2-2072. Cf. O. Dilschneider, "Mythus?!," 153f.

260. In the background stands the lack of paper caused by the War and the effective prevention of the distribution of paper for theological publications on the part of the National Socialist state from February of 1942 onward; cf. Wassmann, "Der 'Fall Bultmann,'" 141n8.

261. To be sure, the majority of the convention members had not even read Bultmann's text.

fundamental principles the world of Christ stood "opposed to the saeculum, with its radio, telephone, and airplane," and Bultmann could not become a conversation partner *intra muros* of the Confessing Church.[262] Wolf immediately lodged a protest against Asmussen's vehement polemic, since it failed to deal with Bultmann's theological distinctions in a way that effectively came to grips with his program of demythologizing. Wolf also rejected Asmussen's attempt to arrange for the Confessing Church's censorship of uncomfortable theological views. To be sure, neither Wolf nor Bultmann succeeded in persuading the rigid and pugnacious theologians who took their stand on the Confessions to engage in a substantive debate.[263] And, like Asmussen, Hans Joachim Iwand flatly rejected Bultmann's lecture as a "symptom of senility."[264]

But other theologians in the Confessing Church disavowed such verdicts, and when leading representatives of the Confessing Church in Kurhesse demanded that Bultmann's statements be rejected for contravening the Confessions in their denial of the central salvation beliefs of the Christian faith,[265] Hans von Soden stepped onto the field. To be sure, he felt certain of Bultmann's Alpirsbach formulations and the borrowings from Heidegger to be problematic, but he deemed the theological concern for demythologizing to be absolutely justified. He also judged that in addition to Asmussen's and Dilschneider's complete misjudging of the seriousness of the problems Bultmann had addressed, their attempt to silence theological dialogue was not only unacceptable due to the form it had taken, but also dangerous for the Confessing Church. "The way Bultmann's lecture has been received in the C[onfessing] C[hurch] gives me serious worries, not for my friend

262. H. Asmussen to E. Wolf, 21. 3. 1942, in E. Konukiewitz, *Hans Asmussen*, 236.

263. Bultmann declared himself prepared for a discussion with Asmussen under *one* condition. Asmussen would have unambiguously to declare as false the conduct of the Berlin convention in its condemnation of Bultmann's Alpirsbach lecture without most of its members having read it. Cf. UB Tübingen, RB est., RB to H. Asmussen, 21. 1., 17. 2. and 6. 3. 1943, Mn 2-2126. Asmussen turned back from taking an unambiguous position. For this reason, the discussion did not take place. Cf. UB Tübingen, RB est., H. Asmussen to RB, 24. 1., 13. 2., and 12. 3. 1943, Mn 2-376. In the Oldenburg State Church, E. Osterloh made himself the legal advisor for Bultmann's demythologizing program over against H. Asmussen and H. Kloppenburg. Cf. P. Zocher, *Edo Osterloh*, 115–18.

264. UB Tübingen, RB est., H. J. Iwand to E. Wolf, 30. 3. 1942 (copy of letter), Mn 2-2997; cf. also H. J. Iwand to G. Bornkamm, 16. 3. 1942, in J. Seim, *Hans Joachim Iwand*, 271f.

265. Cf. the correspondence of B. Heppe and Bultmann of 1940–42, Mn 2-972 (with carbon copies of the positions of the Council of Brothers of the Confessing Church of Kurhessen-Waldeck of June and from 30. 9. 1942) and Mn 2-2243 in UB Tübingen, RB est.

Bultmann, but rather for the C[onfessing] C[hurch]. I fear that, in this case—and unfortunately, not for the first time—it might be led to deny itself the intellectual and spiritual consideration of a serious question and, by doing so, be led into internal divisions. . . . The C[onfessing] C[hurch] is in danger of fostering theological untruthfulness, which is to say, the fear of truth that has hollowed out our state churches from within."[266]

On September 30, 1942, in a vote on demythologizing, the Council of Brothers of the Confessing Church in Kurhesse recommended discussing further in fraternal fashion the questions Bultmann had raised. Pastor Friedrich Hochgrebe (of Gemünden/Wohra) had earlier approached Bultmann with a request for detailed discussions in a study group for pastors and religious teachers in order to examine the possibilities and problems of demythologizing in the praxis of churches and schools. Bultmann accepted this request forthwith, since it was in perfect accord with his intentions for existentialist interpretation.[267] First in Kassel, then, and soon once a month in the *Philippshaus* in Marburg, a group of interested theologians met with Bultmann to do exegesis and discuss recent theological literature. Bultmann led the discussion, with Pastors Hochgrebe and Franz Berthoud of Rauschenberg presiding until 1956, when Pastor Helmut Adamek of Marburg assumed the chair. For more than two decades the *Philippshaus* study-group served as a forum of fruitful exchange between academic theology and theological efforts in school and community and moreover offered Bultmann a place to discuss his plans for publications and lectures.[268]

Among the theologians of the Confessing Church who early on took Bultmann's side in the debate over demythologizing was Dietrich Bonhoeffer. In 1942 he declared the commentary on John and the Alpirsbach lecture to be among the most important recent theological publications,[269] and expressed his pleasure that with his venture Bultmann had begun an intellectually honest discussion of a problem that many had suppressed. In Asmussen and Dilschneider's "arrogance" and the "Pharisaism of belief" Bonhoeffer

266. H. von Soden to District Pastor B. Heppe (of Cölbe), 31. 5. 1942, in E. Dinkler-von Schubert, *Theologie und Kirche*, 343, 345; cf. also H. von Soden to E. Dinkler, 12. 9. 1942, in E. Dinkler-von Schubert, *Feldpost*, 85.

267. Cf. UB Tübingen, RB est., RB to F. Hochgrebe, 2. 9. 1942, Mn 2-3085; RB to G. Bornkamm, 15. 12. 1942, Mn 2-2147.

268. Cf. H. Adamek, "Aus der Tätigkeit." Among others who gave papers were Peter Biehl, Marie-Luise Keller, and Walter Schmithals.

269. Cf. E. Bethge, *Dietrich Bonhoeffer*, 799.

saw "a real disgrace for the Confessing Church."[270] To be sure, he could not endorse Bultmann's position completely. "I would like to speak with Bultmann about this, and I would like to expose myself to the breeze that emanates from him. But then the window will have to be closed again. Otherwise, those who are delicate will too easily catch a chill."[271] Later, during his imprisonment in Tegel, Bonhoeffer came to think that Bultmann had not gone far enough, and that it was necessary to subject not only mythological but all religious concepts to a nonreligious interpretation.[272]

In the early debate over Bultmann's demythologizing lecture, the inquiries and objections of his critics focused on a few themes that would also play a central role in the debate after 1945. His student Jochen Niemöller, the oldest son of Martin Niemöller, raised the point that the closed worldview developed by natural science was accepted only by a few who "keep a tight rein on their *ratio* [thinking]."[273] Even the literary critic Max Kommerell, who was friends with Bultmann, doubted that "all of us" are persuaded by the worldview of natural science.[274] Bultmann replied to such criticism by observing that science axiomatically presupposes this closed worldview and its method proceeds from this premise "whether the individual scientist is clear about this or not." And that presupposition has informed the daily life of people since the sixteenth century—and therefore that of Christians as well.[275] Like Kommerell, the author Marie Luise Kaschnitz also expressed

270. D. Bonhoeffer to E. Wolf, 24. 3. 1942, in D. Bonhoeffer, *Konspiration*, 248; D. Bonhoeffer to W. Krause, 25. 7. 1942, in D. Bonhoeffer, *Konspiration*, 344f; D. Bonhoeffer to E. Wolf, 13. 9. 1942, in D. Bonhoeffer, *Konspiration*, 358. E. Wolf made Bultmann a copy of the passage from Bonhoeffer's letter of 24. 3. 1942. Cf. UB Tübingen, RB est., E. Wolf to RB, 30. 3. 1942, Mn 2-2072.

271. D. Bonhoeffer to W. Krause, in D. Bonhoeffer, *Konspiration*, 345.

272. Cf. D. Bonhoeffer, *Widerstand und Ergebung*, 414; somewhat differently, D. Bonhoeffer, *Widerstand und Ergebung*, 482. In view of Bonhoeffer's fragmentary statements on demythologizing, Bultmann later regretted extraordinarily "that one can no longer have a discussion with Bonhoeffer" (UB Tübingen, RB est., RB to G. Harbsmeier, 25. 6. 1956, Mn 2-2232). Cf. G. Harbsmeier, "Die 'nicht-religiöse Interpretation,'" 74–91.

273. Cited from RB to J. Niemöller, 21. 3. 1943, in E. Dinkler-von Schubert, *Feldpost*, 153f.

274. UB Tübingen, RB est., M. Kommerell to RB, 26. 3. 1942, Mn 2-1181. "'We all' know scientific particulars in greater or lesser fashion. . . . Basically, however, we see tree, sea, bird, clouds, and so on—but also the human figure, and human feelings—and above all, what we name 'cosmos,' a bit with scientific dilettantism, but for the most part poetically, mythologically, with enthusiasm, with sympathy—the poets and the religious of all times taking up lodging in our body and accommodating the half worked-through ideas. We only really think scientifically when we consult something in the dictionary of conversation." This letter is found in C. Weber, *Max Komerell*, 516–23, not taken into consideration.

275. RB to J. Niemöller, 21. 3. 1943, in E. Dinkler-von Schubert, *Feldpost*, 154.

rather instinctive reservations concerning Bultmann's concept of demythologizing. To be sure, she admitted, she was somewhat religiously unmusical. She would first "have to seek to attain a level of inward uprightness and unconditional truthfulness" equal to that of Bultmann. "And perhaps a person who had felt only the vaguest concept of religious experience has not even the right to talk about these things."[276]

A clear clash of interests arose over the concept of myth. In Alpirsbach, Bultmann had defined myth laconically "as research in history of religions understands it."[277] Paul Althaus and Ernst Lohmeyer complained that Bultmann's definition of myth turned out to be too broad and too formal to serve as a useful basis for what he was attempting.[278] In this regard, Bultmann from the beginning showed little inclination to accept any definition of myth other than the one that even in the ancient world had become laden with highly divergent connotations. For to him, the relatively neutral framing of the concept seemed especially well suited to clarifying the hermeneutical problem that most acutely concerned him—and that was how to help people today understand the New Testament message in spite of its foreignness.[279]

Bultmann undertook in print a detailed debate with Helmut Thielicke, who accused him of eliminating the historical element from the Christ-occurrence and handing over Christian theology to a particular philosophy.[280] But state restrictions upon church politics rendered public debate less and less possible.[281] Bultmann regretted that no second edition of his

276. UB Tübingen, RB est., M. L. Kaschnitz to RB, 1. 4. [1942] (no year), Mn 2-1101; cited inexactly in P. Wagner, "Jesus als Spiegelbild," 64f. Bultmann and Marie Luise Kaschnitz knew each other through their membership in the same reading group; see below 358f.

277. RB, *Neues Testament und Mythologie*, 22f, n. 20. On the possible origin of Bultmann's concept of myth, cf. W. Schmithals, "Zum Problem der Entmythologisierung," 170–78.

278. Cf. P. Althaus, "Neues Testament und Mythologie," 337f; as well as M. Meiser, *Paul Althaus*, 367–70. Cf. E. Lohmeyer, "Die rechte Interpretation," in H.-W. Bartsch, *KuM*, vol. 1, 140f; as well as D. Kuhn, *Metaphysik und Geschichte*, 52–57.

279. Cf. RB to P. Althaus, 22. 1. 1943, in E. Wolf, *Mythologie und Kerygma*, 91; UB Tübingen, RB est., RB to E. Lohmeyer, 21. 10. 1944, Mn 2-2287. Cf. also W. Schmithals, "Zum Problem der Entmythologisierung," 170f.

280. Cf. H. Thielicke, "Von der Entmythologisierung," 129–31; as well as RB, "Zur Frage der Entmythologisierung," 3f (also in *KuM*, vol. 1, 221–26).

281. It is probably on this account that Bultmann's reply to Althaus' criticism, "Neues Testament und Mythologie," 342–44—namely, that the demythologizing of eschatology leads to an inadmissible elimination of an end-time eschatology which, for its part, remains dependent on mythological representations—was first published in 1945. Cf. RB to P. Althaus, 22. 1. 1943, in E. Wolf, *Mythologie und Kerygma*, 91. In this letter, Bultmann insisted upon a unity of the eschatological action of God and of a definite historical occurrence "by means of

recently out-of-print "Revelation and Salvation-Occurrence" could appear, for then he would have been able to deal with objections and criticisms of his demythologizing lecture.[282] Instead, he found himself burdened by the difficulty of receiving and answering numerous inquiries and criticisms by letter. "I often heave a sigh over this and would rather go on quietly with my own work."[283] Of course, he received many letters from people who understood him, but "on the whole, [he gained] . . . the impression of a complete blindness to the problem—that is to say, a desperate flight in the face of the truth."[284]

He was therefore all the more grateful for Ernst Lohmeyer's critical appreciation of the concept of demythologizing, offered in a lecture in Breslau on January 9, 1944. Bultmann discovered that unlike most of his previous critics, his friend had grasped the real nature of the hermeneutical problem.[285] In his posthumously published lecture, Lohmeyer agreed with Bultmann that myth requires interpretation—to recognize the truth of which one needs only "to understand myth as the way in which God reveals himself."[286] For this reason, demythologizing can interpret myth historically, even as it is the reciprocal task of theology "to create myth anew," to "do away with" its forms that have become untenable and "to recreate" its true and living possibilities for a new religion.[287] For myth is "the language of all religions."[288] In his reply, Bultmann traced his divergences from Lohmeyer to differences in their understanding of theology. He reaffirmed his view that existentialist interpretation was clearly justified by the twofold intention of myth to speak of human existence and of deity as determining this. In addition, he stressed that regardless of specific problems of understanding, he

which faith wholly renounces the demand to have this event drawn for it in visible, worldly fashion, as does myth, which can conceive the action of God only as a breaking into the continuity of natural or historical occurrence." Besides, Bultmann reproached Althaus for not having sufficiently noted that the resurrection of Christ is *at once* the basis *and* object of faith (RB to P. Althaus, 22. 1. 1943, in E. Wolf, *Mythologie und Kerygma*, 92).

282. Cf. RB to J. Niemöller, 1. 3. 1943, in E. Dinkler-von Schubert, *Feldpost*, 152.

283. UB Tübingen, RB est., RB to H. Bousset, 17. 1. 1943, Mn 2-2148; RB to G. Bornkamm, 15. 3. 1942, Mn 2-2147.

284. PhAU Konstanz, RB to W. Kamlah, 19. 7. 1942.

285. Cf. UB Tübingen, RB est., RB to E. Lohmeyer, 21. 10. 1944, Mn 2-2287.

286. E. Lohmeyer, "Die rechte Interpretation," 144; cf. as well as D. Lührmann, "Ernst Lohmeyers," 83–85; D. Kuhn, *Metaphysik und Geschichte*, 52–54, 65f.

287. E. Lohmeyer, "Die rechte Interpretation," in H.-W. Bartsch, *KuM*, vol. 1, 147f.

288. E. Lohmeyer, "Die rechte Interpretation," in H.-W. Bartsch, *KuM*, vol. 1, 140: ". . . for this reason, to demythologize a religious proclamation, of whatever sort it might be, is to condemn that religion to becoming mute and, thereby, to ceasing to be."

was in general agreement with Lohmeyer in understanding that myth must be interpreted.[289]

As a result of the increasing intensity of the Second World War, the debate over Bultmann's program of demythologizing came to a standstill. Both his partisans and his understanding critics acknowledged his determination in taking responsibility for the truth of the New Testament message in the face of the modern understanding of reality.[290] Speaking at Alpirsbach in 1941, Bultmann himself had noted that everything he said about the *task* of demythologizing could have been said thirty or forty years earlier.[291] His *accomplishment* of that task resulted from his previous theological work.[292] Bultmann was certainly not the only Protestant theologian of the twentieth century to make a determined effort to think through the Christian faith in the context of modern perplexities, but probably no other attempt combined the radical theology and widespread impact on the joint realm of academy and church as did his program of demythologizing. This was to play itself out in the two decades following the end of the Second World War in the continued controversy over this controversial issue.

5. The Preacher

> *Bultmann's sermons speak consciously of God, in that they speak of the human being. Barth's sermons speak just as consciously of the human being and to the human being, in that they speak of God. Barth speaks directly of God and indirectly only of the human being. Bultmann speaks directly of the human being and indirectly of God. For this reason, his sermons are also only indirectly "Christ-sermons." However, they are and mean to be Christ-sermons and nothing other than this!*[293]

289. Cf. UB Tübingen, RB est., RB to E. Lohmeyer, 21. 10. 1944, Mn 2-2287; as well as E. Lohmeyer to RB, 6. 11. 1944, in U. Hutter, "Theologie als Wissenschaft," 159: "Now as before, the main difference seems to me to lie in questions of method. How is theology as a critical study possible on the basis of faith?" (correction from the original, Mn 2-1315.)

290. Cf. P. Althaus, "Neues Testament und Mythologie," 340; E. Lohmeyer, "Die rechte Interpretation," in H.-W. Bartsch, *KuM*, vol. 1, 139.

291. Cf. RB, *Neues Testament und Mythologie*, 24.

292. This is the case, without prejudice to the question of when Bultmann first used the term "demythologizing." The term was probably coined by H. Strathmann, rev. of W. Herrmann, *Ethik*, though Bultmann might have taken it from H. Jonas, *Augustin*, 68. Cf. also the suggestions in H. Jonas, "Heidegger," 640. Bultmann probably used the expression for the first time in 1934. Cf, RB, rev. of H.-D. Wendland, "Die Eschatologie des Reiches Gottes bei Jesus," in RB, *Theologie also Kritik*, 309. On this matter cf. also RB, "Die Bedeutung des Alten Testaments," *GuV* (1st ed.), vol. 1, 315f.

293. G. Harbsmeier, "Gedruckte Predigten," 229.

In December 1935 Bultmann approached Karl Barth with a request to publish two of Bultmann's own sermons in *Theological Existence Today!* In doing so, Bultmann hoped that despite the considerable difference between them, including the two sermons in Barth's series might highlight the shared beliefs that bound them together in the struggle "for the same cause."[294] Barth declined. In Bultmann's sermons he saw "not really Christ preached, but rather . . . the believing person made explicit," and he found them simply "boring." Barth traced his continuing strong differences with Bultmann to the "difference over the relation of christology and anthropology."[295] Likely foreseeing that Barth would not accede to his request, Bultmann had previously described Barth's sermons as hardly bearable: "When you ask questions of the text, it is according to a dogmatic recipe; the text does not speak with its own voice. After a few sentences, one already knows everything that you will say and only asks oneself now and again how he is going to get that out of the words of the text that follow. . . . This exegesis doesn't grip me; the text does not address me; rather, the blanket of dogmatics is spread out over it." To put it in a positive way, he proposed as the goal of preaching "that, under the auspices of the word, the listener's existence is made transparent to him."[296]

Bultmann's way of interpreting the biblical text for the kind of content-driven preaching that he contrasts to Barth's approach can thus be seen to serve as the primary criterion for Bultmann's judgment of giving and hearing sermons. For being above all a hearer and presenter of sermons, he thoroughly disapproved of the elitist attitude of one of his theological friends who went to the University Church only when he was himself to be the preacher. He regularly attended the worship of his congregation in the Lutheran parish church, particularly in the years between 1936 and 1951, when he held the office of head of the parish council.[297] Especially during the years when the National Socialist state was taking an increasingly confrontational stance toward both church administration and worldview, Bultmann conscientiously performed his official service to the church and even took up the offerings. Both his fellow members and his students took this as a silent sign that perfectly reflected the theology professor's loyalty to the Confessions and his devotion to the church. However, if a poor sermon was to be expected, Rudolf and Helene Bultmann would sometimes content

294. RB to K. Barth, 10. 12. 1935, in B. Jaspert, *Barth-Bultmann Briefwechsel*, 159f.
295. K. Barth to RB, 22. 12. 1935, in B. Jaspert, *Barth-Bultmann Briefwechsel*, 162f.
296. RB to K. Barth, 10. 12. 1935, in B. Jaspert, *Barth-Bultmann Briefwechsel*, 161.
297. Cf. UB Tübingen, RB est., the communication of the parish council of the Lutheran parish church of Marburg, 5. 2. 1936, telling of Bultmann's election to it, Mn 2-3049.

themselves with reading a sermon aloud to each other at home. When they were both over seventy, the two would still occasionally make the arduous trip by bus, train, and then footpath to hear the preaching of Dr. Hans Schimmelpfeng, the leader of the Hephata Institutes, whom they held in high esteem.[298]

From time to time—for instance on his vacation in Todtnauberg in 1926, or during his therapeutic spa treatments in Wiesbaden—Bultmann also attended Catholic worship services. What he heard there often said more to him than did many a Protestant sermon.[299] As Bultmann assessed such an experience in 1939, the preaching was "at least up-to-date—a task that for most Protestant preachers exceeds their capacities. . . . Why don't they read more texts aloud and not limit themselves to a few explanations of texts and brief applications!"[300] Thus it is no surprise that the homiletical challenge of making the Christian message understandable within the context of the modern sense of truth became one of the major motifs of his demythologizing lecture in Alpirsbach two years later.[301] In offering a critical appreciation of two sermons that the Marburg preacher Helmut Adamek delivered in 1954, Bultmann outlined his view of a successful sermon. The preacher must first of all discover the theological content of a biblical text, but his sermon must do much more than express dogmatic correctness; it must go on to explain the existential meaning of the theological statements, so that the congregation finds itself involved in a learning process that transports it from the experience of the law to the experience of the gospel.[302]

Bultmann's participation in worship services and his own preaching practice both reflected his view that the sermon, as proclamation of the word of God, belongs at the center of all theological activity. And in this regard he knew he was in fundamental agreement with Karl Barth and the other representatives of dialectical theology; they recognize that theology provides both the sermon's orientation and its purpose.[303] For there is a mutual rela-

298. Cf. E. Hauschildt, *Rudolf Bultmanns Predigten*, 270. For Bultmann's admiration for the sermons of Schimmelpfeng, cf. already RB to G. Krüger, 19. 11. 1939, in F. Lilie, "Bultmann-Krüger Briefwechsel," *ZNThG* 5, 143.

299. Cf. RB to G. Krüger, 13. 7. and 19. 8., 1926, in F. Lilie, "Bultmann-Krüger Briefwechsel," *ZNThG* 4, 292, 294; 19. 11. 1939, in F. Lilie, "Bultmann-Krüger Briefwechsel," *ZNThG* 5, 143.

300. RB to G. Krüger, 19. 11. 1939, in F. Lilie, "Bultmann-Krüger Briefwechsel," *ZNThG* 5, 143.

301. See above 325f.

302. Cf. UB Tübingen, RB est., RB to H. Adamek, 9. 5. 1954, Mn 2-2121; as well as E. Hauschildt, *Rudolf Bultmanns Predigten,* 265f.

303. Cf. RB to K. Barth, 8. 6. 1928, in B. Jaspert, *Barth-Bultmann Briefwechsel,* 81.

tion between the word of God and the church, one that Bultmann described from an ecclesiological perspective in 1929. On the one hand, the church is constituted by the Christian kerygma as "community of worship," as "eschatological fact" and as "a congregation called through the deeds and words of the deity and therefore bound to a history." On the other hand, the essential task of the church consists in witnessing to and passing on God's word of salvation that has appeared in Jesus Christ. Word of God and church are inseparably related to each other, for the church is constituted through the word, and the word is its authorized tradition. And since the primary role of the word is to make present the eschatological salvation-occurrence in the church, then as Bultmann expresses it in somewhat exaggerated fashion, "Jesus Christ is accessible only in the sermon."[304]

The central significance of the sermon for faith and theology can also be stated from a soteriological perspective. To make the eschatological salvation-occurrence and the forgiveness of sins a present reality requires a form of mediation that is structurally analogous to forgiveness itself. Since forgiveness occurs only in encounter, it can be promised only in the word and accepted only in faith. This being so, neither forgiveness as such nor the claim of the word of forgiveness to make present the eschatological occurrence either can or may be humanly proven or legitimated. Christian theology is thus limited by the fact that we cannot dispense with God and still claim his self-revelation—or the truthfulness of the Christian proclamation.[305]

Following his time as a tutor from 1907–16, Bultmann no longer had any regular preaching responsibilities, and his attempt to institute a new plan for academic worship services in Marburg in the early 1920s foundered at first. This meant that Bultmann could not actively participate in the university worship, because the two university preachers had a prior claim. By necessity, then, he satisfied himself for more than a decade with minor homiletical opportunities. He spoke at end-of-the-week devotions held in the *Michelchen*, the chapel on the mountain slope opposite the Elizabeth Church. Further, he led regular Bible studies as well as devotions and worship services at the beginning of the semester and Advent, all for an audience made up predominantly of students.[306]

304. RB, "Kirche und Lehre," *GuV* (1st ed.), vol. 1, 153f, 180.

305. Cf. E. Hauschildt, *Rudolf Bultmanns Predigten*, 117.

306. Cf. the bibliography of Bultmann's sermons and religious talks in E. Hauschildt, *Rudolf Bultmanns Predigten*, xiii–xix, corrected by K. Hammann, "Rudolf Bultmann und der Universitätsgottesdienst," 90n19. To be added to Hauschildt's list is the wedding sermon that Bultmann gave at Eberfeld on 30. 11. 1927 for Heinrich Schlier and Erna, née Haas. Cf. UB Tübingen, RB est., Mn 2-3435.

When the university preacher Friedrich Niebergall died in Marburg on September 20, 1932, and his homiletic colleague Karl Bornhäuser was made emeritus the following March, the positions they had long held were not filled. This opened the way for the remaining members of the theological faculty to adopt a rotational schedule for leading future academic worship services. This especially suited Bultmann and von Soden, and on July 2, 1933, Bultmann inaugurated the series of university worship for which the whole theological faculty would thereafter be responsible with a sermon on 1 John 4:7–12.[307] The community was straightaway treated to an eminently political sermon. Bultmann showed how, amidst the intoxication of the "national uprising" of 1933, one could draw a sober assessment of the current situation from the message of the New Testament. As he saw it, such an incorruptible source of judgment bestowed the power to refuse ethical and legal validity to certain measures of the new government.[308]

The academic worship of Marburg became his favorite preaching venue until his retirement in 1951. In addition, he occasionally led worship services in his own parish church, and he continued his past practice of leading devotions and Bible studies for students. And he took on casual speaking assignments on behalf of suffering family members, friends, and students. During the Second World War, the schedule of weddings and especially funerals at which Bultmann was asked to preach often became overcrowded. In nearly all cases, these involved people who had some close connection to him and who, like him, belonged to the milieu of the academically educated upper middle class. After he became emeritus, Bultmann led devotions or gave sermons only sporadically—for instance, during his stays abroad in Cambridge, England, in 1953, and Syracuse, New York, in 1959,[309] as well as at the founder's day celebration of his fraternity *Igel* in 1954 at Tübingen. Apart from all this, during the early years of the Federal Republic he made increasing use of a different medium—newspapers and magazines, by means of which he was able to share his religious observations with a wider public.[310]

According to the recollections of witnesses at the time, the Marburg worship services at which Bultmann preached were for the most part well attended.[311] The congregation was comprised of various groups. In the pews

307. Cf. K. Hammann, "Rudolf Bultmann und der Universitäts Gottesdienst," 114f.

308. Cf. RB, "Sermon on 1 John 4:7–12." *VW*, 247–60; see also above 267 and 270.

309. Cf. RB, "Sermon, Hendricks Chapel, Syracuse, NY," 26. 4. 1959, in H. Gollwitzer and H. Traub, *Hören und Handeln*, 47–51.

310. Cf. H. U. Gumbrecht, "Zorn."

311. The impressions that follow are based on the recollections of those who heard Bultmann, given by E. Hauschildt, *Rudolf Bultmanns Predigten*, 261–63.

of the University Church, which in Marburg was the church for the upper classes, the preacher had an educated public before him: students, members of the university, and the bourgeoisie of the city. During the Third Reich, here and in the main Lutheran parish church, it was primarily members of the Confessing Church who attended the worship services that Bultmann conducted. In any case, Christians loyal to the Confessions determined the church life in Marburg between 1933 and 1945, and the majority of pastors in Marburg belonged to the Confessing Church.[312] And besides the academically educated, other members of the community naturally sought out community worship in the main Lutheran parish church—civil servants, workers in the trades, businesspersons, and the young women from the surrounding rural area who were employed in the bourgeois households of the university city. When Bultmann used the homiletical "we" in his sermons, he did so, as it were, as a representative and spokesperson for the urban bourgeoisie, the Confessing Church, and his students. It was to this congregation that he interpreted the biblical texts, and together with it that the preacher joined in the process of coming to understand, in the effort to achieve a new self-understanding.

Bultmann prepared his sermons with care. As extant manuscripts show, the texts of his sermons were fully worked out before he presented them in the service. Here and there he went on to supply them with marginal additions or corrections, and in the early days of his preaching he also wrote down the overall structure of the sermon in the margin or on an extra sheet of paper.[313] Usually, as it were, to check it over himself, he would read the prepared text aloud to his wife at home, before delivering it to the congregation. And although he kept to the manuscript, he apparently read the sermon aloud so skillfully as to give the impression that he was presenting his thoughts extemporaneously.

In the pulpit Bultmann maintained essentially the academic style of presentation that his students had become familiar with in the lecture hall, but he did not weigh the congregation down with a scholarly burden. Calmly and to the point, with a voice that became ever quieter, he pursued a sort of dialogue with his audience. Some of these found his sermons to be dry; while others, like his students Marie Veit and Erich Vellmer, for instance,

312. Among others, there were the Lutheran pastors Gottfried Schmidmann, Dr. Friedrich S. Geller, Otto E. Waltemath, Franz Bücking, Dr. Hans Schimmelpfeng, and the pastor of the Reformed congregation, D. Karl-Bernhard Ritter. Only the Reformed pastor Karl Veerhof joined the "German Christians."

313. Cf. E. Grässer, "Einleitung," in RB, *VW*, xiif.

found them moving and inspiring precisely in their simplicity. One critical reader later detected in the printed "Marburg Sermons" an air of "the distinctively restrained, cool North German climate of this proclamation."[314] In any event, Bultmann refrained from any rhetorical tricks to lend emphasis to particular sermonic points. Just as foreign to him was oratorical pathos. As it was, his repertoire of effects might have been too limited in this respect, and he could have been more rhetorically brilliant in the pulpit; but with his manner of preaching he fulfilled the homiletical postulate stressed by the theology of the word of God: that, as witness to the gospel, the preacher is to retire behind that to which he witnesses, and under no circumstances was he to present himself in the pulpit as a religious virtuoso who used his personal gifts to vouch for the gospel's credibility and its claim to truth. To be sure, even in the simplicity of the way he spoke, Bultmann remained authentic. For this was the formal analogue to his theological view that the aim of proclamation is to display the kerygma in its existential significance for the speaker. To that end, however, one must radically confront the kerygma, whether to free it from myth, from the uncertain historicity of particular biblical happenings, or from being swamped by metaphysics.[315]

In 1957 Bultmann took issue with the published Goethe- and Schiller-sermons that the Bremen pastor Julius Berggraf had given at the beginning of the twentieth century. Such sermons on lyrical texts conveyed at best general truths; they were not proclamation in the proper sense. For the character of the sermon as proclamation consists in the authoritative "form of address of the word of God, which in paradoxical fashion is spoken through a human being, even through the preacher." The sermon is characterized more precisely by the fact that it is an interpretation of a text of Holy Scripture.[316] Only in his early days did Bultmann occasionally give sermons that were not tied to a biblical text, two such examples being the 1914 sermon "This- and Otherworldly Religion" and the 1922 devotion "Night" based on a verse of Nietzsche, that he presented in the *Michelchen*. Karl Barth, who on the occasion of a visit to Marburg took part in this form of worship, later referred to the arrangement in mockingly ironic fashion in a circular letter as a production of "the little Michael cult."[317] After 1922, however, Bultmann invariably based his sermons on biblical texts.

314. K. Ihlenfeld, "Marburger Predigten," 192.

315. Cf. J. Konrad, "Zu Form," 487f.

316. Cf. RB, "Allgemeine Wahrheiten," in *GuV* (1st ed), vol. 3, 166f.

317. Cf. Barth's circular letter of 26. 2. 1922, in E. Thurneysen, *Barth-Thurneysen Briefwechsel*, 48.

But being bound to a text did not provide any guarantee that a sermon was thereby appropriate to scripture. Bultmann did indeed recommend this form of the homily to his students "in view of the corruption of thematic sermons and on pedagogical grounds," but he disputed Barth in favoring the equal rights of homily and thematic sermon. "Appropriateness to scripture is not guaranteed by the form of the homily, nor is the authority of scripture abandoned by the form of the thematic sermon."[318] Accordingly, Bultmann availed himself of both homiletical genres. The conviction that "interpretation and detailed discussion of thematic subject matter are meant to coincide"[319] permitted him to make use of the homily form as well as that of the thematic sermon. On December 12, 1943, he gave a close homiletic reading of the Beatitudes (Matt 5:3–10) while at the same time speaking to the unifying Advent theme of promise and expectation.[320] Conversely, after delving briefly into a single Bible verse, Bultmann could develop in detail an overarching theme in its present significance for his listeners. On May 9, 1937, he started from Gen 8:22 and dealt in this way with Christian faith in creation and with the joy in the presence of God in nature. In doing so, he resolutely separated himself from the contemporary idolizing of nature, blood, and the people, as well as from any sort of natural theology.[321] And at the end of the summer semester of 1938, amidst the besetting lack of freedom and unrest of the time, he took up Jesus' farewell to his disciples (John 14:27) to announce—in contrast to peace as the world gives it—the peace of eternity as the word of Jesus promises it.[322]

To discover and analyze the relation of the biblical message to reality was at that time one of the central tasks of Christian preaching. Especially during the Third Reich and the years immediately following the War, this problem presented itself with increasing intensity. Bultmann spoke to existing needs and cares, and addressed the situations of the time: the National Socialists' seizure of power, the distress of Christianity under the ideology of "the people," the outbreak of war, and the collapse of the Third Reich.[323] As he did so, he exercised little or no self-restraint, and therefore frequently earned public criticism for criticizing developments in the life of the nation and society, and even more for attacking the injustice of the regime. From time to

318. RB to K. Barth, 10. 12. 1935, in B. Jaspert, *Barth-Bultmann Briefwechsel*, 160.
319. Konrad, "Zu Form," 485.
320. RB, *MP*, 180–88.
321. Cf. RB, *MP*, 26–40.
322. Cf. RB, *MP*, 79–86.
323. See also above, 267, 270, 285–87, and below, 371f.

time, he couched his charges in subtle hints, allowing his hearers, who had daily been exposed to the direct pressure of the dictatorship, to discern what the political implications of these sermons might be.

The calm level-headedness with which Bultmann brought the events and issues of the time into his sermons while at the same time relativizing them, not only came from his steady temperament but also reflected that particular freedom from the world with which readiness for God's future equips the believer. The dialectic of eschatological existence that Bultmann had since 1909 recognized in the Pauline ὡς μή—the "having, as if one had not" of 1 Cor 7:29–31—embraced at the same time distance from and closeness to the world. As Bultmann preached on June 22, 1941—just as the beginning of the war with Russia was announced—whoever allows God to call him out of our unsettled world into his world will immediately experience the blessing of God's coming into this earthly, provisional life.[324] Whoever is ready to allow himself to be freed by the power of love from himself and from every tie to the world is enabled to understand himself anew as a future possibility of God; and this applies both to other people and to the world, even if this world can never be more than the setting for life that is provisional and unfulfilled.[325]

After being particularly stimulated by Gogarten's work, Bultmann had rediscovered a number of Luther's texts, and from about 1921 onward increasingly included citations of Luther in his sermons. They functioned not merely as decorative accessories but rather served to anchor in the great reformer's theology the claims he made in his own sermons. Bultmann gave prominence to the *pro me* character of the salvation-occurrence, demarcated fiduciary faith from mere *fides historica* [historical faith], understood the human being as *simul iustus et peccator* [both justified and a sinner], and placed the offense of the word of the cross at the center of his proclamation. He based his own independent reinterpretation of the Lutheran doctrine of the justification of the sinner by faith alone on the contrast between work and gift,[326] and thus followed Luther's "doctrine" of law and gospel in his preaching as well. What Luther had declared the highest art of the theologian, the ability to distinguish correctly between law and gospel, Bultmann displayed with innovative variations in his sermons. Since he also sought to interpret the Christian message existentially in the pulpit, he found the dis-

324. Cf. RB, *MP*, 132–36 (sermon on Luke 14:16–24).

325. Cf. RB, *MP*, 66–70 (sermon on Rom 8:18–27, tied into 1 Cor 7:29–31).

326. On the individual stages of this process of coming to understand on Bultmann's part, cf. E. Hauschildt, *Rudolf Bultmanns Predigten*, 16–155.

tinction between law and gospel indispensable in two ways. For one thing, the preaching of the law—in Luther's sense of *usus theologicus legis* [theological application of law]—was functionally subordinated to the preaching of the gospel. In the light of the gospel, the role of the law—whether the universal moral law or the specific demand of the revealed will of God—was to prepare hearers for the proclamation of the gospel and thereby for the irrevocable possibility of Christian existence. And yet the concrete form of the law was liable to historical change, and therefore if preaching intended to make Christian faith understandable in the present, it had to relate itself to the exigencies of the law in the present. Working outwards from Luther, Bultmann took the law as a symbol of the historicity of the human being.

It was to this formal horizon of understanding, to the reality of the modern person, that the business of communicating the gospel had to relate itself, and it must do so by way of both connection and contradiction. Therefore, in his sermons Bultmann could uninhibitedly and critically emphasize both Christian faith's close relation to and its distance from the ambivalent realities of the newly-promoted religion of the day,[327] from nature-piety,[328] and from idealism,[329] and although he invariably brought the gospel to bear as a critical corrective to human failure and human self-alienation, this did not prevent him from shining a powerful light on the positive potentialities and the successful accomplishments of human existence—what might be called the pre-dawn rays of the gospel.

Related to this subject is the intensive use he made of literature, a practice that even in the context of twentieth-century preaching lent a thoroughly distinctive note to Bultmann's sermons. Not invariably, but with unusual frequency, Bultmann's sermons cited texts from Christian literature, tales, proverbs, philosophical texts, hymns, and above all poetry. After 1935 Bultmann seems to have kept two notebooks, one with Greek texts from classical antiquity[330] and the other with texts of nineteenth- and twentieth-century authors.[331] Using categories that for the most part were related to theology, he listed citations from German literature under 398 headings from "superstition" [*Aberglaube*] to "doubt" [*Zweifel*]. He drew on this literary bank account to good purpose, as for instance in a sermon on Mark

327. Cf. RB, *MP*, 1–13 (sermon of 7. 6. 1936, on Acts 17:22–32).

328. Cf. RB, *MP*, 26–40 (sermon of 9. 5. 1937, on Gen 8:22).

329. Cf. RB, *MP*, 189–200 (sermon of 17. 6. 1945, on 2 Cor 4:6–11).

330. Cf. RB, quotations from great literature, n.d.

331. Cf. RB, quotations from great literature, n.d.; as well as T. Kucharz, *Theologen und ihre Dichter*, 185–87.

13:31–33 that he preached on July 25, 1950. In this one sermon, in addition to citations from the Psalms and Ecclesiastes, Bultmann wove together not fewer than eleven literary witnesses from antiquity and modernity: texts from Tibullus and Horace, Pascal and Johann M. Usteri, Friedrich Hebbel, Hugo von Hoffmansthal and Count Paul Yorck von Wartenburg, Wilhelm Raabe, Friedrich Rückert and Ludwig Tieck, Marcel Proust, and finally Gerhard Tersteegen.[332] And even without relying on his notebooks, he was able to draw on the rich fund of his reading, as he did in a 1937 sermon based on Gen 8:22. In this literary dialogue between the Christian belief in creation and forms of nature piety, Bultmann employed eleven mostly lyrical texts in which he allowed five popular authors to speak: Goethe, Schiller, Joseph von Eichendorff, and Wilhelm Raabe, as well as Friedrich Gottlieb Klopstock.[333]

This substantial homiletical use of literature might suggest that the preacher, long steeped in humanistic and literary culture, had become a sophisticated guarantor of the culture of his predominantly bourgeois community.[334] Had not Paul become a Jew to the Jews for the sake of the gospel and behaved as one without law for those who were without law (cf. 1 Cor 9:19–23)? Bultmann's homiletical use of literature certainly did not aim primarily at achieving accord with the cultured community through a shared aesthetic inheritance. Rather, he helped himself to the poetic tradition because he found experiences of life and meanings of human existence brought to particularly rich expression there. It was precisely for this reason that literary texts were suited to elucidating human historicity on the level of the law, as well as illustrating aspects of real life against the background of the gospel. In literature, Bultmann saw reflections of humanity's knowledge of its transitoriness as well as its encounter with and search for God in nature—reflections that he found as profoundly meaningful as the individual's dialectical relation to self and world, the specifically Christian experience of God, or other features of a believing existence.

Almost without exception the first reviewers of his "Marburg Sermons" found it noteworthy that Bultmann included relatively little explicit discussion of demythologizing. To be sure, so great was both the surprise over this omission[335] and its appreciative defense,[336] that both sides may have failed

332. Cf. RB, *MP*, 216–26; as well as E. Hauschildt, *Rudolf Bultmanns Predigten*, 159–83; T. Kucharz, *Theologen und ihrd Dichter*, 206–11.

333. Cf. RB, *MP*, 26–40; as well as T. Kucharz, *Theologen und ihre Dichter*, 201–5.

334. Cf. T. Kucharz, *Theologen und ihre Dichter*, 220.

335. Cf. K. Ihlenfeld, "Marburger Predigten," 192f; J. Konrad, "Zu Form," 485.

336. Cf. G. Harbsmeier, "Gedruckte Predigten," 226f.

to recognize that Bultmann saw demythologizing as merely a special case of existentialist interpretation. Meanwhile, he was dealing with the same problem in the pulpit. On July 13, 1941, a few weeks after the Alpirsbach lecture, he provided an example of the truthfulness he had demanded when he preached on the pericope of Peter's huge catch of fish (Luke 5:1–11). In order not to leave the congregation in any uncertainty, Bultmann declared that he regarded the story "a pious fiction."[337] The Christian faith demands of no one the *sacrificium intellectus* of taking as historical facts those New Testament wonders that are contrary to all experience; rather, Christian faith in the miraculous consists in accepting Jesus Christ as liberator from the law and from death. And having faith in God the creator in and of itself implies trust in the wonders of God and his wondrous creative activity. This far-from-simple faith can be grasped by one who is sure of himself when he says, "I believe that God has created *me*, together with all creatures."[338] It is from this faith in wonder that the actual miracle in the story of Peter's haul of fish also derives, for as Jesus enlists the sinful man Peter in his service and thus makes him new, so "the word of the redeeming grace of God that encounters us in Jesus makes us new," by "liberating us . . . from ourselves."[339]

Just as Christian faith in wonder needed to be released from the miraculous features of the New Testament wonder stories,[340] so Bultmann sought also to free Christian hope for the future from mythological pictures taken from apocalypticism's arsenal of images. On Rogation Sunday in 1943 he preached on John 16:22–23, a passage from Jesus' farewell discourse. Bultmann understood the eschatological promise of Christ to his disciples, ". . . I will see you again, and your hearts will rejoice," not literally, nor as a representation of an actual event. For to give a name to the object of that future joy would amount to an inappropriate objectification of the inexpressible, eschatological joy in worldly terms. It is precisely the uncertain joy of freedom from the world together with freedom from ourselves that in its intrinsic openness is like faith as risk.[341] In thus challenging the mythical picture of bidding farewell by definitively uniting the ascended Christ and

337. RB, *MP*, 140.

338. M. Luther, "Der Kleine Katechismus," 510, 33f; cited in modernized form in RB, *MP*, 142.

339. RB, *MP*, 146. For Bultmann, the liberating work of Christ applied to the whole person, not just, as it were, to the "soul." Cf. the position he takes to D. Meyer, "Sermon on Mark 7:31–37" (in U. H. J, Körtner, *Jesus im 21. Jahrhundert*, 202–6), in RB to D. Meyer, 10. 10. 1952, in U. Körtner, *Jesus im 21. Jahrhundert*, 207f.

340. Cf. RB, "Zur Frage des Wunders," *GuV* (1st ed.), vol. 1, 214–28.

341. Cf. RB, *MP*, 169–79 (sermon on John 16:22–33, delivered 30. 5. 1943).

the believer, Bultmann had at the same time released the Christian hope for the future, for its basis and content is the Christ who promises himself.[342]

By transforming an objectified future expectation into the present-centered existentialist eschatology of the decision of faith, Bultmann had finally forged a radical conclusion for a long theological development. The crisis caused by the conflict of an end-of-history eschatology that had been gaining ground during the modern period and its practical elimination by Bultmann and other twentieth-century theologians had resulted in a "night without any pictures"[343] that could not possibly remain as Christian theology's last word for the hope of faith. But on what other theologian, what preacher could one seriously confer what is in any case the dubious honor of having said the last word?

6. Life among Family and Friends

> *Circumstances had utterly destroyed the earlier forms of academic collegiality, and only a few public institutions still offered any framework for this at all. To these belonged the Association of the Friends of the Humanistic Academy, of which Bultmann became the chair, and whose activities continued unaltered.*[344]

In the early 1930s, the Bultmanns decided to build their own house. They acquired a piece of land on Calvin Street, in a desirable residential area of Marburg. There, on the steep slope between the Dammelsberg and the Schlossberg, the new residence was built in 1934. The planning and oversight of the construction was completely in the hands of Helene Bultmann, who brought to the job the necessary ingredient of her practical common sense. In keeping with her overall view and financial concerns, the building was erected as a duplex. When on June 22, 1934, her very busy husband first set foot on the property, it was to join her in celebrating the completion of the building. The move from Bismarck Street to 14 Calvin Street took place from September 26–29.[345]

Helene Bultmann saw to it that the new premises were suited to the various needs of the family. Like each of the three daughters, grandmother Luise Feldmann, who had lived as a member of her daughter's family since 1922,

342. Cf. J. Konrad, "Zu Form," 489, 493f.
343. E. Hirsch, *Das Wesen*, 17.
344. H.-G. Gadamer, *Philosophische Lehrjahre*, 55.
345. All dates in this section are given according to RB, *Chronik 1917–1945*.

Plate 32: The House on 14 Calvin Street, built in 1934

also had her own room. Thus, Leni's mother was able to take part in family and social life but also could when necessary, as when Rudolf and Leni might wish to be alone together for an evening, retire to her own living area. The office and the library of the head of the house lay on the top floor, and at his insistence were painted in blue and red, the Oldenburg colors. As it happened, the painter had mistakenly chosen a Pompeian red, but this served Bultmann as a visual reminder of how far he was from his Oldenburg homeland.[346] Also according to his wish, the windows opened outwards, as they did in northern Germany. This was so that he could more easily tend his flowers on the inside window sill. From his office, the view extended far over the roofs of the southern quarter of Marburg to the valley of the Lahn and to Cappel, with the foothills of the Lahn mountains on the one side and, on the other, Gisselberg, including the Weimar and the Hasen Peaks.

Wilhelm and Marie Therese Mommsen occupied the adjoining house with their four sons, Karl, Friedrich Jens, and the twins Wolfgang Justin and Hans. Wilhelm Mommsen, a grandson of the famous Nobel Laureate for Literature Theodor Mommsen, had been appointed to the chair for medieval and modern history in Marburg in 1929. The relationship between Bultmann and Mommsen got off to an easy start. In 1929, the two wrote the readers' reports for the dissertation that Bultmann's student Hildegard Astholz submitted to the philosophy department, a work on Johann Gustav Droysen's understanding of history.[347] In the doctoral supervision of the

346. Cf. W. Schmithals, "Das wissenschaftliche Werk," 19f; as well as (in retrospect on the building of the house) RB to E. Käsemann, 30. 8. 1959, Mn 2-2251, in UB Tübingen, RB est.

347. Cf. H. Astholz, *Das Problem 'Geschichte.'*" In her dissertation, the author oriented herself to the understanding of Christianity and history developed by Bultmann. Cf. H. Astholz, *Das Problem 'Geschichte,'"* 28.

Jewish student, Friedemann Boschwitz, which the National Socialist overseer of students Rudolf Kluge had in vain sought to prevent, Mommsen, the advisor, and Bultmann as the other reader again worked together in collegial fashion in 1934.[348] But in the period that followed, increasing tension strained relations between the two neighbors. As his teacher Friedrich Meinecke had done, and as he himself was a liberal Rational Democrat, Wilhelm Mommsen had endorsed the German Democratic Party. Following the party's dissolution in 1930, Mommsen joined the German State Party, and when the Third Reich came into being, the politically ambitious historian soon became a convinced supporter of National Socialism.[349] Having Mommsen for a neighbor became increasingly dangerous for Bultmann. It was easy enough to decline Mrs. Mommsen's repeated invitations for the Bultmann daughters to join in listening to the speeches of the "Führer" on the Mommsens' radio. But dealings with Mommsen himself and his involvement with the National Socialist state proved far more difficult.

Overall, Bultmann felt a heightened sense of family responsibility during the National Socialist regime. This was clear to him from the outset. In the summer of 1934, he visited his home in Oldenburg, and on August 20, 1934 he performed the wedding of his student, Kendrick Grobel, and his niece, Marianne Pleus, in Dedesdorf on the Lower Weser. His fiftieth birthday also fell on that day, and this "brought clearly enough to mind . . . how rich and fortunate have been the 50 years that lie behind me." However, Bultmann perceived just as clearly the shadows "that the concerns for state and church and family are casting over these days." But concerning his own person he had "no worry to match that of the menacing future; naturally, I have to turn my thoughts to wife and children," he confided to von Soden.[350] For during the Third Reich, family and social life for the Bultmanns went on under conditions that from the outset did not allow things to continue as a private idyll remote from political realities.

Rudolf and Helene Bultmann refrained from exerting any sort of pressure on their daughters' religious education. This was particularly the case since in the Elizabeth School, Antje, Gesine, and Heilke were not subjected

348. Cf. UB Tübingen, RB est., W. Mommsen to RB, 1. 6. 1934, Mn 2-1417. On the proceedings, see above 300.

349. On the backgrounds, cf. A. C. Nagel, "'Der Prototyp der Leute, . . .'" 55–91; P. Köpf, *Die Mommsens*, 44–63, 121–46, 166–83, 193–212; as well as, critically, S. Rebenich, "Die Guten und die Bösen," 16.

350. UB Tübingen, RB est., RB to H. von Soden, 21. 8. 1934 (from Dedesdorf), Mn 2-2385. The wedding sermon Bultmann gave in Dedesdorf on 20. 8. 1934 is reprinted in *VW*, 274–78.

to the propaganda of the National Socialist regime. In 1933 Antje was confirmed in the Lutheran parish church by the Rev. Dr. Friedrich S. Geller, a highly cultured theologian, whose sermons Bultmann admired.[351] But the Bultmanns were less in agreement with the rigid educational methods that Geller employed in Antje's confirmation class, particularly on the young ones. For this reason, Gesine and Heilke went for their confirmation instruction to Dr. Karl Bernhard Ritter, the pastor of the Reformed congregation in the University Church. Like Geller and most of the other Marburg pastors, Ritter belonged to the Confessing Church. He understood how to make his instruction appeal to young people. Ritter, who had founded the Protestant Brotherhood of Michael in 1931, also introduced new and unfamiliar features into the Marburg worship services. He confirmed Gesine in 1935 and Heilke in 1939.

At home, the Bultmanns practiced such conventional religious forms as saying grace at table as a matter of course. The church year also offered enough occasions to celebrate the religious dimension of life from time to time. Other firm family traditions developed, with Bultmann reading aloud Psalm 90 on New Year's Eve and Psalm 103 on New Year's Day. Still, Bultmann was no friend of pious affectation. So, when on appropriate occasions he did make use of religious language, it took on all the more weight. When during the War Gesine went on a dangerous trip with her student chamber orchestra, her father sent her on her way with a "Go with God!" And when, during an air-raid, anxious folk gathered in the local shelter, he offered the brief prayer, "May God protect us now!"

The annual high-point of family life arrived with the Christmas celebrations. No demythologizing went on under the Bultmann Christmas tree, for the family celebrated much as did other families of the academic upper-middle class. When in 1939 the newly married Antje spent Christmas away from home for the first time, Bultmann described the celebrations in a six-page letter: going to church, the final preparations in the house, the best clothes that the family members wore, getting together in mother's room, reading the Christmas story aloud, the lighting of the candles on the tree and "then—wouldn't you know it!—the little clock strikes! 'Oh come, little children!' 'Oh, how joyfully!' And then the light and the smell of the Christmas tree enveloped us again, and we were so happy, even if we did have a nostalgic thought for the missing Antje." There followed the giving out of presents, first downstairs, then upstairs with Grandma, and then dinner,

351. Cf. UB Tübingen, RB est., RB to A. Bultmann Lemke, 28. 12. 1939, Mn 2-3452.

which because of the War, was more modest than usual, and finally, opening and inspecting the presents. Bultmann thanked Antje for the cigars that she had given him, along with a citation from the diary of Count Yorck which, *mutatis mutandis*, also applied to himself: "In possession of my tobacco *and, so, utterly personally content. . . .*" Christmas Day was then given over to reading, singing, and making music. As their Christmas gift to the household, Gesine and Heilke performed a piece of music that they had advertised on a large sheet of paper on the parents' Christmas gift-table:

> **One-time only performance of famous artistes!**
>
> On December 25, 1939, from 10–11 a. m. in the dining room of the Bultmann home. 1. Bach Invention No. 4, 2. Invention by Joh. Seb. Bach No. 8 Cello and Flute. Performers: Gesine Bultmann, Flute; Heilke Bultmann, Cello. Admission Free!

On the day after Christmas, Bultmann began by taking the worship service in the parish church, and the rest of the day offered the opportunity for exchanging visits among friends. In 1939 the married couple of Birtner and Steinmeyer along with Lorenz Krüger came over to the Bultmanns and sang a number of Christmas carols. But this was not enough: "We had resolved to celebrate December 27th as a third proper Christmas Day." And once again the extended celebration featured a program of lectures, music, singing, and visits—this time from the Reidemeisters.[352]

As early as 1933, Bultmann noticed "the destruction of a substantive communal life in the family and society."[353] As he saw it, the National Socialist state was completing the process of the destruction of true community that had already begun: with the help of organization, propaganda, and technology, it was creating what was at best a false substitute for community.[354] Among the forms of true human community that ultimately had their roots in the religious community of faith, Bultmann counted art, literature, and music. These were accorded a correspondingly high value in the family and social life of the Bultmanns. This was true of music in particular. Bultmann put himself in the right mood for the day by playing on the piano each morning a chorale by Johann Sebastian Bach. Among composers he admired Mozart above all, and in this he was in agreement with Karl Barth, but unlike Barth he did not make this personal preference public as an article

352. Cf. UB Tübingen, RB est., RB to A. Bultmann Lemke, 28. 12. 1939, Mn 2-3452.
353. RB, "Zur Frage der Reform," *GuV* (5th ed.), vol. 2, 295.
354. RB, "Formen menschlicher Gemeinschaft," *GuV* (5th ed.), vol. 2, 266f.

Plate 33: The Bultmann Family, March 1936: Antje, Helene, Heilke, Rudolf, and Gesine Bultmann

of theological (self-)interpretation. When he was alone at home, Bultmann occasionally sang such sections of Mozart operas as Sarastro's arias from *The Magic Flute*. His wife had a beautiful alto voice, and was often a soloist in evenings of sacred music and church concerts that the university music director Hermann Stephani put on in Marburg and elsewhere. A friendship with the family of the music scholar Herbert Birtner arose as the result of music. Over time, accompanied by Birtner on the piano, Helene Bultmann studied many of Schubert's songs, and captivated early on by the musical atmosphere of their parents' home, Antje (violin), Gesine (flute), and Heilke (cello) soon saw to it that hardly a sociable evening at 14 Calvin Street went by without music being made. In his chronicle, Bultmann meticulously recorded all the concerts at home and in public that saw his wife and daughters, especially Gesine, take part as soloists.[355]

Bultmann also recorded in his chronicle the outings, hikes, and trips that he took with his wife and early on with his daughters, along with the routes they traveled and the most important stops; and he also recorded the trips that Antje, Gesine, and Heilke set off on as they began to go on their own. In his old age, probably to remind himself, he put together a list of his

355. Cf. RB, *Chronik 1917–1945*.

Plate 34: Helene and Rudolf Bultmann in Marburg, August 1957

foreign trips.[356] To the extent that these had to do with his scholarly activities, these will receive special notice.[357] The three- or sometimes four-week vacation trips following the summer semester were chiefly for the purpose of relaxation but provided cultural enrichment as well. To his many correspondents Bultmann described joyfully and in detail the experiences that he and his wife had in their travels as well as his impressions of landscapes, cities, monuments, works of art, and people. If occasionally no scenic postcard was to be had, he would simply draw one himself, as he did in 1943 while on what was for some time his last recuperative stay in the Black Forest, with the caption, "Badenweiler, View into the Plain of the Rhine and out onto the Vosges."[358] If a trip took him to Oldenburg or to southern Germany, he took the opportunity to pay visits to the many branches of his relatives in his homeland and to the spas in Baden. He also made regular stops to see theologian friends. During trips to Switzerland, he made a habit of seeking out the Old Testament scholar Walter Baumgartner in Basel. Baumgartner was a teetotaler, a choice his wife Maria honored, and Bultmann knew this. Once

356. Cf. the appendix, "Trips" in *Chronik 1917–1945*, 50.
357. See below 430–42.
358. UB Tübingen, RB est., RB to A. Bultmann Lemke, 17. 9. 1943, Mn 2-3452.

during a visit in Basel, evening drew near and as was customary the guests sat around without a drink. Bultmann excused himself, saying he had to go back to the train station, where he had agreed to meet a friend. Upon his return, Baumgartner asked him the name of the friend he had met in the station. Bultmann was quick to reply, "His name is *Châteauneuf-du-Pape*. . . ."

Probably the most unforgettable of the impressions that Bultmann and his wife took away from their travels were those from a trip to Italy and Sicily in the early autumn of 1938. Zürich, Bologna, Naples, Messina, Palermo, Agrigentum, Syracuse, Taormina, Messina, Paestum, Naples, Rome, Milan, and Basel were the stops on this trip particularly devoted to culture. Along the way Bultmann shared his impressions with Gerhard Krüger: The streets of Palermo were "filled with an atmosphere that was a mixture of gasoline and baked fish, cheese and perfume (but much more penetrating than Nivea). . . . But it makes one dizzy . . . to see how the monuments of history stand side by side here: Greek antiquities (the metropes of Selinunte!!), Moorish, Byzantine art, Spanish Baroque." From Syracuse, the city of Archimedes, there was less to report. "The tongue sticks to the roof of one's mouth, and what the locals drink is not suited to slake an Oldenburger's thirst." Then came the trip across to Capri "on a packed steamer . . . enveloped in the smog of ship's oil and cigarettes; bawled at by gramophone music. A choppy sea, the ship lurched from side to side, and we were offering sacrifices right and left to Poseidon. . . . So far as our situation allows us to judge, Capri certainly, and the Gulf of Naples in general are marvelously beautiful." Finally, what stood out as the "high point of our trip" was "a classical day" in Rome. "We were in the Tivoli Gardens, and here the Italy of Goethe disclosed itself to us in captivating splendor. The return trip through the campagna, with the sun setting behind it, was magnificent."[359] To be sure, as impressive as Italy had been, it did not manage to unsettle Bultmann's scale of values. His summary of Rome was well-attested in family lore: "It is beautiful here, almost as beautiful as in Oldenburg!"

The four-week spa treatment that Bultmann took at regular two-year intervals in Wiesbaden served to refresh body and soul. There the "spirits of the hot springs, of the Rhine and of wine and of the sounds of strings and of song"[360] hovered around him. The treatment, with its daily regimen—bathing, dancing, sleep, going for a walk to Biebrich or Eltville for a glass

359. RB to G. Krüger, 25. 9., 30. 9., 10. 10., 16. 10. 1938, in F. Lilie, "Bultmann-Krüger Briefwechsel," *ZNThG* 4, 302–5.

360. RB to G. Krüger, 5. 3. 1932, in F. Lilie, "Bultmann-Krüger Briefwechsel," *ZNThG* 4, 297.

of Rheingau Riesling, reading, doing nothing much—allowed Bultmann, as he discovered, to exist "in substantially physical fashion."[361] The stay in Wiesbaden helped to relieve his hip trouble noticeably. Beyond that, he found the spa location at Taunus particularly attractive because he was able to indulge his passion of attending the opera here. In the realm of musical theatre, Mozart and Verdi were his clear favorites, while he had no use for Wagner, whom the National Socialist cultural politics had helped to become the dominating presence on opera stages both here and in Wiesbaden.[362] On the train platform in Marburg, as he left for the spa, one could often hear him say, alluding to Dante's *Divine Comedy*, "Now comes the train of the blessed!" From the warm climate of the Rheingau, the "train of the damned" then brought him back to Marburg, which seemed to him to have too many days of fog and rain.

Within the University of Marburg, Bultmann had lively contact with the philosopher Erich Frank during the early years of the Third Reich. With this former student of Jaspers he met weekly in the castle café for friendly and scholarly exchange. Frank, who was a bachelor, also eagerly shared in the social life of the Bultmanns. There was further opportunity for interdisciplinary conversation at the table reserved for regulars in the "Sun" in the marketplace, where Bultmann, the Old Testament scholar Emil Balla, the biologist Jürgen Harms, the physician Felix Klewitz, and the historian of literature Friedrich Carl Sell got together once a week in the evening. After Frank, Friedländer, and Sell had emigrated, Bultmann was at first able to continue what he considered the important scholarly dialogue about the limits of his own discipline only with Gerhard Krüger.[363] The published correspondence between the two conveys, despite the edition's shortcomings, a vivid impression of the close human and scholarly relationship between the philosophically interested theologian and the theologically interested philosopher. Now that Heinrich Schlier, Günther Bornkamm, and Hans-Georg Gadamer had long left Marburg, Krüger remained the only participant in Bultmann's once flourishing *Graeca* to carry on reading the classical texts of Greek literature with his friend; and when Krüger accepted a call to Münster

361. RB to G. Krüger, 2. 3. 1936, in F. Lilie, "Bultmann-Krüger Briefwechsel," *ZNThG* 4, 299.

362. Cf. RB to G. Krüger, 12. 3. 1936 and 2. 3. 1938, in F. Lilie, "Bultmann-Krüger Briefwechsel," *ZNThG* 4, 300f; 22. 3. and 29. 3. 1940, in F. Lilie, "Bultmann-Krüger Briefwechsel," *ZNThG* 5, 274f; UB Tübingen, RB est., RB to A. Bultmann Lemke, 10. 3. 1938, Mn 2-3452.

363. Cf. UB Tübingen, RB est., RB to A. Bultmann Lemke, 11. 2. 1940, Mn 2-3452.

in 1940, Bultmann had to continue the reading on his own,[364] though now and again with Max Kommerell and Wilhelm Anz.[365] But his *Graeca* never regained its former stability, because the fluctuation of participants and their differing capabilities were too great. Kommerell, for instance, had to struggle with the philosophical side of the reading matter.[366]

Bultmann's involvement with the Friends of the Humanistic Academy represented the interface of university and public culture in the city. Kurt Steinmeyer, who had taken over the directorship of the school in 1932, brought a fresh spirit to the venerable institution, founded as was the University of Marburg by Landgrave Philipp the Magnanimous in 1527. During the period of the National Socialist dictatorship, Steinmeyer strove with some success to maintain the *Gymnasium Philippinum* as a place of cultural and intellectual freedom, and persuaded Bultmann to become the chair of the Association of the Friends of the Humanistic Academy. Under Bultmann's leadership, the Association experienced "a unique flowering."[367] The National Socialist policy towards secondary schools had within a very short time crushed the traditional community institutions of academic culture, but the lecture evenings of the Association offered a partial substitute. The hall of the Philippinum became a forum for independence of the spirit. Here a life of the mind supported by humanistic traditions was able to stand against the political indoctrination and worldview of National Socialism.

Bultmann invited the speakers and led the ensuing discussions, which according to the recollection of Arthur Henkel he was able to move along "with astute questions and knowledgeable objections."[368] And it was here

364. Cf. RB to G. Krüger, 3. 3., 26. 3. 1941, in F. Lilie, "Bultmann-Krüger Briefwechsel," *ZNThG* 5, 287f; DLA Marbach, RB to H.-G. Gadamer, 22. 1. 1941.

365. Cf. RB to G. Krüger, 6. 12. 1941, in F. Lilie, "Bultmann-Krüger Briefwechsel," *ZNThG* 5, 295.

366. M. Kommerell to K. Reinhardt, 10. 1. 1943, in I. Jens, *Max Kommerell*, 410: ". . . I turn up regularly at Bultmann's for *Graeca*, Greek poetry; sometimes pleasurable and always tough—at the moment, he and the three in the group, the teacher Antz[!], are stuck into the gluey Theognis, who never wants to finish, whose relation to poesy I can't figure out, and who at every minute brings enlightenment to the other two, in extending the hand of Plato and Nietzsche—I feel myself banished and brood meekly over the words. Between his love of battle and my weariness of it, aesthetic discussions with Bultmann have now been given up, and we live in the peaceful delight of reciprocal incomprehensibility." Cf. RB to G. Krüger, 27. 1. 1942, in F. Lilie, "Bultmann-Krüger Briefwechsel," *ZNThG* 5, 297f; 27. 8. 1944, in F. Lilie, "Bultmann-Krüger Briefwechsel," *ZNThG* 6, 136: ". . . our *Graeca* vegetates on."

367. A. Henkel, "Die erste," 15.

368. A. Henkel, "Die erste," 15. Cf. also on what follows H.-G. Gadamer, *Philosophische Lehrjahre*, 55.

that Bultmann first presented his investigations of the ancient symbolism of light, which were published years later.[369] Karl Löwith spoke on "Kierkegaard and Nietzsche"; Karl Reinhardt interpreted the riddles of Heraclitus; Max Kommerell, who was then still teaching in Frankfurt, took part in the lectures with a presentation on the topic of Helen in *Faust II*; and Hans-Georg Gadamer ventured into a wider public with his "Plato and the Poets." In 1934, he published this study under Goethe's trenchant epigraph, "Whoever philosophizes disagrees with the way of thinking of those before him and those around him."[370] This motto more or less applied to all the evening lectures that took place under the aegis of Bultmann and Steinmeyer. Bultmann regarded these lectures as necessary, because despite the variety of their subject matter, they were unified in spirit by the indispensable quest for the blessing and the questioning nature of humanism. In contrast, he found that the lectures in the realm of the university "had gotten out of control . . . came to be more and more a plague that was completely ruining education. Why don't people—and above all, students—just sit down in their room and study in organized fashion one unified area of knowledge or interest? They would get more out of that than [from] continual 'stimulation'!"[371]

A literature group that formed around Bultmann and Steinmeyer provided yet further inspiration. It met one afternoon a week, usually at 14 Calvin Street but occasionally at the home of the Steinmeyers on Rollwiesenweg. Like-minded folks gathered to share with one other an interest in literature and their rejection of National Socialism. Kurt and Jane Steinmeyer, Rudolf and Helene Bultmann, as well as the mathematician Kurt Reidemeister and his wife Annemarie were the early members of this private reading group. They were later joined by Wilhelm and Margarete Anz, the German literature student Arthur Henkel, the author Marie Luise Kaschnitz and her husband, the archaeologist Guido Kaschnitz-von Weinberg, as well as by the literary historian Max Kommerell and his wife Erika.[372] Parceling out the roles among themselves, they read theatrical works by Shakespeare and Hugo von Hofmannsthal, Molière's *Tartuffe*, Werner Bergengruen's *Der Grosstyrann und das Gericht* [*The Great Tyrant and the Court*], and

369. Cf. RB, "Zur Geschichte der Lichtsymbolik," *Exegetica*, 323–55.

370. Cf. H.-G. Gadamer, *Plato und die Dichter*, 5; as well as J. Grondin, *Hans-Georg Gadamer*, 189–92; on Kommerell cf. C. Weber, 533f.

371. UB Tübingen, RB est., RB to A. Bultmann Lemke, 20. 1. 1938, Mn 2-3452.

372. Cf. on what follows RB to G. Krüger, 9. 2. 1941, in F. Lilie, "Bultmann-Krüger Briefwechsel," *ZNThG* 5, 285f; D. von Gersdorff, *Marie Luise Kaschnitz*, 116, 208; T. Kucharz, *Theologen und ihre Dichter*, 167.

other works by authors forbidden by the Nazis. Marie Luise Kaschnitz later acquainted the group with the lyric poetry of Paul Celans, which at that time was completely unknown in Germany. They read and discussed what they had read and in this way constructed for themselves a bright spiritual alternative to the leaden reality of the National Socialist state.

Now and again, Antje, Gesine, and Heilke Bultmann took part in the afternoon readings. Reading together fit in well with Bultmann's pronounced desire to exchange ideas about literature with others and to reflect on his own and others' impressions of the reading. At the same time, his contact with literature was directed by his interest in examining through literature and art in general the full range of existential possibilities for discovering the true in the beautiful.[373] It was less the formal and aesthetic perspective than the material and existentialist approach that shaped his responses to art, literature, and music. When Marie Luise Kaschnitz presented him with the gift of two poems, Bultmann thanked her with an attempt at interpretation: "The 'Pietà,' which I had not known before, seems to me so concentrated in its essence, rather more beautiful than the 'Semele,' which, as you read it aloud, made such a strong impression on me. It is very remarkable how you reduce both subjects, the Greek as well as the Christian, as it were to the same motif: Tragedy, which for womanly life (but one might well generalize to say for human life, which achieves its purest form in that of woman) springs from the fact that the divine will enters its sphere of life in its imperious way."[374]

In the Marburg arts scene, Rudolf and Helene Bultmann established a series of relationships with painters, all of whom opposed National Socialism and its racial and nativist cultural policies. An especially intimate friendship developed between the Bultmann and Bantzer families. The Bultmanns and their daughters not only spent the afternoon of New Year's Eve each year with this family—the painter and university drawing teacher, Karl Francis Bantzer, his wife Elsita, and their children Christoph, Veronika, Franziska, Claus and Effi—but also did many other things together.[375] Karl Francis' father, the "elder" Bantzer, had gained a more than regional reputation for Hessian painting through such genre paintings as *Lord's Supper in a Hessian Village Church* (1892) and *Schwälmer Dance* (1897–98), but also through

373. Cf. T. Kucharz, *Theologen und ihre Dichter*, 229–34.

374. DLA Marbach, M. L. Kaschnitz est., RB to M. L. Kaschnitz, 26. 5. 1939; the poems "Pieta" and "Semele" are reprinted in M. L. Kaschnitz, *Gesammelte Werke*, vol. 5, 34, 70f; cf. also P. Wagner, "Jesus als Spiegelbild," 59–63.

375. Cf. also the correspondences between the two families, Mn 2-399–401, 2-573, 2-2130 in UB Tübingen, RB est.

his naturalistic landscapes and portraits. Bultmann admired the art of Carl Bantzer[376] and led the painter's funeral service, which took place in his studio on December 23, 1941. In his address on Psalm 90 and Matt 5:8, Bultmann recalled that Bantzer had portrayed the essence of the Hessian homeland, the beauty of its landscape and people. Above all, however, in his pictures and portraits—especially in the likenesses of peasants and old women—he had directed one's view to the essence of the human being placed before eternity with its light pouring out to meet him.[377] While Bultmann was speaking, six farmers from Willingshausen entered the studio, dressed in the clothes they wore to the Lord's Supper. The deceased had frequently painted in Willingshausen, the oldest German artists' colony. Now these *Schwälmer* had come to Marburg to pay their last respects to the elder Bantzer,[378] and their mere appearance touchingly underscored Bultmann's words.

In Bultmann's guest book is the sketch of a head of Zeus in front of a Doric temple and under it the comment, "We owe our being together here to the old man."[379] With these words, the painter Franz Frank and his wife Erika alluded to the fact that, in the beginning of February 1939, before they went to Sicily, they had inquired about the Bultmanns' experiences the year before in Italy. Franz Frank, a grandson of the important Erlangen theologian Franz Hermann Reinhold Frank, had moved to Gossfelden with his family after the closing of the Pedagogical Academy of Kassel in 1932. There the Franks took up residence in the house of the painter Otto Ubbelohde, who had died in 1922. The National Socialists pensioned off Frank from the civil service in 1933 and repeatedly either prohibited or closed exhibitions of his work in the period that followed. Since the National Socialists had branded his work as "degenerate art" and had banned it from public showings, Frank found himself in a difficult situation professionally and personally. Rudolf and Helene Bultmann purchased two of his paintings: a landscape, *Field of Poppies in the Swabian Alps,* and a city-view of Marburg with the *Schwanallee*, the old tobacco factory, and the house in which Martin Heidegger had lived. Frank, Bultmann, and Gerhard Krüger maintained friendly social contacts on a sporadic basis.[380] Gesine Bultmann and Elsita Bantzer posed for the painter when in 1938 he undertook a cycle of twelve drawings based on the *Odyssey*, a work that he first showed in 1964. During

376. Cf. UB Tübingen, RB est., RB to C. Bantzer, 10. 8. 1937 (draft of letter), Mn 2-2131.

377. Cf. Bultmann's memorial address for C. Bantzer of 23. 12. 1941, *VW*, 305–10.

378. Cf. B. Küster, *Carl Bantzer*, 315.

379. Entry by F. and E. Frank in Bultmann's guestbook, 10.–12. 2. 1939, Mn 2-3041.

380. Cf. R. Zimmermann, *Franz Frank*, 184.

a leave from the front in the winter of 1940, Frank on his own initiative did portraits of Bultmann and Krüger.[381] Though his real strength did not lie in portraiture, the portrait of Bultmann, in its depiction of his "insistent and sage countenance,"[382] might be said to belong among Frank's most successful works in this realm. The picture shows Bultmann in his study, the material context of his life indicated by the background of a bookshelf and a wall painted in Oldenburg blue on which hangs a colored lithograph seascape. With hands folded and lightly leaning on a writing desk, Bultmann radiates a profound inner calm. The firm glance of his clear eyes seems to indicate that in the temporality of existence he is at the same time opening himself to a transcendent reality. The Marburg University Museum acquired the portrait from Frank in 1964, and today it is on loan from the museum and hangs in the office of the Dean of the Protestant theological faculty in Marburg.[383]

The inner calm of Bultmann that Frank captured in his painting was exposed to many stresses as the Second World War went on. In the weeks following the beginning of the War, Bultmann was still able to find himself amazed at how quickly "people" accustomed themselves to such basic changes in the circumstances of life; it seemed like a fairytale that he had been in Italy exactly a year before! In talking with Gerhard Krüger, Bultmann strained to work out the philosophical and theological aspects of this "becoming-accustomed" and other overarching existential questions that the War raised. What were the meanings of all the themes that they knew so well from the ancient texts, but that now defined peremptory encroachments on their lives: surrendering to the will of God, bearing up under fate, the μίμησις [imitation] of the suffering of Christ, and, in general, the question of the meaning of life?[384]

These questions became even more pressing for those who had been torn from the previous settings of their lives and conscripted into the armed forces. In October of 1939, members of the Protestant student community from Marburg established a connection between the soldiers in the field and the professors and students back home through a regularly distributed circular letter. A circle of friends around Hans von Soden carried out this illegal activity despite the personal risks it entailed. First Erich Dinkler, and after he was called up to the armed forces, his wife Erika Dinkler-von Schubert

381. Entry by Bultmann in his *Chronik 1917–1945*: "21 February–1 March [1940] Frank is painting the head of the house."

382. Herbert von Buttlar, 1950, cited in R. Zimmermann, *Franz Frank*, 146.

383. The portrait of Bultmann is reproduced in R. Zimmermann, *Franz Frank*, 81.

384. Cf. the Bultmann-Krüger correspondence of 16. 10., 2. 11., 9. 11., 22. 11., 28. 11. 1939, in F. Lilie, "Bultmann-Krüger Briefwechsel," *ZNThG* 5, 138–50.

put together the circular letters, composed of soldiers' letters from the front, sermons, and greetings from academic teachers. Bultmann supported this remarkable initiative from the outset. He repeatedly turned to the task of bringing church proclamation to bear pastorally and theologically in words of greeting for students serving in the field.[385] His sermon of June 22, 1941, the day German forces invaded the Soviet Union, and his demythologizing lecture of the same year, together with texts of von Soden, Gerhard von Rad, and Erich Dinkler, were intended to show the gratitude of the Protestant student community in Marburg to those who wore the uniform. It constituted an impressive witness to the Christian literature of edification in a challenging time.[386]

All the while, Wilhelm Mommsen was active in "intellectual deployment for war." By means of numerous addresses in front of officers in the armed forces, in barracks and sick bays, on SS bases and in front of National Socialist units, he was seeking to strengthen the military power of the troops and the populace. This involvement brought him admission into the party in 1941, and the War Service Cross, second class in 1943.[387] On the "home front," Bultmann's neighbor was active as air defense watch officer in his residential area. During training evenings he incessantly instructed the residents of his block on the importance of air defense, and put into practice in Calvin Street and in Rotenberg what had been taught in major air defense exercises.[388] Bultmann took part in four of the evening air defense courses. He found that "what little that was of use" that he experienced there could as well "have been set down in a short leaflet and would have saved a lot of time."[389] Thereafter Bultmann was again and again absent from the air defense training sessions with the result that neighbor Mommsen reported him to the appropriate air defense official.[390] Luckily for Bultmann, this report was not pursued further. That he and his family were in jeopardy also became evident in March of 1942, when Helene Bultmann was summoned for questioning by the criminal police because a letter from a friend from Africa placed her under suspicion as a spy. After several hours, the matter was cleared up in her favor.[391]

385. Cf. Bultmann's greetings of 22. 11. 1939, the beginning of February 1940, New Year 1941, in E. Dinkler-von Schubert, *Feldpost*, 25f, 30f, 142–45.

386. The texts are published in E. Dinkler-von Schubert, *Feldpost*. Cf. also RB to E. Dinkler, 20. 12. 1942, 9. 5. 1945, in E. Dinkler-von Schubert, *Feldpost*, 10f.

387. Cf. A. C. Nagel, "'Der Prototyp der Leute, . . .'" 79f; P. Köpf, *Die Mommsens*, 206–11.

388. Cf. UB Tübingen, RB est., RB to A. Bultmann Lemke, 25. 7. 1944, Mn 2-3452.

389. UB Tübingen, RB est., RB to A. Bultmann Lemke, 24. 7. 1940, Mn 2-3452.

390. Cf. P. Köpf, *Die Mommsens*, 243, 246.

391. Cf. UB Tübingen, RB est., RB to A. Bultmann Lemke, 20. 3. 1942, Mn 2-3452.

Occasionally Bultmann received reports of what was actually happening in the theaters of the war—accounts that differed greatly from the announcements of National Socialist propaganda.[392] Ernst Lohmeyer, whose correspondence with Bultmann during the War gradually intensified, had shattering things to report from Poland and Belgium.[393] Bultmann underlined many passages in Lohmeyer's letters with a red pencil. Where his friend wrote of "the many riff-raff" with whom one had to fight a running battle, Bultmann noted down, "doubtless, the S. S. and S. A. are what is meant!"[394] From Poland Lohmeyer wrote, "What has happened in the occupied territory is so impossible and unspeakable, that it would have been a thousand times better if it had never started. Force against force, barbarity against lesser barbarity . . . morally speaking, we have lost everything in these territories."[395] In Belgium as well, he could only bemoan the "degrading harshness of the War, the emergence of all the dull meanness that easily attaches itself to it."[396] In 1941, Lohmeyer thanked Bultmann with a box of cigars for sending him the last installment of the commentary on John. He did not believe, he added, "that I will ever smoke cigars with you again."[397] This foreboding was to be fulfilled in tragic fashion.

As the war went on, the everyday life of the Bultmanns, like that of most Germans, was marked by considerable privations. The shortage of food, the nearly complete disappearance of semi-luxury items such as coffee, tobacco, and wine—all this signified more than just a loss of a certain quality of life. At the order of the office of housing, Heilke had to move out of her room in March of 1944 to make way for people who had been bombed out.[398] The devastating air raid on Kassel on October 22, 1943, further brought this issue home to the head of the house,[399] since due to the lack of gas and coal for cooking, his wife had to share Mrs. Mommsen's stove until the end of the war.[400] The war burdened all family members with additional responsibilities. During the temporary closing of the university for the winter semester of 1939–40, Bultmann was assigned to teach Greek and Latin for nine weeks at

392. Cf. on the events in Italy RB to A. Bultmann Lemke, 27. 8. 1943, Mn 2-3452 in UB Tübingen, RB est.

393. On Lohmeyer's active service, cf. A. Köhn, *Der Neutestamentler Ernst Lohmeyer*, 104–13.

394. UB Tübingen, RB est., E. Lohmeyer to RB, 18. 9. 1939, Mn 2-1315.

395. UB Tübingen, RB est., E. Lohmeyer to RB, 8. 11. 1939, Mn 2-1315.

396. UB Tübingen, RB est., E. Lohmeyer to RB, 26. 6. 1940, Mn 2-1315.

397. UB Tübingen, RB est., E. Lohmeyer to RB, 25. 1. 1941, Mn 2-1315.

398. Cf. UB Tübingen, RB est., RB to A. Bultmann Lemke, 5. 3. 1944, Mn 2-3452.

399. Cf. UB Tübingen, RB est., RB to A. Bultmann Lemke, 12. 11. 1943, Mn 2-3452; RB to G. Krüger, 13. 11. 1943, in F. Lilie, "Bultmann-Krüger Briefwechsel," *ZNThG* 5, 307.

400. Cf. UB Tübingen, RB est., RB to A. Bultmann Lemke, 4. 3. 1945, Mn 2-3452.

the Philippinum. He accepted the new pedagogical challenge gladly, but he regretted that he had lost the five early mornings each week that he had used for his scholarly work.[401] Helene Bultmann did service at the Red Cross, and Gesine and Heilke were repeatedly obliged to do the war work that was assigned to students. Working in the munitions factories in Allendorf, Heilke was especially exposed to the dangers of air raids.

Far heavier than these burdens was that of the loss in human life, which the Bultmann family also had reason to lament. Particularly painful for Gesine, but for her parents as well, was the fate of the musicologist Werner Wegner, whom Herbert Birtner had sponsored for his doctorate. Gesine and Wegner had become engaged on New Year's Day of 1940, and now he had been missing in Russia since December 1941. After weeks of hope and worry, it was learned that he had been taken to a Russian prison severely wounded and had died there. The sad news came to Bultmann via von Soden from Dinkler, to whose division Wegner had belonged.[402] In September 1942, Wegner's mentor, Herbert Birtner, also fell in Russia. On October 31st, Bultmann performed the memorial service for the musicologist who, knowing that music connects the human being with the invisible world of God, had dedicated himself to Heinrich Schütz and the Protestant musical tradition.[403]

Bultmann's eldest daughter, Antje, had married the physician and psychiatrist Rudolf Lemke immediately prior to the war,[404] but the marriage was ill-fated, and they were divorced after two years. After completing her training at the University of Leipzig library, she found a position at the Thuringian public library in Jena. There, at a musical evening in the home of Gerhard von Rad, in which she joined the Old Testament scholar and his wife Luise in making music, she got to know the writer Ricarda Huch. Having soon made friends with the poet, her daughter Marietta Böhm, and her husband Franz Böhm, Antje went in 1944 to live with Ricarda Huch in Jena at 72 Philosophenweg. Over the years that followed, she became an indispensable

401. Cf. RB to G. Krüger, 19. 9. 1939, in F. Lilie, "Bultmann-Krüger Briefwechsel," *ZNThG* 5, 136; 5. 11. 1941, in F. Lilie, "Bultmann-Krüger Briefwechsel," *ZNThG* 5, 293. Furthermore, after Nazi educational authorities had banned religious education in the schools, Bultmann took part in a team for religious education to pupils of higher grades of grammar school in Marburg. Cf. UB Tübingen, RB est., W. Brand to RB, 6. 4. 1949, Mn 2-3463.

402. Cf. UB Tübingen, RB est., H. von Soden to RB, 8. 2. 1942, Mn 2-2385; cf. also RB, "Bericht," in H. G. Göckeritz, *Bultmann-Gogarten Briefwechsel*, 309.

403. Cf. Bultmann's sermon on Rom 8:31, 35, 37–39 at the memorial celebration for H. Birtner on 31. 10. 1942, Mn 2-147.

404. Cf. Bultmann's wedding sermon for R. Lemke and A. Bultmann of 24. 11. 1939, Mn 2-136; as well as RB, "Bericht," in H. G. Göckeritz, *Bultmann-Gogarten Briefwechsel*, 209f.

support to the aged poet, who was losing her sight.[405] Antje introduced Ricarda Huch to her father when he visited Jena in May of 1940.[406] He admired her poetry, and especially her book, *Luthers Glaube* [*Luther's Faith*]; he also admired her for her humanity and uncompromising conduct during the National Socialist dictatorship.[407]

Gesine completed her training as a flautist in Berlin, and much to the delight of her parents lived from the summer of 1944 until the end of the war in Marburg.[408] Upon graduating from high school, Heilke at first took up the study of philology in Marburg, largely because Max Kommerell's teaching encouraged her to follow this path. But in the long run, Heilke's "passion for music" proved "too strong," and she gave up her studies to prepare herself to become a cellist.[409] After they had left home, Bultmann made it a habit to write to his daughters on a regular basis and to delight them with art postcards and poems. Before the end of his life, Antje had received no fewer than 61 cards and 1054 letters—a rich treasure trove for anyone interested in a chronicle of his life.

As Bultmann's sixtieth birthday approached in the summer of 1944, the premature death of Max Kommerell threw a dark shadow over the circle of his friends. Bultmann had given enduring support to Kommerell's appointment at the university in Marburg,[410] and after the literature scholar had come to Marburg in 1941, he was soon one of Bultmann's closest friends. Kommerell's exceptional poetic and interpretative gifts, which occasionally led him to use unconventional ways of speaking that alienated others, made him a stimulating and therefore valued conversation partner of Bultmann's.[411] The already close relationship between the theologian and the literature scholar was further intensified by the letters they exchanged in the final

405. Cf. C. Koepcke, *Ricarda Huch*, 261, 269–83; B. Bronnen, *Fliegen mit gestutzten Flügeln*, 63–65, 129–32, 159–64. R. Huch to H. Bultmann, 29. 12. 1942, in R. Huch, *Briefe*, 260: "Antje surrounds me in particular with a solicitude to which I am scarce accustomed. I do not want to accuse my relatives with this—my daughter knows full well that, despite my old age, I am still healthy and strong—thank God for this!—my somewhat shrunken outside attracts more of Antje's attention . . ."

406. Cf. RB, *Chronik 1917–1945,* 40 (11. 5. 1940).

407. Cf. UB Tübingen, RB est., RB to A. Bultmann Lemke, 19. 7. 1964, Mn 2-3452. Cf. also R. Huch to RB, 20. 8. 1946, Mn 2-1027.

408. Cf. RB, "Bericht," in H. G. Göckeritz, *Bultmann-Gogarten Briefwechsel*, 309.

409. RB, "Bericht," H. G. Göckertiz, *Bultmann-Gogarten Briefwechsel*, 310.

410. Cf. DLA Marbach, RB to M. Kommerell, 3. 5. 1939; as well as DLA Marbach, RB to H.-G. Gadamer, 22. 1. 1941; cf. C. Weber, *Max Komerell*, 367f.

411. Cf. RB to G. Krüger, 9. 2. and 6. 7. 1941, 27. 1. 1942, in F. Lilie, "Bultmann-Krüger Briefwechsel," *ZNThG* 5, 285, 295, 297. Cf. M. Kommerell to RB, 3. 5. 1944, in I. Jens, *Max Kommerell*, 445–47; cf. also DLA Marbach, RB to E. Kommerell, 24. 9. 1944.

phase of Kommerell's serious illness. Bultmann commented on Kommerell's interpretation of Goethe's poems with the sort of insight[412] that Kommerell "had only very rarely come across."[413] For his part, Kommerell directed to the theologian a cautious question: ". . . to your mind, is not the partly indifferent, but partly deeply respectful attitude of the aging Goethe toward Christ, and the immediacy with which he receives him when he can, preferable to, and fundamentally more Christian than the terribly hybrid and in its own way misguided christology of a Hölderlin or a Novalis?" Of course, the dialogue was only superficially about the problem of how Goethe's poetry might be made to exhibit its magic anew in the present. In truth, the two partners were after the much deeper question of the right way for them to deal with Kommerell's serious illness.[414] Throughout this ordeal, Bultmann proved to be an empathetic companion and chaplain to his critically ill friend, for whom Bultmann's "truly fatherly tenderness and concern . . . really has touched my heart."[415] Bultmann felt the loss of Kommerell as a serious blow—not only personally, but also because of Kommerell's success in teaching and his positive influence on young people in the university as well.[416] In conducting the funeral service on July 29, 1944, Bultmann paid tribute to the person and accomplishments of his friend—works that his own guild of colleagues misjudged and that showed him to be, after Walter Benjamin, perhaps the most important literary scholar of his generation. "Whoever knew

412. Cf. DLA Marbach, RB to M. Kommerell, 4. 6. 1944, 3: ". . . after, following your lead, I went back more deeply into Goethe's poems, I became obsessed with them, and I have become at once your and Goethe's victim. . . . What will be the end of it, I do not yet know." Bultmann is referring here to M. Kommerell, *Gedanken*.

413. M. Kommerell to RB, 7. 6. 1944, in I. Jens, *Max Kommerell*, 450; cf. also M. Kommerell to RB, 7. 6. 1944, in I. Jens, *Max Kommerell*, 451: ". . . seeing that I have never denied that our trains of thought often travel on widely divergent tracks, I now take pleasure in the fact that you now walk under the old tree, laden with fruit and bestowing shade, and interpret along with me—it is good to linger here awhile!"

414. Cf. DLA Marbach, RB to M. Kommerell, 4. 6. 1944, 3; as well as M. Kommerell to RB, 4. 6. 1944: "In response to your personal questions about whether my illness is anything more than something merely to be borne, I cannot say much in reply. It is hard to get through the gray times of the nights, but that is so much due to fever that there is no point grousing about it. Otherwise, I inquire of many a quiet hour, as well as of many a difficult one, what it wants of me, but the answer remains unclear. If it becomes clearer, I expect to hear, 'become invisible, nameless, odorless, forget, and above all, worry that you are forgotten.'"

415. DLA Marbach, M. Kommerell to RB, 7. 6. 1944, 3, 450; cf. also M. Kommerell to RB, 26. 6. 1944, in I. Jens, *Max Kommerell*, 453.

416. Cf. RB to G. Krüger, 27. 8. 1944, in F. Lilie, "Bultmann-Krüger Briefwechsel," *ZNThG* 6, 136; RB, "Bericht," in H. G. Göckeritz, *Bultmann-Gogarten Briefwechsel*, 312.

him experienced the wisdom of his being and now sees this more clearly in the light of the majesty of death—a wisdom that makes itself known as much in a goodness that understands as in a skeptical question, or again in the angry protest against all too certain opinions and big words, and just as much in smiling humor, or even in playing the fool. As we look back, it is as if his motto were, 'Whoever among you thinks he is wise should become a fool in this world, that he might become wise'" (cf. 1 Cor 3:18–23).[417]

Three weeks later Bultmann turned sixty. August 20, 1944, "was a refreshing day in this dark time," a day that made him acutely aware of the love he had experienced in his life. Bultmann felt great gratitude for the companionship of his family, the devotion of friends and students, among whom Günther Bornkamm, Ernst Fuchs, Hans-Georg Gadamer, Ernst Käsemann, Gerhard Krüger, and Heinrich Schlier sent greetings on his birthday, with concern for how his scholarly work was going. Emil Balla, the Reidemeisters, and the Steinmeyers came to Calvin Street to extend their greetings. Hedwig von Soden brought congratulations from her husband, who due to a bad heart could no longer make the uphill trek to his friend's house. Ricarda Huch had "in touching fashion" contributed the coffee, and the celebration brought back many an amusing memory. In the evening, Bultmann, Leni, and Heilke paid a visit to the grave of Max Kommerell in the Ockershäuser cemetery.[418]

In the autumn of 1944, the Bultmanns took Uta Heinemann, the seventeen-year-old daughter of Gustav and Hilda Heinemann, into their household. Uta's mother had studied with Bultmann during the twenties. Bombed out in Essen during the War, Hilda Heinemann found a temporary place for her four daughters and herself in Winterberg. Bultmann and his wife responded without delay to Hilda's request so as to get Uta back to normal schooling in Marburg. Thus, Uta was part of the Bultmann family until the end of the war. For her, this was an unforgettable time. Among other things, she enjoyed the advantage of private study with Bultmann for two hours each Tuesday and Friday afternoon. Among other assignments,

417. Bultmann's funeral sermon for M. Kommerell of 29. 7. 1944, Mn 2-151 in UB Tübingen, RB est.; as well as E. Hauschildt, *Rudolf Bultmanns Predigten*, 242f; and C. Weber, *Max Komerell*, 539–42. On Kommerell, cf. H.-G. Gadamer, *Philosophische Lehrjahre*, 93–110; W. Busch and G. Pickerodt, *Max Kommerell.* On Kommerell's belonging to the circle around Stefan George (until 1928), cf. T. Karlauf, *Stefan George, passim*; C. Weber, *Max Komerell*, 50–64.

418. RB to G. Krüger, 27. 8. 1944, in F. Lilie, "Bultmann-Krüger Briefwechsel," *ZNThG* 6, 134f.

she was given Plato to translate, and the professor explained to her the Greek philosopher's world of ideas.[419]

At the beginning of March 1945, following a long winter of hunger and freezing cold, Bultmann heard "a muffled roar from far away, presumably from the front, with the approach of which one was going to have to reckon."[420] Marburg had been only partly destroyed during the war. To be sure, two air raids had caused damage in the vicinity of the train station, in the hospital quarter, in Weidenhausen, and at the Friedrichsplatz, but they had largely spared the old city of Marburg—and also Bultmann's residential area. Then, on the morning of March 28, 1945, it was all over: American troops took the city without a struggle. Looking out of his office, Bultmann could see how the Americans were coming up the Lahn Valley from Giessen and moving into Marburg. Rudolf and Helene Bultmann greeted their entry "as deliverance and liberation . . . from the criminal rule of the Nazis."[421]

419. Cf. U. Ranke-Heinemann, *Nein und Amen*, 9–11. Later, Ranke-Heinemann, a theologian who converted to the Roman Catholic Church in 1953, also appealed to Bultmann with regard to her criticism of dogma and church. To be sure, she remained in this light-years removed from Bultmann's ways of posing these problems

420. UB Tübingen, RB est., RB to A. Bultmann Lemke, 4. 3. 1945, Mn 2-3452.

421. RB, "Bericht," in H. G. Göckeritz, *Bultmann-Gogarten Briefwechsel*, 308f.

VI. Time of Harvest (1945–ca. 1953)

1. The End of the Third Reich as Liberation and Obligation

The blindness concerning the necessity for holding accountable for what happened even those party members who did not personally commit any crime (that is, if they were not under pressure to join the party and they promoted its "ideals" by entering it) appears to be incurable. From the trials in Nürnberg [Nuremberg] and especially now that the proceedings against the concentration camp physicians in Germany have not called forth greater horror and repugnance, one can see that most people are too taken up with their own personal troubles. But it is still sad . . . all the horror in history up to now cannot be compared with the sins that have been committed here—because these were perpetrated systematically, and not out of passion, but rather according to plan, out of raw cynicism.[1]

On the afternoon of September 7, 1945, Bultmann received an unexpected visit. When the doorbell rang, his wife opened the door and in front of her stood a foreigner with a cap on his head, a British sergeant in his khaki-colored uniform. It took but a second or two for her to recognize the foreigner: "Mr. Jonas! Mr. Jonas, is it really you?!" She broke out into a flood of tears and words and took the visitor to her husband's study. "Rudolf, you have a visitor!"[2] Hans Jonas has relived the scene of the reunion innumerable times since their enforced separation twelve years earlier and has described it in moving words: Bultmann was sitting, as always, in his study "at the desk, pale and emaciated, collar and clothes too big now, but with a countenance full of peace. In the moment of recognition, he rushed into the middle of the room towards me. And there, barely through the hasty exchange of a first hello, scarcely over the shock of the unexpected reunion, with both of us still standing there, he said something that explains why I am telling this highly personal story. I had come from Göttingen and was holding a book under my arm that Ruprecht Publishers had given me for Bultmann. He pointed to this and asked, "May I hope that this is the second volume of *Gnosis*?" At that moment, there entered into my soul—still torn apart by the unspeakable

1. UB Tübingen, RB est., RB to F. C. Sell, 24. 4. 1947, Mn 2-2380.
2. H. Jonas to RB, 12. 5. 1973, in A. Grossmann, "'Und die Gnosis,'" 30.

things that I had first experienced in my own homeland, the fate of my mother and innumerable others—for the first time, something like peace. In the face of the steadfastness of being thought about and of a loving concern, beyond the collapse of a world, I suddenly realized that one can pick things up and go on with that for which one needs a belief in human beings."[3]

Unlike most Germans in 1945, Bultmann perceived the end of the Second World War as liberation from the tyranny of National Socialism,[4] but the surprising reunion with Hans Jonas showed that this newly acquired freedom would provide a fundamental and long-forbidden prerequisite for the revitalization of relationships. Following the entrance of the United States into the War near the end of 1941, the National Socialist authorities had returned Bultmann's letters to friends in exile in America as undeliverable. Now, in the summer of 1945, he succeeded in reestablishing through correspondence connections with Erich Frank, Paul Friedländer, and Friedrich Carl Sell. At the beginning of December 1945, he sent them a full report of what his family was going through, developments in the university following the end of the war, descriptions of the present state of public life, and reflections on the way forward for society and the university.

Bultmann's portrayal of the complexity of the needs—of the lack of foodstuffs, clothing, and the necessities of life, as well as of the cold due to the lack of fuel—covered a wide range of problems. Nonetheless, he moderated the Jeremiads concerning his own distress during the months immediately following the War. Quartering two families and other homeless in his house made him aware of the more acute misery of those who had been bombed out or had fled from the East and were now completely without means. In January of 1946, an American officer whose unit had recently come to Marburg wanted to take over Bultmann's house on two hours' notice, a demand that was fortunately averted at the last minute through the intervention of Samson Benjamin Knoll and Edward Yarnall Hartshorne, two officers of the American military government.[5] To be sure, living conditions and shortages of food, fuel, and electricity remained calamitous in Marburg, as elsewhere, for months, and even years to come. That students and local

3. H. Jonas, "Im Kampf," in O. Kaiser, *Gedenken an Rudolf Bultmann*, 44f; cf. also H. Jonas, *Errinerungen*, 234–37.

4. Cf. RB to F. Gogarten, 10. 6. 1945, in H. G. Göckeritz, *Bultmann-Gogarten Briefwechsel*, 232; RB, "Bericht über unser Ergehen in Marburg," in H. G. Göckeritz, *Bultmann-Gogarten Briefwechsel*, 308f.

5. Cf. UB Tübingen, RB est., RB to F. Bultmann, 20. 1. 1946, Mn 2-3418; as well as W. Bernsdorff and M. Vialon, "Vom Um-Erzieher," 36; E. Y. Hartshorne to E. F. Hartshorne, 18. 1. 1946, in J. Tent, *Academic Proconcul*, 242.

residents increasingly blamed these conditions on the American occupying power, Bultmann regarded as a fatal development.[6] For he was convinced that only an easing of the economic situation would permit the establishment of a stable political order that could provide a better future.

Although the University of Marburg remained closed in the summer of 1945, the theological faculty recommenced university worship services at the end of May. On June 17, 1945, only a few weeks after the surrender, Bultmann preached on 2 Cor 4:6–11 at a service in the Reformed church for both the city and the university. In his sermon, he interpreted the paradox of the cross of Christ as the symbol of the Christian life. Concerning the question that dominated the present time, that of "how to emerge from our poverty, how to build a better future,"[7] he considered the most important issue to be how to find security and peace *amidst* distress. "Paul's strength comes from the fact that he lives in two worlds—not only in the visible world of transitoriness, of tears, and of death, the world in which we 'are afflicted in every way,' in which 'we are perplexed,' but also in the invisible world in which there is no anxiety and no despair."[8] Bultmann saw the Christian, the existential individual, as forever existing in both of these worlds. To be sure, he was also aware of voices that in response to the depressing poverty of the first weeks following the war would exchange the newly recovered spiritual freedom for the old regime's chimera of external well-being. Such a wish, he insisted, bespoke a sinking back into the lowest level of human existence.[9] It was precisely the past years that showed all too clearly that Germany had brought upon itself both inward and external catastrophe, since "[its] faith in the world of the spirit and obedience to its claim" had been lost.[10]

This was the leitmotif of Bultmann's analysis of the worldview of National Socialism, which he was able to view only as "the final, radical consequence" of a development that was already under way in the nineteenth century.[11] Nationalistic will to power, utilitarian ideas, a life-style oriented purely to economic success, and the instrumentalization of knowledge for the sake of politics and technology had bundled themselves together into the National

6. Cf. UB Tübingen, RB est., RB to F. C. Sell, 21. 11. 1946, Mn 2-2380; as well as J. Gimbel, *Eine deutsche Stadt*, 47–50, 78–81, 102–16. E. Y. Hartshorne judged of Bultmann's report, "The longer letter from Professor Bultmann seems to me one of the finest expressions of 'the good German' I have seen" (E. Y. Hartshorne to E. F. Hartshorne, 17. 12. 1945, in J. Tent, *Academic Proconcul*, 227).

7. RB, *MP*, 189; cf. A. Lippmann, *Marburger Theologie*, 450f.

8. RB, *MP*, 190.

9. Cf. RB, *MP*, 197.

10. RB, *MP*, 194.

11. RB, *MP*, 194.

Socialist ideology. This transformation destroyed centuries of achievement by human civilization in the areas of law, morality, truth, beauty, and of course religion—and put in their place the drive for self-assertion and the will to power of race or nation. In view of this destructive turn, it was necessary that life be turned once again through the word of the grace of God towards the invisible, spiritual world. "A life that is successful only in practical terms is by no means a life that deserves to be called genuinely human."[12]

What form academic life in Marburg was to take on had in no way been worked out in June of 1945. Although the American military government forced through measures that made it possible to reopen the university on September 25, 1945,[13] the resumption of teaching in the theological faculty was overshadowed by the death of Hans von Soden.[14] His health, compromised as it was by a congenital heart defect, had gradually worsened during the war, and he had found it necessary to restrict his work on the committees of the Confessing Church since 1940. Ultimately, even summoning up all of his physical strength, he was able to perform his teaching duties only at home, often lying on the sofa. Through his tireless activity on behalf of theology and church, von Soden had proven himself a dependable counselor and an invaluable spiritual guide for his students and the pastors of the Confessing Church in Kurhessen-Waldeck—a truly priestly figure.

On October 2, 1945, Bultmann visited von Soden in his home,[15] just a week after an emergency synod in Treysa had approved new rules of governance for the Protestant Church in Kurhessen-Waldeck, a constitution that was largely attributable to von Soden's efforts. And on this October day, filled with joy, he read aloud to Bultmann the letter that President Friedrich Happich had sent him to report on the adoption of the new church constitution, an act which, as it were, crowned von Soden's work on behalf of the Protestant Church. It was during the subsequent conversation with Bultmann that he suffered the heart attack that led to his death an hour later. The loss of his friend brought Bultmann profound grief. And although it was "not easy" for him, he honored the wish of Hedwig von Soden and presided over the funeral of Hans von Soden in the University Church on October 8,

12. RB, *MP*, 195.

13. In the American zones of occupation, the universities of Marburg, Erlangen, and Heidelberg reopened courses of study for all faculties in WS 1945–46.

14. Cf. RB, "Hans Frhr. Von Soden."

15. What follows is according to Bultmann's report shortly afterwards to G. Harbsmeier, 14. 10. 1945, Mn 2-2237 in UB Tübingen, RB est.; see, somewhat differently, E. Dinkler, Introduction, in E. Dinkler and E. Dinkler-von Schubert, *Theologie und Kirche*, 33f.

1945.[16] In his funeral address, Bultmann cited the words of Paul in 1 Cor 4:1–4 in drawing a very personal picture—not of his friend's life and work, but rather of the inner *essence* of the deceased, who as theologian and person had sought in the multifarious concerns of his life to be nothing other than a "servant of Christ and steward of God's mysteries" (1 Cor 4:1).[17]

The tragic fate of his friend Ernst Lohmeyer likewise affected Bultmann deeply. At the beginning of March 1946, he received a postcard sent by Melie Lohmeyer from Greifswald on February 18. It contained the news that Lohmeyer had been imprisoned. His wife carefully muted her plea for help on account of postal censorship in the Soviet zone of occupation: "Unfortunately, Uncle Ernst . . . had to take an apparently long, uncomfortable journey on the fifteenth. We are very concerned about him. He absolutely must go to a different zone of activity with a better climate. But today, this is difficult."[18] Bultmann understood. He offered to assemble evidence from the letters that her husband had written to him that Lohmeyer had decisively rejected militarism and National Socialism.[19] Further, Bultmann immediately contacted Martin Dibelius to discuss how Lohmeyer might best be helped,[20] and with Dibelius undertook various attempts to this end.[21] In addition to Bultmann, Dibelius, and his family, other scholars close to him sought to obtain his release: they included Martin Buber, Hans von Campenhausen, Ernst Joseph Cohn, Rudolf Hermann, Richard Hönigswald, and Julius Schniewind. But their appeals were unsuccessful, as were those of such church leaders as Otto Dibelius, Martin Niemöller, and Theophil Wurm, whose representations did not resonate with the Soviet authorities. Only years later did it become known that in the face of unspecified charges and under unclear circumstances, Lohmeyer had been unjustly condemned to death by a Soviet military tribunal and executed in Greifswald on September 19, 1946.[22] Bultmann contributed an exegetical study of the First

16. UB Tübingen, RB est., RB to G. Harbsmeier, Mn 2-2232.

17. Cf. RB, "Am Sarge," in Dinkler and Dinkler-von Schubert, *Theologie und Kirche*, 347–51; several formulations from this sermon are taken up in RB, Foreword, in H. von Soden, *Urchristentum und Geschichte*, v–ix. High-ranking church representatives had had von Soden in mind for the position of bishop of the Protestant Church in Kurhessen-Waldeck, as well as for the presiding chair of the newly formed Protestant Church in Germany.

18. UB Tübingen, RB est., M. Seyberth to RB, 17.–18. 2. 1946, Mn 2-1314. Lohmeyer's wife probably wrote under her maiden name on account of the censor.

19. Cf. GstA PK Berlin, Lohmeyer est., RB to M. Lohmeyer, 1. 3. 1946, no. 6/3.

20. UB Tübingen, RB est., Bultmann's notes of 1. 3. and 2. 3. 1946 on M. Seyberth to RB, 17.–18. 2. 1946, Mn 2-1314.

21. Cf. GstA PK Berlin, Lohmeyer est., RB to M. Lohmeyer, 20. 4. 1946, no. 6/7.

22. Cf. A. Köhn, *Der Neutestamentler Ernst Lohmeyer*, 137–56.

Letter of John to the 1951 memorial volume for Lohmeyer edited by Werner Schmauch.[23] At the request of Melie Lohmeyer, he accepted his friend's work, *Gottesknecht und Davidsohn* [*Servant of God and Son of David*], for publication in 1953 in the series *Studies of the Religion and Literature of the Old and New Testament.*[24]

The American military government had a strong interest in resuming classes at Marburg, since the university was earmarked to play an important role in the reeducation of those Germans living in the American occupation zone. It was hoped that the universities would promote the democratization and spiritual-moral renewal of German society. Edward Yarnall Hartshorne, the officer in charge of the university, was a former Harvard sociologist now responsible for the colleges and universities in the U.S. Zone. He had studied in Berlin with Friedrich Meinecke and was extremely knowledgeable concerning conditions in the German universities following 1933.[25] To set in motion a discussion about the future of these institutions and their role in a democratic polity, Hartshorne initiated the Marburg university discussions, which took place June 12–15, 1946.[26]

As in his sermon of June 17, 1945, in his report for the university discussions, "Hochschule, Antike und Christentum" ["University, Antiquity and Christianity"], Bultmann saw in the National Socialist ideology the consequence of modern relativism, which from the nineteenth century on had left its mark in many ways by dissolving the ideas of the true, the good and the just.[27] To be sure, the practical consequences of that profoundly anti-human

23. Cf. RB, "Die kirchliche Redaktion," *Exegetica*, 381–93.

24. Cf. E. Lohmeyer, *Gottesknecht und Davidsohn*; as well as UB Tübingen, RB est., M. Lohmeyer to RB, 28. 2. 1952, Mn 2-1314. Bultmann supported M. Lohmeyer with foodstuffs, coffee, etc.; cf. M. Lohmeyer to RB, 11. 1. 1950 and 28. 2. 1952, Mn 2-1314.

25. Cf. E. Y. Hartshorne, *The German Universities.* On the effects of Hartshorne's work, cf. J. Tent, *Academic Proconcul.*

26. Among others who took part in these discussions, in addition to the chancellors of the Hessian universities of Darmstadt, Frankfurt, Giessen, and Marburg, were the physician Victor von Weizsäcker, the social philosopher Alfred Weber, the sociologist Alexander Mitscherlich, the medievalist Gerd Tellenbach, the classical philologist Bruno Snell, the historian of literature Ernst Beutler, the philosopher Gerhard Krüger; from Marburg, Professors Balla, Benz, Bultmann, Frick, and Heiler (theology), Hamann (history of art), Reidemeister (mathematics), and Versé (pathology); and alongside these also foreign scholars such as the Italian philosopher of religion Enrico Castelli and his philosophical colleague Ernesto Grassi. On Castelli's notes on his trip to Germany in June of 1946, cf. F. R. Hausmann, "Heidegger," 36. On the later fortune of the discussions regarding the Marburg institutions of higher education, the function of which was taken over by the conference of rectors following 1947, cf. A. Lippmann, *Marburger Theologie*, 417f, n. 68.

27. Cf. RB, "Hochschule," 137–43.

development had been ended by the collapse of the Third Reich, and yet the younger generation in particular continued to be threatened by the nihilism that regime had created. It still clung to some of the "values" inculcated through education under National Socialism, and found some degree of refuge in the rigid dogmas of the church. On the other hand, as a generation that had already been deceived once, the young harbored strong reservations about any form of indoctrination. For this reason, Bultmann called for academic instruction that would instill habits of independent and critical thinking. To do this, the humanism that had come out of antiquity and Christianity would have to join in the struggle against relativism. Humanism would need Christianity, "so that reason does not remain in the sphere of theory, but rather becomes knowledge that is existential." Christianity, in turn, would need humanism, since "this makes clear that the will of God is the true, the good, and the just, and makes for its recognition as binding law."[28]

University studies oriented to such principles presupposed a faculty unburdened of the National Socialist past and able to ensure the necessary new beginnings in research and teaching. With this in mind, the Americans in the summer of 1945 set up a planning committee which, while it had no authority to make decisions, was to advise the Special Branch of the Division of Public Safety that was responsible for denazification by presenting reports on the political views and activities of Marburg university lecturers during the Third Reich.[29] This planning committee included theologians Emil Balla and Rudolf Bultmann, the philosopher Julius Ebbinghaus, the art historian Richard Hamann, the Romance languages scholar Werner Krauss, the psychiatrist Ernst Kretschmer, and the mathematician Kurt Reidemeister. According to Hartshorne, the officer for the university, Bultmann's name had from the first been on the American "pre-occupation White List of Marburg"—"a theologian, a liberal, an active supporter of our policies and program."[30] The Americans named Ebbinghaus Acting Rector of the university after the first Rector, theologian Heinrich Frick, resigned his office for health reasons in September of 1945. As Bultmann commented on the situation, Ebbinghaus would now be able "to confirm the Platonic claim that things will go better for the state when the philosophers are kings."[31]

28. RB, "Hochschule," 142.

29. On what follows cf. A. Lippmann, *Marburger Theologie*, 426f; A. C. Nagel, "'Der Prototyp,'" 81f.

30. E. Y. Hartshorne to E. F. Hartshorne, 18. 1. 1946, in J. Tent, *Academic Proconcul*, 242.

31. RB, "Bericht über unser Ergehen in Marburg," in H. G. Göckeritz, *Bultmann-Gogarten Briefwechsel*, 312.

Unfortunately, just as Plato's attempt to exercise political influence in Syracuse had come to naught, Ebbinghaus' rectorate also foundered.

During the Third Reich, Julius Ebbinghaus had adopted Kant's moral philosophy and withdrawn from public life. In the summer of 1945 he won the trust of the Americans,[32] who hoped with his help to "purify" the university faculty.[33] In fact, a first wave of dismissals removed sixty lecturers, more than a third of the teaching personnel, though by exercising their right to protest, thirty-four of them soon gained reinstatement. Within the university, Ebbinghaus, Bultmann, Krauss, and Reidemeister, were among those who approved of a comprehensive denazification of the professorial ranks, but early on a majority of the Marburg faculty affected by the plan registered their opposition to it. They were led by members of the law faculty, who sought to employ legal briefs to exonerate the large number of their colleagues who had been so charged. Bultmann perceived conservative, nationalistic attitudes among those who either resisted or rejected the Americans' efforts at reform, and believed them to have mistakenly judged that "Hitler's politics were only the end of the road that had been taken with the politics of Bismarck."[34] Facing this strong opposition in December of 1945, Hartshorne wanted to pull back, if just for a while: "The reactionaries there are getting on my nerves."[35]

In January 1946, Hartshorne asked Ebbinghaus to dismiss Fritz von Hippel, the dean of the faculty of law and political science, since through his activity in providing expert opinions von Hippel was purposely hindering the purging of the faculty. Von Hippel promptly registered his protest, and the battle over the denazification of the University of Marburg soon aroused the whole city. The university senate voted Ebbinghaus, who favored a thorough ideological purification, out of office in July 1946, and in his place chose the archaeologist Friedrich Matz as the new rector. Bultmann looked "worriedly at the future" of the university—not so much on account of the new rector, whom he regarded as a person of integrity—as because of the unyielding ultra-conservative tendencies of the professoriat.[36] At this early point it had

32. Cf. Hartshorne's journal entries from 1. 5. 1945, in J. Tent, *Academic Proconcul*, 38f, 58f, 63, 66, 75, 77, 92.

33. Cf. Hartshorne's entry of 20. 7. 1945, in J. Tent, *Academic Proconcul*, 75–77.

34. RB, "Bericht über unser Ergehen in Marburg," in H. G. Göckeritz, *Bultmann-Gogarten Briefwechsel*, 313; cf. also UB Tübingen, RB est., RB to F. Bultmann, 20. 1. 1946, Mn 2-3418; ÖBU Basel, W. Baumgartner est., RB to W. Baumgartner, 22. 11. 1946 and 13. 7. 1947.

35. E. Y. Hartshorne to E. F. Hartshorne, 19. 12. 1945, in J. Tent, *Academic Proconcul*, 229.

36. RB to F. C. Sell, 21. 11. 1946, Mn 2-2380; cf. RB to G. Krüger, 19. 8. 1946, in F. Lilie, "Bultmann-Krüger Briefwechsel," *ZNThG* 6, 142.

already become apparent that the original American plans to remove all of the politically accused university lecturers from the Marburg faculty had foundered.

By way of contrast to this development, Bultmann experienced a certain relief following the establishment of procedures for a university senate, since he was now freed from the time-consuming work of the planning committee.[37] But in two instances he did remain involved beyond 1946 in the process of denazification. One concerned the modern historian Wilhelm Mommsen, one of the first Marburg professors to have been dismissed in November 1945. A report on Mommsen drawn up by Samson Benjamin Knoll, Chief Interrogator of the American military government in Marburg in the early summer of 1945, formed the basis of this action.[38] In addition to Mommsen himself, Knoll questioned ten witnesses and consulted three of the historian's publications from the time of the Third Reich. All those questioned gave extremely unflattering testimony regarding Mommsen and called for his expulsion from the university.[39] Most vehement on this point were Ebbinghaus and Reidemeister, who characterized the historian as the "prototype of the people who ought to be expelled."[40] In his report, Knoll also showed that the once liberal democrat had conformed to the ideas of the new rulers, both in his publications and also in his teaching. Knoll's conclusion was as unambiguous as it was unequivocal. Mommsen, the "dishonorable grandson of a renowned grandfather," was to be dismissed from service to the university on the basis of his role in National Socialism.[41]

37. Cf. RB to G. Krüger, 19. 8. 1946, in F. Lilie, "Bultmann-Krüger Briefwechsel," *ZNThG* 6, 142.

38. Cf. A. C. Nagel, "'Der Prototyp,'" 60–67; the presentation in P. Köpf, *Die Mommsens*, 236–63, 280–93 is problematic; see, in a critical vein, S. Rebenich, "Die Guten und die Bösen," 16.

39. Knoll questioned Bultmann, Ebbinghaus, Kretschmer, the sociologist Max Graf zu Solms, and Reidemeister, as well as from outside the university milieu the attorney Hans Natorp, the book dealer Otto Roppel, Mayor Eugen Siebecke, headmaster Kurt Steinmeyr, as well as an intentionally unnamed female student, who, like Bultmann and Natorp, lived in Mommsen's neighborhood.

40. Cited according to A. C. Nagel, "'Der Prototyp,'" 67.

41. A. C. Nagel, "'Der Prototyp,'" wonders why Knoll "came to the sort of dismissive judgment that he did." It may be remarked that there was not a single exonerating feature that might have qualified Knoll's grave assessment of Mommsen. One may in addition draw attention to the still little known biography of Knoll, cited by A. C. Nagel, "'Der Prototyp,'" 60n15. Samson B. Knoll, a Jew born in Galicia, studied history and German literature in Berlin from 1930–33 and was a student of Kurt Breysig's while there. Following the National Socialist seizure of power, he emigrated to the U.S. by way of Paris and London. Cf. W. Bernsdorff and M. Vialon, "Vom Um-Erzieher," 23f.

Bultmann was first questioned about Mommsen in April 1945 by Lieutenant Richard J. Eaton, who had been billeted in his house for several days, but as a neighbor to the historian he did not share any derogatory information.[42] At a later official interrogation by Knoll, Bultmann—who of course was not responsible for the way his statements were represented in the report—admitted that he saw in Mommsen's dealings during the Nazi rule an "absence of character without equal." Bultmann meant thereby to dismiss the political implications of the air-defense affair in which Mommsen had brought a legal proceeding against him, and insisted to Knoll that his criticism of Mommsen was not to be regarded as a denunciation. Still, he insisted, Mommsen was no longer to be considered a teacher of youth, especially since having formerly been a liberal democrat, he joined the National Socialist party, "and that at a time when the character of this party had to have been clear for a long time to a man like [Mommsen], especially as the atrocities of the persecution of Jews of 1938 had already occurred."[43] Bultmann saw Mommsen's opportunistic posture as determined by anxiety, but he focused his assessment primarily on the man's ideological promotion of the injustice of the National Socialist regime, and the fact that he accepted it with approval.[44]

In the denazification proceedings against Mommsen, Bultmann was but one prosecution witness among many, but he played a major role in the case of the social ethicist Georg Wünsch.[45] The former Religious Socialist and opponent of National Socialism had moved closer to "German Christian" positions after 1933 and, in his *Evangelische Ethik des Politischen* [*Protestant Political Ethics*], he had merged basic Christian ideas with central elements of the National Socialist worldview.[46] Following an initiative by Bultmann, the American military government called for the immediate dismissal of Wünsch from university service, but an investigative committee established by the city of Marburg and the university did not reach a clear result. Although

42. What follows is according to RB to W. Mommsen, 30. 12. 1948, Mn 2-2309, in UB Tübingen, RB est. This letter was occasioned by Mommsen's inquiry of Bultmann whether the statements of Bultmann's reproduced in Knoll's report of 1945 had in fact been made by him. Cf. W. Mommsen to RB, 29. 12. 1948, Mn 2-1417; on the facts of the matter, cf. A. C. Nagel, "'Der Prototyp,'" 84f.

43. UB Tübingen, RB est., RB to W. Mommsen, 30. 12. 1948, Mn 2-2309.

44. This in A. C. Nagel, "'Der Prototyp,'" 84, 91; see above, n. 1. On Mommsen's efforts after 1945 to have his dismissal annulled and to get back his professorship, cf. A. C. Nagel, "'Der Prototyp,'" 83–89.

45. On what follows cf. in detail A. Lippmann, *Marburger Theologie*, 427–35; M. Wolfes, "Wünsch, Georg," 130f.

46. Cf. G. Wünsch, *Evangelische Ethik*.

the university representatives judged Wünsch's publication as currying favor with the National Socialist Party and the theological faculty also criticized the statements that Bultmann had denounced, they found that his book as a whole was not determined by National Socialist thought. The legal scholar Fritz von Hippel, one of the most productive workers in the local "factory of fellow travelers,"[47] then supplied Wünsch with a legal brief supporting his exoneration. On the basis of von Hippel's summation, the university senate on April 30, 1947, acquitted the social ethicist of the charge of having supported National Socialism.

Bultmann was unable to consent to this verdict, and published his brief on Wünsch's *Protestant Political Ethics* in the form of a review. In his analysis he argued that Wünsch had sought to harmonize the ideology of National Socialism—including its constituent elements of the Führer principle, the totalitarian state, the relativizing of justice, race-based thought, and depriving the individual of his rights—with the idea of Christian love. In this way, Wünsch had equated the "religious worldview of National Socialism" with the Christian belief in creation, the belief specified in the first article of the Apostles' Creed.[48] To Bultmann, the social ethicist had thereby become unacceptable as a theological teacher.[49] Since the American military government sided not with the judgment of the senate but rather with Bultmann's position, Wünsch was not able to return to his position until 1950.[50]

Taken as a whole, the denazification of the universities in the American zone of occupation was anything but a success story. Under the existing circumstances, a rigorous denazification like that for which Bultmann and Ebbinghaus strove in Marburg was unable to gain a majority within the university. And Bultmann also represented the minority position within the

47. On this concept, cf. L. Niethammer, *Die Mitläuferfabrik.*

48. RB, rev. of G. Wünsch, *Evangelische Ethik*, in RB, *Theologie als Kritik*, 435. K. Löwith, *Mein Leben*, 74, made an assessment in 1940 of the book and the political position of Wünsch during the Nazi period that was similar to that of Bultmann later on.

49. F. von Hippel took a position on Bultmann's review (see n. 48) in "Nochmals," in RB, *Theologie als Kritik*, 517–19. Hippel referred to the outcome of the proceedings of the Senate against Wünsch and to the opinion of the senate that, in his report, Bultmann had torn citations out of context, and that behind the whole business there lay hidden a fundamental theological and personal antagonism between Bultmann and Wünsch. Von Hippel did not go into the substance of Bultmann's review. Cf. also Bultmann's reply to von Hippel's statements in RB, *Theologie als Kritik*, 519f.

50. For details, see A. Lippmann, *Marburger Theologie*, 429. Lippmann asks whether the Senate would also have come to the judgment it did, if it had given consideration to a sermon of Wünsch's from 1941, in which the one-time pacifist argued for the National Socialist war policy. Cf. on this sermon A. Lippmann, *Marburger Theologie*, 397–401.

theological faculty.[51] In the unhappy situation of being "completely isolated" in his own faculty throughout the last years of his teaching, he was helped by his experience "that as a loner, one can also be more significant to the students—or at least to the better of them—than can the rest."[52] Even if others were able to view the Third Reich as an accident of German history and quickly return to business as usual, Bultmann remained loyal to his conviction that a genuinely new beginning required the readiness of those involved to assume responsibility for what had happened.[53]

On June 30, 1956, the New Testament scholar Georg Bertram, who had taught at Giessen until 1945, called on Bultmann. Bertram, an early adherent of the form-critical method, had spread anti-Semitic hatred in his publications during the Third Reich. Now, of all things, he hoped for a professorship in Old Testament in Frankfurt. Would Bultmann be able to intercede on his behalf? To begin with, Bultmann found it incomprehensible that the Protestant Church in Hessen-Nassau had accepted Bertram as a pastor in 1945; now, due to his behavior in the period of National Socialism, Bultmann found himself "unable to regard him as qualified [to hold] a professorship in a theological faculty again." Bertram's objection that one must surely be able to forget after ten years only strengthened Bultmann in his posture of rejection.[54]

In the years just after the Second World War, Bultmann noticed "a widespread reactionary and nationalistic ethos" and a disinterest in politics among the Marburg student body, a spiritual fatigue[55]—in any case, not the independent thinking and questioning that had marked the generation following the First World War. The students, it seemed to him, were interested only in beginning a career as quickly as possible.[56] Nationalistically-minded students announced their presence loudly, as when Hans Asmussen spoke on humanism and the gospel in front of the Marburg student body in December of 1945. They applauded enthusiastically when Asmussen fiercely criticized the Allies. Bultmann, on the other hand, heard "an unbelievably superficial and primitive talk. It was real propaganda-talk in the Nazi style, meant to rally

51. Cf. E. Benz to W. Krauss, 30. 12. 1947 and 19. 5. 1948, P. Jehle, *Werner Krauss*, 400, 457f. Due to his decisive attitude on the denazification question, Ebbinghaus was even a target of several slander campaigns.

52. UB Tübingen, RB est., RB to E. Käsemann, 12. 3. 1954, Mn 2-2251.

53. Cf. similarly in the matter M. Dibelius, *Selbstbestimmung*, 34–48.

54. UB Tübingen, RB est., RB to A. Bultmann Lemke, 1. 7. 1956, Mn 2-3452.

55. UB Tübingen, RB est., RB to F. C. Sell, 11. 2. 1947, Mn 2-2380; cf. RB to G. Krüger, 21. 1. 1946, in F. Lilie, "Bultmann-Krüger Briefwechsel," *ZNThG* 6, 141.

56. UB Tübingen, RB est., RB to F. C. Sell, 16. 12. 1946, Mn 2-2380.

a church of Storm Troopers."[57] Bultmann considered the re-authorization of student fraternities and their traditional heraldic colors, originally banned in 1945, to be another example of an unhealthy policy of restoration. "July 20th was celebrated tastefully by the fraternities (in their colors) having a morning drinking party in the market place—at the invitation of the city!"[58] What Bultmann's friend, Erich Frank, who had emigrated to the United States, got to hear from postwar Germany made it difficult for him even to think about paying a visit to the country.[59] When the Marburg philosophical faculty under the deanship of Kurt Reidemeister resolved to re-extend to Erich Auerbach the offer of the Professorship of Romance languages that had become vacant by the departure of Werner Krauss to Leipzig, Bultmann warned Auerbach, who had been teaching in the U.S. in the meantime, not to return to Marburg. On the one hand, he felt that for "Marburg (and especially for our circle of friends)" it would certainly be desirable if Auerbach received and accepted the offer. On the other, Bultmann felt obligated to advise Auerbach to remain in the U.S. because the atmosphere at the university in Marburg was, as the denazification procedures had shown all too clearly, a "most unpleasant" one.[60] The attitudes and events that Bultmann had experienced since 1945, as well as the complex of occurrences that had led to "the new starting point" evidently called for serious reflection on how the future life of the nation and society was to take shape, and in what direction it was to move.

57. RB to G. Krüger, 16. 12. 1945, in F. Lilie, "Bultmann-Krüger Briefwechsel," *ZNThG* 6, 140; cf. RB to E. Käsemann, 16. 12. 1945, Mn 2-2251, and RB to F. Bultmann, 20. 1. 1946, Mn 2-3418, in UB Tübingen, RB est. As a consequence of the incidents attending Asmussen's lecture, the Rector withdrew the right of the student body to hold lectures in university buildings. Cf. A. Lippmann, *Marburger Theologie*, 458.

58. UB Tübingen, RB est., RB to F. C. Sell, 3. 8. 1952, Mn 2-2380.

59. Cf. UB Tübingen, RB est., E. Frank to RB, 28. 7. 1947, Mn 2-760. Frank was fearful of being exposed to resentments in Germany against Jewish emigres; cf. F. C. Sell to RB, 15. 1. 1947, Mn 2-1816. Yet in 1949, Frank decided to come to Germany, chiefly in order to visit Bultmann and his own teacher K. Jaspers. Cf. E. Frank to H. Bultmann, 29. 5. and 7. 6. 1949, Mn 2-2821. When, after crossing the sea, he stepped onto European soil in Rotterdam for the first time in eleven years, he suffered a heart attack (17. 6. 1949). Cf. H.-G. Gadamer, rev. of E. Frank, *Philosophical Understanding*, 260. Cf. DLA Marbach, RB to K. Jaspers, 2. 7. 1949, 4: "In the same fashion—I think—do we find ourselves shaken by the sudden death of our mutual friend Erich Frank. Only a few days ago, we (my wife and I, that is) received yet another letter full of joy over a reunion. And what we had expected from this reunion and from the exchange it would bring! I have known few persons of the same nobility of soul and goodness of heart. . . . Like me, aside from the personal loss, you will lament that of substance, as well."

60. DLA Marbach, RB to E. Auerbach, 18. 6. 1948; as well as M. Vialon, "Erich Auerbach und Rudolf Bultmann," 183–87.

2. Contributions to the Reorientation of Culture

> *. . . [N]either the Protestant nor the Catholic Church will prove to be a cultural force. I have no other advice than to retrieve what binds Christianity in a tension-filled unity with humanism; and, going from there, Karl Jaspers' challenge of tackling the problems of modern technological life as well in a philosophical fashion seems to me a valid one (*The Idea of the University*), even if I don't yet see how this is actually going to happen.*[61]

Two new publications in 1946 seemed worth noting: Friedrich Meinecke's *Die deutsche Katastrophe* [*The German Catastrophe*] and Alfred Weber's *Abschied von der bisherigen Geschichte* [*Farewell to Previous History*]. Bultmann was well aware that the Dean of German historiography and the Heidelberg scholar of culture and society, respectively, were presenting what amounted to totally different diagnoses of recent German history, but it seemed to him more important that the two books agreed in exposing the disastrous alliance of culture and power in the nineteenth century and in their criticism of the concept of the power-state as reflected in Bismarck and Prussian militarism. In this regard, Bultmann found nothing novel in Meinecke's explanation of National Socialism in terms of the history of political ideas, but he hoped that Meinecke's book would contribute to self-criticism among the cultured German upper-middle class, especially the group that shared a Prussian and nationalistic orientation. Of greater substantive interest to him was Weber's far-reaching analysis of Western history. Weber's exposition of nihilism as the ultimate and decisive presupposition of National Socialism together with his challenge to achieve a new relation to 'transcendence' might seem theologically vague; all the same, Bultmann found his interpretation of the German catastrophe in the context of a modern Europe defined by the discoveries of natural science and technological innovations to possess a high degree of plausibility.[62]

61. UB Tübingen, RB est., RB to F. C. Sell, 16. 12. 1946, Mn 2-2380.

62. Cf. UB Tübingen, RB est., RB to F. C. Sell, 11. 2. 1947, Mn 2-2380; as well as RB to G. Krüger, 26. 1. 1947, in F. Lilie, "Bultmann-Krüger Briefwechsel," *ZNThG* 6, 143f. Cf. F. Meinecke, *Die deutsche Katastrophe*; A. Weber, *Abschied*. In his correspondence of the years 1945–47, Bultmann mentions further Anna Seghers' successful novel, *Das siebte Kreuz* [*The Seventh Cross*], which presented a vivid picture of the National Socialists' mechanisms of suppression and persecution. Cf. UB Tübingen, RB est., RB to F. C. Sell, 24. 4. 1947, Mn 2-2380. Despite differences on particular points, Bultmann declared himself "on the whole in complete agreement" with K. Barth's "Voice of a Swiss." Without holding himself out as an expert on the subject, he did, however, think that Barth's understanding of Luther was all too

Combining individual details of the historical process that had led to National Socialism into a concise model of explanation was not Bultmann's thing. He left it to those whose profession gave them the competencies to develop historiographical theories for the multi-layered genesis of the Third Reich. Nor did he follow the lead of Karl Jaspers and occupy himself during the postwar period as a political writer. Finally, unlike his Heidelberg New Testament colleague Martin Dibelius, Bultmann drew up no memorandum adopting explicit positions on the question of guilt following 1945 and the political reordering of Germany.[63] In contrast to these, he gave lectures on the pressing problems of the postwar period, and for him these all came back to the single key question of the spiritual sources from which both individual and social life might be able to create new strength and direction following the catastrophe of the Third Reich. Bultmann published his lectures not in theological journals, but rather in literary periodicals devoted to the task of contributing to a new spiritual orientation, periodicals without disciplinary boundaries, such as *Merkur* [*Mercury*], *Studium generale* [*General Studies*], *Universitas* [*University*], or *Die Wandlung* [*The Metamorphosis*].[64]

The first volume of the monthly *Die Wandlung*, edited by Dolf Sternberger with the assistance of Karl Jaspers, Werner Krauss, and Alfred Weber, appeared in November of 1945. Bultmann entitled his contribution to this volume, "Adam, Where Are You?" This was the summons by which, according to the biblical myth of the fall, God called the first human being out of hiding (Gen 3:9). Thus Bultmann was asking where amidst the ruins of the present one might find the individual to whom the call of God pertains, and how to describe him. The Old Testament and Greek mythology regard "all people in their humanness—and that means in relation to the transcendent God"—in their frailty and creatureliness *as equal*.[65] But while Greek thought considers the individual to be part of cosmic nature, the biblical tradition conceives history to be the reality in which the human being encounters God. If Hellenism pictures the rationally constructed polis as the paradigmatic form of human community, for the Bible it is the people of God, the community created by God alone, that offers the ideal picture of communal life. To be sure, the "tragedy of the history of Israel and of

greatly colored "by the picture of the epigones of Lutheranism" (RB to G. Harbsmeier, 25. 11. 1945, Mn 2-2232). Bultmann also distanced himself from Barth's study, *Rechtfertigung und Recht*. Cf. RB to G. Krüger, 16. 12. 1945, in F. Lilie, "Bultmann-Krüger Briefwechsel," *ZNThG* 6, 140. Cf. K. Barth, *Eine Schweizer Stimme 1938–1945*.

63. Cf. M. Dibelius, *Selbstbesinnung*; as well as S. Geiser, *Verantwortung*, 225–76.

64. Cf. H. U. Gumbrecht, "Zorn."

65. RB, "Adam, wo bist du?" *GuV* (5th ed.), vol. 2, 108.

Judaism" consists in the fact that equating the people of God with the concrete people existing in history was bound to founder on its internal contradiction.[66] In thinking through the Christ-occurrence, the New Testament had separated the relation to God "from belonging to a particular, historical people."[67] The founding document of Christianity proclaims that all the differences among human beings in the visible world are fundamentally done away with in Christ. Therefore, the New Testament does not propagate an illusory program of political or social leveling, but calls all existing inequalities into question. Above all, faith makes it possible to discern despite those inequalities "the ultimate inner equality" that has its irreversible foundation in defining the individual in terms of the *imago Dei*,[68] and hence this radical equality can never be relativized by falsely alleging the original inequality of persons, races and peoples. This is how the summons, "Adam, where are you?" pertains to the human being as God intends him.

National Socialism had exploited for its own interests the existentially and inherently valuable individual. The danger in such a program is that "the human being will increasingly be abused as a means to ends . . . and thereby be deceived as to the meaning of his life." And this danger has not been exorcised by the elimination of National Socialism, for it still threatens humanity as a permanent side effect "of a world that is increasingly technologized and organized down to the last detail."[69] For this reason, Bultmann declares in 1948 that it is the common task of humanism and of Christian faith to join forces against the systematic erosion of consciousness of oneself as a person. He comes out against the widespread misunderstanding in church circles that humanism, with its belief in the absolute autonomy of the human being, first gave birth to modern relativism and nihilism. In fact, rooted as it is in Greek antiquity, genuine humanism struggles against the arbitrariness of subjectivism by binding the individual to the pervasive law of the cosmos and thereby to the law-giving divine power as well.[70]

But Bultmann also underscores the differences between humanism, which as a spiritual attitude makes "*the world into a home for human beings*," and Christianity, for whose dialectical relation to the world is expressed in 1 Cor 7:29–31, "*the world is* [intrinsically] *a foreign place*,"[71] by means of a systematic comparison of the humanistic ideas of the true, the good, and the

66. RB, "Adam, wo bist du?" *GuV* (5th ed.), vol. 2, 111.
67. RB, "Adam, wo bist du?" *GuV* (5th ed.), vol. 2, 114.
68. RB, "Adam, wo bist du?" *GuV* (5th ed.), vol. 2, 116.
69. RB, "Humanismus und Christentum," *GuV* (5th ed.), vol. 2, 147.
70. Cf. RB, "Humanismus und Christentum," *GuV* (5th ed.), vol. 2, 145f.
71. RB, "Humanismus und Christentum," *GuV* (5th ed.), vol. 2, 134f.

beautiful with the Christian understanding of these ideas. He sees the decisive difference in the fact that the humanist endeavors to realize the truth of his life by his own actions, whereas the person of faith allows himself to accept this truth ever anew through the justifying word of God's forgiveness of him, the sinner.[72] But one may not totally separate humanism and Christian faith on the basis of this continuing contrast. Even if the two frameworks of existence do not ultimately require each other, it is nevertheless an indelible inheritance of Western history that they have formed a fruitful relation, with each enriching and critically delimiting the other. If Christianity might rightfully have emphasized its distance from humanism in earlier periods, Bultmann regards it a present necessity for Christian faith and humanism to struggle together against a false understanding of human autonomy and to speak out for the indestructible dignity of the human person.[73]

How can Christianity and humanism best give expression to their elective affinities? In the face of the catastrophe that has descended upon Western culture, they need first and foremost to discover anew the highest good of their common tradition, the idea of freedom, to analyze how it has gone wrong in modernity, and to show to the fullest advantage its genuine content by contrasting it to the present political and social dangers it faces. Towards the end of the 1940s, Bultmann is not primarily concerned with countering certain tendencies within the church, but he does this as well by contrasting Christian freedom to all forms of clericalism, to the newly emerging ecclesiastical bureaucracy, and to an understanding of Christian teaching as a rigid, "orthodox" system dominated by the traditional confessions.[74] Moreover, the call to reinvigorate the idea of freedom is intended not for the church alone, but is meant to include the self-understanding of Western culture for the sake of its meaning and future.

The concept of spiritual freedom, an inheritance from Greek antiquity that Christianity transformed and an idea whose internal quality of restraint

72. Cf. RB, "Humanismus und Christentum," *GuV* (5th ed.), vol. 2, 135–41.

73. Cf. RB, "Humanismus und Christentum," *GuV* (5th ed.), vol. 2, 142–45. I cannot here discuss in detail the relation of Bultmann's concept of humanism to M. Heidegger's "Letter on Humanism," published in 1947. Cf. M. Heidegger, *Brief über den 'Humanismus'*; as well as G. Krüger, "Martin Heidegger und der Humanismus." Bultmann represented a singular position in the contemporary theological discussion of how to specify the relation of humanism and Christianity. To simplify somewhat, one might say he pursued a middle way between Roman Catholic conceptions, which conceived Christianity as an ideal-typical elevating of humanism to a new level, and the model favored in the Protestant realm, especially among representatives of the theology of the word of God, according to which humanism was to be negated on the basis of the self-revelation of God as the allegedly self-assertive expression of human religion.

74. Cf. RB, "Für die christliche Freiheit."

was thought by Bultmann to have been lost since the nineteenth century, faces a serious new danger today. Now, in the early period of the Federal Republic, Germany is engaged in political, economic, and social developments that threaten the idea of freedom. In general, people are endeavoring to fashion patterns of life that will make the state into a bearer of culture and prosperity, to regulate economic life, and to view culture itself as something to be created.[75] To be sure, organization can never by itself prepare the way for freedom. The individual has to seek this out for himself. He will find it if he provides a place for that which transcends the useful and usable in human life, for the freedom of celebration, the leisure of play, and for self-consciousness and reflection on history in order to gain freedom from the past and in the present. Experiences such as these, and not least religious awareness of the connection between freedom and faith in God the creator, may lead the individual into solitariness. He will also experience freedom in the risk of becoming what God has made him.[76]

In the years following the War, controversial public discussions arose in both ecclesiastical and political spheres over the question of whether state-sponsored schools should teach religion along confessional lines. In this context, Bultmann had the opportunity to develop ideas on putting his humanistic ideal of education into practice in the area of religious instruction. In Oldenburg, Edo Osterloh, the current chairman of the Church Council for School Affairs and a student of Bultmann's, in 1947 presented a policy aimed at giving churches the responsibility for teaching about Christianity in the schools. Osterloh did not want to reintroduce the religious supervision of schools that had been unofficially terminated in 1919, but his plan more or less corresponded to the program of Protestant [church] instruction that Helmuth Kittel had also developed in 1947.[77] While Osterloh's draft elicited violent opposition, it also received the lively approval of the teachers of Oldenburg.[78] In the spring of 1948, Bultmann was asked to take part in the discussion as a kind of expert on the subject.[79]

75. Cf. RB, "Die Bedeutung des Gedankens der Freiheit," *GuV* (5th ed.), vol. 3, 283–87. Bultmann delivered this lecture in Göttingen on 12. 7. 1950. Cf. RB, *Chronik 1946–1961*, Mn 2-225, sheet 11.

76. Cf. RB, "Die Bedeutung des Gedankens der Freiheit," *GuV* (5th ed.), vol. 3, 286–93.

77. Cf. H. Kittel, *Vom Religionsunterricht.*

78. On the particulars, cf. G. Eberhard, *Existentiale Theologie*, 123–26; R. Rittner, "Die evangelische Kirche," 763–67; P. Zocher, *Edo Osterloh*, 177–85.

79. It has to remain an open question whether E. Osterloh or another participant in the discussion sought out Bultmann to take a position on the issues. Cf. P. Zocher, *Edo Osterloh*, 185n250.

Bultmann's remarks on Osterloh's draft, and on two further proposals in the Oldenburg controversy of May 7, 1948, focus on three subject areas: the kind of religious instruction, the definition of the idea of education, and the importance of making religious instruction transparent.[80] First, Bultmann distinguishes between the church of faith and its institutional form. The church as it is presently constituted ought not to be the subject of instruction in religion in the schools, because any appearance of clericalism should be avoided. Instead, the church of faith, which is the proper subject of religious instruction, should become present in the school in the figure of the teacher of religion. In any case, the school must not abrogate the right of the church to have high expectations and a degree of responsibility for instruction in religion.[81]

For this purpose, a concept of education is needed in order to define the task of religious instruction in schools. Bultmann agrees with Osterloh that forming the character of students is a central concern of schools, and must therefore serve a basic educational purpose. For Bultmann, this must be the humanistic idea of the formation of the whole person, which today can be understood only with an eye to the challenge of technology.[82] Humanistic formation requires more than the communication of certain teachings, for it must be modeled on "the Platonic way of philosophizing."[83] In order to teach religion in school, knowledge of the Christian religion is indispensable to an understanding of Western history and literature. What is more, the existential questions that humanistic instruction arouses are the same ones that motivate the Christian religion. On the basis of these premises, Bultmann assigns to instruction in religion the maieutic task of bringing forth "the spirit and, therewith, the existential questioning of students."[84] But religious instruction does not mean directly proclaiming the gospel. Bultmann argues against such an ecclesiastical conception of instruction on the basis of pedagogical considerations and the theological axiom that the reality of God cannot be disclosed through any human effort, and therefore not through

80. Bultmann's text, not published in 1948, is reprinted in G. Eberhard, *Existentiale Theologie*, 332–36; H. Stock, "Ein religionspädagogischer Nachtrag," 166–71.

81. H. Stock, "Ein religionspädagogischer Nachtrag," 172, points to the fact that, at the time when Bultmann assigned instruction in religion to the school, the basic law of the Federal Republic of Germany, with its Article 7, Section 3, did not yet exist.

82. Cf. RB, "Einige Bemerkungen," in G. Eberhard, *Existentiale Theologie*, 333; H. Stock, "Ein religionspädagogischer Nachtrag," 168, with reference to K. Jaspers, *Die Idee der Universität*. See above n. 61.

83. RB, "Einige Bemerkungen," in G. Eberhard, *Existentiale Theologie*, 333.

84. RB, "Einige Bemerkungen," in G. Eberhard, *Existentiale Theologie*, 334; H. Stock, "Ein religionspädagogischer Nachtrag," 169.

Christian instruction. Bultmann's expert counsel in the Oldenburg debate on religious instruction had little effect,[85] but his text can be seen as an early attempt to formulate the conceptual foundations of a hermeneutical approach to religious instruction.[86] Incidentally, this humanistic ideal of formation that Bultmann presented in his proposal of 1948 was one he adhered to for the rest of his life.[87]

The various thematic strands in Bultmann's contributions to the postwar reorientation of culture came together in his reflections on a new relationship between the German people and Israel, an article published in *Merkur* for 1952. In this essay, Bultmann took up a discussion to which Leo Baeck had issued an invitation seven years after his liberation from [the concentration camp] Theresienstadt.[88] Agreeing with the Jewish theologian, Bultmann viewed the radical self-assessment of Jews and Germans as a necessary beginning for a genuine peace between the two peoples. Also necessary would be insight into the true nature of the human being, the nation, and the state, perceptions that had been grossly distorted by National Socialism. Bultmann again put forth his oft-repeated view that National Socialism represented the conclusion of a development that had begun in the nineteenth century. Its distinguishing marks, he reiterated, were the abandoning of the understanding of the human being as person and of the world as a divine ordinance, the illusion of being able to extend human rule even over destiny and history, and the exploitation of human beings for political and economic purposes—a dehumanization effected by the totalitarian power-state under the guise of utilitarianism.[89] Given this context, Bultmann posed the question whether one element of Judaism might not be partly responsible for these destructive developments—namely, those Jews who may not have represented "a true and pure Judaism."[90] To be sure, he stressed the incomparably greater guilt

85. Cf. P. Zocher, *Edo Osterloh*, 188.

86. Thus, H. Stock, "Ein religionspädagogischer Nachtrag," 174. It is not by chance that M. Stallmann and H. Stock, the two main representatives of hermeneutical pedagogy in religion, were students of Bultmann's.

87. Cf. RB, "Ist humanistische Bildung zeitgemäss?" RB, "Erziehung und christlicher Glaube," *GuV* (3d ed.), vol. 4, 52–55; RB, "Ein Wort über Bildung," 4–6.

88. Cf. L. Baeck, "Israel und das deutsche Volk," 50–61; on what follows cf. also K. Hammann, "Rudolf Bultmanns Begegnung," 35–38.

89. The criticism of modernity that Bultmann had earlier voiced during the Third Reich was a variant based on the theology of creation of M. Heidegger's criticism, likewise developed during the Third Reich and published after 1945, of the modern era and its tendency to total power over the world and the instrumentalizing of the human being through technology, science, and organization. Cf. M. Heidegger, "Die Zeit des Weltbildes," 75–96; as well as K. Hammann, "Rudolf Bultmanns Begegnung," 38n15.

90. RB, "Das deutsche Volk und Israel," *GuV* (1st ed.), vol. 3, 57.

of the Germans towards Judaism, a factor that Bultmann thought was inadequately represented by the concept of collective guilt. For the theological understanding of "guilt" involves guilt before God, which can apply only to individual people. Still, among the critics of the concept of collective guilt, Bultmann was one of the few who spoke of a collective responsibility of the German people towards Judaism. "There certainly is a collective responsibility, however, in which the innocent takes upon himself the guilt of the guilty. Whoever is a German is liable for what was done to the Jews in the name of Germany, even if he was not personally involved in it."[91]

In his answer to Leo Baeck, Bultmann adduced as a further source of guilt Germany's having disowned the Old Testament-Jewish tradition. He had in 1949 taken up this subject in two lectures presented in Bremen and Munich. In this regard, he stressed the significance of the Old Testament for the Jewish-Christian understanding of history and for insight into the historicity of human existence. To these closely related ideas he added the concept that the individual's personhood is grounded in its relation to God and the total acceptance in the Jewish-Christian tradition of God's transcendence.[92] At the same time, he maintained the qualitative priority of the Christ-occurrence compared to Old Testament-Jewish history as regards fulfillment and prophecy.

In the interpretations of the relation between the Old and New Testament that he presented in several places in 1949, Bultmann responded critically to a thesis that Johann Christian Konrad had developed from the Hegelian philosophy of history. In it Konrad proposed that Christ, as the goal of the history of Israel prophesied in the Old Testament, is the culmination of the history of salvation.[93] In contrast to this Bultmann emphasizes the eschatological character of the Christ-occurrence, to which Old Testament-Jewish history as a whole serves as prophecy. To be sure, it is only by virtue of its New Testament fulfillment that this history can be seen as promise, and then only "*in its internal contradiction, in its foundering.*"[94] This contradiction derives from Israel's understanding of itself as God's chosen people. To be sure, Israel's self-understanding is based on the transcendent God, but it sees God's activity as depicted in the empirical history of its own people. And

91. RB, "Das deutsche Volk und Israel," *GuV* (1st ed.), vol. 3, 58. On the contemporary discussion, cf. K. Jaspers, *Die Schuldfrage*; M. Dibelius, *Selbstbesinnung*, 34–48; M. Greschat, *Die Schuld der Kirche*.

92. Cf. RB, "Das Christentum als orientalische," *GuV* (5th ed.), vol. 2, 187–210; RB, "Die Bedeutung der altestamentlich-jüdischen Tradition," *GuV* (5th ed.), vol. 2, 236–45.

93. Cf. RB, "Weissagung und Erfüllung," *GuV* (5th ed.), vol. 2, 168–71.

94. RB, "Weissagung und Erfüllung," *GuV* (5th ed.), vol. 2, 183.

by doing so, it misunderstands the radically eschatological meaning of the activity of God. Nor can the central Old Testament ideas of the covenant, the kingship of God, and the people of God be realized inwardly, for until its New Testament fulfillment, this history of a *tragic* foundering[95] can be seen only as promise. Bultmann defines the relation between Old and New Testament in the framework of the Pauline distinction of law and gospel. Only that person who comprehends the law as a false path that leads to foundering can recognize faith as an exclusive path to salvation that is opened up solely through the gospel. "Just as faith, in order to be truly justifying faith, must contain within itself the permanent overcoming of the law, so too, in order to be eschatological, a way of living must overcome all attempts to permanently identify a worldly occurrence with an eschatological one."[96]

The theological work that Bultmann pursued in the postwar years in trying to reorient culture following the collapse of the Third Reich, could not remain an undertaking for individuals. In order to establish a dialogue among theological scholars as well as between those academics and the theologians engaged with the churches or schools, Bultmann had been planning since the autumn of 1946 to return the *Theologische Rundschau* to publication. On January 1, 1944, the Association of National Literature had ordered the merging of the periodical with *Deutsche Theologie* [*German Theology*], but only one volume could be published that year. In October of 1946, while attending a meeting of the Gesellschaft für evangelische Theologie [Society for Protestant Theology] in Bad Boll, Bultmann presented his plans for the *Theologische Rundschau* to Madame Hoffet, the French military government censor for Protestant theological publications.[97] The project faced serious difficulties due to lack of paper[98] and a long delay in obtaining authorization for scholarly publications from the censor's office in Baden-Baden.[99] To expedite the journal's publication, Bultmann pointed out to Madame Hoffet that the periodical had made no concessions of any kind to officials of the Third Reich, and that unknown to the Nazi censors it had published numerous contributions by Jewish authors and articles that disagreed with National Socialist views.[100] Bultmann's goal was for the *Theologische Rundschau* to assume an important role in reestablishing the international scholarly exchange

95. RB, "Adam, wo bist du?" *GuV* (5th ed.), vol. 2, 111.
96. RB, "Weissagung und Erfüllung," *GuV* (5th ed.), vol. 2, 186.
97. Cf. UB Tübingen, RB est., RB to F. C. Sell, 21. 11. 1946, Mn 2-2380.
98. Cf. UB Tübingen, RB est., RB to F. C. Sell, 16. 12. 1946, Mn 2-2380.
99. Cf. also F. W. Graf, "Nachwort des Herausgebers," in M. Dibelius, *Selbstbesinnung*, 83–88.
100. Cf. UB Tübingen, RB est., RB to Mme. Hoffet, 2. 12. 1946, Mn 2-2127.

that had been almost completely suppressed during the Third Reich.[101] And, as he had hoped, when the periodical reappeared in 1948 several foreign scholars were among the first contributors.[102]

Another enterprise that Bultmann followed from its start was the initiative of Gerhard Ebeling and Hanns Rückert to found a new journal for historical theology. This was especially interesting to him inasmuch as Ebeling and Rückert had spoken up decisively for the historical method in theology during the quarrel that had erupted at the end of the 1940s over Bultmann's program of demythologizing.[103] In 1950, in the first issue of this new journal that purposely carried the name of an earlier publication, *Zeitschrift für Theologie und Kirche* [*Journal for Theology and Church*], readers came upon two contributions that in somewhat different ways outlined the agenda to which the editors and collaborators of the journal had committed themselves: Gerhard Ebeling's definitive essay, "The Significance of the Historical-Critical Method for Protestant Theology and Church," and Rudolf Bultmann's equally foundational study, "The Problem of Hermeneutics."[104]

Critically expanding on the contributions of Friedrich Schleiermacher and Wilhelm Dilthey to a theory of the art of interpretation, Bultmann in this latter essay unfolds the hermeneutical implications of the existentialist interpretation of biblical texts. The interpretative analysis "*of the biblical writings is subject to no other conditions of understanding than those that apply to any other literature.*"[105] The imperative presupposition for any real understanding is the life-relation of the interpreter to the subject matter expressed in the text.[106] And from the fact that the text and the interpreter are thus bound together, there follows a definite pre-understanding of the subject matter at issue. Yet from the subject matter's inherent interest and the interpreter's

101. Cf. RB, Preface, *ThR*.

102. Among others, Walter Baumgartner (Basel), Aage Bentzen (Hellerup), Kendrick Grobel (Vanderbilt), Paul Kahle (Wadhurst/Sussex), Friedrich C. Sell (Wellesley).

103. Cf. J. Wallmann, "Die Wiedergründung," 506f, 508f.

104. Bultmann had presented a lecture with the same title and underlying theme as this essay on 6. 8. 1948 in Hermannsburg bei Celle before a working group of teachers of religious pedagogy, on 23. 2. 1949 in Göttingen at the invitation of the department of theology, and during the first meeting of the "old Marburgers" following the Second World War. This gathering took place 10.–14. 10. 1949 in Herborn.

105. RB, "Das Problem der Hermeneutik," *GuV* (5th ed.), vol. 2, 231; on what follows, cf. also J. Grondin, "Gadamer und Bultmann."

106. RB, "Das Problem der Hermeneutik," *GuV* (5th ed.), vol. 2, 221f, thus represented, along with Schleiermacher and Dilthey, the view that works of poetry and art could of course also disclose possibilities for existence to the interpreter.

Plate 35: Meeting of the "Old Marburgers," October 10–14, 1949 in Herborn. Displayed, from left to right: Front row, seated: Erna Schlier, Helene Bultmann, Rudolf Bultmann, Irmgard Feussner, Hildegard Urner-Astholz. Second and third row: Hermann Diem, Götz Harbsmier, Werner Kohleick, Hans-George Gadamer, Ulrich Henn, Gerhard Ebeling, Ernst Käsemann, Marie Veit, Hanna Grothmann, Ilse Buschfranz, Walter Kohlschmidt, Gerhard Krüger, Karl Linke, Doris Faulhaber, Günther Bornkamm, Friedrich Luncke, Ernst Fuchs, Ulrich Finckh, Walter Klaas. Fourth and fifth row, standing: Ruth Comann, Thomas Dell, Herta Fromme, Herbert Schneider, Philipp Vielhauer, Alfred Habermann, Margarete Dell, Werner Flentje, Else Köppe, August Dell, Martin Stallman

pre-understanding grows an interpretive problem that can be taken in any direction whatever. Bultmann contends that in the case of poetic, philosophical, and religious texts, the appropriate hermeneutical principle is "*the question of human existence, as that of one's own existence.*"[107] For understanding is inherent in human existence.

It follows from this that the interpretation of biblical texts presupposes a pre-understanding of what "can in a general sense be described as what God does"[108] as opposed to what human beings do. In Bultmann's view the individual person's questions about chance, salvation, the meaning of events,

107. RB, "Das Problem der Hermeneutik," *GuV* (5th ed.), vol. 2, 228.
108. RB, "Das Problem der Hermeneutik," *GuV* (5th ed.), vol. 2, 231.

and the authenticity of his existence, always express an existential knowledge of God. In the case of the New Testament, of course, the question of understanding must include the readiness to correct one's pre-understanding of the subject matter while in the act of listening to the text. What is essential in the critical interpretation of biblical writings is the appropriate construction of the question directed to the text at issue—that is, it must be a question directed at the human understanding of existence. For the person who is moved by the question of God asks about nothing other than "about the truth of human existence."[109]

3. Primitive Christianity in its Contemporary Setting [Das Urchristentum im Rahmen der antiken Religionen]

> *If it is a concrete and pressing problem for theology today to specify the Christian understanding of existence in its relation to that of idealism, and to find the right concepts with which to make the Christian understanding of existence explicit, it is also an urgent task to investigate our traditional conceptuality's origin in antiquity and to make clear the understanding of existence that it implies.*[110]

In 1949, Bultmann published his first postwar book, *Primitive Christianity in its Contemporary Setting* (hereafter, *Primitive Christianity*), in the Erasmus-Bibliothek of the Artemis-Verlag press of Zurich, which was under the care of Walter Rüegg. Bultmann had become acquainted with the Swiss sociologist during the Marburg university discussions in 1946–47. Rüegg's discussions with Bultmann centered on the question of what role the humanistic tradition of antiquity might play in the process of cultural reorientation following the catastrophe of National Socialism. Out of this dialogue emerged the plan for the Erasmus-Bibliotek to publish the lecture that Bultmann had last given in the summer semester of 1947, *Das Urchristentum im Zusammenhang der antiken Religionen* [*Earliest Christianity in its Connection with the Religions of Antiquity*].[111] Bultmann's work, "a showpiece in the comparative study of religion,"[112] characteristically began by presenting the earliest historical

109. RB, "Das Problem der Hermeneutik," *GuV* (5th ed.), vol. 2, 233.

110. RB, rev. of W. Jaeger, *Die geistige Gegenwart der Antike*, in RB, *Theologie als Kritik*, 243.

111. Cf. UB Tübingen, RB est., W. Rüegg to RB, 18. 1. 1947; 19. 10. 1947; 12. 3. 1948, Mn 2-1661. Indeed, Bultmann had already expressed the wish in 1940 to publish this lecture as a book at some point. Cf. RB to G. Bornkamm, 28. 3. 1940, Mn 2-2147.

112. G. Klein, "Rudolf Bultmann," 188.

material on Christianity then available. In order to present a profile of earliest Christianity drawn from its complex historical interweaving with the religions and worldviews of antiquity, Bultmann employed the history of religions perspective with the intention of making these historical religious realities accessible to an existentialist interpretation. In doing so, any "apologetic purpose was far from his mind." Nor did he wish to present Christianity along the lines of the Hegelian philosophy of history—for instance, "as the crowning achievement of the ancient history of religion"—nor did he pursue the goal of demonstrating the truth of Christianity by analyzing the reasons for its success in world history. But he certainly did set himself the task of presenting "the phenomena of past history . . . as also possibilities for an understanding of existence in the present." Here his interest was especially focused on whether and to what extent earliest Christianity developed a "new possibility for human beings to understand existence."[113]

At the time his book on earliest Christianity appeared in the spring of 1949, Bultmann was staying with his cousin, Fritz Bultmann, in Ganderkese. When he left, he wrote in his cousin's guest book a poem that expresses the concept of existence that Bultmann regarded as distinctive of earliest Christianity.[114]

We are born on time's relentless stream,
Our present passes ever on.
And so is all but a fading dream?
And we, with it, forlorn?

Take heart, for in this flow of time
Our freedom from ourselves we win,
And in what comes we e'er shall find
Ourselves renewed again, again.

Thus says the Word, and if you're open
And ready for what may come or be,
In faith and love you may find hope,
And find in time eternity.

In the Introduction to his disquisition on earliest Christianity, Bultmann emphasizes that he is not attempting to provide a contribution to the kind of historical research that is merely a reconstruction of the events of religious

113. RB, *Das Urchristentum*, 7f.

114. Entry by RB in the guestbook of F. Bultmann, Ganderkese, 3.–7. 3. 1949, in R. Rittner, *Rudolf Bultmann und Oldenburg*, 16.

history. His interpretation of the understanding of existence found in ancient religions does, however, presuppose such research,[115] and the picture of earliest Christianity that he drew in his 1949 book is to be understood with reference to the specific points he made in the course of both adopting and initiating elements of this research in the field of earliest Christian history.

In the decades around the turn of the twentieth century, research in this field had reached a zenith marked by the several and varied works of Carl Weizsäcker, Otto Pfleiderer, Rudolf Knopf, and Johannes Weiss. The classic document of that heyday of reconstruction was Carl Weizsäcker's *Das apostolische Zeitalter der urchristlichen Kirche* [*The Apostolic Age of the Christian Church*].[116] Bultmann regarded this survey, in which Weizsäcker modified the understanding of earliest Christianity developed by his teacher Ferdinand Christian Baur, as a prime example of historical-critical analysis of the New Testament.[117] In his lexicographic article, "Urgemeinde" ["Earliest Community"] of 1913, Bultmann had remained largely within the framework of the Baur-Weizsäcker view of history, although even then he strongly emphasized the eschatological mood of the earliest community. To be sure, the ethical spirit of the earliest community was closely tied to its eschatological stance—as shown by its conflicted attitude toward the law—and thus remained curiously ambivalent. "It saw itself as the true Israel, and it was a Jewish sect" is how Bultmann put it.[118] "Since the gentile church does not represent the organic continuation of the earliest community," that history is broken off. And thereupon Bultmann brought into play Ferdinand Christian Baur's criterion that in the apostolic age "the idea, the principle of Christianity that arises from seeing Jesus as a person, actually enters into consciousness and thus realizes itself." However, the earliest community had not yet adopted this idea of Christianity, since it had not yet moved forward "to freedom from the law, to overcoming of national barriers, to the understanding of Christianity as a moral religion of salvation." Therefore the historical significance of the earliest community consists in the fact that it unknowingly kept alive the spirit of Jesus and passed the gospel tradition on to the gentile church.[119]

115. Cf. RB, *Urchristentum*, 8.

116. Cf. C. Weizsäcker, *Das apostolische Zeitalter*; cf. also W. G. Kümmel, *Das Neue Testament*, 72f.

117. Bultmann reckoned Weizsäcker's work among the six books that were of decisive significance for his own path as a theologian and interpreter of the New Testament. Cf. RB, "Milestones in Books," 125; also in RB, *Theologie als Kritik*, 513.

118. RB, "Urgemeinde, christliche," 1520.

119. RB, "Urgemeinde, christliche," 1523.

As a member of the history-of-religions school, Bultmann was encouraged in his relativizion of the weight of the earliest community, as this served as a remarkable model of the newly equalized relations among the currents of early Christianity. Wilhelm Heitmüller had developed the distinction between the earliest community in Palestine and Hellenistic Christianity in 1912 in the context of examining the relation between Jesus' proclamation and Paul's theology. The essential elements of Pauline theology stem from Hellenistic Christianity and must therefore be regarded as a further link in the chain that connects Jesus and the apostles.[120] Soon afterwards, Wilhelm Bousset's book *Kyrios Christos* presented the thesis that Hellenistic-gentile Christianity first worshipped Jesus as Kyrios and understood Christianity as a religion of salvation. Both the cultically stamped religion of Paul and the spiritually shaped mysticism of the gospel writer John must therefore have grown from the rootstock of that earliest Hellenistic Christianity, each at a considerable historical distance from Jesus' simple gospel of the forgiveness of sins.[121]

In 1919, Bultmann had rated the Bousset-Heitmüller distinction between earliest Palestinian and Hellenistic Christianity "as the most profound realization concerning the history of earliest Christianity." To be sure, the problems raised by this insight into the emergence of the Christian religion on Hellenistic soil were neither solved nor at the time even recognized,[122] but a year later in his Wartburg lecture "Ethical and Mystical Religion in Earliest Christianity," Bultmann made a first attempt at solving them.[123] Contrary to what liberal theology had claimed, it was not the historical Jesus and his religion that had been historically influential, but rather the Christ-myth and -cult of the Hellenistic community that had been historically influential. Following Ernst Troeltsch's description of the sociological structure of earliest Christianity, Bultmann was then able to place Jesus and the earliest community in Palestine within the typology of ethical religion and locate earliest Hellenistic Christianity within the mystical-cultic typology. Seen from the perspective of the history and sociology of religion, Jesus and the earliest Palestinian community belonged within Judaism—as "a Jewish sect, if you like." In contrast, "'Christianity' first begins in the Hellenistic community as an independent historical entity, as a religious

120. Cf. W. Heitmüller, "Zum Problem," 330.

121. Cf. W. Bousset, *Kyrios Christos.* Bultmann paid tribute to the significance of this book more than fifty years after it first appeared. Cf. RB, Preface, in W. Bousset, *Kyrios Christos*, vf.

122. RB, "Die neutestamentliche Forschung," *Theologie als Kritik*, 102f.

123. Cf. RB, "Ethische und mystische Religion," 29–47; as well as the interpretation in M. Evang, *Rudolf Bultmann*, 290–332.

community with its own form of myth and cult and community life."[124] Without explicitly discussing the issue, Bultmann mentioned at the end of his essay "that transitions and combinations"—indeed, a profound affinity between the ethical and mystical type of religion—pointed to a possible higher unity of the two types.[125]

In the years that followed, authors such as Eduard Meyer, Adolf Deissmann, Karl Holl and Hans Lietzmann subjected Bultmann to the harshest criticism, since they misjudged his view of the constitutive importance of Hellenistic Christianity for the beginnings of the Christian religion.[126] For him, the "Hellenism-thesis" was not merely a marginal problem for history or the history of religions, for he viewed the relation between the early Palestinian and Hellenistic communities as "the basic problem of the history of earliest Christianity."[127] Indeed, he saw its clarification as the *conditio sine qua non* [indispensable condition] for constructing a coherent picture of earliest Christianity. But the "synthetic historical presentation"[128] that this required had to make it historically plausible that Christianity specifically began with the belief in Jesus Christ as eschatological mediator of salvation.[129] Likewise, in attempting to analyze Christianity's historical development it had to determine "what is specifically Christian in the materials" by examining earliest Christianity's understanding of existence against the background of other ancient religions and worldviews.[130]

Bultmann had described one side of this two-sided task at the beginning of April 1921, in his answer to Hans von Soden's challenge: "whether [or not] world history might have made the mistake of taking for [the author] and hero of the most highly developed ethical religion a person who himself did not at all reach this level: . . . [H]istory has surely made *one* mistake by taking Jesus of Nazareth as hero of the Christian religion, whereas in truth it is the Κύριος Χριστός [Christ the Lord] of the cult, whose person enriches from within his own goodness in all epochs of the development.

124. RB, "Ethische und mystische Religion," 36.

125. RB, "Ethische und mystische Religion," 46.

126. Cf. the following in *Theologie als Kritik*: RB, "Eduard Meyers Werk," 113; RB, "Aus der Geschichte des Urchristentums," 124; RB, rev. of A. Deissmann, 130; RB, "Urchristentum," 154–56; RB, "Urchristentum und Religionsgeschichte," 270–73; RB, rev. of H. Lietzmann, *Geschichte der alten Kirche 1,* 295f.

127. RB, "Eduard Meyers Werk," *Theologie als Kritik*, 113.

128. RB, "Urchristentum," *Theologie als Kritik*, 154.

129. Cf. also Bultmann's impressive criticism of Holl in "Urchristentum und Religionsgeschichte," *Theologie als Kritik*, 269–83.

130. Cf. also—and already in terms of an existentialist theological conceptuality—Bultmann's debate with H. Lietzmann in his review in RB, *Theologie als Kritik*, 295.

Luther and Schleiermacher do not, as they think they do, stand under the influence of Jesus of Nazareth, but rather under the influence of the Christ of the church, of the Pauline (Hellenistic) Christ-myth, of the Gospel of John."[131] The other side of the task Bultmann outlined to Karl Barth in December of 1922. The empirical facts of the history of ancient religions were not, he insisted, the primary background in terms of which one should attempt to understand such specific statements as, for instance, those of Paul. Rather, Bultmann conceived those facts to be "representative of particular spiritual attitudes which, in wrestling with their sources, the research scholar draws into conversation with them and poses decisive questions through them."[132]

Bultmann actively pursued this conversation in his teaching in Marburg, and from the summer semester of 1921 on, he treated history-of-religion topics in the history of earliest Christianity with increasing intensity.[133] He also employed the questions that were directing him in these matters in his critique of the first two volumes of Hans Lietzmann's *Geschichte der alten Kirche* [*History of the Ancient Church*]. Should not a presentation of the beginnings of Christianity make clear "the meaning of the kerygma on the basis of an analysis of the empirical historical facts?" Was it not also to be made clear on the basis of "what the meaning of *church* is?" Must not such a presentation "bring more forcefully to the consciousness of today's reader the '*tua res agitur*' [matters that concern him] than Lietzmann manages to do?"[134] Does not the historian of the beginnings of the church have to conceive his task as a theological one as well, and therefore pose the question of truth within his historical presentation? Does he not also have to ask what is to be considered the real meaning of Christian faith?[135]

Lietzmann was well pleased with Bultmann's inquiries concerning his understanding of history,[136] but he disarmingly confessed to agreeing with Leopold von Ranke's classical description of historiography as an attempt "simply to explain 'how it actually was.'" It went without saying for Lietzmann that this had to be done in a methodically reflective and controlled way, and in hopes of being able to discern the working of God

131. UB Tübingen, RB est., RB to H. von Soden, 3. 4. 1921, Mn 2-2385.

132. RB to K. Barth, 31. 12. 1922, in B. Jaspert, *Barth-Bultmann Briefwechsel*, 15.

133. Cf. the overview in B. Jaspert, "Sachgemässe Exegese," 210–21.

134. RB, rev. of H. Lietzmann, in RB, *Theologie als Kritik*, 295f.

135. RB, rev. of H. Lietzmann, *Geschichte der alten Kirche 2,* in RB, *Theologie als Kritik*, 380f.

136. Cf. H. Lietzmann to RB, 23. 2. 1935, in K. Aland, *Glanz und Niedergang*, 808.

in history.[137] Bultmann saw the difference between himself and this student of Harnack in the fact that Lietzmann meant "to separate the believing and judging conception of history from critical investigation of it . . . and to let it go at that," whereas he himself "thought that historical and 'theological' investigation of history [had] to proceed as one." Of course, this did not imply pursuing historical-critical exegesis of the Bible from a predetermined standpoint, but exegesis, like research into church history, had to be driven by questions related to both the texts and the historical connections.[138] In their dialogue, Bultmann and Lietzmann treated one another's viewpoint with obvious respect, for such was the scholarly protocol to which they felt duty-bound.

From the summer semester of 1931 onwards, Bultmann had repeatedly presented a required course of public one-hour lectures that was at first entitled "Earliest Christianity and the History of Religion," and from the summer semester of 1944 onwards, "Earliest Christianity in History, Specifically in Connection with the Religions of Antiquity." Like this lecture-course, the 1949 book that grew out of it was also directed at the general educated public. Bultmann dedicated the book to the friends who had been driven out by the National Socialists, the same ones to whom the dedication of the commentary on John had already been directed in 1941: Erich Frank, Paul Friedländer, and Friedrich Carl Sell. They had been teaching in the U.S. in the meantime, and received this token of Bultmann's friendship with gratitude and real joy. At the time, Frank "called to mind the wonderful hours" before the war during which Bultmann had read and discussed with him the texts dealt with in the book.[139]

In keeping with his existentialist approach, Bultmann deals only in passing with the external development of the religions and cultural currents of antiquity, and with their religious expressions in worship, myth, social structure, and law. Like the rest of the history-of-religions school, he understands earliest Hellenistic Christianity as a syncretic phenomenon.[140] This characterization of Hellenistic Christianity as a form of syncretism

137. H. Lietzmann to RB, 20. 5. 1939, in K. Aland, *Glanz und Niedergang*, 962.

138. RB to H. Lietzmann, 21. 6. 1939, in K. Aland, *Glanz und Niedergang*, 967.

139. UB Tübingen, RB est., E. Frank to RB, 29. 4. 1949, Mn 2-760; cf. also P. Friedländer to RB, 24. 4. 1949, Mn 2-787. The "old witch's house" was the small house on the castle mount in Marburg in which Frank had lived prior to emigrating in 1939. Regarding Bultmann's lectures, cf. also K. Oehler, *Blick aus dem Philosophenturm*, 40–42.

140. RB, *Urchristentum*, 195–200; on the application of the concept of syncretism to earliest Christianity, cf. RB, *Urchristentum*, 255n1; as well as H. Gunkel, *Zum religionsgeschichtlichen Verständnis*, 35–95.

provides an effective starting-point for the book. This is because Judaism and pagan Hellenism, the cultural and religious forces and forms that decisively influenced earliest Christianity, both preserve traditions without which their own world of ideas as well as that of earliest Christianity could not be understood. With this in mind, the overall plan of the book becomes transparent. Bultmann leads up to the comparatively brief examination of earliest Christianity in the fifth chapter by presenting a chapter on Judaism and one on Hellenism, each of which is accompanied by a chapter on its foundational heritage: the Old Testament and ancient Greece, respectively.

In the first chapter, Bultmann deals with the religion of ancient Israel according to the literary record in the Old Testament. The presentation is organized around the motifs of "God and the World," "God and the People," and "God and the Person." This is why the whole reads much like a brief theology of the Old Testament. To be sure, Bultmann intends from the outset to weave together comparative religion and existentialist interpretation. Thus, he emphasizes the overall distinctive contours of the religion and faith of Israel and their contrast with the Greek world of ideas. The idea of creation in the Old Testament and the belief in Yahweh as the ruler of the world and of human beings differs in significant ways from the Greek idea of a cosmos harmoniously ordered according to an eternal law. Similarly, the faith of Israel understands history as the "real domain of God"; whereas in writing history the Greeks concentrate on the past "in order to discern the unchanging laws of historical occurrence," the Old Testament presentation of history is directed towards the future, and treats specific events according to their relation to God's established goals.[141]

God's action in history is accomplished specifically by placing himself in relation to his people, by making Israel his chosen people; but the people's intended loyalty to God can be demonstrated only by the individual. And since this kind of obedience fails to take place, the concept of the covenant increasingly takes on an eschatological quality. For "the covenant cannot be realized in history as it actually is; its realization is conceivable only in a mythical future of perfect well-being."[142] As with the complete fulfillment of God's covenant, so, too, must Israel finally project the idea of the holy people "into a mythical future." In Bultmann's view, through these anticipations of the eschatological future, Israel has in fact abandoned the idea of "God as the one who comes," and as "the lord of history."[143] As the normal

141. RB, *Urchristentum*, 17–19.
142. RB, *Urchristentum*, 41.
143. RB, *Urchristentum*, 46.

understanding of each of these two anthropological constructs reveals, the Old Testament concept of the person differs fundamentally from the Greek idea. Unlike the Greek ethics of duty and virtue, the Old Testament does not start out from an ideal image of the person; instead, the Israelite ethic teaches that the will of God aims at an obedient society—and ultimately at radical personal obedience. Even when through obstinacy and arrogance—the ultimate "sin of ingratitude to God"—the individual fails to realize "his proper role as a creature," he nonetheless knows himself to be dependent on the forgiving grace of God. To be sure, Israel also expects the complete forgiveness of sin only in the eschatological future.[144]

In the presentation of post-exilic Judaism, Bultmann explains each of the religious ideas of Palestinian and Hellenistic Judaism in its own right. Thus, it was not so much this structure of the second chapter as it was the decision to treat the proclamation of Jesus in the context of Palestinian Judaism that caused a fuss among the first readers of the book. Assigning the message of Jesus to the worldview of Palestinian Judaism offered a number of explosive discussion topics. Nonetheless, this way of proceeding could have seemed odd[145] only to someone who was unaware of Bultmann's previous publications on the subject.

The popular form of Jewish hope was focused on the restoration of the Davidic Empire under a messianic king. Alongside this traditional nationalistic hope, a cosmological eschatology established itself, and because of its dualistic and pessimistic worldview, supplied Judaism with such new ideas as the resurrection of the dead. From time to time, the nationalistic and the cosmological pictures of the future combined to create diverse variations.[146] Following the exile, Judaism linked itself to history by linking itself to scripture. But loyalty to the sacred book led to God being no longer thought of "in a genuine sense [as] the God of history, and as . . . the one who is always coming." Indeed, Judaism no longer experienced God in the present, but at most continued to read about his revelatory deeds in the past.[147] Characteristic of Judaism, of course, is the high value it places on the law. Cultic holiness therefore came increasingly to be accommodated to the life of the community under the law. However, Judaism was able to summon up no more than formal obedience to the law; it did not push forward to radical obedience involving the whole person in response to the claim of God. Since

144. RB, *Urchristentum*, 56–59.
145. Cf. as an example W. G. Kümmel, rev. of RB, *Urchristentum*, 734.
146. Cf. RB, *Urchristentum*, 88–96.
147. RB, *Urchristentum*, 64.

the Jewish authorities maintained a legal conception of obedience to the law, they increasingly paved the way for both soteriological insecurity and pious self-righteousness. Here, no doubt, Bultmann has partially misrepresented the Torah observance of post-exilic Judaism under the problematic heading, "Jewish Legalism."[148] In doing so, he lagged behind his own positive assessment of Jewish piety with regard to the law—as, for instance, in the essay "Christ the End of the Law" (1940). Even he seems to have been unable to free himself completely from old burdens imposed by Protestant theology.

[In *Primitive Christianity*,] Bultmann's portrayal of Jesus' proclamation is essentially an abridged version of the Jesus-book of 1926. Jesus' preaching is "a great *protest against Jewish legalism*," and replaces the traditional view of divine justice with the idea that God's will manifests itself in the demand of love. As do the Old Testament and Judaism, Jesus understands God as the creator, but only Jesus knows God as the transcendent one who forever approaches human beings. In contrast to Judaism's view, God's will can no longer be discerned in the history of the people, but like Judaism, Jesus removes God from history. In his case, however, this removal from the world is not artificially mediated through the law, but is rather grounded in the concrete nearness of the munificent and demanding God in everyday life.[149] Taking up Judaism's apocalyptic-cosmological expectation of the future, Jesus proclaims the nearness of the reign of God. His eschatological preaching designates the present as the time of decision. Even if Jesus did not proclaim himself the messiah, he nonetheless embodies "*in his person* the 'sign of the times.'" For through his word he calls all to radical decision for the inbreaking reign of God. To be sure, his expectation of the end of the world in the near future was mistaken. At the same time, his message is taken over by the Christian community insofar as it brings to expression the one who proclaims God's reign to be near as the one who is proclaimed.[150]

Bultmann explains his treatment of Jesus' proclamation in the context of Jewish religion by a statement that clearly echoes a famous dictum of Julius Wellhausen's:[151] "Jesus was not a 'Christian,' but a Jew, and his preach-

148. Cf. RB, *Urchristentum*, 71f: "These regulations went into detail to the point of absurdity . . . the precision of the scribal jurists was a typical expression of Jewish legalism." Cf. also, however, the qualifications in the same passage: "All the same, we should not exaggerate this side of the matter [of the crushing burden of commandments]." The pious Jew experiences the cultic commandments "as not a burden at all."

149. RB, *Urchristentum*, 78–88.

150. RB, *Urchristentum*, 96–103.

151. J. Wellhausen, *Einleitung*, 113: "The gospel means just as much as Christianity. Jesus was no Christian, but a Jew."

ing moves within the thought forms and imagery of Judaism, even where it stands in opposition to traditional Jewish religion."[152] Werner Georg Kümmel, however, came out vehemently against this locating of Jesus within the history of the Jewish religion, arguing that while Jesus was surely no Christian, by his messianic self-consciousness and his eschatological view of history, he smashes the framework of Jewish belief in revelation.[153] This objection could hardly be convincing to Bultmann, for in his view it was specifically in his eschatological and ethical preaching that Jesus remained fully within the framework of the history of Jewish religion. Jesus could not have escaped this context even if he had tried to pass himself off as the Messiah—a notion Bultmann deemed unlikely. What is more, in his book on earliest Christianity, Bultmann unequivocally expressed Jesus' authoritative personal claim much as he had in coining the idea of implicit christology in 1929.[154]

Bultmann had for decades studied the Greek classics, and was thoroughly familiar with the authoritative interpretations of Greek philosophy—especially those of his friends Erich Frank, Paul Friedländer, Gerhard Krüger, and Hans-Georg Gadamer.[155] All this was useful for his summary of the Greek heritage in the book's third chapter, in which he draws a sweeping panorama from the essence of the polis to the Greek worldview and Greek science. Because the justice and law of the polis find their basis in the divinity, the citizen's religion ultimately consists in his relation to the polis. But inasmuch as people bend the laws more and more to their own advantage and become part of the sophistic enlightenment, a belief in fate increasingly takes the place of εὐσέβεια, the "*awesome reverence for the divine powers.*"[156] Along with this, science emerges from the womb of Ionian philosophy, which inquires after the ἀρχή, the origin of all things. And thus Socrates represents a new departure in redirecting the nature-oriented perspective of natural philosophy back to the human being. Onto the ancient position of the religious undergirding of the polis, Plato now superimposes the concept

152. RB, *Urchristentum*, 78.

153. Cf. W. G. Kümmel, rev. of RB, *Das Urchristentum*, 735; W. G. Kümmel, *Das Neue Testament*, 76.

154. Cf. RB, "Die Bedeutung des geschichtlichen Jesus," *GuV* (1933 ed.), vol. 1, 204f; RB, *Urchristentum*, 98–100.

155. Cf. the footnotes in RB, *Urchristentum*, 245–49; also the reference there (246) to Bultmann's own essay, "Polis und Hades," *GuV* (5th ed.), vol. 2, 20–31. To be sure, W. Kamlah ("Die Theologie und das 'griechische Denken,'" 688) thinks that Bultmann erred in thinking that Platonic reason was "rationally controlling, rather than, to the contrary, perceptive reason." Cf. also Bultmann's reflective reaction in RB to G. Krüger, 28. 1. 1951, in F. Lilie, "Bultmann-Krüger Briefwechsel," *ZNThG* 6, 288.

156. RB, *Urchristentum*, 123.

that the world of ideas represents what is eternal. The human being now seeks increasingly to understand his existence within the cosmos by directing his life according to the ideals of the beautiful and the good, and thus seeing the individual life in analogy to the cosmos—that is, perceived as a work of art. Virtue and culture help him to perfect himself both in life's varied activities and as a member of society.[157]

Hellenism continues the classical Greek tradition, modifies it, and enriches it with new motifs. This happens in the *stoa*, which presents an otherworldly existence as the ideal for leading life. To be sure, Stoic wisdom does not restrict itself to the individual person but assumes ethical responsibility for society as well. In comparison with Christianity, which regards temporality as constitutive for the essence of being human, the trouble with Stoicism is that it thinks otherworldliness can be achieved by eliminating temporality from human existence.[158] During the period of the empire, solar pantheism and fatalism penetrate the Greco-Roman world through oriental star worship. Bultmann had previously examined these events and their religious impact in a study of the symbolism of light in the ancient world.[159] Just as astrology assumes the role of predicting the future by means of the heavenly bodies, many other voices offer messages of salvation to those who feel themselves subjected to forces that fate has imposed on them. Although the Hellenistic mystery religions that thus mediate salvation (σωτηρία) are much alike in their cultic forms, they are not grounded in a uniform theology, and therefore do not possess a uniform understanding of existence.[160]

But such an understanding does develop in Gnosticism, which Bultmann characterizes as "a religious movement of pre-Christian origin."[161] The Gnostic myth of the redeemed redeemer—which he appropriates from the work of Richard Reitzenstein and Wilhelm Bousset, and from Hans Jonas' studies in the phenomenology of religion—is paradigmatic for Gnosticism. In this system the individual is aware of his being alone in the world because the true self is not at home in the corporeal and psychic sphere. The individual can be liberated from bondage to the terrible anxiety of this imprisonment only through an eschatological-mythical occurrence—the separation from body and soul that the self experiences in death. Only a communication that comes from "the other side" can mediate this sort of redemption.

157. Cf. RB, *Urchristentum*, 115–48.
158. Cf. RB, *Urchristentum*, 151–62.
159. Cf. RB, "Zur Geschichte der Lichtsymbolik," *Exegetica*, 323–55.
160. Cf. RB, *Urchristentum*, 163–80.
161. RB, *Urchristentum*, 181.

Consequently, Gnostic existence realizes itself in hearing the call of this revelation, in believing the truth of this saving word that is preached. From the "gnosis" of what it means to be human there thus develops the "gnosis" found in the vision of God. In moving between these two conditions, the Gnostic exists in a radically otherworldly way. His behavior, like the ethic that grounds it, takes on a radically negative orientation by way of demonstrating his having been utterly removed from the world.[162]

The picture of Gnosticism that Bultmann draws here, a brief sketch intended to recapitulate his prior statements on the subject, received very different notices from the reviewers of *Primitive Christianity.* Wilhelm Kamlah and Werner Georg Kümmel found Bultmann's portrayal of Gnosticism especially valuable, since it explained his hermeneutical interest in the way Gnostic motifs were adopted and modified by early Christian proclamation.[163] In contrast, the Harvard religious historian Arthur Darby Nock anticipated later objections to Bultmann's understanding of Gnosticism by registering fundamental doubts as to whether pre-Christian Gnosticism was in fact a systematic religious worldview. Nock also judged that Paul had been much less influenced by specific Gnostic ideas than Bultmann alleged.[164]

Thus Bultmann sees, particularly through the prism of the sociology of religion, that the earliest community in Palestine is fundamentally a Jewish sect; and therefore the various threads from the history of the religions of antiquity really entwine for the first time in earliest Hellenistic Christianity. Therefore, this form of earliest Christianity seems, at least at first glance, to be a syncretic amalgam that has selected, adopted, and modified a manifold array of motifs and ideas from the religious traditions of Judaism and Hellenism. More precise analysis will therefore be required to determine whether, because of a new and unique understanding of existence, earliest Christianity differs significantly from the religious formations that influenced it. Bultmann's way of addressing this question is to understand earliest Christianity by presupposing that it is principally Paul and John who offer authoritative interpretations of the Christian understanding of existence.[165]

Earliest Christianity understands the core of being human to consist in the exercise of free will that in its very occurrence amounts to a rebellion against

162. Cf. RB, *Urchristentum*, 181–92.

163. Cf. W. Kamlah, "Die Theologie und das 'griechische Denken,'" 689f; W. G. Kümmel, rev. of RB, *Das Urchristentum*, 735.

164. Cf. A. D. Nock, rev. of RB, *Das Urchristentum*, 37–39. Bultmann's friend A. Fridrichsen had Nock record this conversation. Cf. A. Fridrichsen to RB, 4. 6. 1949, Mn 2-783.

165. Cf. RB, *Urchristentum*, 195–200.

God. However, the human individual cannot, as the Greeks think, overcome this power of evil on his own through reason and culture. Nor as Judaism imagines can he become free from sin by fulfilling the law. Because the individual is one with and defined by his willing of evil, he can be freed only by God, and this occurs when he gives up boasting before God as a way of protecting himself and radically entrusts himself in faith to the grace of God. Faith presents as a gift the "radical openness for the future" that makes up the quintessential freedom of the Christian. Thus freed by the grace of God from the power of sin and from his own past, a person is able to open himself in freedom "for the future, for the encounters in which he will experience God's grace ever anew as the grace that comes to meet him."[166] But the New Testament does not give consistent expression to this understanding of existence, since it "drags along" with it the Jewish apocalyptic expectation of a utopian state of affairs at the end of time. Nevertheless, God now no longer speaks to us out of the empirical history of Israel, "*but rather through Christ* who is the end of history, and through the word that proclaims him." The proclamation of the grace of God individuates the person before God, for the word always calls the individual to the decision to permit himself to be freed for the authenticity of existence that results from surrender to the divine grace.[167]

The New Testament gives priority to Gnostic ideas in order to make it clear that by living in the world, the individual is enslaved by cosmic forces. In spite of this Paul—though differently from Gnosticism—conceives of the situation not simply as a fated disaster, but at the same time the result of guilt on the part of the person. For in willing to constitute his own being, the individual guiltily and inescapably gives himself up to the powers of flesh, the law, sin, and death. The person can be redeemed from the alienation of the world he has himself helped constitute only because in the cross of Christ, God "renders judgment on the world" and "shatters to pieces all boasting" in order thus to demonstrate his grace as "*his permanent futurity*, his permanent being out ahead."[168] For its interpretation of the redemption that has taken place in Christ, earliest Christianity also falls back on various ideas from out of its religious and pagan environment. In this regard, it refers especially to the Gnostic redeemer myth, by means of which conceptuality it is able to express the eschatological event of salvation "as an occurrence that is beginning to take place in the present." In distinction from

166. RB, *Urchristentum*, 206f.
167. RB, *Urchristentum*, 207–10.
168. RB, *Urchristentum*, 210–18.

Gnosticism, which locates the coming of the redeemer in a mythical prehistory, Christian belief identifies the eschatological occurrence with a historical event: the advent and crucifixion of Christ. The Christian understanding of the eschatological occurrence differs from that of Gnosticism in that it takes place ever anew in the proclaimed Word, the Word in which the redeemer is present and to which faith opens itself. It is precisely this faith—because it affords the individual freedom from himself and for himself and therein a new self-understanding—in which we find expressed the fact "that the New Testament understands *human existence as historical existence*." The decision of faith does not constitute a demonstrable possession, but rather grounds all genuine life-decisions of the Christian. To the extent that these concern his relation to the world, they are stamped by the dialectic between inner distance and loving participation described by 1 Cor 7:29–31. In large part because the Christian actualizes the unworldliness of his existence through love in the present, the fundamental openness of Christian existence mirrors the future of the coming God.[169]

Primitive Christianity did not have as great an impact on New Testament scholars as Bultmann's other books had.[170] Concern with the history of religions was not exactly *en vogue* among Protestant theologians during the middle of the twentieth century. Karl Barth's criticism, which was based on a theology of revelation, of religion as the supposedly self-assertive attempt of the human being to justify himself in the face of God's original design, was especially telling. This attack generated a climate that dissuaded New Testament scholarship from turning *en masse* to the history of ancient religions. Nevertheless, Bultmann's book provided a highly original and advantageous display of the legacy of the history of religions school. And undertaking an existentialist interpretation of the New Testament necessarily included an awareness of earliest Christianity's contextual place within the history of religions. For both ancient Judaism and Hellenism—and especially the latter by leaving its mark on the popular philosophy of Stoicism, the mystery religions, and mythological Gnosticism—formed the background of language and ideas against which earliest Christianity brought to light what was distinctive in Christian faith.

Among those for whom it was written, educated readers who were not versed in theology, Bultmann's book apparently fulfilled its purpose; for the

169. RB, *Urchristentum*, 218–33. On the content of the book cf. also E. Dinkler, rev. of RB, *Das Urchristentum*, 67–75.

170. These numbers are symptomatic: Bultmann's commentary on John met with sixty-three reviews, that on earliest Christianity only five.

first edition of 4,400 copies[171] was sold out in a few years,[172] and by 1998, six hardcover editions had appeared,[173] as well as three in paperback and seven foreign language versions.[174] In addition to the content itself, the striking language and the clear historical and systematic organization of the book may have contributed to its success. Furthermore, Bultmann gave a poetic flavor to his work by weaving into his presentation significant amounts of literature representing the religions and worldviews of antiquity. These texts did more than provide scholarly decoration, for they gave authentic and vivid expression to the understandings of existence they reflected. Ernst Beutler, the Goethe scholar, praised Bultmann's expositions for their "sober clarity."[175] Arthur Darby Nock found *Primitive Christianity* a remarkable book that touches and moves the reader as does a piece of music—as does, one might even say, a piece by Wagner.[176] For Bultmann's friend Ernst Moering, the book "proved once more that what is true is also beautiful."[177] And finally, the Heidelberg Academy of Sciences named the book as the specific reason for nominating its author for the 1957 Reuchlin Prize.[178]

4. The End of Academic Teaching

> *Lord, I am not worthy of the least of all the steadfast love and the faithfulness that you have shown to your servant. (Gen 32:10)*
>
> *What do you have that you have not received? And if you received it, why do you boast as if you had not received it? (1 Cor 4:7)*[179]

During his last regular semester at Marburg, Bultmann interpreted Paul's Second Corinthians in a course of lectures. Lecturing on this letter, which

171. Cf. UB Tübingen, RB est., Artemis-Verlag to RB, 12. 8. 1949, Mn 2-2440.

172. Cf. UB Tübingen, RB est., Artemis-Verlag to RB, 20. 7. 1953, Mn 2-2440.

173. The book came out through its fifth edition in the Artemis-Verlag Press up until 1986 and in the Patmos-Verlag in its sixth in 1998.

174. Notable paperback editions include: Rowohlts Deutsche Enzyklopädie 157/158 (1962), Deutscher Taschenbuch-Verlag 4580 (1992), and Patmos Paperback (1998; 2005, 4th ed). Moreover, the book appeared in the following languages: English, French, Danish, Italian, Hungarian, Portuguese, and Japanese.

175. E. Beutler to A. Schweitzer, 24. 4. 1949, in W. Zager, *A. Schweitzer*, 83.

176. Cf. A. D. Nock, rev. of RB, *Das Urchristentum*, 39.

177. UB Tübingen, RB est., E. Moering to RB, 22. 10. 1950, Mn 2-1410.

178. See also below 502f. To see Bultmann's view, cf. also the critique of the classical philologist H. Langerbeck, rev. of RB, *Das Urchristentum*, 15–17; as well as the eight-page reply by Bultmann in RB to H. Langerbeck, 12. 7. 1955, Mn 2-2277; and RB, "Christentum und Antike," 10n1.

179. Biblical citations with which Bultmann concluded his farewell lecture in Marburg on 24. 7. 1951.

probably left a stronger mark on Bultmann's theology than any other New Testament writing,[180] "had always been especially dear" to him.[181] For the Second Letter to the Corinthians provided themes that were central to his theological thinking: the word of proclamation as eschatological event, the grounding of the apostolic office in the Christ event, the paradox that this eschatological event marking God's reconciliation of the world has taken place in the historical fact of the cross and becomes present again from time to time in proclamation, as well as the exemplary significance of apostolic existence for the faith and life of the Christian. In the seminar, Bultmann dealt with the topic of "Paul and Gnosticism." On July 16, 1951, he concluded "the final session of the seminar of the semester with the observation that Paul was, of course, not only a Gnostic, but that it is necessary to come to understand Paul in connection with all the religious and spiritual movements of his time."[182]

Before becoming emeritus, Bultmann presented his farewell lecture on July 24, 1951, to an overflow house in the largest lecture hall.[183] A representative of the student body presented him with an edition of the collected works of Georg Christoph Lichtenberg as a sign of thanks and respect. Günther Bornkamm assessed the theological work of the teacher, whose wide-ranging research had borne fruit in pioneering works. Bultmann had not contented himself with the mere historical reconstruction of past facts, but had always sought to understand what the New Testament message was about in the context of a contemporary understanding of truth. In his word of thanks, the Dean of the Marburg theological faculty, Emil Balla, emphasized

Plate 36: During the Final Lecture in Marburg, 1951

180. Cf. E. Dinkler, Foreword, in RB, *Der zweite Brief an die Korinther*, 11f.
181. RB, *Der zweite Brief an die Korinther*, 7 (Foreword).
182. B. Jaspert, "Sachgemässe Exegese," 160.
183. All dates in this section are given according to RB, *Chronik 1946–1961.*

Bultmann's extraordinary success as a teacher. Thousands of young theologians had gone through his classes. It would be difficult to find a successor to the man who was Protestantism's most significant New Testament scholar. Bishop Adolf Wüstemann, himself a former Bultmann student, spoke on behalf of the two churches of Hesse. Wüstemann thanked Bultmann for his courageous and uncompromising involvement in the Confessing Church and even more for the service he had performed, and no doubt would continue to perform, for the Protestant Church through his unwavering search for responsible knowledge of the truth. Bultmann thanked his audience and the speakers with simple words and expressed his gratitude for more than thirty years of teaching in Marburg through two biblical passages, Gen 32:10 and 1 Cor 4:7, in which he found expressed the primary motifs of his theological existence.[184]

Bultmann was "very happy"[185] about becoming emeritus, a status that the Hessian Minister of Education made effective on October 1, 1951.[186] The new situation held out the happy prospect of being freed from the duties of teaching and academic committee work, and thus of being able to dedicate himself to research projects that had long been put off. After all, the *Theology of the New Testament* was still not finished, and new editions of the *History of the Synoptic Tradition*, the Jesus-book, the commentary on John and the first volume of *Faith and Understanding* needed to be prepared. In addition to these, a second volume of *Faith and Understanding* was due for printing, not to mention the demands on his time arising from the increasingly heated debate over the demythologizing program. To be sure, the leisure that all these activities would require was not immediately forthcoming. The business of finding his replacement made only halting progress. And so in the summer semester of 1952 he let himself be persuaded to make up for a portion of the shortage of New Testament staff by taking on a two-hour lecture course.[187]

In spite of the incessant responsibilities, Bultmann was able to free himself up for what might be called two trips into his own past. One took him and his wife during the Pentecost vacation to his beloved Oldenburg. There he visited relatives and placed memorial flowers on his parents' grave. Once

184. See above n. 179. Cf. Kl., "Dank"; O. Kaiser, "Worte des Dedenkens," 41.

185. Cf. G. Diesselhorst collection, Hessian Minister for Education and National Culture to RB, 29. 6. 1951.

186. RB to G. Krüger, 8. 7. 1951, in F. Lilie, "Bultmann-Krüger Briefwechsel," *ZNThG* 6, 289.

187. Cf. UB Tübingen, RB est., RB to F. C. Sell, 3. 8. 1952, Mn 2-2380.

again, he showed Leni the Ammerland with his birthplace of Wiefelstede, and Rastede, where he had first gone to school; and he traveled back to his childhood and youth "to the Geest landscape, with its cornfields and oak groves, its hedgerows and farmhouses."[188] Thereupon exciting cultural experiences beckoned, as Bultmann, his wife, and daughters Gesine and Heilke visited Italy from September 5th to October 3rd, 1952. With Basel soon behind them, the Bultmanns enjoyed stays in Bologna, Ravenna, Florence, Pisa, Lucca, Siena, and San Gimignano. The impressions gained from standing in front of the paintings and other works of art in the Uffizi Galleries, the Pitti Palace, and the churches and museums outside of Florence were as overwhelming as they had been on Bultmann's first trip to Italy as a student in 1904. And yet because of "the racing traffic and the noise associated with it," Florence and the other cities they visited seemed to have lost the peculiar charm they had exercised on him nearly fifty years before. It seemed to Bultmann "that in Italy at least half of the inhabitants are sitting on motorcycles." He thus found all the more pleasant the quiet that he experienced in the medieval town of San Gimignano.[189]

In the summer of 1952, Werner Georg Kümmel, who had gone from Zürich to Mainz the year before, accepted the appointment to Bultmann's chair in Marburg. And when difficulties arose in filling the New Testament vacancy in Zürich, the theological faculty there asked Bultmann to take over Kümmel's chair during the winter semester of 1953–54. Bultmann agreed to this request, since from his earliest days as a scholar he had had friendly relations with the Swiss theologians Walter Baumgartner in Basel and Walter Gut and Ludwig Köhler in Zürich. Besides, he had been invited to Switzerland to lecture many times.[190] A further reason for his willingness to assume the teaching job was that the duties connected with it were kept within bounds. He was to offer a four-hour lecture course on Paul's letters to the Galatians and the Philippians, as well as a two-hour seminar on the concept of faith in the New Testament.[191]

In Zürich, Bultmann took up quarters in the Augustine Hotel on 8 St. Peter Street, where he prepared to live as "a proper hermit again" in his room and in the university.[192] He enjoyed the work with students, especially

188. UB Tübingen, RB est., RB to A. Bultmann Lemke, 15. 6. 1952, Mn 2-3452.

189. UB Tübingen, RB est., RB to A. Bultmann Lemke, 7. 10. 1952; cf. also 19. 7. 1952, Mn 2-3452.

190. Cf. H. Urner-Astholz, "Errinerungen," 206.

191. Cf. G. Diesselhorst, Ministry of Education of the Canton of Zürich to RB, 23. 6. 1953.

192. UB Tübingen, RB est., RB to A. Bultmann Lemke, 13. 1. 1954, Mn 2-3452.

with those who were prepared to entertain his ideas.[193] And his existence as a hermit was repeatedly interrupted by invitations from his friend Ludwig Köhler, the Old Testament scholar Hans Wildberger, and Walter Rüegg, the editor of the Erasmus-Bibliothek of the Artemis-Verlag press. Thanks to his good relations with Rüegg, Bultmann succeed in getting the posthumous essays of Erich Frank published in the Erasmus-Bibliothek. In the foreword that the publisher asked him to write for this collection of essays, he pointed to the fragmentary character of his friend's work in philosophy, but insisted that the anthology served as a legacy to Frank's passionate interest "in clarifying the basic issues of contemporary consciousness, the questions about what it means to live and to be a person."[194] Since his teaching duties were not particularly strenuous, Bultmann's time in Zürich seemed to him "almost like a vacation in Wiesbaden,"[195] for he even had time enough to go to the opera and the theater.[196]

In addition, Bultmann was occasionally sought out for lectures and other forms of service that went beyond his teaching job. Once, when the Zürich church council extended an invitation to the theological faculty, he gave "a little report" on his theological career.[197] And when the *Neue Zürcher Zeitung* asked him for a written reflection to include in its Christmas edition of 1953, Bultmann took the opportunity to set forth the Christmas message: "We are not who we seem to be, or who we imagine that we are. We are who we are in the light of the grace of God. Indeed, we are what we never are here and now, but what we never are here and now—*precisely that is our true being.* That is the faith of Christmas."[198] While in Zürich, Bultmann came to recognize the degree to which the Swiss had been spared the experience of the two World Wars, but even so "the feeling of security that the wealth in the stores or the theatre presented" seemed "something uncanny" to him.[199] Yet even the outward contentment of life in Switzerland could not hide the fact that the "political and economic confusions" of the postwar period represented the "uncanniness and darkness of the world" and strikingly reflected a structural secularism on the part of human beings. Two

193. Cf. UB Tübingen, RB est., RB to A. Bultmann Lemke, 7. 3. 1954, Mn 2-3452; as well as P. Biehl and P. Schulz, *Autobiographische Miniaturen*, 50f.

194. RB, Foreword, in E. Frank, *Wissen, Wollen, Glauben*; cf. also RB, "Zum Thema: Christentum und Antike," 220–22, 224–26.

195. UB Tübingen, RB est., RB to A. Bultmann Lemke, 5. 11. 1953, Mn 2-3452.

196. Cf. UB Tübingen, RB est., RB to A. Bultmann Lemke, 24. 1. 1954, Mn 2-3452.

197. UB Tübingen, RB est., RB to E. Käsemann, 31. 12. 1953, Mn 2-2251.

198. RB, "Weihnachten," *GuV* (1st ed.), vol. 3, 79; cf. also H. U. Gumbrecht, "Zorn."

199. UB Tübingen, RB est., RB to E. Käsemann, 31. 12. 1953, Mn 2-2251.

Plate 37: Rudolf Bultmann, ca. 1955

contributors to this were the "demonic power" of technology and the world of work, which does not allow "those who are possessed by it" to find authenticity in their existence. The genuine light of Christmas, a symbol that Bultmann interpreted through the fourth stanza of Luther's chorale "Be ye praised, Jesus Christ," shone not least in order that human beings might be enabled by faith to become children of light, free persons who were capable of love.[200]

In January of 1954, Bultmann presented his thoughts on "History and Eschatology in the New Testament" in Basel at the invitation of the theology faculty there. The presentation was part of the preparations for the Gifford Lectures, which he was scheduled to give in Scotland in the spring of 1955, where his topic would be "History and Eschatology."[201] In the Basel lecture, Bultmann first argues the need to understand both the Old Testament concept of history and Jewish apocalyptic thought in order to recognize the redefinition of history that is carried out in the New Testament under the auspices of eschatology. It is neither the national history of Israel nor the entirety of world history that forms actual history. Rather, historical insight takes place when the kerygma allows the individual to free himself from his past and to be re-situated into the eschatological existence that is open to the future. This is precisely what Paul and John in particular make clear in the New Testament by no longer interpreting the eschaton as occurring at the end of history, but rather as occurring in the present.[202] Even Karl Barth made an appearance at Bultmann's

200. RB, "Weihnachten," *GuV* (1st ed.), vol. 3, 77–79.

201. See below 440–42.

202. Cf. RB, "Geschichte und Eschatologie im Neuen Testament," *GuV* (1st ed.), vol. 3, 91–106.

lecture, but he did not take part in the discussion that followed. While in Basel, Bultmann visited his old friend, Walter Baumgartner, someone with whom he always found it profitable to talk.[203]

On February 16, 1954, Bultmann gave another lecture in the largest auditorium of the Zürich Technical University. Adopting the framework of a *studium generale*, he spoke about "Science and Existence." In the same venue two weeks earlier, Martin Heidegger had lectured on "Science and Consciousness," a performance that Bultmann found linguistically and rhetorically "a splendid achievement," but one that produced no new thoughts. "One is beginning to figure out that objectifying, systematic science does not penetrate to the meaning of life."[204] To be sure, Bultmann stressed this same idea in his own lecture and went on to extend his understanding of the historicity of human existence to numerous other ideas he had earlier developed. The novel element in this presentation was that, contrary to the Introduction to his Jesus-book, Bultmann no longer shared the assumption of classical physics that the natural sciences were able to achieve objective knowledge of experiential perceptions. Rather, he gave favorable notice to the insights of Niels Bohr and Werner Heisenberg concerning the change in elementary particles under the influence of experimental intervention, and thus conclusively bade farewell to that sort of objectifying thinking and speaking in the realms of history and theology.[205]

Contact with Heidegger was first renewed on February 3, 1954, in the context of a gathering in the house of Medard Boss, a friend of Heidegger's who was a psychiatrist in Zürich. A day later, Heidegger sought out Bultmann in his hotel, and a memorable discussion occurred.[206] Bultmann gave an explicit report of it to his eldest daughter, who was living in the United States: "In the morning of that day, Heidegger called on me in the Augustine Hotel, and we began with an enjoyable conversation about matters of substance. He, too, is indignant over Jaspers' attack on me. Then I explained to him why I had not taken part in the *Festschrift* for him[207] and told him that in my opinion he would ultimately have to make retractions and go public with his transgressions during the Nazi period. He was not impervious to this and claimed that he, too, had already considered this,

203. Cf. UB Tübingen, RB est., RB to A. Bultmann Lemke, 30. 1. 1954, Mn 2-3452.

204. UB Tübingen, RB est., RB to A. Bultmann Lemke, 6. 2. 1954, Mn 2-3452.

205. Cf. RB, "Wissenschaft und Existenz," *GuV* (1st ed.), vol. 3, 107–21.

206. The presentation of the scene in H. Jonas, *Errinerungen*, 302, now needs to be corrected in numerous respects in light of Bultmann's report, closer to the time that follows.

207. Cf. [W. F. Otto et al.,] "Anteile."

but that he had not been able to decide to do it, because it went against the grain for him to bring back up so many details; so many things that had been said were slanders. I said that if he were now to confess his transgressions, he would not have to defend himself; rather, he simply had to admit his transgressions publicly. Now I'm wondering whether he will decide to do this."[208] Bultmann's hope that Heidegger would publicly confess his failures during the Nazi period was not to be fulfilled.[209]

As the semester in Zürich drew to a close, Bultmann was able to look back on months of undisturbed work and many productive encounters. Leaving Zürich was difficult for him, especially as the students had welcomed him with singing as he entered the lecture hall for the last time on February 25, 1954. Indeed, Walter Gut opened his farewell address with the sentence, "There is only *one* Rudolf Bultmann, and he has been ours!" This filled the one so honored with emotion.[210] He was also pleased that a delegation of the Zürich theological faculty made up of Fritz Blanke, Ludwig Köhler, and Victor Maag made a special call on him to try to get him to extend his occupancy of the chair through the summer semester of 1954. But after weighing all the considerations, he felt it necessary to decline the Zürichers' requests.[211]

During the summer of 1954, while Bultmann did further work on the Gifford Lectures, he found a welcome diversion in two events that allowed his thoughts to wander back to scenes of long ago. First, on July 12, 1954, the Hessian Residence for Scholarship Students celebrated its 425th anniversary with a ceremony in the knights' hall of the Marburg castle. Under Heinrich, the first Director following the War, as the regular seminary for scholarship students, the *Collegium Philippinum,* had found a new home in what was once the royal stables of the castle.[212] Bultmann, who had been tutor from 1907–16 at the venerable educational institution founded by Landgrave Philipp the Magnanimous, gave the celebratory address at the anniversary on the topic "History and Eschatology in the New Testament." The ceremony took a turn that had not been anticipated. First, it began late because of a choir rehearsal, and then, the number and length of the greetings ran on excessively. When Bultmann finally began his lecture, over an hour late, some of the guests had already left to eat, and all he could do

208. UB Tübingen, RB est., RB to A. Bultmann Lemke, 6. 2. 1954, Mn 2-3452.
209. Cf. H. Jonas, *Erinnerungen*; on the problem, R. Safranski, *Ein Meister*, 480–88.
210. UB Tübingen, RB est., RB to A. Bultmann Lemke, 27. 2. 1954, Mn 2-3452.
211. UB Tübingen, RB est., Bultmann to A. Bultmann Lemke, 7. 3. 1954, Mn 2-3452.
212. Cf. T. Siegfried, "425 jähriges Jubiläum," 5.

was to shorten his remarks and speak as fast as he could.[213] At any rate, the anniversary introduced him to the new medium of television, for the Hesse broadcasting network asked the former tutor for a report on the task and the history of the Residence.

The celebration of the founding of his fraternity *Igel*, held in Tübingen on July 24–25, 1954, went better for him. That Sunday, Bultmann conducted the worship service in the Tübingen castle church in memory of the fraternity brothers who had died or had fallen in war.[214] Afterwards, the members and their wives drove to the nearby Cistercian cloister at Bebenhausen and to Hohenentringen, where the beauty of the valleys of the Ammer and the Neckar came into view. The celebration concluded in Niedernau, near Rottenburg. Between coffee and the evening meal there was dancing, "beautiful music, and a merry stage performance, in which the gods of Olympus came on stage and protested their being demythologized." Bultmann was happy to have joined in the celebration of the founding, to have seen old acquaintances again, and to have made new ones. Since he was among the oldest of the members of the fraternity to have attended, the celebration also highlighted for him the inexorable law of the passage of time.[215]

And though it was a happier occasion, his seventieth birthday on August 20, 1954, also indicated that he had now entered the final phase of his life. To be sure, his birthday was not the quiet one that he himself had actually wished for, but he did play a willing part in a good celebration. A Mozart string quartet put him in the mood for the day, one during which numerous well-wishers appeared at 14 Calvin Street. Walther Eltester presented him with a *Festschrift*, and the governmental department head Willy Viehweg bestowed the Goethe plaque of the State of Hesse. Heinrich Schlier gave the following delayed report of the day: "Bultmann was well feted by relatives, friends, teachers, and officials. One sees how close he is to people. Yet at the same time he retains a moral severity that old age has moderated only somewhat."[216] For Bultmann himself, it was "not least . . . the supportive presence of friends from near and far that made the day special."[217]

While he was still writing thank-you notes for the more than 260 written letters of congratulation on his birthday, he had to turn to his next obliga-

213. Cf. UB Tübingen, RB est., RB to A. Bultmann Lemke, 18. 7. 1954, Mn 2-3452.

214. Cf. RB, *VW*, 342 (sermon no. 124).

215. UB Tübingen, RB est., RB to A. Bultmann Lemke, 1. 8. 1954, Mn 2-3452.

216. H. Schlier to E. Peterson, 19. 10. 1954, cited in R. von Bendemann, *Heinrich Schlier*, 90n334.

217. RB to G. Krüger, 29. 8. 1954, in F. Lilie, "Bultmann-Krüger Briefwechsel," *ZNThG* 6, 298.

tion, the final preparations for the ninth annual conference of *Studiorum Novi Testamenti Societas* that would take place in Marburg September 7–10, 1954. Because Vincent Taylor, the President of the Society, was unable to attend this meeting, organizing and leading it fell to Bultmann. As chairman of the conference, he opened the sessions with a devotional reflection,[218] but beyond that he confined himself to leading the discussions that followed the presentations and to overseeing the social and cultural program of the conference.[219] Though long acknowledged as the doyen of New Testament scholarship,[220] he left it to younger colleagues to come forward with new insights and to lead discussion of particular exegetical issues. It might have seemed to some that Bultmann intended to make a gentle withdrawal to a retirement cottage within the grounds of theological scholarship. Had he not already said pretty much all he had to say when he finished the *Theology of the New Testament* in 1953?

5. Theology of the New Testament [Theologie des Neuen Testaments]

> *It is not necessary to praise this work; the way it deals with the material speaks for itself. The impression of detailed work, of the thoroughness of the way the material is treated, and of the precision with which questions are posed is strongest precisely where critical questions emerge. The presentation is masterful in its organization and style.*[221]

Following the *History of the Synoptic Tradition* and the commentary on the Gospel of John, Bultmann worked from 1948 to 1953 to produce a further *magnum opus*, his *Theology of the New Testament.* The book contains no less than the sum total of his decades of work to set forth the meaning of the New Testament message. As Nils Alstrop Dahl recognized in retrospect, ever since the 1920s Bultmann's efforts to interpret the New Testament had proceeded with an intrinsic consistency towards this comprehensive presentation.[222] The book appeared in the series Neue theologische Grundrisse [New

218. Cf. RB, *VW*, 342 (sermon no. 125).

219. Cf. G. H. Boobyer, "The Ninth General Meeting."

220. Bultmann was the President of the *Studiorum Novi Testamenti Societas* for 1953–54 and had already led its eighth annual meeting of 8.–10. 9. 1953 in Cambridge. Cf. G. H. Boobyer, "The Eighth General Meeting."

221. H. Conzelmann, rev. of RB, *Theologie des Neuen Testaments*, 151; cf. also M. Barth, "Methode," 1.

222. Cf. N. A. Dahl, "Die *Theologie des Neuen Testaments*," 22.

Outlines in Theology] from Mohr Siebeck in Tübingen, and was edited by Bultmann himself. The publisher's contract, dated December 6, 1929, and signed fourteen days later by the author, provided for the volume to include twenty-five printed sheaves. As an honorarium, for every one thousand copies per edition, Bultmann was to receive sixty Reichmarks for each sheaf of sixteen printed pages. The deadline for the submission of the manuscript was set for December 31, 1932.[223]

But in fact, Bultmann first began work on the transcript of the typesetting copy immediately following the end of the Second World War, when the closing of the University of Marburg provided him the free time required for this.[224] In June of 1945 he indicated that he hoped "to be able to bring the text to completion in a few weeks."[225] This was not to be. Lack of food and the extraordinary cold of the first winters following the war hindered any appreciable progress on the work.[226] So it was that the first offering of his *Theology of the New Testament* did not appear until 1948. The second offering followed it in 1951, and the third in 1953.[227] The first edition consisted of eight thousand copies.[228] The publisher was happy to honor Bultmann's wish to append an epilogue to the original text.[229]

In the Epilogue, Bultmann provides an orderly account of his understanding of the *task* of a New Testament theology, and seeks to justify his approach in this book by critically examining its place in the history of New Testament scholarship and to locate this in the history of theology. Partly adopting the view of Ferdinand Christian Baur, Bultmann assigns to New Testament theology the task of making conceptually explicit the self-understanding inherent in faith—that is, to depict faith as it interprets

223. Cf. UB Tübingen, RB est., the contract for publication of 6.–21. 12. 1929, Mn 2-2485.

224. Cf. RB, "Bericht über unser Ergehen in Marburg," in H. G. Göckeritz, *Bultmann-Gogarten Briefwechsel*, 311. Bultmann had begun preparations for the composition of the *Theology of the New Testament* after concluding the manuscript of the commentary on John. Cf. UB Tübingen, RB est., RB to G. Bornkamm, 3. 8. 1940, Mn 2-2147.

225. RB to F. Gogarten, 10. 6. 1945, in H. G. Göckeritz, *Bultmann-Gogarten Briefwechsel*, 233.

226. Cf. RB, "Bericht über unser Ergehen in Marburg," in H. G. Göckeritz, *Bultmann-Gogarten Briefwechsel*, 310–12.

227. Bultmann had finished the text of the final part on 31. 12. 1952. Cf. RB to G. Krüger, 28. 1. 1953, in F. Lilie, "Bultmann-Krüger Briefwechsel," *ZNThG* 6, 294.

228. Cf. UB Tübingen, RB est., H. G. Siebeck to RB, 3. 5. 1948, Mn 2-2500. The French military government in Baden-Baden agreed to paper checks for five thousand copies. The Evangelical Welfare Organization made available the paper for three thousand copies.

229. Cf. UB Tübingen, RB est., RB to H. G. Siebeck, 7. 1. 1953, Mn 2-2624; H. G. Siebeck to RB, 9. 1. 1953, Mn 2-2504.

itself, not simply as the object of faith. And since in the New Testament faith refers itself to "*the kerygma* that speaks of God's dealing in the human being Jesus of Nazareth," then what is to be presented in the theology of the New Testament is "the kerygma and the self-understanding it manifests in which faith unfolds itself."[230] This cannot be achieved by simply reproducing the theological statements of the New Testament, for such statements cannot constitute the object of faith inasmuch as they are conditioned by their situation and incomplete. As more or less appropriate explications of the believer's self-understanding, they are subject to continual criticism of what they are about, a practice Luther applied in exemplary fashion to individual New Testament writings.[231] In particular, through such a content-critical distinguishing between the kerygma and theological statements, it is necessary above all to investigate the very kerygma that provides the self-understanding of faith as "a possibility of human self-understanding."[232]

Bultmann sees the central problem in *presenting the material* to be that of weighing the two reciprocally related interests of historical reconstruction and interpretation that bears on the present. As a document of history, it is self-evident that the New Testament is to be investigated in historical-critical fashion and in terms of the history of religions. So far as this is concerned, Bultmann realizes that with regard to a number of individual historical questions and indeed for the outline of his *Theology of the New Testament*, he is indebted to the history of religions school and to its chief representatives, William Wrede and Wilhelm Bousset.[233] To be sure, he goes beyond the historian of religions by understanding that historical work must be boldly used to interpret the New Testament writings "on the assumption that these have something to say to the present."[234] In order to grasp the contemporary significance of the New Testament, it is never enough to reconstruct the history of earliest Christianity or the development of certain doctrines as matters of the past. Rather, the theology of the New Testament must always employ historical reconstruction to make clear the self-understanding of faith in its relation to the kerygma.

This program is reflected in a concise way in the layout of Bultmann's *Theology of the New Testament*. The proclamation of Jesus, the kerygma of

230. RB, *Theologie des Neuen Testaments* (4th ed.), 587; cf. O. Merk, "Biblische Theologie II," 464f; J. Frey, "Zum Problem," 18, 29–32.

231. Cf. RB, *Theologie des Neuen Testaments* (4th ed.), 586f.

232. RB, *Theologie des Neuen Testaments* (4th ed.), 589.

233. Cf. O. Merk, "Biblische Theologie II," 463, 465.

234. RB, *Theologie des Neuen Testaments* (4th ed.), 599.

the earliest community, and the kerygma of the Hellenistic community prior to and aside from Paul are treated in the first part as "presuppositions and motifs of New Testament theology." The second part presents the actual theology of the New Testament, an exposition that can be confined to Paul and John because only these two witnesses, each in terms of its own distinctive conceptuality, have expounded the self-understanding of faith in its relation to the kerygma. One can discern a great deal of common ground in the contemporary religious atmosphere they share. Their material closeness to each other is unmistakable. This is for Bultmann sufficient reason to place Paul and John next to each other at the center of New Testament theology, even though the two are not related to each other historically.[235] Only in the "Development toward the Ancient Church," which the third part examines, and even then only to a limited degree and in isolated cases, does one find the self-understanding of faith explicated in ways that are more or less adequate.

The sentences that introduce the book, and probably its most important ones, draw a striking conclusion from the understanding of theology sketched in the "Epilogue."

> *The proclamation of Jesus* is a presupposition for the theology of the New Testament rather than a part of that theology itself. For New Testament theology consists in the unfolding of those ideas by means of which Christian faith ascertains its own object, basis, and consequences. But Christian faith did not exist until there was a Christian kerygma: i.e., a kerygma proclaiming Jesus Christ—specifically Jesus Christ the crucified and risen one—to be God's eschatological act of salvation.[236]

Bultmann's picture of the proclamation of Jesus corresponds in its essence to the content of the Jesus-book and to the chapter of the book on earliest Christianity that deals with Jesus. To be sure, Bultmann here treats at greater length the problem of the messianic consciousness of Jesus, a question that for obvious reasons suggested itself in the context of a theology of the New Testament.

Jesus proclaims the reign of God as near, breaking in, and as the one whose coming faces the human being with the decision between God and worldly goods. The eschatological message of Jesus corresponds fundamentally to his ethical proclamation. For even if Jesus interprets more radically than contemporaneous Judaism God's demand that culminates in the com-

235. Cf. RB, *Theologie des Neuen Testaments* (4th ed.), 357–62.
236. RB, *Theologie des Neuen Testaments* (4th ed.), 1f.

mand to love, he remains in both his ethical and his eschatological proclamation fundamentally within the framework of Judaism. The two sets of ideas form a unity, for "the fulfillment of God's will" represents in an absolute rather than an external sense "the condition for participation in the salvation of his reign."[237] As concerns his *person*, Jesus is the bearer of this proclamation. He does not present himself as the eschatological bringer of salvation; he does not demand faith in his person. Nevertheless, as the final prophetic voice of God before the end of time, he personally represents "the demand of decision,"[238] and belief in him exists only because of and together with the kerygma—and therefore in the community. For this reason, the interests of faith can also be kept completely free from the historical question concerning the messianic self-consciousness of Jesus. If I acknowledge Jesus as the bringer of salvation, I perform an act of faith, and that personal decision cannot depend on how the historical question concerning Jesus' self-understanding might ever be answered.[239] Bultmann regards William Wrede's explanation of the historical findings as completely plausible. The earliest community did not deduce its faith in Christ from the self-consciousness of Jesus. The oldest layer of what is handed down in the synoptic tradition and the oldest kerygma do not understand the life and work of Jesus as messianic. In Hellenistic Christianity, it is the evangelist Mark who first undertakes the posthumous attempt to reconcile the earliest Christian confession of Jesus Christ and the reality of the unmessianic life of Jesus—to which end he employs the literary device of the messianic secret.[240]

The earliest community elevates the proclaimer to being the proclaimed by awaiting Jesus as the coming messiah, as the Son of Man. In this, to be sure, it still operates in consonance with the eschatological hope of Judaism, which it also retains by understanding itself to be the eschatological congregation of the end-time. On the basis of the Easter faith and in its light, the first Christians realize that it is not the teaching of Jesus but "the fact of his coming that is the decisive eschatological occurrence."[241] If "Jesus' call to decision" implied "a christology,"[242] this only now begins to become explicit in the earliest community. It interprets the significance of Jesus for faith with honorific titles—fashioned, in fact, by the community—which speak of his having come or having been sent. On the basis of the Easter faith,

237. RB, *Theologie des Neuen Testaments* (4th ed.), 20.
238. RB, *Theologie des Neuen Testaments* (4th ed.), 8.
239. Cf. RB, *Theologie des Neuen Testaments* (4th ed.), 27.
240. Cf. RB, *Theologie des Neuen Testaments* (4th ed.), 33f.
241. RB, *Theologie des Neuen Testaments* (4th ed.), 45.
242. RB, *Theologie des Neuen Testaments* (4th ed.), 46.

the earliest community goes on to formulate initial interpretations of Jesus' scandalous death on the cross, a death that it declares necessary for the history of salvation and that it understands early on as an expiatory sacrifice for sin. The figure of Jesus is given a present meaning especially where honorific titles—taken for the most part from the Jewish tradition—are ascribed to it. However, both Bultmann and Wilhelm Bousset deem it improbable that the earliest community had already characterized Jesus as κύριος [lord]. At the very least, it did not yet worship Jesus as its lord.[243] Due to its connection to the Jewish synagogue, the earliest community's cultic and organizational forms are undeveloped, for only baptism and common meals—which do not yet constitute the Lord's Supper—provide points at which the emerging cult can attach itself. At first, the leadership of the group consists of the twelve, who function primarily to represent the congregation of the end-time as the true Israel. The "elders" exercise a proper office of leadership, which is bound to the proclamation of the word but not yet regulated through an institutionally determined succession. The questions left open by the kerygma and forms of life of the earliest community need to be understood as such, and as demanding future answers.

This happens gradually in the Hellenistic community, which according to the picture created by Wilhelm Heitmüller and Wilhelm Bousset constitutes an independent stage between the earliest community and Paul. Going far beyond Bousset's *Kyrios Christos*, Bultmann offers a detailed delineation of the developments and motifs of Hellenistic Christianity that partly leave their mark on Paul's theology and partly bypass it.[244] As he does so, he reconstructs the complexities of the Hellenistic community from the Pauline letters and other New Testament texts, as well as from extracanonical New Testament writings. Form-critical analysis and investigations into the history of concepts carefully shape his analyses, and he also leans on lexical investigations that he and others deposited in the *Theological Dictionary of the New Testament* edited by Gerhard Kittel.

The Hellenistic community answers its call to make the kerygma understandable beyond Palestine by missionary preaching. For one thing, it brings monotheism home to pagans by way of language stamped by the Hellenistic synagogue and Hellenistic philosophy, in particular that of the *stoa*. For another, it reveals the significance of Christ by modifying the honorific titles it

243. Cf. RB, *Theologie des Neuen Testaments* (4th ed.), 54f.

244. Cf. RB, *Theologie des Neuen Testaments* (4th ed.), 66–68; as well as H. Conzelmann, rev. of RB, *Theologie des Neuen Testaments*," 153; N. A. Dahl, "Die *Theologie des Neuen Testaments*," 33; H. Braun, "Überwindung," 54–57.

has taken over. The substantive εὐαγγέλιον [good news], which, used in an absolute sense, can be derived from neither the Old Testament-Jewish nor Hellenistic-pagan traditions, comes to serve as a *terminus technicus* [technical term] for the Christian proclamation.[245] Acceptance of the message is characterized by the words πίστις [faith] or πιστεύειν [believing]. Even if the concept of belief does not yet include a personal relationship with God, as the central term for characterizing the relation between the human being and God, it nevertheless takes on a meaning that in the religious environment of antiquity it had not previously had.[246] The Hellenistic community further develops the consciousness of being a church in the eschatological sense, and exists at a distance to the world. It relativizes the cultic commandments of the Old Testament, but it retains its ethical directives. On top of this, it develops initial cultic forms, so that baptism and the meals of the earliest community achieve a sacramental character along the lines of the mystery religions. To be sure, many motifs still exist uneasily alongside one another: a good example is the idea of the spirit, which on the one hand is given as an eschatological gift of the community, and on the other becomes reified in particular experiences and situations.

From the point of view of the history of religions, Hellenistic Christianity especially has to assert its dominance over Gnosticism, its closest relative and most dangerous competitor. It "exists in the whirlpool of the syncretistic process. The genuinely Christian motif is wrestling with others; 'orthodoxy' does not exist at the outset, but rather has to work itself out for the first time."[247] Hellenistic Christianity's relationship to the Gnostic movement is marked as much by theological delimitation from Gnosticism as by the adoption of Gnostic concepts and motifs. This is also how Paul is to be situated historically. By raising the theological motifs and questions of the Hellenistic kerygma "to the degree of clarity that characterizes theological thinking . . . and by [driving them] to the point of decision," he became "the founder of a Christian theology."[248]

Bultmann picks up many of the threads he has spun earlier and in the third part of his presentation treats them chronologically. He tracks the transition of earliest Christianity to the ancient church with the aid of three themes: the formation of church order, the development of doctrine, and the problem

245. Cf. also already (against J. Schniewind) RB to G. Bornkamm, 19 May 1937, Mn 2-2147, in UB Tübingen, RB est.

246. Cf. RB, *Theologie des Neuen Testaments* (4th ed.), 89–93; RB, "Πιστεύω."

247. RB, *Theologie des Neuen Testaments* (4th ed.), 175 (in connection with Walter Bauer).

248. RB, *Theologie des Neuen Testaments* (4th ed.), 188.

of Christian living. Agreeing with Rudolf Sohm and contrary to Adolf von Harnack, he emphasizes that the church initially understood itself as an eschatological entity constituted by the spirit. But one may not play spirit and law against each other, as does Sohm. Rather, one ought, like Karl Holl, to begin with the idea that the spirit is capable of creating a regulative system of laws.[249] The gradual development of proper offices and the convergence between charismatic proclaimers of the word and permanently installed communal officials ultimately leads to congregational office becoming not a regulative but a constitutive feature of the church—and one that increasingly takes on the character of a sacramental institution of salvation. The Christian way of life gradually becomes a condition for participating in salvation in the future. Christianity, bound up into world history, understands itself as a new religion alongside Judaism and paganism.

Doctrine becomes exceedingly multiform as it increasingly comes to be defined over against heresy. As he surveys the various motifs and themes that can be thus identified, Bultmann is guided by the question of whether the dialectical character of Christian existence is recognized and brought to bear. This applies to the relation of faith and history, the paradox of *paradosis*—which understands the eschatological occurrence to be at the same time a historical one—and the dialectic between indicative and imperative as the hallmark of the Christian life. Measured by these particulars, the writings of Ignatius are the best expression within early Christian literature of the existential relevance of the eschatological orientation of Christian faith. Next best are the Deutero-Pauline and the Pastoral epistles of the Pauline school. In Hebrews, 2 Peter, Jude, and 1 Clement, on the other hand, the paradox of Christian existence has largely been lost, and in the Shepherd of Hermas, James, Didache, and Revelation, completely so. These judgments on Bultmann's part are based on the premise that in the New Testament the self-understanding of faith finds its highest degree of expression in Pauline and Johannine theology.

The exposition of Pauline theology constitutes the most extensive chapter in Bultmann's *Theology of the New Testament*; indeed, it is the book's real core. Originating in Hellenistic Judaism, the Christian theology of Paul is materially related not to the Palestinian Jesus-tradition, but rather to the kerygma of the Hellenistic community. Bultmann has no interest whatever in the "personality" of the apostle or in his historical location except as such information aids in understanding his theology.[250] Following the structure

249. Cf. RB, *Theologie des Neuen Testaments* (4th ed.), 446–52.
250. Cf. RB, *Theologie des Neuen Testaments* (4th ed.), 187–90.

of his *RGG* article "Paul," Bultmann employs the same program he had sketched out in 1930.[251] The existentialist interpretation starts out from the assumption that Paul's theology deals not in speculative fashion with God, the human being, and the world each considered separately, but rather with the human person and the world in relation to God. "Every assertion about God is simultaneously an assertion about the human person and vice versa. For this reason and in this sense *Paul's theology is, at the same time, anthropology.*" However, since God's relationship with human beings and the world realizes itself in his historical dealing with them, Paul speaks of Christ as the one through whom God "is working for the salvation of the world and of human beings. Thus, every assertion about Christ is also an assertion about human beings and vice versa; and *Paul's christology is simultaneously soteriology.*" In accord with its anthropological and soteriological approach, Paul's theology is best presented as anthropology.[252] Certain consequences for the arrangement of the presentation stem directly from this. First to be analyzed is the human being prior to the revelation of πίστις [faith], followed by the analysis of the human being under πίστις. In order better to understand the human relation to God, Bultmann first delineates—by way of the anthropological concepts Paul employs—the ontological structure of human existence. And although Paul invariably describes the existence of the human being prior to faith from the standpoint of faith, it nonetheless aids in understanding his anthropological statements to make clear the particular structures of human existence.[253]

The effort he expends on developing the concept of σῶμα indicates its central role in Paul's thinking. By σῶμα he means the whole person, who has a relationship to himself and who bears responsibility for his existence. However, as the anthropological concepts ψυχή [soul], πνεῦμα [spirit], ζωή [life], νοῦς [mind], συνείδησις [consciousness], and καρδία [heart] show, the fulfillment of existence is not simply to be found in the present, but rather is always before one. Σῶμα therefore points to the possibility of a person's gaining or losing himself.[254] This basic ontological structure of human existence forms the presupposition for constituting oneself ontically. Paul views human existence prior to faith, as it appears from the perspective of faith, as having always already missed its mark. Under the heading,

251. See above 196–200; cf. O. Merk, "Paulus-Forschung 1936–1985," 43–48.

252. RB, *Theologie des Neuen Testaments* (4th ed.), 192.

253. RB, *Theologie des Neuen Testaments* (4th ed.), 193. Bultmann speaks here of the "formal structures" of human existence. As is well known, these are for him theologically neutral.

254. Cf. RB, *Theologie des Neuen Testaments* (4th ed.), 193–226.

"Flesh, Sin, and World," Bultmann offers detailed analyses of the history of the concepts σάρξ [flesh], καυχᾶσθαι [boasting], ἁμαρτία [sin], κόσμος [the world], and νόμος [law] in order to reconstruct Paul's views on the individual's fallen state prior to faith—a condition due to the powers of flesh, sin, and death—and on the disclosure of this connection by means of the law.[255]

The "transition from the old existence to the new does not take place as a mental development from sin to faith; rather, faith is decision with regard to the χάρις [grace] that encounters a person in the proclaimed word." This word confronts the individual, the sinner, with the question of "whether or not he is willing to understand himself anew and to receive his life from the hand of God."[256] Bultmann then turns to consider the human being living under πίστις [faith] from the point of view of the central features and concepts of Paul's theology. Implicitly dissociating himself from the history-of-religions school, he begins his account with the doctrine of justification. As a forensic-eschatological concept, δικαιοσύνη θεοῦ [God's justification] describes the salvation that the sinner receives as a gift from God. Χάρις, the basis of justification, means not a quality of God, but rather the eschatological act of God's grace accomplished in the death and resurrection of Christ. However, the salvation-occurrence becomes present in the word of proclamation that confronts the hearer with the decision as to whether he will abandon his self-understanding up to now and understand himself anew on the basis of God's grace. Πίστις, instead of works of the law, forms the "condition for receiving δικαιοσύνη."[257] Utterly unlike performing an action, πίστις is "the free act of obedience, in which the new self constitutes itself in place of the old one. As this sort of decision, it is a *deed* in the true sense: the doer himself is inseparable from it, while in an ἔργον [action, work] he stands side by side with what he does."[258] This exposition of life in faith and its eschatological character leads into the development of Paul's ethical and eschatological views. Under the generic term ἐλευθερία [freedom], Bultmann concludes by treating the freedom granted with πίστις to the believer—freedom from the powers of sin, law, and death, as well as the existence in the spirit that grows out of this freedom, love as fulfillment of the law, and the presence of the life of the future.

In addition to Paul, John is also to be counted as an authentic representative of New Testament theology. Second only to the exposition of the theol-

255. Cf. RB, *Theologie des Neuen Testaments* (4th ed.), 226–70.
256. RB, *Theologie des Neuen Testaments* (4th ed.), 270.
257. RB, *Theologie des Neuen Testaments* (4th ed.), 315.
258. RB, *Theologie des Neuen Testaments* (4th ed.), 317; cf. K. Hammann, "Der Glaube als freie Tat des Gehorsams."

ogy of Paul, the interpretations of the Johannine thought-world serve as a further high point of the book as a whole. What holds true of Bultmann's picture of Paul is true here as well: ". . . in presenting John, Bultmann presents his own theology."[259] He is able to presuppose and to summarize his critical analysis of the Johannine writings in both the commentary on John and his contribution to the commemorative volume for Jülicher, not to mention his other exegetical studies and investigations into the history of ideas on the subject.[260] Concerning the historical location of the author of the gospel, Bultmann declares the question irrelevant just as he did in his commentary. The great distance of John from the synoptics both historically and thematically is obvious. The religious environment in which he works can be recognized as oriental Christianity, a Jewish Christianity of Hellenistic character with Gnosticizing tendencies. John portrays the figure of Jesus in the forms of the Gnostic redeemer myth. He shows no direct relation to Paul, nor has he appropriated specifically Pauline terminology. The points of contact and correspondences between Paul and John that are especially apparent in their dualistic conceptuality stem from the Gnosticizing Hellenism in which both can be found.[261] Despite their deep kinship from a material point of view, the two principal witnesses of New Testament theology differ from each other in significant ways. "For John *the central topic for discussion is not what it is for Paul: what is the way to salvation?* For John *the central topic is salvation itself.*"[262] For this reason, the structure of the presentation of Johannine theology must also be different from that of Pauline variety, particularly if and when each is interpreted in existentialist fashion. Bultmann begins by introducing John's thinking through its distinctive form of dualism. He thereupon describes the revelation occurrence in its working as the κρίσις [judging] of the world, and faith as both the perceptive hearing to which the revelation discloses itself, and the essence of eschatological existence. As it is for Paul, John's goal is to present a theological explication of the basic situation of the individual, faced as he is with the decision between unfaith and faith as the two alternative possibilities of existence.[263]

259. H. Conzelmann, rev. of RB, *Theologie des Neuen Testaments*, 155, who, to be sure, adds that his statement is "no argument against the correctness" of Bultmann's presentation of the Johannine theology.

260. See above 310–23.

261. Cf. RB, *Theologie des Neuen Testaments* (4th ed.), 354–66.

262. RB, *Theologie des Neuen Testaments* (4th ed.), 427.

263. Cf. RB, *Theologie des Neuen Testaments* (4th ed.), 375f; as well as N. A. Dahl, "Die *Theologie des Neuen Testaments*," 45f; J. Frey, "Zum Problem," 30f; H. Braun "Did Paradoxie der Offenbarung," 26f.

"The cosmological dualism of Gnosticism becomes in John a *dualism of decision.*" The contrasting pairs of concepts of light and darkness, truth and falsehood, life and death that stem from Gnostic dualism have an existentialist meaning: they "depict the double possibility of existing humanly—either from God or from the human being himself."[264] The κρίσις of the world is brought about through the eschatological event of the coming of Jesus, and is accomplished not by way of a cosmic drama, but rather as revelation in history. The revealer appears in the concrete historical person Jesus of Nazareth. His words are identical to his work; one need recall only that its content is limited to the "that" of his sending. His statements about himself, the pregnant assertions that are formulated by ἐγώ εἰμι [I am], combine to show that Jesus as revealer "*reveals nothing but that he is the revealer.*"[265] To be sure, the "that" of the revelation does not remain an empty category, for the revelation is "represented as the negation of all human self-assertion and all human norms and evaluations."[266] For faith, however, such negation represents the fulfillment of the human longing for authentic life. Faith is the only way to salvation. It overcomes the offense of ὁ λόγος σὰρξ ἐγένετο ["the Word became flesh"] (John 1:14) by deciding for God and against the world. To be sure, the decision of faith does not rest on this-worldly motives, for it is the working of God that brings it about. Because the believer is removed from the world, faith is understood as being taken out of the world. In eschatological existence, the believer is granted the δόξα [glory] that consists in the knowledge of God as the sole reality, and that includes freedom and love, peace and joy as characteristics of a way of existing that is transparent to itself.

Martin Heidegger rejoiced "in the clear and crisp breeze" that blew throughout Bultmann's presentation. But to his credit, Heidegger added a remark indicative of his own position: "I can't stand the zealous counterfeiting of theologians today and for that reason, I don't pay any attention to it."[267] The early reviewers unanimously praised Bultmann's *Theology of the New Testament* as a masterful achievement that marked a new departure in the history of the discipline,[268] and saw the book's appearance as "an event in the history of theology."[269] Apart from questions regarding exegetical

264. RB, *Theologie des Neuen Testaments* (4th ed.), 373.
265. RB, *Theologie des Neuen Testaments* (4th ed.), 418.
266. RB, *Theologie des Neuen Testaments* (4th ed.), 420.
267. M. Heidegger to RB, 22. 12. 1948, in A. Grossman and C. Landmesser, *Bultmann-Heidegger Briefwechsel*, 205.
268. Cf. H. Conzelmann, rev. of RB, *Theologie des Neuen Testaments,* 151; H. Braun, "Geschichte," 173f, O. Michel, rev. of RB, *Theologie des Neuen Testaments*, 147f.
269. N. A. Dahl, "Die *Theologie des Neuen Testaments*," 21.

details, critics raised a number of objections that persisted in the discussion that followed. Hans Conzelmann questioned the decision to classify the proclamation of Jesus among the presuppositions of the theology of the New Testament. Even if Jesus' call to decision implied a christology, the question remained whether a christology did not also arise from a historical picture of Jesus.[270] And while Nils Alstrup Dahl did not call into question Bultmann's overall reconstruction of earliest Christianity, he sided with Arthur Darby Nock in questioning the existence of a unified pre-Christian Gnostic movement.[271] And this construct, especially in the form of the postulated Gnostic redeemer myth, clearly functioned as a heuristic background for Bultmann's interpretation of Paul and John. Nonetheless, Dahl acknowledged Bultmann's presentation of Paul "as a very great achievement,"[272] Conzelmann pointed to the fact that the obverse of the enticing unity of Bultmann's picture of Paul was its neglect of such topics as salvation history, predestination, and the relation between the church and Israel. It also seemed to Conzelmann that in spite of Romans 7 and Philippians 3, Bultmann's analysis of human existence prior to faith had indicated that it had much greater importance for him than it possessed in the letters of Paul.[273] The first reviewers all praised Bultmann for finding fruitful ways of raising important new questions and also stimulated further discussion of substantive issues. This had, of course, been Bultmann's specific hope, for he had no intention that his *Theology of the New Testament* should become the *theologia perennis* [final word] on the subject.[274]

270. Cf. H. Conzelmann, rev. of RB, *Theologie des Neuen Testaments*," 153; similarly M. Barth, "Methode," 7f; O. Michel, rev. of RB, *Theologie des Neuen Testaments*, 148; also O. Merk, "Biblische Theologie II," 465; E. Lohse, "Rudolf Bultmann als lutherischer Theologe," 52. See also below 455–64.

271. Cf. N. A. Dahl, "Die *Theologie des Neuen Testaments*," 34; also later E. Lohse, "Rudolf Bultmann als lutherischer Theologe," 51f.

272. N. A. Dahl, "Die *Theologie des Neuen Testaments*," 38.

273. Cf. H. Conzelmann, rev. of RB, *Theologie des Neuen Testaments*, 154f; as well as, in contrast, H. Braun, "Überwindung," 65; later O. Merk,"Biblische Theologie II," 465; E. Lohse, "Rudolf Bultmann als lutherischer Theologe," 52.

274. RB, *Theologie des Neuen Testaments* (4th ed.), 585f, explicitly emphasizes "that it . . . is not possible to accomplish the theological task in a definitive way. . . . The continuity of theology through the ages consists not in maintaining once-formulated claims, but rather in the ongoing liveliness with which faith copes in an understanding way with its ever new historical situation on the basis of its origin." M. Barth, "Methode," 1, 6, 26, failed to understand this point. Cf. also H. Langerbeck, rev. of RB, *Theologie des Neuen Testaments*; as well as Bultmann's eight-page reply in UB Tübingen, RB est., RB to H. Langerbeck, 12. 7. 1955, Mn 2-2277; and RB, "Christentum und Antike," 10n1. Cf. also Bultmann's notes upon getting the English translation (by K. Grobel) of *Theologie des Neuen Testaments* (Vanderbilt Univ. Nashville Library, RB to K. Grobel, 16. 1. And 2. 12. 1949, 21. 4. and 23. 4. 1951).

The first edition of the book was sold out several months after being published in its entirety, and the publisher was obliged bring out a second edition in 1954.[275] The work went through nine editions by 1984, far more than any other New Testament theology in the twentieth century.[276] Bultmann's *Theology of the New Testament* went on to become not only a standard work in teaching and research, but, because of its unequalled conceptual unity, a true classic of theological scholarship.[277]

6. Lecture Tours

All scholarly exchanges of thought and discussions, in Marburg as well as in other countries, helped me not only in my work on the New Testament but also in my theological thinking in general.[278]

In the autobiographical remarks that he wrote in January of 1956 in Marburg, Bultmann referred to several of the trips abroad that had taken him to Scandinavia, Switzerland, the Netherlands, England and Scotland, and the United States. He greatly appreciated and enjoyed these lecture tours and the personal and scholarly exchange with foreign scholars that they made possible. This was no accident, because Bultmann found dialogue with his New Testament colleagues as well as representatives of other scholarly disciplines to be enormously significant for his life and work. As his extensive correspondence documents, his theological life involved lively communication with numerous prominent conversation partners. In addition to this, the number of invitations he received to give guest lectures in other European countries and the United States further testified to his international reputation.

Between the theological faculty at Marburg and those of Groningen and Leiden in the Netherlands, there arose occasional contacts between 1923 and 1933. Bultmann took part in this joint work by giving a lecture to a group studying on holiday in Langewissche in 1929,[279] and by speaking on the meaning of Jesus for Christian faith in Groningen, Amsterdam,

275. Cf. UB Tübingen, RB est., H. G. Siebeck's announcement to RB of 10. 4. 1953, Mn 2-2504; RB to H. G. Siebeck, 13. 4. 1953, Mn 2-2624.

276. Cf. RB, *Theologie des Neuen Testaments* (9th ed.; revised and expanded by O. Merk).

277. Cf. O. Merk, "Biblische Theologie II," 465; J. Frey, "Zum Problem," 32; C. Lauer, "*Theologie des Neuen Testaments,*" 730; U. H. J. Körtner, "Rudolf Bultmann."

278. Bultmann's autobiographical remarks of 28. 1. 1956, in B. Jaspert, *Barth-Bultmann Briefwechsel,* 308.

279. Cf. RB, *Chronik 1917–1945,* Mn 2-224, 16. The topic of the lecture is not known.

Utrecht, and Leiden at the end of March 1933.[280] The workshop character of these theological presentations was similar in style to the many talks that Bultmann gave at pastors' conferences, meetings, and the retreats offered each semester by the Marburg theological staff. In contrast to these duties, which Bultmann regularly undertook out of responsibility for the church's proclamation, stood the international speaking engagements that focused more directly on specific issues in his discipline.

In Denmark, Bultmann often addressed a group of pastors interested in dialectical theology who had formed a theological working group associated with the periodical *Tidehverv*. This group sought to keep alive and relevant the legacy of Søren Kierkegaard, and it was Bultmann's Jesus-book, with its continual references to Kierkegaard's dialectic of existence, that had induced these Danish theologians to ask Bultmann to lecture. As a result, in Hindsgavl, near Middelfort on Fünen, at the end of August 1928, he presented to the group three lectures on the coming of the reign of God in the proclamation of Jesus.[281] At the summer meeting of the *Tidehverv* group from August 8–10, 1939, Bultmann gave several talks on "The Proclamation of the New Testament and Christian Mythology," which probably presaged his Alpirsbach lecture of 1941. Finally, July 26–30, 1949, he took up topics related to the debate on demythologizing in three lectures before the Danish theologians in the Krabbesholm Höjeskole near Skive. Bultmann was especially glad to accept the invitations of the *Tidehverv* group because the common affinity for Kierkegaard offered a good basis for productive conversations.[282] Over time, friendly relationships developed with several of the younger Danish theologians: with Tage Wilmjelm and Børge Krag Diderichsen, both of whom had participated as guest auditors in Bultmann's courses in Marburg at the beginning of the 1930s, as well as with Kristoffer Olesen Larsen and Knud Ejler Løgstrup. Rudolf and Helene Bultmann often stayed at the rural pastorate of Tage and Tove Wilhjelm in Praestholm. Following their visit from July 30–August 10, 1949, Bultmann expressed his thanks in the guestbook of the Wilhjelms with the following poem:[283]

280. Cf. RB, *Chronik 1917–1945*, Mn 2-224, 23; H. G. Göckeritz, *Bultmann-Gogarten Briefwechsel*, 205n2.

281. Cf. RB, trans. N. O. Jensen, "Guds Riges Komme i Jesu Forkyndelse"; as well as H. G. Göckeritz, *Bultmann-Gogarten Briefwechsel*, 138n8; T. Bramming, *Tidehvervs historie*, 21–23. On Bultmann's interpretation of Kierkegaard, cf. W. Anz, "Zur Wirkungsgeschichte," 460–66.

282. Cf. RB to F. Gogarten, 8. 9. 1949, in H. G. Göckeritz, *Bultmann-Gogarten Briefwechsel*, 239 and n. 6; T. Bramming, *Tidehvervs historie*, 71f.

283. UB Tübingen, RB est., Bultmann's entry in the guestbook of Tage and Tove Wilhjelm, 30. 7.–10. 8. 1949, Mn 2-2419.

From Marburg, t'was, they called me here,
In study enterprising,
To figure out and make it clear,
This "*de*mythologizing."

I let them know as best I could—
What would it be comprising?
I learned: They well already know
About *my*thologizing!

The land where milk and honey flow—
Is't just a myth of old,
As it with dreaming's wish doth go—
A legend now grown cold?

Oh, no! I saw—to me it's clear
That here does myth persist;
You know the paradox right here:
Mythically to exist!

Myth can—I've always said it's so—
Reality contain.
The right interpretation, though,
It takes, it to explain.

But *here*, reality's the place
Where myth we all can find.
What method must we now embrace,
Its meaning to unbind?

It's love and loyalty of friends
That we with thanks have savored,
In the land of myth, with dividends
Of milk and honey favored.

Bultmann went on a longer trip through Scandinavia October 10–21, 1930. His friend Anton Fridrichsen had organized the trip and helped him arrange the lecture topics.[284] In Uppsala, Oslo, and Copenhagen Bultmann repeated the lecture on the "Concept of the Word of God in the New Testament" that he had recently delivered at the third meeting of German theologians on October 6, 1930, in Breslau.[285] In addition to this, he pre-

284. Cf. UB Tübingen, RB est., A. Fridrichsen to RB, 27. 3., 15. 4., 13. 7., 23. 8., 27. 9. 1930, Mn 2-783.

285. Cf. RB, "Der Begriff des Wortes Gottes im Neuen Testament," *GuV* (1st ed.), vol. 1, 268–93.

sented his thoughts on the "Christology of the New Testament".[286] He sounded a different note in the lecture he gave in Uppsala, Stockholm, Oslo, and Lund, which dealt with "Earliest Christianity and the History of Religions." In it, he developed his view of earliest Christianity as a problem for the history of religions by critically engaging Karl Holl's identically entitled work of 1925. Bultmann agreed heartily with Holl in assigning a central function to the doctrine of justification in the theology of Paul despite the low regard in which this was held by the history-of-religions school. But he just as strongly disputed Holl's attempt to depict the historical character of earliest Christianity by tracing the history of the idea of God represented either by Jesus or by Paul. In this case, Bultmann argued, the insights of Heitmüller and Bousset into the significance of earliest Hellenistic Christianity for the genesis of genuine Christian faith had gone unrecognized. Above all, Holl had not grasped the decisive problem for the history of religions: namely, that earliest Christianity had based the individual's relationship to God on the person of Jesus as the eschatological fact of salvation. Thus the distinctive peculiarity of earliest Christian religion consisted in the eschatological character of both Jesus' preaching and the theology of Paul and John.[287] Since Scandinavian biblical exegesis had traditionally shown a strongly historical-critical character, Bultmann's use of the history of religions to locate earliest Christianity met with great interest among his hearers. Also, the Scandinavian trip reunited him with Fridrichsen, and when Archbishop Nathan Söderblom invited him to lunch in Uppsala and in Oslo, Bultmann was able to witness the conferral of the doctoral degree upon his student, Ragnar Asting. In addition, he made what proved to be the useful acquaintance of the exegetes Lyder Brun and Sigmund Mowinckel (Oslo), Erling Eidem (Lund), and Frederik Torm (Copenhagen),[288] colleagues whose work he acknowledged by including articles on them in the second edition of the *RGG*.[289]

During the Third Reich, opportunities for German scholars to lecture abroad had dwindled, especially for those who were not loyal to the system. Still, Bultmann succeeded in getting approval to lecture in Basel and Zürich in 1937. To be sure, the trip to Switzerland was hedged with restrictions: he

286. Cf. RB, "Die Christologie des Neuen Testaments," *GuV* (1st ed.), vol. 1, 245–67.

287. Cf. RB, "Urchristentum und Religionsgeschichte," *Theologie als Kritik*, 269–83; K. Holl, "Urchristentum und Religionsgeschichte."

288. Cf. RB, *Chronik 1917–1945*, Mn 2-224, 18; as well as RB to G. Krüger, 16. 10. 1930, in F. Lilie, "Bultmann-Krüger Briefwechsel," *ZNThG* 4, 297.

289. Cf. RB, "Brun, Johann Lyder," 1287; RB, "Eidem, Erling," 55; RB, "Fridrichsen, Anton Johnson," 784; RB "Torm, Frederik," 1232.

had to report to the German consulates immediately upon his arrival in Basel and Zürich and there make contact with the foreign branches of the NSDAP [National Socialist German Workers' Party].[290] He accepted these burdensome duties and agreed to provide "information" on the dominant political voices in Switzerland as concerned their relations to Germany. Naturally, he remained true to himself, for in his report he bluntly told the Reich- and Prussian Minister for Science, Education, and Popular Culture that his colleagues in Basel and Zürich "cannot summon up an understanding of the German government's handling of church-related questions."[291]

On November 22, 1947, Bultmann spoke in the assembly hall of the University of Basel on the "Understanding of the World and the Human Being in the New Testament and in Hellenism." A day later, he repeated this lecture in the Zürich Polytechnic. With the topic of his lecture he took up an issue that had always been a part of his thinking and concerning which he was to undertake at least nine further examinations in the coming decades. How could one so relate the two great traditions from which Western culture had drawn its strength that the Christian could both exist eschatologically and find a way of living responsibly in the world? In Bultmann's view, an unambiguous solution of this issue was excluded by the Christian's eschatological existence. But—and this was aimed at the political situation in Germany—at least this situation provided boundaries against the demonic striving to treat the state and critical scholarship as instruments of an unbridled effort to take over control of the world.[292] Bultmann showed himself as pleased with the active participation in discussions following each of the lectures as he was with the personal exchange with his hosts—his old friend Walter Baumgartner in Basel, and his equally long-standing friend in Zürich, Ludwig Köhler.[293]

Both the National Socialist regime's restrictive policy towards scholarship and the Second World War made such lectures beyond the borders of the German Reich increasingly difficult. All the more joyful, then, was Bultmann's response when, following the end of the Third Reich, the Swedish Institute for Cultural Exchange invited him to Sweden for

290. Cf. G. Diesselhorst collection, Chancellor of the Philipps-University of Marburg to RB, 19. 7. and 9. 9. 1937.

291. G. Diesselhorst, RB to the Reich- and Prussian Minister for Science, Education, and National Culture, 27. 11. 1937.

292. Cf. RB, "Das Verständnis von Welt und Mensch im Neuen Testament und in Griechentum," *GuV* (5th ed.), vol. 2, 59–78.

293. Cf. Bultmann's report in G. Diesselhorst, RB to the Reich- and Prussian Minister for Science, Education, and National Culture, 27. 11. 1937.

scholarly work and lectures during the autumn of 1947.[294] As in 1930, Anton Fridrichsen made the preparations[295] for the upcoming stay in what Bultmann found to be a hospitable and cheerful country.[296] And again this time Bultmann delivered several lectures—in Uppsala and Stockholm, and on his way home, in Lund and Copenhagen.[297] He also spent time on his own research, which he was able to pursue in the outstanding collections of the library of the University of Uppsala. Here he had access to Anglo-Saxon and Scandinavian literature that had been unavailable in National Socialist Germany. Working with Fridrichsen in his New Testament seminar and in conversations with other colleagues in his discipline, it became clear to Bultmann that Scandinavian research was less interested in issues of hermeneutics and theological principles than in historical issues and in those posed by the history of religions.[298]

Once he had been made emeritus, Bultmann and his wife set off on September 22, 1951, for a three-month trip to the United States. Because he anticipated the likelihood of strained relationships, he had viewed the undertaking with some anxiety, but contrary to expectation, the Bultmanns not only endured the crossing well, but found it relaxing. And far stronger than the feeling of liberation from his previous duties was the tangible humanity of the informality and the hearty friendliness towards guests that he experienced in the United States—an atmosphere that Bultmann considered largely responsible for the success of the trip.[299] Of all his lecture trips, this one became for him the most extraordinary experience.[300] Following a stormy crossing on the liner Westerdam, the Bultmanns reached New York on the morning of October 2nd, greeted by the upraised torch of the Statue of Liberty and by the silhouette of Manhattan that seemed to them like a "fantasy of the *Gralsburg* [castle of the Holy Grail]."[301] The first

294. Cf. Bultmann's autobiographical remarks of 28. 1. 1956, in B. Jaspert, *Barth-Bultmann Briefwechsel*, 307.

295. Cf. RB to G. Krüger, 23. 10. 1947, in F. Lilie, "Bultmann-Krüger Briefwechsel," *ZNThG* 6, 146f.

296. Cf. UB Tübingen, RB est., A. Fridrichsen to RB, 13. 5. 1947 and n. d., Mn 2-783.

297. Cf. RB, *Chronik 1946–1961*, Mn 2-225, 4f.

298. Cf. RB to G. Krüger, 19. 12. 1947, in F. Lilie, "Bultmann-Krüger Briefwechsel," *ZNThG* 6, 147f.

299. Cf. RB to F. Gogarten, 5. 1. 1952, in H. G. Göckeritz, *Bultmann-Gogarten Briefwechsel*, 243f; Vanderbilt Univ. Nashville Library, RB to K. Grobel, 10. 2. 1952.

300. On what follows, cf. the details in Bultmann's itinerary in B. Jaspert, *Barth-Bultmann Briefwechsel*, 286f; as well as his report drawn up for the Marburg theological faculty in B. Jaspert, *Barth-Bultmann Briefwechsel*, 287–90. In even greater detail, RB, "Bericht über unsere Amerika-Reise."

301. RB, "Bericht über unsere Amerika-Reise," 1.

fourteen days in America were spent recuperating in New Haven, where he saw to the editing of the English versions of his lectures. Erich Dinkler and Paul Schubert, both of whom were then teaching at Yale Divinity School, provided valuable help with this. Thereupon began a veritable lecturing marathon, which took Bultmann to sixteen different cities. Besides the single lectures "Humanism and Christianity" and "The Meaning of the Idea of Freedom for Western Culture," he also delivered the several-hour course of lectures "Jesus Christ and Mythology."[302] This series he delivered at Yale University as the Shaffer Lectures and at Vanderbilt University as the Cole Lectures, and also at other universities, colleges, and seminaries of widely varied denominations.

In "Jesus Christ and Mythology," Bultmann develops his program of demythologizing by returning to the eschatological form of the message of Jesus. Jesus proclaimed the coming of the reign of God in the expectation of its imminent breaking in. And yet the in-breaking of the reign of God that Jesus and earliest Christianity interpreted in apocalyptic images as a cosmic drama of the end did not take place. However, it is not only the actual course of history that has contradicted Jesus' expectation of the imminence of the reign of God, for the modern worldview has clearly superseded the mythological world-picture that undergirded the preaching of Jesus as well as the earliest Christian proclamation of Jesus Christ, and shown them to be untenable. Of course, this finding does not suggest that one must eliminate completely the mythological statements of Jesus' eschatology and of earliest Christianity, but rather means that the mythological representations of the New Testament need to be demythologized, which is to say, reinterpreted. To this end, Bultmann appeals to the New Testament itself. For Paul and, even more radically, John, have already demythologized eschatology.

By detaching the Christian message from an obsolete worldview, demythologizing "removes a false stumbling block and brings into focus the true one, namely, the word of the cross."[303] For this reason, the objection that demythologizing turns the Christian message into a form of rationalism amounts to a mistake, for in fact it opens up the true meaning of the divine mystery. Demythologizing makes clear that the word of God frees the individual from the striving for security caused by anxiety and worry, and

302. Cf. RB, "Humanismus und Christentum," *GuV* (1st ed.), vol. 3, 61–75; RB, "Die Bedeutung des Gedenkens der Freiheit," *GuV* (5th ed.), vol. 2, 274–93; RB, "Jesus Christus und die Mythologie," *GuV* (3d ed.), vol. 4, 141–89.

303. RB, "Jesus Christus und die Mythologie," *GuV* (3d ed.), vol. 4, 157.

bestows on him true freedom—freedom from the world and freedom for the future of God. In this connection, Bultmann again explains the hermeneutical necessity of employing the kind of existentialist analysis that he adopted from Kierkegaard and the early Heidegger. For him, the philosophical analysis of existence is a purely formal matter, since it fails to consider the relation between the human being and God. For precisely this reason, however, it is well suited as a hermeneutical strategy because it makes "the human being open to the word of the Bible."[304] Finally, in the interest of consistency Bultmann considers whether his approach might imply that even talk of God as acting must be demythologized. But this would be necessary only if one saw divine action as a miraculous occurrence that violated the natural order of causation; and such wholesale demythologizing is quite unnecessary insofar as faith perceives the action of God as hidden within worldly events. As it is, this acting takes place in such a way as always to be a matter for my self and my existence. And here Bultmann emphasizes once more in agreement with Wilhelm Herrmann that we therefore cannot speak in an objectifying manner of the action of God and of God himself, "but rather only of what he does to us and with us."[305]

At most of the academic institutions that he visited in the United States, Bultmann encountered a high standard of scholarship. The discussions and conversations following his lectures took place in a friendly and refined atmosphere. Those who had criticisms of his expositions of demythologizing made them without any polemical or opinionated tone. People showed themselves especially receptive to his thought where historical-critical research had traditionally been held in high regard, for instance at Drew University and Hartford Theological Seminary. This was the case also at Wellesley College in Boston, where Louise Pettibone Smith, who, together with Erminie Huntress, had translated the Jesus-book into English in 1934, was now able to take part in theological discussions with the author.[306] And since Bultmann had taken some pains to dissociate himself from the notion that like Karl Barth he was one of the chief representatives of "neo-orthodoxy," a few people were able to differentiate the two. At Vanderbilt University he was known primarily as the author of the *History of the Synoptic Tradition,* while following his lecture and the ensuing discussion at the conservative

304. RB, "Jesus Christus und die Mythologie," *GuV* (3d ed.), vol. 4, 170.
305. RB, "Jesus Christus und die Mythologie," *GuV* (3d ed.), vol. 4, 181.
306. Cf. P. Lehmann, "Louise Pettibone Smith, Rudolf Bultmann, and Wellesley," in E. C. Hobbs, *Bultmann, Retrospect and Prospect*, 91–101.

Presbyterian seminary in Princeton, its President spoke of "what the church owes to the heretics and how the most important stimuli for theology have always come from the heretics."[307]

During the three months in the United States, Bultmann met a large number of scholars, among them Martin Buber and Paul Tillich, the orientalist William Foxwell Albright and the sociologist of religion Joachim Wach, the historian Hajo Holborn, as well as the church historians Roland Herbert Bainton and Wilhelm Pauck, the systematic theologians Paul Lehmann and Amos Wilder (the brother of Thornton Wilder), the philosophers Fritz Kaufmann, Richard Kroner, and Leo Strauss, as well as the brothers Reinhold and Richard Niebuhr. Those among them who had been obliged to leave Germany during the National Socialist period were especially concerned to express during their conversations with Bultmann their great sympathy "over the fate of today's Germany."[308] This theme naturally characterized as well the reunions and exchanges with the friends and colleagues from his more intimate circle who had emigrated during the Third Reich—Karl Löwith and Friedrich Carl Sell, the students of Romance languages Erich Auerbach and Leo Spitzer, as well as the classical philologist Ludwig Edelstein. Because of his joy at being with them, it was especially painful not to be able to visit Paul Friedländer in distant Los Angeles.[309]

His American hosts did everything they could to make the stay of Bultmann and his wife in the United States as pleasant as possible. They showed them great cities and landscapes that in Indian summer were decked out in the brilliant colors of autumn; they took them to museums and concerts. Still it seemed to Bultmann that they failed to understand his wish to become acquainted with "the American way of life" outside of the college and university milieu. Even so he acquired many rich impressions, a few of which may be shared here in no particular order. Bultmann was astonished at the "terrific automobile traffic, which, incidentally, is splendidly organized."[310] He enjoyed the marvelous spectacle of the Smoky Mountains, a view that was made possible by the first airplane flight of his life as he traveled from Washington to Nashville. And especially when illuminated in the evening, the buildings of downtown Chicago and of New York with its Empire State Building, seemed to him like the palaces of a city in

307. RB "Bericht über unsere Amerika-Reise," 289f.

308. RB, report for the Marburg theological faculty in B. Jaspert, *Barth-Bultmann Briefwechsel*, 289f.

309. Cf. RB, "Bericht über unsere Amerika-Reise," 8.

310. RB, "Bericht über unsere Amerika-Reise," 1.

a fairytale—"magnificent, but still at the same time almost preternatural." He thought of the Tower of Babel and recorded with a start "how far life shaped by technology has gotten from its origins in nature."[311] Bultmann was alienated by the gaming machines and jukeboxes that filled restaurants with songs such as "You Are My Star" or "Sweet Girl, Let Me Kiss You." It annoyed him that in many public spaces the television, a technologically superior "apparatus for seeing and hearing at a distance," was left permanently on.[312] He appreciated American cuisine to a degree, but was glad for the opportunity to enjoy German fare in the Hofbräuhaus in New Haven. So as to enjoy a beer before going to bed, he had to obtain a small supply of beer in cans—no simple matter in several places that were dedicated to the duty of being "dry." He was introduced to the "race problem," with which he had not previously been personally confronted, by being taken for a drive through a "Negro neighborhood."

The Statue of Liberty at the entrance to New York harbor seemed to Bultmann "to be a genuine symbol of the spirit of the country."[313] His overall positive picture of the United States stood out against the background of his experiences during the National Socialist period. When sometime later pastor Karl-Bernhard Ritter denounced America's materialism, its striving for success, and its absence of tradition in an article in the local Marburg paper, Bultmann reacted indignantly in a letter to the editor. He did not dispute that in the United States, as elsewhere, there were egoists and materialists, but he defended the country from these simplistic generalizations. He mentioned the role that the United States had played in Germany since 1945, and above all the nation's great respect for personal freedom and tolerance that reflected a tradition important in North America since the eighteenth century.[314]

With increasing age, Bultmann saw himself less and less in a position to take on guest lecturing in foreign countries. He had to decline an invitation to Columbia University for the spring of 1958 for reasons of health.[315] Only the urging of his daughter Antje was able to persuade him to lecture

311. RB, "Bericht über unsere Amerika-Reise," 7.

312. RB, "Bericht über unsere Amerika-Reise," 14.

313. RB to F. Gogarten, 5. 1. 1952, in H. G. Göckeritz, *Bultmann-Gogarten Briefwechsel*, 244; cf., similarly, Vanderbilt Univ. Nashville Library, RB to K. Grobel, 10. 2. 1952.

314. Cf. RB, "Der 'traditionslose' Amerikaner." This letter to the editor brought in several abusive letters to Bultmann. Cf. UB Tübingen, RB est., RB to F. C. Sell, 3. 8. 1952, Mn 2-2380.

315. Cf. RB to G. Krüger, 21. 1. 1957, in F. Lilie, "Bultmann-Krüger Briefwechsel," *ZNThG* 6, 305f.

at Syracuse University in the spring of 1959 and to receive an honorary doctorate there.[316] Four years earlier, from February 7th to March 2nd, 1955, he had delivered the Gifford Lectures in Edinburgh, his last large series of lectures outside Germany. The stay in Scotland was strenuous, for despite harsh cold and severe winter storms, the frugal Scots who ran Bultmann's hotel contented themselves with open fires. At least he and his wife rewarded themselves for all their tribulations with stops on the return journey in Durham, York, London, and Canterbury.[317]

In the Gifford Lectures, Bultmann sets out his understanding of history in the context of the successive formation of the diverse views of history from antiquity onwards. Eschatology in particular, with its idea of an end of all things, provided the presupposition and possibility for seeking to discover an overall meaning of history. Jewish apocalypticism still envisioned an end that transcends history. In earliest Christianity, the longer the parousia was delayed, the greater was the yearning for it, with the result that some came to set purely chronological limits on the period between the present and the return of Christ. The church as a sacramental institution of salvation took on functions that eschatology had dealt with. The historicizing of eschatology, which expressed itself in an interest in the history of the church and its relation to world history, led to a teleological view of history, which sought to give meaning to the entire course of history according to a divine plan of salvation. Bultmann shows how the teleological conception of history was secularized in the Enlightenment and later by idealism and Marxism—a chronology essentially along the lines of Karl Löwith's studies on the topic.[318] As the culmination of this process, historicism naturalized history. The premises of a philosophy of history that conceives of history unfolding as permanent progress had to be given up.

Along with Erich Auerbach, Bultmann sees the historicity of the human being grasped for the first time, if also only dimly, in the realism of the modern novel.[319] He also credits Karl Jaspers' desire to overcome historicism, even though Jaspers is at last able to construct a picture of history as a whole

316. Cf. RB to F. Gogarten, 28. 9. 1958, in H. G. Göckeritz, *Bultmann-Krüger Briefwechsel*, 259; as well as G. Vahanian, "Rudolph [*sic*] Bultmann at Syracuse," 57–65.

317. Cf. RB to F. C. Sell, 9. 10. 1955, Mn 2-2380.

318. Cf. RB, *Geschichte und Eschatologie*, 65–83; K. Löwith, *Weltgeschichte und Heilsgeschehen*. To be sure, Bultmann's private judgment was that Löwith "had not actually understood the meaning of eschatology, nor that of history, either" (RB to F. Gogarten, 26. 9. 1954, in H. G. Göckeritz, *Bultmann-Gogarten Briefwechsel*, 248).

319. RB, *Geschichte und Eschatologie*, 116–22 ; cf. E. Auerbach, *Mimesis*; as well as RB to F. Gogarten, 9. 1. 1955, in H. G. Göckeritz, *Bultmann-Gogarten Briefwechsel*, 249. Cf. also F. Gogarten's study dedicated to RB, "Das abendländische Geschichtsdenken," 270. On

only by taking up a position outside history.[320] In contrast, Bultmann sees R. G. Collingwood's approach to the philosophy of history as taking one a step further, for Collingwood recognized clearly the reciprocal connection between historical process and historical knowledge. The only trouble is that his understanding of history does not accord to human responsibility its due.[321] From the point of view of Christian faith, to be sure, the individual does not himself dispose of the freedom that is given to him as responsibility with the historicity of his existence. For the individual's past determines his life in such a way that his authentic self remains taken from him, and therefore freedom is bestowed upon him strictly as a gift through the proclamation of the grace of God. The proclamation of Jesus Christ understood as the eschatological occurrence is aimed at enabling the person addressed by it to make the decision of faith. In the act of faith, I confirm the truth of "a new understanding of myself as one having been freed from himself through the grace of God and, as a gift, having been made a new person."[322] This is why Bultmann insists that the meaning of history must always lie in the present, not in history as a general idea. The meaning of history is realized to the extent that the present is experienced in its "possibility of being the eschatological moment."[323]

An alternative approach to Bultmann's concept of history as historicity of human existence, but also to the "consequent eschatology" of Albert Schweitzer and his students, had already been presented by Oscar Cullmann in 1946. Starting from a linear understanding of time, the Basel New Testament scholar developed in his book, *Christus und die Zeit* [*Christ and Time*], an eschatology that is closely related to the history of salvation. Within world history, the history of salvation proceeds in a linear process from the creation to the end of history. The Christ-event forms the midpoint of salvation history and, as the turning-point of history, it designates the time of the church as a time of salvation between the "already now" and the "not yet."[324]

Bultmann's diverse references in the Gifford Lectures to Auerbach's *Mimesis*, cf. M. Vialon, "Erich Auerbach und Rudolf Bultmann," 198–204. See also below 508, n. 50.

320. Cf. RB, *Geschichte und Eschatologie*, 148–54; K. Jaspers, *Vom Ursprung und Ziel der Geschichte*. For a critical view of Bultmann's criticism of Jaspers, cf. W. Lohff, rev. of RB, *Geschichte und Eschatologie*, 69.

321. Cf. RB, *Geschichte und Eschatologie*, 155–63; R. G. Collingwood, *The Idea of History*; cf. also RB to G. Krüger, 2. 1. and 3. 6. 1954, in F. Lilie, "Bultmann-Krüger Briefwechsel," *ZNThG* 6, 295–98.

322. RB, *Geschichte und Eschatologie*, 181.

323. RB, *Geschichte und Eschatologie*, 184.

324. Cf. O. Cullmann, *Christus und die Zeit* (1st ed).

Bultmann undertook a comprehensive criticism of this interpretation of the earliest Christian witness in terms of the history of salvation in 1948. He reproached Cullmann for improperly attributing to the New Testament authors a uniform conception of salvation history and likewise for having ignored the problem of setting them in their historical contexts. Above all, the New Testament does not represent Christ as the midpoint of a temporally developing event, but rather as "*the end of history and salvation history.*"[325] Because Cullmann misjudged the theological problem "to have grown out of the delay of the parousia," he was from the outset unable to understand "the historicity of Christian existence" as its eschatological hallmark.[326]

325. RB, "Heilsgeschichte und Geschichte," *Exegetica*, 366.

326. RB, "Heilsgeschichte und Geschichte," *Exegetica*, 367. For further discussion of Cullmann's concept of salvation history, cf. O. Cullmann, *Christus und die Zeit* (3rd ed.), 9–27.

VII. Old and New Debates (ca. 1947–ca. 1970)

1. The Controversy over Demythologizing

> *Many letter-writers want to instruct me in a way that I can only characterize as arrogant. They point me to Bible passages without considering that these have long been familiar to me, and without supposing that, owing to my profession, I have already reflected on their meaning. Therefore, they don't think that I am capable of any conscientiousness, but rather reproach me with irresponsible thoughtlessness. I take this to be as impertinent as it is arrogant. And if it might also seem touching that many letter-writers assure me that they are praying for my conversion, it is the same arrogance that is hiding behind this. I hardly need to give any assurances that all this does not touch me, so far as concerns my own person. But it does concern me, because it is symptomatic of a certain churchy atmosphere, and combined with pity for those who have been led astray by blind guides of the blind is anger over the iniquity of this atmosphere.*[1]

On May 7, 1947, the right-wing Marburg pastor Hans Bruns served a petition to the Council of the Protestant Church in Germany to consider establishing additional church colleges and universities. The church was no longer to leave the education of young theologians to the theological faculties, by whom young people were being let astray and into error. In Marburg, he complained, Bultmann in particular was causing damage by denying facts that were central to salvation.[2] The President of the Council of the Protestant Church in Germany, State Bishop Theophil Wurm, immediately recognized the theologically and ecclesiastically explosive nature of the question regarding the interpretation of the belief in resurrection and of the story of the empty tomb that Bruns had specifically cited. To assist the Council in forming an opinion on this matter, Wurm asked Karl Barth for a statement regarding it.[3] In his reply, Barth strongly advised against his own becoming involved in a debate with Bultmann's theology along the lines and for the reasons indicated by Bruns. With his "shouting like a monk,"

1. RB, "Ein Rückblick," 8.

2. Cf. H. Bruns to the Council of the Evangelical Church of Germany, 7. 5. 1947, in B. Jaspert, *Barth-Bultmann Briefwechsel*, 268–70.

3. Cf. the President of the Council of the Evangelical Church of Germany, T. Wurm, to K. Barth, 20. 5. 1947, in B. Jaspert, *Barth-Bultmann Briefwechsel*, 271–75.

Bruns had failed to see that the specific phrases he had cited as evidence to incriminate Bultmann reflected nothing more than already accepted conclusions. If one wished to pursue the whole issue properly, one would need to combat Bultmann's fundamental heresy, which was in tying theology "to a certain philosophical ontology."[4] However, the church cannot effectively do this by issuing verdicts of censure or pronouncing judgments on doctrine, but only by testifying faithfully to its belief in the risen one.[5]

After repeated discussions of the matter, the Council of the Protestant Church in Germany declared that it did not have the authority to put an end to the controversy that had recently flared up over Bultmann's program of demythologizing by issuing a doctrinal finding.[6] In its first phase, lasting from 1948 until about 1954, the controversy over demythologizing soon developed an enormous and unforeseen dynamic of its own. The elevated pitch of the quarrel had as much to do with the highly divergent levels on which the argument was conducted as it did with the various interests, motives, and starting-points of those who played leading roles in the debate. Representatives of academic theology, theologians serving as pastors and in positions of church leadership, and the laity all became involved with the demythologizing issue. Spokespersons of right-wing and pietist factions as well as representatives of confessional Lutheranism took positions. Supporters of the theological approaches of Barth and Bultmann likewise entered the debate, along with individual philosophers and even Catholic theologians. The complexity of the discussion was further reflected in the variety of journalistic media in which opinions were presented and expounded, criticized and combated: scholarly publications, official church and synodal pronouncements, memoranda and reports, newspaper articles, community and church leaflets, handbills, brochures, and broadsides. The sometimes harsh and irreconcilable partisanship of the fight over demythologizing also mirrored the deficiencies and ongoing difficulties of academic theology in communicating to the broad church public the meaning and the results of its work—particularly in the areas of historical-critical research and biblical in-

4. K. Barth to T. Wurm, 29. 5. 1947, in B. Jaspert, *Barth-Bultmann Briefwechsel*, 280.

5. Cf. also his reaction in RB to G. Krüger, 10. 8. 1947, in F. Lilie, "Bultmann-Krüger Briefwechsel," *ZNThG* 6, 145: "You will know that I have been accused of heresy before the Council of the Evangelical Church in Germany and that Karl Barth, who was asked for an expert opinion by Wurm, has certified my heresy to me."

6. Cf. C. Nicolaisen and N. A. Schulze (compilers), "Die Protokolle des Rates," vol. 2, 181, 204f, 456, 573, 575f, 587, 647; as well as (also on what follows) H. Günther, *Die ausserakademische Entmythologisierungsdebatte*, 99f.

terpretation. Ultimately, although these systemic problems never came even close to being resolved, the argument over demythologizing functioned as a lightning-rod in the struggle over the fundamental issue of how Protestant Christianity would and should understand itself in relation to a modernity that was characterized by the norms of the Enlightenment.

For those of the right wing, the answer to this question was unambiguous. In a pastoral letter, the Lüdenscheid pastors Paul Deitenbeck and Walter Köllner explained to their congregations on Easter in 1950 that Bultmann's theology attacked the foundations of the church, and that it had sent the church into the final spiritual struggle of the end of days. In February of 1951, the Board of the Gnadauer Association challenged all theologians in responsible positions to reject demythologizing, since it voids the cross and resurrection of Jesus Christ as the center of the New Testament message.[7] The leaders of the Association, who during the Third Reich had not exactly distinguished themselves by the courage of their convictions, now took up the role of guardians of pure Christian doctrine. In doing so, they frequently spread downright travesties of Bultmann's theological concerns in their pronouncements. Displaying a highly toxic mixture of self-righteousness and intellectual naivete, they eagerly painted Bultmann and his students as heretics. But in their zeal to protect what they depicted as objective facts of salvation from the supposedly subversive effects of historical criticism, they never even approached the level of theological discussion appropriate to what they glibly labeled "demythologizing."

Meanwhile, there was scarcely a single German state church in which this subject was not discussed. Individual leaders requested expert opinions from theological faculties in order to focus debates arising in congregations and church bodies over Bultmann's program of demythologizing. In 1952 the Bethel Theological School presented a statement it had formulated at the request of the leadership of the Protestant Church of Westphalia.[8] Especially heated were the debates over demythologizing in the State Church of Württemberg, which was strongly inclined to pietism. Here, a memorandum of the Tübingen theological faculty, authored by Hanns Rückert with the help of Gerhard Ebeling, sought to smooth out the waves of agitation and to steer the debate, which had been dominated by exaggerated polemic and simplistic polarizing, onto a steady course of serious theological

7. Cf. H. Stratmann, *Kein anderes Evangelium*, 1633; E. Busch, "Pietismus," 538f.
8. Cf. U. H. J. Körtner, "Noch einmal Fragen," 159–80.

consideration.[9] In May of 1951 the synod of the Protestant Church in Hessen-Nassau had to act on a motion presented on behalf of pietistic groups that the state church should exclude Bultmann from its examining committee and condemn his theology. The church President, Martin Niemöller, who favored a constructive way of dealing with the problem, made a decisive contribution to the proceedings that led the synod to turn down the motion.[10] Bultmann took the decision of the synod as a propitious sign for the future of the discussion.[11] In the Protestant Church of Kurhessen-Waldeck, Bishop Adolf Wüstemann, a student of Bultmann and von Soden, prevented the synod from taking a position in opposition to the critical theology that Bultmann represented. Wüstemann had early on become involved as a moderator of the demythologizing conversation within the church—one in which, incidentally, Bultmann had been included from the very beginning.[12]

Despite such hopeful signs that the controversy was becoming depersonalized, alarming side effects sometimes continued to accompany the debate. Bultmann had to deal with an extensive correspondence on the demythologizing question, a business that took up a great deal of his working time but that gave him little joy.[13] Worse yet, he also received many letters containing threats and defamations. A court of inquisition self-instituted by a number of fundamentalist groups and a few church leaders initiated diverse actions against him. In 1950 the Bavarian Protestant Press Association refused to advertise Bultmann's *Theology of the New Testament* in the Bavarian church newspaper since, their argument went, the authorities of the state church had rejected his theology.[14] Ernst Fuchs, who supported the necessity of existentialist interpretation of the New Testament, received an ecclesiastical prohibition from preaching for several months as a reward for his involve-

9. Cf. UB Tübingen, RB est., G. Ebeling to RB, 4. 2. 1952 and to Dean T. Dipper, 4. 2. 1952 (duplicate copy), Mn 2-669; H. Rückert [and G. Ebeling], "Für und wider," 404–33; as well as H. Wassmann, "Der 'Fall Bultmann,'" 167–72; cf. also Bultmann's letter of thanks to the Tübingen faculty of 13. 3. 1952, in H. Rückert, "Für und wider," 171.

10. The thoughtful opinion of K. Herbert, "Zur Frage der Entmythologisierung," which the Evangelical Church in the Rhineland also made its own a year later in 1951, shaped the formation of opinion in this state church.

11. Cf. UB Tübingen, RB est., RB to S. Hamm, 5. 5. 1952, Mn 2-3479.

12. Cf. RB to G. Krüger, 27. 1. 1949, in F. Lilie, "Bultmann-Gogarten Briefwechsel," *ZNThG* 6, 152f, as well as the retrospect of A. Wüstemann to G. Ebeling, 18. 6. 1954, Mn 2-3044, 23–26, in UB Tübingen, RB est.

13. Cf. RB to G. Krüger, 29. 1. 1952, in F. Lilie, "Bultmann-Krüger Briefwechsel," *ZNThG* 6, 292.

14. Cf. J. Wallmann, "Wiedergründung," 506n29.

ment. When Fuchs was to be called to a New Testament professorship in Bonn, the leadership of the Protestant Church in the Rhineland prevented the appointment by getting an expert opinion that like his teacher Bultmann, Fuchs represented heretical views.[15]

In April of 1952 the General Synod of the United Evangelical-Lutheran Church of Germany marked the nadir of the campaigns directed against Bultmann's theology. In the run-up to the Synod, the Münster systematic theologian, Ernst Kinder, passed out a collection of essays by Lutheran theologians on demythologizing, a document that church leaderships sent out to their pastors and that was also meant to set the mood for the members of the General Synod. The contributions to that policy document on behalf of Lutheran theology were of quite diverse quality, but all were committed to the goal "of recognizing and of overcoming a disease of Protestant theology which, long in preparation, now appears to be reaching its acute stage."[16] The Erlangen systematic theologian Walter Künneth's diagnosis of the disease was as coarse as it was polemical. Bultmann was pursuing the "self-dissolution of theology into an atheistic philosophy" and was robbing the kerygma of its objective foundation.[17] Given these findings, Künneth was only being consistent in exclaiming at the end of his text the *status confessionis* [affirmation of accepted doctrine].

At the General Synod, which met in Flensburg April 24–29, 1952, quite a number of Synod members demanded an official condemnation of Bultmann's theology by the Lutheran church. Nevertheless, some theologians and bishops advised against such a doctrinal decision. The resolution adopted by the Synod avoided a formal condemnation of Bultmann,[18] but the Synod's *manner* of dealing with the subject of demythologizing amounted to a public repudiation of his theology. At this session, which took place among a great crowd of the public in the Flensburg Mary Church on April 27, 1952, only opponents of demythologizing such as Künneth got to speak. The Synod had invited neither Bultmann himself nor any other theologian who could have represented his concerns. And this was how, to

15. Cf. G. Schunack, "Einleitung," ixf.

16. E. Kinder, *Ein Wort lutherischer Theologie,* 5; cf. also G. Bornkamm, "Die Theologie Bultmanns," 201–16. F. Gogarten turned against the Lutheran position and the announcements of the United Evangelical-Lutheran Church of Germany on demythologizing in *Entmythologisierung und Kirche*; cf. also G. Bornkamm, "Die Theologie Bultmanns," 211–14.

17. W. Künneth, "Bultmanns Philosophie oder Heilswirklichkeit," in E. Kinder, *Ein Wort lutherischer Theologie*, 84; cf. also 88–90.

18. Cf. the decision of the General Synod in H.-W. Bartsch, *KuM* (1st ed.), vol. 2, 6f; as well as E. Lohse, "Die evangelische Kirche," 183–86.

Bultmann's great regret, ecclesiastically constituted Lutheranism bid a hasty farewell to public theological discourse.[19]

The General Synod remanded to its conference of bishops the task of bringing about a clarification of the questions raised by demythologizing. The conference of bishops discharged this task by passing in Tutzing on September 30, 1953, a declaration that was to be read aloud as a pronouncement from the pulpit in all congregations on the Sunday before Advent of that year. The declaration avoided mentioning Bultmann's name, but in the guise of a rhetorical question it declared that by engaging in demythologizing of the texts of the New Testament, some theological teachers stood in danger of "diminishing or even losing the content of the proclamation." These theologians would have to ask themselves whether they had not denied the facts attested in scripture. "Men of the church" would no longer "have to debate with these teachers of theology"; the language was no longer that of a conversation with theologians who had supposedly fallen away from the confession of Jesus Christ.[20] Bultmann reacted with sarcasm when he heard of the pulpit pronouncement ordered by the bishops' conference, and suggested that if the document were officially delivered to him, he might just burn it in the Marburg marketplace, as Luther had once dealt with the bull threatening excommunication.[21] Helene Bultmann was saddened that the Lutheran bishops misjudged one of the "most important of the life's works" of her husband: namely, that of re-opening the way to Christianity for many to whom it had been closed off. "And how Pharisaical is this action of the church—of damning my husband precisely on the Sunday before Advent [the memorial Sunday for the dead and the commemoration of the last judgment]!"[22]

19. Cf. UB Tübingen, RB est., RB to S. Hamm, 5. 5. 1952, Mn 2-3479: "I believe that, after all, it is less the will for *power* than simple *anxiety* that is blinding so many church leaders and pastors—that is, the anxiety that the church might have its foundation taken out from under it. Since one wishes to have God come to one's aid, one uses the means of ecclesiastical authority, thus forgetting what genuine trust in God and Christian freedom are."

20. Declaration of the conference of bishops of the United Evangelical-Lutheran Church of Germany of 30. 9. 1953, in H.-W. Bartsch, *KuM* (3d ed.), vol. 1, 11; cf. also E. Lohse, "Die evangelische Kirche," 185f.

21. Cf. UB Tübingen, RB est., RB to A. Bultmann Lemke, 5. 11. 1953, Mn 2-3452.

22. UB Tübingen, RB est., H. Bultmann to E. Käsemann, 29. 10. 1953, Mn 2-2933. In Tutzing, the Hanoverian State Bishop Hanns Lilje had distanced himself from the pulpit pronouncement of the United Evangelical-Lutheran Church of Germany. Lilje also prohibited the reading of the pronouncement in the congregations of the Hanoverian church. This gladdened Bultmann. Cf. RB to A. Bultmann Lemke, 11. 4. 1954. Mn 2-3452. On Lilje's engagement with Bultmann's program of demythologizing, cf. J. J. Siegmund, *Bischof Johannes Lilje*, 136, 308f, 595.

During the years that the United Evangelical-Lutheran Church of Germany was declaring the demythologizing of the New Testament to be irreconcilable with church teaching, Bultmann joined twice in the agitated public discussion. In a statement in 1952 he replied to various critical contributions that appeared after 1948, taking the opportunity to make clear once more his position in the demythologizing debate. In doing so, he did not content himself with simply repeating what he had said in the Alpirsbach lecture of 1941. Rather, in light of the critical queries that had been directed at him, he sought to investigate the most important aspects of the theological problem and to clarify the meaning of his own ideas. For this reason, he systematically focused on the key matters at issue: the meaning of myth and of demythologizing, the relation of existentialist interpretation to philosophical analysis of existence, and the meaning of "God acting." Because demythologizing excluded as inappropriate any attempt to objectify God in thought or speech, Bultmann took issue with those representatives of Lutheran piety who sought to remove the title "Lutheran" from his theology. He pointedly offered this formulation:

> *[R]adical demythologizing is parallel to Paul's and Luther's doctrine of justification by faith alone apart from works of the law. Or rather, it is its consistent application to the realm of knowing.* As does the doctrine of justification, it destroys any false security and any false demand for security on the part of the human being, whether that security grounds itself in good works or in a kind of knowing that provides proof.[23]

Because it was a matter of importance to Bultmann to explain the subject of demythologizing to those who lacked formal training in philosophy and theology, together with Günther Bornkamm and Friedrich Karl Schumann he organized a series of three lectures and a concluding panel discussion for South German Broadcasting in 1953.[24] In his lecture Bultmann provided an illustration of demythologizing by inviting his audience to imagine the picture-book on Christian hope with which they were all familiar. It was not his intention to eliminate from the modern individual's faith the biblical depictions of hope from the faith simply because they contained mythological elements drawn from Jewish or Gnostic sources. Rather, he wanted to inquire into the understanding of human existence made explicit in the New Testament's various mythological visions of the future. Had not Christianity

23. RB, "Zum Problem der Entmythologisierung," 207; cf. also E. Hauschildt, "Was heisst 'lutherisch'?"

24. Cf. G. Bornkamm, RB, and F. K. Schumann, *Die christliche Hoffnung*, 7.

in its long history already demythologized the worlds in which it depicted its hope by secularizing, or spiritualizing, or aestheticizing them? "The meaning of the mythological depictions of hope that is laid bare by means of demythologizing is this: that they speak of the future of God as they do of the fulfillment of human life." For Bultmann, faith in the future of the coming God included doing without all wish-induced depictions of an after-death existence.[25]

Theology students all over Germany took keen note of what they heard and read in the argument over demythologizing. In places like Württemberg, for instance, they actively followed the theological controversies,[26] and students in Basel were able to get Karl Barth to deal with the theme of "Kerygma and Myth" in his seminar in the winter semester of 1951–52.[27] When Barth and Bultmann got together once again in the Basel pub The Charon on April 18, 1952, they had a friendly discussion on several questions concerning existentialist interpretation. That summer, Barth produced a literary summary of the seminar he gave the previous winter in an effort to understand Bultmann better. "Oh angel, forgive me . . .!" With this citation from *The Marriage of Figaro*, Barth presented a summary of his manuscript to the one whose thinking had prompted his recent efforts at understanding.[28] To be sure, this attempt had been undertaken under the proviso of his limited understanding, but it slid by degrees into a fundamental disagreement with Bultmann's theological approach.[29] In brilliantly argumentative style, Barth expressed his doubts about the methodology of the one who had once been his partner in developing dialectical theology. In retrospect, however, it appears that Barth's criticism of Bultmann's hermeneutical assumptions, of the implications of his biblical interpretation, and of his notion of the relation between theology and anthropology, christology and soteriology, were not well suited to helping the reader understand the contested issues.

In 1952 the two adversaries had very modest hopes of reaching a common definition of the nature and task of theology—or even how to work toward such an agreement. Bultmann replied to Barth not by publishing

25. RB, "Die christliche Hoffnung und das Problem der Entmythologisierung," *GuV* (1st ed.), vol. 3, 90.

26. Cf. H. Wassmann, "Der 'Fall Bultmann,'" 158–61, 166f, H. F. Geisser, "Barth und Bultmann im Streit," 297–315.

27. On what follows, cf. E. Busch, *Karl Barths Lebenslauf*, 401–5.

28. Cf. RB to K. Barth, 11.–15. 11. 1952, in B. Jaspert, *Barth-Bultmann Briefwechsel*, 167n1. Cf. K. Barth, *Rudolf Bultmann. Ein Versuch ihn zu verstehen.*

29. Cf. also G. Bornkamm, "Die Theologie Bultmanns," 224f.

something, but rather in a letter—an extensive one, to be sure—in which he began by taking critical issue with numerous positions and statements of Barth's. Then he went on to note—with considerable astonishment—that Barth obviously completely failed to recognize that his primary concern was to discover the possibilities for understanding the biblical message, and therefore stressed the necessity for ontological reflection on such concepts employed by theology as "event," "revelation," "being," and "actuality."[30] Bultmann concluded his letter with the continuation of the citation from *Figaro* that Barth had used: "How could I then be angry? My heart speaks for you!"—and to these he added Figaro's final line: "[Let] grief be banned forevermore!"[31] For his part, Barth saw in Bultmann's reaction a confirmation of his own opinion that they represented very different understandings of the central theological task. To be sure, Barth expressed his hope that the points on which they were now irreconcilably opposed would be resolved in the eschaton. But for the time being, he said, the two would simply have to accept the fact that they lacked the key to understanding each other—much like a whale and an elephant who encountered each other to their mutual astonishment and yet were unable to communicate with each other.[32]

And just when this attempt at understanding had reached an amicable stand-off, Bultmann found himself challenged by another unexpected opponent—Karl Jaspers. The philosopher took issue with Bultmann's demythologizing program at the 1953 Swiss meeting of theologians, knowing full well that he was setting forth "like a wayfarer in a foreign land."[33] Unlike many other criticisms, this attack was painful to Bultmann;[34] indeed, Martin Heidegger and Hannah Arendt found him despondent following Jaspers' attack.[35] Nor could the two comprehend their colleague's violent attack on

30. Cf. RB to K. Barth, 11.–15. 11. 1952, in B. Jaspert, *Barth-Bultmann Briefwechsel*, 168–71.

31. RB to K. Barth, 11.–15. 11. 1952, in B. Jaspert, *Barth-Bultmann Briefwechsel*, 190f.

32. Cf. K. Barth to RB, 21. 12. 1952, in B. Jaspert, *Barth-Bultmann Briefwechsel*, 192. The disagreement that the two theologians experienced found its expression in their interpretation of Rom 5:12–21, as well. Cf. K. Barth, *Christus und Adam nach Röm 5*; RB, "Adam und Christus nach Römer 5," *Exegetica*, 424–44; as well as K. Barth to RB, 18. 12. 1959, in B. Jaspert, *Barth-Bultmann Briefwechsel*, 198–201. On the particulars, cf. M. Wolter, "'Christus und Adam' oder 'Adam und Christus'?" 15–36.

33. K. Jaspers, "Wahrheit und Unheil," in K. Jaspers and RB, *Die Frage der Entmythologisierung*, 29.

34. Cf. DLA Marbach, RB to K. Jaspers, 15. 6. 1953, 5.

35. Cf. M. Heidegger to H. Arendt, 21. 4. 1954; and H. Arendt to M. Heidegger, 8. 5. 1954, in U. Ludz, *Arendt-Heidegger Briefwechsel*, 141, 146, respectively.

Bultmann,[36] for the *sole* motivation of this criticism was the philosopher's personal ill-will towards the theologian.[37] At an encounter in Heidelberg in February of 1930, Jaspers had obliquely attempted to coax from Bultmann a statement that would clearly demonstrate his "Christian soul, for his own greater good." Bultmann, however, reacted "perfectly obliviously, or with justification, by exercising the prerogative of ignoring [me]." Thus, Jaspers arrived at the assessment that his student Erich Frank subsequently passed on to Bultmann: "He's an Oldenburger, immovable as a granite block, only superficially demonstrative—one never knows what's going on inside him."[38]

In line with this, Jaspers brought out the heavy artillery in 1953 in order to smash the "granite block." Bultmann, he now proposed, lacked an adequate understanding of the modern forms of knowledge. He understood nothing of philosophy, and worse yet based his entire existentialist interpretation on a *single* book, Heidegger's *Being and Time*. By insisting that myth must be given an existentialist interpretation because it derives from an obsolete worldview, Bultmann shows that he has misunderstood the nature of mythical thinking. Such a thought-pattern is not exclusively a phenomenon of bygone times, nor is it a genre that can simply be translated; indeed it is essential not to transform the encoded message of myth by rendering it in the language of objective reality. For myth conceals in symbolic language the mystery of the formless God, the absolute transcendence that due to its "encompassing" nature, eludes direct approach. Thus, in the name of enlightened liberalism Jaspers rejected as a relic of outdated orthodoxy both Bultmann's idea of revelation and "that of justification by faith alone . . . [an idea] that is most alienating to our philosophizing."[39]

In the course of his vehement plea for the *nobilitas ingenita* [innate nobility] of the individual, Jaspers placed no particular value on entering into

36. Cf. (on Heidegger) UB Tübingen, RB est., RB to A. Bultmann Lemke, 4. 2. 1954, Mn 2-3452; H. Arendt to K. Jaspers, 13. 7. 1953 and 6. 10. 1954, in L. Köhler and H. Saner, *Arendt-Jaspers Briefwechsel*, 257–59, 286.

37. Cf. the suggestions of K. Jaspers, "Erwiderung auf Rudolf Bultmanns Antwort," in K. Jaspers and RB, *Die Frage der Entmythologisierung*, 138.

38. K. Jaspers (in retrospect on the encounter of 1930) to RB, 3. 1. 1939, Mn 2-1067. Whether and why Bultmann did not open himself up to Jaspers can no longer be determined. In an analogous case, Bultmann declined to make a public confession of his personal faith. This request grotesquely failed to see that his personal faith was of no concern to anyone. Moreover, making his faith public would not help those who took offense at his theological work. The value of his theological work would prove itself if it contributed to clarifying the meaning and the point of faith. Cf. RB, *Theologie und Glaube*, 273f.

39. K. Jaspers, "Wahrheit und Unheil," in K. Jaspers and RB, *Die Frage der Entmythologisierung*, 47.

dialogue with the one he was quick to call his opponent.[40] Bultmann did not find it easy to react in an appropriate manner to Jaspers' words, issued as they were *ex cathedra* against the claim to absoluteness of Christian faith.[41] He tried to do so by undertaking to make transparent to the philosopher the genuine theological meaning of demythologizing: it did not mean reducing what the modern person might believe, but rather clarifying the meaning of Christian belief. However, this was a hermeneutical task that Jaspers had misrepresented with his talk of the ciphers of transcendence. In criticizing the absolute nature of Christian belief in revelation, Jaspers had misjudged the Bible's actual claim of revelation. He failed to recognize that one could not acknowledge this claim until after he had assured himself of its truth. For what the doctrine of justification by faith makes explicit is that *as faith occurs* the individual opens himself to revelation by experiencing himself in the context of God's grace, and so comes to a new understanding of himself. "The person lives not from the *idea* of the grace of God, but rather from *each granting of grace to him*."[42] It may have been this emphasis on the necessity for the theologian to *interpret* the biblical message that had a positive resonance among students in Basel at the time.[43]

The waves produced by the argument over demythologizing abated noticeably after 1954. New Testament scholars and systematic theologians in the academy increasingly turned their interest to the new question concerning the historical Jesus. Meanwhile, church theology and the church itself became more and more concerned with topics that were not directly connected to the biblical message and its meaning for the present: sociopolitical problems and questions of social ethics, current political issues, and the demand for structural reform of the church. In a sense, the public debate over demythologizing had also exhausted itself. Once the essential arguments had been exchanged, it did not seem very promising to pursue what had been placed at issue under the unfortunate rubric of "demythologizing."[44]

40. Cf. also in correspondingly critical fashion, H. Fahrenbach, "Philosophische Existenzerhellung," 80–85.

41. Cf. RB, "Zur Frage der Entmythologisierung," in K. Jaspers and RB, *Die Frage der Entmythologisierung*, 83f.

42. RB, "Zur Frage der Entmythologisierung," in K. Jaspers and RB, *Die Frage der Entmythologisierung*, 95f.

43. H. Glossner, "Basel, 1953," 12: "Jaspers was not able to convince me and many of my fellow-students of that time; Bultmann had the greater truthfulness, the more powerful engagement with the issues on his side."

44. On the origin of the term, see above, chap. 5, n. 292. In a critical vein, cf. H. Rückert [and G. Ebeling], "Für und wider," 420; as well as, later, RB, "Jesus Christus und did Mythologie," *GuV* (3d ed.), vol. 4, 146.

The expression had encouraged the misunderstanding that it was about the elimination of the mythological statements of the New Testament. Bultmann tirelessly reminded people that demythologizing as a hermeneutical method was not intent on liquidating myth, but rather on interpreting it in an appropriate way; nevertheless, the mistaken impression remained—as did the widespread confusion resulting from the public demythologizing debate that had in large measure been caused by that unsuitable term.[45]

Around 1961, various evangelical right-wing factions within the church took up the fight against "modern theology" with renewed vigor.[46] They came together in January 1966 in the "Confessional Movement 'No Other Gospel.'" Its attacks were no longer directed against Bultmann alone, but more generally against critical theology as such, and especially against the critical interpretation of the Bible practiced by such exegetes of the Bultmann school as Herbert Braun, Ernst Fuchs, Ernst Käsemann, Günter Klein, and Willi Marxsen. Since it was now his students who bore the primary burden in the debate with the so-called Confessional Movement, Bultmann could pull back from the front line of the conflict. At a mass rally on March 6, 1966, in the Westphalian Hall in Dortmund, the Confessional Movement rounded up twenty-two thousand supporters who repudiated all "unbelieving" tendencies in the Protestant Church and its theology. The news magazine *Der Spiegel* took this occasion to conduct an interview with Bultmann, in which he once again—this time in response to the Confessional Movement—sought to indicate the intentions and consequences of demythologizing.[47] In view of the protracted and violent debates over the demythologizing program, it appears that Martin Heidegger's wish in 1964 found little fulfillment; for he hoped that Bultmann's "whole work [would] not be entirely obscured in the future by the label 'demythologizing.'"[48]

Bultmann remained occupied up to his last years with answering letters of inquiry from Christians who were either troubled or simply asking for enlightenment. Right up to the end, some letter writers still felt compelled to demand that he turn from his "false path" and finally become converted to Jesus Christ. "It would," a nephew once-removed let him know in 1974, "certainly be the best decision if you, too, would give honor to our crucified and risen savior Jesus Christ *alone*, who shed his blood and gave his life for us sinners. . . . This necessary change in your view you would certainly not

45. Cf. E. Lohse, "Die evangelische Kirche," 182f.

46. Cf. H. Stratmann, *Kein anderes Evangelium*, 34–169; E. Busch, "Pietismus," 539–43.

47. Cf. [RB,] "Ist Jesus auferstanden wie Goethe?" 42–45.

48. M. Heidegger to RB, 17. 8. 1964, in A. Grossmann and C. Landmesser, *Bultmann-Heidegger Briefwechsel*, 224.

have had to regret for eternity."[49] What Bultmann thought of these sorts of pieces of advice he had already put on record in 1960.[50] At any rate, the visit he received on May 12, 1972, from the Hanoverian state bishop Eduard Lohse was highly gratifying. His colleague in New Testament studies had convinced the conference of bishops of the United Evangelical-Lutheran Church of Germany that it owed Bultmann an expression of its regret over the shameful statements that representatives of the Lutheran churches had once launched against his theology. When Lohse communicated this during his visit in Marburg, Bultmann "was noticeably moved by and grateful for his words."[51]

2. The New Quest for the Historical Jesus

It is when the learner risks
Following the call of the subject,
That he honors the teacher most of all;
Then his voice remains close to him.[52]

In 1951 Bultmann's Jesus-book appeared from the Tübingen publisher Mohr Siebeck in a third and only slightly revised edition, a printing that increased its total press run from thirteen to fourteen thousand copies.[53] Ernst Käsemann hailed the reappearance of the book—and especially the freshness of its presentation in the current situation—tried and tested for over a quarter century, but still not superseded in its basic conception. To be sure, its approach was also what was problematic about Bultmann's classic interpretation: in his view, "Jesus" could be spoken about only in quotation marks even though the oldest layer of what was handed down in the synoptic tradition could if necessary be reconstructed more or less plausibly because of its proximity to Jesus. From the collapse of the life-of-Jesus research, Bultmann rightly decided to put the quest for the earliest kerygma in place of the search for the historical Jesus that had been central for liberal theology. But this decision had in no way settled the problem of the relevance of the historical Jesus for Christian faith.[54]

49. UB Tübingen, RB est., M. Trentepohl to RB, 17. 10. 1974, Mn 2-2728.

50. See above, n. 1.

51. E. Lohse, "Die evangelische Kirche," 186; E. Lohse, *Erneuern und Bewahren*, 163.

52. Epigram by Johannes Wallmann, with which the New Testament seminar of Ernst Fuchs at the Church College of Bethel paid its respects to Rudolf Bultmann on the occasion of his 75th birthday, in August 1959, cited in W. Harnisch, "Theologie der Verkündigung," 11.

53. Cf. W. Schmithals, "Jesus verkündigt das Evangelium" 390f.

54. Cf. E. Käsemann, "Ein neutestamentlicher Überblick," 197.

Two years later, Käsemann once again placed the quest for the historical Jesus on the theological agenda. Among Bultmann's students he was the first to challenge the dominant consensus within dialectical theology that investigation of the historical Jesus had little chance for success, and in any case was theologically illegitimate. Form-critical analysis of the synoptic tradition had confirmed Bultmann in his doubts that a compilation of biblical statements could be used to reconstruct a life of Jesus. And, like Karl Barth, he rejected above all on the basis of theological principle any attempt to ground faith in Jesus Christ on historical facts. Theology "may not go back behind the kerygma . . . in order to reconstruct . . . a 'historical Jesus'. That would be merely the Χριστὸς κατά σάρκα [Christ according to the flesh], who is no more. Not the historical Jesus, but rather Jesus Christ, the one who is preached, is the Lord."[55] But Käsemann nonetheless insisted that theology may not leave matters at this contrast between the historical Jesus and the kerygmatic Christ. He presented his plea for renewing the quest for the historical Jesus at the meeting of the "old Marburgers" in Jugenheim on Bergstrasse on October 20, 1953.

In the discussion at that time, Käsemann makes three points to counter Bultmann's radical view that the historical Jesus has no relevance for Christian faith. For one thing, the Synoptics contain far more authentic tradition than radical historical criticism was willing to admit. Recognizing this, one may regard the oldest passion and Easter traditions in the gospels as reliable; and this implies that, like the tradition it communicates, the kerygma also passes along actual events. Third, one can move from the relevance of the historical Jesus to a systematic conceptualization of salvation history that possesses its own laws and continuity in parallel with a world history that is both embedded in and separate from it.[56]

First of all, Käsemann knows himself to be at one with Bultmann in holding that the life-of-Jesus research of the nineteenth century cannot be revived. He also rejects the attempt of liberal theology to ignore the New Testament's witness to Christ and to use historical criticism to promote Jesus of Nazareth as the ground of faith. The gospels are not to be misunderstood as factual reports having greater or lesser historical reliability. And yet, in the gospels earliest Christianity consciously combined its kerygma with the message of its Lord. Paradoxically, it protects the historical continuity with Jesus by largely replacing the story of his life with its message of Jesus Christ. By identifying the earthly Jesus with the exalted Christ, earliest Christianity

55. RB, "Die Bedeutung der *geschichtlichen* Jesus," *GuV* (1st ed.), vol. 1, 208.
56. E. Käsemann, "Das Problem des historischen Jesus," *Exegetische Versuche*, vol. 1, 189.

shows that it cannot limit its faith to a presentation of Jesus' life. But at the same time it thereby shows its unwillingness to allow "a myth to take the place of history, a heavenly being that of the Nazarene."[57] Without exception the gospels view the history of Jesus from the perspective of Easter, but they attribute to it a constitutive significance for faith. Once earliest Christianity had acknowledged, believed in, and proclaimed the crucified and risen Christ as its Lord, it in effect employed the gospels to get back to the history of the earthly Jesus.

Still, as Käsemann concedes, the historical-critical method cannot provide a totally accurate reconstruction of what the Nazarene said and did, for historical criticism has created different and partly contradictory pictures of Jesus. In view of the confusing muddle caused by these supposedly reliable pictures of Jesus, it will require a radical form of criticism that is aware of the problems inherent in the subject-matter to point the way to the earthly Jesus. And this calls for a set of methods for ascertaining with relative certainty the authentic Jesus-tradition in the gospels. At this point, Käsemann applies to the entire gospel tradition what was later called the criterion of double difference, a tool that Bultmann had effectively used in analyzing Jesus' parables in his *History of the Synoptic Tradition*.[58] This method indicates a high probability of authentic Jesus-material where a tradition can neither be inferred from Judaism nor assigned to earliest Christianity.[59] The character of Jesus' earthly mission appears in paradigmatic fashion in the authentic antitheses of the Sermon on the Mount, in his pronouncements on the Sabbath, and in his criticism of the Jewish purity laws. As the "Amen" used frequently at the beginning of his speeches also demonstrates, Jesus makes the unheard of claim of announcing and establishing the reign of God—and with God's own unmediated authority. Even if he denies the title of Messiah, the sovereignty of his preaching goes beyond the scope of contemporary Jewish piety. Thus, however imprecise the history of Jesus may be, those contours of his proclamation with which earliest Christianity combined his own message still stand out, and therefore Käsemann sees the quest for the historical Jesus to be "legitimately the question about the continuity of the gospel amid the discontinuity seen in the chronological settings and the variations of the kerygma."[60]

57. E. Käsemann, "Das Problem des historischen Jesus," *Exegetische Versuche*, vol. 1, 196.

58. Cf. RB, *Die Geschichte der synoptischen Tradition*, 22; see above, 113.

59. Cf. E. Käsemann, "Das Problem des historischen Jesus," *Exegetische Versuche*, vol. 1, 205.

60. E. Käsemann, "Das Problem des historischen Jesus," *Exegetische Versuche*, vol. 1, 213.

Käsemann's lecture triggered a lively debate in Jugenheim.[61] The discussion involved the understanding of history. What significance did Jesus' life story have for belief in Christ? Two positions collided directly with each other. Bultmann, supported by Friedrich Gogarten, held that the essence of history cannot be discovered by any sort of empirical procedure like a historiography that engages in chronicling or one that outlines the history of ideas. In order to credit the historical continuity between the earthly path of Jesus and the earliest Christian kerygma of Christ, it suffices to recognize the "that" [or factuality] of the history of Jesus. Against this, Käsemann and the young Wolfhart Pannenberg insisted that the kerygma not only presupposes the pure "that" of Jesus' having come, but also is related to the content of Jesus' message. Käsemann even suspected that Bultmann was thinking of the "that" not as an occurrence that could be located in space and time, but rather as the eschatological event. And even though Bultmann naturally rejected this distinction as inadmissible, for him the eschatological event coincided with a particular historical occurrence.[62]

Bultmann regretted that it had not been possible to settle the difference that had arisen between him and Käsemann in Jugenheim. After all, one of his students had disagreed with him on a point that was hardly trivial. And while Bultmann was not really distressed by this, he was nonetheless slightly irritated. Still, he hoped that scholarly exchange and personal friendship with Käsemann would not suffer from the disagreement that had broken out.[63] In August of 1954 Bultmann offered several provisional observations to Käsemann's lecture that by now had been published. He said that he now largely agreed with the first five parts of the essay. His reservation primarily concerned the sixth section, Käsemann's exposition of Jesus' claim to authority. Bultmann employed both historical and exegetical viewpoints to dismiss the authenticity of the texts that his student had claimed to validate the otherwise unattested sovereignty of Jesus. Jesus' manner and eschatological message by no means went beyond the scope of the Jewish religion

61. Besides Bultmann and Käsemann, Wilhelm Anz, Günter Bornkamm, Herbert Braun, Hans Conzelmann, Hermann Diem, Friedrich Gogarten, and Wolfhart Pannenberg took part in the discussion.

62. Cf. UB Tübingen, RB est., minutes of the meeting of the Marburg theologians in Jugenheim on Bergstrasse, 20. 10.–23. 10. [1953], Mn 2-3079.

63. Cf. UB Tübingen, RB est., RB to E. Käsemann, 8. 11. 1953, Mn 2-2251. The portrayal of the Jugenheim meeting in P. Biehl and P. Schulz, *Autobiographische Miniaturen*, 63, is supported neither by the minutes of the meeting (see n. 62 above) nor by the correspondence between Bultmann and Käsemann connected to the meeting.

in any fundamental way.[64] Bultmann was able to go only so far as to consider "that in Jesus' proclamation, the preaching of the law *turns into* that of the preaching of the gospel."[65]

Käsemann's venture let loose a flood of publications on the problem of the historical Jesus. Students of Bultmann as well as theologians who had earlier been in general disagreement with his thinking—German, Anglo-Saxon, and Scandinavian New Testament scholars—joined in the discussion. In contrast to the argument about demythologizing, the debate concerning the quest for the historical Jesus remained largely within the boundaries of academic theology. Since Bultmann was occupied with both the demythologizing debate and preparing the Gifford Lectures for 1955, it was a long time before he was able to present his own view of the matters recently set in motion. For the time being, he simply published in the *Theologische Rundschau* a synopsis of the discussion that his teaching assistant Peter Biehl had prepared.[66] When in 1957 Ernst Käsemann dedicated to Bultmann the second edition of his commentary on Hebrews, the teacher's reflection on his relationship to his student expressed his thanks for this sign of loyalty: "Naturally, it is a joy to every teacher when his student's relationship with him is a lasting one. It is all the greater, the more he can rejoice in the closeness with those students who have attained their own independence and individuality, and whose criticism is also important to himself. And this is just what I have experienced with you."[67]

In the spring of 1959 Bultmann presented a seminar at Syracuse University on the quest for the historical Jesus. This arrangement offered one last opportunity to examine what would also be the topic of a lecture scheduled for a short time later at the Heidelberg Academy of Sciences.[68] In the lecture, which he delivered on July 25, 1959, an extremely hot day in Heidelberg,[69] he took into consideration the most important contributions to the discussion that had appeared up to that time. In the printed version

64. Cf. UB Tübingen, RB est., RB to E. Käsemann, 7. 8. 1954, Mn 2-2251.

65. UB Tübingen, RB est., RB to E. Käsemann, 23. 8. 1954, Mn 2-2251.

66. Cf. UB Tübingen, RB est., RB to E. Käsemann, 29. 10. 1956, Mn 2-2252; P. Biehl, "Zur Frage nach dem historischen Jesus," 54–76; as well as P. Biehl and P. Schulz, *Autobiographische Miniaturen*, 63.

67. UB Tübingen, RB est., RB to E. Käsemann, 2. 6. 1957, Mn 2-2251; cf. E. Käsemann, *Das wandernde Gottesvolk*, 3, also 4.

68. Cf. UB Tübingen, RB est., RB to G. Bornkamm, 12. 5. and 18. 6. 1959, Mn 2-2147.

69. Cf. UB Tübingen, RB est., Bultmann's report to A. Bultmann Lemke, 2. 8. 1959, Mn 2-3452.

of the Heidelberg Academy lecture, Bultmann was able for the first time to discuss essays, by Hans Conzelmann, Gerhard Ebeling, and Ernst Fuchs, dedicated to him on the occasion of his 75th birthday, that had appeared in the first supplement to the *Zeitschrift für Theologie und Kirche*.[70]

In his Academy treatment, Bultmann seeks to show that the historical and material relation between the historical Jesus and the earliest Christian kerygma are to be distinguished from one other. Since the kerygma identifies the eschatological event with the history of Jesus and thus with a historical occurrence, it self-evidently presupposes the activity of the historical Jesus. If Jesus is to be included within Judaism—and this Bultmann maintains over against Käsemann[71]—the question arises whether "*the historical Jesus is identical with the Christ of the kerygma*."[72] Both Paul and John show, though each in a different way, that in their proclamation they presuppose nothing more than the "that" of the story of Jesus. The Synoptics, on the other hand, in combining historical report and kerygmatic christology, show no intention of "legitimating the Christ-kerygma by means of history, but on the contrary of legitimating the messianic concept of Jesus by setting it in the light of kerygmatic christology."[73] But in any case the kerygma does not attest to its own credibility by referring to the "what" and "how" of Jesus' activity. Bultmann reaffirms his view that both Jesus' eschatological message and his manner implied a christology. But proving historically that the kerygma is related to Jesus' activity and his special claim still does not imply anything with regard to a material continuity between the proclamation, the activity of Jesus, and the early Christian message of Christ.[74]

In Bultmann's view, the theologians who are now asking afresh about the historical Jesus are not really getting beyond the empirical or objective record of Jesus' activity.[75] What is necessary would be an existentialist interpretation of history that remains open to the possibility of a new self-understanding in the encounter with what Jesus says and does.[76] In this hermeneutical approach to the proclamation and activity of Jesus, asking

70. Cf. UB Tübingen, RB est., RB to G. Bornkamm, 27. 10. 1959, Mn 2-2147; cf. G. Ebeling, *Die Frage nach dem historischen Jesus*, 1959.

71. RB, "Das Verhältnis," *Exegetica*, 449, brings to bear in addition to the aforementioned grounds "that modern Jewish theologians lay claim to Jesus for themselves."

72. RB, "Das Verhältnis," *Exegetica*, 449.

73. RB, "Das Verhältnis," *Exegetica*, 453.

74. Cf. RB, "Das Verhältnis," *Exegetica*, 457f.

75. RB, "Das Verhältnis," *Exegetica*, 459–65, joins in discussion with works of E. Fuchs, G. Ebeling, G. Bornkamm, E. Käsemann, and J. M. Robinson in particular.

76. Cf. RB, "Das Verhältnis," *Exegetica*, 459; as well as, already, the Introduction to the Jesus-book; see above 190–92.

"Why did the proclaimer become the proclaimed?" proves to be not "the question of the causality of the historical sequence of events, but rather that of inner necessity."[77] In addressing this central question, Bultmann appropriates reflections of James M. Robinson and Hans Conzelmann as well as a formulation of Ernst Käsemann: "The solution to the problem lies in the fact that the kerygma has transformed the 'once' of the historical Jesus into a 'once for all time.'"[78] In the story of Jesus, earliest Christianity recognized with increasing clarity the definitive eschatological occurrence, which in contrast to mere historical events that fall victim to the past, continues to be present in the proclamation. By proclaiming Jesus as the eschatological event, the kerygma "has put itself in the place of the historical Jesus."[79] For this reason, faith in Christ is always also faith in the church as the bearer of the witness to Christ.[80] And Jesus is raised into the kerygma to the extent that "it is *his* word that the hearer meets in the kerygma."[81] Bultmann sees the meaning of the Easter faith in its being precisely faith in the Christ who is present in the kerygma.

Karl Barth read Bultmann's Heidelberg Academy treatise with profound agreement on the substance of the matter: "A true cemetery of honor, in which you there solemnly buried your students together, each one with a small cross, helmet, and nameplate!"[82] But these students were not able to accept the argument of their teacher without further comment. Among them, Ernst Fuchs attempted to pursue the quest for the historical Jesus by focusing on the hermeneutical relevance of language for disclosing and understanding reality. In the context of his teaching about the language of faith, Fuchs developed a profound understanding for the constitutive character of the word of God that becomes a speech-event in proclamation. As it takes place in speech, God's love becomes word; it happens as God's "yes" to the person. Taking this route, Fuchs discovered new insights into the significance for faith of what the historical Jesus said and did. Jesus' conduct proves to be the enacting of care just as his message gives voice to a word of love. For Fuchs, the faith that is ignited at Jesus' word contains a linguistic prize;

77. RB, "Das Verhältnis," *Exegetica*, 465.

78. RB, "Das Verhältnis," *Exegetica*, 467f; E. Käsemann, "Das Problem des historischen Jesus," *Exegetische Versuche* (6th ed.), vol. 1, 200f.

79. RB, "Das Verhältnis," *Exegetica*, 468.

80. RB, "Das Verhältnis," *Exegetica*, 468n80, explicitly points to the fact that here he has in view the church not as an institution but as eschatological occurrence. Cf. also UB Tübingen, RB est., RB to E. Käsemann, 9. 9. 1960, Mn 2-2251.

81. RB, "Das Verhältnis," *Exegetica*, 469.

82. K. Barth to RB, 3. 1. 1961, in B. Jaspert, *Barth-Bultmann Briefwechsel*, 201.

for in the "yes"-word of God that Jesus pronounces in an original way, the believer is enabled to discover the love that constitutes and bears up his life.[83]

In 1962 Gerhard Ebeling summarized the most important objections to Bultmann's argument in his work, *Theologie und Verkündigung* [*Theology and Proclamation*]. First, he was doubtful about Bultmann's view that the historical continuity between Jesus and the post-Easter kerygma was confined to the "that" of Jesus' having come. For every knowing about the "that" of a historical event presupposes an acquaintance with the "what" and the "how" of that occurrence, and vice versa.[84] To this extent, restricting historical continuity to the pure "that" separates the person of Jesus of Nazareth from the concrete reference of the kerygma. Here Ebeling referred to the fact that contrary to Bultmann's interpretation, the New Testament witnesses invariably displayed an interest, however minimal, in the historical "what" and "how" of Jesus' nature.[85] And as for the person of Jesus—to which, after all, the kerygma does refer—if it were not possible to provide him with a historically specific description, the kerygma would be a mere myth.[86] Ebeling agreed with Bultmann that in its claim to truth, Christian belief neither could nor should be validated by so-called historical facts, and therefore not by the historical Jesus. Nevertheless, the kerygma must be related to what Jesus said and did, for it understands Jesus as the basis of faith and makes explicit precisely what is implied by Jesus' person, manner, and proclamation. The implicitly christological kerygma deals with the "word-event in which Jesus' encounter with God . . . comes to be spoken in such a way that this encounter . . . becomes the event that validates faith."[87]

Thereby Ebeling not only adopted Bultmann's distinction between the christology implied in Jesus' words and deeds and made explicit through the kerygma, but he constructively developed it.[88] Ernst Käsemann, in contrast, reacted with evident irritation to Bultmann's contribution to the debate over the new quest of the historical Jesus. He engaged Bultmann's Academy analysis with the conviction that defending the truth of theology required him to resume the bitter dispute with his teacher and to face the personal

83. Cf. E. Fuchs, *Zur Frage nach dem historischen Jesus.* Bultmann took a good look at the basic intention of the concept of the speech-event used by (Ebeling and) Fuchs, above all in UA Tübingen, G. Ebeling est., RB to E. Fuchs, 8. 3. 1960 (carbon copy).

84. Cf. G. Ebeling, *Theologie und Verkündigung*, 68f; also A. Beutel, *Gerhard Ebeling*, 265–67.

85. Cf. G. Ebeling, *Theologie und Verkündigung*, 69, 125–27; also H. Diem, *Ja oder Nein*, 277–79.

86. Cf. G. Ebeling, *Theologie und Verkündigung*, 63.

87. G. Ebeling, *Theologie und Verkündigung*, 81.

88. E. Jüngel, *Paulus and Jesus*, is also to be noted in this connection.

tensions that would result.[89] Bultmann in turn took up the gauntlet that the most pugnacious of his students had thrown down before him. He sought at first to parry the attack with an eight-page letter that he shortly afterward published in a slightly modified form as "Answer to Ernst Käsemann."[90]

Käsemann was unable to accept Bultmann's view that it was only the "that" of the history of Jesus that identified the gospel for earliest Christianity. The question that stood at the center of the controversy—whether the New Testament "reckoned the earthly Jesus as its own criterion"—was to be answered in the affirmative. Even Paul understands that despite all the "overflowing mythology" determined by its genre, the hymn in Phil 2:5–11 portrays Christ as the irreplaceable figure of the earthly Jesus and ties the kerygma to this.[91] To be sure, the gospel writers avoided writing biographies of Jesus in order to ward off the danger of Docetism, and yet their gospels were etched with the unmistakable features of the Nazarene. In this way, the gospels represent a critical reaction to enthusiastic tendencies in earliest Christianity. But Bultmann was unable to adopt this thesis regarding the origin of the gospels; as he had done earlier, he denied that Paul and John had any interest that would qualify as going beyond the "that" of the story of the historical Jesus.[92]

Käsemann further sharpened his position in the course of criticizing a statement in support of Bultmann by Herbert Braun, who proposed that for earliest Christianity the self-understanding of the believer was the constant and christology the variable.[93] Against this, Käsemann objected that in the New Testament, the believer's belonging to Christ was the decisive constant, whereas "nothing [seems] so variable as the self-understanding of the believer."[94] Bultmann did not recognize this criticism as valid, for in his view Käsemann had reduced the self-understanding of the believer to an empirical feature of human beings that could be objectively observed and defined. From a theological perspective, however, the self-understanding of the individual includes reference to a transcendent reality.[95]

89. Cf. E. Käsemann, "Sackgassen im Streit um den historischen Jesus," *Exegetische Versuche* (3d ed.), vol. 2, 42.

90. Cf. UB Tübingen, RB est., RB to E. Käsemann, 2. 4. 1965, Mn 2-2251; RB, "Antwort an Ernst Käsemann," *GuV* (3d ed.), vol. 4, 190–98.

91. E. Käsemann, "Sackgassen im Streit um den historischen Jesus," *Exegetische Versuche* (3d ed.), vol. 2, 53.

92. Cf. RB, "Antwort an Ernst Käsemann," *GuV* (3d ed.), vol. 4, 195f.

93. Cf. RB, "Das Verhältnis," *Exegetica*, 463.

94. Käsemann, "Sackgassen im Streit um den historischen Jesus," *Exegetische Versuche* (3d ed.), vol. 2, 45.

95. Cf. RB, "Antwort an Ernst Käsemann," *GuV* (3d ed.), vol. 4, 195.

Käsemann ultimately found theologically unacceptable his teacher's thesis that faith in the Christ present in the kerygma always implied faith in the church as the bearer of the kerygma. Ultimately, he argued, the distinction drawn by Bultmann to safeguard this distinction between the church as an institution and as an eschatological occurrence amounts to an unhistorical dualism. For to the extent that the eschatological occurrence plays itself out in what is earthly, it always requires the substrate, the embodiment of institutional forms. Furthermore, whoever would say *credo in ecclesiam* [I believe in the church] would thereby relinquish the possibility of critical encounter with the tradition of the church. It is Christ alone who is to be seen as the criterion of the individual Christian's belief as well as that of the community of believers, and this Christ is not only present in the kerygma but has also exalted himself over us.[96] Bultmann agreed with Käsemann's assertion that Christ alone is the ground and lord of the church, but he pointed out that the Christ so understood still encounters the believer solely in the word of proclamation that the church addresses to him. For this reason, Bultmann conceived the relation between the church as institution and as eschatological occurrence not as a dualistic, but rather as a dialectical one.[97]

The exchange of blows between Käsemann and Bultmann was not free from redundancies and misunderstandings on both sides. Teacher and student were not able to agree on the theological meaning of the quest of the historical Jesus.[98] In the long run, the insight that belief in Jesus Christ had to be grounded in both the proclamation and the activity of Jesus prevailed over Bultmann's extreme position. Nevertheless, Käsemann's solution to the problem of the historical Jesus with its criterion of double difference did not provide a final answer either. Thus, the ongoing course of the debate over the historical Jesus seems to confirm the famous saying with which Albert Schweitzer once concluded his *The Quest of the Historical Jesus.* "As One unknown, without a name," Jesus comes to each generation "as of old, by the lake-side, He came to those who knew Him not." But those who obey his call to discipleship will, in fellowship with him, "experience as an ineffable mystery Who He is."[99]

96. Cf. Käsemann, "Sackgassen im Streit um den historischen Jesus," *Exegetische Versuche* (3d ed.), vol. 2, 61–64.

97. Cf. RB, "Antwort an Ernst Käsemann," *GuV* (3d ed.), vol. 4, 198.

98. The persistence with which Bultmann defended the position he had come to early on in the controversy over the relevance of the historical Jesus for Christian faith may have encouraged Käsemann in slogging away at other areas of the theology of his teacher, as well.

99. Cf. A. Schweitzer, *Geschichte der Leben-Jesu-Forschung*, 630.

3. Relations with Theological Contemporaries

What we do when we try out other solutions is itself a problem that you have posed. I have never written a line and seldom delivered a lecture without thinking of you as I do, and will probably never do so in the future. Our differences are essentially a function of other relationships, and you have been the force behind these as well. That you have personally kept faith with me through it all is most profoundly reciprocated by me.[100]

In 1963, Günther Bornkamm published in the *Theologische Rundschau* a report on the discussion that Bultmann's theological work had initiated—especially the demythologizing program, but also the hermeneutic that it was based on. This collective review was preceded by a bibliography compiled by Egon Brandenburger containing no fewer than 453 titles.[101] The enormous compass of the literary citations, which made no pretense at completeness, was like a seismograph showing the breadth and intensity of contention that Bultmann's theology had unleashed. The public debate over demythologizing carried Bultmann's name far beyond the realm of church and theology; undoubtedly he had become a famous man.

The media did their best to satisfy the interest of a broader public in obtaining all the details about the thought and the person of the controversial Marburg theology professor. Between 1958 and 1963, several radio stations carried a series of six lectures by Bultmann on various topics.[102] On August 23, 1964, South German Radio aired on its second program an interview between Hans Fischer-Barnicol and Bultmann.[103] Against the background of the Confessional Movement's violent attacks against his "heresy" under the title "No Other Gospel," the news magazine *Der Spiegel* questioned him in the summer of 1966 about the content and the aims of his theological thinking.[104] But Bultmann was determined not to expose himself to media attention, and for years turned down requests for television interviews. Only under pressure from Heinz Zahrndt, the publisher of the *Sonntagsblatt*

100. UB Tübingen, RB est., E. Käsemann to RB, 4. 2. 1970, Mn 2-1083.
101. Cf. G. Bornkamm, "Die Theologie Bultmanns," 173–84.
102. Cf. the compilation of audio tapes in UB Tübingen, RB est., Mn 2-317–22.
103. Cf. H. Fischer-Barnicol, "Freiheit zur Zukunft," Mn 2-323.
104. Cf. [RB,] "Ist Jesus auferstanden wie Goethe?" The title of the interview came not from Bultmann, but rather from the *Spiegel* editor Werner Harenberg, who saw the interview through to publication with Bultmann.

[*Sunday Edition*], did Bultmann make an exception and took on the ordeal of a television interview on January 9, 1969. The proceedings confirmed him in his opinion: "Never again!"[105] It was a comparatively painless matter when painters or photographers did portraits of him.[106] The photographer Paul Swiridoff, from *Schwäbisch Hall*, succeeded in taking one of the most expressive portraits of Bultmann—"it's the eyes!"—in accordance with his maxim that the observer must be able to read a face captured in a photograph as one would a landscape. Swiridoff also included his 1965 portrait of Bultmann in the exhibition he assembled of ninety "portraits of cultural Germany."[107] In Marburg during July of 1956, Bultmann acceded to a request from the American theologian Schubert Miles Ogden and wrote down autobiographical remarks for the sake of his American readers.[108] In 1958 he assembled for the *Expository Times* a list of the six books that he recognized as having had decisive significance for his work as a theologian and interpreter of the New Testament:[109]

1. Carl Weizsäcker, *Das Apostolische Zeitalter der Christlichen Kirche* [*The Apostolic Era of the Christian Church*], 1886 (1st ed.)
2. William Wrede, *Das Messiasgeheimnis in den Evangelien* [*The Messianic Secret in the Gospels*], 1901 (1st ed.)
3. Johannes Weiss, *Die Predigt Jesu vom Reiche Gottes* [*Jesus' Preaching of the Kingdom of God*], 1900 (2d ed.)
4. Wilhelm Herrmann, *Ethik* [*Ethics*], 1904 (3d ed.)
5. Karl Barth, *Der Römerbrief* [*The Epistle to the Romans*], 1922 (2d ed.)
6. Martin Heidegger, *Sein und Zeit* [*Being and Time*], 1927 (1st ed.)

In view of the great influence that Bultmann's thought exercised on theological discourse during the first two decades after 1945, it was inevitable that scholarly research would turn to his work as a whole or to individual aspects of it. Even while he was himself still actively engaged in his work, his theo-

105. RB to G. Krüger, 17. 1. 1969, in F. Lilie, "Bultmann-Krüger Briefwechsel,"*ZNThG* 7, 163; cf. also RB to G. Krüger 21 January 1969, Lilile, *Bultmann-Krüger Briefwechsel*, 164. The interview recorded by H. Zahrnt for North German Radio (cf. UB Tübingen, RB est., Mn 2-234), was not aired for reasons that are no longer possible to work out.

106. The Universitätsmuseum für Kunst und Kulturgeschichte Marburg [Marburg University Museum for Art and History of Culture] preserves painted portraits of Bultmann by Effi Bantzer (1962) and Gerhard Stengel (1965). An oil painting from 1974 by Bernd Jaspert is reproduced as the frontispiece in B. Jaspert, *Rudolf Bultmanns Werk und Wirkung*.

107. Cf. P. Swiridoff, *Das Gesicht*, 64 (illustration); P. Swiridoff, *Porträts aus dem geistigen Deutschland*, 178 (illustration) and 179 (text).

108. Cf. B. Jaspert, *Barth-Bultmann Briefwechsel* (2d ed.), 302–11.

109. Cf. RB, *Milestones in Books. IV*, 125; also in RB, *Theologie als Kritik*, 513.

logical approach and the paths of thought he pursued became the object of numerous critical investigations. Young theologians pursued doctoral studies on such issues as the status of the eschatological in Bultmann's theology, his conception of the relation of faith and history, the significance of Wilhelm Herrmann or of Martin Heidegger for his thinking.[110]

Before the Second World War Bultmann had already found a following outside of Germany as a representative of dialectical theology, especially in the Anglo-Saxon and Scandinavian countries. The full scope of his international reputation emerged after 1950, when the Glasgow systematic theologian John Macquarrie published two books that acquainted Scottish theologians with Bultmann's basic ideas. Macquarrie defended the inherent legitimacy of existentialist interpretation of the kerygma, sought to explain the limits set by the demythologization of the kerygma, and emphasized that myth contains both existential and ontological dimensions.[111] Bultmann's interpretation by the Catholic theologian René Marlé proved significant for the French-speaking world. The Jesuit gave a sympathetic introduction to Bultmann's interpretation of the New Testament. The critical questions that Marlé directed towards Bultmann got their bite from Catholic theology's opposition to the Lutheran doctrine of justification and the understanding of the individual made explicit therein.[112] Bultmann saw that the real value of Marlé's criticism consisted in the clear exposition of this basic contrast upon which he based his attack on the subject-matter.[113]

Bultmann also recognized the contributions of the American systematic theologian Schubert Miles Ogden as a constructive engagement with his theology, and especially his book *Christ without Myth*. Ogden affirmed the basic thrust of Bultmann's theological work but thought it was not carried through consistently. Bultmann rightly understands that divine revelation sets the individual free for authentic existence, but unnecessarily restricts revelation to the particular historical event of the life and death of Jesus. The vulnerability of existentialist interpretation to the threat of subjectivism both can and must be minimized by a metaphysical theology that directly attests

110. Cf. (as a selection) J. Körner, *Eschatologie und Geschichte*; H. Orr, *Geschichte und Heilsgeschichte in der Theologie Rudolf Bultmanns*; F. W. Sticht, *Die Bedeutung Wilhelm Herrmanns*; G. Noller, *Sein und Existenz.*

111. Cf. J. Macquarrie, *An Existentialist Theology*; J. Macquarrie, *The Scope of Demythologizing.*

112. Cf. R. Marlé, *Bultmann et l'interpretation du Nouveau Testament.*

113. Cf. RB, "In eigener Sache," *GuV* (1st ed.), vol. 3, 185–89; as well as RB, rev. of [the German translation of] R. Marlé, *Bultmann und die Interpretation des Neuen Testamentes*, 440. Cf. also P. Corset, Correspondance Rudolf Bultmann-Rene Marlé, 537–42. Cf. also RB to A. Malet, A. Malet, *Mythos et Logos*, [ixf].

not only faith as a phenomenon of human existence, but also and above all knows God as the reality in which faith is grounded. For this purpose Ogden recommended an appeal to the process philosophy of Charles Hartshorne.[114] Bultmann, however, regarded Ogden's concept of a "philosophical theology" as deeply problematic. Bultmann did address once again the question of how one may properly speak of God, yet could not indicate precisely the direction he might take in thinking further about this issue.[115] Nor did Bultmann accept Ogden's reproach of inconsistency. The New Testament kerygma is in no way to be reduced to a picture of Jesus "as a symbol of authentic existence." One must rather recognize the nature of Christ's message as having the character of event and decision. For it is reflective of the fundamental stumbling-block [*skandalon*] of the kerygma that this message directs itself in personal address to its hearers in the word.[116]

Bultmann's theological work had an astonishing resonance in the Catholic academic milieu. The atmosphere at the conclusion of the Second Vatican Council and precisely the loosening of the shackles that had long restrained Catholic exegesis made for a climate that was conducive to Catholic theologians' dealing with Bultmann's thinking. The constructive role that the Protestant theologian assigned to philosophy, or even his view that, as the bearer of the word, the church belongs henceforth to the eschatological occurrence, seemed to hold ecumenical potential. Thus, Catholic exegetes and fundamental theologians began to deal with Bultmann's work in an objective openness that the old, unproductive model of controversy and debate had eschewed.[117] To the extent that Bultmann became aware of the results of these investigations, he acknowledged them as contributions not only to the interpretation of his own theology but also to the ecumenical conversation.[118] He gave special recognition to the careful and sympathetic presentation of his thought by Gotthold Hasenhüttl, whose book *Der Glaubensvollzug* [*Making Faith Real*] signified a breakthrough in the Catholic reception of Bultmann—one that not accidentally occurred shortly after Vatican II.[119] Hasenhüttl's rich and subtle analysis, dialogical as it was,

114. Cf. S. M. Ogden, *Christ without Myth*.

115. Cf. RB, "Zur Frage einer 'Philosophischen Theologie,'" *GuV* (3d ed.), vol. 4, 104–6.

116. Cf. RB, rev. of S. M. Ogden, *Christ without Myth*, in RB, *Theologie als Kritik*, 507; cf. also RB, "Reply," 271–73.

117. Cf. (as a selection) F. Theunis, *Offenbarung und Glaube bei Rudolf Bultmann*; K. Hollmann, *Existenz und Glaube*; M. Boutin, *Relationalität also Verstehungsprinzip bei Rudolf Bultmann*.

118. Cf. RB, "Zum Geleit," 9.

119. Cf. G. Bornkamm, "Die Theologie Bultmanns," 246–59; H. Hering, "Ungeliebter Kronzeuge," in B. Jaspert, *Werk und Wirkung*, 380f.

opened up new and fruitful perspectives and brought out the relationship between basic insights of the Reformation and the Catholic understanding of faith. Although agreement on the part of the Protestant theologian and his Catholic interpreter extended over nearly all relevant topics, both were conscious of continuing disagreement in the understanding of the church. But Bultmann could not possibly go along with Hasenhüttl's proposal that the dialectical relation between visible and invisible church be understood and recognized as a paradoxical sign of the identity of the visible church represented through the papacy and that which it represented: the *ecclesia invisibilis* as eschatological phenomenon. He did not believe any ecclesiastical office or legal apparatus to be constitutive of the church.[120]

Bultmann had his doubts about the efforts of younger German Protestant dogmaticians to follow new paths in various areas of systematic theology. To be sure, he affirmed Helmut Gollwitzer's conception of God as a reality standing over against the human being and therefore understanding revelation as an occurrence arising out of the freedom of God; however, he found far from convincing *the way* that Gollwitzer made the case for this in his book, *Die Existenz Gottes im Bekenntnis des Glaubens* [*The Existence of God in the Confession of Faith*]. He responded to Gollwitzer's criticism of his theology with an explicit statement that blunted the attack by tracing those disparagements to their author's serious misunderstandings of particular statements and concepts.[121] As he had rejected Ogden's demand for a philosophical theology, Bultmann now rejected Gollwitzer's postulate that theology must first of all postulate God's being-in-and-for-itself and only later take up the meaning of God's being-for-us.[122] Bultmann reacted with similar reserve to Wolfhart Pannenberg's little book, *Was Ist der Mensch?* [*What Is Man?*]; he found Pannenberg's discussion of Marxism quite fine, but the chapter dealing with the individual's role in history rather superficial. As a whole, Bultmann found in the book "an awkward apologia," since Pannenberg had "simplistically [inferred] the human being's relatedness to God from his openness to the world and to the future."[123]

In contrast, Bultmann rejoiced in the theological work of Gerhard Ebeling, in which he felt his own thinking was carried forward "in freedom

120. Cf. RB, Foreword, in G. Hasenhüttl, *Der Glaubensvollzug*, 10f; RB, "Reply," 276–78.

121. Cf. UB Tübingen, RB est., RB to H. Gollwitzer, 26. 7. 1963, Mn 2-3449; as well as H. Gollwitzer, *Die Existenz Gottes.*

122. Cf. UB Tübingen, RB est., RB to H. Gollwitzer, 26. 7. 1963; also E. Jüngel, *Gottes Sein ist im Werden*, 113f, 117.

123. UB Tübingen, RB est., RB to E. Dinkler, 21. 12. 1963, Mn 2-643; cf. W. Pannenberg, *Was ist der Mensch?*

and with a fruitful yield."[124] Ebeling, as he had already assured Bultmann in 1949, understood himself "as in the first instance your student,"[125] and his teacher returned the compliment when in 1961 he vigorously beseeched Ebeling to accept a call to Marburg: "*You* are the man!"—that is, the systematician who, in view of the reconstruction of the Marburg theological faculty that is in prospect, "is able to ensure the unity of doing theology."[126] It goes without saying that in this case, as in others, shared theological intentions could on occasion include criticism on the part of both parties.[127]

Bultmann found a promising contribution to the question regarding God in John A. T. Robinson's book, *Honest to God.* Taking up the thought of Dietrich Bonhoeffer, Rudolf Bultmann, and Paul Tillich, the Anglican bishop made a case for finally bidding farewell to the theistic picture of God. The traditional supernatural understanding of God, as a consequence of which God is represented as a being outside the world, whether spatially or metaphysically or spiritually, must be demythologized. In order to make the thought of transcendence credible to the modern person, Robinson adopted Tillich's language of God as the foundation or depth of being and to Bonhoeffer's demand that the transcendence of God as such be understood to be in the midst of our life. On this basis, Robinson understood God as the reality of love as this comes to expression in personal relationships between persons. And to be sure, love as the final reality is revealed in the person Jesus of Nazareth. For, as "the man for others," Jesus makes transparent the divine reality of love in the midst of our life.[128]

In a contribution to the German discussion of Robinson's book requested by the weekly news magazine *Die Zeit* [*Time*],[129] Bultmann declared himself in agreement with the concern for finding a new formulation of the idea of God, because the theistic picture of God had become untenable in the modern world. Therefore, theology must reimagine the idea of God's tran-

124. UA Tübingen, G. Ebeling est., RB to G. Ebeling, 20 September 1959, 633/616. Bultmann made reference here to G. Ebeling, *Das Wesen des christlichen Glaubens.*

125. UB Tübingen, RB est., G. Ebeling to RB, 17. 8. 1949, Mn 2-669. On what follows, cf. A. Beutel, *Gerhard Ebeling*, 263–70.

126. UA Tübingen, G. Ebeling est., RB to G. Ebeling, 12 December 1961, 633/626. Ebeling elaborated in detail his doubts about accepting the call in a seven-page letter; cf. UB Tübingen, RB est., G. Ebeling to RB, 18. 12. 1961, Mn 2-669.

127. Bultmann harbored doubt to some degree over Ebeling's understanding of language. Cf. UA Tübingen, G. Ebeling est., RB to G. Ebeling, 21. 12. 1964, 633/616; as well as several drafts of letters to G. Ebeling, n. d. [1971], Mn 2-2189. Cf. from the other direction, G. Ebeling, *Theologie und Verkündigung.*

128. Cf. J. A. T. Robinson, *Honest to God.*

129. Cf. UB Tübingen, RB est., RB to E. Käsemann, 23. 5. 1963, Mn 2-2251.

scendence that is indispensable for Christian faith in God—that is, it must resolve the dialectic between transcendence and immanence, the paradox of the presence of the transcendent God in the world. Still, in Bultmann's view, Robinson would have been able to express this intention more convincingly if he had taken into account core testimonies of New Testament eschatology—the paradoxical identity of a historical event with the eschatological occurrence, and the idea of the church as an eschatological phenomenon.[130] Moreover, Bultmann suggested that he had already found the topics dealt with by Robinson discussed in highly stimulating fashion in the French theologian Gabriel Vahanian's book, *The Death of God*.

On June 21, 1963, in the context of the Marburg University celebration, Bultmann spoke on the topic, "The Idea of God and the Modern Person."[131] Starting out from the "death of God" language of Jean Paul and Friedrich Nietzsche, in both of which cases atheism is understood as nihilism, Bultmann examined in detail the effects of nihilism on the Christian idea of God. The atheism that projects a nihilistic image has to be understood as a consequence of the secularization of the world. Since this secularization—in the sense of a "de-divinizing" and a "worldifying" of the world—has taken place as a legitimate result of Christianity,[132] it can be said that in the case of modern atheism an adversary to the Christian belief in God has, as it were, sprung from its own shoot. In this context, Bultmann echoes Vahanian's examination of the "death of God" in the culture of modernity. As Vahanian demonstrates with regard to the history of North America, and especially to the process whereby the originally eschatological faith of the Puritan fathers became more and more this-worldly, one can see that an exclusive emphasis on the otherworldliness of transcendence has been responsible for the transformation of Christianity into a this-worldly religion. Vahanian describes the absence of God thus produced in modern American culture as a "death of God." Where the individual replaces Christian belief in revelation with his own religiosity, the transcendence of God gets lost in the secularism of modernity, and we find ourselves in a post-Christian era.[133]

In Bultmann's view, Vahanian's call to free Christian faith from its secular alienation bore a certain parallel to the battle Karl Barth had waged in

130. Cf. RB, "Ist der Glaube an Gott erledigt?" *GuV* (3d ed.), vol. 4, 110. Bultmann had reservations about Robinson's exegetical work. Cf. RB, rev. of J. A. T. Robinson, "Twelve New Testament Studies," 359f.

131. Cf. M. Vogtmann, "Das Jenseits als geistiger Ort."

132. Cf. RB, "Der Gottesgedanke und der moderne Mensch," *GuV* (3d ed.), vol. 4, 116–18, with reference especially to F. Gogarten, *Verhängnis und Hoffnung der Neuzeit.*

133. Cf. G. Vahanian, *The Death of God.*

his *Epistle to the Romans* against Schleiermacher and any such religion of experience.[134] This is precisely what makes it necessary to restore the connection to transcendence that the modern person has lost through excessive reflection on the dialectical relation between worldliness and faith. To this end, Bultmann takes up Bonhoeffer's relevant though fragmentary hints that God is to be discerned as our transcendence in the midst of our this-worldliness. He also regards Ernst Barlach's language of the transformations of God as helpful, since it is about understanding God as the one who shares himself as the unconditioned in the conditional. In whatever way theology and philosophy seek to clarify this matter of concern,[135] the modern person can open himself "*for encounters with God in the world, in time.*" For himself, Bultmann above all finds in Jesus' parable of the final judgment (Matt 25:31–46) testimony to the message of the "transformations" of God and the presence of eternity in time.[136]

His contribution to the Marburg University celebration of 1963 was to be Bultmann's final public address. "As the great old man of Marburg theology left the hall following his lecture, accompanied by the Chancellor and those of his party, the audience rose in a spontaneous act of reverence, in which gratitude, solidarity, and deep respect found silent and noble expression before a person and his achievement"—thus the local newspaper concluded its report of the occasion.[137] Karl Barth did not receive the printed version of the lecture so positively, for in his letter of thanks for it he was content to note with a cheerful coolness the differences that remained between himself and Bultmann—in particular in their assessment of Robinson's book.[138] Since like Vahanian Bultmann took the concept "death of God" as a cipher for the God-forgetfulness of Western civilization, he felt no need to follow the later aberrations of the so-called Death of God theology. Nor would it fall to him to work out the christological origin and good theological sense of the death of God talk.[139]

134. Cf. RB to G. Vahanian, n. d. [12. 8. 1962], in G. Vahanian, *Kultur ohne Gott?* 155f; RB, "Der Gottesgedanke und der moderne Mensch," *GuV* (3d ed.), vol. 4, 119f; cf. M. Arnold, "Gabriel Vahanian et Rudolf Bultmann," 59–76.

135. RB, "Der Gottesgedanke und der moderne Mensch," *GuV* (3d ed.), vol. 4, 123–25, names, as examples, the philosophy of history of Ernst Troeltsch, Hans Jonas' myth of the suffering God, and Schubert M. Ogden's identification of the eternity of God as his temporality and historicity.

136. RB, "Der Gottesgedanke und der moderne Mensch," *GuV* (3d ed.), vol. 4, 126f.

137. M. Vogtmann, "Das Jenseits als geistiger Ort."

138. Cf. K. Barth to RB, 28. 12. 1963, in B. Jaspert, *Barth-Bultmann Briefwechsel* (2d ed.), 202f.

139. Cf. also E. Jüngel, "Vom Tod des lebendigen Gorres," 105–25; later E. Jüngel, *Gott als Geheimnis der Welt.*

Bultmann never let go of the question of what sense it makes to speak of God in the face of the challenge of atheism. In one of his last texts, he distinguished between the unconscious atheism that does not even pose the question of a transcendent reality and the conscious atheism that can find expression in various forms. Bultmann now added to the "transformations of God" formula that had been employed in 1963 the idea developed by Eberhard Jüngel that "God's being is in becoming," using the concept as Jüngel had applied it to the inward growth of awareness of God's revelation.[140] The individual is always moved by the question of the authenticity of his existence. The belief in the "unconditioned in the conditioned" that comes to life in that question does not yet correspond to the Christian belief in God, but the proclamation of the church can become poignantly understandable for the person who is moved by the question regarding God. The word of God proclaimed by the church ever anew invites one to grasp belief in God and to give it voice in personal confession. And in so doing, the faith that renews life can entrust itself to the word of Christ witnessed to by Paul in 2 Cor 12:9: "My grace is sufficient for you; for power is made perfect in weakness."[141]

During the last decades of his life, Bultmann found his preeminence in the realm of New Testament exegesis especially challenged by the critical prowess of his former student Ernst Käsemann. In 1957 when the debate over the quest of the historical Jesus was still in progress, Käsemann wrote a comprehensive essay in which he proposed that undertaking a thorough-going analysis of Bultmann's entire work was the "most pressing task of the present generation of New Testament scholars in Germany."[142] For Käsemann, the paramount position of his teacher in the recent history of New Testament scholarship was beyond question. With regard not only to the Synoptics, but "also to Paul and John," Bultmann had introduced "a new epoch of research."[143] As no other exegete of his generation, he combines historical erudition and awareness of systematic issues. He has uninhibitedly exposed the theological crisis that has accompanied Protestantism for more than two centuries and at the same time opened up possibilities for assimilating the

140. Cf. RB, "Die protestantische Theologie und der Atheismus" (Ital. 1970; Ger. 1971), *Neues Testament und christliche Existenz*, 296; as well as (with another intention) E. Jüngel, *Gottes Sein ist im Werden, passim.*

141. RB, "Die protestantische Theologie und der Atheismus," *Neues Testament und christliche Existenz*, 298; cf. UA Tübingen, G. Ebeling est., RB to G. Ebeling, 1. 3. 1971, 633/616.

142. E. Käsemann, "Neutestamentliche Fragen von heute," *Exegetische Versuche* (3d ed.), vol. 2, 19. Cf. U. H. J. Körtner, "Über Bultmann hinaus," 205–16.

143. E. Käsemann, "Neutestamentliche Fragen von heute," *Exegetische Versuche* (3d ed.), vol. 2, 22.

problems that historical criticism has raised. Now, however, it is Bultmann's students who must scrutinize the historical presuppositions of his conception of theology. To Bultmann belongs the rare credit of having trained his students for such truthful analysis—even if it should be aimed at him. In taking stock of the pertinent issues for investigation in 1957, Käsemann placed on the agenda items that were absolutely central to Bultmann's work. In addition to the problem of the historical Jesus, it was necessary to look critically at Bultmann's interpretation of John and Paul. Even the matter of locating earliest Christianity as a historical religion required renewed attention.

Among Bultmann's students, Käsemann was the most consistent in his exegetical and theological efforts to show his independence from his teacher. In 1968 a younger theologian who was also close to Bultmann noted acerbically that some of his students were spending their lives "cutting the umbilical cord to the great teacher."[144] Käsemann found the remark, which doubtless referred to him, extremely painful,[145] especially since he had enjoyed a multifaceted relationship with Bultmann. Indeed, the correspondence between the two theologians bears impressive witness to the complex nature of their association. In 1965 Käsemann employed his characteristic style to inform Bultmann that "deep respect, gratitude, and—may I say?—love may no longer stand in the way of an attack that might mar our relationship, that makes me appear ungrateful, and that gives pleasure to those who oppose us both." He had followed Bultmann unconditionally for thirty years, and now he, too, was slowly reaching the end of his journey and had to take stock of "what it all amounted to" for him.[146]

Käsemann developed his interpretation of John by commenting on the points that Bultmann had made in analyzing the meaning of the Fourth Gospel.[147] For instance, he regarded Bultmann's hypothesis that the gospel writer had appropriated, edited, and commented on a Gnostic source of revelation discourses to be not only indemonstrable, but even unworthy of belief.[148] Bultmann replied that Käsemann would have to prove that such a source could not be presupposed, and went on to insist on the decisive significance of *how* the gospel writer John comments on the source and

144. W. Schmithals, "Herausforderung zu selbstständigem Denken," 51.

145. Cf. E. Käsemann, *Jesu letzter Wille nach Johannes 17* (3d ed.), 8.

146. UB Tübingen, RB est., E. Käsemann to RB, 17. 4. 1965, Mn 2-1083. By the "attack," Käsemann was alluding to E. Käsemann, "Sackgassen im Streit um den historischen Jesus," *Exegetische Versuche* (3d ed.), vol. 2, 31–68.

147. On the particulars, cf. J. Frey, *Die johanneische Eschatologie*, vol. 1, 160–70; M. Rese, "Käsemanns Johannesdeutung."

148. Cf. E. Käsemann, "Neutestamentliche Fragen von heute," *Exegetische Versuche* (3d ed.), vol. 2, 25.

points out the true intention of the ἐγώ εἰμι [I am]-sayings.[149] Bultmann and Käsemann then recognized that the primary difference between their interpretations of John lay in their evaluations of the christology of the Fourth Gospel. Käsemann saw in John 1:14c ("and we have seen his glory") the key to understanding the gospel, the aim of which is to testify to the *praesentia dei* [presence of God] in Christ and, for this reason, understands Jesus as the epiphany of the God who walks on earth.[150] For Bultmann, this interpretation failed to recognize the paradox of Word becoming flesh, and he therefore maintained his view that the Gospel of John was to be understood on the basis of John 1:14a ("and the Word became flesh").[151] Despite this contrast and other differences in exegetical detail, Käsemann and Bultmann were in complete agreement on many issues of Johannine interpretation.[152] Perhaps for this reason as well as the exegetical difficulties presented by the Fourth Gospel, Bultmann did not comment in print on his student's interpretation of John.

It was a different matter when Käsemann declared apocalypticism to be the "mother of all Christian theology."[153] This thesis contained two features that stood in direct opposition to Bultmann's understanding of the history of earliest Christian theology. First, Käsemann located the origin of historical consciousness in apocalypticism because its strong orientation towards the future of God had first made possible the understanding of history as a linear process with a beginning and a goal. Second, he emphasized the expectation of future salvation by which apocalypticism indelibly shaped earliest Christianity by serving to undergird and to sustain Christian existence. With its view of the world as a battleground of powers and human existence as a modality of being under one rule, apocalypticism provided for Käsemann a context within which to interpret earliest Christian theology, John, and especially Paul.[154] Bultmann argued against Käsemann's assessment of apocalypticism as the mother of Christian theology in numerous letters as well as one essay.[155]

149. Cf. UB Tübingen, RB est., RB to E. Käsemann, 22. 7. 1957, Mn 2-2251.

150. Cf. E. Käsemann, "Aufbau und Anliegen des johanneischen Prologs," *Exegetische Versuche* (3d ed.), vol. 2, 171–77.

151. Cf. UB Tübingen, RB est., RB to E. Käsemann, 22. 7. 1957, Mn 2-2251.

152. Cf. also UB Tübingen, RB est., RB to E. Käsemann, 11. 12. 1966, Mn 2-2251, on E. Käsemann, *Jesu letzter Wille nach Joh 17.*

153. Cf. E. Käsemann, *Exegetische Versuche* (3d ed.), vol. 2: "Die Anfänge christlicher Theologie," 100, and "Zum Thema der urchristlichen Apokalyptik," 130.

154. Cf. at length B. Ehler, *Die Herrschaft des Gekreuzigten*, 291–99.

155. Cf. UB Tübingen, RB est., RB to E. Käsemann, 16. 1. and 16. 5. 1961, 23. 5. 1963, Mn 2-2251. Passages from the letter of 23. 5. 1963 are taken up—in part, word for word—in RB, "Ist die Apokalyptik die Mutter der christlichen Theologie?" *Exegetica*, 476–82.

He justified his rejection of this thesis primarily by reference to Paul. To be sure, present and future eschatologies appear alongside one another in Paul, but he attaches a greater weight to the present eschatology than to the apocalyptic expectation of the end. Pauline thinking has thus created a brilliant new teleological understanding of history, one that can be seen as "coming not out of apocalypticism, but rather out of anthropology—that is, out of an understanding of human existence."[156] Paul does take from apocalypticism the motif for the eschatological view of present and future, but the way he formulates this relates it solely to the new understanding of existence on the part of the sinner to whom grace has been shown.

The dispute over the status of apocalypticism touched on the central matters at issue between Käsemann and Bultmann: Paul's theology—especially his teaching on justification—and his anthropology. Käsemann expressed early reservations regarding Bultmann's interpretation of the Pauline teaching on justification in his sketch of the issues between them in 1957.[157] He provoked the guild of New Testament scholars in 1961 with a new interpretation of the concept δικαιοσύνη θεοῦ. By the "righteousness of God," he proposed, Paul denotes not only the eschatological gift of salvation, but also the inseparable concept of the lordship of God over the entire cosmos at the end of days, the proof of power revealed in Christ by means of which the creator God asserts his right over the creation that has fallen away from him.[158] For this reason, Käsemann regards it as imperative to readjust the traditional interpretation of the Pauline teaching on justification. The "righteousness of God" does not refer primarily to the individual, but rather implies the salvation of the entire world. Instead of thinking of Pauline theology in terms of anthropology, one must give priority to christology. Bultmann flatly rejected this new approach to interpretation. Because Käsemann is "captivated by his picturing of Christ as the kosmokrator and by the cosmic extent of redemption," the Pauline teaching on justification and his (Käsemann's) interpretation of it appears from the outset "in a false light."[159] Bultmann did not believe that either Käsemann or his student Peter Stuhlmacher had substantiated the claim that "the Pauline concept of God's righteousness" presents "a radicalizing and universalizing of the Jewish idea of the righteousness of

156. RB, "Ist die Apokalyptik die Mutter der christlichen Theologie?" *Exegetica*, 481.

157. Cf. E. Käsemann, "Neutestamentliche Fragen von Heute," *Exegetische Versuche* (3d ed.), vol. 2, 24.

158. Cf. E. Käsemann, "Gottesgerechtigkeit bei Paulus," *Exegetische Versuche* (3d ed.), vol. 2, 187, 192.

159. UB Tübingen, RB est., RB to E. Käsemann, 22. 7. 1957, Mn 2-2251.

God."[160] Paul had not taken over a previously coined *terminus technicus* [technical term], but rather had initiated the concept δικαιοσύνη θεοῦ and established its genuine meaning.[161] As little as a uniform linguistic usage was available to Paul, just as perfectly did the character of "gift" suit the righteousness of God, for here the gift is inseparable from its giver, and certainly places those who receive it under the lordship of Christ. In short, Bultmann rejected his former student's argument and followed Luther's teaching on justification and probably that of the majority of exegetes[162] in maintaining that the righteousness of God exclusively constitutes the gift of salvation of the merciful God proclaimed through the gospel and to be grasped in faith.

After having raised the issue in 1957, Käsemann focused his criticism on Bultmann's carefully planned attempt to understand and present Pauline theology as anthropology. As a result, Bultmann was impelled to place falsely individualizing limits on the thinking of the apostle who had "given expression to the reality and the radicality of Christ's seizing of power as kosmokrator."[163] Ernst Käsemann's thinking was fundamentally concerned with the structures of power and control over earthly existence. He fought against all attempts to reduce Christ's lordship over the entire universe to the private sphere of the pious individual. Permanently affected by his experiences during the Third Reich,[164] Käsemann rigorously expanded relevant items from the text of the New Testament into an enormous panorama that portrayed a cosmic drama of the creator-God locked in battle with malevolent powers. And into this conflict between the two supernal realms, the individual had been dragged. Only in faith, in obedience to Christ as Lord, could Christians bring about the change of lordship that would effect their salvation and that they also owed in loving service to the world. Bultmann distanced himself from this interpretive approach from the outset. Concepts employed by Käsemann such as "seizing control" or "Christ as kosmokrator" were

160. UB Tübingen, RB est., RB to E. Käsemann, 26. 3. 1964, Mn 2-2251: Bultmann did, however, value Stuhlmacher's monograph for its work on the background in the history of religions of the Pauline concept of the righteousness of God. (Käsemann had put Stuhlmacher's work at Bultmann's disposal before its publication.)

161. Cf. UB Tübingen, RB est., RB to E. Käsemann, 23. 5. 1963, Mn 2-2251. Passages from this letter are taken up in RB, "ΔΙΚΑΙΟΣΥΝΗ ΘΕΟΥ," *Exegetica*, 474f.

162. Cf. also E. Lohse, *Der Brief an die Römer*, 78n24 (literary).

163. Cf. E. Käsemann, "Neutestamentliche Fragen von Heute," *Exegetische Versuche* (3d ed.), vol. 2, 23.

164. On the significance of these experiences for Käsemann's theological thinking, cf. B. Ehler, *Die Herrschaft des Gekreuzigten*, 283. One must also reckon with the long-term influence of E. Peterson on Käsemann's understanding of the person as the object of cosmic powers struggling with each other. Cf. G. Sellin, "Sturz der Götzen," 21.

completely un-Pauline. They showed that Käsemann had inadmissibly absolutized Paul's statements about the lordship of Christ, a concept that in any case primarily concerned human beings. At this juncture, the problem of adequately understanding the concept of σῶμα [body], central to Pauline anthropology, became a virulent one.[165]

Contrary to Bultmann's view that by σῶμα Paul means the whole person in his relation to himself, Käsemann understood this term to express the individual's connection to the world. "For the apostle, it is the person in his worldliness, thus in his capacity for communication."[166] Käsemann thereafter took Bultmann's category of self-understanding to render "the Christian in reality a nonpolitical being" and reduces "his responsibility to personal, inward relations."[167] Bultmann quite rightly rejected this accusation of his student as unjustified, a stand that a later commentator on his dispute with Käsemann confirmed to him.[168] He was able to show that in more than one instance he had said that the person as σῶμα always exists in a historical connection. In Bultmann's mind, the concept of self-understanding that Käsemann had made the object of his incriminating charge included the entire social existence of the individual and his connection to the world.[169] Just as fully as Käsemann, and indeed before him, Bultmann had realized that one must speak of the supra-individual powers and forms of connectedness that fatefully monopolize the person in such a way that he experiences himself as physically dependent on alien powers.[170] Bultmann similarly described the new situation of grace "into which believers . . . have been transplanted" as entering into the "realm of the divine activity."[171] Conversely, he portrayed Paul's view of the cosmos as "the territory of demonic powers,"[172] and as the anti-divine power constituted by people's concerns and actions that exercises control over those who have fallen under its sway.[173] For this reason, Bultmann also saw no reason to revise his own view of things on the basis of what he saw as a number of "aggressive and

165. Cf. UB Tübingen, RB est., RB to E. Käsemann, 22. 7. 1957, Mn 22251.

166. E. Käsemann, "Zum Thema der urchristlichen Apokalyptik," *Exegetische Versuche* (3d ed.), vol. 2, 129f.

167. E. Käsemann, "Zur paulinischen Anthropologie," *Paulinische Perspektiven* (1st ed.), 48f.

168. Cf. with numerous examples G. Klein, "Rudolf Bultmann," 617f; critically of Käsemann also O. Merk, "Paulus-Forschung 1936–1985," 36.

169. Cf. UB Tübingen, RB est., RB to E. Käsemann, 22. 7. 1957, Mn 2-2251.

170. Cf. RB, *Theologie des Neuen Testaments* (4th ed.), 197, 245.

171. RB, *Theologie des Neuen Testaments* (4th ed.), 290.

172. RB, *Theologie des Neuen Testaments* (4th ed.), 258 (printed there with emphasis).

173. Cf. RB, *Theologie des Neuen Testaments* (4th ed.), 257.

provocative claims" in Käsemann's essay "Zur paulinischen Anthropologie" ["On Paul's Anthropology"] that appeared in 1969.[174] Rather, he who had recently turned eighty-five rejected as unjustified the accusation that he remained excessively concerned with his interpretation of what he called "the abhorrent subject-object dichotomy" and Käsemann's analysis of the concept of self-understanding.[175]

Thus, the differences between the two theologians over central features of the exegesis of Paul remained. When Ernst Käsemann published his commentary on Romans, Bultmann congratulated him: "[T]ruly a great opus." To be sure, along with the admiration he paid Käsemann for his achievement, he did let drop the remark that while he was listening to the commentary being read, "a few questions" had occurred to him.[176]

4. Late Exegetical Fruits

What unites us exegetes despite various theological attitudes is obligation to the text. In this commentary [on the three Letters of John], Bultmann displays anew his exegetical accountability and mastery. One can only hope that we are not so inundated by the present-day wave of hermeneutical interpretations that theological discussion detaches itself from the texts. For Bultmann, this is not the case.[177]

With increasing age, Bultmann's strength for work clearly declined. From this situation, which he himself made note of, he drew the logical conclusions. He decided to focus the capacities that remained to him in working through his commentary on the Letters of John and put other scholarly plans aside. He assigned some of them to Erich Dinkler, whom he charged with going over the manuscript of his lectures on Second Corinthians and preparing it for the press, as well as readying for publication his lecture course on theological encyclopedia. Other materials, such as lecture manuscripts, notes and excerpts on various New Testament writings and subjects, he entrusted to those among his students who were dealing with related topics in their

174. UB Tübingen, RB est., RB to E. Käsemann, 27. 1. 1970, Mn 2-2251, on E. Käsemann, "Zur Paulinischen Anthropologie," *Paulinische Perspektiven* (1st ed).

175. UB Tübingen, RB est., RB to E. Käsemann, 27. 1. 1970, Mn 2-2251.

176. UB Tübingen, RB est., RB to E. Käsemann, 8. 8. 1973, Mn 2-2251, on E. Käsemann, *An die Römer*. Since Bultmann could no longer read for himself, H. Leipold read aloud to him "some crucial excerpts" from the commentary.

177. R. Schnackenburg, rev. of RB, *Die drei Johannesbriefe*, 587.

own scholarship.[178] And yet three new exegetical works appeared in the last decade of his life: the collection of essays entitled *Exegetica*, as well as commentaries on the Letters of John and on Second Corinthians.

The initiative for publishing a volume of Bultmann's most important exegetical essays came from Erich Dinkler. He also consulted with the author in selecting the studies that were reprinted in *Exegetica*.[179] This collection was not meant to resemble a museum archive or to provide a glimpse into Bultmann's research on the New Testament that would be "of interest to biographical scholarship or the history of theology."[180] Instead, Dinkler selected exegetical works and studies in the history of religions that he regarded as relevant to contemporary scholarly discussion. To be sure, the twenty-four contributions fully documented developments and high points that summarized the nearly half a century during which they were written. Reprinted in chronological order, the studies illustrate their original contexts: Bultmann's work on a commentary, a monograph, or a set of issues that was important to him. Thus, the seven studies on the Johannine conceptual world and theology form a sort of introduction to the commentaries on the Gospel and the Letters of John. Nine contributions underscore in a purely quantitative way the importance that Bultmann attached to Pauline theology. Additional essays deal with the synoptic tradition, especially with topics surrounding the issue of the significance of the historical Jesus.

In his Introduction, Erich Dinkler explained in detail the context in which each of the individual studies had come to be written, and their position in the history of research. In doing so, he called special attention to how solidly Bultmann's specialized exegetical investigations were based in the history of religions. Taken as a whole, they let one see once again the degree to which Bultmann's historical-critical analysis and his theological interpretation of the New Testament were inextricably bound together.[181] Bultmann took up the editor's cue in his own Foreword when he noted that it had always been a particular concern of his "to strive for the unity of exegesis and theology and, to be sure, in such a way that the primary role belonged to exegesis."[182]

178. E. Dinkler received Bultmann's lectures on *Romans*; O. Merk, materials on the synoptics and the lectures on *First Thessalonians*; and H. Thyen, writings on the *Gospel of John* and Johannine theology.

179. Cf. UB Tübingen, RB est., E. Dinkler to RB, 4. 5. and 13. 5. 1966, Mn 2-643; RB to E. Dinkler, 17. 5. 6. 7. and 13. 7. 1966, Mn 2-2176.

180. E. Dinkler, Introduction, in RB, *Exegetica*, ix.

181. Cf. E. Dinkler, Introduction, in RB, *Exegetica*, xxi–xxiii; cf. also W. Schmithals, rev. of RB, *Exegetica*, 500.

182. RB, *Exegetica*, vii.

Dinkler included his reminder of Bultmann's insistence on the constitutive connection of exegesis and theology not only to facilitate an understanding of his work, but he also meant to establish a strong contrast to certain tendencies within contemporary Protestant theology. For in the closing years of the 1960s, a number of theologians thought they could account for the Christian faith—or at least for its social and political implications—without grounding their interpretations on biblical texts.

As early as 1918 Bultmann had taken on the task of producing for Meyer's Kritisch-Exegetischer Kommentar über das Neue Testament [Critical-Exegetical Commentaries on the New Testament] a new interpretation of both the Gospel and the Letters of John.[183] Now, following his eightieth birthday, he set his hand to the long-postponed project of writing a commentary on the Letters of John. And despite the long delay, he was able to go back to the preparatory studies he had done. In 1927 he had written for the Jülicher celebratory volume a literary-critical analysis of the First Letter of John, and relying primarily on critical observations regarding literary style, concluded that the author had both made use of a source and then commented on it.[184] Thereafter, Bultmann sought in the 1951 memorial volume for Ernst Lohmeyer to demonstrate that an ecclesiastical redaction had given the First Letter of John its final literary form by using various interpolations and additions in a way comparable to what had occurred in the case of the Gospel of John.[185] Taking on the *RGG* article on the Johannine letters offered the opportunity to look back on the state of research up until 1959 and to give a collective overview of the Letters of John.[186] Finally, the explanation of the three letters proposed by the Catholic New Testament scholar Rudolf Schnackenburg stimulated Bultmann to reexamine and critically test his own view of the literary character and theological content of the Letters of John.[187]

Although after 1964 Bultmann concentrated on this commentary, he made only slow progress on it. Because of the decline in his powers and weather-related problems with his health, the end of the task was a long time in coming.[188] Thanks to the support of his personal assistant Otto Merk

183. Cf. M. Evang, *Bultmann*, 72f; see above 311.

184. Cf. RB, "Analyse des ersten Johannesbriefes," *Exegetica*, 105–23.

185. Cf. RB, "Die kirchliche Redaktion des ersten Johannesbriefes," *Exegetica*, 381–93.

186. Cf. RB, "Johannesbriefe," 836–39.

187. Cf. RB, rev. of R. Schnackenburg, *Die Johannesbriefe*, in RB, *Theologie als Kritik*, 507–10.

188. Cf. RB to G. Krüger, 8. 1. 1967, in F. Lilie, "Bultmann-Krüger Briefwechsel," *ZNThG* 7, 154.

in procuring literature and reading corrections,[189] he at last managed to finish the writing by the end of 1966 and to complete the editing in the late summer of 1967.[190] The book appeared in October 1967 in an edition of ten thousand copies. Due to the high demand for it, a further printing was needed within two years.[191]

Plate 38: Rudolf Bultmann, 1964

In the succinct Introduction to the Commentary, Bultmann begins by discussing the relation of the First Letter of John to the Gospel of John. He regards the hypothesis that the two writings come from one and the same author as implausible, for while the Gospel takes aim against the unbelieving cosmos as represented by the unbelieving Jews, the Letter opposes heretics within the Christian community. Thus, the Letter must be assigned to a time later than that of the Gospel. The kinship in ideas and language between the two writings can be explained by the author of the First Letter's having made use of the Gospel in the sense in which the ecclesiastical tradition had entrusted it to him.[192] With this in mind, Bultmann readopts in only slightly modified form the view he had previously taken on literary-critical grounds: that 1 John 1:5–2:27 reflects an originally independent writing, the themes of which the author of the Letter appropriated and on which he composed

189. Cf. UB Tübingen, RB est., RB to E. Dinkler, 20. 6. and 7. 11. 1967, Mn 2-2176.

190. Cf. RB to G. Krüger, 15. 9. 1967, in F. Lilie, "Bultmann-Krüger Briefwechsel," *ZNThG* 7, 156.

191. Cf. RB, *Die drei Johannesbriefe*.

192. Cf. RB, *Die drei Johannesbriefe*, 9f.

Plate 39: Rudolf Bultmann in Marburg, August 1968

variations in the sections that follow.[193] So, too, Bultmann goes on to reckon with further ecclesiastical redaction, a process to which he ascribes the concluding section, 1 John 5:14–21, a series of formulations that have the sense of the traditional apocalyptic eschatology (1 John 2:28; 3:2; 4:17), and statements of an atonement christology (1 John 1:7b; 2:2; 4:10b).

As for the relationship of the three Letters of John to one another, Bultmann strikes a distinctive note by viewing the second as not really a letter. In issuing to a congregation a forceful warning against heretics, the author imitates the content and style of the First Letter, and the form and concluding greetings of the Third Letter.[194] Other than that, Bultmann regards as probable the view represented by Ernst Käsemann that the author of the Third Letter of John seeks to safeguard the theological authority of the old Johannine tradition against the subsequent formations of early Catholicism.[195] Finally, because the First Letter lacks essential features of the New Testament epistle genre, Bultmann argues for seeing it as an apostolic letter of admonition or a manifesto.

193. This hypothesis at first found sweeping agreement from exegetes such as H. Braun and H. Preisker (cf. RB, *Die drei Johannesbriefe*, 10f). However, it was not unable to sustain itself in the long term. Cf. already E. Haenchen, "Neuere Literatur zu den Johannesbriefen," *Die Bibel und wir*, 243–46; R. Schnackenburg, rev. of RB, *Die drei Johannesbriefe*, 586; W. Schmithals, *Johannesevangelium und Johannesbriefe*, 129f.

194. Cf. RB, *Die drei Johannesbriefe*, 10, 105, 109f.

195. Cf. RB, *Die drei Johannesbriefe*, 10, 98–100.

While in his commentary Rudolf Schnackenburg emphasizes the impress of the Old Testament and Jewish tradition on the Letters of John, Bultmann regards Gnostic conceptions as the intellectual horizon for these writings, as he does for the Gospel of John. In both cases, however, Gnostic motifs are modified as the Christ-occurrence is reflected upon. Thus as 1 John 1:5–7 shows, the cosmological dualism of Gnosticism has been historicized into a dualism of decision, which requires the believer to choose between two possibilities of being.[196] The First Letter of John also speaks repeatedly of the true knowledge of God, but in contrast to Gnosticism it thereby understands "not a theoretical or speculative cognition of God," but rather a relation to God in which the knower—who is necessarily a believer—allows himself to be determined by God in both his existence and his doings (cf. 1 John 2:3–11).[197] Just as love is inseparably bound to faith, so it must realize itself in life (cf. 1 John 3:14). This sure and specific knowledge on the part of faith that the eschatological gift of life is already present in the Christian community constituted by love therefore relativizes the traditional statements of futuristic eschatology. To be sure, the author is aware that the ultimate vision of the glorified Son of God is reserved for the future, and that in this future vision the believers ultimately become those who know who they already are—namely, children of God (cf. 1 John 3:2).

With regard to individual details of exegesis, Bultmann often reached conclusions similar to those of Schnackenburg. The Protestant and the Catholic theologians also gave one another's commentary a very favorable review.[198] To be sure, Schnackenburg was unable to adopt Bultmann's theses regarding literary criticism and the history of tradition, but he assessed his colleague's interpretation as a "ripe work of old age" that attended carefully to the texts, avoiding one-sided judgments, and dealing with other exegetical options in a conciliatory fashion.[199]

It was not in such a ripened form that Bultmann's interpretation of Second Corinthians appeared in 1976, the year of his death. The peculiar pre-history of this commentary was such that it presented merely the philological and historical materials that Bultmann had outlined between 1940 and 1951 as the basis of his lecture-course on Second Corinthians.[200] After procuring the

196. Cf. RB, *Die drei Johannesbriefe*, 23–25.

197. RB, *Die drei Johannesbriefe*, 31.

198. Cf. RB, rev. of R. Schnackenburg, *Die Johannesbriefe*, in RB, *Theologie als Kritik*, 507–10; R. Schnackenburg, rev. of RB, *Die drei Johannesbriefe*, 586f. Cf, also C. Brütsch, rev. of RB, *Die drei Johannesbriefe*, 470f.

199. R. Schnackenburg, rev. of RB, *Die drei Johannesbriefe*, 586, also 587.

200. On the prehistory of the commentary, cf. E. Dinkler, Foreword and Introduction, in RB, *Der zweite Brief an die Korinther*, 9f.

manuscript of Bultmann's lectures, Erich Dinkler was prevented by other duties from developing them into a true commentary, and after consulting with Bultmann, the Göttingen publisher and Dinkler agreed to publish the manuscript of his lectures along with a bibliography, index, etc., as a special volume of the Meyer Commentaries. Bultmann, who had recently turned 91, laconically informed Dinkler that this procedure certainly did not accord with earlier arrangements with the publisher, but was "personally of no consequence" to him, for at his advanced age important matters were no longer important: he "was only vegetating now."[201]

In his commentary, Bultmann does not deal explicitly with the literary- critical issues connected with Second Corinthians, but he does proceed from the view that the writing contains pieces from two originally independent letters of Paul. He thus attributes 2 Cor 2:14–7:4, 10–13, and 9 to an intervening letter "C," in which the apostle Paul defends himself against Gnosticizing pneumatics—probably not, as some held, Judaizers (2 Corinthians 10–13). The sections 2 Cor 1:1–2; 2:13; 7:5–16, as well as 8 he assigned to letter "D." Although the Second Letter to the Corinthians is therefore to be viewed as a composite, it exhibits a unified theme: the apostolic office and the word of proclamation.[202]

Since the commentary reproduces the pattern of Bultmann's lectures, it offers primarily philological elucidations of individual concepts and history-of-religions parallels that reflect Paul's Hellenistic environment. Gnostic motifs contribute to a better understanding of what it means to perceive the apostolic proclamation as "fragrance of knowledge" (2 Cor 2:14),[203] and allusions drawn from the realm of Hellenism illustrate the idea of a transformation through vision (cf. 2 Cor 3:18).[204] Further, Paul's debate with opponents who long to be made naked in death (cf. 2 Cor 5:3) becomes comprehensible only when one consults comparative material from Gnosticism.[205]

As for the analysis of textual details that Bultmann undertakes in an ongoing adversarial conversation with the older commentaries of Hans Lietzmann and Hans Windisch, his explication of theological problems and connections does not come off at all badly; for he resolutely interprets the Second Letter to the Corinthians on the basis of its core topic, the apostolic office, the

201. UB Tübingen, RB est., RB to E. Dinkler, 29. 10. 1975, Mn 2-2176.

202. Cf. RB, *Der zweite Brief an die Korinther*: 21–23, also the Foreword and Introduction by E. Dinkler, 11f.

203. Cf. RB, *Der zweite Brief an die Korinther*, 69f.

204. Cf. RB, *Der zweite Brief an die Korinther*, 93–99.

205. Cf. RB, *Der zweite Brief an die Korinther*, 138f.

performance of which consists exclusively in the service of the proclamation. Everything that Paul has to say in this writing with regard to his person is self-referential only to the extent that the apostolic office of the proclamation of the Word has been conferred upon him.[206] And therefore Paul shapes the defense of his apostleship to conform to the exposition of what the Christian proclamation is meant to and does accomplish: it proclaims the Christ-occurrence as that event in which God has reconciled the world to himself. Since the apostolic office communicates the word of reconciliation, it allows the salvation that has occurred in Christ to become present. Only in the sermon and in the faith that embraces it does this reconciliation become actual for us today. And as the office of reconciliation is established together with the act of reconciliation, so also the proclamation belongs to the eschatological occurrence (cf. 2 Cor 5:14–21; 6:2).[207]

Tying together statements about the apostle and sayings about the community, especially in 2 Corinthians 3–5, emphasizes the point that apostolic existence is to be understood as a model of Christian existence. In the central section, 2 Cor 5:16–21, Paul characteristically describes the basic features of Christian existence not by speaking of the individual "I," but rather by speaking of a "we" that includes all believers. Being ἐν Χριστῶ [in Christ] (2 Cor 5:17) signifies more precisely "the thoroughgoing determination of life through Christ, . . . not . . . a mysterious quality, a higher nature."[208] Believers are able to understand themselves as a new creation to the extent that, existing eschatologically, "by virtue of appropriating the death of Christ, they have come to authentic life."[209]

Bultmann's interpretation clearly displayed the powerful influence that the Second Letter to the Corinthians had exercised on his theological thinking—though to be sure unsettled dogmatic points sometimes predetermined particular exegeses. For instance, Bultmann regarded 2 Cor 5:16 as documentary proof of the theological illegitimacy of the quest of the historical Jesus: "The Χριστὸς κατὰ σάρκα [Christ according to the flesh] is Christ as he was discernible in worldly fashion, before death and resurrection."[210] Despite such debatable issues of interpretation, in sending his thanks to Bultmann, Eduard Lohse, the Bishop of the State Church of Hannover,

206. Cf. RB, *Der zweite Brief an die Korinther*, 21.

207. Cf. RB, *Der zweite Brief an die Korinther*, 152–71, esp. 162.

208. RB, *Der zweite Brief an die Korinther*, 100 (on 2 Cor 3:18).

209. RB, *Der zweite Brief an die Korinther*, 154 (on 2 Cor 5:15); cf. also 158f (on 2 Cor 5:17).

210. RB, *Der zweite Brief an die Korinther*, 156; cf. also, critically, J. Eckert, rev. of RB, *Der zweite Brief an die Korinther*, 461f.

deemed the commentary "a legacy not only to us New Testament scholars, but beyond that, to the Protestant Church."[211] With his clarification of the Second Letter to the Corinthians, Bultmann had produced an "impressive witness for the theology of the Word" in the tradition of the Reformers. "Just as his scholarly work once began with an investigation of Pauline theology, so it ends after more than six decades with the interpretation of the apostle's message of Christ."[212] Ernst Käsemann expressed the hope that the commentary might be able to make transparent for people today, in whom its memory was fading more and more, the dialectical theology that had guided Bultmann on his theological path. His interpretation of the Second Letter to the Corinthians once again stimulated controversial discussion. And Käsemann struck a conciliatory note in his last letter to his teacher: "It is perhaps the case that I have never come closer to you than here."[213] The text of his lecture-course on the Second Letter to the Corinthians, a presentation that marked the end of his official teaching activity at Marburg in 1951, Bultmann had published *gratis* as a parting gift to his audience.[214]

5. Political Theology?

> *[T]he love that knows what it has to do knows about the situation of the moment and its demand; and this can fully manage the planning and designing of an order for human life. Whether a concrete design is the task of a Christian ethics one may well doubt. I think (and I believe I am at one with Gogarten in this regard) that human reason suffices for this purpose, in which realm, however, falls the knowledge of law and justice.*[215]

During the 1960s, a profound social transformation was taking place in the German Federal Republic. The change in the cultural climate resulted in student protests against the establishment, against the institutions of society, and especially against what were perceived as the encrusted structures of the universities. Bultmann, who had long since become emeritus, was not touched personally by the student revolt. From Werner Georg Kümmel he

211. UB Tübingen, RB est., E. Lohse to RB, 23. 2. 1976, Mn 2-1317.
212. E. Lohse, rev. of RB, *Der zweite Brief an die Korinther*, 353.
213. UB Tübingen, RB est., E. Käsemann to RB, 23. 2. 1976, Mn 2-1083.
214. Cf. RB, *Der zweite Brief an die Korinther*, 7; cf. Bultmann's lecture on 2 Corinthians and R. Slenczka, untitled report, 81.
215. UB Tübingen, RB est., RB to D. Sölle, 16. 6. 1965, Mn 2-2386.

heard of the actions of a group of radicalized students who interfered with the Marburg theological faculty's teaching.[216] When he blamed this student unrest principally on a "lack of upbringing," which in turn resulted from the lowering of the university's entrance standards, it was clear that he was not aware of the complex social and political causes of the student protests. His perspective was largely restricted to the university, and he regarded as disastrous the current threat of the university's transition into academic institutions of applied sciences.[217] Bultmann signed the "Marburg Manifesto of April 17, 1968," in which fifteen hundred German teachers in higher education renounced the "politicizing and so-called democratizing" of the universities.[218]

The Kahl case also confronted Bultmann with some of the symptoms of radical change. During his theological studies, the acid bath of historical criticism had etched Joachim Kahl with the suspicion that he had been inwardly drifting away from Christian faith since about 1965. But in 1967 this suspicion led him to follow the unprincipled course of taking his degree in Marburg with a work on Gogarten and immediately announcing his resignation from the church. In an interview with a left-leaning Marburg student newspaper, Kahl sought to justify his unusual actions by presuming upon his university studies in Protestant theology to claim that Bultmann's program of demythologizing was "pure bluff, a robbing of dead people, a crime against disagreeable texts."[219] Thereupon, the Dean of the theological faculty demanded that Kahl apologize for this slanderous statement regarding Bultmann.[220] Kahl refused to do this and merely wrote Bultmann a wounded letter, in which he insinuated that "only a misunderstanding" could have placed his "criticism of demythologizing on this personal level."[221]

Bultmann thanked the theological faculty for having defended his work "against the slanderous statements of Mr. Kahl" and recommended that it not regard Kahl as deserving of a reply. In any case, he would not take part in any discussion of the matters concerning Kahl. Bultmann added by way of explanation: "For me, the conduct of my former Grand Duke of Oldenburg is exemplary. During my time as a student in Oldenburg, the police arrested

216. Cf. UB Tübingen, RB est., RB to E. Dinkler, 21./22. 12. 1967, Mn 2-2176.

217. UB Tübingen, RB est., RB to E. Dinkler, 27. 8. 1968, Mn 2-2176.

218. Cf. "Marburger Manifest," 42.

219. M. Buckmiller, "Theologischer 'Kahl'-Schlag," 14.

220. Cf. UB Tübingen, RB est., Dean of the Marburg theological faculty to J. Kahl, 21. 12. 1967, Mn 2-1953.

221. UB Tübingen, RB est.: J. Kahl to RB, 3. 1. 1968, Mn 2-1085; and J. Kahl to the Marburg theological faculty, 3. 1. 1968, Mn 2-1085.

a tramp on account of slanderous remarks he had made against the Grand Duke. When this was communicated to him, he said, 'Let him go immediately! He cannot slander me!' This is the example I should like to follow."[222] This is also how he acted when Kahl accused Bultmann's theology of irrationality and dogmatism in his pamphlet, "The Poverty of Christianity." Kahl's "Plea for a Humanity without God" was an insipid rehash of the nineteenth-century criticism of religion, expanded by way of a tendentious "real balance-sheet of the history of theology" and a "debate" with modern Protestant theology that ignored the basic rules of scholarship. His sorry effort was eagerly gobbled up in half-educated circles of left-leaning criticism of the church but even then did not constitute sufficient reason for Bultmann to stoop to responding to Kahl's polemic.[223]

Dorothee Sölle's criticism of Bultmann's theology was a different matter. Gogarten's former student had established a dialogue with Bultmann at the meetings of the "old Marburgers," but there had been reservations among the "old Marburgers" about whether Sölle ought to appear as a speaker at the get-togethers. Wilhelm Anz and Erich Dinkler were fearful that if this were to happen, the discussions might then "get even more into the channel of [Ernst] Bloch's *Prinzip Hoffnung* [*Principle of Hope*]." Bultmann, however, spoke up for giving Sölle the opportunity to make a presentation.[224] Her early writings—for instance, *Stellvertretung. Ein Kapitel Theologie nach dem 'Tode Gottes'* [*Christ the Representative: An Essay in Theology after the 'Death of God'*] (1965) and *Leiden* [*Suffering*] (1973)—thoroughly impressed Bultmann,[225] chiefly because of the sensibility expressed in them together with Sölle's ability to incorporate literary texts into theological discussion. Nevertheless, how to specify the relation between faith and moral responsibility and between theology and ethics was from the first a matter of controversy for the two theologians. Sölle charged in particular that Bultmann reduced the historicity of human existence to the momentary event of decision. Bultmann countered that he understood human existence quite comprehensively as a life of responsibility for the inheritance of the past as well as for the future. The question boiled down to whether it is the task of Christian preaching or of Christian ethics to create a comprehensive

222. UB Tübingen, RB est., RB to the Dean of the Marburg theological faculty, 13. 1. 1968, Mn 2-2403.

223. Cf. J. Kahl, *Das Elend des Christentums*, esp. 98–100; and, critical of it, J. M. Lohse, *Menschlich sein mit oder ohne Gott?*

224. UB Tübingen, RB est., RB to E. Dinkler, 7. 11. 1968, Mn 2-2176.

225. Cf. UB Tübingen, RB est., RB to E. Käsemann, 12./13. 1. 1976, Mn 2-2251.

template for the ordering of human life. Should it not suffice for Christian preaching to arouse in the individual a sense of urgent responsibility for such an ordering?[226]

In a private dialogue with Götz Harbsmeier in 1952 concerning German remilitarization, Bultmann had already taken a similar position. He could grant a political mandate to the church only in the exceptional circumstance of a totalitarian state. In a democratic state, the church and other institutions supported by spiritual interests—for instance, the university—had at most an indirect political function. Individual Christians should of course engage in and be responsible for political decisions, but in doing so they must orient themselves to secular points of view. Bultmann deemed it unacceptable to justify either support or rejection of rearmament by deploying an allegedly Christian ideology.[227]

Again dealing with an issue of political ethics in 1958, Bultmann offered a carefully articulated argument along the same lines on the occasion of the debate over the use of nuclear energy and the acquisition of nuclear arms by the German Federal Republic. He was convinced that the church must decisively reject the assumption that it wished to issue concrete rulings on specific political issues. For the business of the church is "to proclaim the word of God, but not to deliver political judgments. A political judgment in a specific political situation is not the word of God. Theology must keep close watch that there be no mixing of Christian faith with a political program." As strictly as Bultmann rejected any kind of politicizing clericalism, he stressed with equal insistence the political responsibility of the individual Christian. To observe this responsibility in the spirit of *libertas Christiana*, the Christian must acquire expertise and, especially in a pluralistic society, must form an independent judgment in discourse with others in order to arrive at political judgments based on good political sense. Theology and the church must make this political responsibility transparent and inculcate it, but it is not their "task to set up politically binding rules and thereby take away from the individual person responsibility for his own decision."[228]

Bultmann took Ernst Käsemann's *Ruf der Freiheit* [*Jesus Means Freedom*] as his student had initially meant it: it was a call to critical and indeed polemi-

226. Cf. UB Tübingen, RB est.: D. Sölle to RB, 13. 7. 1964 and 22. 12. 1965, Mn 2-1834; RB to D. Sölle, 16. 6. 1965, Mn 2-2386.

227. Cf. UB Tübingen, RB est., RB to G. Harbsmeier, 15. 5. 1952, Mn 2-2232. On the acute problem, cf. J. Vogel, *Kirche und Wiederbewaffnung*.

228. RB, "Gedenken über die gegenwärtige theologische Situation," *GuV* (1st ed.), vol. 3, 195f. This position was probably induced by the demand on the part of the church brotherhoods directed at synod of the Evangelical Church of Germany of 1958 in Berlin to attend theologically to the arming of the Federal Republic with atomic weapons.

cal debate with "No Other Gospel," the so-called confessional movement, with populist contentment in the church, and with the current ecclesiastical and theological dogmatism of insisting on right doctrine.[229] To be sure, a number of the author's sweeping judgments led Bultmann to issue a reminder that not every theologian in a position of church leadership ought to be made responsible for things having gone off course. He named as exemplary leaders Bishop Erich Vellmer (of Kurhessen-Waldeck) and President Joachim Beckmann (of Rhineland), but also praised individual pastors who in the exercise of their office were witnessing to Christian freedom without allowing themselves to be paralyzed by fear of official ecclesiasticism. In the course of his response to Käsemann's polemic, Bultmann once again discussed various exegetical and systematic options his student had taken. Here and there, for instance, he confessed to not having "made the most of the significance of the lordship of Christ and of 'freedom' for the whole world," for instance. To be sure, he found that once again Käsemann had put too much stress on the relatively few statements in the New Testament regarding the lordship of Christ.[230] Bultmann agreed with the opinion that, *given certain conditions*, Christians were to "turn away from or even to set themselves over against the state and the nation."[231] Nevertheless, he maintained that despite its misuse by some elements of Protestantism, Luther's teaching of the two kingdoms provided the best way to understand how the gospel referred to politics and the difference between both entities.

Unfortunately, Bultmann's 1958 warning against politicizing the church and mixing law with gospel was, to the great detriment of theology and church, ignored or consciously passed over in the following decades by segments of German Protestantism. A number of "progressive" forces once again dealt simplistically with the relations of theology and society, the church's proclamation and political-social reality. Many a pulpit became a religious platform from which social-critical and directly political agitation was promoted. Certainly, the increasing tendency to give theological legitimation to particular political views, claims, and judgments was in part a result of

229. Cf. UB Tübingen, RB est., RB to E. Käsemann, 27. 1. 1968, Mn 2-2251, on E. Käsemann, *Ruf der Freiheit*; as well as RB to G. Krüger, 28. 1. and 3. 3. 1968, in F. Lilie, "Bultmann-Krüger Briefwechsel," *ZNThG* 7, 160f.

230. Cf. UB Tübingen, RB est., RB to E. Käsemann, 27. 1. 1968, Mn 2-2251; and see above 474–79.

231. RB to E. Käsemann, 27. 1. 1968, Mn 2-2251, 143. Bultmann expressed heartfelt concern for Ernst Käsemann's worries about his youngest daughter Elisabeth, who was involved politically in South America, first in Montevideo and later in Buenos Aires (cf. E. Käsemann to RB, 15. 8. 1968, 6. 7. and 17. 8. 1975, Mn 2-1083; and RB to E. Käsemann, 15. 9. 1968, 13. 4. 1975, Mn 2-2251).

inadequacies that church and theology had brought upon themselves during the postwar period. There was a far-reaching lack of innovative thinking in social ethics, and in view of the processes of social change and pressing global problems in the 1960s, more attention to such issues might have pointed out the political implications of Christian faith. Thus, it seemed to many an opportune time to develop concepts of a "political theology." To be sure, the half-life of these sketches proved comparatively short, and not only due to their narrow dependence on Neo-Marxist philosophy. The protagonists of political theology agreed in demanding that the privatizing tendencies underlying the theology of the word of God had to be corrected.[232]

Dorothee Sölle put forward her version of political theology in 1971 in the form of a discussion with the thought of Rudolf Bultmann.[233] Relying on Gogarten, she concluded that Bultmann's view of the historicity of human existence was all but predestined for a broadening of its perspective through a political theology. Bultmann had not recognized that possibility inherent in his own approach because he had individualized salvation and had treated it in a selectively existentialist fashion, and by doing so had obscured the degree to which human existence is bound up in society. Moreover, she proposed, Bultmann's thought was "pre-sociologically bourgeois"; he lacked as "an essential presupposition of contemporary political theory . . . the distinction of state and society."[234] Sölle agreed with Johann Baptiste Metz that it was now time to abandon the individualistic narrowing and privatizing of faith and boldly realize theology's functional power to critique and to change society. The Enlightenment's intention in giving rise to the historical-critical method had to be consistently realized through a political-social hermeneutic of the gospel. Critique of ideology must expose not only the mythical worldview of the Bible, but also the deformations of Christianity, the structures of society, and their ideological superstructure. To do so, political theology had to orient "its understanding of truth in the direction of the unity of theory and praxis that has not yet appeared." On this basis, Sölle issued as "the criterion of verification of every theological statement . . . the praxis that the future makes possible." Theological statements contained only "so much truth as they can practically employ in changing reality."[235] As the critical norm of this political theology, Sölle lifted up the historical Jesus,

232. Cf. W. Schmithals, "Gesellschaftliches Engagement der Christen," 21–25; G. Klein, "Rudolf Bultmann—Ein Lehrer der Kirche," 616–18; H. Fischer, *Protestantische Theologie im 20, Jahrhundert*, 189–95.

233. Cf. D. Sölle, "Hoffnung verändert die Welt," 15–20; D. Sölle, *Politische Theologie*.

234. D. Sölle, *Politische Theologie*, 58f.

235. D. Sölle, *Politische Theologie*, 96f.

whom she believed she could commend to her readers as the political Jesus, the initiator of the exodus out of unjust structures of power.

Since Bultmann himself was no longer able to read, he had Bernd Jaspert read three selected chapters of Sölle's book aloud to him.[236] Due to his weakened state of health, the now eighty-seven-year-old confined his personal reply to his critic to a few succinct observations on her *Political Theology*.[237] That Sölle denounced the concept of being taken out of the world because she had misread his own dialectic, and had summarily labeled his theology as apolitical, Bultmann considered an aggravating misunderstanding and an inappropriate narrowing of the implications of his thinking. The way Sölle discredited the concept of authority and imposed the verdict of decisionism on the kerygma seemed to him a fundamental theological mistake. For, by doing so, she had rescinded not only the word of God that encounters one and that authoritatively demands faith in the kerygma, but also the possibility of grasping this faith in its distinctiveness as that act which for the first time constitutes the believing subject in his relation to God and to himself.

In particular, Bultmann censured Sölle's view that faith, understood as being taken out of the world, is "oriented to the understanding of the fatedness of circumstances and of the way things are ordered" and demands the "surrendering of social, political reason, which the world takes as unalterable."[238] On the contrary, Bultmann insists that faith grants "the freedom to change the world." However, to connect theory and praxis with each other is not somehow the task of a "political" theology, but rather "of theology in general," which must also "take into consideration the *responsibility* of faith for the structures of the contemporary world."[239] In this regard, however, the realizing of "an authentic life for all people . . . in the context of societal hopes"[240] that Sölle understands as a postulate of the gospel is, on Bultmann's view, a challenge for *law*—which is fully affirmed by faith. For the "inward freedom that makes faith independent of political structures does not release it from this responsibility [for societal structures and, as the case may be, for changing them], but rather demands it."[241] However—and

236. Cf. D. Sölle, *Politische Theologie*, 71–89 ("5. Political Theology as Hermeneutic"), 105–16 ("7. The Political Interpretation of Sin"), and 117–34 ("8. The Political Interpretation of Forgiveness").

237. Citations of what follows are from RB to D. Sölle, August 1971, Mn 2-2386, in UB Tübingen, RB est.

238. D. Sölle, *Politische Theologie*, 79.

239. UB Tübingen, RB est., RB to D. Sölle, August 1971, Mn 2-2386.

240. D. Sölle, *Politische Theologie*, 77.

241. UB Tübingen, RB est., RB to D. Sölle, August 1971, Mn 2-2386.

Bultmann regarded this to be insufficiently dealt with by his critic—each envisaged societal change *in concreto* requires careful reflection, for if it is to appear as legitimate from the perspective of faith, realizing it still invariably necessitates concrete decisions of the believing individual.

In this connection, Sölle's "political interpretation" of sin as a collective failure of conduct due essentially to political and social structures especially drove Bultmann to do some re-thinking. He did not dispute that communal life can be burdened with compulsions that can cause such transgressions, but what Sölle characterized as sin—for instance, collaboration "with structurally grounded, mostly anonymous injustice"[242]—Bultmann thought should simply be subsumed under the concept of guilt. He insisted on his "individualistic" view so as to avoid any talk "of sin that is caused by the compulsions of social structures." As personal transgression in conduct, sin must be quite precisely distinguished from guilt or collective guilt that has arisen through compulsion of whatever kind.[243] Bultmann certainly agreed with Sölle that in the concept of sin, "compulsion and freedom" are to be thought of "as related to each other dialectically," and that the contradiction between compulsion and freedom can be resolved "only in the whole person becoming new in a new world."[244] Nevertheless, he objected, "the becoming new of the world" is a mere utopia if it is not conceived "as a permanent task," as the changing of people's ways that is to be achieved in the world. In addition, Bultmann decisively opposed Sölle's assertion that in his theological approach the transition from existentialist to political theology was a matter of concern. And going beyond the points mentioned above, he also asserted as a basic difference between them the fact that he was interested in "the dialectical relation between an otherworldly, transcendent reality and this-worldly reality," while for Sölle, this problem evidently did not exist at all, since she occupied herself exclusively with this-worldly reality.[245]

Sölle did not feel impelled to consider either these objections of Bultmann's or Hans Hübner's critical discussion of her position[245] or indeed to revise her political theology.[246] Immediately following his reaction to her book, she did, to be sure, make an "existential observation" to him on the

242. D. Sölle, *Politische Theologie*, 112.

243. UB Tübingen, RB est., RB to D. Sölle, August 1971, Mn 2-2386.

244. D. Sölle, *Politische Theologie*, 112.

245. Cf. H. Hübner, *Politische Theologie und existentiale Interpretation*. For a critique of Sölle, see also B. Jaspert, *Sackgassen im Streit mit Rudolf Bultmann*, 93–112.

246. Cf. D. Sölle, "Rudolf Bultmann und die politische Theologie," in StA Oldenburg, 62–79. One may doubt that Sölle understood Bultmann's theological objections to her political theology at all. This is shown clearly in D. Sölle, *Gegenwind*, 54–60.

subject of being taken out of the world. Having just then failed in her first attempt to become qualified to teach in Cologne, she meekly conceded, "the point of Christian distance from the world did become clear to me once more. To be able to lose ὡς μὴ [as if not], one learns from such events." Thus "by a few detours" she had come "to prune back some of" her criticism of Bultmann.[247] But this readiness for self-critical modesty did not last long. For his part, Bultmann showed himself to be increasingly concerned over the politicizing of the church's proclamation and the increasing disregard for New Testament exegesis that was also being propagated by Sölle.[248] In the conflicts of the following years, the disastrous consequences of the uninhibited transformation of the gospel into direct instruction in political conduct gave him the right to insist that theology was always well advised to practice the necessary art of distinguishing, and especially of distinguishing between the eternal salvation and the earthly well-being of human beings.

247. UB Tübingen, RB est., D. Sölle to RB, 10. 9. 1971, Mn 2-1834.
248. Cf. UB Tübingen, RB est., RB to E. Lohse, ca. April 1971 (letter draft), Mn 2-2288.

VIII. Finale (ca. 1964–1976)

1. Honors

> *If I may give expression to my feelings in the language of your Swabian homeland, with which I became so familiar during my time as a student in Tübingen, I would like to say, "This is downright embarrassing."*[1]

On what was for Bultmann the "unforgettable morning of August 19th," 1964, one day before his eightieth birthday, Erich Dinkler, Ernst Fuchs, Werner Georg Kümmel, and Hartwig Thyen appeared at 14 Calvin Street in order to present the honoree with the thank-you gift of *Zeit und Geschichte* [*Time and History*].[2] As Hans Jonas had done in his speech in honor of the birthday boy on August 20th,[3] so also in his words of greeting at the presentation of the *Festschrift*, Erich Dinkler emphasized that through his research and teaching, Bultmann had disclosed to many more than his friends, colleagues, and students the freedom of faith and the character of Christian existence as risk. He had always made a habit of underscoring his view of the inherently unfinished nature of theology with the insistence that one should go beyond one's own findings for the sake of the subject-matter.[4] Dinkler himself supplied an example of the student's freedom from the teacher's ideas with his analysis of the Caesarea pericope of Mark 8:27–9:1.[5] Bultmann reacted in characteristic fashion to this study, which subjected his own understanding of Peter's confession to criticism: he found Dinkler's argumentation plausible and accorded it lively agreement.[6]

In other respects, as well, the celebratory gift did not reflect a "Bultmann School" hermetically sealed off from new insights and critical inquiries, for its combined contributions by forty-five authors documented manifold stimuli and effects that had come out of Bultmann's theological work. It

1. UB Tübingen, RB est., RB to President of the Republic T. Heuss (in expressing his thanks for the bestowal on him of the Superior Cross of the Federal Order of Merit), 28. 7. 1959, Mn 2-3074.

2. UB Tübingen, RB est., RB to E. Dinkler, 13. 9. 1964, Mn 2-2176.

3. Cf. UB Tübingen, RB est., the fragment of the draft of Hans Jonas' address, Mn 2-3444.

4. Cf. E. Dinkler, *Zeit und Geschichte*, vii.

5. Cf. E. Dinkler, "Petrusbekenntnis und Satanswort," *Zeit und Geschichte*, 127–53.

6. Cf. UB Tübingen, RB est., RB to E. Dinkler, 13. 9. 1964, Mn 2-2176.

took Bultmann several weeks to thank the collaborators on the *Festschrift* for their contributions and to respond to the numerous letters of congratulations for his birthday. He thanked all whose names were recorded on the *Tabula Gratulatoria* for the support they had shown him through their good wishes. "But I am also ashamed, and I can only conclude my thanks by bringing to mind the biblical words with which I once also concluded my lecture on the occasion of my departure from my teaching position: Gen 32:10 and 1 Cor 4:7."[7] The two texts together gave expression to the leitmotif of Bultmann's theological existence. Now, looking back on the eight decades of his life, he found his theological work summed up in them:

> "[Lord], I am not worthy of the least of all the steadfast love and all the faithfulness that you have shown to your servant." (Gen 32:10)[8]
>
> What do you have that you did not receive? And if you received it, why do you boast as if it were not a gift? (1 Cor 4:7)

It was not inconsistent with this inveterate personal modesty that Bultmann rejoiced heartily in the success of the *Festschrift* as a publication, especially as he took it to indicate recognition of the involvement of those who had collaborated in it.[9]

Zeit und Geschichte was the third anthology to appear in Bultmann's honor. His friends and students had previously planned to dedicate a celebratory volume to him on the occasion of his sixtieth birthday in 1944, but the confusion of the war prevented its publication. At any rate, Bultmann had at the time thought that his seventieth birthday would be the earliest appropriate occasion for such a scholarly gift. Naturally, he hoped that a *Festschrift* that had been prepared ahead of time might appear on that date; but this was not so much for his sake as because he hoped that the work of his friends and students, and "also the reemergence of scholarly work and the possibility of it in general," might thus become apparent following the anticipated end of the War.[10] This *Festschrift* was then presented to him on his sixty-fifth birthday, five years later than originally planned. As the initiator of the project, Ernst Wolf paid tribute in his foreword to Bultmann's concern to place historical criticism that was guided by the spirit of truthfulness in the service

7. Bultmann's letter of thanks is cited in RB, *VW*, vi.

8. Bultmann reproduced the text according to the verse-numbering of the old Luther Bible.

9. From August to December 1964, the *Festschrift* "sold so well . . . that Siebeck wanted to have a further 1500 copies printed" (RB to E. Dinkler, 18. 12. 1964, Mn 2-2176).

10. RB to G. Krüger, 27. 8. 1944, in F. Lilie, "Bultmann-Krüger Briefwechsel," *ZNThG* 6, 135.

of the freedom that was witnessed to by the New Testament. Bultmann had "at the same time thereby managed to affirm in a most impressive way what the Confessing Church was all about."[11]

Although the contributions to the *Festschrift* of 1949 represented all the theological disciplines from Old Testament to practical theology, the circle of authors was still limited to Bultmann's German students and colleagues. This restriction caused by the War and the postwar turmoil resulted in a second *Festschrift* on the occasion of Bultmann's seventieth birthday. Numerous theologians from outside of Germany also contributed to this, and their collaboration reflected the international standing of his scholarly work. In order to keep the scope of this volume within limits and representative of Bultmann's theological interests, the authors contributed only exegetical New Testament studies to the *Festschrift,* which was edited by the Marburg New Testament and patristics scholar Walther Eltester.[12]

Nor did Bultmann have any reason to complain about a lack of academic honors. The Marburg theological faculty had already awarded him the distinction of *D. theol. h.c.* in 1920, though this award had a rather prosaic background. Bultmann had received the *Lic. theol.* at Marburg in 1910, but not the *D. theol.*, since in the German theological faculties of that time the *Lic. theol.* was its equivalent. Yet the Giessen theological faculty, to which Bultmann had belonged since the winter semester of 1920–21, allowed only holders of the doctoral degree to participate in qualifying candidates for the doctorate. For this reason, on November 1, 1920, the Dean of the Giessen faculty, Martin Schian, requested the Marburg theological faculty to confer on Bultmann the distinction of a *D. theol. h. c.* The Marburg faculty acceded to this request and granted Bultmann the honorary doctorate on December 24, 1920—both as a deserved honor and a Christmas present at the same time. He dedicated his *Geschichte der synoptischen Tradition* [*History of the Synoptic Tradition*] to them in gratitude for it.[13] When Bultmann was to be honored with the Doctor of Divinity by the University of St. Andrews in Scotland in 1935, he was unsure how he was to conduct himself at the ceremony. He asked Karl Barth, who had earlier already received the Doctor of Divinity from Glasgow, for "instructions regarding proper conduct." Was

11. E. Wolf, Foreword, *Festschrift Rudolf Bultmann*, v.

12. Cf. W. Eltester, *Neutestamentliche Studien für Rudolf Bultmann.*

13. Cf. the letter of the Dean of the Giessen theological faculty to the Marburg theological faculty of 1. 11. 1920, the copy of Bultmann's doctoral citation of 25. 12. 1920, Bultmann's letter of thanks to the Marburg theological faculty of 5. 1. 1921, as well as his announcement of 14. 2. 1921 of his intention to dedicate the *History of the Synoptic Tradition* to the Marburg theological faculty, in UA Marburg, Honorary Doctorates 1921–24.

he to give a speech? What about the difficult question of dress? "Should one appear in tails? Does one have to buy doctoral dress there? All or only part of it? Or does it suffice to rent the garb? (An offer from a shop in Edinburgh has already arrived.)"[14] Barth provided the information eagerly and humorously,[15] so that Bultmann got through the degree ceremony without embarrassment on June 28, 1935.[16] He received other honorary doctorates from Syracuse University and from the philosophical faculty of the University of Marburg in 1959. Apart from this, several scholarly societies elected Bultmann to their membership, among them the Academy of Sciences in Oslo in 1932 and the *Academia Nazionale dei Lincei* in Rome in 1968. The Society of Biblical Literature and Exegesis [shortened to the "Society of Biblical Literature" in 1962] named him an Honorary Member in 1950,[17] and the Wissenschaftliche Gesellschaft für Theologie [Society for the Academic Study of Theology] bestowed honorary membership on him in 1969. The Academia Goetheana in Sao Paolo (1949), as well as the Academies of Sciences of Heidelberg (1958) and Göttingen (1960), appointed him to corresponding membership.

To these academic honors were added diverse public honors on the part of the state. In 1954 the state of Hesse awarded Bultmann the Goethe plaque in acknowledgement of his "exceptional contributions to the cultural life of the state of Hesse," particularly with regard to the reputation of the University of Marburg in Germany and abroad.[18] He received the Order of Merit of the Federal Republic of Germany in the grades of the Superior Cross of Merit (1959), with star (1964) and shoulder sash (1974).[19] The Hessian President, Albert Osswald, bestowed upon Bultmann the Superior Cross of the Order of Merit with star and shoulder sash a day before his ninetieth birthday. In the speech that he gave on the occasion, Osswald paid an extremely well-

14. RB to K. Barth, 29. 3. 1935, in B. Jaspert, *Barth-Bultmann Briefwechsel* (2d ed.), 157f.

15. K. Barth to RB, 31. 3. 1935, in B. Jaspert, *Barth-Bultmann Briefwechsel* (2d ed.), 158f.

16. Cf. also UB Tübingen, RB est., University of St. Andrews to RB, 12. 6. and 20. 6. 1935, Mn 2-1963.

17. Bultmann took this up in the following fashion: ". . . I greet it with a smile, since it takes place at the time when my work is exposed to the most vehement attacks (which, for the rest, doesn't trouble me)" (RB to A. Bultmann Lemke, 22. 4. 1951, Mn 2-3452, in UB Tübingen, RB est).

18. Cf. the award certificate of 20. 8. 1954, as well as the congratulatory letter of the Hessian Minister for Education and Popular Culture Arno Henning of 19. 8. 1954, Mn 2-3072, in UB Tübingen, RB est.

19. Cf. the documents in UB Tübingen, RB est., Mn 2-3074, -3075, -3077.

informed tribute to Bultmann's theological work,[20] for through his staff, the President had acquired the necessary background information from the chapter-head of the Limburg Cathedral, Werner Böckenförde.

Bultmann accepted all these honors with extraordinary modesty. To be sure, he did not conceal the fact that he took a degree of satisfaction from the public acknowledgement of his scholarly work, especially in the face of the numerous attacks against his theology and his person by fundamentalist and other church groups.[21] This was even more the case when the awarding of the Superior Cross of the Federal Order of Merit in 1959 led the "Evangelical" faction to intensify the campaign against the Marburg "heretic." One Dr. Richard vom Baur, chair of the Mannheim publishing house Philadelphia, wrote to the President of the Republic, Theodor Heuss, that Bultmann's activity had long been "a growing outrage for millions of Bible-believing Protestant Christians in Germany," for he denied "the entire official confession of belief of the Protestant Church." Baur asked the President of the Republic to inform him of the considerations that comprised the basis for awarding the Order to Bultmann lest "a nationwide protest in both the spoken and written word begin over this affair."[22] Heuss reacted in magisterial fashion to this perfidious attempt to disparage the integrity of the one he had honored. He had no intention of commenting on the honoring of Bultmann, a scholar of international rank, "to persons who write to me." Moreover, bestowing the Order was not a religious or ecclesiastical but a secular event, and that precluded his applying a dogmatic test to it. Finally, Heuss unequivocally rejected the concluding section of Baur's letter. That sort of "intimidation, even threat," was precisely not Christian. The advertised protest against Bultmann represented rather "the announcement of an organized ('nationwide'!) Phariseeism," which Heuss found "in plain terms, simply contemptible."[23] As Bultmann noted with contentment when he learned of the whole affair, the President of the Republic had answered that pious zealot "briefly and splendidly."[24]

Among the various honors bestowed upon Bultmann, the Reuchlin Prize of 1957 and acceptance into the Order *Pour le mérite* in 1969

20. Cf. A. Osswald, "Ansprach anlässe der Verleihung . . ." ["Remarks on the occasion of the bestowal of the Superior Cross of the Federal Order of Merit with Star and Shoulder Sash upon Prof. D. Dr. Rudolf Bultmann, 19. 8. 1974, Marburg"], 133f.

21. Cf. H. Stegemann, "Bultmanns Entmythologisierung," 6.

22. UB Tübingen, RB est., R. vom Baur to Federal President T. Heuss, 11. 8. 1959 (copy), Mn 2-3074.

23. UB Tübingen, RB est., T. Heuss to R. vom Baur, 13. 8. 1959 (copy), Mn 2-3074.

24. UB Tübingen, RB est., RB to A. Bultmann Lemke, 23. 8. 1959, Mn 2-3452.

played especially important roles. The city of Pforzheim had established the Reuchlin Prize in 1935, on the occasion of the 500th birthday of the Hebraist and humanist Johannes Reuchlin, and after the historian Werner Naf, Bultmann was only the second recipient of this prize. But shortly before the scheduled presentation of the honor, he received from Pforzheim an anonymous threatening letter "from one who means well and speaks for many," and who warned him, "It will not give you joy!" Bultmann ignored the warning.[25] The orientalist Adam Falkenstein gave the reasons for the proposal of the Heidelberg Academy of Sciences to award the Reuchlin Prize to Bultmann: his life's work spanned all areas of the history and literature of early Christianity and of classical and late antique culture and religion, and his historical studies were distinguished by striving "to make the historical past truly present, which does not exhaust itself in a mere reconstruction of what has been." Furthermore, Bultmann had made an outstanding contribution to research and to the understanding of both Christianity and Greco-Roman antiquity, the two great movements that have put their stamp on Western culture up to the present. In particular, his book *Primitive Christianity in Its Contemporary Setting* opened up in equal measure to scholars in the field and to lay people new approaches to a central epoch of the history of religion and culture.[26]

Plate 40: The Holder of the Order *Pour le mérite,* 1969

Mayor Dr. Johann Peter Brandenburg presented the Reuchlin Prize to Bultmann on March 22, 1958, in the Pforzheim city theatre. The Southwest

25. Cited according to RB to A. Bultmann Lemke, 23. 8. 1959, Mn 2-3452, in UB Tübingen, RB est.

26. Explanation of the proposal of the philosophical-historical section of the Heidelberg Academy of Sciences, signed by A. Falkenstein, n. d., Mn 2-3073, in UB Tübingen, RB est.

German Chamber Orchestra, under the direction of Friedrich Tilegant, provided the musical setting for the celebration. In his lecture, Bultmann spoke about the ancient and the Christian understanding of freedom.[27] The constitutive differences between the two go back to differences in their view of the human being. While Greek antiquity understands the individual as a being who by means of reason is able to understand himself as a member of the harmoniously ordered cosmos, the Christian tradition sees what is distinctive of the individual in his historical sense, which emerges from the will and expresses itself in responsibility for history. Characteristically, one encounters neither in the Old Testament nor in Jesus' proclamation a word that corresponds to the Greek concept of "freedom." Paul is the first to have taken this concept over from Hellenistic into Christian usage, though he modified it in important ways as he did so.

The manifold ways in which the idea of freedom is shaped in Greek antiquity exhibit a commonality. Freedom is regarded as a quality that the individual person, being endowed with reason and self-control *per se*, possesses and realizes on the basis of his own strength. In contrast, the idea of freedom in Christianity, especially in Paul, is historicized. Here, freedom signifies a possibility that can become event only but always in the decision of the person. But as Paul knows, the individual is always bound through his past to his old self, and by affirming this bondage, he allows himself to be enslaved by the power of sin, from which he can be freed only through the grace of God, which again and again becomes event in faith. The grace of God frees the human being from himself for the first time, and thereby makes him a new person, who receives himself as a gift of God's grace and seeks to live out the freedom that has been bestowed in love.[28]

In connection with the awarding of the prize in Pforzheim, Paul Kuder, the Chair of the Reuchlin Society, contacted Bultmann in order to persuade him to present an additional lecture.[29] Thus, on February 18, 1960, in Pforzheim, Bultmann renewed the dialogue between antiquity and Christianity, concentrating this time on the subject of the differences in their worldviews. As he had done in the book on *Primitive Christianity in Its Contemporary Setting*, he traversed the entire terrain of the history of ancient religion and culture, from the Old Testament and Judaism, classical Greece,

27. The South German Radio Network broadcast the talk that Bultmann gave again in Heidelberg on 21. 12. 1958 on its First Program.

28. Cf. RB, "Der Gedanke der Freiheit," *GuV* (3d ed.), vol. 4, 42–51.

29. Cf. the correspondence between P. Kuder and RB, Mn 2-1607 and -2342, in UB Tübingen, RB est.

the *stoa*, the Hellenistic mystery cults and star worship, to Gnosis, and on into earliest Christianity. In its beginnings in the proclamation of Jesus, but above all in the Gospel of John and the theology of Paul, Christianity's uniquely dialectical relation to the world comes into view. In the paradoxical eschatological existence of faith, which understands itself in time from beyond time, the need to choose between an optimistic and a pessimistic view of the world is obviated.[30]

Besides the Reuchlin Prize, Bultmann also accorded a special value to being accepted into the Order *Pour le Mérite*. For this award also indicated that lay people outside of the milieux of the academy and the church had given public recognition to his theological work. King Frederick William IV of Prussia, the founder of the Order *Pour le Mérite* for sciences and arts (the so-called Peace Class of the Order of Frederick the Great), had in the constitution of the Order in 1842 planned that "theological scholarship . . . in accordance with its spirit" would preclude its representatives from membership in the Order,[31] and although this proviso had been rescinded, its membership included few theologians. After Adolf von Harnack, Albert Schweitzer, and Gerhard von Rad, Rudolf Bultmann was the fourth Protestant theologian to have been elected to the Order.[32]

Its Chancellor, the Göttingen historian, Percy Ernst Schramm, conferred the insignia of the Order upon Bultmann in a simple ceremony in Braunlage on June 23, 1969.[33] Since Bultmann was already eighty-four when he became a member of the Order, he was no longer able to take part in the gatherings of the chapter of the Order, and therefore he became an emeritus member in 1970. Since he had taken over the seat of the Catholic philosopher of religion Romano Guardini, he was succeeded by Karl Rahner, in turn a Catholic Jesuit theologian. Bultmann welcomed the election of Rahner to the Order as a sign of an ecumenical ethos. To be sure, he regarded the hope for a unification of the two Christian confessions as illusory, but he saw it as fruitful when confessional differences were dealt with in mutual understanding and respect.[34] Even as an emeritus member, Bultmann took a lively inter-

30. Cf. RB, "Optimismus und Pessimismus in Antike und Christentum," *GuV* (3d ed.), vol. 4, 69–90. Despite the statement of the "1959 Annual Report of the Reuchlin Society Pforzheim, Inc., to its members" (see the note on p. 69 therein), the lecture was delivered for the first time in 1960.

31. Cited according to H. Fuhrmann, *Pour le mérite*, 52. On the background of the proviso, cf. pp. 52–55.

32. Julius Wellhausen belonged to the Order as a historian and orientalist.

33. Cf. Orden Pour le Mérite, *Reden und Gedenkworte*, vol. 9, 195.

34. Cf. RB to the Chancellor of the Order, P. E. Schramm, 21. 7. 1970, in Orden Pour le Mérite, *Reden und Gedenkworte*, vol. 10, 195.

est in the fortunes of the Order and its members. For example, he conveyed his best wishes to "my dear Sister-in-the-Order" Marie Luise Kaschnitz on her seventieth birthday, and in doing so recalled the time they had shared in their literary group during the years of the First World War. Since then, Bultmann and his wife had followed the journey of the poet with great interest. Bultmann now expressed his respect for her work by confessing that he felt clearly "the superiority of artistic creativity to scholarly work."[35]

According to the founding statutes of 1942, the Peace-*Pour le Mérite* was to be awarded for "outstanding services in the area of science and art."[36] As with his other honors, Bultmann received this Order for his services in the area of theological scholarship. For a Protestant theologian, problematic connotations adhered to the concept *le mérite* (in Latin, *meritum*), because Luther had repeatedly and sharply attacked the concept of *meritum*, which scholastic theology had introduced into the doctrine of grace by means of the very subtlest of distinctions. In the "Small Catechism"—even in the interpretation of the first article concerning creation—he brought to public attention that the justification of the sinner takes place through faith alone, "out of pure, fatherly, and divine goodness and mercy, without any merit [*sine ullis meis meritis*] or worthiness on my part."[37] The Augsburg Confession of 1530 states just as categorically that no human being can become righteous before God "*propriis viribus, meritis aut operibus*" ["on account of his own wishes, merits, or works"].[38] Bultmann interpreted the faith that makes for righteousness along these lines in its contemporary meaning as the radical "opposite of καύχησις [boasting]."[39] Even if a person has accomplished something meaningful in his life by means of the powers given to him, we still may not "bring this boastfully before God, before whom human greatness can lift up no claim." For as the insight of 1 Cor 4:7 declares, "What do you have that you have not received? And if you received it, why do you boast as if it you had not received it?" In faith, the individual abandons all high-handedness based on one's works, accomplishments, and merits in order "to surrender himself in trust to the grace of God."[40]

35. DLA Marbach, Kaschnitz est., RB to M. L. Kaschnitz, 30. 1. 1971.

36. Cited according to H. Fuhrmann, *Pour le mérite,* 55; cf. also the carefully formulated specification of Frederick William IV that, in the selection of those who bear the Order, those are to be thought of "who have acquired an excellent reputation through the widespread acknowledgement of their merits" (56).

37. M. Luther, "Der Kleine Katechismus (1529)," 511, 3–5.

38. [P. Melanchthon,] "Die Augsburgische Konfession (1530)," 56, 2f.

39. RB, *Theologie des Neuen Testaments*, 281.

40. RB, "Worte . . ." ["Words spoken over the coffin of Katharina Kippenberg"], 5.

Bultmann was thus protected from the danger of attaching to his merits an importance that in accordance with faith in justification could not belong to them. The embarrassing position in which he was placed by the awarding of the Federal Cross of Merit in 1959 consisted only in the matter of properly expressing his thanks for this honor.[41] And precisely because he recognized that it was utterly impossible for an individual to possess any merits *coram Deo* [before God], he was able to rejoice over the acknowledgement of his merits *coram mundo* [before the world]. But even then Bultmann drew back, for in giving thanks for his awards, he never failed to point out that along with his work, that of his theological teachers was also being honored. He had merely endeavored to continue the scholarly tradition he had entered.[42]

2. Family and Personal Matters, Friendships

Yes, one can say that faith exhibits the hidden fellowship of all human beings. For the individual is created to be himself and, indeed, to be himself in the receiving and granting of fellowship.[43]

In December of 1945 Bultmann had bemoaned the fact that under National Socialism and especially during the War "young people had to do without all of the opportunities for their lives that under other conditions, give youth all of its substance and its joy."[44] Meanwhile, following the end of the Third Reich, the circumstances of life gradually but slowly returned to normal. Thus, new perspectives on education and on constructing a professional life opened up for the younger generation. In 1952 Bultmann's eldest daughter Antje, who had worked as a librarian in Jena in the years following the War, decided to go to the United States, where she became a music librarian at the Syracuse University Library. After completing further study in library sciences, she taught in this department at Syracuse University from 1960 on. In the autumn of 1945, Gesine Bultmann was engaged as first flute of the Freiburg Symphony Orchestra, as well as a soloist in the chamber orchestra that performed with the Freiburg Bach Choir. Heilke, the youngest of the

41. Cf. UB Tübingen, RB est., RB to T. Heuss, 28. 7. 1959, Mn 2-3074.

42. Cf. UB Tübingen, RB est.: RB to T. Heuss, 28. 7. 1959, Mn 2-3074; RB to Federal President H. Lübke, 8. 9. 1964, Mn 2-3075; and RB to the theological faculty of Marburg, 14. 11. 1960, cited in H. Stegemann, "Bultmanns Entmythologisierung," 6.

43. RB, "Formen menschlicher Gemeinschaft," *GuV* (5th ed.), vol. 2, 273.

44. RB, "Bericht über unser Ergehen in Marburg," in H. G. Göckeritz, *Bultmann-Gogarten Briefwechsel*, 310.

Bultmann daughters, studied cello at the conservatory in Heidelberg and at music schools in Detmold and Freiburg. From 1952 on, there hung resplendent on the door of the house on Calvin Street displayed a shining brass plaque: "Heilke Bultmann, State-Certified Cello Instructor."[45]

Helene and Rudolf Bultmann followed with natural interest and satisfaction the paths in life their daughters pursued. The family circle began to expand when Gesine married law student Malte Diesselhorst in 1953. Bultmann's son-in-law graduated from Freiburg in 1956, received his teaching qualification at Göttingen in 1966, and served there as Professor of Civil Law from 1970 on. Three children were born to Gesine and Malte Diesselhorst: Jan, Annette, and Viola. The grandchildren brought a great deal of joy to their grandparents both by the fact of their being and their beaming cheerfulness. Bultmann sang old student drinking songs to the three-year-old Jan, who quickly learned to transcribe them on the desk that sat before him—even one in Latin. "So, he has already made a start in Latin to boot," the grandfather noted down, amused and delighted.[46] He eagerly undertook all sorts of grandfatherly duties, telling the grandchildren fairy tales he himself made up and drawing for them pictures that over time turned into a proper picture-book. When Jan and Annette were somewhat older, he looked at pictures with them when they had their early evening drink, and engaged them in conversations on historical subjects or biblical stories.[47] Bultmann followed his grandchildren's development in school and in music with lively interest.[48]

Because the possibilities for taking vacation trips were limited during the early postwar years, Helene and Rudolf Bultmann gratefully accepted invitations of their friends for visits in Switzerland in 1948, 1949, 1950, and 1953. The Bultmanns were able to stay with Walter Baumgartner in Basel and with Walter Gut and Ludwig Köhler in Zürich. They stayed for a week or two at a time with Hans Urner and Hildegard Urner-Astholz in the parsonage at Burg im Stein on the Rhine, with Pastor Alfred Vögeli in Nussbaumen (in Thurgau), as well as with Christoph Senft, a student and relative by marriage of Bultmann's, in Fleurier, near Neuchâtel. During vacations in Switzerland,

45. UB Tübingen, RB est., RB to F. C. Sell, 18. 1. 1953, Mn 2-2380.

46. RB to G. Krüger, 28. 1. 1957, in F. Lilie, "Bultmann-Krüger Briefwechsel," *ZNThG* 6, 306.

47. Cf. RB to G. Krüger, 24. 5. 1961, 8. 1. and 26. 3. 1967, in F. Lilie, "Bultmann-Krüger Briefwechsel," *ZNThG* 7, 152–55.

48. Cf. RB to G. Krüger, 28. 1. and 3. 3. 1968, in F. Lilie, "Bultmann-Krüger Briefwechsel," *ZNThG* 7, 159, 162; UB Tübingen, RB est., RB to E. Dinkler, 18. 4. 1971, Mn 2-2176.

Bultmann was able to combine relaxation and intellectual exchange with his hosts. Reading important new publications such as Erich Auerbach's *Mimesis* or Martin Heidegger's *Holzwege* [*Off the Beaten Track*] led to intensive discussions that included such other guests as Hans Conzelmann, Walter Gut, the Zwingli expert Gottfried W. Locher, and the Japanese classical philologist, Goro Mayeda.[49] Seldom had Bultmann read "a book as fascinating" as Erich Auerbach's major work that came out of his exile in Istanbul between 1942 and 1945: "Frank's *Philosophical Religious Truth* and your *Mimesis* are the most impressive books I have come across in years."[50] In addition to such welcome and impressive reading, the favorable living conditions in Switzerland compared with those of postwar Germany naturally also contributed to Bultmann's well-being.[51]

To be sure, the "economic miracle" soon made vacation trips within Germany possible once again, and in August of 1951 Bultmann spent a week in Rothenburg on the Tauber, Nördlingen, and Dinkelsbühl with his wife. A vacation on Wangeroog in 1956 rekindled in Bultmann memories of his youth. From Karlshafen in September of 1960, the couple visited the Roman churches in Bursfelde, Lippoldsberg, and Corvey. A vacation spot that he and his wife particularly enjoyed in 1958, 1962, 1963, and 1964, once together with Antje, was the Hotel Spielweg in Obermünstertal. For here, in the Bavarian Black Forest, all the prerequisites for relaxing seemed to him to come together: good weather for the most part, beautiful, panoramic

49. Cf. Bultmann's poem of 3. 10. 1948 in the guestbook of the Urners (copy), Mn 2-2409, in UB Tübingen, RB est.; as well as H. Urner-Astholz, "Erinnerungen an Rudolf Bultmann," *Spiegelungen*, 208f. C. Senft was married to Emma Senft, a daughter of Bultmann's cousin Friedrich Bultmann. In October of 1948, on their return journey from Switzerland, at the Notschrei between Oberried and Todtnau, the Bultmanns met for a few hours with Martin and Elfride Heidegger. This was probably the first reunion after the period of the Third Reich. Cf. M. Heidegger to E. Blochmann, 26. 10. 1948, in J. W. Storck, *Heidegger-Blochmann Briefwechsel*, 97.

50. DLA Marbach, RB to E. Auerbach, 16. 10. 1948: Bultmann took Auerbach's presentation of Western realism as reflected in literature as the occasion for asking Auerbach "whether the specifically Western type of humor doesn't go back to a secularization of the Christian understanding of suffering." Cf. M. Vialon, "Erich Auerbach und Rudolf Bultmann," 187–91; on Auerbach, cf. K. Barck and M. Treml, *Erich Auerbach*. Cf. also RB, "Das Christentum als orientalische und als abendländische Religion," *GuV* (5th ed.), vol. 2, 206–10. M. Vialon, "Erich Auerbach und Rudolf Bultmann," 191–95, has shown this as well as how Auerbach followed Bultmann's suggestion in the attention he pays to realistic humor in the second edition of the *Mimesis*. Cf. the inserted chapter "Die verzauberte Dulcinea" ["The Enchanted Dulcinea"] in E. Auerbach, *Mimesis*, 319–42; as well as the dedication to Bultmann in E. Auerbach, "Dante's Address to the Reader," *Gesemmelte Aufsätze*, 145.

51. Cf. RB to G. Krüger, 23. 12. 1950, in F. Lilie, "Bultmann-Krüger Briefwechsel," *ZNThG* 6, 157; VUN Library, Bultmann to K. Grobel, 23. 9. 1950.

environs, peace and quiet, and last but not least, a "quarter" [quarter-liter] of Markgräfler wine.[52] The couple's final foreign trip, to Menaggio on Lake Como in the spring of 1962, stood in sharp contrast, and largely on account of bad weather was more an exhausting than a relaxing undertaking.[53]

In an effort to alleviate his leg pain, Bultmann underwent spa-treatments several times in Wiesbaden (in 1951, 1955, 1966, and 1967) as he had done before the Second World War, and because it was near Gesine's family, who were living in Freiburg at the time, in Bad Krozingen (in 1957 and 1958). With increasing age, he had to deal with severe headaches, migraines, tiredness, and attacks of dizziness,[54] which he blamed on the frequent changes of weather and the "depressing Marburg fog."[55] What weighed on him still more than the complaints of old age, however, was that his wife was afflicted by attacks of dizziness that proved to be symptoms of Ménière's disease,[56] an ailment for which no effective therapies existed in the 1960s. Thus, anxiety for his wife attended Bultmann from this time on, but Rudolf and Helene Bultmann's love and affection for each other never waned. For their golden wedding anniversary on August 6, 1967, Bultmann composed a couplet that expressed their long and happy companionship: "God has blessed us all our days/On both our bright and shadowed ways."[57] He dedicated a number of other occasional poems to his wife, like this one written for New Year, 1965:[58]

A *wonder* we once each other found,
A *wonder* that us in love has bound.
Has through many a common hour,
The wonder given up its power?
What once was wonder—is it now just ordinary?
No! *The ordinary is now extraordinary.*

After becoming emeritus, Bultmann was determined to keep up his established contacts with friends and colleagues in the University of Marburg.

52. Cf. UB Tübingen, RB est., RB to E. Dinkler, 5. 9. 1962, Mn 2-2176.

53. Cf. RB to G. Krüger, 1. 6. 1962, in F. Lilie, "Bultmann-Krüger Breifwechsel," *ZNThG* 6, 309f; UB Tübingen, RB est., RB to E. Käsemann, 4. 9. 1962, Mn 2-2251.

54. Cf. for example RB to F. Gogarten, 10. 1. 1957 and 20. 10. 1963, in H.-G. Göckeritz, *Bultmann-Gogarten Briefwechsel*, 254, 260f.

55. RB to G. Krüger, 3. 12. 1967, in F. Lilie, "Bultmann-Krüger Briefwechsel," *ZNThG* 7, 158; cf. also 152, 154, 157, etc.

56. Cf. UB Tübingen, RB est., RB to E. Dinkler, 19. 6. 1959, Mn 2-2176.

57. RB, "For 6 August 1967," Poems, 11.

58. RB, "New Year 1965," Poems, 7.

Weekly luncheons at the "Sun" with the Old Testament scholar Emil Balla and the zoologist Jürgen Wilhelm Harms, as well as with the two physicians Paul Haendly and Felix Klewitz, served as entertaining breaks in the daily routine. In 1953 Bultmann sought to breathe new life into his *Graeca*, which after flourishing at first had been discontinued during the War. And once again the reading group made promising beginnings, but its changing membership did not sustain the *Graeca* in the long term.[59] Bultmann was in constant and largely controversial conversation with the philosopher Julius Ebbinghaus, but the sworn Kantian and the convinced existentialist theologian seldom reached agreement. Bultmann and his wife were able to indulge their passion for literature in the reading group they hosted every two weeks with three other couples: Wilhelm and Margarete Anz, Arthur and Elisabeth Henkel, and Kurt and Jane Steinmeyer. But what with calls to other universities, and above all the death of some of the conversation partners, the Marburg circle of friends gradually dwindled away.[60]

Literature remained the elixir of Bultmann's life up into his old age. In the last letters he wrote, he discussed literary works and his impressions from recent reading with his friends Walther Fischer and Gerhard Krüger.[61] In a radio interview with Hans Fischer-Barnicol in 1964, Bultmann indicated the importance for theology that he attributed to literature. When his students asked what books to get for themselves, he advised them to spend half of their book money on works of theology and half on literature, for anyone who meant to talk about the existence of the modern person had to see how the individual is understood in contemporary poetry, drama, and novels.[62] Bultmann himself often picked up *den Griffel der Calliope* [Calliope's stylus] both to write poems for concrete occasions within the circle of family and friends and simply to express his own thoughts and experiences of natural phenomena, the heavenly bodies, the seasons of the year, or recollections of the past. To be sure, he made no artistic claims for his poetic creations.[63]

59. At that time, besides Bultmann, the New Testament scholars Walther Eltester and Werner Georg Kümmel, the Greek scholar Friedrich Müller, as well as the two Latinists Hellfried Dahlmann and Carl Becker belonged to his *Graeca*.

60. Cf. UB Tübingen, RB est., RB to F. C. Sell, 5. 8. 1956, Mn 2-2380; RB to G. Krüger, 3. 6. 1954, 28. 1., 1. 5., and 21. 12. 1955, in F. Lilie, "Bultmann-Krüger Briefwechsel," *ZNThG* 6, 297, 300, 303f. Cf. also J. Ebbinghaus, untitled article, 46f.

61. Cf. UB Tübingen, RB est., RB to W. Fischer, 10. 11. 1967 and 17. 2. 1969, Mn 2-2198; as well as T. Kucharz, *Theologen und ihre Dichter*, 183f; RB to G. Krüger, 17. 11. 1967, in F. Lilie, "Bultmann-Krüger Briefwechsel," *ZNThG* 7, 157f.

62. Cf. H. Fischer-Barnicol, "Freiheit zur Zukunft."

63. Cf. for example [RB,] "Variationen über ein Thema"; on Bultmann's authorship of some of the poems printed here, cf. E. Dinkler, "Rudolf Bultmann als Lehrer und Mensch,"

Bultmann did not have a high opinion of postwar German literature as a whole. The year 1957 saw the publication of answers by eighteen writers in response to Karlheinz Deschner's question, "What do you make of Christianity?"[64] These statements left a depressing impression on Bultmann, for it seemed to him that hardly a single one of the authors had grasped what Christian faith actually is. To the extent that they did refer their criticism to the historical phenomenon or to a definite notion of Christianity, they saw Christianity in terms of their own idea of humanity. What is disconcerting about Christianity, its distinctive view of the historical character of human existence, and the nature of Christian existence as decision that comes from it—these crucial factors were what all the writers failed to recognize. Only a Catholic author, Stefan Andres, recognized the real stumbling-block [*skandalon*] of Christian faith: namely, the paradox that the historical event of the coming and going of Jesus, of his cross, is the eschatological occurrence. This paradox is forever reiterated in proclamation, which is both a human and divine word, and one that without needing or being capable of any prior legitimation, poses for the hearer the decision of whether he can and will actualize the new understanding of himself that it discloses to him.[65]

At least some of the writers who had a chance to speak with Deschner grasped the second disconcerting feature of Christian faith. This concerns the dialectical understanding of the world achieved through the eschatological existence of the believer who has been taken out of the world according to 1 Cor 7:29–31. There is a connection between the two forms of disconcertedness, since "*both are an offence to the human striving for security.*"[66] Because Bultmann's reaction to the positions of the eighteen writers made clear above all his understanding of the disconcerting character of Pauline and Johannine Christianity, any possibility of dialogue with those authors was burdened with predictable limitations.[67]

Im Zeichen des Kreuzes, 429–31. Numerous of Bultmann's poems are preserved; see RB, Poems. Cf. also Bultmann's poem, "Es war einmal," in RB to M. Heidegger, 20. 9. 1975, in A. Grossmann and C. Landmesser, *Bultmann-Heidegger Briefwechsel*, 258.

64. Cf. K. Deschner, "Was halten Sie vom Christentum?"

65. Cf. RB, "Das Befremdliche des christlichen Glaubens," *GuV* (1st ed.), vol. 3, 198–207. Bultmann makes reference to his controversy with K. Jaspers, especially to his demand that the Christian proclamation must first of all prove its claim to be revelation. Jaspers thanked Bultmann for sending him the essay, but did not go into his criticism any further. Cf. UB Tübingen, RB est., K. Jaspers to RB, 17. 7. 1959, Mn 2-1067.

66. RB, "Das Befremdliche," *GuV* (1st ed.), vol. 3, 211.

67. Cf. T. Kucharz, *Theologen und ihre Dichter*, 225–29, who points to the fact that Bultmann did, however, know how to appreciate English-language and French existentialist authors (Albert Camus, T. S. Eliot, Jean Giraudoux, Jean Paul Sartre, and Thornton Wilder).

Personal and scholarly connections between Bultmann and his students were maintained by correspondence or visits, but a serious strain on the friendship between teacher and student occurred in the case of Heinrich Schlier. Schlier had hinted to Bultmann in August of 1947 that he was considering converting to Roman Catholicism because Protestantism's understanding of the church, the sacraments, and tradition contained grave errors.[68] On November 8, 1953, Schlier informed his teacher—characteristically, perhaps, on a postcard from Rome—that based on many years of careful deliberations he had taken the logical step of becoming a member of the Roman Catholic Church.[69] For one thing, Bultmann felt that Schlier's informing him of the conversion by postcard showed a grave lack of class; for another, he could not believe the reasons that Schlier cited for the step he had taken.[70] Thereafter, contact between teacher and student did not cease completely, but it became sporadic and decidedly chilly.

It was otherwise with the relationship between Bultmann and Hans Jonas after 1952.[71] Despite the great distance—Jonas taught from 1949 on in Montreal and Ottawa and after 1955 in New York—the two regularly saw each other during Bultmann's stays in the United States in 1951 and 1959 and Jonas' frequent visits to Europe. The teacher-student relationship between the theologian and the philosopher grew in time into an intense friendship.[72] Bultmann took a lively interest in the progress of Jonas' studies of Gnosticism and his philosophical work, and their conversations focused on the philosophical and theological issues they both found of vital importance. In order to be able to think about God at all after his stay in Auschwitz, Hans Jonas followed the ancient Jewish doctrine of zimzum, which hypothesized God's self-contraction to create space for the creation, in an attempt to understand creation of the world and of life as an act of self-limitation and self-divesting.[73] In reply, Bultmann wondered whether the responsibility

68. Cf. R. von Bendemann, *Heinrich Schlier*, 88–90.

69. Cf. UB Tübingen, RB est., H. Schlier to RB, 2. 11. 1953, Mn 2-1726. Contrary to the assertions in R. von Bendemann, *Heinrich Schlier*, 90n334, the correspondence between Bultmann and Schlier did not end in 1950, but continued until 1970.

70. Cf. (already in the approaches to Schlier's conversion) RB to H. Urner-Astholz, 15. 4. 1949, Mn 2-2409 in UB Tübingen, RB est. How Bultmann reacted to Schlier himself at his conversion one can no longer say precisely. For, in accordance with a codicil to Schlier's will, all the letters from his literary remains directed to him were destroyed following his death.

71. Cf. H. Jonas to RB, 11. 12. 1952, in A. Grossmann, "'Und die Gnosis,'" 23–25.

72. Cf. UB Tübingen, RB est., RB to H. Jonas, 15. 3. 1959, Mn 2-3451; H. Jonas, *Erinnerungen*, 237.

73. Cf. H. Jonas, "Unsterblichkeit und heutige Existenz," *Zwischen Nichts und Ewigkeit*, 55–58; later H. Jonas, "Der Gottesbegriff nach Auschwitz," 61–84.

for God that followed from this myth did not expect too much of human beings. Besides, Jonas' attempt to employ myth to explain the puzzle of existence and to solve the theodicy question seemed dubious to him. For to assure those who suffer and those they leave behind that their suffering is "a meaningful occurrence in the fate of deity" could scarcely impart comfort. Moreover, the myth of the fate of deity involved an objectifying way of looking at things. Still, it was necessary to pose the question of the meaning of being specifically as an issue regarding the "meaning of *my own* being."[74] Bultmann and Jonas likewise discussed such subjects as the problem of what the authenticity of human existence consists of and how it is to be attained.[75]

Hans Jonas was genuinely devoted to Bultmann, who was the only teacher he had bidden farewell to before emigrating.[76] The visit with Rudolf and Helene Bultmann in the summer of 1945 had "allowed him at the end of the great darkness . . . to see light again in Germany for the first time."[77] In 1960 Bultmann supported his Jewish student's being offered a chair in philosophy at Marburg, but in view of the shadows cast over his fate by more recent German history, Jonas could not see his way to follow Bultmann's wish and accept the call to Marburg.[78] Later, a recommendation by Bultmann proved a decisive contribution to the state of Hesse's granting Jonas a small pension in compensation for failing to allow him to qualify as a university teacher in 1933.[79] In 1964 during one of his stays in Germany, Jonas presented a lecture entitled "Heidegger und die Theologie" ["Heidegger and Theology"], which received a great deal of attention, in which Jonas engaged in especially severe criticism of Heidegger's later work and the theology that had grown out of it. In doing so, the Jewish philosopher warned Christian theologians not to be led astray by supposing that Heidegger's profoundly pagan view that "the human being is the shepherd of being" comports with the plain and simple biblical directive that the individual must be "his brother's keeper" (Gen 4:9).[80]

74. RB to H. Jonas, n. d. [1963], in H. Jonas, *Zwischen Nichts und Ewigkeit*, 66f, also 67–72.

75. Cf. UB Tübingen, RB est.: H. Jonas to RB, 23. 12. 1962, Mn 2-3444; RB to H. Jonas, 6. 5. 1963, Mn 2-3451.

76. Cf. the fragment of the address that H. Jonas delivered in Marburg on 20. 8. 1964 on the occasion of Bultmann's 80th birthday, Mn 2-3444 in UB Tübingen, RB est.

77. H. Jonas' entry in Bultmann's guestbook, 19. 12. 1962, Mn 2-3041. See above 369f.

78. Cf. also A. Grossmann, "'Und die Gnosis,'" 21f.

79. Cf. RB, "Erklärung"; as well as H. Jonas' thanks to Bultmann (fragment), n. d. [ca. 1973], Mn 2-3444, in UB Tübingen, RB est.

80. H. Jonas, "Heidegger und die Theologie," 639.

Martin Heidegger and Rudolf Bultmann maintained their continuing friendship through letters at Christmas, the New Year, and on each other's birthdays. With advancing age, Heidegger especially came to recall their extraordinary time together from 1923–28 as a precious gift the special nature of which revealed itself in the act of giving thanks.[81] In 1969 Heidegger sent Bultmann the French edition of the lecture "Phenomenology and Theology" that he had given in Tübingen and Marburg in 1927–28 and accompanied it with a characteristic note: "It might be doubted whether today such basic considerations are still reflected on—and reflected on together."[82] To the extent that he learned of it from his theologically interested brother Fritz, Heidegger regarded contemporary theology as having taken a wrong turn in allying itself with political science, psychology—especially psychoanalysis—and sociology.[83] He dedicated the German version of his lecture to "RUDOLF BULTMANN . . . in friendly memory of the Marburg years 1923 to 1928."[84] Bultmann reacted to Heidegger's publication with several "thoughts and questions" that he wrote down between October and December of 1970 and sent to Heidegger on December 15, 1970.[85] In these he interpreted as dialectical the relation between objectifying and non-objectifying thinking and speaking in theology. For him, this corresponded to the paradoxical structure of faith, the event of which was, to be sure, something that took place in one's existence, but for which as an objectively perceptible occurrence no evidence could be given. But in this context Bultmann did not follow Heidegger's suggestion to seek in poetry for paradigmatic traces of a non-objectifying way of thinking and speaking. Clearly, theology must not allow its speaking of God to be prejudiced by comparing it to the poetic language of a Hölderlin or a Rilke.[86]

81. Cf. for example M. Heidegger to RB, 17. 8. 1974, in A. Grossmann and C. Landmesser, *Bultmann-Heidegger Briefwechsel*, 252, etc.

82. M. Heidegger to RB, 27. 11. 1969, in A. Grossmann and C. Landmesser, *Bultmann-Heidegger Briefwechsel*, 233.

83. Cf. M. Heidegger to RB, 12. 10. 1954 and 2. 1. 1975, in A. Grossmann and C. Landmesser, *Bultmann-Heidegger Briefwechsel*, 208, 255; as well as A. Grossmann, "Zwischen Phänomenologie und Theologie," 58.

84. M. Heidegger, *Phänomenologie und Theologie*, 5; cf. M. Heidegger to RB, 24. 10. 1970, in A. Grossmann and C. Landmesser, *Bultmann-Heidegger Briefwechsel*, 237.

85. Cf. RB to M. Heidegger, 15. 12. 1970, in A. Grossmann and C. Landmesser, *Bultmann-Heidegger Briefwechsel*, 237–45.

86. Cf. also A. Grossmann, "Zwischen Phänomenologie und Theologie," 58f, esp. n. 69; O. Pöggeler, "Heidegger und Bultmann," 51.

Plate 41: Meeting of the "Old Marburgers," October 17–21, 1960 in Bethel: Heinrich Ott, Martin Heidegger, and Rudolf Bultmann

Bultmann took part in the annual fall meetings of his students that continued from 1949 through 1962, but after that his age and unstable health prohibited his joining in with the "old Marburgers."[87] In 1965 he had recourse to verse in regretfully declining to attend the meeting in Höchst:[88]

Yet again it's my sad greeting
Not to join you in your meeting.
I, lonely at my writing table,
While all heatedly you're able
Words to brandish without fear,

87. Cf. UB Tübingen, RB est., RB to E. Dinkler, 21. 10. 1963, Mn 2-3491. M. Heidegger also took part in the meetings of the "old Marburgers" in Höchst/Odenwald (1959), Bethel (1960), and Marburg (1962). On 29. 10. 1959 in Höchst, he led an exercise on the theme "Christian Faith and Thought," and on 25. 10. 1962 in Marburg gave a paper on "Time and Being." Cf. M. Heidegger, "Zeit und Sein."

88. UB Tübingen, RB est., RB to the "Old Marburgers," 25. 10. 1965, Mn 2-3491.

As friendly foes to make things clear.
Taking part I'd love to be,
Yet you can manage without me.
To know that what we once began
Superbly yet continue can
Does make me thankful, and
If it's to solitude I'm banned,
To you I'm still most surely bound,
And spread my richest wishes round.

As a rule, it was Erich Dinkler who sent the absent Bultmann reports on how things went at the meetings of the "old Marburgers," but other students did so as well.[89]

Two of Bultmann's professional colleagues—Werner Georg Kümmel and Ernst Fuchs, who had accepted Marburg appointments in 1961 and were still there—maintained their connection through regular visits to 14 Calvin Street.[90] Bultmann also kept in touch with his out-of-town students Günther Bornkamm and Ernst Käsemann, as well as with Erich Dinkler, who, though Hans von Soden's student, increasingly became Bultmann's trusted theological conversation partner. Dinkler and Kümmel, who bore the primary burden of the editorial work for the *Theologische Rundschau*, still included Bultmann in the work of assigning book reviews and surveys of literature to reviewers.[91] Thus, advanced in years as he was, he was still able to feel himself to be the real editor of the *Theologische Rundschau*.

As emeritus, Bultmann was no longer entitled to employ the services of assistants on the Marburg theological faculty, but Erich Grasser, 1954–55, and Peter Biehl, 1956–61, the latter of whom had full-time charge of a group home for Marburg youth, helped him with his scholarly work by running errands, obtaining literature, and proofreading publications.[92] Just as Hans von Soden had once freed up his assistant Werner Georg Kümmel to help out Adolf Jülicher, from 1963 on Kümmel saw to it that his assistant Otto Merk provided similar help to his predecessor, Bultmann. Since Merk obtained his qualification for academic teaching in the Department of New Testament during those years, Bultmann

89. Cf. UB Tübingen, RB est., E. Dinkler to RB, 14. 10. 1968, Mn 2-3487.

90. Cf. UB Tübingen, RB est., RB to E. Dinkler, 27. 8 1968, Mn 2-3491; G. Schunack, Introduction, xii.

91. Cf. for example UB Tübingen, RB est., RB to E. Dinkler, 27. 8. 1968, Mn 2-3491.

92. Cf. P. Biehl and P. Schulz, *Autobiographische Miniaturen*, 66–75.

had at his disposal a competent personal assistant whose work he greatly appreciated.[93]

From about 1964 onwards, reading became increasingly difficult for Bultmann due to failing eyesight. From then on, it became necessary for his private assistant to report on new publications each Friday afternoon and to read aloud selected passages from offprints that he had received.[94] Both Bultmann and his reader came to attach great importance to these sessions. Bultmann was accompanied by his wife, and Merk sat across from them at a small, round table: Bultmann would have a schnapps first and then a beer, while smoking his pipe or a cigar, while Merk enjoyed a glass of Madeira or port. Bits of conversation were injected into what was being read, for Bultmann broke in from time to time, especially with the mention of names. It was not unusual for him to have a box on the table with photographs of people he was close to, his academic teachers and colleagues among others. In this way, by looking at the portrait of one or another of them, he was able to bring to mind old recollections. When Otto Merk took up a call to Erlangen in 1964, his friend Heinrich Leipold, the assistant of the systematician Hans Grass, took over the job of reading aloud, and thus enabled Bultmann to participate in the ongoing course of theological work even during his last years.[95]

Following his eightieth birthday, Bultmann began sifting through his papers and documents and destroying a good many of them. He did not think that letters and sermons needed to be preserved and certainly not published, since they had been written at a particular time and had been meant for particular people and occasions. Friends and his family nevertheless sought to convince him that such documents, tied to a particular context as they were, could be interesting and have significance for posterity. Recognizing the validity of this argument, Bultmann thereafter left to those close to him the decision of what portions of the extensive material should be preserved.[96] In 1965 Bultmann sold most of his library to the Protestant theological faculty of the University of Bochum. He had already left quite a few selected books

93. Cf. UB Tübingen, RB est., RB to E. Dinkler, 7. 11. 1967 and 18./19. 4. 1971, Mn 2-3491.

94. For Bultmann, it was an important matter of academic and human concern to thank the authors personally for sending these and to respond to their texts, whether critically or by acknowledging them.

95. Bernd Jaspert, who lived in the Bultmann house for several years, also regularly read aloud to Bultmann.

96. Cf. A. Bultmann Lemke, "Der unveröffentliche Nachlass von Rudolf Bultmann," 11; B. Jaspert, *Barth-Bultmann Briefwechsel* (2d ed.), n. 14, viif.

to Ernst Käsemann in 1951, and had reduced his stock of books still further by selling parts of it to the Protestant theological faculty of the University of Mainz from 1951 to 1954.[97] He retained merely a small personal library consisting primarily of works vital for his work on the commentary on the Letters of John and for the topic of "Christianity and Antiquity," with which he was very interested. The departure of the books filled him with a certain melancholy, and it made him even more melancholy that he had to give up the long-cherished plan of writing his memoirs from his correspondence: ". . . but for that I have now become too old and tired."[98]

In his conversations with Otto Merk, Bultmann returned to the subject of the transcendence of human life. For a long time the reproduction of a painting by Caspar David Friedrich, the representation of the cross of Christ on a rock in a mountainous landscape, had stood on his desk. In his old age, Bultmann discovered a new view of Friedrich's religious landscape painting, which he had not liked at all in his younger years. Among hymns, he regarded particularly highly the evening hymn of Matthias Claudius, "The Moon Has Risen" (*Evangelisches Gesangbuch* [*Lutheran Hymnal*], 482). He had already emphasized its middle stanzas as giving expression to his faith and theological thinking, and had also said that after the Lord's Prayer it was the finest prayer in Christendom.[99] At the end of his life, its fifth stanza became especially important to him. He reflected upon it each evening with his wife:[100]

God, look on us, your wholeness send,
Our trust in nothing fleeting spend,
Nor joy in what is vain.
Becoming simple, so may we
On earth before you children be,
Sincere and glad and plain.

97. Cf. UB Tübingen, RB est.: the documents in Bultmann's library, Mn 2-3967-3071; as well as RB to E. Dinkler, 1. 2. and 10. 3. 1951, Mn 2-2176; RB to E. Käsemann, 27. 5. and 10. 9. 1951, Mn 2-2251; E. Käsemann to RB, 1. 6. and 3. 8. 1951, Mn 2-1083.

98. UB Tübingen, RB est., RB to A. Bultmann Lemke, 1. 8. 1965, Mn 2-3452; cf. RB to G. Krüger, 8. 8. 1965, in F. Lilie, "Bultmann-Krüger Briefwechsel," *ZNThG* 7, 151.

99. Cf. W. Schmithals, "Das wissenschaftliche Werk Rudolf Bultmanns," 28. The verses intended were 4 ("Wir stolzen Menschenkinder . . .") and 5 ("Gott, lass dein Heil uns schauen . . .").

100. Cf. RB to M. Heidegger, 30. 1. 1970, in A. Grossmann and C. Landmesser, *Bultmann-Heidegger Briefwechsel*, 234; reproduced there in trivially different form than in the *Evangelisches Gesangbuch*, 482, 5; my translation. Cf. also F. Peerlinck, "Rudolf Bultmann und das Kirchenlied," 292, 296f.

3. Leave-Taking, Death, and Burial

The only thing certain about the human future is that death stands before every human being. For the person who is open to every future as the future of the coming God, death has lost its terror. He will do without imagining the future that God grants in death, for all pictures of a glory following death can only be imaginary ideals; and doing without imaginary ideals belongs to the radical openness of faith in God's future.[101]

Whoever becomes old can expect many farewells. Bultmann became very old. The list of friends, conversation partners, and companions from whom he had to take his leave in the last decade of his life was correspondingly long. On Friedrich Gogarten's eightieth birthday, not long before his death in the autumn of 1967, Bultmann was able to express his thanks for what Gogarten had given him and his joy over their shared theological achievements.[102] Karl Barth, to whom Bultmann likewise sent greetings on his eightieth birthday "from the old Marburg" and wished "reassuring courage,"[103] died on December 10, 1968. Paul Friedländer's death fell on the same day in faraway Los Angeles. In view of the long, intense, and—especially during the period of Nazi rule—tried and tested friendship with the classical philologist, Bultmann felt the loss of Friedländer particularly painfully.[104] Years before, two friends who had likewise emigrated to the United States during the Nazi period had also departed this life: the literary historian Friedrich Carl Sell in 1956 and the student of Romance literature Erich Auerbach in 1957.[105]

Karl Jaspers, Bultmann's philosophical adversary in the controversy over demythologizing, died in February 1969. In August of the same year, Bultmann learned of the demise of his friend Walther Fischer, news that he described as "a hard blow." As he recalled in his letter of condolence to Hanna Fischer, he had been "bound in heartfelt friendship" with the physician for

101. RB, "Die christliche Hoffnung," *GuV* (1st ed.), vol. 3, 90.

102. Cf. RB to F. Gogarten, 11. 1. 1967, in H.-G. Göckeritz, *Bultmann-Gogarten Briefwechsel*, 263.

103. RB to K. Barth, 9. 5. 1966, in B. Jaspert, *Barth-Bultmann Briefwechsel* (2d ed.), 203.

104. Cf. RB to G. Krüger, 25. 1. 1969, in F. Lilie, "Bultmann-Krüger Briefwechsel," *ZNThG* 7, 164.

105. Cf. UB Tübingen, RB est., F. C. Sell to RB, 16. 8. 1956, Mn 2-1815; DLA Marbach, RB to M. Auerbach, 10. 11. 1957; as well as M. Vialon, "Erich Auerbach und Rudolf Bultmann," 177f.

decades, a relationship that had begun in 1903, when Bultmann took up his studies in Tübingen. In the *Igel* fraternity Fischer belonged "to the elite of the organization, distinguished through his cultivation and his spirit, loved by all for both his humor and wit." At the time Bultmann felt it a blessing that the older fraternity brother "bestowed his friendship, which had held fast for decades right up to today," even if the communication between them finally became restricted to correspondence.[106] On January 31, 1970, Walter Baumgartner passed away in Basel. A good friend of the Old Testament scholar since his time as a lecturer in Marburg, Bultmann devoted an obituary to his friend in the *Theologische Rundschau,* of which Baumgartner had been an editor since the journal's reappearance in 1929.[107]

Bultmann had more and more taken on the active role in the relationship with Gerhard Krüger, especially following Krüger's serious stroke in 1953. He thus enabled his friend of decades to share in personal and family affairs, and kept him posted on his scholarly work, discussed what was being published in philosophy and theology, and last but not least acted as the *curator animae* [spiritual advisor] of the philosopher, whose health had been in decline. This friendship of so many years ended with the death of Krüger on February 14, 1972. Bultmann likewise outlived Heidegger's students, Karl Löwith and Hannah Arendt. Hans Jonas sent Bultmann the memorial address for the Jewish philosopher that he had given on December 8, 1975, four days after her death.[108] Hannah Arendt had, to be sure, "not been bound in friendship so long and so intimately" as had Jonas, but Bultmann held her in high esteem "not only on account of her friendliness, but also on account of her spirit and character."[109] And then Martin Heidegger went the way of all that is temporal on May 28, 1976, eight weeks before Bultmann, who probably did not learn of the conversation with Heidegger, "Nothing But a God Can Save Us," that *Der Spiegel* had recorded in 1966 and by prior arrangement first published on May 31, 1976, in the edition following Heidegger's death. By this time, Bultmann's own physical powers had considerably weakened, but in any case Heidegger could not bring himself even in that posthumously published interview to offer the public repudiation of his political conduct in 1933 that during their encounter in Zürich on February 4, 1954, Bultmann had challenged him to make.[110]

106. UB Tübingen, RB est., RB to H. Fischer, 10. 8. 1069, Mn 2-2197.

107. Cf. RB, E. Dinkler, W. G. Kümmel, "Walter Baumgartner," 93. On Bultmann's authorship, cf. Mn 2-265 in UB Tübingen, RB est.

108. Cf. Mn 2-1076 (copy) in UB Tübingen, RB est.

109. RB to H. Jonas, 12. 2. 1976, in A. Grossmann, *Bultmann-Jonas Briefwechsel*, 31.

110. Cf. [M. Heidegger,] "Nur noch ein Gott kann uns retten."

Despite the yearning for an irretrievable past evoked by the termination of all these relationships, Bultmann's feeling was chiefly one of gratitude for having encountered these departed friends and for the precious gift of sharing intense experiences with them.[111] To be sure, those bereavements and his increasing solitariness also quietly reminded him of his approaching death.[112] The death of his wife, resulting from the increasingly restricted circumstances of her life in old age, had trenchant meaning for him. During her last years, Leni Bultmann suffered severely from bouts of depression and dizziness, typical symptoms of Ménière's disease for which she had to seek medical and psychiatric treatment. Stays in sanitoriums in Wiesbaden (1967) and Braunlage (1967, 1969) provided only occasional short-term relief, and hospital treatments in Giessen, Hofgeismar, and Marburg were unable to remedy her suffering. For as long as he was in a position to do so, Bultmann read aloud sermons and light literature to her on her sickbed. Helene Bultmann died in a Marburg hospital on April 1, 1973, in her eightieth year.

Bultmann had the words of 2 Cor 4:18 placed at the head of her death announcement: "For what can be seen is temporary, but what cannot be seen is eternal."[113] Pastor Dr. Christian Zippert also based his sermon in the funeral service for Leni Bultmann on April 4, 1973, on this text. He wove into his words a passage from the *Marburg Sermons* that Rudolf Bultmann had once dedicated to his "dear wife."[114] Bultmann did not take part in the burial service of his devoted partner due to his difficulty in walking, and perhaps also his increasing self-consciousness. Pastor Zippert visited him before and after the interment, and at the end of the latter visit he delivered an extemporaneous prayer that he ended with the two final stanzas from Paul Gerhardt's hymn, "O Sacred Head, Now Wounded" (*Evangelisches Gesangbuch*, vv. 9 and 10):

My Savior, be Thou near me
When death is at my door;
Then let Thy presence cheer me,
Forsake me nevermore!

111. Cf. M. Dorhs, *Über den Tod hinaus*, 79–85.

112. Cf. RB to M. Heidegger, in A. Grossmann and C. Landmesser, *Bultmann-Heidegger Briefwechsel*: "Now, I do not belong to those people who cannot bear solitude. Indeed, it is a preparation for the final hour, which for me, in fact, cannot be very far off" (14. 7. 1969, 231f); "Indeed, I am so old that I have to think about leave-taking, and I take leave from a life that was rich in work and joy, in love and friendship—a farewell full of gratitude" (15. 12. 1970, 237–39).

113. Cf. Oberhessische Presse of 3. 4. 1973; as well as AEKR Boppard, W. Mundle est., RB to H. Mundle, 24. 5. 1973, no. 907.

114. Cf. C. Zippert, "Begräbnispredigt für Helene Bultmann."

When soul and body languish,
Oh, leave me not alone,
But take away mine anguish
By virtue of Thine own!

Be Thou my Consolation,
My Shield when I must die;
Remind me of Thy Passion
When my last hour draws nigh.
Mine eyes shall then behold Thee,
Upon Thy cross shall dwell,
My heart by faith enfold Thee.
Who dieth thus dies well!

When Zippert said goodbye a few months later before assuming the directorship of the homiletics seminar in Hofgeismar, Bultmann gave him this advice to take along with him: "Tell your candidates that they should learn the old chorales. It is good to have them in one's memory when one's eyes no longer permit one to read. These are what keep me going now." Bultmann said something similar to Leipold as well. Following his wife's death, Bultmann received what was probably the most moving letter of sympathy from Hans Jonas. With tears flowing as he wrote, the student and now long-time friend remembered Helene Bultmann with the empathy that was typical of him: "She was such a tender, sensitive soul, and as no one else I have ever known, an *anima naturaliter Christiana* [naturally Christian soul]." And Jonas recalled the unforgettable reunion with the couple in the summer of 1945 following the twelve dark years of separation, a meeting that he relived time and time again.[115]

After Heilke Bultmann had moved to Murnau am Staffelsee, Auguste Luksch took over her room. As housekeeper, she was now in charge of Bultmann's care and saw to the preparation of meals. Anna Schlienbecker also performed household tasks on an hourly basis. Her son Jürgen Schlienbecker and Helgard Weiss took up residence in the attic apartment of 14 Calvin Street beginning in 1973, and Jürgen helped get Bultmann up and dressed after his afternoon nap and escorted him to his study. The law student also read aloud to Bultmann each Sunday morning at 10:00 a sermon taken from collections by contemporary theologians. Helgard Weiss also looked after Bultmann, delighting him with flowers and reading aloud to him each day for an hour late in the afternoon.

115. H. Jonas to RB, 12. 5. 1973, in A. Grossmann, *Bultmann-Jonas Briefwechsel*, 30f.

Bultmann's day remained highly disciplined even in his final years. He seldom left his house unless a visit to the doctor was scheduled. Old age now prevented him from playing the obligatory Bach chorale that had formerly begun each day. He spent the morning at his desk until noon, where he maintained his extensive correspondence up to the final weeks of his life. Using a magnifying glass to read and to write, he laboriously sought to be fair to all who wrote to him. As always, questions about demythologizing particularly needed going into.[116] After lunch, he rested until 3:00 p.m., and in the afternoon he received such guests as Marburg theological faculty members Georg Kümmel and Ernst Würthwein, or Elsita Bantzer, Maria von Boxberger, or Lotte Grüneisen, friends of his wife, who often came to Calvin Street to read aloud to him. With Erich Dinkler, Günther Bornkamm, and other theological colleagues who traveled to Marburg at intervals, Bultmann discussed the progress of New Testament scholarship. Erich Vellmer, the bishop of the Evangelical Church of Kurhessen-Waldeck, repeatedly sought out his teacher to discuss questions of church work in detail. On July 6, 1973, Cardinal Franz König, a high-ranking representative of the Roman Catholic Church, paid his respects to the Protestant theologian who was controversial in his own church. Of course, the stream of visitors to the "place of pilgrimage at Calvin Street"[117] ebbed a bit after 1973, but Bultmann was still able to carry on the personal and scholarly theological exchange with other people that was important to him.

Naturally, he also received regular visits from his daughters—Antje from the United States, Gesine, who once a month came for the weekend with her youngest daughter Viola, and from Heilke. From time to time, Bultmann renewed old memories of the carefree days of youth in the Hammelwarden parsonage with his cousins, Anni Thurmann and Maxi Cold. He felt exceeding gratitude for all such personal contacts that were still possible in his extreme old age, and meeting with young people was especially important to him. It made him glad when his young lodgers dropped by to see how he was doing or just to say hello. If Jürgen Schlienbecker and Helgard Weiss had a party on the top floor, he was never bothered, for as he told them, he was always glad when there was life in the house. And if ever he had no afternoon visitors, he became happily engrossed in looking at picture postcards and illustrated books of the places where he and his wife had traveled. He especially recalled this way his travels to Italy and Sicily, and if visitors who

116. Cf. for example UB Tübingen, RB est., RB to C. A. Frazier, June 1973, Mn 2-2201; reprinted also in A. Bultmann Lemke, "Der unveröffentliche Nachlass," 24.

117. H. Stegemann, "Bultmanns Entmythologisierung," 6.

stopped in mentioned these, he was glad to recount his travel experiences. Now and again he made imaginary trips in foreign lands, for which he made such thorough preparations by studying history and art history he was able to make a sort of game out of picturing the routes he would take and the trains and hotels he would book.[118] Like the beer that he regularly drank from a pewter tankard with his meals—a glass of schnapps (usually made from corn) and a cigar or his pipe were among the pleasures of the flesh that he enjoyed into extreme old age. Immediately after dinner at 7:00 p. m., he retired to bed.

Old and tired, Bultmann was now no longer in a position to produce scholarly work, and one also senses from the last texts to come from his pen—a short study of the history of interpretation of the parable of the sower (Mark 4:3–9) and a posthumous biographical sketch of his friend Paul Friedländer—that writing these had been a struggle for him.[119] In place of works of scholarship for *Festschriften* for the Marburg church historian Winfried Zeller and Hans Jonas, he contributed only brief words of greeting.[120] For an anthology on the history of culture, he gave his student Hildegard Urner-Astholz a preface to take with her.[121]

Bultmann spent his ninetieth birthday, August 20, 1974, in the circle of his family. In a small ceremony on the previous day, Hessian President Albert Osswald had bestowed upon him the Superior Cross with star and shoulder sash of the Order of Merit of the Federal Republic of Germany. Bishop Erich Vellmer and the Mayor of Marburg, Dr. Hanno Dreschler, honored Bultmann with their participation in the celebration. Apart from the pains of old age, Bultmann enjoyed good health, and alertly received the congratulations that the representatives of the Marburg theological faculty and several students and friends personally delivered to him on his birthday.[122] Among the presents, he found especially welcome a new cushion for his desk chair—above all it was a genuinely useful present, but it also came accompanied by a poem composed by Claus Bantzer and recited by Elsita Bantzer:[123]

118. Cf. H.-G. Gadamer, "Gedenkworte," 134.

119. Cf. RB, "Die Interpretation von Mk 4:3–9 seit Jülicher," 30–34; RB, "Paul Friedländer (1882–1968)," 91–95.

120. Cf. RB to W. Zeller, in B. Jaspert and R. Mohr, *Traditio—Krisis—Renovatio*, x; RB to H. Jonas, in B. Aland, *Gnosis*, 13.

121. Cf. RB, Foreword, in H. Urner-Astholz, *Mosaiksteine*, 9.

122. Cf. H. Stegemann, "Bultmanns Entmythologisierung," 6.

123. C. Bantzer, "Dase neue Kissen spricht" (poem for R. Bultmann's 90th birthday), 1974, Mn 2-2652, in UB Tübingen, RB est.

Plate 42: Awarding of the Superior Cross with Star and Shoulder Sash of the Order of Merit of the Federal Republic of Germany on August 19, 1974: Bishop D. Erich Vellmer, President Albert Osswald, Rudolf Bultmann, and Lord Mayor Dr. Hanno Drechsler

The new cushion speaks:
Today, a time of joy so great,
I find I am in such a state
That I myself now offer can
To you, most great and honored man,
Albeit just a humble seat
For your haughty knowledge great!
. . .
On me one can sit so long,
Sharpen pencils, think thoughts strong,
For the spiritual outflow
That on paper just must go!
And yet, this cushion is not shy,
In face of thinker's thoughts so high—
Oh no, our master's lofty word
I from here do undergird!

In his birthday greeting Martin Heidegger recalled with gratitude and as an inestimable gift the five years they taught together, the meetings, and the sharing of friendship. "Its effect, both in secret and in public, is incalculable. True charisma remains a mystery, is not of our own merit, but nevertheless belongs to the course of our life and, because of that, demands that we bring it to mind and decide for it ever anew. Thanks follow you and remain with you to whatever great age you attain."[124] Heinrich Leipold later read aloud to Bultmann several articles and letters that were dedicated to him and to his work on the occasion of his ninetieth birthday.[125] He modestly received all these expressions of honor and made no fuss over them, but a birthday letter from Eduard Lohse and an essay in which his colleague the Hanoverian state bishop paid him express tribute as a Lutheran theologian did him visible good—coming as they did after much ecclesiastical hostility and many an uncomprehending synodal resolution on demythologizing.[126] The honoree also took grateful note of Eberhard Jüngel's homage to the "Clarity of the Theology of Rudolf Bultmann."[127] After he had listened to the text of the Tübingen theologian, Bultmann said to Leipold that Jüngel had understood him best of all. Overall, Bultmann especially admired Eberhard Jüngel among the younger theologians. And when on his ninetieth birthday a word of thanks reached him from a pastor for whom his theology had conveyed and sustained the joy of preaching, Bultmann spontaneously remarked, "I wanted nothing else!"

In the spring of 1976 Bultmann's physical powers again deteriorated noticeably. To be sure, he was mentally alert, but from April on he was obliged "with a sad heart" to dispense with the services of Heinrich Leipold, as he could no longer recall "from one week to the next what had been read aloud to him."[128] Bultmann, now very weak, faced death stoically. In June, in his final letter to Antje, he movingly described his physical condition without illusions. Mrs. Luksch had now "not only to tie [his] shoes," but "also help [him] with getting dressed and undressed." "I am so old and have become so clumsy that I cannot manage alone any longer. Unfortunately, I often suffer from severe pains at night, which the ointment Dr. Ferlemann has

124. M. Heidegger to RB, 17. 8. 1974, in A. Grossmann and C. Landmesser, *Bultmann-Heidegger Briefwechsel*, 252.

125. Cf. among 37 newspaper and journal articles, e. g. W. Harnisch, "Theologie der Verkündigung"; E. Schulz, "Das Christentum," 19; B. Jaspert, "Das Lebenswerk Rudolf Bultmanns"; G. Klein, "Rudolf Bultmann," 614–19.

126. Cf. E. Lohse, "Rudolf Bultmann als lutherischer Theologe," 49–54; E. Lohse, private collection, RB to E. Lohse, 23. 10. 1974: "For me it is a great joy that you recognize me as a Lutheran theologian."

127. Cf. E. Jüngel, "Redlich von Gott reden," 475–77.

128. H. Leipold, private collection, A. Bultmann Lemke to H. Leipold, 10. 8. 1976.

prescribed only partly helps." At the same time, the old man, now in his ninety-second year, let his daughter know "How greatly I set my hopes on your coming in August, and that I will indeed be here for it—and for Christmas, too? Hopefully! . . . In love, Your Father."[129] Bultmann's wish was not to come true. Following a hospital stay from June 26 to July 12, he had ten more "relatively good days at the desk and with good conversations" at home, but on July 23 he fell into a coma from which he did not awaken.[130] In his final days and hours, his daughters took turns being with him. Due to his great age, they came to an agreement with his physician, Dr. Johannes Ferlemann, that he should not be transferred to a hospital again and be artificially nourished there. Rudolf Bultmann died peacefully in his home on the morning of July 30, 1976. His eldest daughter, Antje, held his hand as he took his final breath.

Bultmann was buried in Marburg on August 4, 1976. At the wish of his daughters, the Director of the seminar on preaching in Hofgeismar,

129. UB Tübingen, RB est., RB to A. Bultmann Lemke, 19. 6. 1976, Mn 2-3452.
130. UA Tübingen, G. Ebeling est., A. Bultmann Lemke to G. Ebeling, 12. 8. 1976, 633/616.

Plate 43: The Grave of Helene and Rudolf Bultmann in the Marburg City Cemetery

Dr. Christian Zippert, who had been the pastor responsible for Bultmann's district, held the funeral service in the Ockershäuser St. Matthew's church near the cemetery. To the astonishment of many and to the disconcertment of some, the congregation at the funeral did not get to hear a sermon. The deceased had intended this. There was to be no sermon and certainly no obituary. Not all the mourners understood this. Immediately before the service, a few of them still sought to wrest permission from the liturgist to give spoken tributes, and they had difficulty understanding why Bultmann had made these arrangements. Apparently they had not grasped the essence of his theology. Bultmann had intended to prevent any attempt to honor him as a person or as a theologian lest any καύχησις [boasting] over his coffin might obscure the biblical promise. Here a circle was completed, for in 1919 Bultmann's father, Arthur Kennedy, had similarly refused to have a sermon and laudatory obituaries at his funeral.

The form of the funeral service reflected Bultmann's wish "that this time [should] belong entirely to the word of Holy Scripture."[131] Following the opening of the organ chorale "Before your throne . . ." by Johann Sebastian Bach, the choir sang Melchior Franck's motet, "Lord, now let thy . . . ." Two readings from scripture, 2 Cor 4:6–10; 5:1–7; and John 5:21–25, framed by instrumental pieces by Wolfgang Amadeus Mozart and Johann Sebastian Bach followed the greeting and the address to the congregation by the minister. Between the readings, the choir sang the Bach motet, "Jesus, my joy." Then a period of silent prayer was followed by a congregational reading of Psalm 103, a choice that like the scriptural readings and the musical selections, Bultmann's daughters had made based on the personal preferences of their father and family tradition. In closing, the congregation joined in singing Georg Neumark's chorale, "If thou but suffer God to guide thee," a "hymn that meant a great deal to Rudolf Bultmann."[132] Following the funeral service, Bultmann's body was placed in the family grave in the Marburg cemetery next to that of his wife. John 11:25f, the word of promise of the Johannine Christ, the Lord's Prayer, and the benediction concluded the service of interment.

Chiseled into the gravestones of some theologians who have found their final resting places in the Marburg cemetery are epitaphs giving evidence of their faith and life. In the case of Friedrich Christian Vilmar, it is a reference to the Apostles' Creed ("I have believed in the forgiveness of sins, the resur-

131. [C. Zippert,] Rudolf Bultmann Memorial, 1.
132. [C. Zippert,] Rudolf Bultmann Memorial, 3.

rection of the body, and the life everlasting"); in that of Adolf Jülicher, Luke 23:46 ("Father, into your hands I commend my spirit"). Jer 29:13–14 serves as an epitaph for Wilhelm Herrmann. On Rudolf Otto's gravestone, the visitor reads Isa 6:3 ("Holy, holy, holy is the Lord of Hosts"), and on that of Hans von Soden, Cant 8:6 ("Love is strong as death"). Nothing of this sort is to be found on the gravestone of Rudolf Bultmann, for only his name and the dates of his birth and death appear under the name and the dates of his wife's life on the plain marker made of Hessian variegated sandstone. Clearly, any indication of the particular significance of this person was to be avoided. But anyone who visits Bultmann's grave will see several smallish stones placed on his gravestone. This is the custom by which Jews honor their own dead and their non-Jewish teachers. "Taught by history, the Jews have a long memory for their friends."[133] The mute stones on Bultmann's grave marker impressively remind those who can hear their message of the loyalty that the Protestant theologian once showed to his Jewish friends in a dark time.

4. Public Commemoration

When paying tribute to a thinker, one ought perhaps to separate the person from the work and restrict oneself to the memory of his thought alone. In the case of Rudolf Bultmann, this is not possible for me—for reasons that are personally overpowering and also on account of the impartial conviction that this would leave out something too essential and too precious. Bultmann lived what he thought and also thought in such a way that this living for what was thought stood out as its innermost meaning. Above all, there is the fact that he was my teacher and friend, touching my life with a quiet light of meaningfulness that radiated through it. . . . I would love to continue this conversation, begun so, so long ago, with one who is living, and I can do it only with his beloved shadow. A human being of gripping purity has passed away, a fully realized life, always at one with itself. He is not to be mourned, but once again the world has become poorer for one of those from whom its ever-threatened faith can take heart. It is "worth the trouble being a human being."[134]

133. O. Kaiser, "Theologengräber auf dem Marburger Friedhof," 8.
134. H. Jonas, "Im Kampf," in O. Kaiser, *Gedenken an Rudolf Bultmann*, 41, 70.

In view of the outstanding significance of Bultmann's scholarly work in a variety of respects, it went without saying that he and his theological work would be publicly commemorated following his death. Such acts of commemoration had to take account of the fact that it lay utterly outside of Bultmann's own intentions to be elevated as the object of public admiration, whether as a person or even for his "lifetime achievement." Above all, such commemoration must amount to nothing more than an objective recitation of Bultmann's legacy. Also to be avoided was simply assigning his theological insights to a now bygone era in the history of theology and thus merely archiving his work as if in a museum. The various commemorative events that were held following his death and on the occasion of the hundredth anniversary of his birth have, one may now say, largely done justice to these requirements.

This is true, for instance, of the academic commemorative events that took place in the main auditorium of the University of Marburg on November 16, 1976. Approximately eight hundred guests from at home and abroad, representatives of churches and of numerous universities inside and outside of Germany, had traveled to Marburg in order to express their admiration for the great scholar. In his greeting, Otto Kaiser, the Dean of the Department of Protestant Theology, needed eight minutes merely to welcome by name the guests of honor, among whom were Bultmann's one-time student Hilda Heinemann, the widow of the former President of the Federal Republic, Gustav Heinemann. The celebration became a "gathering of the German Protestant intellectual world as had not been seen in such number and in the weight of its names in this century."[135]

In charge of music worthy of the occasion were Prof. Martin Weyer, who played organ works of Johann Sebastian Bach and Johann Nepomuk David, and the Marburg Chamber Orchestra under the leadership of Horst Pusch, which performed an elegy by Paul Hindemith and the *Adagio* from a concerto grosso of Francesco Geminiani. President Rudolf Zingel gave words of commemoration on behalf of the Marburg Philipps-University, as did Bishop D. Erich Vellmer, himself a student of Bultmann's, on behalf of the Evangelical Church of Kurhessen-Waldeck and that in Hessen and Nassau. Jesuit Karl Rahner recalled on behalf of the order *Pour le Mérite* that Bultmann was "one of the very few theologians whom the Order chose for its own"—but observed that Bultmann "honored this Order much more as a member than the Order honored this great theologian by his election."[136]

135. K. A. Odin, "Die Paradoxie des Glaubens," 27.
136. K. Rahner, "Gedenkwort," in O. Kaiser, *Gedenken an Rudolf Bultmann*, 13.

Bultmann's theological student Erich Dinkler gave one of the two lectures of the day. Drawing in part on such yet unedited texts as that of the *Theological Encyclopedia* and on letters to Hans von Soden, Dinkler gave an instructive insight into Bultmann's thinking, the issue of the truth of Christianity, and his understanding of theology as a form of ongoing critical study.[137] At the request of the Bultmann family, Hans Jonas had agreed to give the other lecture. In moving words he recalled personal experiences with the teacher and friend in order to show that Bultmann "lived what he thought." Speaking as a philosopher, Jonas then discussed Bultmann's demythologizing thesis. In what was a sort of posthumous "dialogue with him, from philosopher to theologian, from Jew to Christian, but above all, from friend to friend," he posed the critical question of whether Bultmann had made more concessions than necessary to the critical world-picture of the modern natural sciences. Was not philosophy itself able to keep open the possibility of faith over against this? Should theology rashly submit to natural science's metaphysically excessive claim of the truth of determinism?[138]

Both Dinkler and Jonas made it clear by their lectures that the point of the commemorative celebration consisted not in sadly mourning Bultmann's passing and merely gazing back at his thoughts; rather, the point was to redeem the teacher's legacy by critically continuing on one's own part the dialogue he had begun. On the occasion of the commemorative celebrations, the Department of Protestant Theology of the University of Marburg awarded the honorary doctorate in theology to Hans Jonas. The honor was specifically bestowed on the Jewish philosopher, but in awarding it the Department also acknowledged the extraordinary history of the impact of Bultmann's theology. For along with Martin Heidegger he had once opened the path of inquiry for Heidegger's Jewish student, had kept faith with him in a desperate period, and was bound with him in steadfast friendship through to his life's end.

The hundredth anniversary of Bultmann's birth offered a second opportunity to pay public tribute to his life's work. The previous year, the five-hundredth anniversary of Martin Luther's birth had been commemorated in a divided Germany. Measured by the grand style and huge number of events that had been observed for the Luther anniversary, the public commemoration of the Marburg theologian naturally had a comparatively modest aspect.

137. Cf. E. Dinkler, "Die christliche Wahrheitsfrage," in O. Kaiser, *Gedenken an Rudolf Bultmann*, 15–40.

138. H. Jonas, "Im Kampf," in O. Kaiser, *Gedenken an Rudolf Bultmann*, 41, 70, 68; cf. also H. Jonas, *Erinnerungen*, 237f.

And yet a series of events took place in 1984 that had a far-reaching impact within the world of academic theology.

A scholarly symposium held in Boston by the Department of Religion of Wellesley College dealt with "Bultmann and the Past" and "Bultmann and the Future." Wellesley College had been one of the stops on Bultmann's first trip to the U. S. in 1951. Louise Pettibone Smith, who once translated Bultmann's *Jesus* into English and who had played a leading role in mediating his thought to theology in North America, had taught here for many years. The Wellesley symposium, as Paul Lehmann called to mind, reanimated these old connections.[139] Among those who presented papers were Hans Jonas, one of the first philosophers to be a student of Bultmann's,[140] and Helmut Koester, one of his last New Testamant students, who gave a paper on how Bultmann had categorized earliest Christianity from the point of view of the history of religions.[141] Papers were also delivered by two American theologians who had already taken part in the discussion of Bultmann's theology in the 1960s. Schubert Miles Ogden discussed in detail Bultmann's contribution to the reformulation of christology, and James M. Robinson pursued the references in Bultmann's work to its own time.[142] Antje Bultmann Lemke reviewed and updated the plans being made for editing her father's unpublished works and his letters, and offered a glimpse into the papers he had left behind.[143] Dieter Georgi contributed a supplementary essay on Bultmann's *Theology of the New Testament* to the collection of papers from this symposium.[144] The event made it quite clear that Bultmann had made a considerable and lasting impact in American theological circles. For all this, the valuable documents of the Wellesley symposium scarcely received the attention from German-language theology that they deserved.

The city of Marburg honored Bultmann on the hundredth anniversary of his birth by giving his name to Ortenberg Street. The corresponding resolu-

139. Cf. P. Lehmann, "Louise Pettibone Smith, Rudolf Bultmann and Wellesley," in E. C. Hobbs, *Bultmann, Retrospect and Prospect*, 91–101.

140. Cf. H. Jonas, "A Philosopher Remembers Bultmann," in E. C. Hobbs, *Bultmann, Retrospect and Prospect*, 13–16.

141. Cf. H. Koester, "Early Christianity," in E. C. Hobbs, *Bultmann, Retrospect and Prospect*, 59–74.

142. Cf. in E. C. Hobbs, *Bultmann, Retrospect and Prospect*: S. M. Ogden, "Rudolf Bultmann and the Future of Revisionary Christology," 37–58; J. M. Robinson, "Bultmann and Time," 17–34.

143. Cf. A. Bultmann Lemke, "Bultmann's Papers," in E. C. Hobbs, *Bultmann, Retrospect and Prospect*, 2–12.

144. Cf. D. Georgi, "Bultmann's *Theology of the New Testament* Revisited," in E. C. Hobbs, *Bultmann, Retrospect and Prospect*, 75–87.

tion of the city council put an end to a "lengthy squabble that had preceded it (and one that did not bring credit to all parties) over what street would be suitable for the change of name, a controversy in which opposition in principle to the name 'Bultmann' had definitely played a role."[145] The decision that was finally taken turned out to be more than just a compromise, for in its proximity to Harnack Street and to the Hans von Soden House of the Protestant student community, Rudolf Bultmann Street indicates connections central to the life of its namesake. The municipal authorities of the city of Marburg had asked Heinrich Leipold to formulate a brief caption for the street sign, in order to acknowledge in a sentence Bultmann's concerns and his significance. After great thought Leipold at first came up with this suggestion: "What concerned him was to make the message of the New Testament understandable as a call to faith to people today by means of an existentialist interpretation of mythical thinking." Asked by Leipold what they thought, the Marburg New Testament scholars Wolfgang Harnisch, Dieter Lührmann, and Gerd Schunack came together on a somewhat shorter formulation, which was then incorporated into the caption on the street sign:[146] "Prof. D. Bultmann D.D. (1884–1976) sought to make the Christian message accountable to the modern consciousness of truth." On August 20, 1984, the hundredth anniversary of Bultmann's birth, Mayor Dr. Hanno Drechsler unveiled the new street sign in a small ceremony. Still, this caption for a theologian born somewhere else, and that in the end had to be shortened, aroused harsh criticism.[147] It thus stands as one more among the curiosities of the many misunderstood controversies surrounding Bultmann. The city of Marburg later had a memorial plaque attached to the house at 2 Barfüssertor in which Bultmann had lived from 1910–16.[148]

The Department of Protestant Theology at the Philipps-University of Marburg held a symposium to honor Bultmann on October 26–27, 1984—one that received considerable attention. In his lecture, Walter Schmithals demonstrated that "the certitude of faith in Bultmann's work" is grounded in the historical revelation of God in Jesus Christ and is mediated by the proclaimed word. Gotthold Hasenhüttl, one of Bultmann's Roman Catholic conversation partners, discussed in detail the question that formed one of

145. E. Dettmering, "Ein Name, der sich mit einem Begriff verbindet," 5.

146. H. Leipold, private collection, H. Leipold to the Dean of the Marburg Department of Protestant Theology, 30. 10. 1984.

147. Cf. Oberhessische Presse of 30 October 1984: "Between Pride and Irritation. The Controversies surrounding Rudolf Bultmann Find No End."

148. Unfortunately, the memorial plaque contains two errors.

the central motifs in his theological work: "How is belief in God possible today?" Chamber music, performed by Birgit Sedlatschek, Horst Pusch, Heilke Bultmann, and Roland Knocke, provided the finale to the first day of the symposium in the Old Auditorium.

On the following Saturday, the event reached its climax in the nearly full main auditorium. In his memorial lecture, "Rudolf Bultmann and His Church," Eduard Lohse, the Chief Administrator of the Evangelical Church of Germany, recalled that the Marburg theologian had considered all his scholarly work to be in service of the church and the proclamation that is its task.[149] Eberhard Jüngel presented a lucid interpretation of Bultmann's understanding of theology, "True Theology is Practical: The Knowledge of God and Self-Understanding according to Rudolf Bultmann." In it, he made special reference to Bultmann's course of lectures on encyclopedia, which was just then being edited.[150] A panel discussion featuring the presenters and moderated by Wilfried Härle concluded the symposium. Afterwards, a Marburg professor of theology attempted to discredit the event by writing letters to the editor of the local newspaper in which he charged Bultmann's theology with being uncritical, and reproached him for having "violently distorted the Bible and, above all, the Gospel of John."[151] Nevertheless, this transparently tendentious attack did little or nothing to overshadow the success of the symposium. For the university community had long and disagreeably known that the critic, who had been pushed by student revolts into an irrational fundamentalism, was a colleague who was not to be taken seriously.

A commemoration in Oldenburg honored the hundredth anniversary of Bultmann's birth on September 2, 1984, but except for the remarks of Hartwig Thyen on "Rudolf Bultmann as Historian and Theologian," the talks following the celebration did not attain the level of the Marburg symposium. Apart from Thyen, Siegfried Vierzig spoke on "Rudolf Bultmann and Pedagogy" and Dorothee Sölle on "Rudolf Bultmann and Political Theology."[152]

On the occasion of the twentieth anniversary of Rudolf Bultmann's death, the two Norwegians, Dr. *phil.* Arild Haaland and Dr. *art. kand.* Bjørn Olav Roaldseth from the University of Bergen donated a bust of Bultmann to the Philipps-University of Marburg. Created from one-dimensional images by Hugo Wathne and admittedly bearing scarcely any resemblance to

149. Cf. E. Lohse, "Die evangelische Kirche vor der Theologie Rudolf Bultmanns," 173–91.

150. Cf. E. Jüngel, "Glauben und Verstehen," 16–77.

151. Cf. E.-W. Kohls, "Den Glauben verraten," 10; E.-W. Kohls, "Blinde Blindenleiter," 19.

152. Cf. StA Oldenburg, "Rudolf Bultmann 100 Jahre."

Bultmann, the sculpture was ceremonially unveiled on November 1, 1996, in the inner quadrangle of the old university. The day before, Bishop Dr. Christian Zippert had conducted a worship service for Reformation Day in the university church, after which President Werner Schaal of the Philipps-University opened the academic ceremony in the auditorium of the old university, an event that members of the Bultmann family also attended. Preceded and followed by performances of music by Chopin, Günter Klein presented the celebratory lecture, "Rudolf Bultmann—an Unfinished Theological Legacy."[153] Following the unveiling of the bust, a reception hosted by the President of the University in the cloister of the old university brought the academic ceremony to a close.

Eight years later, at the suggestion of the city council of Oldenburg and with the help of private and public sponsors, Dr. Ekkehard Seeber brought to fruition a plan to complete a collection of the city's noted thinkers with a bust of Bultmann. A commission gave careful attention to this plan, and following a limited competition, it engaged the sculptor Michael Mohns (of Tarnow bei Güstrow) to create a bust of Bultmann with the primary condition that it was to represent the personality of one "in whose essence it lay to wish to be paid no public honor of any kind." The bust therefore had to offer an image appropriate to the personal modesty of the honoree and his unassuming personal demeanor, "as this reflected him and his thought."[154] It seems apparent that those who initiated the project and the artist have succeeded in doing this in marvelous fashion.

Michael Mohns and the firm of Weidner were commissioned to execute the project (Oldenburg), and put the memorial in place on the wall of the theatre on September 5, 2002, in the immediate vicinity of the Marburg Old Gymnasium, the school that Bultmann once took great pleasure in attending. The dedication ceremony took place on September 7, 2002, in the presence of his two daughters, Antje Bultmann Lemke and Gesine Diesselhorst. After Pastor Reinhard Rittner had opened the gathering, Walter Schmithals spoke on "Faith and Understanding. Rudolf Bultmann and the World of Modern Life."[155] Bernd Küster presented the bust of Bultmann and the artist who had created it. Küster began his introduction to the work and its context in art history with words that Bultmann had spoken during the

153. Cf. G. Klein, "Rudolf Bultmann—ein unerledigtes theologisches Vermächtnis."

154. B. Küster, "Die Bultmann-Büste von Michael Mohns," in R. Rittner *Die Bultmann-Büste in Oldenburg*, 16.

155. Cf. W. Schmithals, "Glauben und Verstehen. Rudolf Bultmann und die moderne Lebenswelt," in R. Rittner *Die Bultmann-Büste in Oldenburg*, 5–15.

funeral service for the Hessian painter Carl Bantzer in 1941.[156] In their greetings Bishop Peter Krug of the State Church of Oldenburg, and Lord Mayor Dietmar Schütz recalled Bultmann's significance as a scholar and the example of his life, shaped by the Christian-humanist worldview, as well as his connections to the city of Oldenburg.[157] In addition, at the dedication of the bust, Reinhard Rittner handed out a small booklet with information and sources for further reading about Bultmann's close relationship with his Oldenburg homeland.[158]

A descendant of the working group of the "old Marburgers," the Rudolf Bultmann Society for Hermeneutical Theology was founded in 1998 and took upon itself the task of cultivating and perpetuating the theological work of its namesake. Under the leadership of Ulrich H. J. Körtner (1998–2008) and Christof Landmesser (since 2008), the Society continues Bultmann's initiatives and critical formulations of important questions—the very work that so long impelled him. Thus, the "Rudolf Bultmann Society" does not restrict itself to dealing only with the work of the Marburg theologian, but through its scholarly meetings and publications promotes a comprehensive discussion of the possibilities and the formulation of problems by hermeneutical theology. At the same time, it senses a special obligation to uphold the standards set by Bultmann.

In the meantime, as happened in Marburg, streets in Oldenburg and Rastede have also been named after the theologian whose scholarly work earned an international reputation. And on Pentecost (May 27) of 2007, Bishop Peter Krug of Oldenburg unveiled a memorial plaque to Bultmann on the parsonage in Wiefelstede as part of the celebration of the first 950 years of the existence of St. John's Church in Wiefelstede. Thus, the New Testament scholar who was born on August 20, 1884, in the house that preceded the current parsonage in Wiefelstede and who died in Marburg on July 30, 1976, has in more ways than one returned "as it were, symbolically, to the familiar place of his origin."[159]

156. B. Küster, "Die Bultmann-Büste von Michael Mohns," in R. Rittner, *Die Bultmann-Büste in Oldenburg*, 16–21.

157. Cf. R. Rittner, *Die Bultmann-Büste in Oldenburg*, 22.

158. Cf. R. Rittner, *Rudolf Bultmann und Oldenburg.*

159. B. Küster, "Die Bultmann-Büste von Michael Mohns," in R. Rittner, *Die Bultmann-Büste in Oldenburg*, 16.

Works Cited

Dates are listed in the European format: Date. Month. Year (August 20, 1884 = 20. 8. 1884). German Abbreviations follow S. M. Schwertner, *Internationales Abkürzungsverzeichnis für Theologie und Grenzgebiete*, 1992 (2d ed.), as well as *Redaktion der RGG* (2d ed.), *Abkürzungen Theologie und Religionswissenschaft nach RGG*, 2007 (4th ed). See also the list of abbreviations on p. xi. In addition, the following abbreviations have been employed:

* date of birth

† deceased

Achelis, Ernst Christian. *Lehrbuch der Praktischen Theologie*. Vol. 1. 2d ed. 1898.

Adamek, Helmut. "Aus der Tätigkeit der Theologischen Arbeitsgemeinschaft mit Rudolf Bultmann von 1942–1967." Undated hectography [1967]. Mn 2-3085, pp. 19–32. In UB Tübingen, RB est.

Aland, Barbara, ed. *Gnosis. FS H. Jonas*. Göttingen: Vandenhoeck and Ruprecht, 1978 (P. 13: RB to H. Jonas).

Aland, Kurt, ed. *Glanz und Niedergang der deutschen Universität: 50 Jahre deutscher Wissenschaftsgeschichte in Briefen an und von Hans Lietzmann (1892–1942)*. Berlin: De Gruyter, 1979.

Althaus, Paul. "Neues Testament und Mythologie: Zu R. Bultmanns Versuch der Entmythologisierung des Neuen Testamentes." *ThLZ* 67 (1942): 337–44.

Althaus, Paul. *Paulus und Luther über den Menschen*. 1st ed. Gütersloh: C. Bertelsmann, 1938.

Anz, Wilhelm. "Zur Wirkungsgeschichte Kierkegaards in der deutschen Theologie und Philosophie." *ZThK* 79 (1982): 451–82.

Archive of the Evangelical Church in the Rhineland, Boppard. Letters of RB to H. Mundle, W. Mundle est., 7 NL 124 B, no. 907.

———. Letters of RB to W. Mundle, W. Mundle est., 7 NL 124 B, no. 874.

Archive of the Evangelical Church Parish Essen-Altstadt. Marriage Register, 1917.

Archive of the Evangelical-Lutheran Church Parish Wiefelstede. Baptismal Register, 1884.

Archive of the Evangelical-Lutheran Oberkirchenrat Oldenburg. Confirmation Register Oldenburg, Confirmands, 1899.

Arnold, Matthieu. "Gabriel Vahanian et Rudolf Bultmann." *FV* 95 (1996): 59–76.

Assel, Heinrich. "'Barth ist entlassen ...': Emanuel Hirschs Rolle im Fall Barth und seine Briefe an Wilhelm Stapel." *ZThK* 91 (1994): 445–75.

Astholz, Hildegard. *Das Problem "Geschichte" untersucht bei Johann Gustav Droysen*. HS 231. Berlin: Ebering, 1933.

Auerbach, Erich. *Gesammelte Aufsätze zur romanischen Philologie*. Bern: Francke, 1967.

———. *Mimesis: Dargestellte Wirklichkeit in der abendländischen Literatur.* 1st ed. Bern: Francke, 1946.
———. *Mimesis: Dargestellte Wirklichkeit in der abendländischen Literatur.* 2d ed. Bern: Francke, 1959.
Baasland, Ernst. *Theologie und Methode: Eine historiographische Analyse der Frühschriften Rudolf Bultmanns.* Wuppertal: Brockhaus, 1992.
Baeck, Leo. "Israel und das deutsche Volk (1952)." Pp. 50–61 in *Werke 5. Nach der Schoa—warum sind Juden in der Welt?: Schriften aus der Nachkriegszeit.* Vol. 5. Ed. A. H. Friedlander and B. Klappert. 2002.
Barck, Karlheinz, and Martin Treml, ed. *Erich Auerbach: Geschichte und Aktualität eines europäischen Philologen.* Vol. 2. Berlin: Kulterverlag Kadmos, 2007.
Bartels, Cora. *Kierkegaard receptus.* Vol. 1: *Die theologiegeschichtliche Bedeutung der Kierkegaard-Rezeption Rudolf Bultmanns.* Göttingen: V&R Unipress, 2008.
Barth, Karl. "Abschied." *ZZ* 11 (1933): 536–44.
———. *Christus und Adam nach Röm. 5. Ein Beitrag zur Frage nach dem Menschen und der Menschheit.* 1st ed. ThSt[B] 35. Zollikon: Evangelischer, 1952.
———. "Das erste Gebot als theologisches Axiom." *ZZ* 11 (1933): 297–315.
———. "Das Wort Gottes als Aufgabe der Theologie" (1922). Pp. 197–218 in *Anfänge der dialektischen Theologie I.* 4th ed. Ed. J. Moltmann. München: Kaiser, 1977.
———. *Die Auferstehung der Toten. Eine akademische Vorlesung über 1. Kor. 15.* 1st ed. München: Kaiser, 1924.
———. *Die christliche Dogmatik im Entwurf.* Vol. 1: *Die Lehre vom Worte Gottes. Prolegomena zur christlichen Dogmatik.* München: Kaiser, 1927.
———. *Der Römerbrief.* 1st ed. München: Kaiser, 1919.
———. *Der Römerbrief.* 2d ed. München: Kaiser, 1922.
———. "Der Römerbrief. Vorwort zur dritten Auflage" (1922). Pp. 147–52 in *Anfänge der dialektischen Theologie I.* 4th ed. Ed. J. Moltmann. München: Kaiser, 1977.
———. *Eine Schweizer Stimme 1938–1945.* Zollikon-Zürich: Evangelischer, 1945.
———. Epilogue. Pp. 290–312 in *Schleiermacher-Auswahl.* Ed. K. Barth, H. Bolli, and F. Schleiermacher. München; Hamburg: Siebenstern Taschenbuch, 1968.
———."Kirche und Theologie" (1926). Pp. 302–28 in: *Die Theologie und die Kirche. Ges. Vorträge.* Vol. 2. Ed. Karl Barth. München: Kaiser, 1928.
———. *Rudolf Bultmann. Ein Versuch, ihn zu verstehen.* 1st ed. ThSt[B] 34. Zürich, 1952 .
———. *Theologische Existenz heute!* (1933). 2d ed. Ed. H. Stoevesandt. München: Kaiser, 1984.
Barth, Markus. "Die Methode von Bultmanns 'Theologie des Neuen Testaments.'" *ThZ* 11 (1955): 1–27.
Barth, Ulrich. *Die Christologie Emanuel Hirschs. Eine systematische und problemgeschichtliche Darstellung ihrer geschichtsmethodologischen, erkenntniskritischen und subjektivitätstheoretischen Grundlagen.* Berlin: De Gruyter, 1992.
Bartsch, Hans-Werner, ed. *Kerygma und Mythos.* Vol. 1: *Ein theologisches Gespräch.* 3d ed. ThF 1. Hamburg: Reich, 1954.
———, ed. *Kerygma und Mythos.* Vol. 2: *Diskussion und Stimmen zum Problem der Entmythologisierung.* 1st ed. ThF 2. Hamburg: Reich, 1952.

Bauer, Johannes. *Predigten über Worte Jesu*. Tübingen: Mohr Siebeck, 1903.
Bauer, Walter. *Das Johannesevangelium*. 2d ed. HNT 6. Tübingen: Mohr Siebeck, 1925.
———. "Zur Erinnerung an Anton Fridrichsen." *ZNW* 45 (1954): 123–29.
Baumgartner, Walter. "Rudolf Bultmann. Zu seinem 70. Geburtstag." *ThR* NS 22 (1954): 1f.
Becker, Heinz. *Die Reden des Johannesevangeliums und der Stil der gnostischen Offenbarungsrede*. Phd. diss. FRLANT 68/NF 50. Ed. R. Bultmann. Göttingen: Vandenhoeck & Rupert, 1956.
Beckmann, Joachim, ed. *Kirchliches Jahrbuch für die Evangelische Kirche in Deutschland 1933–1944*. 2d ed. Gütersloh: Bertelsmann, 1976.
Bendemann, Reinhard von. *Heinrich Schlier. Eine kritische Analyse seiner Interpretation paulinischer Theologie*. BEvTh 115. Gütersloh: Kaiser, 1995.
Bernsdorff, Walter, and Martin Vialon. "Vom Um-Erzieher zum Freund. Interview mit Samson B. Knoll—Offizier der amerikanischen Militärregierung in Marburg." Pp. 21–44 in *Aufbruch zwischen Mangel und Verweigerung*. Marburg in den Nachkriegsjahren 2 and Marburger Stadtschriften zur Geschichte und Kultur 68. Ed. B. Hafeneger and W. Schäfer. 2000.
Bertram, Georg. "Die Geschichte der synoptischen Tradition." *ThBl* 1 (1922): 9–13.
Bethge, Eberhard. *Dietrich Bonhoeffer. Theologe, Christ, Zeitgenosse*. 4th ed. München: Kaiser, 1978.
Beutel, Albrecht. *Gerhard Ebeling. Eine Biographie*. Tübingen: Mohr Siebeck, 2012.
Biehl, Peter. "Zur Frage nach dem historischen Jesus." *ThR* NS 24 (1957/58): 54–76.
Biehl, Peter, and Petra Schulz. *Autobiographische Miniaturen. Ein Beitrag zur kommunikativen Religionspädagogik. Lebenswege—Denkwege—Leidenswege*. AHRp 5. Jena: IKS Garamond, 2006.
Biemel, Walter, and Hans Saner, ed. *Martin Heidegger / Karl Jaspers. Briefwechsel 1920–1963*. München: 1990.
Bloch, Ernst. *Das Prinzip Hoffnung*. GA 5. Suhrkamp, 1959.
Bonhoeffer, Dietrich. *Konspiration und Haft 1940–1945*. DBW 16. Ed. J. Glenthøj, U. Kabitz, and W. Krötke. 1996.
———. *Widerstand und Ergebung. Briefe und Aufzeichnungen aus der Haft*. DBW 8. Ed. C. Gremmels, E. Bethge, and R. Bethge, with the assistance of I. Tödt. Gütersloh: Kaiser, 1998.
Bonhöffer, Adolf. *Epiktet und das Neue Testament*. RVV 10. Töpelmann, 1911.
———. "Epiktet und das Neue Testament." *ZNW* 13 (1912): 281–92.
Boobyer, George Henry. "The Eighth General Meeting." *NTS* 1 (1954/55): 69f.
———. "The Ninth General Meeting." *NTS* 1 (1954/55): 227f.
Bornkamm, Günther. "Die Theologie Bultmanns in der neueren Diskussion (1963)." Pp. 173–275 in *Geschichte und Glaube. Erster Teil. Gesammelte Aufsätze*. Vol. 3. BEvTh 48. München: Kaiser, 1968.
———. "*In memoriam* Rudolf Bultmann. *20. 8. 1884 †30. 7. 1976." *NTS* 23 (1977): 235–42.

———. *Mythos und Legende in den apokryphen Thomas-Akten. Beiträge zur Geschichte der Gnosis und zur Vorgeschichte des Manichäismus.* FRLANT 31. Göttingen: Vandenhoeck & Ruprecht, 1933.

Bornkamm, Günther, Rudolf Bultmann, and Friedrich Karl Schumann. *Die christliche Hoffnung und das Problem der Entmythologisierung.* Stuttgart: Evangelischer, 1954.

Boschwitz, Friedemann. *Julius Wellhausen. Motive und Massstäbe seiner Geschichtsschreibung.* Phd. diss. Marburg, 1938.

Bousset, Wilhelm. *Kyrios Christos. Geschichte des Christusglaubens von den Anfängen des Christentums bis Irenaeus.* 1st ed. Göttingen: Vandenhoeck & Ruprecht, 1913.

Boutin, Maurice. *Relationalität als Verstehensprinzip bei Rudolf Bultmann.* BEvTh 67. München: Kaiser, 1974.

Bramming, Torben. *Tidehvervs historie.* Fredericksberg: Anis, 1993.

Braun, Herbert. "Die Geschichte der beginnenden Mißverständnisse." Rev. of R. Bultmann, *Theologie des Neuen Testaments*, part 3, 1953. VF 7 (1953/55): 169–74.

———. "Die Paradoxie der Offenbarung." Rev. of R. Bultmann, *Theologie des Neuen Testaments*, part 2, 1951. VF 6 (1951/52): 25–34.

———. "Die Überwindung des Liberalismus auf der Ebene des Kritizismus." Rev. of R. Bultmann, *Theologie des Neuen Testaments*, part 1, 1948. *VF* 5 (1949/50): 49–67.

Brocke, Bernhard vom. "Marburg im Kaiserreich 1866–1918." Pp. 367–540 in *Marburger Geschichte.* Rückblick auf die Stadtgeschichte in Einzelbeiträgen. 2d ed. Ed. E. Dettmering and R. Grenz. Marburg: Der Magistrat, 1982.

Bronnen, Barbara. *Fliegen mit gestutzten Flügeln. Die letzten Jahre der Ricarda Huch 1933–1947.* Zürich: Arche, 2007.

Brunner, Emil. "Gesetz und Offenbarung. Eine theologische Grundlegung" (1925). Pp. 290–98 in *Anfänge der dialektischen Theologie I.* 4th ed. Ed. J. Moltmann. München: Kaiser, 1977.

Brütsch, Charles. Rev. of R. Bultmann, *Die [drei] Johannesbriefe*, 7th/1st ed., 1967. *ThZ* 24 (1968): 470f.

Buber, Martin. "Offener Brief an Gerhard Kittel" (1933). Pp. 607–10 in *Der Jude und sein Judentum. Gesammelte Aufsätze und Reden.* 2d ed. Gerlingen: Schneider, 1993.

———. *Zwei Glaubensweisen.* Zürich: Manesse, 1950.

Buckmiller, Michael. "Theologischer 'Kahl'-Schlag. Doktor der Theologie tritt aus der Kirche aus. mb-Gespräch." *Marburger Bl.* no. 115 (1967): 13f.

Buggenhagen, Arnold von. *Philosophische Autobiographie.* Meisenheim am Glan: Hain, 1975.

Bühler, Winfried. "Paul Friedländer †." *Gnomon* 41 (1969): 619–23.

Bultmann, Arthur Kennedy. "Die Mission und die sog. moderne Theologie." *Oldenburgisches Kirchenblatt* 12 (1906): 53f.

———. "Die Zeichen der Zeit und ihre Mahnung. Predigt am 2. Adventssonntage." Pp. 12–20 in *Drei Wahlpredigten. Gehalten in der Lambertikirche zu Oldenburg am 1., 2. und 3. Advent 1902.* N. d. [1903].

———. *Staat—Kirche—Religion [-] Schule. Sonderdruck des Oldenburgischen Landeslehrervereins.* 1919.
Bultmann, Rudolf. "Πιστεύω, etc." Sections A, C, and D. *ThWNT* 6 (1959): 174–82, 197–230.
———. "Bemerkungen zur Lehrprobe 'Der Auferstandene.'" *EvErz* 6 (1954): 98–100.
———. "Bericht über unsere Amerika-Reise, 1951," undated manuscript [1952], Mn 2-231. In UB Tübingen, RB est.
———. "Brun, Johann Lyder." P. 1287 in *RGG*. Vol. 1. 2d ed. Tübingen: Mohr Siebeck, 1927.
———. "Christentum und Antike." *ThR* NS 33 (1968): 1–17.
———. *Chronik 1917–1945* [Rudolf Bultmann's diaries], Mn 2-224. In UB Tübingen, RB est.
———. *Chronik 1945–1961* [Rudolf Bultmann's diaries], Mn 2-225. In UB Tübingen, RB est.
———. *Chronik 1962–1974* [Rudolf Bultmann's diaries], Mn 2-226. In UB Tübingen, RB est.
———. *Das Evangelium des Johannes.* KEK 2. Göttingen: Vandenhoeck & Ruprecht, 1941.
———. "Das religiöse Moment in der ethischen Unterweisung des Epiktet und das Neue Testament." *ZNW* 13 (1912): 97–110, 177–91.
———. *Das Urchristentum im Rahmen der antiken Religionen.* 1st ed. ErasB. Zürich: Artemis, 1949.
———. *Das verkündigte Wort. Predigten, Andachten, Ansprachen 1906–1941*, in collaboration with M. Evang. Ed. E. Grässer. Tübingen: Mohr Siebeck, 1984.
———. "Der christliche Sinn von Glaube, Liebe, Hoffnung. Skizze des am 11. Juni 1925 vor der 50. Versammlung evangelischer Religionslehrer an den höheren Lehranstalten der Rheinprovinz gehaltenen Vortrages." *ZEvRU* 36 (1925): 170–72, 197–99.
———. "Der Sinn des christlichen Schöpfungsglaubens." *ZMRW* 51 (1936): 1–20.
———. *Der Stil der paulinischen Predigt und die kynisch-stoische Diatribe.* FRLANT 13. Göttingen: Vandenhoeck & Ruprecht, 1910. 1984 reprint of the 1st ed. with an introduction by H. Hübner.
———. "Der 'traditionslose' Amerikaner." *OP* no. 172 (30. 7. 1952): 6.
———. *Der zweite Brief an die Korinther.* KEK special issue. Ed. E. Dinkler. Göttingen: Vandenhoeck & Ruprecht, 1976.
———. "Die Bedeutung der Eschatologie für die Religion des Neuen Testaments." *ZThK* 27 (1917): 76–87.
———. "Die Bergpredigt Jesu und das Recht des Staates." *Forschungen und Fortschritte. Nachrichtenblatt der Deutschen Wissenschaft und Technik* 12 (1936): 100–102.
———. *Die drei Johannesbriefe.* KEK 14. 7th/1st ed. Göttingen: Vandenhoeck & Ruprecht, 1967.
———. *Die drei Johannesbriefe.* KEK 14. 8th/2d ed. Göttingen: Vandenhoeck & Ruprecht, 1969.

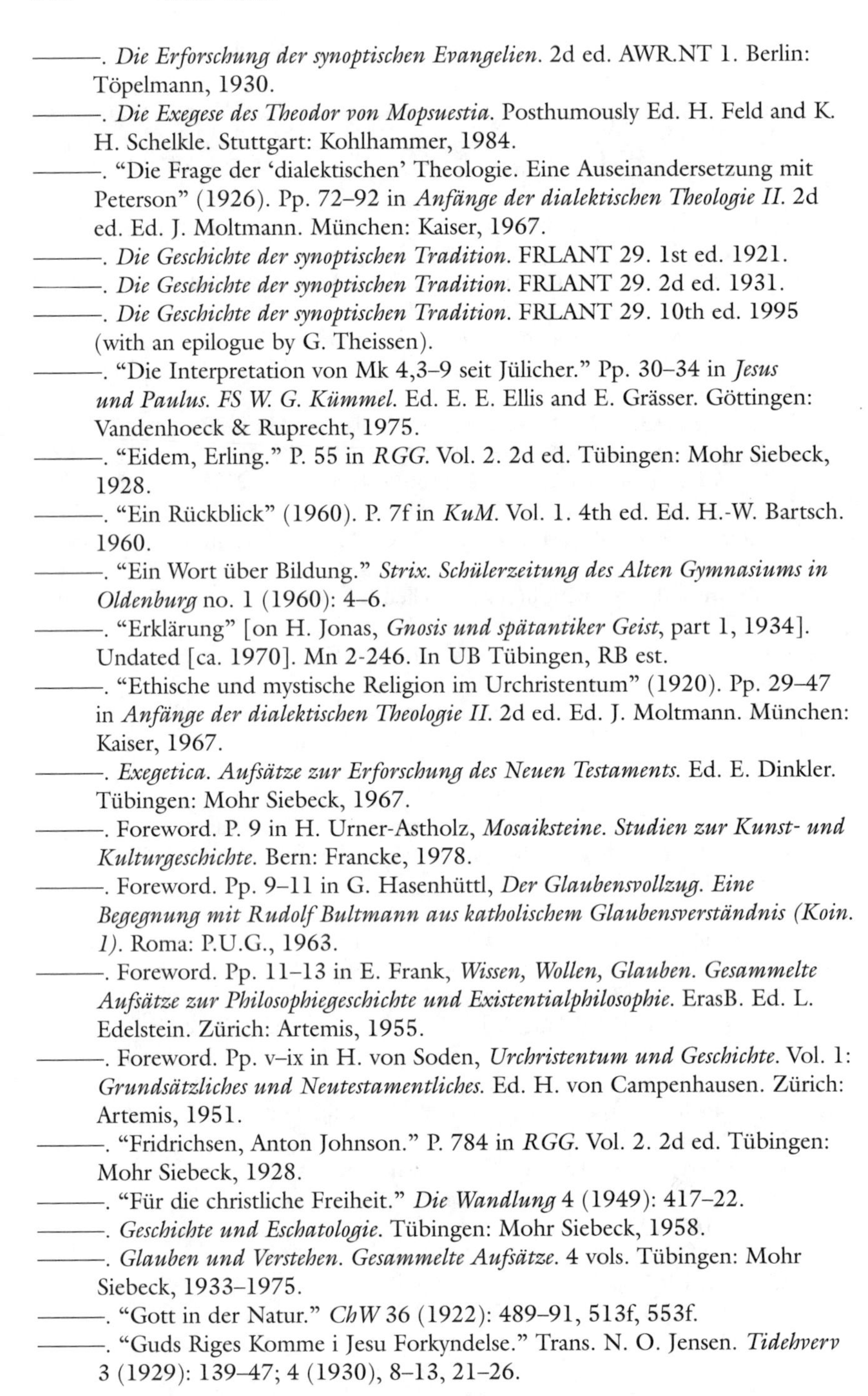

———. *Die Erforschung der synoptischen Evangelien.* 2d ed. AWR.NT 1. Berlin: Töpelmann, 1930.

———. *Die Exegese des Theodor von Mopsuestia.* Posthumously Ed. H. Feld and K. H. Schelkle. Stuttgart: Kohlhammer, 1984.

———. "Die Frage der 'dialektischen' Theologie. Eine Auseinandersetzung mit Peterson" (1926). Pp. 72–92 in *Anfänge der dialektischen Theologie II.* 2d ed. Ed. J. Moltmann. München: Kaiser, 1967.

———. *Die Geschichte der synoptischen Tradition.* FRLANT 29. 1st ed. 1921.

———. *Die Geschichte der synoptischen Tradition.* FRLANT 29. 2d ed. 1931.

———. *Die Geschichte der synoptischen Tradition.* FRLANT 29. 10th ed. 1995 (with an epilogue by G. Theissen).

———. "Die Interpretation von Mk 4,3–9 seit Jülicher." Pp. 30–34 in *Jesus und Paulus. FS W. G. Kümmel.* Ed. E. E. Ellis and E. Grässer. Göttingen: Vandenhoeck & Ruprecht, 1975.

———. "Eidem, Erling." P. 55 in *RGG.* Vol. 2. 2d ed. Tübingen: Mohr Siebeck, 1928.

———. "Ein Rückblick" (1960). P. 7f in *KuM.* Vol. 1. 4th ed. Ed. H.-W. Bartsch. 1960.

———. "Ein Wort über Bildung." *Strix. Schülerzeitung des Alten Gymnasiums in Oldenburg* no. 1 (1960): 4–6.

———. "Erklärung" [on H. Jonas, *Gnosis und spätantiker Geist*, part 1, 1934]. Undated [ca. 1970]. Mn 2-246. In UB Tübingen, RB est.

———. "Ethische und mystische Religion im Urchristentum" (1920). Pp. 29–47 in *Anfänge der dialektischen Theologie II.* 2d ed. Ed. J. Moltmann. München: Kaiser, 1967.

———. *Exegetica. Aufsätze zur Erforschung des Neuen Testaments.* Ed. E. Dinkler. Tübingen: Mohr Siebeck, 1967.

———. Foreword. P. 9 in H. Urner-Astholz, *Mosaiksteine. Studien zur Kunst- und Kulturgeschichte.* Bern: Francke, 1978.

———. Foreword. Pp. 9–11 in G. Hasenhüttl, *Der Glaubensvollzug. Eine Begegnung mit Rudolf Bultmann aus katholischem Glaubensverständnis (Koin. 1).* Roma: P.U.G., 1963.

———. Foreword. Pp. 11–13 in E. Frank, *Wissen, Wollen, Glauben. Gesammelte Aufsätze zur Philosophiegeschichte und Existentialphilosophie.* ErasB. Ed. L. Edelstein. Zürich: Artemis, 1955.

———. Foreword. Pp. v–ix in H. von Soden, *Urchristentum und Geschichte.* Vol. 1: *Grundsätzliches und Neutestamentliches.* Ed. H. von Campenhausen. Zürich: Artemis, 1951.

———. "Fridrichsen, Anton Johnson." P. 784 in *RGG.* Vol. 2. 2d ed. Tübingen: Mohr Siebeck, 1928.

———. "Für die christliche Freiheit." *Die Wandlung* 4 (1949): 417–22.

———. *Geschichte und Eschatologie.* Tübingen: Mohr Siebeck, 1958.

———. *Glauben und Verstehen. Gesammelte Aufsätze.* 4 vols. Tübingen: Mohr Siebeck, 1933–1975.

———. "Gott in der Natur." *ChW* 36 (1922): 489–91, 513f, 553f.

———. "Guds Riges Komme i Jesu Forkyndelse." Trans. N. O. Jensen. *Tidehverv* 3 (1929): 139–47; 4 (1930), 8–13, 21–26.

———. "Hans Frhr. von Soden †." *Marburger Presse* 1, no. 9 (9. 10. 1945): 3.
———. "Heidegger, Martin." P. 1687f in *RGG.* Vol. 2. 2d ed. Tübingen: Mohr Siebeck, 1928.
———. "Hochschule, Antike und Christentum." Pp. 137–43 in *Marburger Hochschulgespräche 12. bis 15. Juni 1946. Referate und Diskussionen.* Frankfurt: Klostermann, 1947.
———."Inselkirchhof." *Nachrichten für Stadt und Land. Zeitschrift für oldenburgische Gemeinde- und Landesinteressen* 37 (11. 7. 1903): no. 160.
———. "Ist humanistische Bildung zeitgemäss?" *Die alte Schulglocke. Mitteilungsbl. des Vereins ehemaliger Schüler des Mariengymnasiums zu Jever Nr. 8.* Jever: Verein, 1954.
———. "Ist Jesus auferstanden wie Goethe? SPIEGEL-Gespräch mit dem Marburger Theologieprofessor D. Dr. Rudolf Bultmann." *Der Spiegel* 20,31 (25. 7. 1966): 42–45. The title of the interview came not from Bultmann but rather from the *Spiegel* editor, Werner Harenberg, who saw the interview through to publication with Bultmann.
———. *Jesus.* UTB 1272. Tübingen: Mohr Siebeck, 1988.
———. *Jesus.* Die Unsterblichen. Die geistigen Heroen der Menschheit in ihrem Leben und Wirken 1. Berlin: Deutsche Bibliothek, n. d. [1st ed. in 1926].
———. "Jesus und Paulus." Pp. 68–90 in *Jesus Christus im Zeugnis der Heiligen Schrift und der Kirche.* BEvTh 2. Ed. K.L. Schmidt. München: Kaiser, 1936.
———. Joke collection, undated, Mn 2-3053. In UB Tübingen, RB est.
———. "Johannesbriefe." Pp. 836–39 in *RGG.* Vol. 3. 3d ed. Tübingen: Mohr Siebeck, 1959.
———. "Johannesevangelium." Pp. 840–50 in *RGG.* Vol. 3. 3d ed. Tübingen: Mohr Siebeck, 1959.
———. "Johannes Weiss zum Gedächtnis." *ThBl* 18 (1939): 242–46.
———. "Karl Barths 'Römerbrief' in zweiter Auflage" (1922). Pp. 119–42 in *Anfänge der dialektischen Theologie I.* 4th ed. Ed. J. Moltmann. München: Kaiser, 1977.
———. Letter to the Reich's Ecclessiastical Committee, 22. 10. 1936. In *Protokoll der Tagung "Alte Marburger" 3–5 January 1994 in Hofgeismar.* N. d. [1995]: 6.
———. *Marburger Predigten.* 2d ed. Tübingen: Mohr Siebeck, 1968.
———. "Milestones in Books. IV." *ET* 70,4 (1958/59): 125.
———. "Mitarbeit an der Strassburger *Revue d'Histoire et de Philosophie religieuses?*" *ThBl* 8 (1929): 251f.
———. "Neueste Paulusforschung." *ThR* NS 6 (1934): 229–46.
———. *Neues Testament und christliche Existenz. Theologische Aufsätze.* Ed. A. Lindemann. Tübingen: Mohr Siebeck, 2002.
———. *Neues Testament und Mythologie. Das Problem der Entmythologisierung der neutestamentlichen Verkündigung.* Reprint of the 1941 edition. Ed. E. Jüngel. BEvTh 96. München: Kaiser, 1988.
———. "The New Approach to the Synoptic Problem." *JR* 6 (1926): 337–62.
———. Obituary for Dr. Leonhard Frank (untitled). *Der Ammerländer* no. 162 (14. 7. 1917): 3.

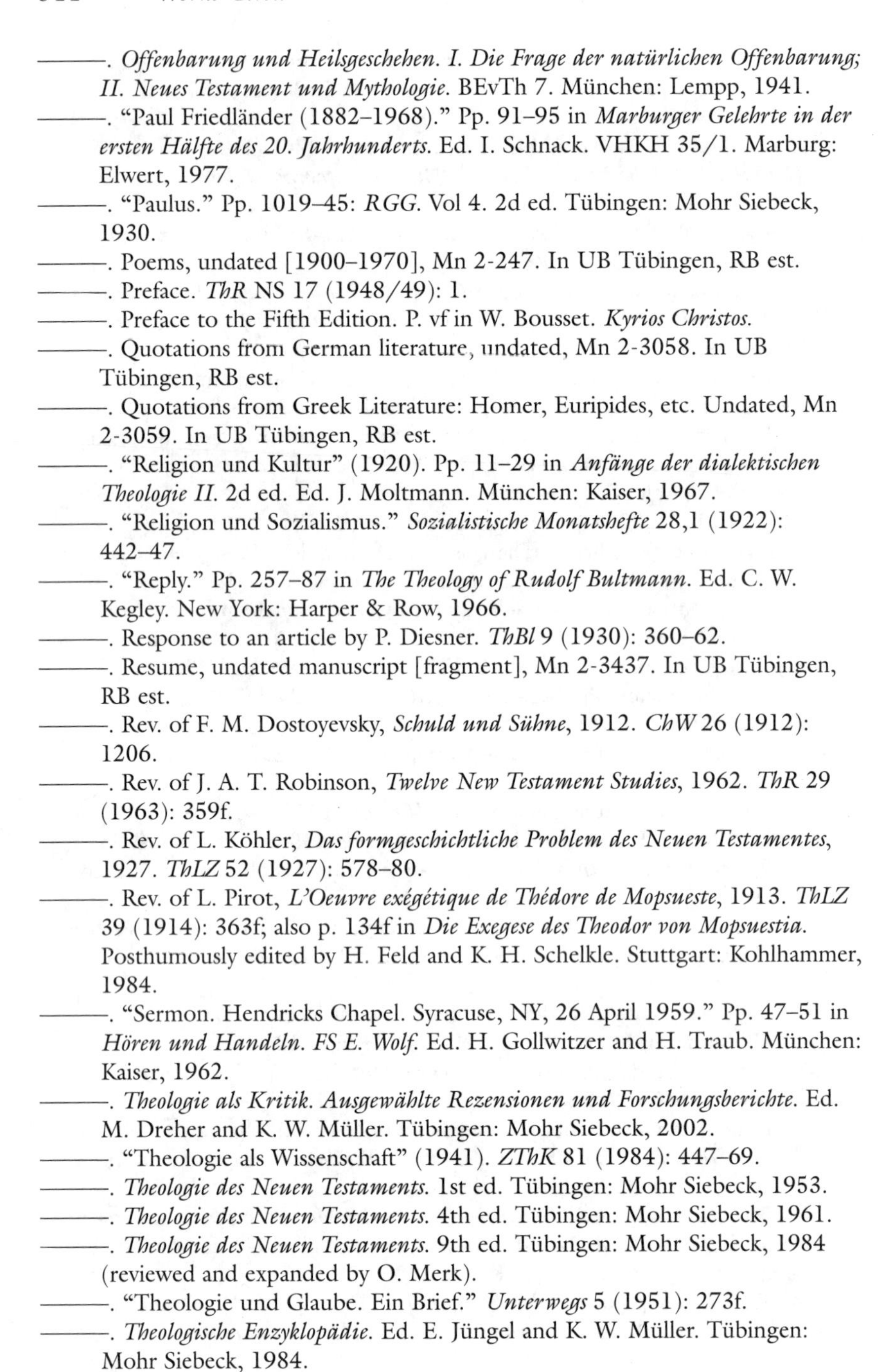

———. *Offenbarung und Heilsgeschehen. I. Die Frage der natürlichen Offenbarung; II. Neues Testament und Mythologie.* BEvTh 7. München: Lempp, 1941.

———. "Paul Friedländer (1882–1968)." Pp. 91–95 in *Marburger Gelehrte in der ersten Hälfte des 20. Jahrhunderts.* Ed. I. Schnack. VHKH 35/1. Marburg: Elwert, 1977.

———. "Paulus." Pp. 1019–45: *RGG.* Vol 4. 2d ed. Tübingen: Mohr Siebeck, 1930.

———. Poems, undated [1900–1970], Mn 2-247. In UB Tübingen, RB est.

———. Preface. *ThR* NS 17 (1948/49): 1.

———. Preface to the Fifth Edition. P. vf in W. Bousset. *Kyrios Christos.*

———. Quotations from German literature, undated, Mn 2-3058. In UB Tübingen, RB est.

———. Quotations from Greek Literature: Homer, Euripides, etc. Undated, Mn 2-3059. In UB Tübingen, RB est.

———. "Religion und Kultur" (1920). Pp. 11–29 in *Anfänge der dialektischen Theologie II.* 2d ed. Ed. J. Moltmann. München: Kaiser, 1967.

———. "Religion und Sozialismus." *Sozialistische Monatshefte* 28,1 (1922): 442–47.

———. "Reply." Pp. 257–87 in *The Theology of Rudolf Bultmann.* Ed. C. W. Kegley. New York: Harper & Row, 1966.

———. Response to an article by P. Diesner. *ThBl* 9 (1930): 360–62.

———. Resume, undated manuscript [fragment], Mn 2-3437. In UB Tübingen, RB est.

———. Rev. of F. M. Dostoyevsky, *Schuld und Sühne*, 1912. *ChW* 26 (1912): 1206.

———. Rev. of J. A. T. Robinson, *Twelve New Testament Studies*, 1962. *ThR* 29 (1963): 359f.

———. Rev. of L. Köhler, *Das formgeschichtliche Problem des Neuen Testamentes*, 1927. *ThLZ* 52 (1927): 578–80.

———. Rev. of L. Pirot, *L'Oeuvre exégétique de Thédore de Mopsueste*, 1913. *ThLZ* 39 (1914): 363f; also p. 134f in *Die Exegese des Theodor von Mopsuestia.* Posthumously edited by H. Feld and K. H. Schelkle. Stuttgart: Kohlhammer, 1984.

———. "Sermon. Hendricks Chapel. Syracuse, NY, 26 April 1959." Pp. 47–51 in *Hören und Handeln. FS E. Wolf.* Ed. H. Gollwitzer and H. Traub. München: Kaiser, 1962.

———. *Theologie als Kritik. Ausgewählte Rezensionen und Forschungsberichte.* Ed. M. Dreher and K. W. Müller. Tübingen: Mohr Siebeck, 2002.

———. "Theologie als Wissenschaft" (1941). *ZThK* 81 (1984): 447–69.

———. *Theologie des Neuen Testaments.* 1st ed. Tübingen: Mohr Siebeck, 1953.

———. *Theologie des Neuen Testaments.* 4th ed. Tübingen: Mohr Siebeck, 1961.

———. *Theologie des Neuen Testaments.* 9th ed. Tübingen: Mohr Siebeck, 1984 (reviewed and expanded by O. Merk).

———. "Theologie und Glaube. Ein Brief." *Unterwegs* 5 (1951): 273f.

———. *Theologische Enzyklopädie.* Ed. E. Jüngel and K. W. Müller. Tübingen: Mohr Siebeck, 1984.

———. "Theologische Wissenschaft und kirchliche Praxis." *Oldenburgisches Kirchenbl.* 19 (1913): 123–27, 133–35.
———. "Torm, Frederik." P. 1232 in *RGG*. Vol. 5. 2d ed. Tübingen: Mohr Siebeck, 1931.
———. "Unruhe und Ruhe." *ChW* 36 (1922): 569f.
———. Untitled article. Pp. 13–17 in *Ockershäuser Blätter*. Vol. 4. Ed. the Akademische Vereinigung. Marburg: Lahn, 1916.
———. Untitled Letter to the Editor [no. 18]. *AdF* no. 29 (1. 8. 1909): 298f.
———. "Urchristentum und Staat. Rede zur Reichsgründungsfeier der Philipps-Universität am 18. January 1928." *Universitätsbund Marburg e.V. Mitteilungen* no. 19 (February 1928), 1–4.
———. "Urchristliche Religion (1915–1925)." *ARW* 24 (1926): 83–164.
———. "Urgemeinde, christliche." Pp. 1514–23 in *RGG*. Vol 5. 1st ed. Tübingen: Mohr Siebeck, 1913.
———. "Variationen über ein Thema." *KiZ* 14 (1959): 289–91. (Bultmann's authorship is only certain for some of the poems printed here.)
———. "Vom Beten." *ChW* 36 (1922): 593f.
———. "Vom geheimnisvollen und vom offenbaren Gott. Pfingstpredigt 1917." *ChW* 31 (1917): 572–79; also pp. 135–47 in R. Bultmann, *VW*.
———. "Vom Schicksal." *ChW* 36 (1922): 609f.
———. *Wachen und Träumen*. Märchen. Edited and introduced by W. Zager. Berlin: Wichern, 2005.
———. "Walter Baumgartner †." *ThR* NS 35 (1970): 93. (This obituary, which was cosigned by E. Dinkler and W. G. Kümmel, was written by Bultmann; cf. Mn 2-265 in UB Tübingen, RB est.)
———. "Was lässt die Spruchquelle über die Urgemeinde erkennen?" *Oldenburgisches Kirchenblatt* 19 (1913): 35–37, 41–44.
———. "Wilhelm Heitmüller." *ChW* 40 (1926): 209–13.
———. "Worte, gesprochen am Sarge Katharina Kippenbergs" (12. 6. 1947). Pp. 4–10 in *Katharina Kippenberg zum Gedächtnis*. Printed privately, n. d. [1947].
———. "Zum Geleit." P. 9 in F. Peerlinck, *Rudolf Bultmann als Prediger. Verkündigung als Vollzug seiner Theologie. ThF* 50. Hamburg-Bergstedt: Reich, 1970.
———. "Zum Problem der Entmythologisierung." Pp. 179–208 in *KuM*. Vol. 2. 1st ed. Ed. H.-W. Bartsch. Hamburg-Volksdorf: Reich, 1952.
———. "Zum Thema. Christentum und Antike." *ThR* NS 23 (1955): 207–29.
———. "Zur Frage der Entmythologisierung des Neuen Testaments." *DtPfBl* 47 (1943): 3f.
———. "Zur Frage der wissenschaftlichen Ausbildung der Theologen." Pp. 34–40 in *Studienbetreuung der Kriegsteilnehmer der Martin-Luther-Universität Halle*. Ed. E. Fascher. Halle: Klintz, November 1944.
———. "Zur Frankfurter Tagung." *AdF* no. 78 (5. 11. 1924): 853f.
———. "Zur Geschichte der Paulus-Forschung." *ThR* NS 1 (1929): 26–59.
Bultmann Lemke, Antje. "Der unveröffentlichte Nachlass von Rudolf Bultmann." Pp. 11–25 in *Rudolf Bultmann (1884–1976). Nachlassverzeichnis*. Ed. H. Wassmann, J. M. Osthof, and A. E. Bruckhaus. Wiesbaden: Harrassowitz, 2001.

———. "Theology for Freedom and Responsibility: Rudolf Bultmann's Views on Church and State." *Syracuse University Library Associates Courier 21* (1986): 3–15.

Busch, Eberhard. "Der Pietismus in Deutschland seit 1945." Pp. 533–62 in *Der Pietismus im neunzehnten und zwanzigsten Jahrhundert.* Geschichte des Pietismus 3. Ed. U. Gäbler et al. Göttingen: Vandenhoeck & Ruprecht, 2000.

———. *Karl Barths Lebenslauf.* 3d ed. München: Kaiser, 1978.

Busch, Walter, and Gerhart Pickerodt, ed. *Max Kommerell. Leben—Werk—Aktualität.* Göttingen: Wallstein, 2003.

Christ, Karl. *Klios Wandlungen. Die deutsche Althistorie vom Neuhumanismus bis zur Gegenwart.* München: Beck, 2006.

Christophersen, Alf. *Kairos. Protestantische Zeitdeutungskämpfe in der Weimarer Republik.* BHTh 143. Tübingen: Mohr Siebeck, 2008.

Cohen, Hermann. *Der Begriff der Religion im System der Philosophie.* PhilArb X/1. Giessen: Töpelmann, 1915.

Collingwood, Robin G. *The Idea of History.* Oxford: Clarendon, 1946.

Colpe, Carsten. *Die religionsgeschichtliche Schule. Darstellung und Kritik ihres Bildes vom gnostischen Erlösermythos.* FRLANT 78. Göttingen: Vandenhoeck & Ruprecht, 1961.

Conzelmann, Hans. Rev. of R. Bultmann, *Theologie des Neuen Testaments,* 1953. *ZKG* 66 (1954/55): 151–57.

Corset, Paul, ed. "Correspondance Rudolf Bultmann–René Marlé." *RSR* 83 (1995): 537–42.

Crystall, Andreas. *Gustav Frenssen. Sein Weg vom Kulturprotestantismus zum Nationalsozialismus.* Religiöse Kulturen der Moderne 10. Gütersloh: Kaiser, Gütersloher, 2002.

Cullmann, Oscar. *Christus und die Zeit. Die urchristliche Zeit- und Geschichtsauffassung.* 1st ed. Zürich: Evangelischer, 1946.

———. *Christus und die Zeit. Die urchristliche Zeit- und Geschichtsauffassung.* 3d ed. Zürich: Evangelischer, 1962.

Dahl, Nils Alstrup. "Die *Theologie des Neuen Testaments.*" *ThR* 22 (1954): 21–54.

Davies, Norman and Roger Moorhouse. *Die Blume Europas. Breslau—Wroclaw—Vratislavia. Die Geschichte einer mitteleuropäischen Stadt.* 1st ed. München: Droemer, 2002.

Dennison, William D. "Rudolf Bultmann: Pastor?" *CTJ* 34 (1999): 179–87.

Deschner, Karlheinz. *Was halten Sie vom Christentum? 18 Antworten auf eine Umfrage.* München: List, 1957.

Dettmering, Erhart. "Ein Name, der sich mit einem Begriff verbindet: Rudolf Bultmann und die Entmythologisierung des Neuen Testaments." *Studier' mal Marburg* (July/August 1984): 5–7.

Deutsches Literaturarchiv Marbach a. N. Letters of RB to E. and M. Auerbach, Bestand A: Auerbach, no ZN number yet assigned.

———. Letters of RB to E. Kommerell, 24. 9. 1944, Bestand D: Kommerell, ZN: HS. 2002.0166.00001.

———. Letters of RB to H.-G. Gadamer, Bestand A: Gadamer, ZN: HS. 2005.0056.

———. Letters of RB to K. Jaspers, Bestand A: Jaspers, ZN: 75.10579/1–5.
———. Letters of RB to M. Kommerell, Bestand A: Kommerell, ZN: 84.1523/1–3.
———. Letters of RB to M. L. Kaschnitz, Bestand A: Kaschnitz/Letters on the death of Guido Kaschnitz of Weinberg, no ZN number yet assigned.
Dibelius, Martin. *Die Formgeschichte des Evangeliums.* 1st ed. Tübingen: Mohr Siebeck, 1919.
———."Ein neuer Kommentar zum Johannes-Evangelium." *ThLZ* 67 (1942): 257–64.
———. *Geschichtliche und übergeschichtliche Religion im Christentum.* Göttingen: Vandenhoeck & Ruprecht, 1925.
———. Rev. of R. Bultmann, *Die Geschichte der synoptischen Tradition*, 1921. *DLZ* 43 (1922): 128–34.
———. Rev. of R. Bultmann, *Die Geschichte der synoptischen Tradition*, 1931 [2d ed]. *DLZ* 53 [NS 3] (1932): 1105–11.
———. *Selbstbesinnung des Deutschen* (1946). Ed. F. W. Graf. Tübingen: Mohr Siebeck, 1997.
———. "Zur Formgeschichte der Evangelien." *ThR* NS 1 (1929): 185–216.
Dieckmann, Bernhard. "Entmythologisierung als Lebensaufgabe. Zur Veröffentlichung von Bultmanns Habilitationsschrift und seinen frühen Predigten." *ThGl* 77 (1987): 88–107.
Diem, Hermann. *Ja oder Nein. 50 Jahre Theologe in Kirche und Staat.* Berlin: Kreuz, 1974.
Diesner, Paul. "Noch einmal: Mitarbeit an der Strassburger *Revue d'Histoire et de Philosophie religieuses*?" *ThBl* 9 (1930): 359f.
Diesselhorst, G. Private Collection. Letters of the Chancellor of the Philipps-University of Marburg to RB, 19. 7. and 9. 9. 1937.
———. Private Collection. Letter of the Hessian Minister for Education and National Culture to RB, 29. 6. 1951.
———. Private Collection. Letter of the Ministry of Education of the Canton of Zürich to RB, 23. 6. 1953.
———. Private Collection. Letter of RB to the Reich and Prussian Minister for Science, Education, and National Culture, 27. 11. 1937.
Dilschneider, Otto. "Mythus?! Gedanken über ein Thema unserer Zeit." *DtPfBl* 46 (1942): 153f.
Dinkler, Erich. *Im Zeichen des Kreuzes. Aufsätze.* Ed. O. Merk and M. Wolter. BZNW 61. Berlin: De Gruyter, 1992.
———. Rev. of R. Bultmann, *Das Urchristentum im Rahmen der antiken Religionen*, 1949. *VF* 5 (1949/50): 67–75.
———. "Veröffentlichungen von Rudolf Bultmann." Pp. 483–507 in R. Bultmann, *Exegetica. Aufsätze zur Erforschung des Neuen Testaments.* Ed. E. Dinkler. Tübingen: Mohr Siebeck, 1967.
———, ed. *Zeit und Geschichte. Dankesgabe an Rudolf Bultmann zum 80. Geburtstag.* Tübingen: Mohr Siebeck, 1964.
Dinkler, Erich, and Erika Dinkler-von Schubert, ed. *Theologie und Kirche im Wirken Hans von Sodens. Briefe und Dokumente aus der Zeit des*

Kirchenkampfes 1933–1945. 2d ed. AKIZ.A 2. Göttingen: Vandenhoeck & Ruprecht, 1986.

Dinkler-von Schubert, Erika, ed. *Feldpost: Zeugnis und Vermächtnis. Briefe und Texte aus dem Kreis der evangelischen Studentengemeinde Marburg/Lahn und ihrer Lehrer (1939–1945).* Göttingen: Vandenhoeck & Ruprecht, 1993.

Dorhs, Michael. Über den Tod hinaus. *Grundzüge einer Individualeschatologie in der Theologie Rudolf Bultmanns.* EHS.T 665. Frankfurt am Main: Lang, 1999.

Dreher, Matthias. *Rudolf Bultmann als Kritiker in seinen Rezensionen und Forschungsberichten. Kommentierende Auswertung.* BVB 11. Münster: Lit, 2005.

Ebbinghaus, Julius. Untitled article. Pp. 1–59 in *Philosophie in Selbstdarstellungen.* Vol. 3. Ed. L. J. Pongratz. 1977.

Ebeling, Gerhard. *Das Wesen des christlichen Glaubens.* 1st ed. Tübingen: Mohr Siebeck, 1959.

———. *Die Frage nach dem historischen Jesus.* ZThK series. Supplement 1. Tübingen: Mohr Siebeck, 1959.

———. *Evangelische Evangelienauslegung. Eine Untersuchung zu Luthers Hermeneutik.* 3d ed. München: Evangelischer, 1991.

———. *Mein theologischer Weg.* Hermeneutische Bl. [series]. Sonderheft, 2006. Pp. 5–66.

———. *Studium der Theologie. Eine enzyklopädische Orientierung.* 1st ed. UTB 446. Tübingen: Mohr Siebeck, 1975.

———. *Theologie und Verkündigung. Ein Gespräch mit Rudolf Bultmann.* 2d ed. HUTh 1. Tübingen: Mohr Siebeck, 1963.

———."Zum Verständnis von R. Bultmanns Aufsatz: 'Welchen Sinn hat es, von Gott zu reden?'" Pp. 343–71 in *Wort und Glaube II. Beiträge zur Fundamentaltheologie und zur Lehre von Gott.* Tübingen: Mohr Siebeck, 1969.

Eberhard, Gertraud. *Existentiale Theologie und Pädagogik. Das Beispiel Rudolf Bultmanns.* TW 4. Bern: Lang, 1974.

Eckert, Jost. Rev. of R. Bultmann, *Der zweite Brief an die Korinther*, 1976. *ThRv* 73 (1977): 460–62.

Ehler, Bernhard. *Die Herrschaft des Gekreuzigten. Ernst Käsemanns Frage nach der Mitte der Schrift.* BZNW 46. Berlin: De Gruyter, 1986.

Eltester, Walther, ed. *Neutestamentliche Studien für Rudolf Bultmann. Zu seinem 70. Geburtstag am 20. August 1954.* BZNW 21. Berlin: Töpelmann, 1954.

Engagement announcement of Helene Feldmann and Rudolf Bultmanns. *ChW* 30 (1916): 655.

Evang, Martin. *Rudolf Bultmann in seiner Frühzeit.* BHTh 74. Tübingen: Mohr Siebeck, 1988.

Fahrenbach, Helmut. "Philosophische Existenzerhellung und theologische Existenzmitteilung. Zur Auseinandersetzung zwischen Karl Jaspers und Rudolf Bultmann." *ThR* NS 24 (1957/58): 77–99, 105–35.

Feine, Paul. *Theologie des Neuen Testaments.* 2d ed. Leipzig: Hinrichs, 1911.

Fischer, Hermann. *Protestantische Theologie im 20. Jahrhundert.* Stuttgart: Kohlhammer, 2002.

Fischer-Barnicol, Hans. "Freiheit zur Zukunft: Der Glaube an das Wort bei Rudolf Bultmann. Ein Porträt im Dialog" (radio interview from 23. 8. 1964), Mn 2-323. In UB Tübingen, RB est.

Flashar, Hellmut. *Inszenierung der Antike. Das griechische Drama auf der Bühne der Neuzeit 1585–1990.* München: Beck, 1991.

Foerster, Erich. "Kirche wider Kirche." Rev. of F. Heiler, *Im Ringen um die Kirche,* 1931. *ThR* NS 4 (1932): 131–70.

———. "Rudolf Bultmanns Jesusbuch." *ZThK* NS 9 (1928): 28–50.

Frenssen, Gustav. *Dorfpredigten.* Full collection. Göttingen: Vandenhoeck & Ruprecht, n. d. [Vol. 1, 9th ed., 1905; Vol. 2, 8th ed., 1906; Vol. 3, 5th ed., 1905].

Frey, Jörg. *Die johanneische Eschatologie.* Vol. 1: *Ihre Probleme im Spiegel der Forschung seit Reimarus.* WUNT 96. Tübingen: Mohr Siebeck, 1997.

———. "Zum Problem der Aufgabe und Durchführung einer Theologie des Neuen Testaments." Pp. 3–53 in *Aufgabe und Durchführung einer Theologie des Neuen Testaments.* WUNT 205. Ed. C. Breytenbach and J. Frey. Tübingen: Mohr Siebeck, 2007.

Fridrichsen, Anton. *Le problème du miracle dans le christianisme primitif.* EHPhR 12. Strasbourg, Paris: Libraire Istra, 1925.

Friedländer, Paul. *Platon.* Vol. 1: *Eidos—Paideia—Dialogos.* 1st ed. Berlin: De Gruyter, 1928.

———. *Platon.* Vol. 2: *Die platonischen Schriften.* 1st ed. Berlin: De Gruyter, 1930.

Fuchs, Ernst. *Christus und der Geist bei Paulus. Eine biblisch-theologische Untersuchung.* Leipzig: Hinrichs, 1932.

———. *Glaube und Tat in den Mandata des Hirten des Hermas.* Marburg: Bauer, 1931.

———. Minutes of the general meeting of the Society for Protestant Theology in Alpirsbach, 1941. Manuscript (1941). Mn 2-3086. In UB Tübingen, RB est.

———. *Wagnis des Glaubens. Aufsätze und Vorträge.* Ed. E. Grötzinger. Neukirchen-Vluyn: Neukirchener, 1979.

———. *Zur Frage nach dem historischen Jesus. Gesammelte Aufsätze.* Vol. 2. Tübingen: Mohr Siebeck, 1960.

Fuhrmann, Horst. *Pour le mérite. Über die Sichtbarmachung von Verdiensten. Eine historische Besinnung.* 2d ed. Sigmaringen: Thorbecke, 1996.

Gadamer, Hans-Georg. "Die neue Platoforschung" (1933). Pp. 212–29 in H.-G. Gadamer, *Griechische Philosophie I.* Tübingen: Mohr Siebeck, 1985.

———. "Einzug in Marburg." Pp. 109–13 in *Erinnerung an Martin Heidegger.* Ed. G. Neske. Pfullingen: Neske, 1977.

———. "Gedenkworte für Rudolf Bultmann." Pp. 131–39 in *Reden und Gedenkworte.* Orden Pour le mérite für Wissenschaften und Künste. Vol. 13. 1976/77.

———. *Philosophische Lehrjahre. Eine Rückschau.* Frankfurt am Main: Klostermann, 1977.

———. *Plato und die Dichter.* Wissenschaft und Gegenwart 5. Frankfurt am Main: Klostermann, 1934.

———. Rev. of E. Frank, *Philosophical Understanding and Religious Truth,* 1945. *ThR* NS 18 (1950): 260–66.

Geheimes Staatsarchiv Preussischer Kulturbesitz Berlin. Letters of RB to E. Lohmeyer, vi. HA Familienarchive und Nachlässe, E. Lohmeyer est. (dep.), no. 5.
———. Letters of RB to M. Lohmeyer, vi. HA Familienarchive und Nachlässe, E. Lohmeyer est. (dep.), no. 6.
Geiser, Stefan. *Verantwortung und Schuld. Studien zu Martin Dibelius.* Hamburger Theologische Studien 20. Münster: Lit, 2001.
Geisser, Hans Friedrich. "Barth und Bultmann im Streit um Stiftlerseelen." Pp. 297–315 in *In Wahrheit und Freiheit. 450 Jahre Evangelisches Stift in Tübingen.* QFWKG 8. Ed. F. Hertel. Stuttgart: Calwer, 1986.
Gerhardsson, Birger. "Anton Fridrichsen, Rudolf Bultmann, Form Criticism and Hermeneutics." Pp. 657–75 in *Geschichte—Tradition—Reflexion. FS für M. Hengel zum 70. Geb.* Vol. 3. Ed. H. Cancik, H. Lichtenberger, and P. Schäfer. Tübingen: Mohr Siebeck, 1996.
Gersdorff, Dagmar von. *Marie Luise Kaschnitz. Eine Biographie.* 2d ed. Frankfurt am Main: Insel, 1993.
Gestrich, Christof. *Neuzeitliches Denken und die Spaltung der dialektischen Theologie. Zur Frage der natürlichen Theologie.* BHTh 52. Tübingen: Mohr Siebeck, 1977.
Gimbel, John. *Eine deutsche Stadt unter amerikanischer Besatzung. Marburg, 1945–1952.* Köln: Kiepenheuer & Witsch, 1964.
Glossner, Herbert. "Basel, 1953. Der grosse Disput mit Bultmann." DASBl no. 8 (25. 2. 1979): 12.
Göckeritz, Hermann Götz, ed. *Rudolf Bultmann–Friedrich Gogarten. Briefwechsel 1921–1967.* Tübingen: Mohr Siebeck, 2002.
Gogarten, Friedrich. "Das abendländische Geschichtsdenken. Bemerkungen zu dem Buch von Erich Auerbach 'Mimesis.'" *ZThK* 51 (1954): 270–360.
———. "Die Krisis unserer Kultur" (1920). Pp. 101–21 in *Anfänge der dialektischen Theologie II.* 2d ed. Ed. J. Moltmann. München: Kaiser, 1967.
———. *Die religiöse Entscheidung.* Jena: Diederichs, 1921.
———. *Einheit von Evangelium und Volkstum?* Hamburg: Hanseat, 1933.
———. *Entmythologisierung und Kirche.* Stuttgart: Vorwerk, 1953.
———. *Gericht oder Skepsis. Eine Streitschrift gegen Karl Barth.* Jena: Diederichs, 1937.
———. "Offenbarung und Zeit." Pp. 20–40 in *Von Glauben und Offenbarung. Vier Vorträge.* Jena: Diederichs, 1923.
———. *Religion weither.* Jena: Diederichs, 1917.
———. *Verhängnis und Hoffnung der Neuzeit. Die Säkularisierung als theologisches Problem.* Stuttgart: Vorwerk, 1953.
———. "Wahrheit und Gewissheit." *ZZ* 8 (1930): 96–119.
———. *Wider die Ächtung der Autorität.* Jena: Diederichs, 1930.
Gollwitzer, Helmut. *Die Existenz Gottes im Bekenntnis des Glaubens.* BEvTh 34. München: Kaiser, 1963.
Graf, Friedrich Wilhelm. "Die 'antihistoristische Revolution' in der protestantischen Theologie der zwanziger Jahre." Pp. 377–405 in *Vernunft des Glaubens. Wissenschaftliche Theologie und kirchliche Lehre. FS zum 60. Geb. von*

Wolfhart Pannenberg. Ed. J. Rohls and G. Wenz. Göttingen: Vandenhoeck & Ruprecht, 1988.

———. "Geschichte durch Übergeschichte überwinden. Antihistoristisches Geschichtsdenken in der protestantischen Theologie der 1920er Jahre." Pp. 217–44 in *Geschichtsdiskurs 4: Krisenbewusstsein, Katastrophenerfahrungen und Innovationen 1880–1945*. Ed. W. Küttler, J. Rüsen, and E. Schulin. Frankfurt am Main: Fischer-Taschenbuch, 1997.

———. "Individualismus, aber bitte nur methodisch. Das Rezept des Rezensenten: Auch Langweiler wusste Rudolf Bultmann geisteserotisch aufzubereiten." *FAZ* no. 93 (22. 4. 2002): 48.

Greschat, Martin, ed. *Die Schuld der Kirche. Dokumente und Reflexionen zur Stuttgarter Schulderklärung from 18./19. Oktober 1945*. Studienbücher zur kirchlichen Zeitgeschichte 4. München: Kaiser, 1982.

Grisebach, Eberhard. *Gegenwart. Eine kritische Ethik*. Halle-Saale: Niemeyer, 1928.

Grondin, Jean. "Gadamer und Bultmann." Pp. 186–208 in *Gadamer verstehen / Understanding Gadamer*. Ed. M. Wischke and M. Hofer. Darmstadt: Wissenschaftliche Buchgesellschaft, 2003.

———. *Hans-Georg Gadamer. Eine Biographie*. Tübingen: Mohr Siebeck, 1999.

Grossmann, Andreas. "Reformatorische Impulse. Heidegger und Luther." Pp. 11–26 in *Heidegger-Lektüren*. Über Kunst, Religion und Politik. Würzburg: Königshausen & Neumann, 2005.

———, ed. "'Und die Gnosis ruft mich immer noch....' Hans Jonas' Denkwege im Lichte seines Briefwechsels mit Rudolf Bultmann." *Journal Phänomenologie* 20 (2003): 18–32.

———. "Zwischen Phänomenologie und Theologie. Heideggers 'Marburger Religionsgespräch' mit Rudolf Bultmann." *ZThK* 95 (1998): 37–62.

Grossmann, Andreas, and Christof Landmesser, ed. *Rudolf Bultmann / Martin Heidegger. Briefwechsel 1925–1975*. With a foreword by Eberhard Jüngel. Frankfurt am Main: Klostermann, 2009.

Gumbrecht, Hans Ulrich. *1926. Ein Jahr am Rand der Zeit*. Frankfurt am Main: Suhrkamp, 2001.

———. "Zorn über die Verdorbenheit der Atmosphäre. Rudolf Bultmanns Zeitungsveröffentlichungen in den frühen Jahren der Bundesrepublik." FAZ no. 68 (21. 3. 2001): N5.

Gunkel, Hermann. *Elias: Jahve und Baal*. RV II/8. Tübingen: Mohr Siebeck, 1906.

———. "Ziele und Methoden der alttestamentlichen Exegese." *MKP* 4 (1904): 521–40.

———. *Zum religionsgeschichtlichen Verständnis des Neuen Testaments*. 1st ed. FRLANT 1. Göttingen: Vandenhoeck & Ruprecht, 1903.

Günther, Hilmar. *Die ausserakademische Entmythologisierungsdebatte in den Jahren 1948–1953. Versuch einer zeitgeschichtlichen, theologischen und semantischen Analyse*. Phd. diss. Leipzig, 1974.

Hackenberg, Oskar. *Bibliographie zu Rudolf Bultmann*. Supplemented by M. Dreher and B. Petri-Hasenöhrl. 2007. http://www.univie.ac.at/bultmann/bilder/Bibliographie_neu.doc.

Haenchen, Ernst. "Das Johannesevangelium und sein Kommentar." *ThLZ* 89 (1964): 881–98.
———. "Neuere Literatur zu den Johannesbriefen" (1960). Pp. 235–311 in E. Haenchen, *Die Bibel und wir. Gesammelte Aufsätze.* Vol. 2. Tübingen: Mohr Siebeck, 1968.
Haering, Hermann. *Theodor Haering 1848–1928. Christ und systematischer Theologe. Ein Lebens- und Zeitbild.* 1963. (P. 400f: RB to T. Haering, n. d. [1927]).
Haering, Theodor. *Das christliche Leben auf Grund des christlichen Glaubens. Christliche Sittenlehre.* 1st ed. Calw & Stuttgart: Vereinsbuchhandlung, 1902.
———. *Der christliche Glaube (Dogmatik).* 1st ed. Calw & Stuttgart: Vereinsbuchhandlung, 1906.
Hahn, Ferdinand. "Die Formgeschichte des Evangeliums. Voraussetzungen, Ausbau und Tragweite." Pp. 427–77 in *Zur Formgeschichte des Evangeliums.* WdF 81. Darmstadt: Wissenschaftliche Buchgesellschaft, 1985.
Hammann, Konrad. "Das abscheuliche Wort 'Apophthegma.' Hermann Gunkel und Rudolf Bultmann. Mit einem Anhang: Rudolf Bultmanns Brief an Hermann Gunkel vom 21. Mai 1922." *JHKGV* 61 (2010): 195–220.
———. "Der Glaube als freie Tat des Gehorsams. Herkunft, Bedeutung und Problematik einer Denkfigur Rudolf Bultmanns." *ZThK* 109 (2012): 206–34.
———. "Die Entstehung von Bultmanns Jesus-Buch." *ZThK* 107 (2010): 191–214.
———. "Der Giessener Universitätsgottesdienst 1917–1936." *JHKGV* 45 (1994): 99–123.
———. "Heinrich Hermelink in Marburg. Kirchenhistoriker in der Weimarer Ära." Pp. 85–106 in *Die Philipps-Universität Marburg zwischen Kaiserreich und Nationalsozialismus.* Hessische Forschungen zur geschichtlichen Landes- und Volkskunde 45. Ed. and pub. Verein für hessische Geschichte und Landeskunde. Kassel: 2006.
———. Private Collection. Letter of H. Koester to K. Hammann, 28. 10. 2005.
———. Private Collection. Letter of H. Leipold to K. Hammann, 29. 7. 2004.
———. Private Collection. Letter of O. Merk to K. Hammann, 2./10. 1. 2006.
———. "Rudolf Bultmann—eine Biographie für die Gegenwart." Pp. 49–68 in *Rudolf Bultmann (1884–1976)—Theologe der Gegenwart. Hermeneutik—Exegese—Theologie—Philosophie.* Ed. C. Landmesser and A. Klein. Neukirchen-Vluyn: Neukirchener, 2010.
———. "Rudolf Bultmanns Begegnung mit dem Judentum." *ZThK* 102 (2005): 35–72.
———. "Rudolf Bultmann und der Universitätsgottesdienst in Marburg." *ZThK* 90 (1993): 87–116.
Hannah Arendt-Zentrum Oldenburg. Letters of RB to H. Arendt, Hannah Arendt Archive.
Harbsmeier, Götz. "Die 'nicht-religiöse Interpretation biblischer Begriffe' bei Bonhoeffer und die Entmythologisierung." Pp. 74–91 in *Die mündige Welt.* 2 vols. Ed. E. Bethge. München: Kaiser, 1956.
———. "Gedruckte Predigten." *MPTh* 46 (1957): 226–35.

Härle, Wilfried. Rev. of Bultmann, Rudolf: *Theologische Enzyklopädie*, edited by E. Jüngel and K. W. Müller, 1984. *RBS* 13 (1986): 162–64.

Härle, Wilfried, and Heinrich Leipold, ed. *Lehrfreiheit und Lehrbeanstandung*. Vol. 1: *Theologische Texte*. 1985.

Harnack, Adolf. *Das Wesen des Christentums, 1905*. GTBS 227. Gütersloh: Gütersloher, 1977.

Harnisch, Wolfgang. "Theologie der Verkündigung. Zum 90. Geburtstag des Marburger Theologen Rudolf Bultmann." *OP* no. 191 (20. 8. 1974).

Hartshorne, Edward Yarnall. *The German Universities and National Socialism*. London: Allen & Unwin, 1937.

Hasenhüttl, Gotthold. *Der Glaubensvollzug. Eine Begegnung mit Rudolf Bultmann aus katholischem Glaubensverständnis*. Koin. 1. Essen: Ludgerus, 1963.

Hasler, Victor. Rev. of R. Bultmann, *Der zweite Brief an die Korinther*, 1976. *ThZ* 33 (1977): 414f.

Hauschildt, Eberhard. *Rudolf Bultmanns Predigten. Existentiale Interpretation und lutherisches Erbe*. MThSt 26. Marburg: Elwert, 1989.

———. "Veröffentlichte Schriften [R. Bultmanns]" [Published Works of R. Bultmann]. Pp. xix–xxxix in E. Hauschildt, *Rudolf Bultmanns Predigten*.

———. "Was heisst 'lutherisch'? Erörtert am Beispiel der Theologie Rudolf Bultmanns." *Luther* 61 (1990): 20–36.

Hausmann, Frank-Rutger. "Heidegger zieht die Hand zurück." *FAZ* no. 106 (7. 5. 2008): 36.

Heidegger, Gertrud, ed. *"Mein liebes Seelchen!" Briefe Martin Heideggers an seine Frau Elfride 1915–1970*. München: Deutsche, 2005.

Heidegger, Martin. "Brief über den 'Humanismus'" (1946). Pp. 313–64 in *Wegmarken*. GA I/9. Frankfurt am Main: Klostermann, 1976.

———. *Der Begriff der Zeit. Vortrag vor der Marburger Theologenschaft Juli 1924*. 1st ed. Ed. H. Tietjen. Tübingen: Niemeyer, 1989.

———. *Die Selbstbehauptung der deutschen Universität* (1933). Rev. ed. Ed. H. Heidegger. Frankfurt am Main: Klostermann, 1983.

———. "Die Zeit des Weltbildes" (1938). Pp. 75–96 in M. Heidegger, *Holzwege*. GA I/5. Frankfurt am Main: Klostermann, 1977.

———. *Logik. Die Frage nach der Wahrheit*. Marburger Vorlesung WS 1925/26. GA II/21. Ed. W. Biemel. Frankfurt am Main: Klostermann, 1976.

[———.] "'Nur noch ein Gott kann uns retten.' SPIEGEL-Gespräch mit Martin Heidegger am 23. September 1966." *Der Spiegel* 30,23 (31. 5. 1976): 193–219.

———. *Phänomenologie und Theologie*. Frankfurt am Main: Klostermann, 1970.

———. *Prolegomena zur Geschichte des Zeitbegriffs*. 1st ed. Marburger Vorlesung SS 1925. GA II/20. Ed. P. Jaeger. Frankfurt am Main: Klostermann, 1979.

———. *Sein und Zeit I*. 1st ed. JPPF 8. Halle: Niemeyer, 1927.

———. "Zeit und Sein" (1962). Pp. 3–30 in M. Heidegger, *Zur Sache des Denkens*. GA I/14. Frankfurt am Main: Klostermann, 2007.

———. "Zur Geschichte des philosophischen Lehrstuhles seit 1866." Pp. 681–87 in H. Hermelink and S. A. Kaehler, *Die Philipps-Universität zu Marburg 1527–1927. Fünf Kapitel aus ihrer Geschichte (1527–1866). Die Universität Marburg seit 1866 in Einzeldarstellungen*. Marburg, 1927.

Heiler, Friedrich. "Wider gröbliche Verkennung unseres evangelischen Denkens. Berichtigung der Kritik Erich Försters 'Kirche wider Kirche.'" *HKi* 14 (1932): 343–49.

Heinemeyer, Walter, ed. *Studium und Stipendium. Untersuchungen zur Geschichte des hessischen Stipendiatenwesens.* VHKH 37. Marburg: Elwert, 1977.

Heise, Jürgen and Ulrich Schoenborn, ed. "Kostproben aus dem Briefwechsel zwischen Ernst Fuchs und Rudolf Bultmann." Pp. 290–322 in *Freude an Gott. Hermeneutische Spätlese bei Ernst Fuchs.* Ed. C. Möller. Waltrop: Spenner, 2003.

Heitmüller, Wilhelm. "Zum Problem Paulus und Jesus." *ZNW* 13 (1912): 320–37.

Henkel, Arthur. "Die erste—und folgenreiche." Pp. 11–20 in *Begegnungen mit Hans-Georg Gadamer.* Ed. G. Figal. 2000.

Herbert, Karl. *Zur Frage der Entmythologisierung.* Publication of the Evangelical Church in Hessen-Nassau. Wiesbaden: 1950.

Herms, Eilert. "Glauben und Verstehen. Gesammelte Aufsätze, Rudolf Bultmann." Pp. 346–48 in *Lexikon der theologischen Werke.* Ed. M. Eckert et al. Stuttgart: Kröner, 2003.

Herrigel, Hermann. "Ein protestantischer Theologe." *FZ* (23. 9. 1934).

Herrmann, Wilhelm. "Der Christ und das Wunder" (1908). Pp. 170–205 in *Schriften zur Grundlegung der Theologie.* Pt. 2. Ed. P. Fischer-Appelt. München: Kaiser, 1967.

———. *Die Wirklichkeit Gottes.* Tübingen: Mohr Siebeck, 1914.

———. *Ethik.* 3d ed. Tübingen: Mohr Siebeck, 1904.

Hess, Jörg. "Jesus, Rudolf Bultmann." P. 413f in: *Lexikon der theologischen Werke.* Ed. M. Eckert et al. Stuttgart: Kröner, 2003.

Hesse, Hermann. *Demian. Die Geschichte von Emil Sinclairs Jugend.* Pp. 5–163 in *Gesammelte Werke.* Vol. 5. Frankfurt am Main: Suhrkamp, 1970.

Hirsch, Emanuel. "Antwort an Rudolf Bultmann." *ZSTh* 4 (1927): 631–61.

———. "Bultmanns Jesus." *ZW* 2 (1926): 309–13.

———. *Das vierte Evangelium in seiner ursprünglichen Gestalt verdeutscht und erklärt.* Tübingen: Mohr Siebeck, 1936.

———. *Das Wesen des Christentums.* Weimer: Deutsche Christen, 1939.

———. *Das Wesen des reformatorischen Christentums.* Berlin: De Gruyter, 1963.

———. "Eine Randglosse zu 1. Kor 7." *ZSTh* 3 (1926): 50–62.

———. *Jesus Christus der Herr. Theologische Vorlesungen.* 1st ed. Göttingen: Vandenhoeck & Ruprecht, 1926.

———. "Stilkritik und Literaranalyse im vierten Evangelium." *ZNW* 43 (1950/51): 128–43.

Hobbs, Edward C., ed. *Bultmann, Retrospect and Prospect: The Centenary Symposium at Wellesley.* HThS 35. Philidelphia: Fortress, 1985.

Hoffmann, Veronika. *Leben und Werk von Walther Fischer.* Phd. diss. med. masch. Rostock, 1999.

Holl, Karl. "Urchristentum und Religionsgeschichte" (1924/25). Pp. 1–32 in *Gesammelte Aufsätze zur Kirchengeschichte.* Vol. 2: *Der Osten.* Tübingen: Mohr Siebeck, 1928.

Hollmann, Klaus. *Existenz und Glaube. Entwicklung und Ergebnisse der Bultmann-Diskussion in der katholischen Theologie.* KKTS 30 Paderborn: Bonifacius-Druckerei, 1972.

Hölscher, L. Private Collection. Hölscher, Gustav. *Aus meinem Leben*. Pt. 2. Undated manuscript [after 1945].

Holtmann, Stefan, and Peter Zocher, ed. *Als Laien die Führung der Bekenntnisgemeinde übernehmen. Briefe aus dem Kirchenkampf von Karl Barth und Karl und Dorothee Stoevesandt (1933–1938)*. Neukirchen-Vluyn: Neukirchener, 2007.

Holtzmann, Heinrich Julius. *Lehrbuch der neutestamentlichen Theologie*. 2d ed. 2 vols. Freiburg: Mohr Siebeck, 1911.

Hübinger, Gangolf. *Kulturprotestantismus und Politik. Zum Verhältnis von Liberalismus und Protestantismus im wilhelminischen Deutschland*. Tübingen: Mohr Siebeck, 1994.

Hübner, Hans. "Bultmanns 'existentiale Interpretation'—Untersuchungen zu ihrer Herkunft." *ZThK* 100 (2003): 280–324.

———. "Der Begriff 'Wahrheit' in der Theologie." *ThLZ* 127 (2002): 576–86.

———. "'Existentiale' Interpretation bei Rudolf Bultmann und Martin Heidegger." *ZThK* 103 (2006): 533–67.

———. *Politische Theologie und existentiale Interpretation. Zur Auseinandersetzung Dorothee Sölles mit Rudolf Bultmann*. Witten: Luther, 1973.

———. Private Collection. Letter of RB to H. Hübner, 5. 6. 1972.

———. "Rückblick auf das Bultmann-Gedenkjahr." *ThLZ* 110 (1985): 641–52.

———. "Rudolf Bultmanns Her-Kunft und Hin-Kunft. Zur neueren Bultmann-Literatur." *ThLZ* 120 (1995): 3–22.

———. "Rudolf Bultmann und das Alte Testament. Zum 100. Geburtstag von Rudolf Bultmann am 20. 8. 1984." *KuD* 30 (1984): 250–72.

———. "Wahrheit und Wort. Heideggers 'Vom Wesen der Wahrheit' und Wahrheit im Johannes-Evangelium." Pp. 139–61 in *Wahrheit und Wirklichkeit. Exegese auf dem Weg zur Fundamentaltheologie. Gesammelte Aufsätze*. Ed. A. Labahn and M. Labahn. Neukirchen-Vluyn: Neukirchener, 2005.

Huch, Ricarda. *Briefe an die Freunde. Ausgewählt und eingeführt von M. Baum*. Münster: Regensberg, 1955.

Hutter, Ulrich. "Theologie als Wissenschaft. Zu Leben und Werk Ernst Lohmeyers (1890–1946). Mit einem Quellenanhang." *JSKG* 69 (1990): 123–69 (Pp. 154–58: E. Lohmeyer to RB).

Hutter-Wolandt, Ulrich. "Rudolf Bultmanns Berufung nach Breslau im Jahre 1916. Bislang unveröffentlichte Quellen." Pp. 345–58 in U. Hutter-Wolandt, *Glaubenswelten. Aufsätze zur schlesischen und Oberlausitzer Kirchengeschichte*. Bonn: Kulturstiftung der deutschen Vertriebenen, 2011.

Ihlenfeld, Kurt. "Marburger Predigten," *EvW* 14 (1960): 192f.

Ittel, Gerhard Wolfgang. "Der Einfluss der Philosophie M. Heideggers auf die Theologie R. Bultmanns." *KuD* 2 (1956): 90–108 (P. 92f: RB to G. W. Ittel, 13. 5. 1955).

Iwand, Hans Joachim. *Theologiegeschichte des 19. und 20. Jahrhunderts. 'Väter und Söhne.'* Nachgelassene Werke NS 3. Ed. G. C. den Hertog. Gütersloh: Kaiser, 2001.

Jaspers, Karl. *Die Idee der Universität*. Berlin: Springer, 1946.

———. *Die Schuldfrage*. Heidelberg: Schneider, 1946.

———. *Vom Ursprung und Ziel der Geschichte*. 1st ed. Zürich: Artemis, 1949.

Jaspers, Karl, and Rudolf Bultmann. *Die Frage der Entmythologisierung*. 2d ed. München: Piper, 1981.

Jaspert, Bernd, ed. "Das Lebenswerk Rudolf Bultmanns." Pp. 11–13 in *Alma Mater Philippina* WS 1974/75; pp. 16–18 in WS 1975/76.

———. *Karl Barth–Rudolf Bultmann. Briefwechsel 1911–1966*. 2d ed. Zürich: Theologischer, 1994.

———, ed. *Karl Barth–Rudolf Bultmann. Briefwechsel 1922–1966*. 1st ed. Zürich: Theologischer, 1971.

———, ed. *Rudolf Bultmanns Werk und Wirkung*. Darmstadt: Wissenschaftliche Buchgesellschaft, 1984.

———. *Sachgemässe Exegese. Die Protokolle aus Rudolf Bultmanns Neutestamentlichen Seminaren 1921–1951*. MThSt 43. Marburg: Elwert, 1996.

———. "Sachkritik und Widerstand. Das Beispiel Rudolf Bultmanns." *ThLZ* 115 (1990): 161–82.

———. *Sackgassen im Streit mit Rudolf Bultmann. Hermeneutische Probleme der Bultmannrezeption in Theologie und Kirche*. St. Ottilien: Erzabtei, 1985.

Jaspert, Bernd, and Rudolf Mohr, ed. *Traditio—Krisis—Renovatio aus theologischer Sicht. FS W. Zeller zum 65*. Marburg: Elwert, 1976. (P. x: RB to W. Zeller, 7. 9. 1973).

Jehle, Frank. *Emil Brunner. Theologe im 20. Jahrhundert*. Zürich: Theologischer, 2006.

Jehle, Peter, ed. *Werner Krauss. Briefe 1922 bis 1976*. Analecta Romanica 65. Frankfurt am Main: Klostermann, 2002.

Jens, Inge, ed. *Max Kommerell. Briefe und Aufzeichnungen 1919–1944*. Olten & Freiburg im Breisgau: Walter, 1967.

Jeremias, Joachim. "Johanneische Literarkritik." *ThBl* 20 (1941): 33–46.

———. Rev. of Rudolf Bultmann, *Das Evangelium des Johannes*, 1941. 10th/1st ed. *DLZ* 64 (1943): 414–20.

Jonas, Hans. *Augustin und das paulinische Freiheitsproblem*. 1st ed. FRLANT 44. Göttingen: Vandenhoeck & Ruprecht, 1930.

———. *Der Begriff der Gnosis*. FRLANT 48. Göttingen: Hubert, 1930.

———. "Der Gottesbegriff nach Auschwitz." Pp. 61–84 in: *Reflexionen finsterer Zeit. Zwei Vorträge von Fritz Stern und Hans Jonas*. Ed. O. Hofius. Tübingen: Mohr Siebeck, 1984.

———. *Erinnerungen*. Ed. C. Wiese after discussions with R. Salamander. Frankfurt: Insel, 2003.

———. *Gnosis und spätantiker Geist*. Vol. 1: *Die mythologische Gnosis*. 1st ed. FRLANT 51. Göttingen: Vandenhoeck & Ruprecht, 1934.

———. "Heidegger und die Theologie." *EvTh* 24 (1964): 621–42.

———. *Zwischen Nichts und Ewigkeit. Drei Aufsätze zur Lehre vom Menschen*. KVR 165. Göttingen: Vandenhoeck & Ruprecht, 1963. (RB to H. Jonas [1963] and H. Jonas to RB [1963]).

Jones, S., and J. Gareth. "'The Play of a Delicate Shadow': Bultmann and Hesse in the Magic Theatre." *JLT* 2 (1988): 96–111.

Jülicher, Adolf. *Die Entmündigung einer preussischen theologischen Fakultät in zeitgeschichtlichem Zusammenhange*. Tübingen: Mohr Siebeck, 1913.

———. "Die Religion Jesu und die Anfänge des Christentums bis zum Nicaenum (325)." Pp. 41–128 in *Die Kultur der Gegenwart.* I/4/1. Ed. P. Hinneberg. Berlin: Teubner, 1906.

———. "Ein moderner Paulus-Ausleger" (1920). Pp. 87–98 in *Anfänge der dialektischen Theologie I.* 4th ed. Ed. J. Moltmann.München: Kaiser, 1977.

Julius-Ebbinghaus-Archiv der Bergischen Universität Wuppertal. Letter of M. Heidegger to J. Ebbinghaus, 4. 1. 1924, H 4.

———. Postcards of RB to J. Ebbinghaus.

Jung, Matthias. "Heidegger und die Theologie. Konstellationen zwischen Vereinnahmung und Distanz." Pp. 474–81 in *Heidegger-Handbuch. Leben—Werk—Wirkung.* Ed. D. Thomä. 2003.

Jüngel, Eberhard. *Barth-Studien.* ÖTh 9. Zürich: Benziger, 1982.

———. "Glaube IV. Systematisch-theologisch." Pp. 953–74 in *RGG.* Vol. 3. 4th ed. Tübingen: Mohr Siebeck, 2000.

———. "Glauben und Verstehen. Zum Theologiebegriff Rudolf Bultmanns." Pp. 16–77 in E. Jüngel, *Wertlose Wahrheit. Zur Identität und Relevanz des christlichen Glaubens. Theologische Erörterungen III.* BEvTh 107. München: Kaiser, 1990.

———. *Gott als Geheimnis der Welt. Zur Begründung der Theologie des Gekreuzigten im Streit zwischen Theismus und Atheismus.* 1st ed. Tübingen: Mohr Siebeck, 1977.

———. "Gott entsprechendes Schweigen? Theologie in der Nachbarschaft des Denkens von Martin Heidegger." Pp. 37–45 in J. Busche et al., *Martin Heidegger. Fragen an sein Werk. Ein Symposion.* Stuttgart: Reclam, 1977.

———. *Gottes Sein ist im Werden. Verantwortliche Rede vom Sein Gottes bei Karl Barth. Eine Paraphrase.* 3d ed. Tübingen: Mohr Siebeck, 1976.

———. *Paulus und Jesus. Eine Untersuchung zur Präzisierung der Frage nach dem Ursprung der Christologie.* 1st ed. HUTh 2. Tübingen: Mohr Siebeck, 1962.

———. "Redlich von Gott reden. Bemerkungen zur Klarheit der Theologie Rudolf Bultmanns." *EK* 7 (1974): 475–77.

———. "Vom Tod des lebendigen Gottes. Ein Plakat" (1968). Pp. 105–25 in E. Jüngel, *Unterwegs zur Sache. Theologische Bemerkungen.* BEvTh 61. 1972.

Kahl, Joachim. *Das Elend des Christentums. oder, Plädoyer für eine Humanität ohne Gott.* 1st ed. Rowohlt, 1968.

Kaiser, Otto, ed. *Gedenken an Rudolf Bultmann mit Beiträgen von R. Zingel, E. Vellmer, K. Rahner, E. Dinkler und H. Jonas.* Tübingen: Mohr Siebeck, 1977.

———. "Theologengräber auf dem Marburger Friedhof." Pp. 7–9 in *Freundeskreis Marburger Theologie. Mitgliederrundbrief* no. 5 (March 2004).

———. "Worte des Gedenkens an Rudolf Bultmann an seinem Grabe anlässlich seines 30. Todestages am 30. Juli 1976 gehalten am 31. Juli 2006." Pp. 40–43 in *Freundeskreis Marburger Theologie, Mitgliederrundbrief* no. 8 (March 2007).

Kamlah, Wilhelm. *Christentum und Selbstbehauptung. Historische und philosophische Untersuchungen zur Entstehung des Christentums und zu Augustins "Bürgerschaft Gottes".* Frankfurt am Main: Klostermann, 1940.

———. "Die Theologie und das 'griechische Denken.' Anmerkungen aus der anderen Fakultät zu: Rudolf Bultmann, Das Urchristentum im Rahmen der

antiken Religionen (Zürich 1949) und Hans von Campenhausen, Glaube und Bildung im Neuen Testament." *StGen* 3 (1950): 686–92.
———. "Zur christlichen Glaubenslehre." Place and date not verified.
Kampmann, Jürgen. "Engagiert—positioniert—wagemutig. Ernst Käsemann und die verfasste evangelische Kirche." Pp. 23–57 in *Dienst in Freiheit. Ernst Käsemann zum 100. Geburtstag.* Theologie interdisziplinär 4. Ed. J. Adam, H.-J. Eckstein, H. Lichtenberger. Neukirchen-Vluyn: Neukirchener, 2008.
Karlauf, Thomas. *Stefan George. Die Entdeckung des Charisma. Biographie.* 4th ed. München: Blessing, 2007.
Kaschnitz, Marie Luise. *Gesammelte Werke.* Vol. 5: *Die Gedichte.* Frankfurt am Main: Insel, 1985.
Käsemann, Ernst. "70 Jahre Theologie in meinem Leben." Pp. 91–104 in *Dienst in Freiheit. Ernst Käsemann zum 100. Geburtstag.* Theologie interdisziplinär 4. Ed. J. Adam, H. J. Eckstein,and H. Lichtenberger. Neukirchen-Vluyn: Neukirchener, 2008.
———. *An die Römer.* HNT 8a. 1st ed. Tübingen: Mohr Siebeck, 1973.
———. *An die Römer.* HNT 8a. 3d ed. Tübingen: Mohr Siebeck, 1974.
———. *Das wandernde Gottesvolk.* 2d ed. FRLANT 55. Göttingen: Vandenhoeck & Ruprecht, 1957.
———. *Der Ruf der Freiheit.* 1st ed. Tübingen: Mohr Siebeck, 1968.
———. *Der Ruf der Freiheit.* 5th ed. Tübingen: Mohr Siebeck, 1972.
———. "Ein neutestamentlicher Überblick." VF 5 (1949/50): 191–218.
———. *Exegetische Versuche und Besinnungen.* Vol. 1. 6th ed. Göttingen: Vandenhoeck & Ruprecht, 1970.
———. *Exegetische Versuche und Besinnungen.* Vol. 2. 3d ed. Göttingen: Vandenhoeck & Ruprecht, 1970.
———. *Jesu letzter Wille nach Johannes 17.* 1st ed. Tübingen: Mohr Siebeck, 1966.
———. *Jesu letzter Wille nach Johannes 17.* 3d ed. Tübingen: Mohr Siebeck, 1971.
———. *Kirchliche Konflikte.* Vol. 1. Göttingen: Vandenhoeck & Ruprecht, 1982.
———. *Leib und Leib Christi.* BHTh 9. Tübingen: Mohr Siebeck, 1933.
———. *Paulinische Perspektiven.* 1st ed. Tübingen: Mohr Siebeck, 1969.
———. *Paulinische Perspektiven.* 2d ed. Tübingen: Mohr Siebeck, 1972.
———. Rev. of Rudolf Bultmann, *Das Evangelium des Johannes,* 1941, 10th/1st ed. *VuF* 3 (1942/46): 182–201.
Kinder, Ernst, ed. *Ein Wort lutherischer Theologie zur Entmythologisierung. Beiträge zur Auseinandersetzung mit dem theologischen Programm Rudolf Bultmanns.* München: Evang. Presseverban für Bayern, 1952.
Kinzig, Wolfram. "Evangelische Patristiker und Christliche Archäologen im 'Dritten Reich.' Drei Fallstudien: Hans Lietzmann, Hans von Soden, Hermann Wolfgang Beyer." Pp. 535–601 in: *Antike und Altertumswissenschaft in der Zeit von Faschismus und Nationalsozialismus. Kolloquium Universität Zürich 14.–17. Oktober 1998.* Texts and Studies in the History of Humanities 1. Ed. B. Näf. Mandelbacktal: Edition Cicero, 2001.
Kisiel, Theodore. *The Genesis of Heidegger's* Being and Time. Berkeley: University of California, 1993.
Kittel, Gerhard. *Die Judenfrage.* Stuttgart: Kohlhammer, 1933[1]; 1933[2].

Kittel, Helmuth. *Vom Religionsunterricht zur Evangelischen Unterweisung*. Wolfenbüttel-Hannover: Wolfenbütteler, 1947.

Kl. (Initials, author not yet identified). "Dank an einen weltbekannten Marburger Gelehrten. Universität, Studentenschaft u. Kirche nehmen Abschied von Prof. Bultmann." *OP* no. 169 (25. 7. 1951): 3.

Klatt, Werner. *Hermann Gunkel. Zu seiner Theologie der Religionsgeschichte und zur Entstehung der formgeschichtlichen Methode*. FRLANT 100. Göttingen: Vandenhoeck & Ruprecht, 1969.

Klein, Günter. "Rudolf Bultmann—Ein Lehrer der Kirche. Zum 90. Geburtstag des Marburger Theologen." *DtPfBl* 74 (1974): 614–19.

———. "Rudolf Bultmann—ein unerledigtes theologisches Vermächtnis." *ZThK* 94 (1997): 177–201.

Klein, Thomas, ed. *Die Lageberichte der Geheimen Staatspolizei über die Provinz Hessen-Nassau 1933–1936*. 2 vols. Köln: Böhlau, 1986.

Knappenberger-Jans, Silke. *Verlagspolitik und Wissenschaft. Der Verlag J. C. B. Mohr (Paul Siebeck) im frühen 20. Jahrhundert*. Mainzer Studien zur Buchwissenschaft 13. Wiesbaden: Harrassowitz, 2001.

Koch, Ernst. *Prinz Rosa=Stramin*. With decorative images by Otto Ubbelohde and an afterword by W. Eckhardt (1834). Marburg: Elwert, 1965 (Photographic reprint of the 1922 ed).

Koch, Hugo. Rev. of H. Jonas, *Augustin und das paulinische Freiheitsproblem*, 1930. *ThLZ* 55 (1930): 469f.

Koepcke, Cordula. *Ricarda Huch. Ihr Leben und ihr Werk*. Frankfurt am Main: Insel, 1996.

Köhler, Lotte and Hans Saner, ed. *Hannah Arendt / Karl Jaspers. Briefwechsel 1926–1969*. 3d ed. München: Piper, 1993.

Kohls, Ernst-Wilhelm. "Blinde Blindenleiter." *OP* no. 278 (28. 11. 1984): 19.

———. "Den Glauben verraten." *OP* no. 261 (7. 11. 1984): 10.

Köhn, Andreas. *Der Neutestamentler Ernst Lohmeyer. Studien zu Biographie und Theologie*. WUNT II 180. Tübingen: Mohr Siebeck, 2004.

Kommerell, Max. *Gedanken über Gedichte*. Frankfurt am Main: Klostermann, 1943.

Konrad, Joachim. "Zu Form und Gehalt der Marburger Predigten Rudolf Bultmanns." *ThLZ* 82 (1957): 481–94.

Konukiewitz, Enno. *Hans Asmussen. Ein lutherischer Theologe im Kirchenkampf*. 2d ed. LKGG 6. Gütersloh: Gütersloher, 1985.

Köpf, Peter. *Die Mommsens. Von 1848 bis heute—die Geschichte einer Familie ist die Geschichte der Deutschen*. Hamburg: Europa, 2004.

Körner, Johannes. *Eschatologie und Geschichte. Eine Untersuchung des Begriffes des Eschatologischen in der Theologie Rudolf Bultmanns*. ThF 13. Hamburg: Reich, 1957.

Korsch, Dietrich. "Religion—ein Bezugsbegriff der liberalen, dialektischen und hermeneutischen Theologie Rudolf Bultmanns." Pp. 119–37 in *Wort Gottes—Kerygma—Religion. Zur Frage nach dem Ort der Theologie*. Ed. U. H. J. Körtner. Neukirchen-Vluyn: Neukirchener, 2003.

Körtner, Ulrich H. J., ed. *Jesus im 21. Jahrhundert. Bultmanns Jesusbuch und die heutige Jesusforschung*. Neukirchen-Vluyn: Neukirchener, 2001. (207f: RB to D. Meyer, 10. 10. 1952).

———. "Noch einmal Fragen an Rudolf Bultmann. Zur Kritik der Theologischen Schule Bethel am Programm der Entmythologisierung." *WuD* 18 (1985): 159–80.

———. Rev. of R. Bultmann, *Theologie als Kritik*, edited by M. Dreher and K. W. Müller, 2002. *ThR* 69 (2004): 228–32.

———. "Rudolf Bultmann, *Theologie des Neuen Testaments*, ED Tübingen 1953." Pp. 289–96 in *Kanon der Theologie. 45 Schlüsseltexte im Portrait.* 2d ed. Ed. C. Danz. Darmstadt: WBG, 2010.

———. "Über Bultmann hinaus: Biblische Hermeneutik bei Ernst Käsemann." *Wiener Jb. für Theologie* 6 (2006): 205–16.

Kroeger, Matthias. *Friedrich Gogarten. Leben und Werk in zeitgeschichtlicher Perspektive—mit zahlreichen Dokumenten und Materialien.* Vol. 1. Stuttgart: Kohlhammer, 1997.

Krüger, Gerhard. "Martin Heidegger und der Humanismus." *ThR* NS 18 (1950): 148–78.

Kucharz, Thomas. *Theologen und ihre Dichter. Literatur, Kultur und Kunst bei Karl Barth, Rudolf Bultmann und Paul Tillich.* Theologie und Literatur 4. Mainz: Matthias-Grünewald, 1995.

Kuhlmann, Gerhardt. "Krisis der Theologie?" *ZThK* NS 12 (1931): 123–46.

———. "Zum theologischen Problem der Existenz. Fragen an Rudolf Bultmann." *ZThK* NS 10 (1929): 28–57.

Kuhn, Dieter. *Metaphysik und Geschichte. Zur Theologie Ernst Lohmeyers.* TBT 131. Berlin: De Gruyter, 2005.

Kümmel, Werner Georg. *Das Neue Testament im 20. Jahrhundert. Ein Forschungsbericht.* SBS 50. Stuttgart: Katholisches Bibelwerk, 1970.

———. Rev. of R. Bultmann, *Das Urchristentum im Rahmen der antiken Religionen*, 1949. *ThLZ* 75 (1950): 733–37.

———. *Römer 7 und die Bekehrung des Paulus.* UNT 17. Leipzig: Hinrichs, 1929.

Küster, Bernd. *Carl Bantzer.* Marburg: Hitzeroth, 1993.

Landmesser, Christof. "Rudolf Bultmann: Religion, Kultur und Existenz." Pp. 121–34 in *Kompendium Religionstheorie.* Ed. V. Drehsen, W. Gräb and B. Weyel. Göttingen: Vandenhoeck & Ruprecht, 2005.

Langerbeck, Hermann. Rev. of R. Bultmann, *Theologie des Neuen Testaments*, pt. 1, 1948; rev. of R. Bultmann, *Das Urchristentum im Rahmen der antiken Religionen*, 1950 (2d ed). *Gn.* 23 (1951): 1–17.

Lattke, Michael. *Register zu Rudolf Bultmanns Glauben und Verstehen Band I–IV.* Tübingen: Mohr Siebeck, 1984.

———. "Rudolf Bultmann on Rudolf Otto." *HThR* 78 (1985): 353–60.

Lauer, Carolin. "*Theologie des Neuen Testaments.* Rudolf Bultmann." Pp. 728–30 in *Lexikon der theologischen Werke.* Ed. M. Eckert et al. Stuttgart: Kröner, 2003.

Leipold, H. Private Collection. Letter of A. Bultmann Lemke to H. Leipold, 10. 8. 1976.

———. Private Collection. Letter of H. Leipold to the Dean of the Faculty for Evangelical Theology Marburg, 30. 10. 1984.

Lemberg, Margret. *"... eines deutschen akademischen Grades unwürdig." Die Entziehung des Doktortitels an der Philipps-Universität Marburg 1933–1945.* Schriften der Universitätsbibliothek Marburg 113. Marburg: UB Marburg, 2002.

Lenin, Wladimir Iljitsch. "Staat und Revolution. Die Lehre des Marxismus from Staat und die Aufgabe des Proletariats in der Revolution." *Werke* 25 (1981; 6th ed.): 393–507.

Lesky, Albin. Rev. of P. Friedländer, *Studien zur antiken Literatur und Kunst*, 1969. *DLZ* 92 (1971): 862–65.

Liebing, Heinz, ed. *Die Marburger Theologen und der Arierparagraph in der Kirche*. Marburg: Elwert, 1977.

———, ed. "Die Marburger Theologische Fakultät im Preussischen Staate." Pp. 261–75 in *Humanismus—Reformation—Konfession. Beiträge zur Kirchengeschichte*. MThSt 20. Ed. with W. Bienert and W. Hage. Marburg: Elwert, 1986.

Lietzmann, Hans. *Ein Beitrag zur Mandäerfrage*. Berlin: Akademie der Wissenschaften, 1930.

Lilie, Frank, ed. "Rudolf Bultmann und Gerhard Krüger. Briefwechsel 1925–1971." *ZNThG* 4 (1997), 281–309; 5 (1998), 133–53, 274–307; 6 (1999), 134–58, 287–313; 7 (2000), 127–50.

Lindemann, Andreas. "Neutestamentler in der Zeit des Nationalsozialismus. Hans von Soden und Rudolf Bultmann in Marburg." *WuD* 20 (1989): 25–52.

———. "Zur Geschichte der Theologischen Rundschau." *ThR* 69 (2004): 1–3.

Lippmann, Andreas. *Marburger Theologie im Nationalsozialismus*. Academia Marburgensis 9. München: Saur, 2003.

Lohff, Wenzel. Rev. of R. Bultmann, *Geschichte und Eschatologie*, 1958. *ThLZ* 86 (1961): 66–69.

Lohmeyer, Ernst. *Gottesknecht und Davidsohn*. 2d ed. FRLANT 61/NS 43. Göttingen: Vandenhoeck & Ruprecht, 1953.

———. *Grundlagen paulinischer Theologie*. BHTh 1. Tübingen: Mohr Siebeck, 1929.

———. Rev. of R. Bultmann, *Jesus*, 1926. *ThLZ* 52 (1927): 433–39.

Lohse, Eduard. "Die evangelische Kirche vor der Theologie Rudolf Bultmanns." *ZThK* 82 (1985): 173–91.

———. *Der Brief an die Römer*. 15th/1st ed. KEK 4. Göttingen: Vandenhoeck & Ruprecht, 2003.

———. *Erneuern und Bewahren. Evangelische Kirche 1970–1990*. Göttingen: Vandenhoeck & Ruprecht, 1993.

———. Private Collection. Letter of RB to E. Lohse, 23. 10. 1974.

———. Rev. of R. Bultmann, *Der zweite Brief an die Korinther*, 1976. *ThLZ* 103 (1978): 352f.

———. "Rudolf Bultmann als lutherischer Theologe. Zum 90. Geburtstag des Marburger Neutestamentlers am 20. August 1974." *Luther* 45 (1974): 49–54.

Lohse, Jens Marten, ed. *Menschlich sein mit oder ohne Gott?* Stuttgart: Kohlhammer, 1969.

Löwith, Karl. "Grundzüge der Entwickelung der Phänomenologie zur Philosophie und ihr Verhältnis zur protestantischen Theologie." *ThR* NS 2 (1930): 26–64.

———. *Mein Leben in Deutschland vor und nach 1933. Ein Bericht* (1940). Stuttgart: Metzler, 1986.

———. "Phänomenologische Ontologie und protestantische Theologie." *ZThK* NS 11 (1930): 365–99.

———. *Weltgeschichte und Heilsgeschehen. Die theologischen Voraussetzungen der Geschichtsphilosophie.* 1st ed. Stuttgart: Kohlhammer, 1952.

Lüdemann, Gerd. "Emanuel Hirsch als Erforscher des frühen Christentums." Pp. 15–36 in *Christentumsgeschichte und Wahrheitsbewusstsein. Studien zur Theologie Emanuel Hirschs.* TBT 50. Ed. J. Ringleben. Berlin: De Gruyter, 1991.

Ludz, Ursula, ed. *Hannah Arendt / Martin Heidegger. Briefe 1925 bis 1975 und andere Zeugnisse.* 3d ed. Frankfurt am Main: Klostermann, 2002.

Lührmann, Dieter. "Der Staat und die Verkündigung. Rudolf Bultmanns Auslegung von Joh 18,28 bis 19,16." Pp. 359–75 in *Theologia crucis—signum crucis. FS E. Dinkler.* Ed. C. Andresen and G. Klein. Tübingen: Mohr Siebeck, 1979.

———. "Ernst Lohmeyers exegetisches Erbe." Pp. 53–87 in *Freiheit in der Gebundenheit. Zur Erinnerung an den Theologen Ernst Lohmeyer anlässlich seines 100. Geburtstages.* Ed. W. Otto. Göttingen: Vandenhoeck & Ruprecht, 1990.

———. "Günther Bornkamm (8. 10. 1905–18. 2. 1990)." *JWKG* 85 (1991): 284–86.

Luther, Martin. "Der Kleine Katechismus" (1529). Pp. 499–542 in *BSLK.* 7th ed. 1976.

———. "Sermon zu St. Michael zu Erfurt getan vom Glauben und Werken" (21. 10. 1522). Pp. 354, 13–24, in *Werke. Kritische Gesamtausgabe.* Weimerar Ausgabe. Vol. 10 Pt. 3. Weimar: Herman Böhlau, 1883–[2007].

Macquarrie, John. *An Existentialist Theology. A Comparison of Heidegger and Bultmann.* LPTh. London: SCM, 1955.

———. *The Scope of Demythologizing.* LPTh. London: SCM, 1960.

Maier-Metz, Harald. "Hermann Jacobsohn: Sein Leben." Pp. 71–80 in *Leben Sie? Die Geschichte der deutsch-jüdischen Familie Jacobsohn.* Ed. R. Verroen, W. Burger and R. Stumm. Marburg: Universitätsbiblioteck Marburg, 2000.

Malet, André. *Mythos et Logos. La pensée de Rudolf Bultmann.* NSTh 14. Geneve: Labor et Fides, 1962. (P. ixf: RB to A. Malet, 14. 2. 1963).

"Marburger Manifest vom 17. 4. 1968." *FAZ* no. 153 (5. 7. 1968): 42.

Marlé, René. *Bultmann et l'interprétation du Nouveau Testament.* Theol[P] 33. Paris: Aubier, 1956.

Martin, Bernd. "Heidegger zwischen Marburg und Freiburg." Pp. 107–22 in *Die Philipps-Universität Marburg zwischen Kaiserreich und Nationalsozialismus.* Hessische Forschungen zur geschichtlichen Landes- und Volkskunde 45. Ed. the Verein für hessische Geschichte und Landeskunde. Kassel: 2006.

Meier, Kurt. *Die Theologischen Fakultäten im Dritten Reich.* Berlin: De Gruyter, 1996.

Meinecke, Friedrich. *Die deutsche Katastrophe. Betrachtungen und Erinnerungen.* 1st ed. Zürich: Aero, 1946.

Meiser, Martin. *Paul Althaus als Neutestamentler. Eine Untersuchung der Werke, Briefe, unveröffentlichten Manuskripte und Randbemerkungen.* CThM.BW, Reihe A, 15. Stuttgart: Calwer, 1993.

[Melanchthon, Philipp.] "Die Augsburgische Konfession" (1530). Pp. 31–137 in *BSLK*. 7th ed. 1967.
Merk, Otto. "Adolf Jülicher als Paulusforscher—anlässlich seines 150. Geburtstages." *JAWG* (2007): 149–64.
———. "Biblische Theologie II. Neues Testament." *TRE* 6 (1980): 455–77.
———. "Paulus-Forschung 1936–1985." *ThR* 53 (1988): 1–81.
———. *Wissenschaftsgeschichte und Exegese. Gesammelte Aufsätze zum 65. Geburtstag*. BZNW 95. Ed. R. Gebauer, M. Karrer, and M. Meiser. Berlin: De Gruyter, 1998.
Meyer, Dietgard. "Predigt zu Mk 7,31–37" (1952). Pp. 201–6 in *Jesus im 21. Jahrhundert. Bultmanns Jesusbuch und die heutige Jesusforschung*. Ed. U. H. J. Körtner. Neukirchen-Vluyn: Neukirchener, 2001.
Meyer, Dietrich. "Zur Geschichte der evangelisch-theologischen Fakultät der Universität Breslau (1811–1945)." *JSKG* 68 (1989): 149–74.
Michel, Otto. Rev. of R. Bultmann, *Theologie des Neuen Testaments*, parts 2 and 3, 1951/53. *ThLZ* 79 (1954): 146–49.
Moering, Ernst. *In ungemessene Weiten. Kanzelreden I/II*. Breslau: Trewendt & Granier, 1922.
Möller, Christian, ed. *Freude an Gott. Hermeneutische Spätlese bei Ernst Fuchs*. Waltrop: Spenner, 2003.
Mörchen, Hermann. "Heidegger und die Marburger Theologie." Pp. 72–85 in *Martin Heidegger—Faszination und Erschrecken. Die politische Dimension einer Philosophie*. Ed. P. Kemper. Frankfurt: Campus, 1990.
Mühling, Andreas. *Karl Ludwig Schmidt. "Und Wissenschaft ist Leben."* AKG 66. New York: De Gruyter, 1997.
Müller, Karl. *Kirchengeschichte*. Grundriss der theologischen Wissenschaften 1/4. 2 vols. Tübingen: Mohr Siebeck, 1892–1919.
Müller, Klaus W. "Rudolf Bultmanns erste Veröffentlichung." *DtPfBl* 102 (2002): 235f.
———. "Zu Rudolf Bultmanns Alpirsbacher Vortrag über 'Theologie als Wissenschaft.'" *ZThK* 81 (1984): 470f.
Müller, Paul-Gerhard. "Altes Testament, Israel und das Judentum in der Theologie Rudolf Bultmanns." Pp. 439–72 in *Kontinuität und Einheit*. Für Franz Mu*ssner*. Ed. with W. Stenger. Freiburg: Herder, 1981.
Mundle, Wilhelm. *Das religiöse Leben des Apostels Paulus*. Leipzig: Hinrichs, 1923.
———. *Die Eigenart der paulinischen Frömmigkeit*. Marburg: Elwert, 1920.
———. "Religion und Sittlichkeit bei Paulus in ihrem inneren Zusammenhang." *ZSTh* 4 (1926): 456–82.
Nagel, Anne Christine. "'Der Prototyp der Leute, die man entfernen soll, ist Mommsen.' Entnazifizierung in der Provinz oder die Ambiguität moralischer Gewissheit." *Jb. zur Liberalismusforschung* 10 (1998): 55–91.
———, ed. *Die Philipps-Universität Marburg im Nationalsozialismus. Dokumente zu ihrer Geschichte*. Pallas Athene. Beiträge zur Universitäts- und Wissenschaftsgeschichte 1. Stuttgart: Steiner, 2000.
———. *Martin Rade—Theologe und Politiker des Sozialen Liberalismus. Eine politische Biographie*. Religiöse Kulturen der Moderne 4. Gütersloh: Kaiser, 1996.

Nichtweiss, Barbara. *Erik Peterson. Neue Sicht auf Leben und Werk.* 2d ed. Freiburg im Breisgau: Herder, 1994.

Nicolaisen, Carsten, and Nora Andrea Schulze, ed. *Die Protokolle des Rates der Evangelischen Kirche in Deutschland.* Vol. 2: *1947/48.* AKIZ.A 6. Göttingen: Vandenhoeck & Ruprecht, 1997.

Niedersächsisches Staatsarchiv Oldenburg. Examination file, Rudolf Karl Bultmann, 250 B. XXIX no. 316.

———. Personnel file, Rudolf Karl Bultmann, 250 B. XXIX a no. 316.

Niethammer, Lutz. *Die Mitläuferfabrik. Die Entnazifizierung am Beispiel Bayerns.* Berlin: Dietz, 1982.

Nock, Arthur Darby. Rev. of R. Bultmann, *Das Urchristentum im Rahmen der antiken Religionen*, 1949. *NSNU* 5 (1951): 35–40.

Noller, Gerhard. *Sein und Existenz. Die Überwindung des Subjekt-Objektschemas in der Philosophie Heideggers und in der Theologie der Entmythologisierung.* FGLP 10,22. München: Kaiser, 1962.

Nowak, Kurt. "Die 'antihistoristische Revolution.' Symptome und Folgen der Krise historischer Weltorientierung nach dem Ersten Weltkrieg in Deutschland." Pp. 133–71 in *Umstrittene Moderne. Die Zukunft der Neuzeit im Urteil der Epoche Ernst Troeltschs.* Troeltsch-Studien 4. Ed. H. Renz and F. W. Graf. Gütersloh: Gütersloher, 1987.

———. *Evangelische Kirche und Weimarer Republik. Zum politischen Weg des deutschen Protestantismus zwischen 1918 und 1932.* 2d ed. Göttingen: Vandenhoeck & Ruprecht, 1988.

———. *Geschichte des Christentums in Deutschland. Religion, Politik und Gesellschaft from Ende der Aufklärung bis zur Mitte des 20. Jahrhunderts.* München: Beck, 1995.

———. "Protestantische Universitätstheologie und 'nationale Revolution.' Ein Beitrag zur Wissenschaftsgeschichte des 'Dritten Reiches.'" Pp. 89–112 in *Theologische Fakultäten im Nationalsozialismus.* AKIZ.B 18. Ed. L. Siegele-Wenschkewitz and C. Nicolaisen. Göttingen: Vandenhoeck & Ruprecht, 1993.

Obituary. "Kirchenrat Bultmann." *Oldenburgisches Kirchenblatt* 25 (1919).

Odin, Karl Alfred. "Die Paradoxie des Glaubens. Gedenkfeier für Bultmann." *FAZ* no. 261 (19. 11. 1976): 27.

Oehler, Klaus. *Blick aus dem Philosophenturm. Eine Rückschau.* Olms: Hildesheim, 2007.

Oelke, Harry. "Bultmann und Weimar. Rudolf Bultmanns wissenschaftliches Wirken in den zwanziger Jahren aus kirchenhistorischer Sicht." Pp. 77–117 in *Wort Gottes—Kerygma—Religion. Zur Frage nach dem Ort der Theologie.* Ed. U. H. J. Körtner. Neukirchen-Vluyn: Neukirchener, 2003.

Öffentliche Bibliothek Universität Basel. Letters and postcards of RB to W. Baumgartner. W. Baumgartner est.

Ogden, Schubert Miles. *Christ without Myth.* New York: Harper, 1961.

Orden Pour le mérite für Wissenschaften und Künste. *Reden und Gedenkworte. Reden und Gedenkworte.* Vol. 9 (1968/69). Heidelberg: Schneider, n. d.

———. Vol. 10 (1970/71). Heidelberg: Schneider, 1973. (P. 195: RB to P. E. Schramm, 21. 7. 1970).

Osswald, Albert. "Ansprache anlässlich der Verleihung des Grossen Bundesverdienstkreuzes mit Stern und Schulterband an Professor D. Dr. Rudolf Bultmann, 19. August 1974, Marburg." *HMH* 50 (1974/75): 133f.
Ott, Heinrich. *Geschichte und Heilsgeschichte in der Theologie Rudolf Bultmanns.* BHTh 19. Tübingen: Mohr Siebeck, 1955.
Ott, Hugo. *Martin Heidegger. Unterwegs zu seiner Biographie.* Frankfurt am Main: Campus, 1988.
Otto, Rudolf. *Das Heilige.* Über das Irrationale in der Idee des Göttlichen und sein Verhältnis zum Rationalen. 1st ed. Breslau: Trewendt & Granier, 1917.
[Otto, Walter F., et al.] *Anteile. Martin Heidegger zum 60. Geburtstag.* Frankfurt am Main: Klostermann, 1950.
Pannenberg, Wolfhart. *Problemgeschichte der neueren evangelischen Theologie in Deutschland. Von Schleiermacher bis zu Barth und Tillich.* Göttingen: Vandenhoeck & Ruprecht, 1997.
———. *Was ist der Mensch? Die Anthropologie der Gegenwart im Lichte der Theologie.* 1st ed. KVR 139/140A. Göttingen: Vandenhoeck & Ruprecht, 1962.
Peterson, Erik. *Theologie und Theologen. Briefweschel mit Karl Barth u.a., Reflexionen und Erinnerungen.* Ausgew. Schr. 9/2. Ed. B. Nichtweiss. Würzburg: Echter, 2009.
Paulus, Rudolf. "Wahrheit und Gewissheit." *ChW* 43 (1929): 1018–26.
Peerlinck, Franz. "Rudolf Bultmann und das Kirchenlied." *MuK* 41 (1971): 290–97.
Peterson, Erik. *Was ist Theologie?* Bonn: Cohen, 1925.
Philosophisches Archiv der Universität Konstanz. Bultmann, Rudolf. Notes on W. Kamlah, *Christentum und Selbstbehauptung*, 1940, Undated manuscript [1941], Wilhelm-Kamlah-Sammlung, WK 2-13-2.
———. Letters of RB to W. Kamlah, Wilhelm-Kamlah-Sammlung, WK 2-13-2.
———. Postcards of RB to W. Kamlah, Wilhelm-Kamlah-Sammlung, WK 2-12-2.
Pöggeler, Otto. "Heideggers Weg von Luther zu Hölderlin." Pp. 167–87 in *Heidegger und die christliche Tradition. Annäherungen an ein schwieriges Thema.* Ed. N. Fischer and F.-W. von Herrmann. Hamburg: Meiner, 2007.
———. "Heidegger und Bultmann. Philosophie und Theologie." Pp. 41–53 in *Heidegger—neu gelesen.* Ed. M. Happel. Würzburg: Köningshausen & Neumann, 1997.
———. *Neue Wege mit Heidegger.* Freiburg, Alber, 1992.
———. *Schicksal und Geschichte. Antigone im Spiegel der Deutungen und Gestaltungen seit Hegel und Hölderlin.* München: Fink, 2004.
Rade, Martin. "Eine ungehaltene Diskussionsrede." *AdF* no. 94 (5. 11. 1929): 1098f.
———. "Eisenach 1929." *AdF* no. 92 (15. 3. 1929): 1059f.
———. "Missio canonica für die evangelischen Fakultäten?" *ChW* 44 (1930): 170f.
———. Untitled article. *AdF* no. 78 (5. 11. 1924): 854.
———. "Zur Orientierung für die nächste Vorstandssitzung des BGC." *AdF* no. 94 (5. 11. 1929): 1099f.
Ramsauer, Helene. "Johannes Ramsauer, geb. 28. Mai 1790, gest. 15. April 1848, Lehrer und Prinzenerzieher." *Oldenburger Jb.* 74 (1974): 33–45.

———. "Johannes Ramsauer und Pestalozzi." *Oldenburger Jb.* 83 (1983): 49–86.
———. "Rudolf Bultmann als Mensch und Lehrer." Pp. 11–17 in *Gedenkfeier für Rudolf Bultmann 1884–1976.* Ed. the Stadt Oldenburg. Oldenburg: Holzberg, 1985.
Ramsauer, Peter. *Zieh aus deines Vaters Hause. Die Lebenswanderung des Pädagogen Johannes Ramsauer im Bannkreis Pestalozzis.* Oldenberg: Isensee, 2005.
Ranke-Heinemann, Uta. *Nein und Amen. Mein Abschied vom traditionellen Christentum. Ergänzte Taschenbuchausgabe.* München: Heyne, 2002.
Rathje, Johannes. *Die Welt des freien Protestantismus. Ein Beitrag zur deutsch-evangelischen Geistesgeschichte. Dargestellt an Leben und Werk von Martin Rade.* Stuttgart: Klotz, 1952.
Rebenich, Stefan. "Die Guten und die Bösen. Peter Köpf banalisiert die Geschichte der Familie Mommsen." *Süddeutsche Zeitung* no. 259 (8. 11. 2004): 16.
Regulations for the Residence for Scholarship Students at Marburg (11. 2. 1849). N. d. [1849].
Reitzenstein, Richard. *Poimandres. Studien zur griechisch-ägyptischen und frühchristlichen Literatur.* Leipzig: Teubner, 1904.
Rese, Martin. "Käsemanns Johannesdeutung—ihre Vor- und Nachgeschichte." *EThL* 82 (2006): 1–33.
Rittner, Reinhard. *Die Bultmann-Büste in Oldenburg. Eine Dokumentation.* 2002.
———. "Die evangelische Kirche in Oldenburg im 20. Jahrhundert." Pp. 643–787 and 853–74 in *Oldenburgische Kirchengeschichte.* Ed. R. Schäfer et al. Oldenburg: Isensee, 1999.
———, ed. "Ein Brief Rudolf Bultmanns aus dem Jahre 1937." Pp. 7–14 in *Protokoll der Tagung "Alte Marburger" 2–4 January 1995 in Hofgeismar.* N. d. [1996].
———. "Hans Roth und Rudolf Bultmann—oder das Ringen um moderne Theologie." *Oldenburger Jb.* 100 (2000): 137–59.
———. *Rudolf Bultmann und Oldenburg.* Oldenburg: Ev.-Luth. Kirche in Oldenburg, 2002.
Robinson, James M. Foreword. Pp. v–ix in E. Haenchen, *Das Johannesevangelium. Ein Kommentar.* Ed. U. Busse. Tübingen: Mohr Siebeck, 1980.
Robinson, John A. T. *Honest to God.* Philadelphia: Westminster, 1963.
Rohden, Wilhelm von. *Geschichte der "Alten Marburger" bis 1934.* Manuscript (1977). Mn 2-3084. In UB Tübingen, RB est.
Rohls, Jan. "Rudolf Bultmanns frühe Marburger Theologie." Pp. 63–83 in *Die Philipps-Universität Marburg zwischen Kaiserreich und Nationalsozialismus.* Hessische Forschungen zur geschichtlichen Landes- und Volkskunde 45. Ed. the Verein für hessische Geschichte und Landeskunde. Kassel: 2006.
Rückert, Hanns [and Gerhard Ebeling]. "Für und wider die Theologie Bultmanns. Denkschrift der Ev.-theol. Fakultät Tübingen, dem württembergischen Landeskirchentag überreicht am 11. 3. 1952" (1952). Pp. 404–33 in H. Rückert, *Vorträge und Aufsätze zur historischen Theologie.* Tübingen: Mohr Siebeck, 1972.
Safranski, Rüdiger. *Ein Meister aus Deutschland. Heidegger und seine Zeit.* München: Hanser, 1994.

Saner, Hans. *Karl Jaspers in Selbstzeugnissen und Bilddokumenten.* 1st ed. Reinbeck bei Hamburg: Rowohlt, 1970.

Schlatter, Adolf. *Die Theologie des Neuen Testaments.* 2 vols. Stuttgart: Vereinsbuchhandlung, 1909/10.

Schleiermacher, Friedrich. *Kurze Darstellung des theologischen Studiums zum Behuf einleitender Vorlesungen. Kritische Ausgabe.* QGP 10. Ed. H. Scholz. Hildesheim: Olms, 1910.

Schlier, Heinrich. *Christus und die Kirche im Epheserbrief.* BHTh 6. Tübingen: Mohr Siebeck, 1930.

———. "Denken im Nachdenken." Pp. 217–21 in *Erinnerung an Martin Heidegger.* Ed. G. Neske. Pfullingen: Neske, 1977.

———. *Religionsgeschichtliche Untersuchungen zu den Ignatiusbriefen.* BZNW 8. Giessen: Töpelmann, 1929.

Schmidt, Karl-Ludwig. *Der Rahmen der Geschichte Jesu. Literarkritische Untersuchungen zur ältesten Jesusüberlieferung.* 1st ed. Berlin: Trowitzsche, 1919.

———. "Eschatologie und Mystik im Urchristentum." *ZNW* 21 (1922): 277–91.

———. "Evangelisch-Theologische Fakultät und Evangelische Kirche." *ThBl* 9 (1930): 235–40.

———. Rev. of Bultmann, Rudolf: *Die Geschichte der synoptischen Tradition*, 1921. *ThLZ* 47 (1922): 396–98.

Schmithals, Walter, ed. "Aus einem Briefwechsel. Rudolf Bultmann an Hans von Soden." *RKZ* 119 (1978): 228–31.

———. "Das wissenschaftliche Werk Rudolf Bultmanns." Pp. 19–28 in *Gedenkfeier für Rudolf Bultmann 1884–1976.* Ed. the Stadt Oldenburg. Oldenburg: Holzberg, 1985.

———. "Ein Brief Rudolf Bultmanns an Erich Foerster." Pp. 70–81 in B. Jaspert, *Rudolf Bultmanns Werk und Wirkung.*

———. "Ein unveröffentlichter Brief Rudolf Bultmanns." *ThR* 54 (1989): 212–14 (RB to W. de Boor, 22. 3. 1926).

———. "Gesellschaftliches Engagement der Christen—aber wie? Die 'Theologie des Wortes Gottes' und die 'politische Theologie.'" *EK* 4 (1971): 21–25.

———. "Herausforderung zu selbständigem Denken." *EK* 1 (1968): 51f.

———. "Jesus verkündigt das Evangelium—Bultmanns Jesus-Buch" (2001). Pp. 388–428 in *Paulus, die Evangelien und das Urchristentum. Beiträge von und zu Walter Schmithals zu seinem 80. Geburtstag.* AGJU 54. Ed. C. Breytenbach. Leiden: Brill, 2004.

———. *Johannesevangelium und Johannesbriefe. Forschungsgeschichte und Analyse.* BZNW 64. Berlin: De Gruyter, 1992.

———. "Johannes Weiss als Wegbereiter der Formgeschichte." *ZThK* 80 (1983): 389–410.

———. "Kritik der Formkritik." *ZThK* 77 (1980): 149–85.

———. Rev. of R. Bultmann, *Exegetica. Aufsätze zur Erforschung des Neuen Testaments*, edited by E. Dinkler, 1967. *ThLZ* 94 (1969): 500.

———. "Zum Problem der Entmythologisierung bei Rudolf Bultmann." *ZThK* 92 (1995): 166–206.

———. "Zu Rudolf Bultmanns 100. Geburtstag." *ThR* 51 (1986): 79–91.
Schnackenburg, Rudolf. Rev. of R. Bultmann, *Die drei Johannesbriefe*, 1967, 7th/1st ed. *ThLZ* 94 (1969): 586f.
Schneider, Hans. "Marburg, das irdische Paradies der Theologen. Eindrücke des niederländischen Studenten Jonkheer van Lennep im Sommersemester 1933." *Alma Mater Philippina* WS 1995/96: 24–30.
Schnelle, Udo. "Die Begründung und die Gestaltung der Ethik bei Paulus." Pp. 109–31 in *Die bleibende Gegenwart des Evangeliums. FS für O. Merk zum 70. Geb.* MThSt 76. Ed. R. Gebauer and M. Meiser. Marburg: Elwert, 2003.
Schniewind, Julius. "Zur Synoptiker-Exegese." *ThR* NS 2 (1930): 129–89.
Schulenburg, Sigrid von der, ed. *Briefwechsel zwischen Wilhelm Dilthey und dem Grafen Paul Yorck von Wartenburg 1877–1897.* Philosophie und Geisteswissenschaften I. Halle: Niemeyer, 1923.
Schulz, Eberhard. "Das Christentum—hinter dem Vorhang der Mythologie. Zum neunzigsten Geburtstag des Marburger Theologen Rudolf Bultmann." *FAZ* no. 191 (20. 8. 1974): 19.
———. "Die frühe Auslöschung des Mythos. Wieder gelesen: Rudolf Bultmanns 'Jesus'" (1926). *FAZ* no. 245 (21. 10. 1977): 25.
Schulz, Walter. Untitled article. Pp. 270–315 in *Philosophie in Selbstdarstellungen.* Vol. 2. Ed. L. J. Pongratz. Hamburg: Meiner, 1975.
Schunack, Gerd. Introduction. Pp. vii–xl in *Ernst Fuchs Lesebuch. Ausgewählte Texte.* Ed. E. Jüngel and G. Schunack. Tübingen: Mohr Siebeck, 2003.
Schütte, Hans-Walter. *Religion und Christentum in der Theologie Rudolf Ottos.* TBT 15. Berlin: De Gruyter, 1969 (Pp. 130–39: RB to R. Otto, 6. 4. 1918).
Schweitzer, Albert. *Die Mystik des Apostels Paulus.* Tübingen: Mohr Siebeck, 1930.
———. *Geschichte der Leben-Jesu-Forschung.* 9th ed. Berlin: De Gruyter, 1984.
Schwerendt, Rudolf. "Heinrich Schlier als Schüler seiner Lehrer Rudolf Bultmann, Martin Heidegger und Karl Barth in den Jahren 1920–1926." *Cath(M)* 57 (2003): 263–86.
Schwöbel, Christoph, ed. *Karl Barth–Martin Rade. Ein Briefwechsel.* Gütersloh: Mohn, 1981.
Seim, Jürgen. *Hans Joachim Iwand. Eine Biografie.* 2d ed. Gütersloh: Kaiser, 1999.
Sellin, Gerhard. "Sturz der Götzen. Ernst Käsemann hat eine Wende in der Erforschung des Neuen Testamentes eingeleitet." *zeitzeichen* 7 (2006): 19–21.
Siegfried, Theodor. "425 jähriges Jubiläum der Hessischen Stipendiaten-Anstalt." *OP* no. 157 (10. 7. 1954): 5.
Siegmund, Johannes Jürgen. *Bischof Johannes Lilje, Abt zu Loccum. Eine Biographie. Nach Selbstzeugnissen, Schriften und Briefen und Zeitzeugenberichten.* Göttingen: Vandenhoeck & Ruprecht, 2003.
Silberer, Gerhard. "Wilhelm Stern, der Freund Henhöfers, und das badische Lehrerseminar." Pp. 139–53 in *Die Erweckung in Baden im 19. Jahrhundert. Vorträge und Aufsätze aus dem Henhöfer-Jahr 1989.* VVKGB 42. Ed. G. Schwinge. Karlsruhe: Evangelischer, 1990.
Simons, Eduard. "Prediger=Professoren?" *ChW* 31 (1917): 305–9.
Sinn, Gunnar. *Christologie und Existenz. Rudolf Bultmanns Interpretation des paulinischen Christuszeugnisses.* TANZ 4. Tübingen: Francke, 1991.

———. "Existenz durch das Wort. Rudolf Bultmanns Paulusdeutung angesichts der theologischen Gegenwart." *LM* 32 (1993): 27–31.

Slenczka, Reinhard. Untitled article. Pp. 79–100 in *Systematische Theologie der Gegenwart in Selbstdarstellungen.* Ed. C. Henning and K. Lehmkühler. Tübingen: Mohr Siebeck, 1998.

Smend, Rudolf. "Hermann Gunkel. 1862–1932." Pp. 160–72 in R. Smend, *Deutsche Alttestamentler in drei Jahrhunderten.* Göttingen: Vandenhoeck & Ruprecht, 1989.

———. *Julius Wellhausen. Ein Bahnbrecher in drei Disziplinen.* Munich: C. F. von Siemens Stiftung, 2006.

Soden, Hans von. Rev. of U. Stutz, *Das Bonner evangelische Universitätspredigeramt in seinem Verhältnis zu Staat, Kirche und Gemeinde* (SPAW.PH 1921, 171–93). *Korrespondenzblatt des Gesamtvereins der deutschen Geschichts- und Altertumsvereine* 96 (1921): 262–64.

Sohm, Walter. *Territorium und Reformation in der hessischen Geschichte 1526–1555.* 1st ed. VHKH 11,1. Marburg: Elwert, 1915.

Sölle, Dorothee. *Gegenwind. Erinnerungen.* Hamburg: Hoffman & Campe, 1995.

———. "Hoffnung verändert die Welt. Kritische Auseinandersetzung mit der Theologie Rudolf Bultmanns." *EK* 4 (1971): 15–20.

———. *Politische Theologie. Auseinandersetzung mit Rudolf Bultmann.* 1st ed. Stuttgart: Kreuz, 1971.

Stadt Oldenburg, Kulturdezernat, ed. *Rudolf Bultmann 100 Jahre. Oldenburger Vorträge.* Oldenburg: Holzberg, 1985.

Stallmann, Edith. *Martin Stallmann—Pfarramt zwischen Republik und Führerstaat.* SPSGNC 5. Bielefeld: Luther, 1989.

Stegemann, Ekkehard W. "Zwischen religionsgeschichtlicher Rekonstruktion und theologischer Interpretation. Rudolf Bultmanns 'Theologie des Neuen Testaments' in ihrem forschungsgeschichtlichen Kontext." *ThZ* 55 (1999): 136–55.

Stegemann, Hartmut. "Bultmanns Entmythologisierung. Verstehenshilfe für Theologen." *OP* no. 175 (3. 8. 1976): 6.

Steinmann, Alfons. Rev. of R. Bultmann, *Der Stil der paulinischen Predigt und die kynisch-stoische Diatribe*, 1910. *BZ* 9 (1911): 217.

Stephan, Horst. Rev. of Rudolf Bultmann, *Glauben und Verstehen*, 1933. *ZThK* NS 14 (1933): 282f.

Sticht, Friedrich Wolfgang. *Die Bedeutung Wilhelm Herrmanns für die Theologie Rudolf Bultmanns.* Phd. diss. Berlin: Ernst Reuter Gesellschaft, 1965 (P. 35: RB to F. W. Sticht, 11. 3. 1964).

Stier, Ewald. "Bund für Gegenwartschristentum." *AdF* no. 94 (5. 11. 1929): 1078–98.

Stock, Hans. "Ein religionspädagogischer Nachtrag zum Bultmann-Gedenkjahr. Erinnerung an einen vergessenen Text." *JRP* 1 (1984): 165–74.

Stock, Konrad: "Das Ethos des Glaubens nach Rudolf Bultmann." Pp. 69–89 in *Christliche Ethik—evangelische Ethik? Das Ethische im Konflikt der Interpretationen.* Ed. U. H. J. Körtner. Neukirchen-Vluyn: Neukirchener, 2004.

Storck, Joachim W., ed. *Martin Heidegger / Elisabeth Blochmann. Briefwechsel 1918–1969.* Marbacher Schriften. 2d ed. Marbach am Neckar: Deutsche Schillergesellschaft, 1990.

Stowers, Stanley Kent. *The Diatribe and Paul's Letter to the Romans.* SBLD 57. Chico, CA: Scholars, 1981.

Strathmann, Hermann. Rev. of W. Herrmann, *Ethik*, 5th ed., 1913. *ThLB* 37 (1914): 143.

Stratmann, Hartmut. *Kein anderes Evangelium. Geist und Geschichte der neuen Bekenntnisbewegung.* Hamburg: Furche, 1970.

Strauss, David Friedrich. *Das Leben Jesu, kritisch bearbeitet.* 2 vols. Tübingen: Osiander, 1835.

Stuhlmacher, Peter. *Gerechtigkeit Gottes bei Paulus.* 2d ed. FRLANT 87. Göttingen: Vandenhoeck & Ruprecht, 1966.

Sturm, Erdmann. "Rudolf Bultmann über Paul Tillich." *Internationales Jb. für die Tillich-Forschung* 1 (2005): 175–81.

Swiridoff, Paul. *Das Gesicht.* Swiridoff-Bildbände 9. Schwäbisch Hall: Schwend, 1961.

———. *Porträts aus dem geistigen Deutschland.* Swiridoff-Bildbände 14. Pfullingen: Neske, 1965.

Taylor, Vincent. "Die Formung der Evangelienüberlieferung" (1933). Pp. 364–414 in *Zur Formgeschichte des Evangeliums.* WdF 81. Ed. F. Hahn. Darmstadt: Wissenschaftliche Buchgesellschaft, 1985.

Tent, James F., ed. *Academic Proconsul. Harvard Sociologist Edward Y. Hartshorne and the Reopening of German Universities 1945–1946. His Personal Account.* Mosaic: Studien und Texte zur amerikanischen Kultur und Geschichte 5. Trier: Wissenschaftlicher Verlag Trier, 1998.

Theissen, Gerd. "Die 'Formgeschichte des Evangeliums' von Martin Dibelius und ihre gegenwärtige Bedeutung." Pp. 143–58 in *Lese-Zeichen für Annelies Findeiss zum 65. Geburtstag am 15. März 1984.* BDBAT 3. Ed. C. Burchard and G. Theissen. Heidelberg: Wiss.-Theol. Seminar, 1984.

———. "Theologie und Exegese in den neutestamentlichen Arbeiten von Günther Bornkamm." *EvTh* 51 (1991): 308–32.

Theunis, Franz. *Offenbarung und Glaube bei Bultmann.* ThF 19. Hamburg-Bergstedt: Reich, 1960.

Thielicke, Helmut. "Von der Entmythologisierung des Neuen Testaments." *DtPfBl* 46 (1942): 129–31.

———. *Zu Gast auf einem schönen Stern. Erinnerungen.* 4th ed. Hamburg: Hoffmann & Campe, 1984.

Thurneysen, Eduard, ed. *Karl Barth–Eduard Thurneysen. Briefwechsel.* Vol. 2: *1921–1930.* Zürich: Theologischer, 1974.

Titius, Arthur, ed. *Deutsche Theologie. Bericht über den ersten deutschen Theologentag zu Eisenach* (1927). Göttingen: Vandenhoeck & Ruprecht, 1928.

Trautwein, Dieter. *Komm Herr segne uns. Lebensfelder im 20. Jahrhundert.* Frankfurt am Main: Lembeck, 2003.

Troeltsch, Ernst. "Die Mission in der modernen Welt." *ChW* 20 (1906): 8–12, 26–28, 56–59.

———. *Die Soziallehren der christlichen Kirchen und Gruppen.* 3d ed. GS I. Tübingen: Mohr Siebeck, 1923.
Universitätsarchiv Giessen. File regarding the replacement hire for the New Testament chair of the late Dr. Bousset, 1920, PrA Theol 2.
———. Letter of RB to the Dean of the Theological Faculty, 3. 7. 1920, Akten der Theologischen Fakultät, Theol K 11.
Universitätsarchiv Marburg. Academic Sermons. Studentische Seelsorge, 1920–1929, 307a acc. 1950/1 no. 52.
———. Bredt, Johann Victor. *Das Amt des Universitäts-Predigers in Marburg.* Manuscript 1923, 307a acc. 1950/1 no. 52.
———. Hiring files of the Theological Faculty at Marburg 1921–1924, 307a acc. 1962/12 no. 7.
———. Honorary Doctorates of the Theological Faculty at Marburg 1921–1932, 307a acc. 1962/12 no. 8.
———. Letter of H. von Soden to the Prorector of Marburg University P. Gieseke, 3. 10. 1936, 305a acc. 1975/79 no. 728, p. 25f.
———. Letter of RB to the Prorector of Marburg University P. Gieseke, 4. 10. 1936, 305a acc. 1975/79 no. 728, p. 24.
———. PhD thesis file, Rudolf Bultmann, 307a acc. 1950/1 no. 63.
———. Qualifying records, Rudolf Bultmann, 307a acc. 1950/1 no. 24.
Universitätsarchiv Tübingen. Letter of A. Bultmann Lemke to G. Ebeling, 12. 8. 1976. G. Ebeling est., 633/616.
———. Letters of RB to G. Ebeling. G. Ebeling est., 633/616 and 626.
———. Letter of RB to E. Fuchs, 8. 3. 1960 (carbon copy). G. Ebeling est., 633/616.
Universitätsbibliothek Giessen. Letter of RB to W. Fischer, 21. 11. 1958, Hs N. F. 137–18.
Universitätsbibliothek Heidelberg. Letter of RB to M. Dibelius, 21. 4. 1921, and postcard of RB to M. Dibelius, 17. 8. 1930. M. Dibelius est., Heid. Hs. 3814.
Universitätsbibliothek Marburg. Letter of RB and H. von Sodens to F. Heiler, 25. 7. 1932. M. Rade est., Ms. 839/65.
———. Letters of RB to A. Jülicher. A. Jülicher est., Ms. 695/294–96.
———. Letters of RB to M. Rade. M. Rade est., Ms. 839/14–31.
Universitätsbibliothek Tübingen. G. Krüger est. Mn 13. Letter of H. Jonas to G. Krüger, 23. 5. 1929.
———. G. Krüger est. Mn 13. Letter of M. Heidegger to G. Krüger, 15. 9. 1925.
———. R. Bultmann est. Guestbooks of Rudolf and Helene Bultmann, 1: 1917–54; 2: 1954–70. Mn 2-3041.
———. R. Bultmann est. Guestbook of Tage and Tove Wilhjelm, Praestholm (Bultmann's entry, 30. 7.–10. 8. 1949, copy). Mn 2-2419.
———. R. Bultmann est. Lecture notes of R. Bultmann. Mn 2-3090-3107.
———. R. Bultmann est. *Protokolle der Tagung der Marburger Theologen 20. 10.–23. 10. 1953 in Jugenheim an der Bergstrasse.* Undated manuscript [1953]. Mn 2-3079.
———. R. Bultmann est. Recordings of radio lectures by R. Bultmann. Mn 2-317-322.

———. R. Bultmann est. Unpublished letters of R. Bultmann. Mn 2.
———. R. Bultmann est. Unpublished sermons of R. Bultmann. Mn 2-34-169.
Universitätsmuseum für Kunst und Kulturgeschichte Marburg. Bantzer, Effi. Portrait of R. Bultmann, 1962. Inv. 14187.
———. Stengel, Gerhard. Portrait of Prof. Dr. Rudolf Bultmann, 1965. Inv. 14186.
Universitäts- und Landesbibliothek Sachsen-Anhalt in Halle (Saale). Letters and postcards of RB to H. Gunkel. H. Gunkel est. Yi 33 I B 350–82.
———. Letters and postcards of RB to J. Schniewind. J. Schniewind est. Yi 25 I B 6–20.
———. Letter drafts of J. Schniewind to RB. J. Schniewind est. Yi 25 I B 6–20.
University of California Los Angeles Library. Letters of RB to P. Friedländer. Department of Special Collections. Paul Friedländer collection. Collection 1551.
Urner-Astholz, Hildegard. "Erinnerungen an Rudolf Bultmann." Pp. 206–9 in H. Urner-Astholz, *Spiegelungen. Neue Studien zur Kunst- und Kulturgeschichte*. 1984.
Vanderbilt University Nashville Library. Letters and postcards of RB to K. Grobel. Special Collections. William Kendrick Grobel Papers.
Vahanian, Gabriel. *The Death of God. The Culture of Our Post-Christian Era*. New York: Braziller, 1961.
———. *Kultur ohne Gott? Analysen und Thesen zur nachchristlichen Ära*. ThÖ 12. Göttingen: Vandenhoeck & Ruprecht, 1973. (Pp. 155–60: RB to G. Vahanian, n. d. [12. 8. 1962]).
———. "Rudolph [*sic*] Bultmann at Syracuse." *Syracuse University Library Associates Courier* 9 (1972): 57–65.
Vahlenkamp, Werner. *Die Geschichte der Westersteder Juden. Aufstieg und Vernichtung einer kleinen Minderheit*. Westerstede: R.-D. Plois, 1988.
Valerio, Karolina de. *Altes Testament und Judentum im Frühwerk Rudolf Bultmanns*. BZNW 71. Berlin: De Gruyter, 1994.
Vialon, Martin. "Erich Auerbach und Rudolf Bultmann. Probleme abendländischer Geschichtsdeutung." Pp. 176–206 in *Marburger Hermeneutik zwischen Tradition und Krise. Marbacher schriften. Neue folge 3*. Ed. M. Bormuth and U. von Bülow. Göttingen: Wallstein, 2008.
Vischer, Eberhard. Rev. of R. Bultmann, *Der Stil der paulinischen Predigt und die kynisch-stoische Diatribe*, 1910. *ThR* 16 (1913): 259f.
Vogel, Johanna. *Kirche und Wiederbewaffnung. Die Haltung der Evangelischen Kirche in Deutschland in den Auseinandersetzungen um die Wiederbewaffnung der Bundesrepublik 1949–1956*. AKIZ.B 4. Göttingen: Vandenhoeck & Ruprecht, 1978.
Vogel, Lothar, ed. "Die Sondervoten von Rudolf Bultmann und Karl Barth zugunsten Friedrich Gogartens aus dem Jahre 1929. Drei Aktenstücke zur Geschichte der Dialektischen Theologie." *ZNThG* 7 (2000): 127–50.
Vogtmann, Martha. "Das Jenseits als geistiger Ort. Festvortrag von Prof. D. Rudolf Bultmann als Auftakt der Universitätsfeiern." *OP* no. 142 (24. 6. 1963).
Wagner, Petra. "Jesus als Spiegelbild der *conditio humana*. Zum Jesusbild im Werk von Marie Luise Kaschnitz." Pp. 57–72 in *Auf dem Weg zu einer theolo-*

gischen Ästhetik. Eine Freundesgabe für Karl-Josef Kuschel zum 50. Geburtstag. Ästhetik—Theologie—Liturgik 2. Ed. G. Langenhorst. Münster: Lit, 1998.

Wallmann, Johannes. "Die Wiedergründung der Zeitschrift für Theologie und Kirche nach dem Zweiten Weltkrieg." *ZThK* 100 (2003): 497–519.

Walter, Richard. "Ernst Käsemanns Wirken als Gemeindepfarrer im Kirchenkampf in Westfalen 1933–1946." *KZG* 12 (1999): 199–224.

Wartenberg, Günther. "Verpasste Chance oder vergebliche Mühe? Dokumente zu dem Versuch, Rudolf Bultmann Anfang des Jahres 1930 nach Leipzig zu berufen." Pp. 285–301 in G. Wartenberg, *Wittenberger Reformation und territoriale Politik. Ausgewählte Aufsätze.* AKThG 11. Leipzig: Evangelische, 2003.

Wassmann, Harry. "Der 'Fall Bultmann' in Württemberg (1941–1953). Der Alpirsbacher Mythologievortrag im Spannungsfeld von Kirchenleitung und Universitätstheologie." Pp. 137–76 in *Bausteine zur Tübinger Universitätsgeschichte, Folge 4.* Ed. V. Schäfer. Tübingen: Attempto, 1989.

Wassmann, Harry, Jakob Matthias Osthof, and Anna-Elisabeth Bruckhaus, ed. *Rudolf Bultmann (1884–1976). Nachlassverzeichnis.* Vol. 2: *Nachlassverzeichnisse der Universitätsbibliothek Tübingen.* Wiesbaden: Harrassowitz, 2001.

Weber, Alfred. *Abschied von der bisherigen Geschichte.* Überwindung des Nihilismus? Bern: Francke, 1946.

Weber, Christian. *Max Kommerell. Eine intellektuelle Biographie.* Berlin: De Gruyter, 2011.

Weinel, Heinrich. *Biblische Theologie des Neuen Testaments. Die Religion Jesu und des Urchristentums.* Grundriss der Theologischen Wissenschaften 1,3/2. Tübingen: Mohr Siebeck, 1911.

Weischedel, Wilhelm. Untitled article. Pp. 316–41 in *Philosophie in Selbstdarstellungen.* Vol. 2. Ed. L. J. Pongratz. Hamburg: Meiner, 1975.

Weiss, Johannes. *Die Aufgaben der Neutestamentlichen Wissenschaft in der Gegenwart.* Göttingen: Vandenhoeck & Ruprecht, 1908.

———. *Die Predigt Jesu vom Reiche Gottes.* 2d ed. Göttingen: Vandenhoeck & Ruprecht, 1900.

———, ed. *Die Schriften des Neuen Testaments neu übersetzt und für die Gegenwart erklärt.* Vol. 1. 2d ed. Göttingen: Vandenhoeck & Ruprecht, 1907.

———, ed. *Die Schriften des Neuen Testaments neu übersetzt und für die Gegenwart erklärt.* Vol. 2. 2d ed. Göttingen: Vandenhoeck & Ruprecht, 1908.

Weizsäcker, Carl. *Das apostolische Zeitalter der christlichen Kirche.* 1st ed. Freiburg: Mohr Siebeck, 1886.

———. *Das apostolische Zeitalter der christlichen Kirche.* 3d ed. Freiburg: Mohr Siebeck, 1902.

Wellhausen, Julius. *Einleitung in die drei ersten Evangelien.* 1st ed. Berlin: Reimer, 1905.

———. *Israelitische und jüdische Geschichte.* 6th ed. Berlin: Reimer, 1907.

Werner, Martin. "Zwei Schriften zum Christusproblem der Gegenwart." *Kirchenblatt für die reformierte Schweiz* 38 (1923): 29–31, 33–35.

Wilbrand, Wilhelm. Rev. of R. Bultmann, *Der Stil der paulinischen Predigt und die kynisch-stoische Diatribe*, 1910. *ThRv* 10 (1911): 273f.

Windisch, Hans. "Das Problem des neutestamentlichen Imperativs." *ZNW* 23 (1924): 265–81.

Winkler, Heinrich August. *Weimar 1918–1933. Die Geschichte der ersten deutschen Demokratie.* 1st ed. München: Beck, 1993.

Winkler, Robert. Rev. of R. Bultmann, *Glauben und Verstehen*, 1933. *ThLZ* 59 (1934): 164f.

Wittekind, Folkart. "Eschatologie zwischen Religion und Geschichte. Zur Genese der Theologie Bultmanns." Pp. 55–84 in *Die Gegenwart der Zukunft. Geschichte und Eschatologie.* Ed. U. H. J. Körtner. Neukirchen-Vluyn: Neukirchener, 2008.

———. "Gott—die alles bestimmende Wirklichkeit? Zum Verständnis von Bultmanns Deutung der Gottesvorstellung Jesu." Pp. 583–604 in *Denkwürdiges Geheimnis. Beiträge zur Gotteslehre. FS für E. Jüngel zum 70. Geburtstag.* Ed. I. U. Dalferth et al. Tübingen: Mohr Siebeck, 2004.

Wolf, Ernst, ed. *FS Rudolf Bultmann. Zum 65. Geburtstag überreicht.* Stuttgart: Kohlhammer, 1949.

———, ed. *Mythologie und Kerygma. Das hermeneutische Problem evangelischer Verkündigung.* Jahresgabe der Gesellschaft für evangelische Theologie 1946. Hektographie. Göttingen: 1945. (P. 91f: RB to P. Althaus, 22. 1. 1943; also printed on pp. 9f in *Protokoll der Tagung Alte Marburger 3–5 January 1994 in Hofgeismar*, 1994).

Wolfes, Matthias. "Wünsch, Georg." *BBKL* 14 (1998): 103–56.

Wolff, Fritz. "Das Zirkular des Professor D. Dr. Rudolf Bultmann vom 9. November 1925." Pp. 49–59 in *Marburg im Kontext. Gedenkbuch an das Marburger Religionsgespräch.* Monographia Hassiae 7. Ed. G. Bezzenberger. Kassel: Evangelischer, 1980.

Wolter, Michael. "'Christus und Adam' oder 'Adam und Christus'? Karl Barths und Rudolf Bultmanns Interpretation von Römer 5,12–21." Pp. 15–36 in *Existenz und Sein. Karl Barth und die Marburger Theologie.* Ed. W. Schmithals. Tübingen: Mohr Siebeck, 1989.

———. "Das Judentum in der Theologie Rudolf Bultmanns." Pp. 15–32 in *Erinnern—Verstehen—Versöhnen. Kirche und Juden in Hessen 1933–1945.* Didaskalia 40. Ed. B. Jaspert. Kassel: Evangelischer, 1992.

Wrede, William. *Das Messiasgeheimnis in den Evangelien. Zugleich ein Beitrag zum Verständnis des Markusevangeliums.* 1st ed. Göttingen: Vandenhoeck & Ruprecht, 1901.

———. *Paulus.* 1st ed. RV I/5–6. Tübingen: Mohr Siebeck, 1904.

———. Über Aufgabe und Methode der sogenannten Neutestamentlichen Theologie. Göttingen: Vandenhoeck & Ruprecht, 1897.

Wünsch, Georg. *Evangelische Ethik des Politischen.* Tübingen: Mohr Siebeck, 1936.

Young-Bruehl, Elisabeth. *Hannah Arendt. Leben, Werk und Zeit.* Aus dem Amerikanischen von H. G. Holl. 1st ed. Frankfurt am Main: Fischer, 1986.

Zager, Werner, ed. *Albert Schweitzer. Theologischer und philosophischer Briefwechsel 1900–1965.* Albert Schweitzer. Werke aus dem Nachlass. München: Beck, 2006.

———. *Liberale Exegese des Neuen Testaments. David Friedrich Strauss—William Wrede—Albert Schweitzer—Rudolf Bultmann.* Neukirchen-Vluyn: Neukirchener, 2004.

Zastrow, Constantin von. “Die Theologie der Christlichen Welt in Laienbeurteilung.” *AdF* no. 27 (8. 2. 1909): 257–70.

Zimmermann, Rainer. *Franz Frank. Leben und Werk des Malers.* München: Klinkhardt & Biermann, 1985.

Zimmermann, Ruben. “Jenseits von Indikativ und Imperativ. Entwurf einer ‘impliziten Ethik’ des Paulus am Beispiel des 1. Korintherbriefes.” *ThLZ* 132 (2007): 259–84.

Zippert, Christian. Private Collection. Rudolf Bultmann Memorial on 4. 8. 1976. Undated manuscript [1976].

———. Private Collection. Zippert, Christian. Funeral sermon for Helene Bultmann on 2 Cor 4:16–18. Undated manuscript [1973].

Zocher, Peter. *Edo Osterloh—Vom Theologen zum christlichen Politiker. Eine Fallstudie zum Verhältnis von Theologie und Politik im 20. Jahrhundert.* AKIZ.B 48. Göttingen: Vandenhoeck & Ruprecht, 2007.

Photo Credits

PLATE 1: Rudolf Bultmann's Parents, Arthur Kennedy Bultmann and Helene née Stern, ca. 1900. UB Tübingen, RB est., Mn 2-3088 A/2.

PLATE 2: The Bultmann Siblings: Rudolf, Peter, Arthur and Helene, ca. 1901. UB Tübingen, RB est., Mn 2-3088 A/9.

PLATE 3: Rudolf Bultmann as a Graduate. UB Tübingen, RB est., Mn 2-3088 A/12.

PLATE 4: A Drawing of Bultmann's from 1901. UB Tübingen, RB est., Mn 2-3057.

PLATE 5: Eduard Thurmann, Annemarie Bultmann (later Thurmann), Maria Bultmann (later Cold) and Rudolf Bultmann on Wangeroog in 1911. UB Tübingen, RB est., Mn 2-3088 A/15.

PLATE 6: Karl Müller. UB Tübingen, RB est., Mn 3089/41.

PLATE 7: Adolf von Harnack. From A. von Harnack, *Aus der Werkstatt des Vollendeten. Als Abschluss seiner Reden und Aufsätze*, ed. A. von Harnack (Reden und Aufsätze NF 5), 1930; Alfred Töpelmann (Giessen).

PLATE 8: Hermann Gunkel. From R. Smend, *Deutsche Alttestamentler in drei Jahrhunderten*, 1989, 161; Vandenhoeck & Ruprecht (Göttingen).

PLATE 9: Adolf Jülicher. UB Tübingen, RB est., Mn 2-3089/36.

PLATE 10: Johannes Weiss. UB Tübingen, RB est., Mn 2-3089/50.

PLATE 11: Wilhelm Herrmann. UB Tübingen, RB est., Mn 2-3089/33.

PLATE 12: Wilhelm Heitmüller. UB Tübingen, RB est., Mn 2-3089/30.

PLATE 13: The University of Marburg—Assembly Hall and University Church. UB Tübingen, RB est., Mn 2-3088 B/36.

PLATE 14: A Favorite Vacation Spot of Bultmann's (Dammühle near Marburg). UB Tübingen, RB est., Mn 2-3088 B19.

PLATE 15: Rudolf Bultmann as Tutor in Marburg, ca. 1912. Private property of Gesine Diesselhorst.

PLATE 16: "As the picture shows, this is where I have to give my examination-sermon next Sunday evening ..." Drawing of Bultmann's for his Niece, Elisabeth Pleus, July 22, 1912. UB Tübingen, RB est., Mn 2-3455.

PLATE 17: Helene Feldmann, 1916. Private property of Gesine Diesselhorst.

PLATE 18: Rudolf Bultmann, 1916. UB Tübingen, RB est., Mn 2-3088 A/16.

PLATE 19: Professor in Marburg, ca. 1922. UB Tübingen, RB est., Mn 2-3088 A/21.

PLATE 20: Dialectical theology: Friedrich Gogarten, Eduard Thurneysen and Karl Barth at the *Bergli* in the Summer of 1922. UB Tübingen, RB est., Mn 2-3089/2.

PLATE 21: Rudolf Bultmann and Günther Bornkamm in Conversation. Private property of Anna-Elisabeth Conrad (maiden name Bornkamm).

PLATE 22: Erich Dinkler. UB Tübingen, RB est., Mn 2-3089/18.

PLATE 23: Ernst Fuchs, Bonn 1931. Private property of Veronika Schnaufer (maiden name Fuchs).

PLATE 24: Ernst Käsemann, Jugenheim 1958. UB Tübingen, RB est., Mn 2-3089/37.

PLATE 25: Meeting of the "Old Marburgers," October 26–28, 1931 in Marburg: Heinrich Schlier and Rudolf Bultmann in Conversation, Friedrich Gogarten in the Background. UB Tübingen, RB est., Mn 2-3088 A/37.

PLATE 26: Leisure Time for the Marburg Theologians, February 6–7, 1937 in Kirchvers: Gerhard Krüger and Rudolf Bultmann. UB Tübingen, RB est., Mn 2-3088 A/38.

PLATE 27: Hans von Soden. Marburg photo archive.

PLATE 28: Paul Friedländer. Marburg photo archive.

PLATE 29: Martin Heidegger, 1927. UB Tübingen, RB est., MS 2-3089/29.

PLATE 30: Ernst Lohmeyer. From W. Otto (ed.), *Freiheit in der Gebundenheit: Zur Erinnerung an den Theologen Ernst Lohmeyer anlässlich seines 100. Geburtstages, 1990, [3]*; Vandenhoeck & Ruprecht (Göttingen).

PLATE 31: Rudolf Bultmann in Alpirsbach, June 1941 (photo by Antje Bultmann Lemke). Private property of Gesine Diesselhorst.

PLATE 32: The House at 14 Calvin Street, built in 1934. UB Tübingen, RB est., Mn 2-3088 B/40.

PLATE 33: The Bultmann Family, March 1936: Antje, Helene, Heilke, Rudolf and Gesine Bultmann. UB Tübingen, RB est., Mn 2-3088 A/36.

PLATE 34: Helene and Rudolf Bultmann in Marburg, August 1957 (photo by Therese Putnam). UB Tübingen, RB est., Mn 2-3088 A/41.

PLATE 35: Meeting of the "Old Marburgers," October 10–14, 1949 in Herborn (photo by Friedrich Wilhelm Petri). Displayed, from left to right: Front row, seated: Erna Schlier, Helene Bultmann, Rudolf Bultmann, Irmgard Feussner, Hildegard Urner-Astholz. Second and third row: Hermann Diem, Götz Harbsmier, Werner Kohleick, Hans-George Gadamer, Ulrich Henn, Gerhard Ebeling, Ernst Käsemann, Marie Veit, Hanna Grothmann, Ilse Buschfranz, Walter Kohlschmidt, Gerhard Krüger, Karl Linke, Doris Faulhaber, Günther Bornkamm, Friedrich Luncke, Ernst Fuchs, Ulrich Finckh, Walter Klaas. Fourth and fifth row, standing: Ruth Comann, Thomas Dell, Herta Fromme, Herbert Schneider, Philipp Vielhauer, Alfred Habermann, Margarete Dell, Werner Flentje, Else Köppe, August Dell, Martin Stallman. UB Tübingen, RB est., Mn 2-3088 A/42.

PLATE 36: During the Final Lecture in Marburg, 1951. UB Tübingen, RB est., Mn 2-3088 A/44.

PLATE 37: Rudolf Bultmann, ca. 1955. UB Tübingen, RB est., Mn 2-3088 A/56.

PLATE 38: Rudolf Bultmann, 1964. Private property of Konrad Hammann; also in E. Dinkler (ed.), *Zeit und Geschichte: Dankesgabe an Rudolf Bultmann zum 80. Geburtstag*, 1964.

PLATE 39: Rudolf Bultmann in Marburg, August 1968. Private property of Gesine Diesselhorst.

PLATE 40: The Holder of the Order *Pour le mérite*, 1969. UB Tübingen, RB est., Mn 2-3088 A/92.

PLATE 41: Meeting of the "Old Marburgers," October 17–21, 1960 in Bethel: Heinrich Ott, Martin Heidegger, and Rudolf Bultmann (photo by Ernst Keller). UB Tübingen, RB est., Mn 2-3088 A/71.

PLATE 42: Awarding of the Superior Cross with Star and Shoulder Sash of the Order of Merit of the Federal Republic of Germany on August 19, 1974: Bishop D. Erich Vellmer, President Albert Osswald, Rudolf Bultmann, and Lord Mayor Dr. Hanno Drechsler. UB Tübingen, RB est., Mn 2-3088 A/93.

PLATE 43: The Grave of Helene and Rudolf Bultmann in the Marburg City Cemetery (photo by Konrad Hammann). Private property of Konrad Hammann.

Index of Biblical References

Index of People, Places, Institutions and Publications

Index of Subjects

About the Author

Konrad Hammann is Professor of Systematic and Historical Theology and its Didactic in the Evangelical-Theological Faculty of the University of Münster, Germany. Born in 1955, he studied theology in Marburg, Tübingen, Munich and Göttingen. He held an academic assistantship in Munich from 1980–81 and a vicariate in Verden/Aller from 1981–83. He also served as a pastor in Schwalmstadt-Trutzhain from 1984–91, receiving his PhD in 1988. From 1991–2003, he served as pastor in Göttingen, completing his postdoctoral qualification at the University of Göttingen in 1998.